The Blue Guides

M000032503

Albania

Australia

Austria Austria
Vienna

Bali, Java and Lombok

Belgium

Bulgaria

Czech & Slovak Czech & Slovak
Republics Republics
Prague

China

Cyprus

Denmark

Egypt

France France
Paris and Versailles
Burgundy
Loire Valley
Midi-Pyrénées
Normandy
Provence
South West France

Germany Berlin and eastern
Germany

Greece Greece
Athens
Crete
Rhodes and the
Dodecanese

Hungary Hungary
Budapest

Southern India

Ireland

Italy Northern Italy
Southern Italy
Florence
Rome

Jordan

Malaysia and
Singapore

Malta and Gozo

Mexico

Morocco

Netherlands Netherlands
Amsterdam

Poland Poland
Kraków

Portugal

Spain Spain
Barcelona
Madrid

Sweden

Switzerland

Thailand

Tunisia

Turkey Turkey
Istanbul

UK England
Scotland
Wales
Channel Islands
London
Oxford and Cambridge
Country Houses of
England

USA New York
Museums and
Galleries of New York
Boston and Cambridge
Washington

Please write in with your comments, suggestions and corrections for the next edition of the Blue Guide. Writers of the most helpful letters will be awarded a free Blue Guide of their choice.

Bali, Java and Lombok

Gavin Pattison

A&C Black • London
WW Norton • New York

BLUE GUIDE

1st edition, October 2000

Published by A & C Black (Publishers) Limited
35 Bedford Row, London WC1R 4JH

Maps and plans drawn by RJS Associates, © A&C Black

Colour photographs © Gavin Pattison
Illustrations © Peter Spells, except p 74 © Jaideep Charkrabarti, p 136 after W.O.J.
Nieuwnekamp, and p 323 after Oudheidkundige Dienst in Nederlandsch-Indie Uittreksel Uit de
Oudheidkundge Verslagen, 1912–1949.

A CIP catalogue record of this book is available from the British Library.

ISBN 0–7136–3915–6

Published in the United States of America by
WW Norton and Company Inc.
500 Fifth Avenue, New York, NY 10110

Published simultaneously in Canada by
Penguin Books Canada Limited
10 Alcorn Avenue, Toronto
Ontario M4V 3B2

ISBN 0–393–31948–2 USA

The author and the publishers have done their best to ensure the accuracy of all the information
in Blue Guide Bali, Java and Lombok; however, they can accept no responsibility for any loss,
injury or inconvenience sustained by any traveller as a result of information or advice contained
in the guide.

Cover photographs. Main picture: detail of a large *kala* face, Candi Jago, near Malang, east Java;
small pictures: Slopeng sand dunes, Madura, © Gavin Pattison.

Title page illustration: Durga Mahishasuramardini from Candi Jawi.

Gavin Pattison is a journalist and freelance writer who has spent many years exploring southeast Asia, working in Indonesia, Thailand and Cambodia, Vietnam and the Philippines. He read
Southeast Asian studies and language at university and co-authored Blue Guide Thailand. He is at
present working in Uganda.

Printed and bound in England by Butler & Tanner Ltd., Frome and London.

Contents

Introduction 7

Practical information

Planning your trip 11
Getting there 13
Money 15
Where to stay 16
Food and drink 18
Getting around 23
The Indonesian language 28
Health 32
Crime and personal security 37
Postal and telecoms services 38
Sporting and leisure activities 39

Public holidays and annual festivals 40
Additional information 42
  Disabled travellers 42
  Women travellers 42
  Embassies and consulates in
    Indonesia 43
  Opening hours 43
  Film and photography 43
  News media 43
  Local customs and behaviour 44
  Tipping and donations 45

Background information

Physical geography 46
Flora and fauna 47
The people of Java, Bali and Lombok 54
Historical summary 56
Art and architecture 71
  Art and Architecture of Hindu-Buddhist Java, 400–1500,
    by William Southworth 71
  Religion and architecture on Bali 83
  Decorative arts and crafts 87
  Drama, dance and music 92
Further reading 97

The Guide

Bali

Denpasar and the southern resorts 100
Ubud and vicinity 118
East Bali: Bangli, Klungkung and Karangasem 142
North Bali: Batur, Bratan and the coast 160
West Bali: Tabanan, Jembrana and Pulau Menjangan 169

Java

Jakarta 178
Banten, Krakatau and the west coast 209
Bogor, Puncak and Pelabuhanratu 222
Bandung 235
Around Bandung 245
Cipanas, Tasikmalaya and Pangandaran 254
Cirebon and vicinity 264

Baturaden, Wonosobo and Dieng 269
Magelang, Ambarawa and Gedong Songo 278
The north coast: Pekalongan, Semarang and Kudus 285
Yogyakarta 297
Around Yogyakarta 312
Surakarta (Solo) and vicinity 337
Pacitan and Madiun 346
Kediri, Tulungagung and Blitar 350
Malang and the Bromo-Semeru massif 363
Gunung Penanggungan, Trowulan and vicinity 374
Surubaya 382
Madura 388
The eastern salient: Argopuro and Ijen 397

Lombok
West Lombok: Ampenan, Mataram, Cakranegara and Senggigi 407
Central Lombok: Mataram to the east coast 416
North Lombok and Gunung Rinjani 419
South Lombok 425

Glossary 431
Index 435

Maps and plans

Maps of Java, Bali and Lombok at the end of the book

Bali
Denpasar 104
Gunung Kawi 138
Kuta, Legian and Seminyaka 115

Sanur 109
Ubud, Around 128–129
Ubud, Central 126

Java
Bandung, Central 241
Banten Lama 212
Blitar 358
Bogor 225
Bondowoso 399
Candi Borobudur 316
Candi Loro Jonggrang 328
Candi Panataran 360
Cirebon 266
Dieng Plateau 275
Ijen Plateau 401
Jakarta, Centre 193
Jakarta, Kota 198

Kudus 294
Madura and the Kangean archipelago 390
Malang 366
Prambanan 327
Semarang 290
Surabaya 386
Surakarta (Solo) 341
Tasikmalaya 259
Wonosobo 272
Yogyakarta 306
Yogyakarta, Around 313

Lombok
Mataram 410

Introduction

Almost everyone has heard of Bali; far fewer are those familiar with the names of Java and Lombok, let alone Madura. This is not altogether surprising in view of the tourism industry's marketing of these islands: the reader of holiday brochures is frequently left with the perception either that Bali and Indonesia are separate entities or, more commonly, that Bali IS Indonesia. This *Blue Guide* has been written partly in the hope that readers will be encouraged to spend more time exploring Bali's immediate neighbours.

In compiling this guide I have imagined an enthusiastic traveller with a keen interest in art and architecture, history and archaeology, as well as in the people and natural landscape of the islands: a traveller who is sufficiently confident and eager not only to step on the well-trampled paths to familiar, established tourist destinations, such as Yogyakarta, Ubud, Kuta and Bogor, but to explore the back roads, searching out minor but charming temples and splendid landscapes which would otherwise receive just a handful of visitors each year.

Java, with a population of more than 110 million people, is one of the most densely populated islands on earth. It is a marvellous destination for people interested in other people: rarely are you out of sight of others. Like Bali, much of it is extremely beautiful, with a backbone of volcanoes running the length of the island, glorious amphitheatres of terraced rice fields, and high mist-shrouded plateaux inhabited by tough, resourceful farmers.

Though Bali lacks the grandeur of Java, it makes up for it with an astonishingly verdant, compact landscape and an immensely rich religious and social fabric which, because of its easily visualised aspects, has long been a favourite of the tourist trade. Lombok, the lesser known and poorer neighbour, is only now beginning to cater for the increasingly sophisticated tastes of the modern tourist; the visitor here should be prepared to rough it occasionally.

The first part of this *Blue Guide* is a general introduction to the islands, with practical travel information and short sections on art, architecture, history, the people, flora and fauna, and religion. The second, much larger part of the volume is devoted to 29 travel itineraries, each of which can be read as a separate entity. While, in some cases, specific routes are described in detail to assist in finding rather obscure sites, or certain roads are suggested for their particularly fine scenery, I have attempted to stray where practical from the *Blue Guide* tradition of describing linear routes from A to B in the hope that this provides for greater flexibility of travel.

Though this *Blue Guide* is as comprehensive as time has allowed, I am well aware of certain gaps: antiquities left out, and tracks left untrodden. I hope, nevertheless, that there is sufficient here to engage the interests of any traveller, whether visiting the islands for the first or the twentieth time. Comments, criticisms, suggestions and corrections from readers would be greatly welcomed for incorporation in later editions.

In my years of travelling to Indonesia, I have always been able to rely on the wonderful hospitality of Gillian and John Arnold in Jakarta; I am very deeply indebted to them for their assistance, advice, unceasing generosity and excellent company. To my partner, Bella Bird, who many years ago passed on to me her tremendous enthusiasm for Indonesia, I owe a special debt of gratitude. Special thanks also go to Tri and Milka Kumala Soehartoadi: to Milka for providing a base at her family's home in Malang; to Tri for being an always good-humoured travelling companion and skilled mechanic.

In Bali, Rana Helmi very kindly provided wonderful accommodation, thoughtful company and sound advice at her home in Ubud. Nia Fliam and Agus Ismoyo in Yogyakarta were generous with their knowledge of Indonesian art and artists. Esther and Peter Scarborough uncomplainingly squeezed me with their family into their house in Malang, at times with no advance warning. Russell Comer was always happy to track down obscure sites, and has freely given advice based on his years in Yogyakarta and Jakarta. Keith Harris provided detailed knowledge of Gede Pangrango National Park.

In Lombok, I was accompanied for much of the time by Tim Crosskey, the best kind of travelling companion: curious, resilient and always calm in a crisis. In Bali, my work was enlivened by the presence of Farida Shaikh. Rob Dickinson, the world authority on Javanese steam locomotives, gave generously of his advice and time, and provided the information on Java's sugar industry. Filka Puspowinahyu found answers to all my questions about Jakarta and Yogyakarta, keeping me informed of new developments in my absence.

To William Southworth, who took valuable time out from writing his doctoral thesis to contribute the section on early Javanese art and architecture, I offer my heartfelt thanks.

At the outset of this project, Peter Pangaribuan in the Indonesian Department of Tourism, and Hendrati Sukendar Munthe at the Indonesian embassy in London, smoothed my path by assisting with the bureaucratic paperwork. Roger and Jenny Pattison were always willing to search out information in their local library, assist with European language translations, and phone offices on my behalf. Others who have generously assisted me include Dini Djalal, Dr John Miksic, Dr Ed Edwards McKinnon, Alastair Robb, Steve Bensted, Max Arifin, and Christian Winge. To all the above, I give profound thanks.

Gemma Davies has been an unbelievably patient and calm editor, and I owe her immeasurable thanks for her support over the years this volume has been maturing. Ian Kearey very kindly read the proofs from beginning to end in a laborious task which resulted in many improvements. Martin Daly at the London School of Oriental and African Studies very generously gave of his time to check the bibliographic details. Professor Michael Hitchcock offered much sound advice based on his encyclopaedic knowledge of the Indonesian arts. Robert Smith, the book's long-suffering cartographer, achieved the seemingly impossible, transforming my tatty sketches and scribbled notes into clear, accurate maps. To him I owe a huge debt of thanks.

I regret that there are almost certainly names I have forgotten, to whom thanks are owed. It goes without saying that all errors in the text are mine alone.

The economic and political crisis

As of early 2000, Indonesia is an incredibly cheap travel destination for foreign tourists equipped with dollars or pounds. Hotels offer hugely discounted rates; gasoline costs almost nothing; retail prices are astonishingly low; and tourists are relatively few. The downside is that several of the most pleasant hotels have closed or been mothballed in the wake of the economic crisis which hit Indonesia from mid-1997; and with the surging unemployment has come a rise in petty crime. As the long-term fate of these hotels remains uncertain, they are still listed in the guide in the hope that they may reopen in the forthcoming months; travellers should come prepared to find the odd one closed.

Life is increasingly hard for a huge number of Indonesians, who are struggling to make ends meet, so foreigners who flaunt their enormous comparative wealth are not likely to be appreciated. Despite the very difficult times, Indonesians remain extremely hospitable; it behoves the foreign visitor to act with sensitivity.

And a few excuses from the author

In the past decade, telephone numbers have changed with great frequency; the pace of change is now slowing, as six- and seven-digit numbers become more common. However, it is highly likely that several numbers listed in this book have changed between the time of research and publication.

In the mid-1990s, hotels were ordered to change any English name to an Indonesian name. Sometimes this just meant reversing the word order: Miranda Hotel became Hotel Miranda. Sometimes it meant translating the name: Sunrise Bungalows became Bungalo Matahari. Occasionally, bizarre mixtures were created: Regent's Park Hotel became Hotel Taman Regent's. When I researched this book, some hotels had still not changed their names, while others which had were still known to the local taxi and rickshaw drivers by their old name.

Distances given in the text are not absolutely precise, but are my best estimate; they should usually be accurate to a few hundred metres.

Roads are generally very badly signposted, so in parts of the text detailed route descriptions have been written to help those travellers using their own transport. Where possible, this guide makes use of the roadside kilometre posts to make route finding easier.

PRACTICAL INFORMATION

 Planning your trip

When to visit

The islands of Indonesia experience distinct wet and dry seasons, but temperature and relative humidity are fairly constant year-round, varying more between
day and night than between months. Expect minimum temperatures of
22°–24°C (72°–75°F) and maximums of 31°–33°C (88°–91°F); there are occasional frosts in the highlands. The wettest months are during the northwest
monsoon, which generally lasts from November to March; the driest months are
from May to September. Rainfall varies also according to altitude: mountainous
areas experience rain almost all year round and can receive more than 7000mm
per year; other areas – including the north coast of Java's eastern salient, northeast Bali, and the north Lombok coast – have more than eight dry months and
receive less than 1500mm per year.

The rain, when it comes, is usually very heavy and seldom lasts for more than
a couple of hours. Travel in the rainy season does enable the visitor to see the
countryside at its most lush, but it does of course affect hiking, volcano-climbing,
birdwatching and other outdoor activities.

The main tourist seasons generally disregard the weather and are related more
to foreign holiday periods, which fall in July and August, and during Christmas
and the New Year. At these times advance bookings are recommended; expect
hotel rooms and flights to cost more than usual.

Passports and formalities

A passport valid for at least six months is required. Holders of Australian, British,
Canadian and US passports, and nationals from more than 40 other countries,
may enter Indonesia for 60 days without a visa; this visa-free entry is not extend-
able. For longer stays, visitors need a social/cultural visa or a work visa, both of
which entail considerable paperwork and bureaucratic hassles.

On entering Indonesia by air, you should be carrying a ticket out of the country; if you cannot produce this on demand at the immigration desk, expect to be
taken aside. It is not enough to argue that you do not yet know your departure
point or date, nor that you plan to leave by boat to Singapore, nor that you intend
to purchase the ticket in the country. The entry requirements also include funds
of at least US $1000 in cash, credit cards or travellers' cheques.

If arriving from yellow fever endemic zones in Africa and South America, an
International Certificate of Vaccination is required.

Indonesian diplomatic missions abroad

- In **Australia**, the Indonesian embassy is at 8 Darwin Ave, **Yarralumla**, ACT
  2600 (☎ 02 6250 8600). There are consulates at: 236–38 Maroubra Rd,
  Maroubra, NSW 2035 (☎ 02 9344 9933); 45 King William St, **Adelaide**,
  SA 5001 (☎ 08 8217 8288); 72 Queens Road, **Melbourne**, VIC 3004 (☎ 03

9525 2755); 134 Adelaide Terrace, **East Perth**, WA 6004 (☎ 08 9221 5858); and 20 Harry Chan Ave, **Darwin**, NT 0800 (☎ 08 8941 0048).

- In **Britain**, the embassy is at 38 Grosvenor Square, **London** W1X 9AD (☎ 020 7499 7661).
- In **Canada**, the embassy is at 55 Parkdale Ave, **Ottawa**, ON, K1Y 1ES (☎ 613 724 1100). There are consulates at: 129 Jarvis St, **Toronto**, ON, M5C 2H6 (☎ 416 360 4020); and 1455 West Georgia St, 2nd fl., **Vancouver**, BC, V6G 2T3 (☎ 604 682 8855).
- In the **United States**, the embassy is at 2020 Massachusetts Ave NW, **Washington**, DC 20036 (☎ 202 775 5200). There are consulates at 72 East Randolph St, **Chicago**, IL 60601 (☎ 312 345 9300); 10900 Richmond Ave, **Houston**, TX 77042 (☎ 713 785 1691); 3457 Wilshire Blvd, 4th fl., **Los Angeles**, CA 90010 (☎ 213 383 5126); 5 East 68th St, **New York**, NY 10021 (☎ 212 879 0600); 1111 Columbus Ave, **San Francisco**, CA 94133 (☎ 415 474 9571).

The Internet

There are many thousands of web sites with information about Indonesia. A few useful ones to start with include:

- http://indonesia.elga.net.id/ provides links to scores of other pages on various general subjects.
- http://www.indocenter.co.id/ offers the latest news on Indonesian current affairs, updated daily; also hundreds of links to other sites.
- http://www.balivillas.com/ details of magnificent private villas for rent on Bali, and a large amount of other useful information for travellers to Bali.
- http://www.asiatravel.com/ provides room rates and descriptions, and takes bookings for dozens of hotels in Indonesia.
- http://www.ihra.co.id/ Indonesian Hotels & Restaurants Association.
- http://www.iit.edu/~indonesia/jendela/ listings of newspapers and magazines with Indonesian news, and a vast amount of other links.
- http://www.batavianet.com/links another very good links site.
- http://www.bart.nl/~edcolijn/ an excellent site offering information about Indonesian wildlife and flora, national parks and reserves, with links to many related places.
- http://www.dialspace.dial.pipex.com/steam/ for Rob Dickinson's excellent site on Java's steam locomotives and sugar mills.
- http://www.nmnh.si.edu/gvp/ for the Smithsonian Institution's bulletins on recent Indonesian volcanic eruptions.
- http://www.seatrekindonesia.com/ for traditional boat charters through eastern Indonesia.
- http://www.tourismindonesia.com/ for the Indonesian tourism promotion board's news.

Allowances and prohibitions

Luggage checks are usually fairly cursory on arrival. Narcotics, firearms and pornography are prohibited, and law-breakers can expect harsh treatment; the death sentence can be imposed for certain narcotics offences. You can bring any amount of foreign currency in and out of Indonesia. Two litres of alcohol and 200 cigarettes are permitted duty-free.

Things to take

A warm sweater or jacket will be needed for visiting any highland areas. A folding umbrella or a waterproof cape is advised in the rainy season. Heavy jeans which take hours to dry are impratical; light, loose cotton clothing is recommended. Other items to consider include earplugs, flashlight, compass (more useful than you might think, when asking directions), hat, sunglasses, snorkel and mask, rubber sandals, sarong, small padlock (for luggage or cheap hotel rooms) and all but the most basic toiletries.

If you plan to spend time scuba-diving, playing golf, caving, bird-watching, hiking or camping, bring as much of your own equipment as you can because it can be difficult to hire good quality equipment locally.

Indonesians who become your friends would appreciate simple gifts such as postcards from your country or photographs of you and your family.

Tourist information

The government-funded Indonesia Tourist Promotion Board has several overseas offices which can provide general information. These include:

- **Australia**: Level 10, 5 Elizabeth St, Sydney, NSW 2000 (☎ 02 9233 3630).
- **Britain**: c/o Indonesian Embassy, 38 Grosvenor Square, London W1X 9AD (☎ 020 7499 7661; ask for the information department). For brochures, a list of tour operators, and travel tips, ☎ 0900 160 0180; calls cost 60p a minute.
- **USA**: 3457 Wilshire Blvd, Suite 104, Los Angeles, CA 90010 (☎ 213 387 2078).

 Getting there

All three islands are served by **international flights**. While long-haul flights from Europe and North America go to Jakarta or Bali, several Asian-based airlines have direct flights to Lombok and Surabaya.

Flying from Europe to Indonesia, the most direct flights include *Garuda Indonesia* from London or Amsterdam; *Malaysia Airlines* via Kuala Lumpur from London or Paris; *Singapore Airlines* via Singapore from London, Paris or Amsterdam. Many other airlines, including *Emirates* and *British Airways*, fly from Europe to Singapore, with frequent connections from there to on regional carriers to Jakarta.

Many flights from the west coast of the USA are routed via Taipei or Tokyo. *China Airlines* flies from Los Angeles to Jakarta via Taipei, and also offers a direct Taipei-Bali flight. *Eva Air* flies from Los Angeles or San Francisco to Taipei, to connect with *China Airlines*. *Northwest Airlines* and *United Airlines* fly from Seattle to Tokyo to connect with *Japan Air Lines* to Jakarta. *Air Canada* flies from Vancouver to Taipei while *Cathay Pacific* flies from Vancouver to Hong Kong; both connect with *China Airlines* to Jakarta. *Korean Airlines* flies from Chicago to Jakarta via Seoul.

Most flights from the east coast of the USA are routed via Europe; again, the choice of airlines is large.

International airline offices in Indonesia

- *Air France:* The Grand Bali Beach, Sanur, Bali (☎ 0361 288511); Summitmas I, Jl. Sudirman, **Jakarta** (☎ 021 520 2262).
- *Air New Zealand:* Wisti Sabha, Ngurah Rai Airport, Tuban, Bali (☎ 0361 756170); Wisma Metropolitan II, Jl. Sudirman, Jakarta ☎ 021 571 1902).
- *American Airlines:* Satriavi Bldg, Jl. Prapatan 32, Jakarta (☎ 021 231 1132).
- *Ansett Australia:* The Grand Bali Beach, Sanur, Bali (☎ 0361 289636); BDN Bldg, cnr. Jl. Thamrin and Jl. Kebon Sirih, Jakarta (☎ 021 391 5501/4461).
- *British Airways:* World Trade Center, Jl. Sudirman, Jakarta (☎ 021 521 1490).
- *Cathay Pacific:* The Grand Bali Beach, Sanur, Bali (☎ 0361 286001/ 288511); Gedung Bursa Efek Jakarta, Jl. Sudirman, Jakarta (☎ 021 515 1747/2747); Graha Bumi Modern, Hyatt Regency, Jl. Basuki Rachmat, Surabaya (☎ 031 531 7421/7543).
- *Emirates:* Hotel Sahid Jaya, Jl. Sudirman, Jakarta (☎ 021 574 2440).
- *Eva Air:* Wisti Sabha, Ngurah Rai Airport, Tuban, Bali (☎ 0361 751011); Graha Bumi Modern, Hyatt Regency, Jl. Basuki Rachmat, Surabaya (☎ 031 546 5123).
- *Gulf Air:* Wisma Danamon Aetna Life, Menara II, Jl. Sudirman, Jakarta (☎ 021 577 0789/0456).
- *JAL:* The Grand Bali Beach, Sanur, Bali (☎ 0361 287576/7).
- *KLM*: Wisti Sabha, Ngurah Rai Airport, Tuban, Bali (☎ 0361 756126/7); Summitmas II, Jl. Sudirman, Jakarta (☎ 021 252 6730/5, 252 6740).
- *Lufthansa:* The Grand Bali Beach, Sanur, Bali (☎ 0361 288511); Bank Panin Pusat, Jl. Sudirman, Jakarta (☎ 021 570 2005/2015).
- *Malaysia Airlines:* The Grand Bali Beach, Sanur, Bali (☎ 0361 285071); World Trade Center, Jl. Sudirman, Jakarta (☎ 021 522 9682); Graha Bumi Modern, Hyatt Regency, Jl. Basuki Rachmat, Surabaya (☎ 031 531 8632).
- *Northwest Airlines:* Wisma Bumiputera, Jl. Sudirman, Jakarta (☎ 021 520 3152).
- *Philippine Airlines:* Plaza Mashill, Jl. Sudirman, Jakarta (☎ 021 526 7780).
- *Qantas:* The Grand Bali Beach, Sanur, Bali (☎ 0361 288331); BDN Bldg, Jl. Kebon Sirih, Jakarta (☎ 021 230 0277/0655).
- *SAS:* S. Widjoyo Centre, Jl. Sudirman, Jakarta (☎ 021 252 4081).
- *Singapore Airlines:* Bank Bali, Jl. Dewi Sartika 88, Denpasar, Bali (☎ 0361 261666/261669); Plaza Chase, Jl. Sudirman, Jakarta (☎ 021 520 6881, 570 4422); 10th fl., Menara BBD, Surabaya (☎ 031 531 9215–8).
- *SilkAir:* Plaza Chase, Jl. Sudirman, Jakarta (☎ 021 520 8018).
- *Swissair:* Plaza Mashill, Jl. Sudirman, Jakarta (☎ 021 522 9901/9911).
- *Thai:* The Grand Bali Beach, Sanur, Bali (☎ 0361 288141); BDN Bldg, cnr. Jl. Thamrin and Jl. Kebon Sirih, Jakarta (☎ 021 314 0607); Graha Bumi Modern, Hyatt Regency, Jl. Basuki Rachmad, Surabaya (☎ 031 546 3710–12).
- *United Airlines:* Bank Pacific Bldg, Jl. Sudirman, Jakarta (☎ 021 570 7520).

The following have offices in Surabaya, but no flights from there: British Airways, China Southern Airlines, JAL, Lufthansa, Northwest Airlines, Qantas and Saudia, all in Graha Bumi Modern at the Hyatt Regency. Emirates is inside the Hyatt Regency itself; KLM is in the World Trade Center off Jl. Pemuda.

Within southeast Asia, there are flights from Bangkok, Manila and Brunei, while *Qantas* flies from Australia.

The following is a short selection of **UK** tour operators and travel agents who offer flights and accommodation bookings and also pre-arranged holidays.
Travelbag ☎ 01420 88724 (flights and accommodation), *Trailfinders* ☎ 020 77938 3366. *Abercrombie & Kent Travel* ☎ 020 7559 8500 (upmarket organised and tailor made holidays), *Explore Worldwide* ☎ 01252 760100 (specialises in trekking and overland tours), *Imaginative Traveller* ☎ 020 8742 8612, *Kuoni Travel* ☎ 01306 740500 (varied selection of organised holidays), *Bales Worldwide* ☎ 01306 885991 (specialises in organised holidays).

Cruise ships occasionally pass through Indonesian waters, calling at ports on Bali, Java, Lombok and elsewhere in the archipelago.
Noble Caledonia (☎ UK: 020 7409 0376) runs irregular but highly regarded cruises, usually through the islands to the east of Lombok.
Other operators in this region include:
Cunard Line (☎ UK: 01703 716608; USA: 415 391 7444 or 391 8518, 800 929 9595 or 929 4747).
Radisson Seven Seas (☎ UK: 020 7287 9060; USA: 800 333 3333).
Silversea (☎ UK: 020 7613 4777; USA: 954 522 4477 or 800 722 9955).
Swan Hellenic Cruises (☎ UK: 020 7800 2200; US agent: 206 728 4202).

Money

The currency is the **rupiah**. There are notes of 100, 500, 1000, 5000, 10,000, 20,000 and 50,000 rupiah, and coins of 500 and 1000 rupiah; smaller-value coins do exist, but are now virtually worthless and rarely seen.

Banks and money changers
The private banks tend to be more efficient at changing money than the state-owned banks. Among those which can usually be recommended are *Bank Bali*, *BCA*, *BII* and *BNI*.

Money changers can be found near the clusters of guest houses in Yogyakarta and in the main tourist resorts on Bali and Lombok. Exchange rates vary considerably, so it can be worth checking several if you plan to change a large sum. Banks are usually open Mon–Fri 08.00–14.00; and Sat 08.00–12.00; money changers generally open for longer hours. Whether you use a money changer or a bank, always check the amount you are given very carefully before walking away; tricks by sleight of hand or dubious arithmetic have become increasingly frequent, especially among Bali's money changers.

Cash, cheques, credit and debit cards
Visitors are advised to take a mixture of US dollars in cash, travellers' cheques of a well-known brand, and a credit or debit card.

US dollars are far and away the most acceptable foreign currency at banks and money changers, and are vital if travelling off the beaten track. In Bali and the main tourist centres on Java and Lombok, Australian and Canadian dollars and major European currencies may be accepted at some banks and money changers. In all cases, make sure your foreign notes are fairly new and unmarked; torn, dirty and marked notes are often refused, as are old-style US dollars. Larger-value notes ($100 bills especially) often get a better rate of exchange, and small denominations may sometimes be rejected.

Some banks and money changers will only take certain travellers cheques: American Express and Thomas Cook are the best known, though a bank may on occasion refuse even one of these.

In almost every town there is at least one bank which will give a cash advance on a credit or direct debit card; Mastercard and Visa are the most widely accepted. Banks which are known to take them are marked by 'M' and 'V' in the main text (though other banks may do so too); most charge a fixed fee, regardless of the transaction's size. A growing number of ATMs accept foreign cards, but outside Jakarta, Bandung, Surabaya and Bali's resorts, these are still too few to rely on. It is important to keep the machine receipts, as there have been cases of banks inaccurately debiting travellers' accounts back home.

 Where to stay

Some of the world's most wonderful hotels can be found on **Bali**, while the standard of accommodation in **Java**'s main cities and towns has been steadily improving in recent years. In the smaller towns on Java, and further from the beaten track, hotels tend to be rather scruffy and simply furnished; many lack air-conditioning, but have electric fans instead.

Losmen and *penginapan* are simple, cheap hotels, often with rooms arranged round a central courtyard or small garden. These are extremely variable in quality – some of them bright and spotlessly clean, others filthy and unfriendly – but usually have no hot water.

In **Bali**, mid- and low-priced lodgings are often built in the form of a traditional Balinese house compound; this is especially true in Ubud, where there is a huge and excellent choice of accommodation. **Lombok** has the poorest selection of rooms, with few to recommend outside Mataram, Senggigi and the three resort islands off the northwest coast.

Visitors coming to climb volcanoes and hike through some of the national parks should bring **camping equipment**. For ascents of Gunung Rinjani on Lombok and some mountains on Java, such as Gunung Semeru, equipment can be hired locally but may not be especially good quality or lightweight. For most other mountains where an overnight camp is required, such as Gunung Raung, your own equipment is essential.

Hotel tariffs

The official room rates for almost all mid- and high-priced hotels should be seen only as a guide, not the actual amount the hotel realistically expects to charge. Except in the high season (July–August, Christmas and New Year) ,when the best hotels are often full and advance booking is recommended, there is generally a glut of rooms and the price is very negotiable. Discounts of 15–60 per cent should be sought, though you will have to bargain. If you plan to stay several

Hotel price guide

Hotels listed in the main text are priced according to their official tariffs in the following ranges. The wild fluctuations of the rupiah in recent months mean that although the stars may no longer represent the exact values marked, the vast majority of hotels will still be priced in the same range relative to one another.

☆	US$15	UK£10
☆☆	$15–40	£10–25
☆☆☆	$40–75	£25–46
☆☆☆☆	$75–150	£46–93
☆☆☆☆☆	$150	£93

nights, the price per night should drop; further price falls should come when you look as if you are about to walk away in disappointment. It pays to bargain in a polite, friendly tone, not in an aggrieved or angry way.

Always have a look at the room before accepting any price. It is worth checking that water actually flows from the taps in basins and showers; that the lights work; that the air-con unit or electric fan works and is not too noisy; that the door has a secure lock; and that the windows are not vulnerable to thieves.

Beware that many tariffs at mid- and high-priced hotels quote a figure '++'; this means there is a service charge and a government tax (together totalling 21 per cent in 1999) to be added to the bill. Prices at cheap *losmen* are not usually negotiable, but nor do they add service or tax to the bill; the price they quote is what you pay. In such lodgings, a lone traveller must usually pay the same as two people sharing a room, though occasionally there are cheaper, single rooms available; a simple breakfast – sometimes just a glass of tea or coffee, sliced bread, a hard-boiled egg or banana – is usually included in the price, as is a glass of tea or coffee in the afternoon or on arrival.

Bathroom etiquette

Most bathrooms in *losmen* and cheap hotels contain a large basin (*bak kamar mandi*) filled with cold water, which the bather sluices over themselves using a scoop or small bucket provided. This is very refreshing in hot weather, but on cool mornings requires a moment of bravado. You should never climb into the basin, nor drop soap into it. The toilet in such lodgings is usually a squat-type with no cistern and no toilet paper; it is flushed by repeatedly pouring scoops of water from the *bak kamar mandi* until the toilet is clear.

When using the toilet, Indonesians usually clean themselves with soap, water and their left hand, rather than toilet paper. In lodgings used to foreigners' habits, there is often a bucket in the room for waste toilet paper and other bathroom refuse; such items flushed down the toilet are likely to cause a blockage.

Electric current and light

Almost everywhere in Java, Bali and Lombok, electricity is now AC 220–230V; plugs with two round pins are required. If you intend to stay in the cheaper *losmen* and *penginapan*, it is wise to buy locally a 60W threaded bulb to replace the feeble 25W light often found in the room.

Food and drink

While Indonesia cannot boast of having one of the world's great cuisines, eating here can still be a highly enjoyable experience. There is food everywhere you look, and it is usually worth trying everything new at least once. Some of the tastiest and freshest food is the cheapest – served either from an itinerant pedlar with two large baskets hung from a yoke slung across the shoulder, or from *kaki lima* ('five legs'). These are small wooden handcarts (traditionally three-legged) pushed by vendors (the two legs) who walk a regular route several times each day, ringing a bell or banging with a stick to attract attention, and serving just one or two different dishes or snacks. Paradoxically, some of the worst food – and most dangerous to your health – can be the most expensive: bland attempts at European dishes in overpriced tourist restaurants, where the food has grown stale through lack of custom.

In every town you will find simple food stalls (***warung***) set up in clusters along the pavement, each one lit at night by a hissing gas lamp (or, increasingly, fluorescent strip lights powered by a car battery), and run by a woman and her extended family who have been serving the same half-dozen dishes to the same clientele on the same site for years. Usually there is a long communal table, flanked by wooden benches and protected from the outside world by a sheet or old sacking, on which is written the name of the stall or the dishes it serves. Without knowing a word of Indonesian, you can go in, smile, look at the different dishes people are eating, and point to the one you want; better still, try out a few words of Indonesian and see what happens. People may crack the odd joke at your expense, and you may be charged slightly more than a local, but more often than not you will find someone who can speak some English and can help you out. *Warung* servings are often rather small; it is very acceptable to ask for a second, half-portion (*tambah separoh*) to fill you up. The main risk from eating at handcarts or *warung* comes usually not from the food, but from the plates and cutlery, which may have been washed in less than pure water.

Rather more sophisticated than the pedlar and the *warung* is the ***rumah makan*** ('eating house') or café. These usually have longer menus than a *warung* (though many dishes may be unavailable on any particular day), several tables and chairs, and waitress service. Often there will also be a counter selling biscuits, snacks, sweets and drinks to take away.

Found in most Javanese towns are ***rumah makan Padang***, identifiable by a dozen or more bowls laden with different foods, usually piled precariously in the front window. These are cafés serving spicy Minangkabau food from Padang in West Sumatra; the food is usually cold but highly spiced, very tasty, served extremely quickly, and quite expensive. Just pick what you like from the huge array of platters; you will be charged according to what you eat.

The ***restoran*** ('restaurant') is generally smarter and more expensive than a *rumah makan*, is often owned by Chinese, and is where wealthier Indonesians (particularly Chinese) will be found. The food – especially seafood – can be excellent, but the *restoran* caters mainly to groups, and a lone traveller may feel out of place.

Increasing numbers of restaurants serving excellent international food have opened in recent years in Jakarta, Bandung, Yogyakarta, Surabaya and the resorts on Bali, offering fine Japanese and Korean, Tex-Mex, Italian, Spanish and French food. Inevitably, in the same towns and resorts are huge numbers of cafés and restaurants, set up to milk the tourist market, which serve often disgracefully poor versions of staple Indonesian dishes or feeble attempts at European food; eating regularly in such places becomes an immensely depressing experience.

Foreign fast-food chains are also well established in Indonesia, among them *A&W*, *Dunkin' Donuts*, *KFC*, *Häagen-Dazs*, *McDonald's* and *Sizzler*. They attract wealthy middle-class Indonesians, and students who can do their homework in air-conditioned comfort for the price of a coffee. Whether such places will survive the economic recession remains to be seen.

Etiquette

At home and in simple *warung*, Indonesians often eat with their right hand, scooping up balls of food held together with a 'glue' of sauce and rice; in smarter cafés and restaurants they usually often eat with spoon and fork, using the spoon to convey the food to their mouth. Before and after the meal, they will wash their hands with water; usually a jug and bowl are provided.

A guest in someone's house should not drink or eat till invited, even if the food has already been placed in front of them; usually the host will say: '*Silakan!*' ('Please – go ahead!') or just '*Makan!*' ('Eat!') as an invitation to begin. It is also customary for the guest to leave some food on the plate and some drink in the glass to emphasise the generosity of the host; likewise, they should not take the last morsels of food from a common platter. It is considered rude to refuse food prepared by your host; even if it looks appalling, eat just a tiny amount (or pretend to) and then plead fullness. If it is something you cannot eat for dietary reasons – such as pork for a Muslim or meat for a vegetarian – this can be explained apologetically; Indonesians understand well the idea that some foods are taboo for some people.

Rice

Most Indonesians eat three times a day, with white rice – either steamed or fried – the main component of all three meals, supplemented by side dishes of fish, meat or vegetables. *Nasi goreng* (fried rice) may be eaten at breakfast to use up the previous night's *nasi putih* (steamed rice). On the street, as in the home, *nasi goreng* varies enormously: at its simplest, it is little more than rice fried in oil with a few shallots, chillies, sweet soy sauce and a dollop of tomato ketchup; more usually, small pieces of chicken or beef, tiny dried shrimps and shredded cabbage are added. *Nasi goreng istimewa* ('special fried rice') usually comes with a fried egg on top and perhaps some *kerupuk udang* (prawn crackers). *Nasi rames* or *nasi campur*, often seen on menus, is a serving of steamed rice surrounded by a selection of meat and vegetable side dishes, all piled onto one plate; the accompanying dishes vary greatly, but this is a good opportunity to try several different foods. Almost any *warung* can produce a *nasi rames*.

Noodles

Egg noodles are the other main carbohydrate source, usually eaten fried or in a soup. *Bakmi goreng*, *mi goreng* or *mi jawa* are various preparations of noodles which are boiled, then fried with shallots, shrimps, garlic, dark sweet soy sauce, pieces of beef and shredded vegetables; the quality varies hugely. *Mi bakso*, usually bought from a handcart or *warung*, is a common noodle soup containing balls of meat or fish, which can be very delicious or truly awful, depending on the quality of the meatballs and the quantity of monosodium glutamate.

Meat and fish

Pork, forbidden to Muslims, is rarely seen in Java or Lombok, but **babi guling** (spit-roasted, stuffed suckling pig) is one of Bali's delicious specialities. Chicken and beef or buffalo, and less frequently goat, are the main meats of Java and Lombok, often made into thick spicy curries with coconut milk, or an oily soup which in Indonesia is served as a main dish. Intestines and offal are used rather more than in Western cuisine. The more common meat and fish dishes include:

Ayam goreng plain fried chicken, often marinated in a spicy tamarind and soy-flavoured sauce.

Bebek betutu duck wrapped in banana leaves with herbs and spices, then slowly baked; a Balinese speciality.

Gudeg a wonderful Yogyakarta speciality made from chicken cooked with jackfruit in a thick coconut milk known as *santan* (not the 'water' in the young coconut, but a mixture of that and the oils extracted from pressed, grated coconut flesh).

Ikan asam manis fish – usually carp or gourami – marinated in vinegar with chillies, ginger and coriander, then fried and covered with a hot sweet-and-sour sauce.

Kari ikan a fish curry (or *kari udang* – prawn curry) using a curry base of *santan* and tamarind water, flavoured with lemon grass, coriander and garlic.

Opor ayam roasted chicken pieces served in a very mildly spicy *santan* sauce.

Rawon a very dark spicy dish of diced beef flavoured and coloured by *keluak* seeds.

Rendang a Minangkabau dish from Sumatra, but very popular in Java: large chunks of buffalo meat (or beef) simmered in a thick *santan* sauce with onions, chillies, ginger and turmeric for a couple of hours till almost dry.

Sate small pieces of marinated meat impaled on a skewer and grilled over charcoal; usually eaten with **bumbu sate** (a piquant peanut sauce) and **lontong** (cold, compressed blocks of boiled rice). Different meats can be used: *sate kambing* (lamb or goat) and *sate ayam* (chicken) are most common.

Sop buntut oxtail soup cooked with coriander and cumin, chillies and turmeric.

Soto ayam a chicken soup often cooked with garlic, bean sprouts, shrimps, turmeric and ginger.

Soto daging a spicy soup usually made with beef.

Udang bakar tiger prawns marinated in a very hot sauce made from **belacan** (shrimp paste) and *cabai rawit* (tiny chillies), then grilled.

Pulses and vegetables

The vegetarian can eat healthily in Indonesia, though the diet may become rather repetitive. The nutritious soya bean is used imaginatively, and provides a rich supply of protein in the form of **tahu** (bean curd or tofu), **tempe** (*tempeh*: slabs made from split beans fermented with an edible fungus, and consisting of 40 per cent protein), soya bean milk, soy sauce, and **tauco** (salted, fermented and crushed beans). Readily available vegetable- or pulse-based dishes include:

Capcai a Chinese dish of fried vegetables, usually rather greasy and frequently badly made.

Gado-gado salad – usually made from a selection of potato, cabbage, green beans and bean sprouts – added to *lontong*, covered with a slightly spicy peanut sauce, and garnished with cucumber, a hard-boiled egg and *kerupuk* or **emping** (crispy yellow crackers made from deep-fried, crushed *melinjo* nut kernels). A very common dish in Indonesia, its quality varies greatly.

Lalap a platter of raw or lightly cooked vegetables; each mouthful is usually dipped in **sambal**, a very hot chilli relish.

Pecel a salad of lightly cooked vegetables with a spicy peanut sauce.

Sayur lodeh a thin, spicy vegetable stew cooked in coconut milk.

Tahu goreng and **tempe goreng** versions of fried soya bean usually served as side dishes.

Urap a salad made from either cooked or raw vegetables, served in a spicy coconut sauce.

Urap panggang bamboo shoots baked with coconut and eggs.

Herbs, spices and seasonings

Indonesian cuisine relies heavily on several staples for flavouring and seasoning meat and fish dishes, for curry sauces, soups and marinades. Two words worth learning are *pedas* (chilli-hot) and *panas* (temperature-hot). Hot chillies (*cabai* or *lombok*) are used in most recipes; other key ingredients include coriander seeds (*ketumbar*) and cumin (*jinten*), ginger (*jahe*), galangal (*laos* and *kencur*), lemon grass (*serai*), Kaffir lime leaves (*daun jeruk purut*), tamarind (*asam*), turmeric (*kunyit*), soy sauce (*kecap manis*), shrimp paste (*belacan* or *terasi*) and tiny dried shrimps (*ebi*).

Snacks and sweets

Dadar gulung or **kue dadar** sweet, delicious coconut-filled pancakes.

Dodol sticky, log-shaped sweets made from palm sugar, rice flour and coconut, and usually brightly coloured. Garut in West Java is the centre of production.

Es campur a sweet, sticky concoction of fruit syrup, condensed milk, shaved ice, coloured jelly shapes, tapioca and bread cubes; ingredients and quality vary greatly.

Kacang goreng fried peanuts; a snack frequently eaten with beer.

Kue bugis small, sweet, coconut-filled cakes, usually wrapped in banana leaves.

Martabak savoury meat pancakes, or sweet ones filled with condensed milk and sometimes chocolate flavouring; usually bought from handcarts, and made by highly dextrous vendors.

Pisang goreng banana fritters.

Rempeyek kacang (or peyek) peanuts deep-fried in batter to form savoury, peanut-laced crackers.

Fruits

A huge variety of fruit is available, some of which will be unfamiliar to the visitor newly arrived in Asia:

Belimbing (carambola) a yellow, smooth-skinned fruit with longitudinal ridges which, when sliced, produces star-shaped cross-sections of crisp flesh; refreshing, but often lacking flavour.

Durian a large fruit with a thick green prickly skin and a soft, yellow creamy flesh. It has a remarkably pungent smell and flavour which many foreigners find disagreeable, but most Indonesians adore. The smell can linger for hours or days in a confined space. The large seeds can be roasted and eaten.

Jambu air (rose-apple) small white, pinkish or green fruit, with an apple-like taste and crispness.
Jambu biji (guava) crisp, sweet flesh beneath a hard, green skin.
Jeruk bali (pomelo) akin to grapefruit, but with a very thick green skin and a deep layer of pith; very refreshing, tangy-tasting pink or white flesh.
Jeruk manis (tangerine, clementine or orange) sweet-tasting flesh inside a thin green or orange skin; can be rather dry.
Jeruk nipis (lime) small green limes with a very sour juice used to make *air jeruk*, a deliciously thirst-quenching, though often over-sweetened drink.
Jeruk purut (Kaffir lime) a small, knobbly, green-skinned citrus fruit with little juice; its leaves are used in cooking.
Kelengkeng (lychee) small, round fruit with a knobbly red skin, and white flesh round a shiny black seed.
Mangga (mango) a large variety are available; unripe fruits are cooked like vegetables and used in *rujak*, a tart-tasting fruit salad eaten with an accompanying sweet and chilli-hot sauce. The best ones are said to come from near Cirebon and Indramayu in West Java.
Manggis (mangosteen) apple-sized round fruit with purple skin – which stains indelibly – and sweet white flesh in segments. Ideally should be eaten in combination with durian.
Nanas (pineapple) unripe fruits are often added to *rujak* (see above).
Nangka (jackfruit) can weigh more than 20kg; a green-skinned, yellow-fleshed fruit covered in small blunt spines. Unripe fruits are used to make *gudeg* (see above). The sweet, ripe flesh has a rubbery texture and pleasant flavour.
Papaya large green and orange fruit with smooth, soft orange flesh and filled with hundreds of round black seeds.
Pisang (banana) a vast number of varieties are grown, with a wealth of different textures, flavours, colours and sizes. Popular ones include the very small and sweet, thin-skinned, bright yellow *pisang emas* ('golden bananas'); the larger and firmer *pisang raja* ('king bananas'), sometimes used for frying; and the hard, seed-filled *pisang klutuk*, sold while unripe and often used to make *rujak* (see above).
Pokat (avocado) not widely available outside Bali, where it is often used to make a thick fruit juice.
Rambutan small fruit with a hairy red skin and sweet, juicy white flesh.
Salak a small, pear-shaped fruit with a shiny brown, tessellated skin appearing somewhat like snake-skin scales. Dry, crisp white flesh with little flavour; the best are said to grow in Bali and in the Serayu valley round Banjarnegara in Central Java.
Semangka (watermelon) the seeds are dried, roasted and eaten as snacks.
Sirsak (soursop) green knobbly skin with a pulpy, juicy flesh; very refreshing if ripe.

Drinks

Tap water is not safe to drink anywhere; **bottled water** is found almost everywhere, and most cafés and *warung* provide cooled, boiled water for drinking. **Carbonated drinks** are widely available, as is a bottled, sweet, cold black tea (*teh botol*). Several decent lager **beers** (*bir*) are brewed locally, including Bintang, Anker and Heineken. **Wine** is produced in northwest Bali and sold under the Hatten Wines label in Bali's southern resorts.

   Teh manis, a weak, sweet **black tea**, is the most ubiquitous hot drink, and is refreshing when served chilled (*es teh*). **Coffee**, grown throughout the archipelago, is usually served sweet and black: *kopi tubruk* ('collision coffee') is strong black coffee made by boiling coffee grounds with water (and usually sugar); *kopi susu* ('milk coffee'), made with condensed milk, is usually extremely weak, tasteless and relatively expensive. Some of the better hotels and restaurants can provide a good range of coffees from many parts of the country. **Ginger tea** (*teh jahe*), often regarded as a health tonic, is quite widely available, especially in highland areas.

Seasonal **fruit juices** can be excellent, though they are often sweetened too much for the foreigner's palate; *air jeruk* or *es jeruk* (citrus juice) is a favourite, available year-round. In Bali, the delicious *es advokat* or *es pokat* (avocado juice) is made from the fruit pulp blended with condensed milk and palm sugar.

Ice (*es batu*), added to drinks, is a potential health threat but is often too refreshing to do without. In most cafés and restaurants, especially in tourist areas which are used to foreigners' demands, it is made from boiled water and can be safely used; in smaller, rural *warung* it may not be.

Getting around

Maps
The *Java & Bali* map published by Nelles to the scale 1:650,000 is recommended for visitors touring Java. For Bali, the *Bali* map by Nelles to the scale 1:180,000 is generally less accurate than that published by Periplus to the scale 1:250,000; the latter also has several useful street plans. The *Lombok & Sumbawa* map by Periplus is excellent. All the above are widely available in Indonesia and abroad. Maps recommended for specific areas and cities are listed in the main text, and are available in local shops.

By air
In this vast archipelago, a flight can save you hours or days of travel by land and sea; even the short hop from Yogyakarta to Jakarta replaces 8 hours of sitting on a bus or train. Of course, you see and experience less, but you may instead be treated to an unexpected view of volcano peaks poking through the cloud. Flights are reasonably priced, and certain early-morning or late-evening departures are often slightly cheaper than those departing at more suitable times. Tickets bought direct from airlines are sometimes cheaper, sometimes more expensive, than those bought from travel agents; there seems to be little pattern to this. A 5 per cent discount is given on return tickets; children aged two to nine are charged 50 per cent, and younger infants are charged 10 per cent of the fare. Bookings should be made as long in advance as is practical, and a computer print-out of the flight details should be obtained as proof of your reservation. Four carriers operate domestic flights:

• *Bouraq Indonesia* has a small route network, with flights out of a few Javanese cities and Denpasar.

• *Garuda Indonesia*, the state-owned airline, has a few domestic flights, notably between Jakarta and Denpasar.

• *Mandala* is another small operator, which, despite its reputation for tardiness, has had the best safety record of all the carriers for the past ten years.

• *Merpati Nusantara*, the state-owned carrier which took over the vast majority of *Garuda's* domestic routes, has the most extensive network and flies to extremely remote landing strips in the outer islands. It also has the worst safety record (at least 14 crashes in the 1990s), so for travel round Java, Bali and Lombok, where there are alternatives, it may be wise to avoid it, if it is still operating. In late 1999 *Merpati* was technically bankrupt and one proposal being suggested was to re-merge it with *Garuda*.

By sea

The state-owned *Pelni* shipping line currently has c 20 passenger ships criss-crossing the archipelago between Medan in North Sumatra and Jayapura on the north coast of Irian Jaya. Almost all of them call at one or more of Java's north coast ports, Bali's Benoa Harbour or Lembar on Lombok at some point in their journey; most operate on a 14-day circuit, though with the economic downturn of the late 1990s schedules have become less regular and some ports and routes have been cut out altogether. While the lower-class accommodation remains generally miserable, first class (two-bed cabins) and second class (four-bed cabins) are clean and comfortable. The food aboard is variable, so it is wise to take plenty of your own snacks, especially on a long voyage. If you like travelling by ship, and have plenty of time, this can be a very enjoyable way to reach some of the more remote parts of the archipelago. For trips within Java, Bali and Lombok, however, it is far quicker and easier to travel by land, with quick hops on the regular ferries between the islands.

Inter-island ferries

Vehicle ferries between **Java** and **Bali** depart every few minutes from Ketapang, just north of Banyuwangi on Java's east coast, and Gilimanuk on Bali's western tip; the crossing takes up to one hour. For the **Bali–Lombok** crossing, vehicle ferries run between Padangbai on Bali's southeast coast and Lembar, Lombok's western port, departing every two hours; the journey takes c 4 hours. Vehicle ferries cross the narrow strait between **Surabaya** and **Madura** every few minutes, and a daily ferry operates between **Kalianget** in east Madura and **Jangkar**, near Asembagus on Java's north coast. There are fairly regular but infrequent ferries from **Dungkek** in east Madura to the larger islands of the **Kangean archipelago**.

Local cruises and charters

Several Bali-based companies offer cruises to the islands east of Bali. *Sea Trek* (PT Pinisi Duta Bahari) at Jl. Danau Tamblingan 64, Sanur (☎ 0361 286992; fax 286985; e-mail: seatrekdps@denparsar.wasantara.net.id) sails a variety of beautiful custom-built, traditional-style schooners on circuits of 2–10 days through the archipelagoes of Nusa Tenggara and South Sulawesi; tailor-made itineraries for group charters (8–16 passengers) can be easily arranged. Typical rates: $125–160/person/day. *Spice Island Cruises* at Jl. Padang Galak 25, Sanur (☎ 0361 286283; fax 286284) operates cruise ships on three- or four-night circuits to Lombok, Sumbawa and Komodo.

By rail

There are no railways on Bali and Lombok. Java's rail system, after decades of steady decline, has been improved in recent years, with fast, comfortable services now operating between Jakarta and Bandung, Cirebon, Semarang, Surabaya, Yogyakarta and Solo. Travellers have a choice of classes: the cheapest are less expensive than buses; the most comfortable are considerably more expensive. Rail travel can be fun, and always interesting, though services are not terribly frequent. For longer journeys between Java's larger towns and cities, the railway is strongly recommended over the bus: train stations are usually much closer to the city centre than bus stations (especially in Jakarta, Bandung, Yogyakarta and Surabaya), and train travel is generally more comfortable. Ticket sales for the better, faster trains are now computerised; for the others, though, purchasing a ticket can still be a time-consuming hassle. To avoid this, you can usually buy a ticket through a travel agent for a small surcharge.

Different classes are available on different trains: *eksekutif* is the most comfortable, usually with meals provided and an air-con compartment; *bisnis* is usually fan-cooled, but has the advantage of having windows that open; below that is *ekonomi*, which is best avoided unless for very short local journeys, where it may be the only class available. Within trains of the same class, expect variations: newer rolling stock tends to be furnished to a higher standard. Only a very few services have couchettes; one that does is the *Senja Utama Solo*, a useful overnight train between Jakarta, Yogyakarta and Solo.

By bus

Most Indonesians travel by bus. In Java, buses are very frequent and cheap, and can be frighteningly quick (especially at night) with seeming lunatics at the wheel; they nevertheless reach their destination in one piece most of the time. Some routes appear more dangerous than others: Java's north coast highway seems particularly accident-prone. Bus terminals are usually on the outskirts of town, and can be rather miserable places. Touts will usually help you find the correct bus, but you should check that the one you are directed to is in fact the next one departing to your destination, not one that will sit in the terminal for a further hour or two before moving. It is also worth checking the fare with other passengers before departure, as it is not uncommon for the bus conductor to try charging foreigners more than the correct amount.

Long-distance **overnight buses** (*bis malam*) should be booked a day or more in advance. These are usually air-conditioned, sometimes with videos and snacks, and have numbered seats. Booking in advance at the office or agent, you can usually choose the seat you want. The safest seats are in the middle of the bus; the most dangerous are considered to be those at the very front, though for tall foreigners these can have the advantage of extra leg-room.

Local transport

Visitors relying on public transport will quickly discover that there is virtually always some sort of transport available between any two points – though it might be very slow. On the rare occasions where nothing official materialises, you may find yourself being offered a lift on the back of someone's motorcycle in return for a small payment.

Taxis In the larger towns and cities, including Jakarta, Bandung, Surabaya, Yogyakarta, Malang and Denpasar, metered taxis provide the most comfortable way to get around. Always check that the driver resets the meter at the start of the journey. In Jakarta, the passenger pays for any toll-road charges incurred.

City buses A few cities, including Jakarta, Bandung, Yogyakarta and Surabaya, have a network of numbered city bus routes. The buses tend to be extremely full, hot, slow and uncomfortable; they are also the haunt of pick-pockets, and are generally best avoided unless you revel in such a situation.

Becak Found in virtually every town in Java, these pedal-powered tricycles are cheap and fun to use. The fare must be negotiated in advance. In towns like Yogyakarta where hundreds of tourists use *becak*, the starting price is often absurdly high, so hard bargaining is required. But bear in mind that *becak* drivers are poor, the work is hard and hot, and supply always outstrips demand. Hotel staff can usually suggest an appropriate fare between two points.

Bemo, travel, angkot, kolt, mikrolet Different names in different places for minibuses of different shapes and sizes. These are the workhorses of the local transport system in Java, Bali and Lombok. In some towns, such as Bogor, Malang and Mataram, they operate within the city on fixed circuits, with fixed fares, and are numbered (or lettered) according to route. Larger ones are used for short journeys between towns, especially on routes which larger buses cannot manage – such as most mountain routes in Bali and the Wonosobo–Dieng road in Central Java. They are often packed extremely full, and for a tall foreigner can be very uncomfortable; visibility is usually poor, unless you grab the front seat, and drivers can be aggressive in their haste to catch new passengers ahead of the competition. Flag them down anywhere by sticking out your arm and attracting the driver's or loader's eye. They will stop anywhere to let you out; pay as you get out.

Ojek A motorcycle taxi where the paying passenger rides pillion; most common in rural areas. *Ojek* are immensely useful for getting to destinations off the main roads, such as remote candis, waterfalls, volcanoes and national park gates. Licensed *ojek* drivers often wear a brightly coloured waistcoat printed with a number. They tend to gather at junctions on the main road where minor roads are poorly served by other public transport. There is usually a standard price, but this is negotiable; agree the fare before accepting the ride. In more remote areas, where there is no official *ojek* service, it is acceptable to ask a passing motorcyclist for a ride; in such a situation, you should usually offer a fair payment at the end of the journey.

Passengers not used to riding a motorcycle should be aware of the hot exhaust pipe as they mount and dismount; they should also avoid jerky movements which may upset the driver's balance, especially on rough tracks.

Dokar, andong, cidomo, delman Pony-traps of different sizes, with different names, found in several towns. *Dokar* are the small two-wheeled carts found in towns such as Bogor and Denpasar. Larger four-wheeled carriages known as *andong* are found in a few towns. *Cidomo*, found in Lombok, are small carts with two car wheels and pneumatic tyres. Slow and sometimes uncomfortable, these are nevertheless a rather enjoyable way to travel short distances, though not on busy roads in town centres. The price must be negotiated in advance.

Vehicle rentals
You can rent a **car** with or without a driver. The former has obvious advantages, and does not necessarily cost much more. For a single-day rental, it is fairly easy to find a vehicle and driver: in Jakarta, car-and-driver clubs advertise in the

Jakarta Post; in Bogor, vehicles gather at the gates to the Botanical Gardens; in Ubud, Bali, they gather beside the town's main intersection. In most other towns, hotel staff may be able to find a friend with a vehicle which can be chartered for the day, if given sufficient notice. An alternative is to ask a *mikrolet* driver if he is willing to rent himself and his vehicle to you for a day or certain number of hours; another option is to rent through a travel agent (usually for a rather higher price). In each case, negotiate the price in advance, making it extremely clear where you wish to go, for how long you are hiring the vehicle, and whether or not the price includes fuel and the driver's food and drink for the day.

For **self-drive**, the large international firms such as *Hertz* do have offices in Jakarta and Bali, but much better rates can be found with local companies. Recommended is *Toyota Rent a Car*, which has offices in Jakarta, Bandung, Surabaya and Bali and rents vehicles by the day, week, month or year; it can provide insurance and a breakdown recovery service. In Bali there are also scores of small Suzuki jeeps for rent at very low prices. Prices are always negotiable.

Driving in Indonesia is remarkably easy, though it takes a while to become used to it; Western visitors will find that traffic moves more slowly than at home. Always drive defensively and expect anything to happen in front of you: buses overtake on blind corners and vehicles pull out of side roads without pausing to look. Worry less about what happens behind you: that is someone else's responsibility. In an accident, the larger vehicle is almost always considered the guilty party; pedestrians, bicycles and motorcycles are usually considered blameless. There is also a tendency to blame the vehicle driven by the foreigner, though where this is clearly not the case the police will usually behave fairly.

Before renting a vehicle, test-drive it round the block and check carefully for damage to the bodywork and tyres before agreeing to a deal; also ensure the horn, brakes, wipers and lights work properly. To avoid disagreement later, make sure the owner notes down any dents or scrapes the vehicle has already sustained before you set out, and gives you a copy. Check also your responsibilities should the vehicle break down, be stolen, or be damaged in an accident. An international driving permit is required with your national driving licence. At night, the vehicle should ideally be parked in a hotel compound; if left on the street, ensure that the hotel night guard (*satpam* or *penjaga*) watches over it.

While the number of petrol/gas stations (*pompa bensin*) is steadily increasing, they are still rare enough for your tank to run dry if you are careless; if in doubt, fill up. Many old petrol pumps are still operating, whose accuracy is highly dubious; more reliable are the modern digital pumps. In emergency, petrol can be bought from roadside kiosks intended for motorcycles; it is more expensive, and may occasionally be watered down.

Small **motorcycles** can be rented in the main tourist centres – Yogyakarta, Bali, Senggigi and Mataram – and private arrangements can often be made with hotel staff elsewhere. If you are a competent rider, renting a bike can be an ideal way to explore. Costs are low, fuel is cheap and widely available, mechanics are easily found for punctures and simple repairs, and even the smallest bikes can negotiate tracks out of reach to cars. At night you can park them securely inside your hotel compound, or even in your room if necessary. The drawbacks are the other traffic and the problems of travel in the rainy season. A helmet is essential to your safety, and a poor-quality one is usually provided with the bike; if you plan a rental of several weeks, it is worth buying a decent one or even bringing your own from home. An international driving permit valid for motorcycles is a legal requirement. If you are not a regular motorcycle rider, Indonesia is not a good place to learn; incompetent or ill-prepared foreigners on bikes die or suffer serious injuries each year on Bali.

Bicycles can be hired very cheaply in Pangandaran, Yogyakarta, Bali and a few other tourist centres. If you can cope with the climate and traffic, they provide a quick and easy means to travel short distances. Some foreigners – especially Dutch – bring their own. If you do, bring appropriate spares and tools with you; local tyres and tubes may be different sizes.

The rainy season

A single season of unusually heavy rain can destroy a road, reducing smooth asphalt to a cratered moonscape. While main highways are patched up quickly, quiet country lanes may be left unrepaired for a year or more. Be prepared for the roads described in this book to have changed, either for the worse or occasionally for the better.

Street numbers and names

Finding your way to an urban address is not always easy. House numbers are changed frequently, and you may see three different numbers on one building. Sometimes numbering appears to be totally random, and Indonesians often find it easier to use descriptions, not numbers, when giving instructions.

Nevertheless, numbers of offices and hotels, where known, are generally listed in this guide, in the hope that it may make them easier to find. Just do not be surprised if the first '21' you reach is not the one you are seeking; yours may be further along on the other side, between 'no. 174' and 'no. 88'.

Main streets are frequently named after national heroes or other prominent people with long military titles and initials. In the text, such names have been shortened to their briefest common appellation. So Jalan Jenderal Sudirman becomes Jl. Sudirman (or just 'Sudirman' if giving directions to a taxi driver); Jl. Laksamana Laut Martadinata becomes Jl. Martadinata; Jl. Moh. Husni Thamrin becomes Jl. Thamrin. Spelling varies from town to town, and sometimes from one end of the street to another; I have tried to use the spelling most commonly used in any particular location.

The Indonesian language

Bahasa Indonesia ('Indonesian language') is the national language in an archipelago which has hundreds of regional languages and dialects. It is derived from the native language of northeastern Sumatra, which in turn is a descendant of an archaic Malay, dating from the 12C. A huge number of words have been absorbed from elsewhere, especially from other regional languages in the archipelago, such as Javanese. Arabic and Dutch have also provided several thousand words, but the biggest source of new words today is English. The consonants 'f', 'kh', 'sy', 'v' and 'z' all indicate words borrowed from elsewhere.

Pronunciation

Written in the Roman script, Indonesian is easy to read and, apart from a few variations in pronunciation, is fairly simple to speak. Key differences from English include:

- double vowels, whether identical, as '**aa**' in *maaf* (pardon), or different, as '**ae**' as in *daerah* (area), are separated by a glottal stop, so becoming ma'af and da'erah.
- '**ai**' is pronounced somewhere between the English 'ay' in 'bay', and 'uy' in 'buy', as in *pandai* (clever).
- '**au**' is pronounced like the 'ow' in the English 'how', as in *kerbau* (buffalo).
- '**c**' is pronounced 'ch', so the Indonesian word *cat* (paint) is pronounced 'chat'.
- '**e**' represents two different sounds: the neutral 'e' in 'token', as in *empat* (four); and the strong 'e' in 'bet', as in *enak* (delicious). These can only be learnt by usage, as the difference is not shown in the written word.
- '**kh**' is a single phonetic unit, pronounced rather like the soft 'ch' in 'loch'.
- '**ng**' is a single unit pronounced like the 'ng' in 'singing', as in Nganjuk, the East Javan town.
- '**ny**' is a single unit pronounced like the 'ny' in 'canyon', as in the very common Balinese name, Nyoman.
- '**o**' is pronounced like the 'o' in 'moth', and not as the 'o' in 'most'.
- '**r**' is almost always rolled, which for many native English speakers takes a lot of practice.
- '**s**' is always a soft 's', not a hard 'z' sound. Thus *bahasa* (language) is not pronounced 'bahaza'; *rasa* (feeling) is not 'raza'.
- '**sy**' is a single unit, borrowed from Arabic and pronounced 'sh'. Thus *masyarakat* (society) is pronounced much like 'masharakat'.
- '**u**' is pronounced like the 'u' in 'put', and not as the 'u' in 'utter'.

Spelling

A standard, simplified orthography was established in 1972, but old Dutch and pre-1972 Indonesian spellings are still occasionally encountered, particularly in people's names. The old 'tj' ('tjandi') is now written 'c' ('candi'; pronounced 'chandi'). The old 'dj' ('Djakarta') is now written 'j' ('Jakarta'). The old 'oe' ('Soeharto') is now written and pronounced 'u' ('Suharto').

Another confusion is that 'a' in Javanese, when used in the final and penultimate syllables without a final consonant, is pronounced as an 'o'. This is especially relevant to the Javanese names of historical people and places. Thus Prince Diponegoro may be written 'Dipanegara'; the town of Solo is sometimes seen written 'Sala'; and Kartosuro becomes 'Kartasura'. In the text an attempt has been made to spell such words as they are pronounced, though this may mean the transliteration is incorrect.

Learning Indonesian

It is extremely easy to learn a few hundred essential words which can be used to make yourself understood: numbers, greetings, names of food and drinks, question words, and a few general nouns and adjectives can go a long way; your grammar may be nonexistent, but you can communicate to some extent.

For those with the time and determination, several **cassette-based language courses** are available, including those by Berlitz, Linguaphone and Routledge. **Teach-yourself books** can also be found; recommended is the two-volume

Bahasa Indonesia: Introduction to Indonesian Language and Culture by Yohanni Johns (Periplus Editions, Singapore), available in Jakarta and Bali.

An alternative approach is to buy a **phrase book** and a good **dictionary**, and travel through the country with them close at hand. Recommended is the *Kamus Indonesia Inggris* (Indonesian-English Dictionary) by John Echols and Hassan Shadily (3rd ed., Gramedia, Jakarta, 1994) which, with its English-Indonesian companion volume, is available in good bookshops in Java and Bali.

Several **language schools** in Java, especially in Yogyakarta, offer personal tuition at a reasonable price. Standards rise and fall depending on the quality of staff at any one time. Prospective students are advised to visit a couple of schools and speak to current pupils. Schools in Yogyakarta recommended in the past include *Puri* (☎/fax 0274 583789; e-mail:puri@idola.net.id) at Kompleks Kolombo 4, off the east side of Jl. Gejayan on the northeast side of the city; and *Wisma Bahasa* (☎ 0274 588409; e-mail:wisba@yogya.wasantara.net.id) nearby, off Jl. Rajawali.

Some useful words and phrases

Below are a few commonly used words and phrases which you may hear or can easily use yourself.

Greetings and civilities

Good morning (up to about 11.30)	*Selamat pagi*
Good day (11.30–15.00)	*Selamat siang*
Good afternoon (15.00–dusk)	*Selamat sore*
Good evening (after dark)	*Selamat malam*
Goodnight/sleep well	*Selamat tidur*
Welcome	*Selamat datang*
Goodbye (to someone who is leaving)	*Selamat jalan*
Goodbye (if it's you who is leaving)	*Selamat tinggal*
How are you, Salim?	*Bagaimana Salim?*
I'm fine	*Baik*
Excuse me (when seeking attention)	*Permisi*
Sorry	*Maaf*
Please do so/go ahead (an invitation)	*Silakan*
Thank you [very much]	*Terima kasih [banyak]*
Where are you going?	*Mau ke mana?*
Just going for a walk	*Jalan-jalan saja* (a polite response if you don't want to tell a stranger where you are going)
[I'm going] to the market	*[Mau] ke pasar* (a polite response if you are happy to tell the stranger that you are going there)
Do you want to accompany me?	*Mau ikut?* (a polite follow-on question)
Yes, I'll come/no thanks	*Ya, mau/tidak mau*

Simple phrases

Sorry, I don't understand	*Maaf, saya belum paham*
I can't yet speak Indonesian	*Saya belum bisa bicara bahasa Indonesia*
Is there anyone who can speak English?	*Apakah ada yang bisa bicara bahasa Inggris?*

What is your name?	*Nama anda siapa?*
My name is...	*Nama saya...*
Where are you from?	*Anda dari mana?*
I'm from...	*Saya dari...*
Where do you live?	*Anda tinggal di mana?*
I live in...	*Saya tinggal di...*
What do you want to buy?	*Anda mau beli apa?*
I want to buy...	*Saya mau beli...*
How much is it?	*Harganya berapa?*
Wow! Very expensive.	*Aduh! Mahal sekali.*
Can you reduce the price?	*Bisa kurang?*
Yes, I can	*Bisa/boleh*
No, I can't	*Tidak bisa/tidak boleh*
Do you want to eat?	*Mau makan?*
What do you want to eat?	*Mau makan apa?*
I want to eat satay	*Saya mau makan sate*
What do you want to drink?	*Mau minum apa?*
I want to drink iced tea	*Saya mau minum es teh*
I'll have the fried rice	*Saya pesan nasi goreng* (when ordering from a waiter)
Bon appetit!	*Selamat makan!*

Directions

In rural areas especially, directions may be given according to points of the compass; it always pays to know which way you're facing.

Where is...?	*Di mana...?*
Where is the train station/ bus station/airport?	*Di mana stasiun kereta api/stasiun bis/ lapangan terbang?*
Where is the toilet?	*Di mana WC ('way say')?*
Where is the caretaker's house?	*Di mana rumah juru kunci?*
Where is the nearest pharmacy?	*Di mana apotik yang terdekat?*
Over there	*Di sana*
A [very] long way away	*Jauh (sekali)*
About how far from here?	*Kira-kira berapa jauh dari sini?*
About 100m	*Kira-kira seratus meter*
I don't know	*Saya tidak tahu*
North/south	*Utara/selatan*
East/west	*Timur/barat*
You should head south...	*Anda jalan ke selatan...*
On the left side	*Di sebelah kiri*
On the right side	*Di sebelah kanan*
Turn left	*Belok kiri*
Turn right	*Belok kanan*
Straight on (in a general direction)	*Terus*
Straight (without deviating from a straight line)	*Lurus*
Just keep on going straight	*Ikut terus/lurus saja*

Common signs

Open/closed (shop opening hours, etc)	*Buka/tutup*
Ladies/gentlemen (toilets)	*Wanita/laki-laki*
Entrance/exit [gate] (at a hotel, etc)	*[Pintu] masuk/[pintu] keluar*
Parking/car park	*Tempat parkir*
... is forbidden	*Dilarang...*
No parking	*Dilarang parkir*
No entry/Keep out	*Dilarang masuk*
Caution (road sign)	*Awas/Hati-hati*

Time and days

What time does the bus leave?	*Jam berapa bis berangkat?*
At two o'clock	*Jam dua*
Five past six	*Jam enam lebih lima* ('Six o'clock more five')
A quarter past five	*Jam lima seperempat* ('Five o'clock and a quarter')
Half past seven	*Jam setengah delapan* ('Half before eight')
A quarter to nine	*Jam sembilan kurang seperempat* ('Nine o'clock less a quarter')
Ten minutes to eleven	*Jam sebelas kurang sepuluh* ('Eleven o'clock less ten')
Sunday	*Hari minggu*
Monday	*Hari senin*
Tuesday	*Hari selasa*
Wednesday	*Hari rabu*
Thursday	*Hari kamis*
Friday	*Hari jumaat*
Saturday	*Hari sabtu*

 # Health

Outside Jakarta, you cannot expect very sophisticated medical care. Visitors are strongly advised to arrange comprehensive medical insurance which covers repatriation costs in case of serious illness or accident. As a very rough indication, Indonesia is considered a high-risk area for malaria, dengue, rabies (outside Bali and Java) and intestinal worms such as hookworm; and a medium-risk area for typhoid, tuberculosis, diphtheria, polio, hepatitis A and B, typhus, and filariasis. Several of these can be pre-empted with a vaccine before you depart, so it is definitely worth seeking the latest medical advice from your doctor or travel clinic; check too if any vaccinations you may have had previously are in need of an update. **Pregnant women** should seek special advice about all aspects of health care.

Basic precautions

In practice, if you take sensible precautions with food and drink, and with personal hygiene, you will be unlucky to suffer anything worse than a short bout of diarrhoea. Basic common sense applies (though matters are often outside your control): salad vegetables and raw fruit should be washed in clean water, unless peeled or shelled; meat should be thoroughly cooked; non-bottled drinks of uncertain origin should be refused; and ice should generally be avoided, unless you know the water has been boiled prior to freezing. Locally made ice-cream and milk sold by street hawkers are best avoided: properly packaged brands which have been stored appropriately are usually safe.

You should drink plenty of liquid (not beer) to avoid dehydration: at least three or four litres a day is advised. Bottled water is very widely available and is safe to drink, as are bottled, carbonated drinks and beer, drinks in cartons, and hot tea and coffee. You should wash and dry your hands before eating, and aim to eat freshly cooked food; observe the health and hygiene of the cook if eating at a food-stall or handcart; note the popularity of the establishment: a busy place suggests happy, repeat customers and a rapid turnover in food stocks. Food from an expensive hotel is not necessarily safer than that from a handcart: it is often more likely to have been sitting around for longer, gathering flies and bacteria.

Visitors not used to the intense ultraviolet light of the tropical sun should take great care to avoid excessive exposure, which can produce severe sunstroke and sunburn, and can increase the risk of skin cancer; pale skin burns very easily, even in dappled shade. Wear protective clothing, sunglasses and a good sun lotion with both UVA and UVB protection; a wide-brimmed hat can be very useful.

You should wash frequently; Indonesians bathe three or more times each day, and it is a good idea to follow their example. Prickly heat (a very itchy mild rash, found particularly among children and overweight people) is best treated by regular washing in cool water, drying with a talcum powder, and wearing loose cotton clothing. Thrush can be a problem; prevention can be aided by wearing cotton underwear, and keeping the genital area dry and cool. A daily vinegar douche (30ml/litre of water) can relieve the itching; yoghurt may also help. Other fungal infections such as athlete's foot may also be exacerbated by the heat and humidity of the tropics. In cheap hotels especially, where cleaning procedures may be somewhat lax, it is advisable to wear rubber sandals in the bathroom; these are often provided in the room.

Diarrhoea

The most common illness faced by visitors to Indonesia, diarrhoea is most frequently caused simply by a change in diet and water; usually it will clear up by itself after two or three days. Rather less often, it results from bacterial organisms such as *E. coli*, shigella and salmonella, or from intestinal parasites, all of which can be picked up from contaminated food and drink.

In **every** situation, it is extremely important to maintain fluid intake: in the rare situations where diarrhoea is severe enough to be life-threatening, it is your fluid intake which is most crucial to your survival, not treatment with antibiotics or anti-diarrhoeal medicine. Oral rehydration solutions can be bought ready-made (Dioralyte, Rehidrat) or can be made by adding sugar and salt to water, in the ratio of eight level teaspoons of sugar to half a teaspoon of salt in one litre of water.

If diarrhoea persists for longer than five days, or if there is blood in the stool, or if it is accompanied by fever, seek medical advice.

The most common bacteria causing diarrhoea are ***Escherichia coli*** (*E. coli*); an attack rarely lasts more than 48 hours. **Amoebiasis** (amoebic dysentery), caused by a parasitic amoeba in the large intestine, can lead to bleeding and ulceration of the intestine wall. The main symptom is recurrent dysentery, some-times lasting months, with blood and slimy mucus passed with the diarrhoea. Metronidazole (Flagyl), an antibiotic, is the recommended treatment. **Giardiasis** (giardia), caused by a parasite in the small intestine, is also a fairly frequent cause of diarrhoea. Foul-smelling burps, a painfully swollen abdomen, and chronic diarrhoea are symptoms; again, metronidazole is the recommended treatment. If untreated, it can persist for months.

Mosquito-borne illness

Malaria is a parasitic disease which kills c 3 million people worldwide each year, causes acute illness in c 100 million, and infects c 500 million; ignore it at your peril. Risk of infection varies by area: the greatest risk lies in swampy areas, marsh and forest; the risk in cities is less. Malaria is transmitted by the female of several *Anopheles* species of mosquito, which bite at night. They can carry in their saliva a single-celled parasite called *Plasmodium*, four species of which cause disease in humans; the most dangerous is *P. falciparum*, which is usually the cause of cerebral malaria, a potentially fatal disease.

The incubation period for the parasite is usually from about one week to two months, but may be longer, especially if prophylaxis has been used. The main symptoms include fever, chills with sweating, headache and sometimes diar-rhoea. A coma can develop quickly on occasion (especially with *P. falciparum*), so if you have any of these symptoms, insist on having a blood sample taken (even though the cause may be something else entirely). It is wise to act promptly, because the severity of illness is generally related to the number of parasites in the blood. No anti-malarial prophylaxis gives complete protection, so even if you have been taking this as recommended, seek early diagnosis and treatment.

If you think you have malaria, seek medical advice immediately. Preventive behaviour should include:

- Use anti-malarial drugs as recommended by your doctor or travel clinic. The prophylaxis recommended by the WHO for Indonesia is chloroquine (Avloclor, Nivaquine) and proguanil (Paludrine), taken in combination; the chloroquine course should start one week before departure and proguanil one day before; just as importantly, the dosage must be continued for four weeks after you return to a non-malarial zone. As no prophylaxis provides complete protec-tion, the following precautions are also very important.
- Always sleep under a mosquito net, if one is available. Ideally, you should have your own net, impregnated with a pesticide.
- After dark, wear long trousers/pants, a long-sleeved shirt, socks and shoes; put mosquito repellent on exposed skin.
- Sleeping in an air-conditioned room reduces the likelihood of being bitten.
- In a fan-cooled room, burn a mosquito coil (*obat nyamuk bakar*; often provided by the hotel on request) beneath the windows or by the bathroom door.
- A fever which occurs in the year after you return home could be malaria; you must inform your doctor or clinician that you have been in a malarial zone.

Dengue is a virus spread from person to person in both urban and rural environ-ments by the female *Aedes aegypti* mosquito. Dengue has become increasingly prevalent in Java, Bali and Lombok in the past few years. The mosquito bites during the day, so there is little preventive action you can take; there is no vaccine available. After about a week of incubation, there is a sudden onset of fever, headache and severe joint and muscle pains (from which it gets its alternative name, 'break-bone fever'). The initial fever is followed within days by a rash spreading from the trunk of the body to the face and limbs. The fever usually subsides within a week and the victim then recovers; complete rest and frequent fluid intake are advised. To relieve the pain, take paracetamol, *not* drugs like aspirin or ibuprofen, which might aggravate abnormal bleeding.

Dengue haemorrhagic fever, a much more severe form of dengue, is responsible for many deaths in Indonesia, but the chances of a foreign visitor catching it are extremely rare, as it results from recurrent infection by specific strains of the virus.

Viral hepatitis

The different hepatitis viruses all cause illness resulting from acute inflammation of the liver. The first signs may be headache, fever, chills and fatigue, followed a few days later by vomiting, nausea and abdominal pains, dark urine, pale faeces and jaundice; in some cases, complete liver failure and coma may follow.

Hepatitis A, transmitted through faecally-contaminated food and drink, can be prevented by a reliable vaccine; this is strongly advised. If no vaccine is available, an injection of gamma globulin offers short-term protection. **Hepatitis B**, which can be transmitted through sexual activity, needle-sharing, blood transfusion and injections, etc, is also vaccine-preventable; the vaccine is recommended for all frequent travellers to endemic areas (such as Indonesia), health workers, and those resident in endemic areas for more than six months.

Hepatitis E, though not causing chronic liver damage, can be extremely dangerous during pregnancy. There is no vaccine available, so you must rely on the general hygiene precautions listed above.

AIDS and STDs

AIDS – the acquired immunodeficiency syndrome – is the late stage of infection caused by the human immunodeficiency virus (HIV). The virus attacks the immune system, thus reducing the body's ability to fight other infections and cancers. Once infected with HIV, virtually all people will develop AIDS, and all will be potentially infectious to other people.

The virus is found in blood, vaginal fluids and semen, and is passed either as a sexually-transmitted disease (STD), or through blood transfusions, or through blood on unsterilised needles and other skin-piercing instruments. It is *not* spread by social contact, by sharing food utensils, through swimming pools, toilet seats, mosquitoes, or through food-hawkers and restaurant workers infected with HIV.

Protection is gained by abstaining from sex or by practising safe sex with a condom, and by avoiding high-risk activities such as drug-injecting. By practising safe sex, you also greatly reduce the risk of contracting other sexually-transmitted diseases.

Creatures to avoid

Hookworms of various types infect c 600 million people worldwide. The larva usually penetrates the skin through the foot, so you should not walk barefoot on soil, grass or sandy ground. The larva moves through the bloodstream to the lungs, where it can cause a cough, before moving through the air passages and oesophagus to the lining of the small intestine, where it survives by sucking blood. It can grow to c 1cm and live for nine years. A chronic case may cause anaemia, though in a person with an adequate diet it may be many months or even a year or more before this becomes apparent. The worms can be eliminated with drugs: the recommended treatment is mebendazole.

Cockroaches contaminate food with their liquid faeces, which can carry *E. coli*, salmonella and staphylococcus. Of the c 3500 species found in the world, only two are particularly common in Java, Bali and Lombok, but they are extremely robust, numerous and can survive almost anywhere.

The **domestic dog** is the sole known reservoir host to rabies in Indonesia; rabies is rare in Java and, perhaps surprisingly in view of all the stray dogs, extremely rare in Bali. In the early 1980s c 35 deaths from rabies were reported per year in Java – from a human population numbering more than 90 million; the number of deaths has almost certainly declined further since then. Only in Lombok should you take special care to avoid dogs; fortunately, they are few. If you are bitten, wash and disinfect the wound immediately and go straight to a doctor.

Dangerous **snakes** include the ground pit viper and the white-lipped pit viper; king cobra and common cobra; banded krait and Malayan krait; several species of venomous sea snakes; and the reticulated python and rock python, which can kill a human by constriction. The kraits, cobras and vipers are reportedly fairly common in scrub (though I have never encountered one), so if walking in thick bush, wear sturdy shoes and long trousers/pants, and watch the path. If bitten, do not try to suck out or cut out the poison, do not apply a tourniquet, and do not go in search of the snake. If the bite is on a limb, the best action is to straighten the limb, bandage it firmly along the length between the wound and the trunk of the body, and go immediately to hospital; the limb should be moved as little as possible.

Spiders include three species of tarantula, which may look frightening but are not considered dangerous. Several **scorpion** species can be found in houses or under tree bark; all can inflict a painful sting from the tail, but this is seldom fatal. Wash and disinfect the wound at once, take a simple painkiller such as paracetamol, and go straight to a doctor. **Leeches** can be an annoyance in damp rainforest; while not dangerous, they can find their way onto parts of your body you would prefer them not to. They are best removed by applying salt, alcohol, vinegar or a lighted cigarette till they drop off. If pulled off, their mouth parts often remain in the wound, which can become infected. To discourage them, apply insect repellent to skin, clothing and boots, or rub moist, coarse tobacco on the skin of your feet and legs.

Water sports hazards

Divers need to be aware of dangers in the sea, including various **sea snakes**, **jellyfish**, **stingrays**, **morays**, **lion fish** and **scorpion fish**, and perhaps the occasional **tiger shark**; it is always worth heeding local advice about possible dangers. Snorkellers should beware of sunburn on their backs and legs if left exposed while swimming, and the problems caused by coral cuts if not properly cleaned and dressed; they should also wear shoes to avoid the agony of treading on sea urchin spines. Much of Java's south coast is unsafe for swimming because of strong rip currents; before swimming anywhere, seek local advice.

Traffic accidents

Road accidents are the main cause of death among travellers. On public transport, there is little preventive action you can take, except to sit near the centre of the bus or *bemo*, or to actually get off and wait for another if the driver seems particularly suicidal or incompetent. In Bali, most fatal accidents involving travellers are caused by inexperienced tourists riding motorcycles. The winding, congested, mountainous lanes of Bali are not the ideal place to learn to ride a bike.

First-aid kit

While most common medicines can be found in pharmacies locally, they may be hard to find in an emergency. The following items are best brought from home: an anti-diarrhoeal agent such as loperamide hydrochloride (Imodium), which may be used to temporarily stop diarrhoea on long journeys; antiseptic cream; oral rehydration salts; painkillers (paracetamol, ibuprofen, aspirin, etc); malarial prophylaxis; insect repellent (in the UK, non-toxic Mosi-guard Natural is recommended); sun lotion and aftersun cream/gel; calamine (for sunburn and bites); a few needles and syringes; a disinfectant and wound dressings; and condoms. Ideally, visitors should have a dental check before departure.

Diabetics are advised to bring all needles and insulin from home; a letter from your doctor stating that you have diabetes (*diabet* or *penyakit kencing manis*) is also a good idea, in case customs officials question your needles, syringes, tablets, etc. Note that there are few sugar-free cold drinks available except water, and many Indonesian dishes contain sugar. In the UK, the BDA (☎ 020 7 323 1531) can provide information for diabetics visiting Indonesia.

 # Crime and personal security

Theft by stealth is the main problem, although the economic downturn of the late 1990s has led to more frequent crime against foreigners, accompanied, unfortunately, by occasional violence. Pickpockets hang around bus and train stations, and work on crowded buses; hotel staff very occasionally steal from bedrooms. In tourist centres, specially Bali, beware of young bag-snatchers on motorcycles; bags are best held firmly in the hand, with a shoulder strap as extra protection. Don't bring anything you can't afford to lose.

Visitors who flaunt their wealth are bound to attract unwelcome attention: only minimal jewellery should be worn; cameras and other valuables should be guarded at all times. Rooms in cheaper hotels and *losmen* sometimes lock with a padlock; it is advisable to travel with your own.

Money is best carried, not in a wallet in the hip pocket, but as a bundle of loose notes in a buttoned or zipped chest pocket, or at least a front trouser pocket, where you can see if someone is attempting to rob you. For long journeys on buses or trains it can be wise to carry money, passport and air tickets in a money belt round your waist beneath your clothing. At other times, it is usually best to bury them deep in your luggage or deposit them in the hotel safe. Increasing numbers of hotels now have safety boxes in each room, but if the safe is communal, ask the hotel employee to sign a written record of what you are depositing.

Serious crime against foreigners is very rare – but it does happen. Rape and murder of tourists have occurred in the past, and it is important to avoid situations which leave you at risk. Single women are especially vulnerable, and should avoid walking alone late at night. Visitors who get extremely drunk, or interfere with local women, or insult local religious beliefs, are asking for trouble. Ingenious crooks are constantly thinking up new scams. In Bali, beware of people telling you that your hire-car wheels are loose or you've got an oil leak which they can fix.

Postal and telecoms services

The postal service
The system is reasonably efficient, though slow, but it is unwise to post valuable items. Although a registered postal service is available, such items are best sent via a private courier company and should be insured against loss.

If you have the time, it is always safest to take a letter for posting to the post office yourself; ask the clerk to frank it in front of you. An unstamped letter, left together with the money for a stamp, may well go astray from a hotel reception desk, even at a five-star hotel in Jakarta. Good-quality postcards are widely available in the tourist centres, and aerograms can be bought at most post offices. In the resorts of Kuta, Sanur, Ubud and Lovina on Bali, private postal agents provide most of the usual services and are often faster than the post offices. In the larger towns, including Jakarta, Yogyakarta, Bandung and Surabaya, entrepreneurs offer useful parcel-wrapping services outside the post office; you bring the goods, they provide robust wrapping materials for a reasonable fee, and will then, if needed, help you have the parcel weighed, stamped and franked in the post office.

Telecoms
An absurdly high surcharge is often made by hotels for international phone calls, so it might be worth checking the rates before embarking on a long call home. Virtually every town, large or small, has a 24-hour **telecoms office** from which you can make international and long-distance national calls, and there are many privately-run **telephone offices** (*wartel*), which charge the same rates. In most cases, a digital display on the telephone unit tells you how much the call is costing; certain times of day are cheaper than others. For national calls, you can use phone cards in a growing number of public phones; they are sold at a premium, but enable you to avoid queues in the *wartel*. Faxes can be sent from most larger *wartel*; **e-mail** can be sent or received at a growing number of four- or five-star hotels, and – in Bali at least – at a few *wartel* and Internet cafés.

Time zones
Indonesia is spread across three time zones:

GMT+7   **Java**, **Madura**, Sumatra and West Kalimantan.
GMT+8   **Bali**, **Lombok**, Nusa Tenggara, Sulawesi and the rest of Kalimantan.
GMT+9   Moluccas and Irian Jaya.

Sporting and leisure activities

Java, Bali and Lombok offer a huge variety of activities, especially for the outdoors enthusiast. On Bali in particular, there is a wide range of water sports, including surfing, diving, dinghy sailing and windsurfing.

Birdwatching More than 500 bird species are found on the islands, including more than 30 endemic species, and there are many easily accessible birding sites. Contact the office of *BirdLife International* in Bogor (see p 224) for further information.

Caving There are several extensive cave systems in Java, including the Luweng Jaran complex with more than 25km of passages and chambers; a permit is required to visit those caves not open to tourists. Contact Dr. R.K.T. Ko of the Federation of Indonesian Speleological Activities (Finspac) at PO Box 55, Bogor (☎ 0251 254376; fax 255343) for further information.

Diving and snorkelling Bali is an excellent diving centre, with eight or nine main dive sites. Beginners' courses are available, and equipment can be hired at reasonable prices. Several diving companies can arrange boat charters to superb reefs further east. Java has a few good diving areas, notably round parts of the Seribu archipelago off the coast from Jakarta.

Golf There are beautiful golf courses on all three islands; of special note are the *Bali Handara Kosaido Country Club* near Lake Bratan on Bali, and the *GEC Rinjani Country Club* on Lombok.

Surfing Bali, eastern Java and Lombok offer some of the world's finest surfing. Grajagan, on the southeast tip of Java, is a regular fixture on the world surfing championships circuit; the Bukit peninsula on Bali attracts scores of experienced surfers to its many breaks.

Volcano climbing There are more than 30 volcanoes in Java, Bali and Lombok, many of them active, and almost all of them climbable. Visitors planning to climb several should bring their own camping equipment. **A warning**: volcanoes can be **extremely dangerous** and unpredictable; tourists have been killed or severely injured on several occasions in the past few years. Any ascent should be planned carefully, and local police, park rangers or villagers should be consulted for the latest advice. Some volcanoes safe to climb at the time of this writing may have erupted subsequently; others may have returned to a slumbering state. Always tell someone where you are going.

White-water rafting At least half a dozen operators in Bali run half-day rafting trips along various rivers in southern Bali. Others run trips on the Citarik river near Pelabuhanratu in West Java (see p 233), and on the Progo river in Magelang in Central Java (see p 281).

Spectator sports Soccer and badminton are both extremely popular sports nationwide. On Bali you can watch the rather gory spectacle of a cockfight; on Madura and in East Java near Bondowoso you can watch Madurese bull racing. On Lombok, you can occasionally see pony racing at a track near Cakranegara. In the past, Java has hosted international tennis tournaments and motorcycle Grands Prix; these may not continue in the current economic climate.

Public holidays and annual festivals

Indonesia has 12 or 13 national public holidays within one Gregorian calendar year, comprising a variety of secular, Muslim, Christian, Buddhist and Hindu festivals. At such times, trains, flights and inter-city buses become extremely full as people flock home to their families. National holidays include:

- 1 Jan — **New Year's day**
- Late March to late April — **Nyepi** (Balinese new year). First day of the month of Kedasa in the Balinese lunar calendar. **Note**: Nyepi is a day of silence and stillness when everyone in Bali stays at home. **Do not count on exceptions being made for tourists**, who are generally expected to stay within their hotel compound and refrain from making a loud noise.

  On the eve of Nyepi, Balinese lay out offerings to the evil spirits at major road junctions and display crude, larger-than-life-size dolls, *ogoh-ogoh*. From late afternoon, a loud clamour arises through the island as everyone bangs whatever they can to make as much noise as possible; as dusk falls, flaming torches are brandished, and a frenzied uproar begins. The intention is to wake the demons so they might find the offerings laid for them. The silence on Nyepi, New Year's Day, when everyone stays quietly in the home, is seen either as a way to encourage any remaining demons to believe that all the people have left and there is no-one left to torment; or it is a sign of calm relief that the evil spirits have been satisfied for another year.

- March/April — **Good Friday**
- May/June — **Ascension Day**
- mid-May–mid-June — **Wesak** (anniversary of the Buddha's birth, enlightenment and death); celebrated on the full moon
- 17 August — **Independence Day** (*hari proklamasi kemerdekaan*)
- 25 December — **Christmas Day** (*hari natal*)

Festivals governed by the Islamic calendar advance 10 or 11 days each year as the Islamic year has only 355 or 354 days; it is thus possible for any one of these to occur twice within one Gregorian calendar year. The following are all national holidays:

- **Idul Fitri** (marking the end of the month-long fast of Ramadan, and the start of Lebaran). During 2000–2004 it advances from early April to late November. The most important Islamic holiday, celebrated with feasting and visits to friends and relatives. In the days prior to the holiday, public transport is absolutely packed.
- **Idul Adha** (festival of sacrifice, celebrating the submission of Abraham to Allah). During 2000–2004 it advances from late March to early February. Goats are slaughtered at the mosques; the meat is usually given to the poor.
- **Tahun Baru Hijriah** (Islamic new year). During 2000–2004 it advances from early April to late February.
- **Maulud Nabi Muhammad** (birthday of Muhammad). During 2000–2004 it advances from mid-June to early May.
- **Isra Mikraj Nabi Muhammad** (ascension of Muhammad). During 2000–2004 it advances from late October to mid-September.

Regional festivals

Other festivals of special note for visitors include **Galungan** and **Kuningan** in Bali, celebrated every 210 days in the Pawukon 30-week cycle. Galungan, on the Wednesday of Dunggulan, the 11th week (28/2/01, 26/9/01, 24/4/02, 20/11/02, 18/6/03, 14/1/04, 11/8/04), marks the start of a 10-day festival, ending on Kuningan, during which the deified ancestors of the Balinese descend to their former homes to be entertained with offerings and prayers. Shops and schools close in the days before Galungan, and Balinese flock home from Java and other islands; long bamboo poles (*penjor*) are hung with offerings along the roadside, and women make intricate offerings of brightly coloured rice dough which are presented on Galungan; the following day, everyone visits friends and relatives. This is one of the most interesting times to visit Bali.

Also worth noting is Tumpek Landep, which occurs once every 210 days (on the Saturday of Landep, the second week of the 30-week calendar), on which Balinese make an offering to their weapons; today, these include cars, motorcycles and trucks, as well as the more traditional krises. You will see offerings tied to the radiator grills of cars and the mirrors of motorcycles, etc, and owners of valuable krises will present a special offering to their family shrine.

In Yogyakarta, colourful processions take place during the **Garebeg Mulud** festival on the birthday of Muhammad; **Garebeg Puasa** occurs on Idul Fitri, and **Garebeg Besar** on Idul Adha.

Additional information

Disabled travellers

No special provision is made for disabled travellers outside the four- and five-star hotels in the main cities and resorts. Public road transport is virtually impossible to use for people with wheelchairs or those who have difficulty flexing their legs and stooping. To travel in comfort it is really necesssary to hire a car or minivan. A Kijang or one of the many types of minibus is ideal, with better head- and leg-room than a standard sedan. They are easily and cheaply found on Bali and the main tourist centres on Java (including Bogor, Bandung, Yogyakarta, etc); see relevant chapters for details.

For pedestrians and wheelchair users, steps and uneven surfaces are frequent obstacles: pavements often have very high curbs with no ramps; most buildings are raised at least two or three steps above street level, and again, ramps are very rare. The best lodgings and many mid-priced hotels have lifts, though on Bali and Lombok at least (and to a lesser extent on Java) accommodation is very often only one storey high anyway.

In the UK, *RADAR* (☎ 020 7250 3222) sells a guide to air travel for the disabled and can provide some information about a few hotels with facilities for disabled guests.

Women travellers

Western women in Indonesia are occasionally pestered by Indonesian men. This happens more often to women travelling alone, but can happen when with a companion. Usually it takes the form of harmless but persistent staring and occasional catcalling, but men may purposely touch or rub against the woman's breasts – usually in a situation where it can be passed off as accidental, as in a crowded railway carriage corridor or on a shared bus seat. One way to respond is to say, in an offended voice loud enough for others nearby to hear: 'Kurang ajar!' ('How uncivilised!'). Despite such hassles, violence against women is extremely rare – though it has happened.

Tourists can happily wear minidresses, figure-hugging shorts and bikini tops in the beach resorts of Kuta and Sanur, where the locals have become used to it (and where young Javanese men come on holiday especially to appreciate such sights), but to dress like this elsewhere is likely to be seen as highly provocative: away from the beach or night-club, only *filles de joie* expose large areas of bare flesh. Suggested practical clothing includes long cotton skirts or baggy trousers/pants, and loose blouses.

Some Indonesian men, observing the relatively revealing dress of Western women, their capacity and willingness to drink alcohol, and their openness in talking with male strangers, and perhaps influenced by Hollywood seduction scenes, may on occasion misinterpret such behaviour as a come-on, and assume it to be an invitation for a more intimate relationship. This is true especially in the beach resorts of Bali, where beach boys hang out in search of lonely (and comparatively wealthy) Western female companions who may be seeking a romantic tryst. To avoid possible later ill-feeling or embarrassment, make clear your position at the outset, should the conversation turn in that direction. Needless to say, the vast majority of men are extremely polite and friendly.

Embassies and consulates in Indonesia

In case of emergencies, your embassy or consulate may be able to help. If you have broken the law, do not expect sympathy; staff may, however, be able to recommend or provide a lawyer.

Australia: Jl. Rasuna Said, kav. C15–16, **Jakarta** (☎ 021 522 7111); consulate at Jl. Moh. Yamin 4, Renon, Denpasar, **Bali** (☎ 0361 235092/3).

Britain: Jl. Thamrin 75, **Jakarta**; consulates at Jl. Agus Salim 128, **Jakarta** (☎ 021 390 7484); and Standard Chartered Bank, Jl. Sudirman 57, **Surabaya** (☎ 031 520311). In **Bali**, the Australian consulate can assist British citizens.

Canada: Wisma Metropolitan I, 5th fl., Jl. Sudirman, **Jakarta** (☎ 021 525 0709). For emergencies in **Bali**, the Australian consulate at Renon can assist Canadian citizens.

Netherlands: Jl. Rasuna Said, kav. S3, **Jakarta** (☎ 021 525 1515); consulates at Jl. Diponegoro 25, Bandung; Jl. Pemuda 54, **Surabaya** (☎ 031 531 1162); and Jl. Raya Imam Bonjol 599-A, Kuta, **Bali** (☎ 0361 751517).

USA: Jl. Medan Merdeka Selatan 5, **Jakarta** (☎ 021 344 2211); consulate-general at Jl. Dr. Sutomo 33, **Surabaya** (☎ 031 582287/8); and consular agent at Jl. Hayam Wuruk 188, Denpasar, **Bali** (☎ 0361 233605).

Opening hours

Working hours vary enormously. If you have important business at a government office, bank, post office, travel agent or any other office, it is best to visit between 09.00 and 10.30. Government offices generally open Mon–Thur, 08.00–14.00; Fri–Sat, 08.00–11.00 or 12.00. Banks may open at 08.00 or 08.30. Shopping centres usually open daily at 09.00 or 10.00 and close at some time between 19.00 and 21.30. Municipal markets are usually active soon after sunrise.

Film and photography

Colour print film is widely available on Java and Bali, and in Mataram on Lombok. Colour slide film is rather less common, but can be found in the main cities and tourist centres. For black-and-white film, or unusual formats, it is best to bring your own stock. Film purchased locally is best bought from air-conditioned shops where it may not have been exposed to constant heat and humidity; prices are negotiable, especially if buying more than one film. For most situations, standard ISO100/21° film is suitable; check the expiry date on the box.

Processing is generally of a fairly high standard, but can occasionally be disappointing; if the films are valuable to you, it is probably safer to take them home for developing at a lab whose work you know.

The best times for taking photographs are before about 10.00 and after about 15.00; in the middle of the day, the sun is so bright it can leave photos looking very washed out. A polarising filter may improve matters.

News media

The main English-language newspaper is the *Jakarta Post*, a broadsheet which provides generally good coverage of national and international affairs. In the

Suharto era, when outspoken news media were under constant threat of closure, the *Jakarta Post* mastered the art of subterfuge, unerringly conveying its criticisms without spelling them out. Today, in a more liberal climate, its criticisms have become more robust. Greatly inferior are the *Indonesian Times* and the *Indonesian Observer*. The *Jakarta Post* is available in most of the larger towns on Java (though it may arrive in the late afternoon), and in the main tourist centres on Bali. On Lombok, it can be found only in the capital and Senggigi.

There is a huge variety of Indonesian-language newspapers and magazines, and in the main business and tourist centres one can find international papers, including *Newsweek, Asiaweek, International Herald Tribune* and the *Far Eastern Economic Review*.

In Bali, there are several free listings magazines which provide useful coverage of new restaurants, shops, festivals and activities. Titles come and go; current ones include the monthly *Bali Kini* and *Bali Plus*, and the bimonthly *Bali Echo*.

There is little English-language radio or TV, but short-wave radios can pick up Radio Australia, the BBC World Service and Voice of America, and the better hotels have satellite TV.

Local customs and behaviour

There are many things a foreigner might do which can make an Indonesian feel aggrieved, disgusted, or even physically sick. In tourist centres, allowance is made for visitors' uncouth ways; elsewhere, you may upset people unknowingly. To avoid the worst *faux pas*, follow the suggestions below.

- Eat, touch other people, and pass objects or money with your right hand; your left is for cleaning yourself in the bathroom.
- Nudity in public, even on a beach, is considered highly offensive.
- Pointing a finger at someone or something is rude; use your right thumb resting on the clenched fist.
- Standing with legs apart and hands on hips or folded across your chest is considered arrogant and rude; in general, a display of humility and modesty is best.
- A show of anger or impatience towards anyone from whom you seek a service will, in most cases, do your cause more harm than good, especially when dealing with officialdom.
- Avoid insulting anyone's religion; religion plays an extremely important role in people's lives and offence is easily taken. To enter a Balinese temple, visitors must wear a sarong and a sash; to enter a mosque, you must cover your legs and preferably wear a long-sleeved shirt.
- It is very rude to touch someone's head – even that of a child. For many people, it is the abode of the spirits and is to be respected. Equally, it is offensive to point your feet – spiritually, the lowest part of the body – at someone. If sitting cross-legged, check where your raised foot is pointing.
- Take off your shoes when entering someone's home or a mosque.
- Pick your teeth with a toothpick, not your fingers, and cover your mouth with the other hand while doing so; otherwise your companions may feel sick.
- Likewise, blowing your nose in public may sicken bystanders.
- Beckon someone with your fingers pointed downwards, not upwards as would be normal at home.
- When stopping in a vehicle to ask directions, it is rude to call out your question from the car; climb out and walk over to your potential informant. This can be

irritating if stopping every five minutes, but to do otherwise is considered discourteous.

Tipping and donations

Tips are not expected in *warung*, cafés and restaurants, though some smarter ones add a service charge to the bill. In a few top-class hotels, the bellboy may expect a tip for carrying your luggage; this is not normal practice elsewhere. Taxi drivers invariably claim to have no change and expect you to round up the fare to the next 500 or 1000 rupiah. Bus drivers may try the same tactic; it is not so acceptable socially for them to take more than the correct fare, as the bus is traditionally the poor man's transport.

Car drivers especially are often under pressure to tip for all sorts of small services, even if they are not required. A man who cleans your car in the hotel car park without asking is hoping you will feel grateful enough to reward him. With so many people struggling to earn a living, it would be churlish to refuse. Bear in mind also that it is all too easy for an aggrieved person to put a long scratch down the side of the car in your absence.

In some situations it is polite to make a donation. This often happens when visiting *candis* in Java; the caretaker will unlock the site for you and, when you come to depart, may ask you to sign the visitors' book. It is appropriate to leave a reasonable donation tucked inside the book. If caretakers are specially helpful, it is worth being specially generous; they are usually kindly people who are pleased to receive interested visitors, especially from abroad. If no book is produced, a donation (a few small notes, folded together) should still be given.

At the other end of the spectrum is the forced 'donation'. At some popular tourist sites a donation is obligatory, and someone will produce a book in which are written huge sums apparently given by past visitors. Disregard the amounts, and give what you feel the site is worth to you. It is all too easy to add two or three noughts to a number in the book after the donor has left.

Finally, there are 'guides'. At some sites, a young man (or less frequently a woman) will latch on to you through casual conversation, and slowly become your guide. If you want one, this is fine, though you must expect to tip them afterwards. If you prefer to explore the site alone, make this very clear from the outset.

BACKGROUND INFORMATION

Physical geography

The vast archipelagic nation of Indonesia straddles the equator for c 5000km from west to east. A government survey published in January 1997 counted 17,508 islands, of which two-thirds are unnamed and uninhabited; the land mass of the islands covers almost two million square kilometres. **Java**, the largest island described in this book, is the fifth largest in the country, somewhat larger than New York State but slightly smaller than England, and home to nearly 120 million people. Its eastern neighbour, **Bali**, less than one-twentieth as large, covers c 5500 sq km, comparable to Delaware State; **Lombok**, next in line to the east, is slightly smaller.

Indonesia is one of the most volcanically active regions in the world, with 75 historically active volcanoes. One is on Lombok, two are on Bali, and 21 are on Java. All three islands are part of the Sunda Arc, a tectonic plate boundary that stretches more than 3000km from the northwest tip of Sumatra, through Java, Bali and Lombok to the Banda Sea. The volcanism results from the subduction of the Indian Ocean crust beneath the Sunda Plate – part of a series of tectonic plate collisions and separations which produce volcanic belts along the Pacific rim through the Philippines, Japan and Russia's Kamchatka peninsula. Java appeared c 5–26 million years ago as a string of volcanic islands which eventually merged to form a single island. In the Pliocene epoch (1.6–5 million years ago), submarine volcanoes emerged from the sea to form Bali and Lombok.

Cataclysmic eruptions have occurred in historical times, notably from Krakatau in 1883 and from Tambora on Sumbawa in 1815; both caused catastrophic loss of life, but pale into insignificance compared with Toba on Sumatra, which exploded c 71,000 years ago, sending perhaps 2800 cu km of ash into the sky and leaving behind a lake covering more than 1000 sq km.

It appears that Toba's eruption was followed by a six-year-long volcanic winter and a thousand-year period of relentless cold, with temperatures significantly lower than during the last glacial maximum, 18,000–21,000 years ago. Geneticists have suggested the world's hominid population fell to less than 10,000 breeding females at this time.

Despite their huge potential for destruction, Indonesia's volcanoes have also been immensely productive, exuding lava flows and lahars, which over time are eroded and washed onto the plains to produce fertile basaltic soils. Fine volcanic ash, deposited far from the craters, provides a mineral-rich top-dressing. It is in part due to such activity that rice farmers on Java, Bali and Lombok can consistently feed more than 130 million people.

In contrast to the fertile alluvial plains, large areas along the southern coasts of Java, Bali and Lombok are limestone, resulting from the uplift of ancient coral reefs. Today these are some of the poorest and most barren parts of the islands: the Gunung Kidul region southeast of Yogyakarta; the Blambangan peninsula at

Java's southeastern tip; the Bukit peninsula on Bali; Nusa Penida; the Ekas peninsula and the region round Pengantap on Lombok.

 # Flora and fauna

Indonesia straddles the most famous faunistic boundary in the world, known as **Wallace's Line**. The English naturalist, Alfred Russel Wallace (1823–1913), noticed in the 1850s that there appeared to be a major change in fauna – especially avifauna – between the eastern and western islands of the archipelago. He placed the boundary through the Lombok Strait, between Bali and Lombok, and extrapolated it northward between Borneo and Sulawesi. This line was subsequently modified by other naturalists, notably L.F. de Beaufort, who proposed an alternative boundary, Lydekker's Line, through the Timor Sea and Arafura Sea and passing northward between the Moluccas and Irian Jaya.

Further refinements to the theory were made in the 1940s by E. Mayr, who argued that both Wallace's and Lydekker's lines were of similar significance: Wallace's marked the boundary eastward from which Asian faunal species become relatively scarce, while Lydekker's marked the similar frontier for Australian fauna migrating westwards; the area between the two lines was a region of transition where the two faunas met, and where those species most adept at dispersal and most able to appropriate new habitats, could penetrate most deeply. Thus the tiger reached no further east than Bali, while certain beetles spread eastward to New Guinea and the Solomon Islands beyond; cockatoos from Australia reached westward to Lombok, but did not cross the Lombok Strait to Bali, while the cassowary's range extended only to Seram in the Moluccas.

The distribution of flora in Indonesia is rather different: although the archipelago's flora is far from homogeneous, the most striking floristic boundary is not found within the island chain but between Malesia (the biogeographic region stretching from Malaysia to New Guinea, which includes Indonesia) and Australia.

Mammals

There are more than 150 known mammal species in Java, Bali and Lombok, of which about 20 per cent are endemic to one or more of the islands. Almost certainly there are others still unrecorded: a completely new species of fruit bat was discovered in West Java in 1973, and other bats and a rat were found in the early 1990s.

Notable species include the **Javan rhino**, which can weigh two tonnes, and is now found only in Ujung Kulon National Park on Java's southwest tip; only c 50 individuals remain, and because of their extremely slow reproduction rates, it seems almost inevitable that the population will eventually become extinct. Several hundred **leopards** survive in Java's national parks and on the forested slopes of volcanoes, beyond the reach of most humans. Endemic **primates** include the beautiful but very rare Javan gibbon and Javan leaf monkey (*surili*), found mainly in lowland forest in West Java, and the more widespread ebony leaf monkey (*lutung*), whose range extends to mangroves and montane forests; Gunung Halimun National Park provides the best remaining habitat for the gibbon and *surili*. Other primates include the charming, nocturnal slow loris and the very common long-tailed macaque.

Other endemic species include many bats and rats; the **Javan** or **Timor deer**; the dainty **Bawean deer**, known only from the island of Bawean off the north Java coast; and the very rare **Javan pig**, similar in appearance to the common wild boar. In the 19C, the Javan pig was traditionally hunted using bait made with the solid residues left from brewing rice wine; the drunk pig could be easily caught. Today the pigs are usually poisoned. The Javan deer population is steadily dwindling as more of its natural savanna habitat is converted to rice, coffee and sugar cane. In the mid-19C, the German-born naturalist, Junghuhn, reported seeing 50,000 deer on Gunung Argopuro's Yang Plateau, and in a single day counted 75 herds; such numbers will never be seen again. The Bawean deer is one of the world's rarest deer, though visitors may see specimens in some of Java's zoos.

Banteng are a species of large wild cattle weighing nearly one tonne, readily seen in several of Java's national parks and reserves, including Ujung Kulon, Baluran and Alas Purwo. The **wild dog** is present in the same parks, but is much harder to find.

Large **bat colonies** can be seen at several caves and tree roosts in Java and Bali. Several species navigate by highly sensitive, radar-like echolocation, emitting a clicking sound which in some species is audible to the human ear; objects as small as 1mm across can be detected. In defence, some moths can detect echolocating bats from 40m away; the bats in turn may click only intermittently, to give their prey less warning.

The tiger's fate

Both the Bali tiger and Javan tiger are now considered extinct, yet in the 17C and 18C tigers were considered a pest on Java. In 1659, they were reported to have killed 14 woodcutters near Batavia and several slaves at Ancol. A century later, the government paid for the killing of 27 tigers and leopards which had become a menace just outside the city walls. Hunting in the 19C and early 20C by men like the Ledeboer brothers—notorious big-game hunters who claimed to have shot 100 tigers between 1910 and 1940—as well as a steady shrinkage of prime habitat as the human population grew, brought about their demise. By the late 1970s, it was believed only three Javan tigers remained—in Meru Betiri National Park. Subsequently, there have been occasional newspaper reports of individual sightings, notably on the slopes of Gunung Merbabu in 1997, when the national news agency reported a sighting of four tigers forced into the open by forest fires; however, the Meru Betiri population has not been seen for many years, and it is likely that other sightings were in fact of leopards.

The Bali tiger population, first described in 1912, can never have numbered many more than a few hundred individuals at most; as the human population grew and farm land expanded, there was simply no room left. The last known Bali tiger was shot in 1937 for the collection of the Zoological Museum in Bogor, though there were reports in 1963 of villagers finding a tiger corpse in the forest.

Avifauna

More than 500 bird species are found on Java, Bali and Lombok, including more than 20 endemics on Java and one on Bali—the extremely rare **Bali mynah**. (There are more than 20 times as

Rhinoceros hornbill

many Bali mynahs in private American collections as in the
wild.) Several more species are found only on Java and Bali,
while the black-winged starling is unique to Java, Bali and
Lombok. One of the most striking of Java's endemics is the endangered **Javan hawk-eagle**, of which perhaps only 50 pairs survive.

Common coastal birds include the magnificent white-bellied sea
eagle, several heron, egret and stork species, osprey and Brahminy
kite. Seabirds to look out for on boat rides include tropicbirds,
boobies and noddies, terns and frigatebirds.

Grey-billed heron

Reptiles and amphibians

There are five species of **marine turtle** in the waters round Bali, Java and
Lombok: the green, leatherback, loggerhead, hawksbill and olive ridley. All
except the loggerhead are endangered – and protected by law – but the main turtle rookeries have long been exploited by egg collectors, and turtle meat is in
great demand on Bali for ceremonial and religious purposes.

Saltwater crocodiles can still be found in West Java's Ujung Kulon National
Park, and there are occasional reports of **Siamese crocodiles** in the Rawa
Danau nature reserve. The islands also possess c 100 snake species, more than
50 lizards, monitors and skinks, several freshwater turtles, and c 50 amphibians.

Strange creatures

In pools and streams in the limestone caves of the Gunung Kidul region to the
southeast of Yogyakarta lives *Puntius microps*, an **endemic fish** species which is
found in various forms: some specimens have small eyes, some have tiny eyes,
some have none and some have eyes only on one side of the head.

Among Java's **moths** are two of the world's largest: the pale green, long-
winged moon moth *Argema maenas* and the atlas moth *Attacus atlas*; the latter is
remarkable for the four large scaleless windows in its wings. Other moths found
on Java are known to drink tears from humans and other mammals while the latter sleep. Also remarkable is the skin-piercing, blood-sucking *Calyptra minuticor-
nis*, a moth species which lives on deer and cattle.

Four species of **snakehead**, an unusual type of freshwater fish which can
breathe atmospheric air, are found in Java and Bali. Three build bubble-nests in
swamps or slow-moving rivers; the fourth hatches its young in its mouth. They
can slither across fields and roads in search of new habitat, and bury themselves
in mud during a drought. The largest species, *Channa micropeltes*, has been
known to fatally attack humans who approach its fry.

The world's largest **eel**, *Thyrsoidea macrurus*, which grows to almost 2.5m in
length, is found in estuaries in west Java. A tiny **goby**, *Pandaka trimaculata*, measuring just 13mm, is found on Bali's north coast.

The largest of the islands' **beetles** is the three-horned dynastine *Chalcosoma
atlas*, which grows up to 13cm; other species barely reach 0.5mm in length. Best
avoided are some bombardier beetles which can fire a boiling hot secretion from
the abdomen tip if disturbed.

Pomacea canaliculatus, a species of **golden snail** native to South America, was
first found wild in east Java in 1987. It has rapidly become the most serious rice
pest after the brown planthopper, feeding on newly transplanted rice and capable of destroying the entire crop. Its ability to survive at least six months of

drought, by lying dormant in the soil, makes it difficult to control.

Another introduced species, the nocturnal **giant African land snail** *Achatina fulica* from Madagascar, is equally destructive; it can grow to more than 10cm in six months, and feeds on almost any vegetation, including prickly pear cactus and euphorbia. Even in towns, where there is often little lime in the soil to provide the calcium for its shell, the snail survives by scouring whitewash and mortar from buildings. It is now farmed, especially in east Java, where several thousand tons are exported annually, and is used in medicine and as cattle feed.

Flora

Java alone has more than 6500 known plant species, of which 70 per cent are native to the island, and more than 200 species of endemic **orchids**; plant numbers on Bali and Lombok are unknown. Plants of economic or medicinal importance include rattans, several palms, some of Java's 30 bamboo species, gingers and parsleys. Species of the latter two families are widely used in *jamu*, Javanese traditional herbal medicine; most *jamu* are liquid tonics, and may comprise up to 14 different plants mixed in precise proportions.

Among the most remarkable of the islands' native plants are the two parasitic ***Rafflesia*** species—*R. patma*, found in lowland forest along the south coast of west and central Java, and *R. rochussenii*, which has only ever been found on Gunung Salak near Bogor. The *Rafflesia* seed sends its roots into climbing vines, forming flower buds at intervals along the stem of the vine; after 18 months' growth, these open into the world's largest blooms of up to 1m across, reddish-orange in colour and covered in creamy-white blotches that resemble festering sores; the plant emits a powerful stench likened to rotting snakes or rats, which attracts carrion flies and beetles. When the flower dies, it collapses into a black core in which the seeds mature over the next six months, to be dispersed by wild animals.

Floristic habitats

The coasts of Java, Bali and Lombok comprise a mixture of mangrove forest, magnificent towering cliffs and rocky shores, sandy beaches fringed by beach forest, and sand dunes. **Mangrove forest** is found mostly along Java's north coast and in a few scattered parts on the south coast, especially Grajagan Bay in east Java and Segara Anakan in central Java; on the fringe of Bali's Benoa harbour; and on Lombok's east coast. Extensive **sand dunes** can be seen on the north coast of Madura, and on Java's south coast near Parangtritis. **Sea-grass meadows** exist in lagoons offshore from shallowly sloping sand beaches, as at Sanur on Bali.

Coral reefs are found along parts of Java's west coast and the Ujung Kulon peninsula, in the Seribu archipelago offshore from Jakarta, in the Karimunjawa archipelago off Jepara, on the Blambangan peninsula at Java's southeast tip, and in the Kangean archipelago to the east of Madura; Bali's finest reefs are found at the northwest tip, in Bali Barat National Park; the best on Lombok surround the three small islands – Gili Air, Gili Meno and Gili Trawangan – off the northwest coast.

Lowland evergreen rainforest, once found in substantial swathes across west Java, has now been reduced to small remnant patches there and on the south coast of east Java near Gunung Semeru; very little is found on Bali or Lombok. **Seasonal deciduous forest**, such as that found in Baluran National Park, is characterised by thorny plants, and may experience up to six months without rainfall. At Rawa Danau in west Java is the only significant remaining patch of **lowland freshwater swamp forest**, protected as a nature reserve.

In the highlands, at heights from c 1000–1800m, **lower montane forest** is the dominant habitat, characterised by shorter trees and increased numbers of epiphytes such as orchids; oaks, chestnuts and laurels are most abundant. The **upper montane forest**, above 1800m, is characterised by large amounts of moss and lichens, rhododendrons, ferns and lianas. Above this, you find **sub-alpine forest**, with Javan edelweiss, as on Gunung Gede and the Yang Plateau.

Important crops

More than 8000 varieties of **rice** exist in Indonesia, and it is possible that Java alone, which produces more than 60 per cent of all Indonesia's rice, possesses that many; the vast amount of production, however, is confined to just four varieties. Most rice on Java and Bali is grown in irrigated fields, with about one quarter of production grown in rain-fed fields and the rest in dry upland fields; on Lombok, the irrigated proportion is smaller. Irrigated paddy fields are unique in their ability to produce up to two tons of rice per hectare per harvest for centuries, with no fallow period, no decline in yield and no need for chemical fertiliser. Recently-developed high-yield varieties may produce four to six tons per hectare, but require the costly addition of chemical fertiliser and pesticide. Terraced rice fields have almost certainly been under continuous cultivation on Bali and Java for longer than a millennium: an 8C AD royal edict found on Bali refers to irrigation-tunnel builders – no doubt predecessors of the immensely sophisticated *subak* irrigation associations whose networks now criss-cross Bali's rice-growing landscape.

Today, all rice farmers on Bali belong to one of many hundred subak, which are responsible for all aspects of irrigation: the construction and maintenance of canals, aqueducts and weirs; and the equitable sharing of the water supply among members. Some subak networks have evolved into immensely complex systems with many kilometres of canals and tunnels which must be able to cope with a water flow that becomes ten times greater in the rainy season than the dry. Each subak must also cooperate with neighbouring associations to deal collectively with pests and problems of water-supply in times of drought or flood. Farmers growing rain-fed rice or dry upland rice, as in large parts of Madura, southern Lombok and the eastern tip of Bali, obtain smaller yields than those with year-round irrigation, and generally grow only one rice crop per year; they usually practise multiple cropping with cassava, maize and legumes, in an attempt to maximise productivity and minimise loss through drought.

The paddy field not only provides the rice, but gives the farmer and his family a steady supply of protein in the form of fish, frogs, eels, and even dragonflies, which are roasted and eaten by young boys; most paddies also support large duck populations which eat the brown planthopper, a destructive pest which sucks sap from the rice plant.

Other significant crops include sugar cane and rubber, coffee, tobacco and tea. Before 1707, when commercial **coffee** was first grown on Java, Yemen was virtually the only source. Within 20 years, the Priangan coffee estates round Bandung were rivalling the Yemeni crop in quantity and quality. Today, very good-quality coffee is grown throughout much of the Indonesian archipelago, which is the world's third largest producer. In Java and Bali the primary crop is robusta, most of it exported through London to become instant coffee; large estates can be seen on the Ijen plateau. Some arabica is also grown, with the finest quality beans traded in New York; the rest is used in the domestic market.

Native to the Amazon basin, the first **rubber** seedlings were brought to Java in the 1870s, and within 30 years rubber had become a valuable plantation crop. Today Indonesia is the world's largest rubber producer, though Java and Bali account for only about 2 per cent of the country's production and almost none is grown on Lombok. The visitor will see rubber plantations throughout west Java, and also in the vicinity of the Alas Purwo and Meru Betiri National Parks.

Living fossils: the sugar mills of Java

Steam engines used by the sugar cane industry

The use of sugar cane may have originated in New Guinea c 8000 BC, but the earliest references to its use in Java come from Chinese travellers in the 5C and 7C AD. Large-scale cultivation was begun by Chinese immigrants in the early 17C, and by the mid-19C the Javan sugar industry was immensely profitable. In the 1920s and 1930s it was the Dutch East Indies' most valuable crop, and only Cuba produced more sugar than Java. The mills then were state-of-the-art and the export trade was booming.

By the mid-1990s – after several price and production slumps, the Second World War and a revolution against the colonial power – the mills had become antiquated monuments to a bygone era, and Indonesia had become a net importer of sugar. The government had invested only modestly in a few larger mills in the years since independence, and the industry was only capable of producing sugar which cost several times the world price.

The mills remained open, if only to provide much-needed employment and stability in rural areas, but the government was beginning to baulk at the costs. A quarter of all mills were earmarked for closure by the late 1990s, and production was to be shifted to the outer islands of the archipelago.

The economic collapse of 1997–98 earned the mills a brief reprieve: the weakened rupiah raised the price of sugar imports, and the mills could absorb some of the huge numbers of newly unemployed labourers.

But by the end of 1999 the outlook again looked very bleak as the government liberalised sugar imports and the rupiah slowly strengthened once more.

For the moment, sugar is grown along much of Java's north coast between Cirebon and Rembang, and between Pasuruan and Situbondo. Other large estates are found on the fertile plains near Yogyakarta and Solo, Madiun, Kediri,

Malang, Lumajang and Jember. Of the 50 working mills – mostly in central and east Java – the smaller ones are of greatest interest, still using ancient stationary steam engines with huge flywheels, installed c 100 years ago.

The cane is grown in rotation with rice: the labour-intensive sugar harvest usually starts in the west in May and finishes in the east in October; cutting is done manually, though oxen and tractors are used in field preparation on some estates. After the harvest, the cane ridges are flattened and the fields are flooded for rice.

Traditionally, all cane was transported by narrow-gauge railway to the mills; today road transport has taken over in some areas, but most mills still operate railways within their yards, and half of them still bring the cane from the fields by rail. Up to the late 1970s, steam locomotive enthusiasts from around the world flocked to Java to see the main-line steam engines. These have long since been retired, to but enthusiasts still come to see their narrow-gauge cousins soldiering on at the sugar mills. Most of these locos are of German or Dutch origin, and predate the Second World War; some are almost 100 years old. Each season, c 100–150 steam locomotives are put to work; they are remarkably simple to maintain, require no imported spare parts, and most importantly, burn bagasse – the dried remnant of the crushed sugar cane – which is free.

Official permission is normally required to visit the sugar mills themselves, but there are no restrictions on watching the trains at work in the fields; do not be surprised, in east Java especially, to find a train loaded with cane clanking slowly along the roadside at dusk. The mills at Gondang Baru (see p 332) and Kedawung (see p 370) have been designated 'tourist mills', and visitors are welcome. The Gondang mill is home to a Sugar Museum and has some of the oldest steam-powered mill machinery on Java. Casual visitors to other mills will often be permitted entry, sometimes for a small fee. For the steam locomotive enthusiast, the following sugar mills (pabrik gula) are strongly recommended:

- Sragi (see p 286): an extensive system with 22 steam locomotives.
- Pakis Baru (see p 296): magnificently maintained locomotives dating back to 1899, kept busy in the mill.
- Trangkil (see p 296): post-1930 locomotives, including the last steam loco built in the UK.
- Tasik Madu (see p 346): a large fleet used for shunting in the mill.
- Rejosari (see p 350): a fine selection of interesting locomotives.
- Merican (see p 353): a small, very active mill.
- Olean (see p 399): unusually, steam locomotives here bring long trains of cane to the mill in the afternoon; elsewhere, most loaded trains run at night.

While these mills – or any others – can be visited by independent travellers, steam enthusiasts are best served by specialised tours. The most established of these are the highly regarded trips run by Rob Dickinson, a 'ferroequinologist' with 20 years' experience in Java, who can be contacted at 5 Ash Lane, Monmouth, NP5 4FJ, UK (☎/fax 01600 713405; e-mail: rob-dickinson@ dial.pipex.com).

The visitor cannot travel through any of these islands without encountering

coconut palms. These immensely versatile trees, which can provide up to 100 coconuts each year for 40 years or more, are grown either in large commercial plantations or, just as often, as individual specimens owned by a family. They provide food and drink, oil for cooking, leaves for roofing thatch and matting, timber for building and utensils, and charcoal for fuel. The oil is also used commercially to make soap and margarine, candles and cosmetics.

Tea is an important cash crop in west Java, and most visible on the slopes of Puncak east of Bogor, and in the Priangan highlands to the north and south of Bandung; tea factory tours are available on Puncak (see p 228).

Valuable **teak** and **mahogany** hardwoods and **Sumatran pine** plantations are the main commercial timbers grown on Bali, Java and Lombok; the pines can be tapped for their resin, which is distilled to produce turpentine and rosin for use in paint, varnish and the pulp industry. The teak, *Tectona grandis*, was almost certainly introduced from India by Hindus, perhaps as early as the 6C; it is now the most important plantation tree on Java, and accounts for more than 500,000ha. On Madura and Lombok, the **lontar palm** is a useful, drought-resistant tree that provides building and roofing materials; most importantly, it can be tapped for a sweet juice, *tuak manis*, which is reduced by boiling to produce a sweet brown syrup and palm sugar; the syrup can then be fermented to produce a toddy. A mature lontar is capable of producing 200–400 litres of juice per year; a few tress are enough to sustain a family through a year of drought.

Seaweed is cultivated commercially on the coasts of Bali, the Nusa Penida island group, and Lombok to produce agar, used as a thickening agent in processed food such as ice-cream and cottage cheese. Other cultivated seaweed species produce carrageenan, a thicker gelatinous agent used in paint, cosmetics and insecticides.

National parks and reserves

Java's first conservation area was created in 1889 on the slopes of Gunung Gede in west Java, and in the following 50 years most of today's conservation areas were listed. There are now nine National Parks (*taman nasional*) or Marine Parks (*taman laut*) on Java, one on Bali and none on Lombok. Other types of conservation area, including nature reserves (*cagar alam*), wildlife reserves (*suaka margasatwa*) and recreation parks (*taman wisata*), offer varying degrees of protection to flora and fauna, and range in size from 2000–5000ha; tourists generally are not welcome in the wildlife reserves, though many of the nature reserves – especially those with waterfalls and lakes – are open to visitors. Camping is permitted in the National Parks and Marine Parks, as well as some recreation parks; some sort of permanent lodging is also available within the parks, or just outside the park boundary.

The people of Java, Bali and Lombok

Indonesia is the world's fourth most populous country (after China, India and the USA), with c 206 million people in 1999. Officially, the 200 millionth baby was born on Lombok in February 1997 – just one of c 8000 born across the archipelago on the same day. A Lombok infant was singled out for the honour because of the island's effective family planning programme.

Java's population, soon to reach 120 million, is made up primarily of three ethnic groups: the majority **Javanese**, who comprise c 65 per cent of the island's population; the **Sundanese** in the western highlands (c 20 per cent); and **Madurese**, who have migrated from Madura to settle throughout much of eastern Java (c 10 per cent). The Javanese heartland reaches from Gunung Slamet eastwards to Malang; this is the *kejawen*, the part of the island where Javanese mysticism and high culture are most strongly established and refined. Language is at its most elaborate and personal status is of great importance; society is primarily rural, and deeply conservative.

In contrast, the **Javanese** of the north coast – the inhabitants of the *pasisir* – are largely urban dwellers and astute traders; they are louder, brasher and more outspoken than their compatriots inland, and follow a more orthodox and rigorous form of Islam.

Sundanese culture in many ways lies between the *kejawen* and the *pasisir*. The people have adopted art forms similar to the *kejawen*, such as *wayang kulit* and gamelan, but have incorporated their own distinct variations. Sundanese language is more akin to the Malay of southern Sumatra than to Javanese, but like the *pasisir*, orthodox Islam has a very strong influence, and social hierarchies are less pronounced than among the *kejawen*.

Java's eastern salient is dominated by **Madurese** who, since the 18C, have migrated from their own island as mercenaries and maritime traders, and more recently in search of arable land; and by central Javanese who have migrated eastwards since the 19C.

Bali, with three million people, is more ethnically homogeneous than Java. More than 95 per cent of the people are ethnic **Balinese**, and the vast majority of these are Hindu; about 5 per cent are Muslims.

Lombok is dominated by the **Sasak**, who comprise c 90 per cent of the population and call themselves Muslim; Hindu Balinese account for most of the rest. The Islam of the Sasak varies from fairly orthodox practice to a minority practice known as Wetu Telu, which emphasises ancestor worship, traditional *adat* or customary law, and animism, all overlaid with a veneer of Islam. The Wetu Telu do not generally pray five times a day, as orthodox Islam prescribes, and some do not fast for the full month of Ramadan. Inevitably there is an element of friction between the two groups.

Small communities of other ethnic groups are scattered across the islands, among them Bugis from South Sulawesi, whose traditional stilt houses can be seen on the south and east Lombok coasts; Chinese, mostly small merchants, who make up c 3.5 per cent of the country's population but control much of its wealth; and sizeable Arab communities on Java's pasisir coast and Lombok. In West Java several isolated, archaic communities remain, the best-known of whom are the Baduy (see p 216).

Of special note are the c 50,000 **Tenggerese**, hardy rural dwellers in the rugged Tengger highlands round Gunung Bromo and Gunung Semeru in east Java, who traditionally practised a religion known to them as *agama Buda* ('Buda religion'), considered to be the religion of the 13C–15C pre-Islamic kingdom of Majapahit, which incorporated certain elements of Hinduism. Somewhat isolated in the mountains, they alone were able to resist the introduction of Islam into eastern Java in the 18C, and have maintained their own traditions to this day, though many Tengger communities have now officially changed their religion to Hinduism, and identify their beliefs more closely with the Hindu Balinese. Bromo itself is named after the Hindu god, Brahma, who was frequently identified as the god of fire.

 # Historical summary

Prehistory

The oldest known mammal remains found on Java – primitive hippopotamus, deer, and elephant-like mastodon – date from the upper Pliocene epoch (1.6–3 million years ago). Early hominids, *Homo erectus*, are generally thought to have appeared in the middle Pleistocene (130,000–700,000 years ago), although research in the mid-1990s indicates that volcanic pumice found at the sites of some of these fossils is nearly 2 million years old; if this reflects the true age of the fossils, they are almost as old as the earliest *H. erectus* found in Africa.

Until recently, it was believed that *H. erectus* became extinct on Java long before the arrival of early modern man, *Homo sapiens*, whose stone and obsidian tools have been found at several sites on the island. However, research in the 1990s by the American geochronologist, Carl Swisher, indicates that some *H. erectus* fossils are in fact only c 27,000–53,000 years old, implying that *H. erectus* survived on Java perhaps 250,000 years longer than on the Asian mainland and may have co-existed with early *H. sapiens*; although the earliest *H. sapiens* known on Java are less than 10,000 years old, evidence elsewhere in southeast Asia suggests he existed in the region as long as c 40,000 years ago.

Java's original *H. sapiens* were probably Australoids, akin to present-day Australian Aborigines; the latter are thought to have migrated southeastward from the Indonesian islands to Australia c 30,000 years ago. The occupants of Java were later ousted by more sophisticated hunter-gatherers from southeast Asia. In the upper Pleistocene, for a period between 18,000–22,000 years ago, the sea level was c 50–150m lower than at present, and *H. sapiens* could have walked between Java, Sumatra, Borneo and the Malay peninsula, which all lie on the Sunda Shelf (the continental part of the Sunda Plate). Bali would have been cut off by a strait narrower and more easily navigable than today's Bali Strait; Lombok, however, was separated by the deep and turbulent Lombok Strait.

Another immigrant wave, 3000–5000 years ago, brought proto-Malay cultivators (whose descendants may include the Tenggerese of east Java and the Sasak of Lombok). After them came Austronesians (deutero-Malays), who arrived c 1000–3000 years ago via the Malay peninsula and the Philippines from Taiwan and southern China, bringing knowledge of pottery and the cultivation of millet, Job's tears, and rice; there is evidence that irrigated rice farming began on Java more than 1000 years ago. It is their descendants who today dominate western Indonesia.

Protohistory and early history (c 500 BC–5C AD)

Current knowledge of this period on Java and Bali is limited to several archaeological remains, some megalithic ritual sites, and a considerable number of scattered small finds, especially of socketed bronze axes and other metal tools, decorated bronze Chinese-influenced *Dong-son* ceremonial drums from Vietnam, Indian beads and Roman-influenced Rouletted Ware pottery, decorated with dots and lines made by a roulette or comb – the evidence of early trade.

By the 1C AD, a world trading system had been established, linking Han dynasty China, parts of south India and southeast Asia, and the Mediterranean. The coastal communities of north Java and north Bali, and to a lesser extent the islands further east round the Flores Sea, were a significant part of this network, which was dominated initially by Indian merchants. They took cloves from the Moluccas and sandalwood from the islands east of Lombok to the Roman empire, and exported pottery, beads and other goods to southeast Asia.

When Indian trade with Rome declined in the 3C, both the Ikshvakus in southern India, and their 4C successors, the Pallavas, shifted their mercantile focus eastward to China and southeast Asia, and in so doing, brought Buddhism to the region. In the 5C, the establishment of independent, competing, regional states in southern China led to an expansion in trade round the Malacca and Sunda Straits, which directly benefited the coastal ports of Java.

The Chinese were the first to record with any consistency their voyages and descriptions of states and settlements with which they traded. While few ports mentioned in these early sources can now be identified, it is highly likely that most were coastal settlements on Java, Bali, Sumatra, and the Malay peninsula. The earliest evidence of such polities to be found on Java itself comes in the form of stone inscriptions, which mention Purnavarman, the ruler of **Tarumanagara**, somewhere in western Java, in the mid-5C; the site of the kingdom has not been located.

Ho-ling and Mataram (7C–9C)

Chinese documents have revealed that in 640, a Buddhist polity called Ho-ling, probably located on Java's north coast between modern Semarang and Pekalongan, sent its first recorded mission to the Chinese court. For a few decades, this trading and farming state also became a regular transit point for Chinese Buddhist pilgrims travelling to India, and played a dominant entrepôt role in the spice and sandalwood trade in the Java and Banda Seas. However, by c 670, the Chinese pilgrims had begun to break their journey instead at Shrivijaya in southern Sumatra, which replaced Ho-ling as the region's dominant mercantile centre.

Emissaries from Ho-ling nevertheless continued to reach China into the early 9C, and it appears that Ho-ling annexed – or perhaps was annexed by – a neighbouring state in the interior of central Java, forming a union in the early 8C which later became known as **Mataram**.

This is the best known of the early Javanese states, especially from the 9C onward, when inscriptions become more plentiful. They indicate that Mataram eventually became sufficiently organised to collect taxes and impose labour levies, and was governed by a three-tiered administration. **Sanjaya**, an early ruler – probably the first of a line – of this polity, is known from a Sanskrit inscription of 732 found at Candi Gunung Wukir (see p 323). The earliest monumental remains in central Java, including the Shaivite temples of the Dieng plateau (see p 274) and Gedong Songo (see p 283), also date from the mid-8C.

In the second half of the 8C, the Sanjaya dynasty was replaced by the Mahayana Buddhist **Shailendras** as the pre-eminent power in the region. It was at this time that much of Java's magnificent Buddhist architecture was built, including Borobudur and some of the temples near Prambanan (see p 324). The Shailendra court at Mataram established itself as an important international centre of Buddhist learning, but it remains unclear whether the Shailendras were native Javanese or outsiders, perhaps from the Malay peninsula.

In the first half of the 9C, the marriage of a Shailendra queen to a Sanjaya king enabled the Hindu Sanjaya dynasty to become the dominant power once more, though there are many signs from both the monumental architecture and inscriptions that the two religions coexisted in an atmosphere of mutual tolerance, with perhaps considerable syncretism. It is possible that the Shailendra line survived by taking over the kingdom of Shrivijaya in southern Sumatra.

Despite the discovery of numerous inscriptions from the period, and the temples which are scattered across the countryside to the east and west of modern Yogyakarta, no urban settlement from the period has been found in the region. Archaeologists have concluded that society was largely agrarian and dispersed, and government was by a tiny elite of nobles subject to a supreme ruler.

In the late 9C or early 10C, the rulers of Mataram moved their power base eastwards to the upper Brantas valley, somewhere southwest of modern Surabaya. The reason for this move remains a mystery, but the evidence for it is overwhelming. No inscriptions or monuments dating from the 300-year period after 919 have been discovered in central Java, while **Sindok**, the ruler credited with establishing the new centre of power in the mid-10C, has left more than a dozen inscriptions in the east.

An inscription dated to 937 tells how in 928–29, Sindok repulsed an attack by Shrivijaya. Sung dynasty Chinese records tell of further warfare between Shrivijaya and the Javanese state after 960, which only ended when the Cholas of southern India raided the Shrivijayan ports in 1024–25.

Java-Bali relations (10C–11C)

In Bali, the first dated documents appear shortly before the succession of Sindok in Java – in the late 9C and early 10C. They and subsequent inscriptions indicate that while Bali was independent of Java at that time, Balinese society practised both Buddhism and Shaivism, perhaps of Javanese origin, or perhaps brought directly from India. At the end of the 10C, the Balinese ruler was Udayana, whose consort, Mahendradatta, was the great-granddaughter of Sindok of Java. An important result of this marriage was the greater penetration of Hinduism and Javanese culture into Bali.

In 1001, Udayana and Mahendradatta had a son named **Airlangga**, who would later become the ruler of both Java and Bali. As a youth he went to live at the Javanese court, and was there in 1016 when it was destroyed – probably in retaliation for earlier attacks – by an invading force from Shrivijaya. Airlangga took refuge among hermits and in 1019 was crowned king, though his Javanese territory now comprised only a small coastal strip between modern Surabaya and Pasuruhan. It was only after the Cholas had sufficiently weakened Shrivijaya in the 1020s that Airlangga was able to start reconquering the Javanese lands of his mother's ancestors. By the time of his death in 1049, he had succeeded in this, and it appears he had initiated a rapprochement with Shrivijaya by marrying a Sumatran princess; he was buried at Candi Belahan (see p 377).

Kediri, Singosari and Majapahit

Airlangga divided his Javanese kingdom into two, perhaps to avoid a conflict after his death. To the east was Janggala (which included the area of modern Malang, Surabaya, and Pasuruhan), and to the west, Kediri (or Panjalu) which had its capital at modern Kediri (and included the area round modern Madiun). In Bali, his younger brother or brother-in-law became ruler. Very little is known of either the Javanese kingdoms or Bali for the next 150 years, except for the names of rulers which are mentioned in several inscriptions.

We do know that at the start of the 13C Kediri was occupied by a ruler named Kertajaya, while Janggala had come under the control of a brigand named Angrok. In 1221 or 1222, Angrok seized Kediri and thus reunified Airlangga's kingdom, which he governed from a new capital, Singosari (see p 369). Angrok was assassinated in 1227 at the instigation of his stepson, Anushapati, whose father had been murdered earlier by Angrok. Anushapati was in turn killed by Angrok's son, Tohpati, in 1248, followed a few months later by Tohpati himself, put to death by Anushapati's son, whose descendants then succeeded as rulers of Singosari.

Taking advantage of the decline of Shrivijaya, the kingdom of **Singosari** had become extremely powerful by 1275, with considerable influence on Sumatra and the Malay peninsula. Its last ruler, Kertanagara, died in 1292 in battle with a rebellious viceroy of Kediri. There followed a year-long struggle between rival claimants to the throne, involving Chinese and Mongol forces; the eventual winner was a son-in-law of Kertanagara named Vijaya, who founded a new kingdom named Majapahit and took the name Kertarajasa.

The early years of the **Majapahit** kingdom were a time of war and rebellion. Kertarajasa's son, Jayanagara, succeeded him in 1309, and during his rule there emerged Gajah Mada, who became his prime minister in 1331. Gajah Mada is one of the great figures of this period, remembered today through the many streets on Java which are named after him. Under his able leadership, Majapahit spread its influence through Java and in 1343 mounted a successful expedition against Bali – which at that time had once again become independent. Majapahit then maintained influence on Bali through vassals who ruled from Gelgel in the modern regency of Klungkung.

In 1350, the greatest of the Majapahit rulers, **Hayam Wuruk**, began his long reign. By the time of his death in 1389, the kingdom controlled most of the Indonesian archipelago – including Bali and Lombok – and much of the Malay peninsula. After his death, Majapahit fell into decline, a victim partly of the growing political and commercial power of Malacca (in present-day Malaysia), founded in 1403, but also of a debilitating five-year war of succession. Further disputed successions, invasion attempts and rebellions followed in the 15C, and by the 1470s the remnant of the Majapahit empire was coming under threat from the Muslim state of Demak on Java's north coast.

Islam and the growth of Demak

Tombstones found in Sumatra show the presence there of Islam by the late 13C. More significantly, others dating from Hayam Wuruk's reign and belonging to

Javanese nobility – perhaps even members of the ruling dynasty – have been found at cemeteries in the vicinity of Majapahit. The implication is that Hindu-Buddhism and Islam were practised concurrently at the royal court. It seems likely that Islam was brought to the court by Sufis, whose supposedly supernatural powers would have attracted a Hindu-Buddhist élite already used to the mystical practices of their own religion.

At the same time, Islam was reaching the trading centres of Java's north coast, brought by foreign merchants. A Chinese Muslim who visited in 1416 reported the presence of Muslims from the west and China. In the 15C, the Islamic state of Malacca became the region's dominant trading centre, and apparently played an active role in encouraging the spread of Islam in the region.

The earliest reliable account of Islamic penetration into the archipelago was written by a Portuguese named Tomé Pires, who travelled through many of the islands in the early 16C. He found much of Sumatra divided into Islamic states, and attributed this to the influence of Muslim merchants. West Java remained under the control of the Hindu-Buddhist kingdom of Pajajaran, but coastal areas of north Java were Islamised; the interior of east and central Java remained Hindu-Buddhist, as were Madura, Bali and Lombok. Islam, however, had already reached the main trading centres of the Moluccas – the famed 'spice islands' – though it had not reached Timor and Sumba, the centres of the valuable sandalwood trade.

Clearly trade played a role in the spread of Islam, but the process of Islamisation in the archipelago was not simply the result of following the main trade routes. Local legend emphasises the role played by Sufi mystics – and in particular, nine individuals known as the *wali songo* ('nine saints'), who are accredited with the spread of Islam in Java. It seems quite likely that Islam in fact spread through both trade and Sufism, with each providing support for the other.

The origin of the Islamic state of **Demak** on Java's north coast is unclear, but it may have been founded by a Chinese Muslim in the early 16C. Under the leadership of Sultan Trenggana, it expanded aggressively in the 1520s and 1530s, and by Trenggana's death in 1546 had considerable influence across much of the island. Its power was short-lived, but its achievement in spreading Islam was considerable. While Hindu kingdoms survived in eastern Java, they were under increasing pressure, especially with the emergence in the late 16C of a new Islamic kingdom of **Mataram** (in the vicinity of modern Yogyakarta). Many Hindus fled to Bali to escape the tide of Islam.

Mataram and the VOC

As with Demak, the origins of Mataram remain obscure, but an early ruler of the kingdom was Senapati (r. c 1584–1601), under whose grandson, **Agung** (r. 1613–45), Mataram reached its most glorious heights. By 1625, he controlled most of central and eastern Java, and was prepared to attack Batavia in the west, which in 1619 had fallen to the forces of the Dutch-based **VOC** – the **United East India Company**.

The first Dutch expedition in search of the spice islands had reached Java in 1596, calling at Banten on the north coast; the following year it anchored briefly at Bali to replenish supplies. The VOC initially established trading posts at Banten and nearby Jayakarta (modern Jakarta) in the early 17C, and in 1619 seized Jayakarta by force – renaming it **Batavia** – in a bid to control the spice trade to Europe.

Agung mounted an attack on the Dutch in Batavia in 1628, but his force of 10,000 men was defeated by disease and hunger; another assault in 1629 also failed, after which he was never strong enough to try again.

Throughout the 17C and 18C, the relationship between the royal court of Mataram (and of its successors at nearby Plered, Kartosuro, Surakarta and Yogyakarta) and the VOC swayed between war and alliance. The VOC sought influence among the local power-brokers on Java, while the local rulers saw the VOC as a useful ally in regional power struggles – an ally which could then be safely ignored from a position of strength. The VOC could provide valuable military support – at a price, which all too often the royal court could ill afford. The debts could only be paid by raising taxes, which alienated the population and caused unrest.

By the late 18C, however, the VOC was in financial trouble, had lost its valuable monopoly of the clove trade, and was mired in corruption. Furthermore, in 1795, as a result of the Napoleonic wars in Europe, the Dutch were obliged to hand over their Indonesian possessions to the British. On Java they resisted till September 1811, when the Dutch Governor-General surrendered to British forces in central Java. By this time, the VOC had ceased to exist, having been dissolved in 1800 and replaced by a Dutch colonial administration which took over the company's assets.

Meanwhile, Bali remained generally free of direct VOC interference through the 17C and 18C. The island remained under the control of the Gelgel court until its collapse in the mid-17C, when a series of warring kingdoms emerged. By this time, the VOC presence in Batavia had created a large new market for slaves, which the warring Balinese lords exploited by exporting their prisoners and criminals; this in turn provided funds for further fighting. Balinese slaves were in great demand: the men were considered strong and brave, the women beautiful. They were also thought to be faithful and diligent. Thousands were shipped to Java, and further afield – including Mauritius – from the main slave port at Kuta.

By the 1690s, **Buleleng** in northwest Bali had emerged as the strongest kingdom, and had expanded its influence into eastern Java.

In eastern Bali, the kingdom of **Karangasem** expanded eastwards, invading western Lombok at the same time as Makassarese from south Sulawesi were expanding into eastern Lombok. The two invading forces clashed in the late 17C, resulting in a Balinese victory. Karangasem continued to hold sway over Lombok for the next century, until a disputed succession permitted the local Sasak aristocracy to once again assert a degree of independence. By this time, Karangasem had defeated its main rival on Bali, the kingdom of Buleleng, and had become the dominant state in the north of the island.

British rule and Dutch colonialism

Thomas Stamford Raffles, later to found Singapore, was Lieutenant-Governor of Java from 1811–16. He ransacked the Yogyakarta court in 1812 after encountering hostility from the ruler, Hamengkubuwono II, but for the most part was content to administer the island from his palace at Bogor. With the return of the Dutch in 1816, growing tensions led in 1825 to the outbreak of the Java War, a five-year anti-Dutch rebellion which spread rapidly to many parts of the island. One of the ringleaders, Prince Diponegoro, was finally arrested in 1830, and the rebellion fizzled out – but not before the deaths of more than 200,000 Javanese.

1830 marked the true beginning of the **Dutch colonial period** on Java. While the VOC had continually lost money, it now became important to make profits from Java, to pay for the administration of the island and also to generate revenue for the impoverished Dutch government in Europe. The idea of the *cultuurstelsel* ('cultivation system') was introduced, whereby each village was to set aside a part of its land to grow crops for export, which would be sold to the government at a fixed price; with this money, the village would be able to pay its compulsory land tax to the government, and could keep any excess revenue for itself. In theory, this was fine; in practice, it was open to gross abuse by the local officials, who both set the land tax assessment and decided the share of land to be planted with export crops. If the payment for the crops rose, the officials used this to justify higher taxes.

For the Dutch administration, this system produced steady, large profits. For the farmers, however, it frequently produced hardships. By the 1840s, rice shortages and the accompanying price fluctuations, created by the need to use more rice land for export crops such as sugar cane and indigo, were causing famines. By the 1860s, as the problems of the *cultuurstelsel* could no longer be ignored, the Dutch government finally began to change the system; the compulsory cultivation of coffee – the last part to be tackled – was ended in 1919.

Meanwhile, the Dutch had mounted a series of military expeditions against Bali in the 1840s, seeking to end the Balinese wrecking and plundering of Dutch ships. At the third attempt in 1849, the Dutch inflicted a heavy defeat on the Balinese and came to an agreement which gave them sovereignty while allowing the local rajas to rule the small kingdoms on their behalf. This situation persisted till the early 20C, when another shipwreck triggered a Dutch invasion at Sanur in 1906. The Dutch marched on Denpasar, the capital, where the local rulers and their entire entourages performed a series of mass suicides in front of the advancing Dutch (see p 104). By 1909, they controlled the whole island.

The rise of nationalism

By 1920 the first calls for complete independence from the Netherlands had already been heard on Java – much to the shock of the Dutch administration. In the early years of the 20C, the first of the modern agenda-led groups – some of them nationalist in nature – began to establish themselves, among them the Javanese-based Budi Utomo, with a largely white-collar membership, formed in 1908; Sarekat Islam, a populist Muslim organisation founded in 1912 with support from across the archipelago; the Indische Partij, an early nationalist party with an Indo-European membership, whose leaders were quickly exiled; and the Partai Komunis Indonesia (PKI: the Indonesian Communist Party).

In 1927, a Javanese named **Sukarno**, with two Sumatran colleagues, Mohammad Hatta and Sutan Sjahrir, formed the Perserikatan Nasional Indonesia (Indonesian Nationalist Association), which the following year became the Indonesian Nationalist Party, the first purely Indonesian-run, secular party demanding full independence. By the end of 1929, it had 10,000 members. Sukarno and the others were arrested, imprisoned and later exiled to far-flung corners of the archipelago.

Through the 1930s there was little compromise by the Dutch government. In May 1940, as Germany invaded the Netherlands, martial law was declared in Indonesia and all public meetings were banned. On 8 December 1941, the

Japanese attacked Hawaii's Pearl Harbor; on 10 January 1942, they invaded Indonesia. In February, they defeated a combined fleet of Australian, British, Dutch and American ships in the battle of the Java Sea, and in March the Dutch government on Java surrendered to the Japanese.

The Japanese occupation (1942–45)

The Japanese considered Indonesia's natural resources vital to their war effort, and initially they received a warm welcome from many Indonesians, who were happy to see the Dutch interned. About 170,000 Europeans were placed in camps across the archipelago, often in appalling conditions; in the male civilian camps, the death rate was 40 per cent. Initial pleasure at the Japanese arrival was quickly tempered for most Indonesians by their frequent displays of arrogance and brutality. Some nationalist leaders, such as Hatta and Sjahrir, were opposed to fascism and saw the Dutch as the lesser of two evils, but despite attempts to establish underground networks, there was no serious resistance to the Japanese till 1944.

As it became apparent that Japan was losing the war in the Pacific, the Japanese administrators on Java began to search harder for ways to control popular movements, especially the large Islamic organisations, Muhammadiyah and Nahdlatul Ulama. They never succeeded to any great extent, and by February 1944 faced a peasant revolt on Java caused by Japanese rice requisitioning. The rebellion was fiercely crushed, thus provoking the rural Islamic movement into greater opposition.

In September 1944, in what appears to have been one of several increasingly desperate attempts to win Indonesian support as the Japanese position steadily worsened, the Japanese Prime Minister began to promise independence for the East Indies, but no date was given. More and more concessions were made until July 1945, when the Japanese authorities agreed to grant Indonesian independence within a matter of months.

On 6 August the Americans dropped the atomic bomb on Hiroshima; on 15 August the Japanese surrendered. In Indonesia, a power vacuum was briefly created, as there were no Allied forces in the region to take the Japanese surrender. On the night of 16 August, Sukarno, Hatta, and other nationalists drafted a declaration of independence; on the morning of 17 August, Sukarno read this out to a small gathering outside his house in Jakarta.

The revolution (1945–50)

A republican government was quickly created in Jakarta, with Sukarno as President and Hatta vice-president. Now that the Japanese had formally surrendered, many were prepared to assist the Indonesians discreetly; some provided arms, while local Japanese commanders often withdrew their forces to permit the republicans free rein in their neighbourhood.

Allied forces began to arrive in September to take the Japanese surrender. The eastern part of the archipelago – including Bali and Lombok – was taken by Australian and Dutch forces, which in most cases arrived before the local republican administration had been organised. On Java and Sumatra, however, British forces under Lord Louis Mountbatten were required to take control. While Mountbatten had little intention of helping the Dutch regain their colony, and was concerned solely with accepting the Japanese surrender and freeing

European internees, the presence of Allied forces on Java created growing tensions, which exploded in Surabaya in late October. Three days of fierce fighting between Allied forces and the Indonesians for control of the city resulted in the death of more than 6000 Indonesians (see p 385).

The battle of Surabaya, despite being an overwhelming physical defeat for the republicans, was a turning point. The British realised the dangers of taking sides in this conflict; the Dutch, on the other hand, were forced to notice the strength of opposition to their return and to acknowledge the depth of support the republican cause attracted. For the republicans, the battle became a symbol of national resistance.

By November 1946 the Dutch were seeking to negotiate a deal which would create a federal structure, recognising the republic as the authority on Java, Madura and Sumatra, while the Dutch kept control over the rest of the archipelago. An agreement was signed, but was quickly abandoned. In May 1947, the Dutch decided to go to war to win back Java and Sumatra. They attacked in July, seizing key sites across Java and Sumatra, but under pressure from the USA, Australia, Britain, India and the Soviet Union, a ceasefire was called at the end of the month. A new agreement was struck, but again came to nothing.

There followed a year of chaos on Java as the republican movement came close to civil war. By late 1948, a communist rebellion against the republic had begun in Madiun in east Java, only to be crushed by pro-republican forces, with perhaps 8000 deaths.

The Dutch, meanwhile, launched a second strike to finally defeat the republic in December 1948. They quickly took Yogyakarta, the republic's capital, but came under intense international pressure – from the UN and the USA especially – to accept a ceasefire. This was effected on 31 December, but a period of guerrilla warfare followed.

In January 1949, the UN Security Council demanded that the Dutch transfer sovereignty to the republic by 1 July 1950. From August to November 1949, negotiations continued, and finally, on 17 August 1950, the Republic of Indonesia came into being, with its capital at Jakarta.

The Sukarno years (1950–65)

The first two years of independence were dominated by a political power struggle between the civilian government and the military. Although the politicians won, the early period of the republic was one of weak government, considerable economic turmoil, and constant rebellion by militant Muslims.

A high point for the regime came in 1955 when Indonesia hosted the Asian-African Conference at Bandung, which placed Sukarno firmly in the spotlight as a leader of the Afro-Asian world, and which also endorsed Indonesia's claim to Dutch-held West New Guinea. Meanwhile, the resurrected **PKI**, the **Indonesian communist party**, was experiencing massive growth in support. It was not, however, Marxist-Leninist ideas which attracted villagers, but the fact that PKI teams built schools in rural areas, repaired roads, and set up literacy courses.

Elections were held in 1955; the turnout was estimated to be nearly 92 per cent, in what were to be the freest and most politically open elections ever held in independent Indonesia – until those of 1999. There was no clear majority, however, and parliament remained a somewhat toothless institution, with a high turnover of cabinets.

Frustrated by the succession of weak governments, Sukarno began to talk of a 'guided democracy', an Indonesian democracy based on consensus rather than a parliamentary contest between government and opposition parties. Meanwhile, renewed tensions between the government on Java and military officers on the outer islands, who resented the increasingly pronounced concentration of power on Java, resulted in military-led rebellions on Sumatra and in south Sulawesi, supported by local civilians. It increasingly looked as if Indonesia was going to disintegrate.

In March 1957, Sukarno proclaimed martial law. In early 1958 the Javanese-dominated government forces launched attacks on the Sumatran dissidents, who by now were receiving weapons from the USA (and American pilots were dropping bombs from American planes), channelled through Malaya and Singapore. By mid-1958 Jakarta had the upper hand, and American-Indonesian relations had been seriously damaged, while Malaya and Singapore were viewed with suspicion.

In December 1957, after the UN had failed to pass a resolution calling for the Dutch to negotiate with Indonesia over the future of West New Guinea, more than 45,000 Dutch citizens were ordered to leave the country, and their businesses were seized in a wave of anti-Dutch feeling which Sukarno encouraged. The army took over the businesses, but poor management brought economic problems.

In 1962, Sukarno finally won succeeded in winning West New Guinea from the Dutch, when in August the territory was finally transferred to the UN, which would hand it to Indonesia the following year. 1963 also marked the start of Indonesia's 'confrontation' (*konfrontasi*) with Malaysia and Singapore, over objections to Malaysia's plans to incorporate both Singapore and the states of Sabah and Sarawak on the island of Borneo into its federation. A small-scale border war broke out on Borneo, with British and Malaysian forces fighting the Indonesian army, while Indonesian paratroopers were also dropped onto the Malay peninsula.

Domestic political power was increasingly concentrated in two opposing camps – the military, which by 1959 had emerged as the single most powerful force in the country, and the communist PKI. Sukarno himself was attempting to control both sides in an increasingly complex web of intrigue and manipulation, while at the same time his rhetoric was increasingly anti-Western. By late 1963 the PKI had allied itself with China, and had a huge membership among the rural poor as a result of its social welfare programmes. Within the armed forces, the air force came under PKI influence, while the navy sided with the army, although this was itself being increasingly infiltrated by the PKI. At the same time, the Indonesian economy was collapsing under the weight of huge debts and flamboyant expenditure by Sukarno on grandiose building projects, inflation was running at 500–1000 per cent, and his rhetoric grew ever more anti-imperialist.

By 1965, the nation was in a political maelstrom. The armed forces were divided; the country's economic and social structures were nearing collapse; the communists and Sukarno were increasingly vocal in their radical rhetoric. Sukarno announced an anti-imperialist Jakarta-Beijing-Pyongyang-Hanoi axis and a withdrawal from the IMF and World Bank, having earlier withdrawn from the UN in protest at Malaysia being given a seat on the Security Council. Sukarno also seemed on the point of agreeing to the creation of a 'fifth force' of armed workers and peasants (in addition to the army, air force, navy and police), an idea suggested by the PKI as a way to neutralise the power of the army.

The 1965 coup attempt and the rise of Suharto

On 30 September 1965, six generals were kidnapped and murdered by members of the Presidential Guard in what was subsequently presented to the public as an attempted communist coup. The then General Suharto always maintained later that he only found out about the coup attempt the following morning, but one of the convicted ringleaders, Colonel Abdul Latief, has said he told Suharto about the plot on the eve of the generals' abduction; Latief, now in his seventies and only released from prison in 1999, has alleged that Suharto not only knew about it, but was actively involved in the plot.

The son of a minor village official, **Suharto** never completed high school, but at the age of 19 joined the Dutch colonial army. Later involved in the independence struggle of the mid-1940s, he subsequently worked his way quickly through the ranks. At the time of the 1965 coup attempt, he was commander of Kostrad, the strategic reserve force based in Jakarta, which was the only active fighting unit in the capital. In such a key role, it seems scarcely believable that he – of all people – should not have been a target of the coup plotters.

He always maintained that he acted has fast as possible to crush the coup. The generals' murders were used by him as an excuse to ban the communist party and discredit Sukarno. In the following months, a well-orchestrated anti-communist purge swept the country, resulting in c 500,000–one million deaths. By March 1966, Suharto was sure enough of his power base to wrestle political power from Sukarno, whose credibility lay shattered; two years later, Suharto formally became President, inaugurating his 'New Order'.

Suharto's New Order (1967–98)

Despite the widespread corruption and gross nepotism for which he is remembered by young Indonesians today, Suharto did nevertheless lead Indonesia out of abject poverty and political turmoil in the 1960s, when inflation stood at more than 1000 per cent, into an era of high economic growth by the early 1990s. Per capita income under his New Order regime rose on average by 4.3 per cent annually from 1965 to 1988; from 1988, the economy grew by almost 7 per cent per year – according to official statistics, though these figures are considered a government invention by some foreign economists.

If government figures are believed, the regime excelled in poverty alleviation: in 1970, more than 70 per cent of Indonesians lived in poverty; by 1990 the proportion had fallen to 15 per cent. This was achieved thanks to oil windfalls which, despite huge corruption, were still plentiful enough to provide sensible investment in agriculture, transport and education by the President's team of Western-educated technocrats. They ensured that a new generation of more literate farmers (who made up 80 per cent of the population) could take advantage of new agricultural techniques and get their produce to market efficiently. Rice production was successfully increased so that for a while in the 1980s Indonesia became self-sufficient. Coupled with this, Suharto initiated a successful family-planning programme. Together, these resulted in a significant drop in malnutrition and infant mortality.

The New Order's shortcomings

When Suharto finally resigned in May 1998, he had just begun his seventh consecutive, unopposed five-year term as President, his position rubber-stamped by the democratic-sounding house of representatives. In fact, though, there was little democracy in Suharto's New Order.

Suharto, like Sukarno before him, argued that for a young country as geographically and ethnically fragmented as Indonesia, strong government which tolerated little dissent was a suitable approach; democracy in the New Order existed in name only. The 500-member house of representatives, which sat a few times each year, was filled largely with Suharto's minions: initially, 100 seats were reserved for the military, while the remaining 400 members were elected by popular vote. However, the inappropriately named 'Festival of Democracy', held every seven years to elect these 400, was always weighted so heavily in favour of the government party, Golkar, that the two permitted opposition parties never took more than 30 per cent of the total vote. Typical of these 'festivals' was the April 1987 election, when virtually every aspect of the campaign was regulated by the government, including the times of party rallies and the size of the crowds. Speeches had to be submitted in advance, and could discuss nothing but economic development.

Through the 1980s and early 1990s, millions of young, literate, educated Indonesians became newly eligible to vote, only to find their aspirations for change frequently frustrated. Increasing corruption at every level within the government administration, ever more excessive displays of nepotism by Suharto's family, and a continued intolerance by the regime for outspoken critics led to a gradual increase in scenes of public disorder. Most infamous of such incidents was the killing of pro-independence demonstrators in the east Timorese town of Dili in November 1991, but there were many other, smaller signs of dissatisfaction – many of them the result of land-grabbing by politically well-connected businessmen.

In a typical incident of the period, in mid-1995, tobacco farmers in Jember, east Java, went on the rampage in protest at local government officials transferring land – which the farmers had been tending for many years – to a state-owned plantation company. The same year, there were more riots in Dili – a predominantly Catholic town in east Timor – after a Javanese Muslim prison officer there denounced Catholicism as a nonsense religion; and in west Java, anti-Chinese riots followed the alleged mistreatment of a Muslim girl for stealing a chocolate bar from a Chinese-owned shop. Dozens of such disturbances occurred through the 1990s, often triggered by a seemingly petty incident, and frequently taking the form of religious or ethnic unrest. Much more serious was an outbreak of ethnic blood-letting in west Kalimantan in early 1997, which claimed perhaps 1000 lives.

Although the economy was steadily growing, and average per capita income was soaring from little more than $100 in 1970 to $1200 in 1991, the new wealth was not evenly distributed: a vast share went to a tiny group of tycoons and Suharto family cronies, which did little to appease the 800,000 or so frustrated young people who entered the job market each year but could not find full-time employment.

Suharto's family and friends

People's greatest resentment was directed at Suharto's relatives and cronies, who enriched themselves to a staggering degree. His children became multi-millionaires – some of them billionaires – with significant interests in virtually every sector of the economy. On occasion, they squabbled among themselves in their endless hunt for easy riches – most notoriously when the eldest son and daughter battled for control of Busang, a gold mine in East Kalimantan touted as the world's richest gold find, which turned out to be a hoax. By mid-1996, the net worth of the six children was estimated at $6 billion; a CIA estimate of the family's total worth in 1998 was $30 billion.

Suharto's eldest daughter, popularly known as Tutut, owned the vastly profitable toll-roads in Jakarta, as well as dozens of other companies. His second son, Bambang Trihatmodjo, wealthiest of them all, was perhaps the most shrewd and capable business man, earning grudging respect for his acumen, but who nevertheless took full advantage of his privileged position. Greatest disdain was shown for the youngest son, Tommy, who most blatantly abused his position to win the contract to develop a 'national car' and to establish a monopoly in the trade of cloves.

Also close to Suharto were a group of enormously rich tycoons, among them Mohamad 'Bob' Hasan who for many years held a monopoly in the immensely profitable plywood trade, and Liem Sioe Liong, whose conglomerate, Salim Group, in 1991 accounted for five per cent of Indonesia's GNP.

Demise of the New Order

Suharto's eventual departure resulted largely from the regional economic crisis which spread across south-east Asia and began to buffet Indonesia in mid-1997. By October, the rupiah had collapsed and the IMF (International Monetary Fund) was proposing a $33 billion bailout plan to help restore confidence in the economy. The government resisted the plan for several months, while the *rupiah* grew ever weaker and a drought caused by El Niño led farmers to flock to the cities in search of work. The ranks of unemployed were boosted by thousands of Indonesian migrant workers sent home from struggling economies in Malaysia and Saudi Arabia. By February 1998, average per capita income had collapsed to $300, and only 22 of 286 publicly listed companies were still solvent; the *rupiah*, meanwhile, had lost 75 per cent of its value over the past seven months. Increasingly desperate people began to look for scapegoats, and almost inevitably the Chinese community was blamed. Although it makes up about three per cent of the population, the community's economic clout is vastly more significant; consequently, looters began to target Chinese properties in towns across Java.

It now seems likely that much of the anti-Chinese sentiment was in fact stirred up by military elements in an attempt to divert popular criticism away from Suharto's re-election, due in March 1998. In the months preceding the election, pro-democracy activists had begun to disappear, apparently arrested and tortured by Kopassus units – the military special forces. Suharto was duly re-elected unopposed to serve his seventh presidential term, and promptly announced a new Cabinet which included his eldest daughter and several prominent business associates.

With another five years of Suharto now seeming inevitable, and the economy showing no signs of improvement, students began to demonstrate for change on campuses across Java. In early May, four were shot dead by police or soldiers at Trisakti University in Jakarta. This incident triggered waves of rioting and looting across the city in which more than 500 people died. Property linked to Suharto's family and friends was frequently targeted by the furious looters, but again there appears to have been a deliberate attempt, perhaps by renegade army units, to fan racial hatred and encourage the targeting of Chinese premises, and most shockingly, the mass rape of Chinese women and young girls. In the aftermath of Suharto's downfall, nearly two hundred such rape cases were documented – possibly just a proportion of the total.

Habibie's presidency

On 21 May 1998, after 32 years in control, Suharto resigned. Thirty thousand students had invaded the parliament complex the previous week and kept up a vociferous call for him to go. The vice-president, B.J. Habibie, was sworn in as his successor.

Habibie, formerly the Minister for Research and Technology, was a German-trained engineer, who for many years had been one of Suharto's closest protégés. His own family's business empire was worth an estimated $60 million in mid-1998. He quickly distanced himself from the Suharto regime, however. He released several high-profile political prisoners, apologised for the previous government's human rights abuses, and in a radical and highly controversial move, agreed to allow a UN-sponsored referendum on independence for East Timor, the troubled former Portuguese colony invaded by Indonesia in 1975.

Habibie also permitted the formation of new political parties, and for the first time since 1955, authorised competitive multi-party elections for mid-1999, with presidential elections at the end of the year. He further announced the abolition of the special symbol on identity cards formerly required to identify ethnic Chinese, and in August 1998, Golkar – the government party – removed seven of Suharto's relatives, including Tommy, Bambang and Tutut, from their parliamentary seats.

But the economic strife which had swept Suharto from power continued to generate frequent protests by students demanding faster political and social change, and in November, the security forces in Jakarta shot dead more than a dozen demonstrators during clashes near parliament.

Habibie found himself walking a knife edge between the democratic forces unleashed by his reforms and a conservative military wary of losing its huge political clout.

For those promoting the ideals of democracy, the parliamentary elections in June 1999 were generally a success. Almost 50 political parties took part, and 21 of them won at least one seat. But there was no overall majority, and the final results of the ballot were not announced for many weeks – which led to widespread suspicion that the result was being rigged. The government party, Golkar, came second.

Meanwhile, in August, the UN-organised vote on **East Timor**'s future produced a massive majority in favour of independence. With a turnout of nearly 99 per cent, almost 80 per cent voted to leave Indonesia. In the immediate aftermath of the vote, furious pro-Jakarta militia swept across East Timor, systematically destroying the capital, Dili, and several smaller towns, terrorising the population, and killing hundreds, while the Indonesian military stood and watched, offering tacit support to this scorched earth policy.

The UN, seemingly caught unawares, in the end reacted to the world's disgust by sending in a peace-keeping force. It was too late to prevent the wholesale destruction of the territory, but it did quickly put a halt to much of the terror.

The loss of East Timor, however, was not well received by most Indonesians, and especially by the military, who saw it as a threat to the unity of the nation state. Already, other parts of the country were clamouring for their own referendums on independence – especially Aceh and Irian Jaya, at the extreme west and east ends of the country, where secessionists had been waging low key guerrilla wars on and off since the 1940s.

The pragmatic Habibie had done more for democracy in 15 months than his predecessors had done in 40 years, but the result was threatening to tear the country apart. With the nation still reeling from the economic crisis of mid-1997, the political crisis caused by the East Timor vote came at the same time as a bank scandal which threatened to implicate Habibie himself, or at least his close associates.

Facing a hostile parliament, and a military which detested him for what it saw as his meek surrender of East Timor, Habibie pulled out of September's presidential election just before the vote.

The winner was Abdurrachman Wahid, a 59-year-old, partially blind, moderate Muslim cleric who commanded widespread respect, both in parliament and among the population in general, through his chairmanship of the 40-million strong Muslim group, Nahdlatul Ulama.

Abdurrachman Wahid at the helm

Often described by the media as frail, Wahid nevertheless was quick to assert himself. A realist, he withdrew the last of the Indonesian military from East Timor by the end of October, and soon afterwards held meetings with Xanana Gusmao, the de facto leader of the new East Timor state, in an attempt to reconcile the two sides.

In another conciliatory move, Wahid announced he would pardon former president Suharto, should he be found guilty of charges of corruption. His family and friends, however, will not be excused. Meanwhile, the war against corrupt government officials is to continue.

The nation's economy shrank by about 15 per cent in 1998, with further recession forecast for 1999; most economic gains made under Suharto were lost in just a few months. By the end of 1998, up to half of Indonesia's 88 million workers were either jobless or underemployed, and Indonesia had become a major rice importer, buying up to a quarter of the world's traded rice – a far cry from its years of virtual self-sufficiency a decade earlier.

But perhaps Wahid's biggest problems remain the increasingly loud and violent demands for independence from secessionist groups in Aceh, and ethnic blood-letting in the central spice islands of the Moluccas, where Christian fighting Muslim has become an all too familiar occurrence in the past couple of years.

Entering the 21st century, Indonesia looks more fragile than it has at any time since 1950, with huge political, social and economic hurdles to overcome. There are calls by some – albeit mostly foreigners – for a federal type of political system, but it appears the current government will try to prevent further break-up of the nation by instead offering greater autonomy to the provinces on the edge of the archipelago which feel left out of the Javanese-dominated political and economic processes.

Art and architecture

Art and architecture of Hindu-Buddhist Java, 400–1500

by William Southworth

Early period (c 400–732)

The Hindu and Buddhist religions were both introduced into Java at about the beginning of the 5C AD, in a process which was later accompanied by the foundation of temples and monasteries, and complemented by a florescence of religious sculpture; stone relief carvings and statuary were produced according to Indian iconographic models, as well as statuettes and ritual objects of bronze, silver and gold. The earliest known inscriptions, written in Sanskrit – the sacred language of India – using south Indian scripts, also appear from this time.

Early development

Many early scholars, writing during the Dutch colonial period, suggested that these religious ideas were brought directly to Java by Indian colonists, and that the surviving monuments were the work of Indian, rather than indigenous, craftsmen. This view, however, was keenly disputed, and it now appears certain that the initial spread of Indian religion and iconography to Java was essentially a cultural adaptation by the Javanese themselves of new religious ideas which arrived on Java as a result of the growing trade and cultural interaction between India, southeast Asia and China.

Buddhist monks from India certainly travelled on merchant ships to China, stopping in Malaya, Sumatra and Java on the way; Gunavarman, an Indian missionary, is thought to have converted a Javanese king to Buddhism in the 5C. At the same time, pilgrims from China and southeast Asia travelled to the great religious centres of the Indian subcontinent; among them was the Chinese pilgrim, Fa Xian, who travelled throughout central Asia and India in the early 5C, and returned to China via Indonesia.

The increase of popular worship

The international appeal of Indian religious philosophy at this time coincided with a number of radical developments in the practice of the Hindu and Buddhist religions in India itself, particularly in the south.

The complexity of traditional Hindu Brahman ritual and the remoteness of the deities reverenced in the ancient scriptures of the *Vedas*, as well as the non-theistic traditions of Theravada Buddhism, were challenged by an undercurrent of popular worship, which expressed a desire for the tangible presence of the deity, and for the establishment of a direct and personal relationship with them. This was achieved through the founding of free-standing temples within urban areas, in which the deity could be made manifest in the form of aniconic symbols or through stone and bronze statuary. This movement resulted in the development of local legends and religious traditions, yet it was combined also with monistic ideas of a single transcendant deity – identified either with Vishnu as Bhagavata, or Shiva as Pasupata or Maheshvara.

This new combination of religious philosophy, monist cults and popular worship was later formalised in the hymns of the *bhakti* movement of 'personal devotion', and had a profound effect on the spread of both Hinduism and Buddhism throughout southeast Asia.

Early inscriptions and images

The earliest known Sanskrit inscriptions on Java have been found in the west of the island, inscribed onto huge boulders of natural rock (see p 231). Five have been discovered, all bearing inscriptions apparently written on the orders of a king, Purnavarman, and are traditionally dated to the mid-5C. In addition to the lines of text, the inscriptions were accompanied by the outsize imprints of the feet of the king and his war elephant, which were likened respectively to those of the Hindu god Vishnu, and of the elephant Airavata, the mount of Indra.

Several early Vishnu images have also been found in west Java, and dated to the 6C or 7C. They can be directly compared to sculptures of Vishnu of similar date from north and southeast India, southern and central Thailand, Cambodia and southern Vietnam; carved from a single block of stone, they depict Vishnu with multiple arms and wearing a conical crown or mitre, and carrying his common attributes, the conch and discus.

By the 7C, the main centres of Buddhism in Indonesia appear to have developed in southern Sumatra, and belonged to a kingdom known as Shrivijaya. Several inscriptions found near modern Palembang, written in Old Malay and Sanskrit, using south Indian script and dated to the late 7C, attest to the power of this kingdom. Furthermore, the Chinese Buddhist scholar-pilgrim, Yijing, is also known to have studied there in the course of his journeys to and from India in the late 7C; his narrative notes the size and importance of the Buddhist monasteries he visited there.

Large bronze statues of the Buddha have been found throughout Indonesia, some of the earliest in southern Sumatra, eastern Kalimantan, central and east Java, and western Sulawesi. These have proved extremely difficult to date accurately, but are now thought to belong to the 7C or 8C. The Buddha is usually shown standing, with one hand performing the *mudra*, or gesture, of teaching, while the other holds an alms-bowl or the hem of his long robe. The robe itself can be depicted as plain or pleated, although the right shoulder appears always to be uncovered. Known examples display a wide variety of styling, and demonstrate the diversity of Buddhist contacts across Asia at this time.

Central Javanese period (c 732–929)

The earliest known central Javanese king, Sanjaya, dedicated a *linga* to Shiva in 732 after defeating neighbouring princes in war; the inscription narrating this event was rediscovered at Gunung Wukir (see p 323), northwest of Yogyakarta. Almost all the monuments and inscriptions of central Java date from the period 732–929, and thus form a natural grouping for classification and study.

Early Shaivite temples and iconography

The Shiva temples of the **Dieng plateau** (see p 274) and **Gedong Songo** (see p 283) represent an early tradition of Shiva-veneration established before 778, although these sites continued to be developed throughout the central Javanese period. Both sites are situated at high altitude in active volcanic regions, and the temple groups were almost certainly associated with the curative sulphur springs nearby. The buildings themselves represent the Hindu temple at its simplest and most essential form, consisting of a single-cell shrine, capped by a roof or tower made up of two or three diminishing storeys. Each shrine is raised on a platform or foot, and is entered via a short stairway, usually on the west side. Niches on the other three sides would originally have contained votive statues of divinities connected with the worship of Shiva.

Although the wall niches at Dieng and Gedong Songo are now mostly empty, sculptures and relief panels from later temples show a regular pattern of iconography: the niche in the north wall displays Durga, the consort of Shiva, in her role as Mahishasuramardini or 'slayer of the buffalo demon'; in the rear niche (east or west, depending on the temple's alignment) is Ganesha, the elephant-headed son of Shiva; the south niche contains an image of Agastya, the sage accredited with the spread of Shaivism in Java; the two niches flanking the entrance to the sanctum contain Shiva's loyal attendants, Nandishvara and Mahakala.

Shiva temples were also often faced by a secondary shrine containing an image of the bull, Nandi, Shiva's mount and foremost devotee. Unlike the principal temples constructed of stone, secondary shrines were frequently built of brick or wood; these have deteriorated, leaving only brick or laterite foundations, but stone examples still exist at Dieng and Gedong Songo. The temples were sealed by wooden doors, none of which remain.

The iconography of Hindu and Buddhist sculpture

The complete sculptural composition of Shiva, Ganesha, Agastya and Durga can be seen at several sites, including one of the temples at Gedong Songo; Candi Selogriyo (see p 280) near Magelang (though the images here are severely damaged); Candi Sambisari (see p 325) near Yogyakarta; and Candi Shiva in the Loro Jonggrang complex (see p 326) at Prambanan.

According to Indian mythology, **Durga Mahishasuramardini** was a goddess of immense beauty created from the combined *shakti* or 'power' of the gods, as the embodiment of their anger at the usurpation of heaven by the buffalo demon, Mahishasura. This heterogeneous origin is symbolised by her multiple arms carrying the weapons of the various gods, which she uses to defeat and slay the demon.

In Indonesian mythology, however, she was identified as Shiva's consort, **Parvati**, the daughter of the king of the mountain. She is usually portrayed with her lower right hand grasping the tail of the buffalo, while her left arm clutches the hair of the demon, whose spirit emerges from the throat of the buffalo at the moment of death. In her upper six arms she carries an assortment of weapons and martial symbols, including the discus, conch, trident, bow and arrows, sword and shield.

The elephant-god **Ganesha** is the son of Shiva and

Ganesha

*Six of the most commonly seen hand gestures (*mudra*) of the Buddha, all of which can be seen at Borobudur, the magnificent monument in central Java*

Top left: vitarka mudra
Top right: abhaya mudra
Mid left: dharmacakra mudra
Mid right: bhumisparsha mudra
Bottom left: dhyana mudra
Bottom right: varada mudra

Parvati, and in Indian mythology was considered leader of the *gana*, the dwarf attendants of Shiva. In Java, he is often represented in a martial aspect as the army commander of the gods. A very fine statue of Ganesha was found at Candi Banon, near Borobudur in central Java, and is now to be seen at the National Museum in Jakarta. He is shown seated, with the soles of his feet pressed together; his trunk is shown feeding from a bowl of sweets in his lower left hand, while his lower right hand holds his broken tusk. He carries a small axe in his upper left hand, and a rosary in his upper right. These iconographic details varied slightly according to region and time period.

Agastya is shown as a *rishi* or sage – a semi-divine teacher who acted as intermediary between the gods and humankind. He is portrayed as an elderly man in simple clothing, with a long beard and moustache, and a rotund, protruding belly. He is usually depicted wearing the sacred shoulder string of Shiva, and holds a small *kendi* or earthenware jar of sacred water in his left hand, and a rosary in his right. The statue of Agastya from Candi Banon, also in the National Museum in Jakarta, was once flanked by two kneeling figures or disciples, but only fragments of their feet and legs remain.

Shiva himself was often venerated in the form of a *linga* (a stylised phallus, carved from stone, representing both male fertility and the central axis of the universe), and placed on a *yoni* (representing the female sexual organ,

Agastya – the semi-divine teacher

and acting as a repository for the sacred water poured over the *linga* as part of the *puja* ceremony of worship); the combination of *linga* and *yoni* was positioned at the centre of the shrine.

The divine grouping of Shiva, Durga, Ganesha and Agastya has been compared to that of the royal court of king, queen, commander and counsellor. The vast majority of the major lowland temples were royal foundations, and expressed the power and munificence of the king or ruling dynasty, as well as reflecting and paying homage to that of the divinity.

Nandi

Statues of the bull, **Nandi**, usually depict him resting on the ground, with his head raised and alert, and with his legs folded under him. Sculptures of Nandi became increasingly elaborate over time, with the addition of elaborate collars, consisting of strings of bells, flowers and beads, and of layered blankets and saddles. Statues of Nandi can be seen at several sites, including Candi Pringapus (see p 280) near Parakan; Candi Gunung Wukir (see p 323) near Yogyakarta; Candi Nandi in the Loro Jonggrang complex (see p 329); and at the statuary store on the Dieng Plateau (see p 276).

The door guardians, **Nandishvara** and **Mahakala**, are named from later texts, but are clearly distinguished in central Javanese iconography. Nandishvara is placed in a niche to the left of the entrance, and usually has a calm, cultured appearance. He may be shown carrying a trident, *kendi*, rosary or fly whisk in his two hands. In contrast, Mahakala on the right is given a fierce, almost demonic countenance, and usually carries a club and dagger.

Aspects of Javanese sculpture

The iconography of Hindu and Buddhist statuary in Java initially followed Indian models, though greater variation appeared over time. Early Javanese sculpture is distinctive, however, in the modelling of the head and facial expression of anthropomorphic figures, and in the depiction of indigenous forms of dress and jewellery. Furthermore, a clear distinction was made between statues that were used as objects of worship – which were described by the Sanskrit and Old Javanese term *arca*, and denoted specifically the physical form of a deity – and those which performed a purely iconographic, demonstrative function. Images – even of major deities – were only considered *arca* when the statue had been placed within the temple and ritually consecrated by sacred water. A similar distinction is made in modern Bali between *togog* (statues that perform an iconographic but not a ritual function) and *pratima* (those which are believed to be the seat of the deity, and which are elaborately enthroned within the temple compound).

The outer walls of Javanese temples are often sculpted with a wide range of ornamental motifs, some of them possessing important mythological or ritual significance. The most universal are the *kala* and *makara* motifs. They appear on the doorways and niches at Dieng, and continue throughout the Hindu-Buddhist period in Java. The *kala*, a demonic face placed above the entrance or niche, is sometimes identified as the demon Rahu, who is said to have swallowed the universe, only to disgorge it again after being decapitated by the gods. The *makara* are dragon-like creatures, sometimes portrayed with the trunk of an elephant and the tail of a fish; they may perhaps be associated with the oral tradition that rivers or springs emerge from the mouths of crocodiles. *Makara* are usually portrayed on either side of the doorway or niche, with an arc of water, often depicted like foliage, issuing from their jaws and converging in the open mouth of the *kala*. Waterspouts, used to drain excess rainwater from the roof, are also often sculpted in the shape of *makara* heads.

The primary function of all Hindu temples was to house the deity made manifest within them, and to provide for their comfort and well-being. With the *linga* and *yoni* in position, there was often only room within the sanctuary for the *puja*, the rite of worship by the Brahmin priest, while other ceremonies, including music and dance, took place outside. Gold, silver and bronze objects donated by wealthy individuals for use in the *puja* ceremony have survived, including incense burners, dishes for food offerings, and containers for holy water.

Early Buddhism: the Shailendra dynasty

Theravada and Mahayana Buddhism appear to have coexisted during the central Javanese period. The Shailendra dynasty is known from inscriptions to have become the primary ruling power in central Java from c 778 to the mid-9C, and Buddhism undoubtedly flourished under Shailendra rule. The Buddhist temple of Candi Kalasan (see p 325) has been associated with the earliest known Shailendra inscription of 778, though it seems that the temple was rebuilt at least twice in its history, with the present structure perhaps dating from the mid-9C.

The pre-eminent Mahayana Buddhist monument in Java is undoubtedly **Borobudur** (see p 312). It too has been dated to the late 8C–mid-9C, partly on the basis of inscriptions discovered on the hidden foot of the monument; it was probably built over a considerable period, perhaps from c 780–860. As well as being the largest single ancient monument in Java, it is also the most richly decorated, with nearly 1500 panels of narrative relief carving and more than 500 statues of the Buddha.

A huge image of the historical Buddha, Shakyamuni Gautama, in Mahayana philosophy the human manifestation of the 'cosmic' Buddha Vairocana, is contained in Candi Mendut (see p 320), which by its position and alignment seems to be conceptually related to Borobudur. The Buddha is seated on a throne, flanked by the bodhisattvas, **Avalokiteshvara** and **Vajrapani**. Bodhisattvas are semi-divine beings who forego the final attainment of nirvana in order to help others gain enlightenment. The most important bodhisattvas can be easily recognised: Avalokiteshvara, the bodhisattva of compassion, usually carries in his headdress a miniature apparition of Amitabha, the 'cosmic' Buddha of the west; Manjushri, the bodhisattva of infinite wisdom, commonly carries the book of wisdom on a lotus in his left hand, and a sword in his right; Samantabhadra, symbolising the perfection of the bodhisattva's conduct, carries a three-stemmed flower; and Maitreya, the Buddha of the Future living his last existence as a bodhisattva, is portrayed with a miniature *stupa* in his headdress.

Small images of gold, silver or bronze depicting the major bodhisattvas, the cosmic Buddhas and Buddhist emblems have been found throughout Java, and may well have been used for personal veneration. Similar Hindu images have also been found, but only appear to have been produced in large numbers during the 9C and 10C. After the demise of the Shailendra dynasty in the mid-9C, Hindu religion and philosophy again became the predominant tradition among the ruling princes of central Java.

The Trimurti at Loro Jonggrang: Shiva, Vishnu and Brahma

Although Vishnu was clearly venerated in central Java, Shiva was always considered the highest god in central Javanese Hinduism: even in the Old Javanese version of the *Ramayana* (of which the hero Rama is recognised as an *avatar* or earthly incarnation of Vishnu), the pre-eminent position of Shiva is maintained. **Shiva** is central to the group of three main temples of Candi Loro Jonggrang at Prambanan (see p 327), a huge temple complex constructed from the mid-9C to early 10C. The main sanctuary contains a rare anthropomorphic statue of Shiva standing on the *yoni*, and also includes secondary chambers dedicated to Durga, Ganesha and Agastya. Shiva is identified by the third eye in his forehead, and by the symbols of the crescent moon and skull in his headdress. He is usually depicted holding a fly-whisk and rosary, among other emblems.

The central Shiva temple of **Loro Jonggrang** is flanked by temples to Brahma in the south and to Vishnu in the north. The *trimurti* (trinity) of Shiva, Brahma and Vishnu was also worshipped at Candi Banon (near Borobudur) and at Dieng. **Brahma**, the Creator, is identified by his four heads, each facing towards one of the cardinal directions. He is sometimes depicted holding a *kendi*, fly-whisk and rosary, and riding his mount, the sacred goose, Hamsa. **Vishnu** is depicted holding his main emblems, the discus and the conch, in his upper right and upper left hands; his lower hold a club and a sphere or cube. Occasionally, as at Candi Ijo (see p 332) and Candi Loro Jonggrang, he is shown in the form of one of his ten earthly incarnations – sometimes as Narasimha, a man-lion; as Trivikrama, a dwarf; as the hero Rama; or as Krishna, whose cosmic battles with the demonic forces of nature are illustrated in the reliefs at Loro Jonggrang.

Opposite each temple within the central enclosure of Candi Loro Jonggrang is a shrine to the vehicle of the deity: Nandi, the bull of Shiva; Garuda, the bird of Vishnu; and Hamsa, the goose of Brahma.

A recent study has suggested that the entire central enclosure may originally have been flooded, as an earthly reflection of the heavenly Mount Meru at the centre of the Sea of Milk. This idea is supported by the unusual thickness of the enclosure wall and the height of the temple bases, and corresponds roughly to the description of a Shiva temple in the Old Javanese version of the *Ramayana*. Whether or not this was the case at Loro Jonggrang, it is certain that highly complex hydraulic systems were sometimes incorporated into the design of Javanese *candi* and religious complexes.

Outside the central enclosure at Loro Jonggrang is a second courtyard comprising four concentric rings of smaller shrines, now mostly ruined, but originally numbering 224. This type of plan can also be seen at Candi Sewu (see p 329), where four concentric rings of 240 subsidiary shrines surround the central Buddhist sanctuary.

Temple construction

Nearly all the temples of central Java are constructed from andesite, a dark and roughly textured volcanic rock which occurs naturally in the region. In the early temples, small dressed blocks of andesite were used to gradually build up the walls of the temple, but at Loro Jonggrang, Candi Plaosan and Candi Sojiwan, all located near Prambanan (see p 324), huge boulders were used, some weighing up to 600kg. For the interior of these three temples, a type of marl was employed to provide a smoother finish to the walls; all three have been dated to the latest period of the central Javanese style, from the mid- to late 9C.

Some brick temples may also have been constructed in central Java, as brick was commonly used for religious buildings in mainland southeast Asia at this period. Brick and wooden structures, however, are less resilient than those of stone, and many have no doubt been lost.

On the hills south of Prambanan, the remains of what was probably a palace complex have been found. A large walled terrace, laid out with stone pillar bases, was probably the site of a wooden columned hall or *pendopo*, similar to those found at the royal *keraton* of Yogyakarta and Surakarta today.

Cutaway of typical Javanese candi

East Javanese period (c 929–1500)

Around the year 929, the political and religious centre of Java appears to have shifted to the east of the island, encouraging closer commercial and cultural contacts between Java and the eastern islands of Indonesia, especially Bali. Some scholars have also argued that the relative abandonment of the great religious sites of central Java from this time may have been the result of a severe volcanic eruption, most probably from Gunung Merapi, which may have been interpreted as a sign of the gods' displeasure. Important transformations in religious doctrine also seem to have taken place.

During the 11C and 12C, Vishnu was given prominence over Shiva in the court ceremonies of Java, and was part of a renewed spiritual movement contemporary with a similar revival of Vaishnavism in India. Court literature from this period begins with eulogies to Vishnu, and Javanese kings were portrayed as incarnations of the deity. Religious handbooks were also used to give instruction on how to obtain unification with the transcendental forms of the deity through yoga and other means.

The art of east Java is often divided into four sub-periods, based on important political events. The first sub-period, distinguished by renewed conflict with the kingdom of Shrivijaya in Sumatra, is dated from **929 to the death of King Airlangga in 1049**. Airlangga was the son of the Balinese prince Udayana and a Javanese princess, and contacts with Bali were exceptionally close at this time. The bathing places of Jolotundo and Belahan (see pp 376–377), in the foothills of Gunung Penanggungan, are closely associated with Udayana and Airlangga respectively, but few other structures can be stylistically dated to this period with any accuracy. The extraordinary terracotta statue of Vishnu riding his mount, Garuda, discovered at Belahan and now in the Trowulan Museum (see p 380), is the most famous image from this period: while Vishnu, seated in royal ease with his lower hands folded in meditation, retains the serenity of central Javanese sculpture, he is almost dwarfed by the rampant figure of Garuda beneath him, the demonic jaws of the mythical bird appearing to bellow with rage, his right foot crushing the body of a writhing *naga*. This statue is thought to represent the deified form of Airlangga, united with Vishnu after his death.

Before his death in 1049, Airlangga divided the kingdom between his two sons, creating the states of Kediri and Janggala. The period 1049–1222 is therefore described as the **Kediri period**, after the more powerful of these two states.

No surviving temples can be firmly dated to this time, and it is possible either that less durable materials were used, or that buildings were destroyed or rebuilt by subsequent dynasties. The kingdom of Kediri ended in 1222 with the usurpation of a commoner, Ken Angrok, who established a new capital at Singhasari (Singosari, near Malang).

A number of royal foundations associated with particular kings of the **Singosari dynasty** have survived, notably Candi Kidal (see p 368), which was established as the funerary temple of King Anushapati (d. 1248); and Candi Jago (see p 367), which performed the same function for King Vishnuvardhana on his death in 1268. It has been suggested that Candi Jawi (see p 377) and Candi Singosari (see p 369) were perhaps built as the reign temple and funerary temple respectively of King Kertanagara (r. 1268–92), the son of Vishnuvardhana.

The art historian Marijke Klokke has suggested that Java experienced a major break in religious development in the 13C, with fundamental changes occurring under the kingdoms of Singosari (1222–92) and **Majapahit** (1292–c 1500). During this period Hinduism and Buddhism are described as two distinct but equal paths to the highest transcendental reality. This is expressed in the Old Javanese text, *Sutasoma*, as '*bhinneka tunggal ika*' – 'different but essentially one' – which has since become the motto of the Indonesian republic.

The essential form of Javanese temples also began to develop away from the pattern established in central Java, into a more distinctively localised idiom. The 13C shrine of Candi Kidal, dedicated both to Shiva and to King Anushapati of Singosari, retains the square sanctuary and raised platform of earlier temples. The prominence and height of the superstructure is exaggerated, however, by the addition of a heavy, overhanging architrave and an elongated, multi-storeyed tower rising up to a square pinnacle. A huge, rounded *kala* face is placed above the entrance and niches to ward off the influence of malign spirits. This appears more demonic than its central Javanese predecessors, with round, bulging eyes and curving horns above the head. A similar pattern of architectural design can be seen on Candi Jawi and on the dated temple at Panataran (see p 359). Candi Jabung (see p 398), built in the mid-14C, also conforms roughly to this concept, but the walls of the temple body are rounded and raised on a massive base.

Kala face on doorway at Candi Panataran

Candi Jago is one of the few exclusively Buddhist temples from the east Javanese period. The principal image depicts Amoghapasha Lokeshvara, a generalised form of the bodhisattva, Avalokiteshvara; this was originally accompanied by his four companions or *shakti* – elements or reflections of his divine power – Tara, Sudhanakumara, Hayagriva and Bhrikuti. The figure of Amoghapasha also represented the deified form of Kertanagara's father, Vishnuvardhana, and copies of this grouping appear to have been distributed to the king's dependencies. Kertanagara, the last ruler of the Singosari dynasty, followed Tantric forms of Buddhism and Hinduism, including the worship of Bhairava, a demonic aspect of Shiva. Tantric

Kala face at Candi Jago

philosophy of this period encouraged the deliberate breaking of taboos and the super-indulgence of the senses as a means of breaking through the conceptual veil of *maya* or worldly illusion. Cemeteries or burial grounds especially were linked to Tantric ritual, and skulls became common motifs in both Hindu and Buddhist iconography.

Majapahit (1292–c 1500)

After the assassination of Kertanagara in 1292, one of his sons-in-law set up a new ruling dynasty at Majapahit (Trowulan), near the modern town of Mojokerto. Majapahit was the last of the great pre-Islamic kingdoms in Java, and the Majapahit period is generally dated from 1292 to c 1500. The majority of surviving east Javanese temples were constructed during Majapahit's hegemony, and show a clear development in architectural form. While the larger monuments of central Java were built in a concentric plan, with the main temple or structure in the centre, and subsidiary shrines radiating outwards from it, the principal sanctuary of an east Javanese temple is positioned at the far end of a temple complex or compound, with a gradual progression of secondary temples leading up to it. This pattern of progression is emphasised at Candi Jago and Candi Panataran, both of which were rebuilt and extended in the mid-14C. Both are raised on a series of terraces, allowing a gradual ascent to the main sanctuary. This type of plan is still employed in Bali today, with the principal shrines raised at the innermost end of the temple complex.

The shrine of Candi Singosari is unusual in having a two-tiered structure, with a lower series of cellas which once contained Hindu images (one – Bhatara Guru – is still present), and an upper sanctuary which was probably reserved for a Buddhist configuration. This type of dual sanctuary, dedicated both to Hindu and Buddhist worship, is mentioned in the Old Javanese texts of this period.

The translations of Sanskrit and Pali texts into Old Javanese demonstrate the gradual acculturation of Hindu and Buddhist ideas into a local religious context; this was followed by original compositions which formed the basis of an indigenous Javanese literary tradition. The *Negarakertagama*, written in 1365 by Prapanca, the court poet of King Hayam Wuruk (r. 1350–89), contains biographies of the kings of the Singosari and Majapahit dynasties, emphasising their divine origin and their reassimilation to divinity at death. Funerary temples were erected in their memory, and contained an image representing an iconographic fusion of both the deity and the deceased king. According to certain texts, statues of the deceased king unified with the deity were sometimes placed in *prasada* or high tower structures within the palace compound. The *puja* ceremony was intended to bring both to life, with the *dharma* of the deceased king able to exert a powerful influence on the lives of his descendants.

East Javanese sculpture and reliefs

The sculpture of the east Javanese period also became increasingly exaggerated or idealised. Although clearly developed iconographically from those of central Java, religious statues from east Java and Bali appear progressively compacted, as if emphasising their intensity and power. Depictions of Durga Mahishasuramardini become more emboldened, and show the goddess standing with feet apart upon the fallen body of the buffalo demon. Relief carving appears increasingly two-dimensional – with almost flat, lightly engraved figures barely raised above a level background. The shape of the figures also becomes more angular, prefiguring the slender but angular forms of the *wayang kulit* – flat leather puppets in the shadow drama of contemporary Java.

The reliefs depicted on east Javanese temples can often be identified from surviving Old Javanese texts. Among the most popular subjects are the Tantri themes of the *Tantri Kamandaka*, an Old Javanese version of a south Indian narrative cycle. It tells the familiar story of a king who takes a new bride each day, until no more suitable girls can be found. The king's minister finally presents his daughter, Tantri, for marriage, and to maintain the king's interest she narrates to him a complex series of interrelated stories, based on the tale of friendship between a lion and a bull and similar themes. Many of these animal stories are based on wisdom literature, and can be interpreted as political allegories. Representations of them can be seen at Candi Jago, Candi Mirigambar (see p 357), Candi Panataran, Candi Surowono and Candi Rimbi (see p 381).

Durga Mahishasuramardini figure from Candi Jawi

The Indian epic poem, the *Mahabharata*, was used as a rich source of material for Javanese stories and narrative reliefs, and remains the primary source of stories for today's *wayang kulit* performances. In the Old Javanese *Parthayajna* and *Arjunavivaha* versions of this epic, the eldest of the Pandava brothers, Yudhishthira, stakes his siblings' inheritance on a game of chess with the eldest of his cousins, the Kauravas, who wins by cheating. Yudhishthira asks his brother Arjuna to seek the help of the gods, and the stories are based on the tests given to him, including the popular temptation of the seven heavenly maidens. These stories are depicted on Candi Jago, Candi Surowono, Candi Kedaton (see p 398), and in Gua Selomangleng (see p 356) near Tulungagung. Stories from the *Ramayana* cycle, especially those involving the monkey prince Hanuman, and from the *Krishnayana*, showing Krishna's love for Rukmini, were also popular, and are illustrated on the main temple at Panataran.

As well as depicting and adapting stories from the epic Indian cycles, many indigenous legends are also shown. One of the most popular is the story of *Shri Tanjung*, about a beautiful maiden who agreed to elope with her lover Sidapaksha to his home country. The king of this country, however, falls in love with Shri Tanjung and sends Sidapaksha on a dangerous errand to heaven. When he unexpectedly returns, the king deceives him into believing that Shri Tanjung has been unfaithful, and he kills her in his anger before realising his mistake. The soul of Shri Tanjung travels through the underworld to heaven, but is told that the time of her death has not yet come, and upon her being revived by Durga, the lovers are reunited. Scenes from this story are not easy to identify, but the image of Shri Tanjung riding on a fish-like creature through the underworld can be seen on the *pendopo* terrace at Candi Panataran and on Candi Surowono.

In addition to problems of identifying motifs, the placement and sequence of reliefs on east Javanese temples can be confusing. Rather than presenting a clear narrative sequence, scenes, stories and motifs are combined to illustrate qualities or themes appropriate to the deified king to whom the temple was dedicated.

Rituals and ritual objects

Small devotional statuettes made of gold, silver and bronze were produced in large numbers during the central Javanese period, but became increasingly rare from the 10C onwards. In east Java, these are replaced by a wide range of ritual objects including bells, lamps, incense burners and tripods, as well as distinctive four-pronged *vajra* symbols, which appear individually and on staffs and bells.

An important ritual was formulated at this time to sanctify the production of holy water, itself linked to the cult of mountain springs and mountain worship. The *Mahabharata* includes the story of the 'Churning of the Sea of Milk', which tells how the Hindu gods and demons used the *naga* wrapped round Mount Meru to churn the primordial ocean and obtain the elixir of life. In one Javanese version, the gods transport Mount Meru to Java, and it is the mountain itself, not the ocean, which produces the water of life. Bronze vessels have been found with layered necks representing the peaks of the mountain and with spouts cast in the shape of a *naga*; these were almost certainly used as vessels for holy water.

In east Java, the *naga* appears to have replaced the *makara* as the predominant symbol of water in temple architecture. This is evident from the development of architectural forms: the Naga temple at Panataran might have functioned as a storeroom for holy water, its walls and roof tower representing Mount Meru, encircled by the carving of a snake around the dais. The Panataran complex was constructed from the late-12C to the mid-15C, being expanded to house the funerary temples of the Majapahit kings.

The period after 1500

After the fall of Majapahit, c 1500, the Hindu-Buddhist tradition became supplanted in central Java by Islam, which had prospered in the northern coastal ports since the late 13C. The Hindu-Buddhist tradition was maintained for some time, however, in the eastern salient of Java (and still persists in rather altered form in the rugged Tengger highlands round Gunung Bromo). In Bali, the Hindu and Buddhist religions have been combined with the veneration of nature spirits and ancestors to form a syncretic religion, which may well preserve many aspects of the Javanese tradition; many ancient Javanese texts were preserved, copied and adapted in Bali, and Balinese Hinduism was included as an official state religion of Indonesia in the 1950s.

Buddhism has also seen a revival, being reintroduced and practised by Chinese merchant families in particular, who have combined Mahayana Buddhist traditions with Taoist and Confucian beliefs. In 1963, Buddhism was also recognised, as the fifth and last state religion of Indonesia (after Islam, Catholicism, Protestantism and Hinduism).

The monuments established during the great period of Hindu-Buddhist dominance in Java were largely abandoned until the early 19C, when European scholars and officials began to take a new antiquarian interest in them. Early reconstruction programmes were begun at the start of the 20C and have continued up to the present day, with major restoration work being conducted at Loro Jonggrang, Candi Sewu and Candi Barong (see p 332) during the last 15 years; Borobudur was rebuilt in a huge, UNESCO-sponsored project in the 1970s and 1980s. At present, Candi Plaosan (see p 330), Candi Sojiwan (see p 330) and Candi Ijo (see p 332) are being reconstructed. The remains of further *candi* are regularly discovered, although usually in poor condition, and it must be assumed that other treasures are still to be found. To modern Indonesian scholars, the surviving *candi*, sculptures and artefacts of the Hindu-Buddhist period represent ancestral *pusaka* or sacred heirlooms embodying the spirit and strength of the ancient Indonesian people who created and used them.

Religion and architecture on Bali

No-one can visit Bali without coming face to face with Balinese religion: rituals and festivals are so frequent and so ubiquitous that even the most dedicated hedonist, busily concentrating on a holiday in the sun, will at some point cross paths with its practitioners.

The official religion of the Balinese is usually described as Bali-Hinduism. It is not, however, immediately recognisable as the classical Hinduism of India. Bali-Hinduism has evolved since the 16C to combine aspects of the Javanese Hindu-Buddhist traditions and later Hindu influences which arrived directly from India, as well as older, animist beliefs. Thus, the forces of nature are worshipped as deities, as are ancestors; there are deities responsible for the rice harvest, for the irrigation system, for weapons, for trees, for musical instruments and dance costumes, for shadow puppets, for domestic animals, and much else. All benevolent forces are balanced by opposing, malevolent powers; stability is maintained, not by defeating the destructive force, but by balancing it with a positive force of equal power. Maintaining this harmony is fundamental to Balinese beliefs; it is achieved through continual, protective ritual and offerings, prayer and sacrifice.

The Bali-Hindu universe, reflecting this harmony, comprises three levels or realms. Upwards, towards the summit of Bali's highest volcano, Gunung Agung – the direction described as *kaja* – is the abode of the gods and deified ancestors who personify order. Downwards, towards the sea and the opposite of *kaja*, is *kelod*, the direction of demons who personify disorder. In between lies the human world. When, occasionally, the harmony between opposing spiritual forces is lost, a catastrophe, perhaps in the form of a volcanic eruption, a tidal wave or an epidemic, may strike the island. Such an occurrence is interpreted as a failing on the part of the Balinese to provide the correct rituals and sacrifices.

Bali-Hindu gods and demons

To comply with the Indonesian constitution, which demands that all officially recognised religions be monotheist in nature, contemporary Bali-Hinduism accepts a single creator god, known as Sang Hyang Widhi Wasa, of whom all other deities are manifestations. This is a relatively recent concept, dating from the early 1950s: the idea of a unitary creator was largely unknown to commentators writing about Balinese religion in the 1930s, let alone to villagers who had always believed in a multiplicity of gods.

In his anthropomorphic representation, Sang Hyang Widhi Wasa (also known as Atintya) is depicted in meditation, surrounded by flames. To encourage Balinese acceptance of this monotheistic concept, Pura Agung Jagatnatha (see p 103) was constructed in Denpasar; dominating the temple compound is a high *padmasana* or throne dedicated to Sang Hyang Widhi Wasa.

Chief among the other elements of the Bali-Hindu pantheon are the classical Hindu trinity: Brahma, the creator; Vishnu, the preserver; and Shiva, the dissolver or destroyer. Dewi Sri is the much-loved goddess of rice; Saraswati, the consort of Brahma, is the goddess of knowledge and the arts; Dewi Ulun Danu Batur, the goddess of Lake Batur, is considered one of the most powerful, as it is her waters which provide the irrigation for rice cultivation. Ida Bhatara Gunung Agung, the god of Gunung Agung, the island's highest and most sacred peak, is honoured at Pura Besakih, the largest, most important temple complex on Bali. Bhatari Durga, the consort of Shiva in her terrifying aspect, is most often manifest as Rangda, the queen of demons and witches. Deified ancestors are also extremely important, providing every Balinese with a highly personal link to the world of the gods.

Offerings

All spiritual forces, whether good or evil, must be honoured and entertained, or appeased, with rituals and offerings. Many rites have an exorcising or cleansing function; others promote personal spiritual and material well-being; some honour specific deities; others are performed for the dead, to permit the soul to return to the spirit world; and some are to ordain priests.

The visitor to Bali, even if only stepping between hotel room and beach each day, cannot fail to notice such offerings, for they are to be seen everywhere, everyday. Most commonly seen are *canang*, the tiny, ubiquitous, banana-leaf platters pinned with slivers of bamboo, and filled typically with cooked rice grains, flower petals, betel quid and incense. They are renewed each day; their importance is in the ritual, not the material substance, so the visitor need not worry unduly about treading on or driving over an old one. They are left to rot or be eaten by dogs, or may be swept up by the street sweeper on his rounds.

Balinese temples

The *pura*, an area of sacred ground in which shrines dedicated to various gods are placed, is generally, though perhaps somewhat inaccurately, translated as 'temple'. It is not a temple in the common sense of the word, but a space which the gods occasionally visit. There are many thousands of *pura* on Bali: most villages and urban neighbourhoods have at least three, and often several more, each serving a specific purpose. The three found in virtually every village are the *pura desa*, usually found in the heart of the village beside the village hall and serving as the community's main gathering place; the *pura puseh*, usually described as the 'temple of origin' and dedicated to the community's founders, which stands at the *kaja* (mountainward) end of the village; and the *pura dalem*, the 'temple of the great one', which stands at the *kelod* (seaward) end of the village, and which is usually dedicated to Shiva and associated with destruction and death.

Many other *pura* are related to *subak*, the water-sharing associations which manage most aspects of water irrigation for rice cultivation. These *pura* range from regional *pura masceti*, shared by many *subak* associations, to shrines known as *bedugul*, maintained by individual farmers in the corner of the paddy field where the water enters their land. *Pura* will also be found at every spring, lake and river headwater.

Some *pura* are associated with legendary priests and Shaivite-Buddhist sages credited with bringing Hindu beliefs to Bali; others belong to specific ancestral clans and royal families.

Etiquette for visitors

To enter the sacred compound of the *pura*, the visitor **must** be appropriately attired: both men and women must wear a *kamben* (sarong), and a *selendang* (waist sash); the shoulders should be fully covered. At some *pura* which regularly receive regular foreign visitors, signs may illustrate the dress code and appropriate behaviour, and there may be sashes and sarongs for hire; note that menstruating women may not enter. If you attend an *odalan* or temple festival (see below), more formal dress may be required: a buttoned shirt is appropriate, worn with a smart sarong and the waist sash. You should never clamber on the shrines, nor place yourself higher than a priest.

Layout of the pura

The *pura* usually comprises two or three courtyards containing a dozen or more shrines and other structures, but at its simplest may consist of a single compound with a couple of shrines. In most cases the basic layout is similar: the innermost courtyard is the most sacred, and usually will be on the *kaja* side of the complex. Here are found the most important shrines, which may take the form of the multi-tiered *meru* – a pagoda-like structure with between three and eleven tiers (always an odd number) – or they may be the single-storey, pavilion-like structures with small, closed wooden chambers known as *gedong* and *pelinggih*, which house religious artefacts or effigies of particular deities. These tend to line the *kaja* wall of the courtyard and the *kangin* (east) side. At the corner of the two sides will often be found the *padmasana*, a raised stone throne, sometimes rather abstract in design, which is the seat for Sang Hyang Widhi Wasa, the supreme deity. Near the centre of the innermost courtyard is usually an open, roofed pavilion, built as a gathering place for the deities when they descend to the *pura* for festivals.

The roofs of the shrines and pavilions are usually thatched with palm fronds, while the structures themselves are of wood or red brick, sometimes with elaborate carved stone at the base.

The courtyards of the *pura* are separated by often intricately carved stone and brick gateways. Leading into the innermost courtyard is usually a highly ornamented **kori agung**, an arched gateway which is usually closed except during festivals. It is decorated with the grotesque visage of Bhoma, the son of the forest, portrayed with fangs and bulging eyes, who is intended to frighten away evil forces. Beyond the gate there often stands an **aling-aling**, a low wall designed to deflect malevolent spirits, which have difficulty turning corners. Outer gateways may be in the form of the **candi bentar** (split gate).

In a corner of one of the outer courtyards is usually a tower or high pavilion containing the **kulkul** – one or more drums or wooden bells, beaten to summon the community, usually at festival time.

Other structures found in the *pura* include cockpits, where fights may be held during festivals; kitchen pavilions or *paon*, where offerings may be prepared; gamelan pavilions or *bale gong*, where a gamelan orchestra will play during festivals; and sculpted stone guardians known as *raksasa*, which are usually placed in pairs flanking a gateway.

Odalan

The *odalan* is an annual festival held by each *pura* to celebrate its foundation and to pay homage to the deities whose shrines lie within the sacred ground. Most *odalan* last for three days, though celebrations may last longer at some of the more important *pura*. The women of the community, dressed in their finest attire – often brightly coloured brocades – bring to the *pura* elaborate offerings from their household, in the form of towering *gebogan* piled high with artistically arranged fruit, brightly coloured rice cakes, eggs and flowers. These mountainous, seemingly gravity-defying offerings are secured to a hidden banana-trunk core. Ritual dances are usually performed, a gamelan orchestra will play, and there might be cockfights. The shrines and *pura* gates will be decorated with tall bamboo poles called **penjor**, from which are hung elaborate offerings made from plaited palm fronds; brightly coloured umbrellas covered with *perada* cloth (see below) will shade the shrines and offerings from the sun.

The date of the *odalan* varies from *pura* to *pura*, so visitors to Bali have plenty of opportunities to come across one somewhere on their travels round the island. The most important ones are listed in the cheap paper Balinese calendars sold in the main towns; any Balinese can help you interpret these somewhat complex, but highly informative documents. While foreign visitors are usually welcome at such events, they must be suitably dressed (see above).

Ceremonies for the dead

Among the most elaborate and spectacular of Balinese ceremonies are cremations, particularly of members of the former royal households. These can involve a cast of thousands, and require months of planning and preparation. The elements that a foreign visitor is most likely to see are the funerary procession and actual cremation, which occur on the same day.

Cremation is the means by which the soul is released from the human body so that it may be reincarnated. Unlike most Western funerals, a Balinese cremation is not a time for public sorrow, but for banter and boisterous activity, though not outright celebration; nevertheless, the many rituals are taken extremely seriously.

If the deceased is from a royal family, the corpse may have lain for two months or more in a mummified state, awaiting an auspicious day for the funeral. On the day of cremation, the wrapped, embalmed body is laid in a tall, brightly coloured, multi-tiered tower called a *bade*, built of wood, bamboo and paper, and decorated with monstrous faces, including the countenance of Bhoma; this is carried from the palace to the cremation site by scores of men from the local community. Also in the procession will be the *lembu*, a hollow, larger than life-size image of a bull (for men) or a cow (for women), borne aloft on a platform by dozens more men; this is the sarcophagus in which the body will be laid before cremation. The third main element of a royal funerary procession is Naga Banda, a mythical serpent-dragon, perhaps 50m long, representing the *naga* which ties mankind to the human world. This is later ceremonially 'shot' by the priest, thus freeing the soul of the dead.

At the cremation ground, the corpse is transferred from the *bade* to the *lembu*, which is packed with fine cloths and offerings and placed on a funeral pyre of wood soaked in kerosene; the priest pours holy water over the sarcophagus, and finally the entire structure is burnt, as is the magnificent *bade*.

After the conflagration, bone fragments from the corpse are retrieved to be pulverised into an effigy; they are later taken to the coast and cast into the sea. Further purification and deification rituals follow in the coming days and weeks.

Decorative arts and crafts

The Indonesian archipelago contains an incredible wealth of arts and traditional crafts, many of which can be easily found by the visitor to Java and Bali, and to a lesser extent on Lombok. The best-known internationally is Javanese batik, but modern Indonesian painters have in the past 30 years come to the world's attention and established a reputation for high-quality, original work. Detailed below are the most important arts and crafts, and those that visitors will almost certainly encounter on their travels through these islands.

Painting

Western-style painting with oil paints and watercolours was introduced into **Java** by the Dutch during the colonial era. Until c 1920, the European tradition of painting landscapes, portraits and still lifes was the dominant form; the best-known today of the Indonesian artists from this period is Raden Saleh (1810?–80), whose works have regularly sold at auction in the 1990s for several hundred thousand dollars (and in one case, $2 million). Since the 1920s, when less-traditional painting styles and subjects became increasingly dominant, many more Javanese artists have achieved international acclaim. Among the best known of this generation of modern painters are Affandi (1907?–90), Basoeki Abdullah (1915–92), Hendra Gunawan (1918–83), Sudjana Kerton (1922–94) and Widayat (b. 1919?), all from Java, and S. Sudjojono (1914–86) and Hassan Djaafar (1918–95) from Sumatra.

Many from this era are now household names among the region's collectors, and their art works predominate in Java's few art museums and galleries. There are, however, a great many highly talented younger artists, among them Dede Eri Supria (b. 1956), a painter of extreme social realism, Ivan Sagito (b. 1957), the best-known of the surrealists, Heri Dono (b. 1960), and Eddie Hara, who in the past decade have also attracted an appreciative international audience.

Bali has experienced a distinctly different painting movement, one which today is closely tied to the tourist market. Western-style painting was introduced by foreign artists residing on the island from the 1920s; prior to this, Balinese painters traditionally produced works primarily for religious functions, their style derived from the two-dimensional *wayang kulit* – the popular leather-hide puppets – and their themes taken from the *Ramayana* and *Mahabharata* epics. These early works, traditionally painted on long cloth scrolls, and dating back to the 18C (and possibly the 15C), today are known generally as classical or Kamasan-style paintings, after the village of Kamasan near Semarapura in southeast Bali, where the style is still produced today. The Museum of Classical Balinese Painting (see p 146) near Semarapura has a huge collection, while a smaller selection can be seen at the Museum Neka (see p 124) in Ubud. In Kamasan itself (see p 148) the tradition is maintained by scores of artists, who sell their work directly from the studio.

Among the influential European painters who settled in Bali in the early 20C was the German, Walter Spies, who came to Indonesia in 1923, staying first in Bandung, where he worked as a pianist, then in Yogyakarta, where he became conductor in the orchestra of Sultan Hamengkubuwono VIII. He moved to Bali in 1927, living initially in Campuhan on the west side of Ubud, and later moving to Iseh in Karangasem regency. Spies not only painted, but was a talented musician, composer, choreographer, photographer, botanist, archaeologist and linguist. In 1936 he founded an artists' group, 'Pita Maha', with a Dutch painter, Rudolf Bonnet, and the prince of Ubud, Cokorda Gede Agung Sukawati. The group, which attracted a membership of more than 100 local artists, sought to promote the sale of Balinese art while maintaining high artistic standards in the face of growing tourism and the inevitable accompanying commercialism. Bonnet himself had settled in Ubud in 1931, while other foreign artists, among them Miguel Covarrubias, Willem Gerard Hofker and Adrien-Jean Le Mayeur de Merprès, arrived about the same time.

The foreigners popularised styles, techniques and subject matter previously unused by the Balinese, and influenced the development of distinctive 'Ubud' and 'Batuan' styles, named after the centres where they evolved. Sanur, another important painting centre, was home to Covarrubias, Le Mayeur, and to Hans and Rolf Neuhaus, two Dutch brothers who ran a small art gallery and shop in Sanur for Bali's early tourists.

In the late 1950s, the highly distinctive 'Young Artists' style of painting developed in Penestanan, a village west of Ubud, where a Dutchman, Arie Smit, taught local boys how to paint in a somewhat naive, highly colourful style, and provided them with art materials.

Fine examples of all the various styles can be seen at the Museum Neka and other art museums in and near Ubud. Today, the once highly localised styles are much imitated by painters throughout Bali, seeking to cash in on the tourist trade. Furthermore, with the arrival of many other painters from Java and Sumatra, and more foreign artists seeking the paradise romantically reported by their predecessors, painting in Bali is now immensely diverse in nature; among the best known of today's artists are the abstract painter, Made Wianta, and the pointillist, I Gusti Ngurah Gede Pemecutan, both of whom have studios in Denpasar (see p 105).

Sculpture and woodcarving

The tradition of stone **sculpture** on Java probably predates the arrival of the Hindu and Buddhist religions from the 5C; on Bali, it accompanied the growth of Hinduism from the 9C. While a great deal of religious sculpture is still produced today on Bali to adorn renovated temples, most stone carving on both islands is now for the tourist market, both domestic and foreign. The main centres are Muntilan, north of Yogyakarta, and Batubulan on Bali, just northeast of Denpasar. At both places, soft, relatively lightweight volcanic stone is shaped into ornaments or religious icons; popular subjects include Ganesha and Garuda, the mount of the Hindu god, Vishnu.

There is a vast **woodcarving** industry on Bali catering to the tourist market, and dominated by the mass-production of cheap, softwood ornaments. In several villages round Ubud and further north, thousands of people are employed to copy designs for export. The subject matter changes every few years as the taste of the export market changes.

It wasn't always like this. As with stonemasons, artisans proficient in woodcarving have been much sought after for centuries to decorate Bali's numerous temple structures and palaces. Ornamental woodcarving is a concept of the 20C, which has grown as the tourist market for such work has expanded. Traditionally, some of the best work has been produced in Mas (see p 131), north of Denpasar, where several galleries offer a huge selection; although the craft is now practised more widely throughout Gianyar regency, Mas remains an important centre.

As with painting, a great number of today's artisans copy the style and form initiated by the best-known carvers in the 1930s – men like Ida Bagus Nyana (1912–85) from Mas, his son, Ida Bagus Tilem, and I Nyoman Cokot, who became known for his tree-trunks, fabulously carved with mythical demons and anthropomorphic monsters.

Wooden **face masks** carved to represent specific mythical figures are widely used in certain dance-dramas, in particular the *topeng* in Java and Bali, and the *wayang orang* and Barong-Rangda drama in Bali (see below). In Java, they are worn solely for theatrical effect. In Bali, however, masks used for certain ritual performances are believed to be occupied by ancestral spirits or gods, and are considered to be imbued with supernatural powers; the performer who wears such a mask is believed to 'become' the character it represents. The maker of such masks is an immensely skilled and respected artisan, who may take several months to complete a particularly special one.

Painted wooden face mask

Textiles

Textiles have played an important role in the islands of Indonesia since trade with India and China began to expand from the 5C AD, though the art of weaving most likely arrived several centuries before that, probably accompanied by a fledgling trade in textiles. Today, Java, Madura, Bali and Lombok all possess thriving textile traditions, though with the exception of batik, these are generally less well known to outsiders than the magnificent ikat fabrics of Nusa Tenggara and Kalimantan.

Java traditionally has been the principal centre of batik production in the archipelago. Batik today has come to mean cloth coloured by the wax-resist technique, an art which reached its most refined form in the 19C, both at the royal courts of Yogyakarta and Solo in central Java, and at Cirebon and other north coast towns, where Arab, Chinese and Indo-European entrepreneurs in the mid-19C began to fund Indo-European manufacturers to produce batik for the domestic market. These early producers painted the molten wax onto the cloth with a *canting* (the fine-spouted, copper waxing instrument – a 17C Javanese design) and used natural pigment dyes to make beautiful hand-drawn batik cloths known as *batik tulis*; the white cloth itself was imported in the 18C from India, and in the 19C from England, the Netherlands and Belgium. The decoration of a hand-waxed cloth could take a month or more to complete.

Demand for batik grew rapidly in the 19C, both domestically and for export, and by the 1840s producers were starting to use intricately patterned copper blocks known as *cap* to wax the cloths by section, making production faster; 20 cloths could be produced each day with this cheaper method. Most Arab and Chinese entrepreneurs switched to *batik cap* production, leaving the Indo-European factories on the north coast to produce the more expensive *batik tulis*; the latter could not compete economically, and by 1920 *batik tulis* production had largely collapsed. Today *batik tulis* is still produced by a few factories and individuals, but is expensive and usually is bought only for special occasions; the vast majority of batik made on Java today for everyday use is *batik cap*, or even imitation batik produced by screen or machine printing. Large factories in Solo today produce high-quality batik clothing; smaller production centres include Pekalongan, Cirebon and Tuban on the north coast. Yogyakarta is the centre for batik paintings, which are produced cheaply by the hundred for the tourist market; and for magnificent modern batik fine art, usually on silk, which attracts collectors worldwide.

On **Madura**, *batik tulis* remains a cottage industry, with whole villages round Pamekasan in the east, and round Tanjung Bumi on the north coast, producing both traditional, rough and simple red-based designs as well as more flamboyant modern variations.

Bali produces a wider variety of textiles, but is best known for the tie-resist cloths known as *endek*. Woven in cotton, silk or rayon, *endek* is better known outside Bali as weft-ikat, produced by tie-dying only the transverse or weft thread of the cloth; the warp thread (running lengthways) is left monochrome. Traditionally, the weft yarns are first stretched on a frame and tied with dye-resist bindings before dipping in the dye. The process is repeated for the different colours and finally the yarn is woven onto a loom; the monochrome warp thread is then woven into the weft.

Today, increasingly, the yarn is dyed using the much faster *cetak* process, whereby the chemical dye colours are painted onto the required parts of the weft thread and then covered with a tie resist before dipping in a dye bath containing the background colour. The result is not so precise, but several colours can be painted together much more quickly.

Much of Bali's *endek* is produced by small factories in Gianyar (see p 133), using shaft looms equipped with fly-shuttles, which are much faster than the traditional body-tension looms. *Endek* is also produced, on a much smaller scale, in Singaraja (see p 164) on the north coast, and Sideman (see p 159), as well as a few other centres.

Silk – and increasingly, rayon – embroidered with a supplementary weft of gold or silver thread is known as *songket*. Traditionally, *songket* brocades were worn by women of aristocratic families, but the cloth today is increasingly popular as ceremonial dress for whoever can afford it. Sideman is regarded as the source of the best *songket* on Bali.

Equally lavish is *perada*, a ceremonial cloth painted on one side with patterns in gold leaf (or more commonly today, in bronze paint). It is worn primarily by dancers, and can be seen at any performance of the *legong* or *gambuh*, for example, or on parasols at temple ceremonies.

The village of Tenganan Pegeringsingan (see p 152) in east Bali is the only place in Indonesia to produce fabric by the highly complex double-ikat method, in which both weft and warp are resist-dyed separately before being woven together. These remarkable textiles, known as *geringsing*, are woven from cotton on a continuous warp which produces a tubular fabric when removed from the loom. This uncut cloth is considered sacred, and across Bali is presented to the gods and ancestral spirits.

Every visitor to Bali will notice the black-and-white checkered *poleng* cloth seen draped round statues and shrines all over the island; the checks are usually described as representing the balance of positive and negative spiritual forces constantly at work on the island.

Weavers in **Lombok** traditionally use body-tension looms to produce weft-ikat fabrics similar to those of Bali, though large-scale production using semi-mechanised looms is now found in Cakranegara (see p 411) and Sukarara (see p 427); in Pringgasela (see p 417), a cottage industry producing *songket* and weft-ikat employs scores of villagers.

Ceramics

At old mosques on Java's north coast, and on the gateways and drum towers of old temples on Bali, it is not unusual to find Chinese Ming dynasty glazed ceramics decorating the brick walls; many have been lost, leaving an empty hollow, but others have been replaced with more recent 19C Dutch plates. Unlike China, Thailand and Vietnam, there is no tradition of large-scale ceramics manufacture on Java, Bali or Lombok; most early ceramics came here through trade.

Today, Kelampok (see p 271) near Banyumas in central Java is an important production centre, with many galleries lining the main road. In Bandung, the National Crafts Council (Dewan Kerajinan Nasional) at Jl. Braga 15 is responsible for marketing some of the fine ceramics made in Bandung. On Lombok, there are several villages with important cottage industries producing simple pottery. The best known include Banyumulek (see p 413) near Cakranegara; Rungkang (see p 416) and Masbagik Timur (see p 418) in central Lombok ; and Penujak (see p 427) in southern Lombok.

Gold, silver and the kris

The settlement of Kota Gede (see p 311), on the southeastern outskirts of Yogyakarta, is Java's main centre for the production of **silver** ornaments and jewellery. Silversmithing has been practised here for centuries: the first artisans served the royal court of Mataram. Today there are dozens of galleries and workshops producing a wide range of designs.

Bali, too, is an important producer of silver, mainly for export and the tourist market. The road between Batubulan and Celuk, to the northeast of Denpasar, is flanked by scores of small producers of both silver and gold jewellery.

Ancient **gold** hoards have been found at several sites on Java during the past 50 years, and gold implements have frequently been found during the excavation of Hindu-Javanese temples. Although there is little evidence of gold-mining on Java in the past, it is clear that for centuries gold has been considered a highly valued metal. Today there are commercial gold mines on Java, but most gold jewellery and ornaments are fashioned on Bali, round Celuk and Kamasan in particular.

Since at least the 5C, the fabulous **kris** (*keris*), a type of ceremonial dagger, has been forged in Java and elsewhere in the archipelago. The most important krises are believed to hold magical powers which can protect their owner and cause the downfall of enemies; equally, they can turn against their master if mistreated. Older krises are generally considered the more powerful, having absorbed the souls of previous owners into their supernatural strength; some are believed to fly through the air invisibly.

The finest krises, which are often but not always shaped with wavy blades, have individual names and are passed from generation to generation within a family, or presented from one dignitary to another, often accompanied by legends of their special powers. The damascene blades, traditionally made from alternating layers of carbon steel and nickel alloy steel, are laboriously heated, folded and hammered time and again by the expert artisan to give a magnificent multi-hued lustre or *pamor* to the blade surface. Different *pamor* are considered to have different inherent strengths and powers. The hilts, usually of wood (and sometimes of ivory), are often bejewelled, decorated with silver, or intricately carved and polished to a deep sheen; the scabbard too, is often a wonderful work of art, made from beaten gold, perfumed sandalwood, or painted, lacquered wood.

The most coveted krises are those forged in the 16C in the Mataram kingdom of central Java. The use of the kris today is purely ritualistic: they may be exchanged in a marriage alliance, or presented, within the scabbard, as a sign of goodwill and peace. Ancient krises kept in Java's royal palaces are ritually bathed each year with citrus juice and an arsenic compound to refresh and brighten the *pamor*. The guardians at the palaces of Solo and Yogyakarta can be seen with the kris tucked into their waist sash. Very fine antique examples can be seen in museums in Jakarta, Bandung, Yogyakarta, Denpasar and Mataram.

Basketry and bamboo

Throughout the islands of Indonesia, basketry made from palm fronds, rattan vines, pandanus, banana and coconut fibres, bamboo and other natural materials, is still used extensively – particularly in rural areas – for storage and a thousand other tasks, despite the ever-growing use of plastic and metal. You only need to visit Bogor's Ethnobotany Museum (see p 224) to see the amazing range of products. There are scores of different baskets designed for catching fish and for trapping animals; many are specifically designed for a particular species or a particular task, such as carrying a cock to the cockfight or transporting a pig to market. The materials are cheap and easily replaced when worn out, and their production can provide a secondary income for rural farmers. Particularly elegant boxes are made on Lombok from lontar palm fronds, and decorated with tiny shells.

Bamboo is an immensely versatile woody grass which can be made into musical instruments, scaffolding, containers for liquid, pipes for irrigation, weapons for hunting and slaughtering animals, and house frames. The oldest mosques on Lombok are built of bamboo, as are the walls of houses in some of Bali's most traditional settlements.

Drama, dance and music

Of all the islands of Indonesia, Java and Bali have particularly rich traditions of theatre and drama. Bali alone has scores of dance-drama forms; some are sacred rituals, others are purely secular in nature. Many have been reworked and shortened to make them more accessible to tourists. Detailed below are those which visitors to Java and Bali are most likely to encounter.

Wayang kulit

The shadow theatre tradition in Java using two-dimensional leather puppets, *wayang kulit* dates back at least to the 11C and possibly to the 9C. Cut from cured buffalo hide and mounted on a rod of buffalo horn, the puppets have hinged arms and are intricately painted and very carefully shaped to provide the correct characteristics required of a particular individual.

In western Java, most *wayang kulit* stories are adapted loosely from the *Ramayana* and *Mahabharata* Hindu epics, known collectively as *wayang purwa*. A professional *wayang purwa* puppet set contains c 200 puppets, of which perhaps 60 will be used in any single performance; wealthy patrons, who sponsor frequent performances, may own 400 or more.

In eastern Java, the repertoire known as *wayang gedog* – a collection of several cycles of stories set in the late Hindu kingdoms of Singosari, Kediri and Majapahit – is rather more popular. The hero of one of these cycles is Panji, prince of Kuripan, who, like Arjuna in the *Mahabharata*, is considered exceptionally noble and unbeatable in battle and love. Another popular cycle involves Damar Wulan, the stable boy and grass cutter who eventually becomes king of Majapahit.

Wayang kulit has been repeatedly adapted in the 20C to provide an entertaining teaching aid. A form known as *wayang suluh* was developed in the 1940s to narrate the struggle for independence from the Dutch; *wayang wahyu* has been used to narrate stories from the Bible. Present-day puppeteers may incorporate modern characters and ideas into their performance in a bid to maintain the interest of the younger generation.

Performances are usually sponsored by a family or institution, sometimes in connection with a religious ceremony or wedding, or as a gesture of thanks. A typical *wayang purwa* performance may last 8–10 hours, through the night. The puppets are manipulated by the highly skilled *dalang*, the puppeteer who narrates and sings the story, using different voices for the various characters, and providing the tempo for the accompanying gamelan orchestra; he sits with the orchestra behind the screen of white cotton on which the puppets' shadows are cast. The good puppets are ranged on one side of the stage, the evil ones on the other; when not in use, they are arranged to the side of the screen in racks traditionally made from the trunk of a banana plant.

The audience freely wanders from one side of the screen to the other, choosing to watch either the puppets' shadows or the puppeteer at work; it is a tremendously social occasion, with people eating, chatting, laughing and sleeping through the show. Such all-night performances can be seen once a month in Yogyakarta; shorter excerpts are often shown for tourists in theatres and restaurants in Yogya and Bali.

Wayang golek

These three-dimensional, wooden-headed puppets are most popular in west Java, though it is likely that the tradition originated from the north coast in the 16C, influenced by Chinese puppetry. Popular *wayang golek* subjects include *wayang cepak*, which deals principally with local history and legends, heavily interwoven with tales of the arrival of Islam. The cast includes a core of c 60 fairly uniform puppets, with perhaps 150 others, which vary according to local taste; their costumes, often of batik or *songket*, can be exquisite. The main centres for *wayang golek* are Bandung and Bogor, where workshops may be easily visited. The tourist trade accounts for most sales today. Performances are rare, though as with *wayang kulit*, short excerpts designed for tourists may be seen in Yogya and Bandung.

Wayang kelitik or wayang kerucil

These are flat wooden puppets, about 1cm thick, very rarely used today but found in several Javanese museums. They come from east Java, and were traditionally used for the *Damar Wulan* cycle; later they were adapted for the *Ramayana* and *Mahabharata*.

Wayang beber

Probably no longer performed today, Javanese *wayang beber* are stories, usually from the *Panji* cycle, painted on long scrolls of cloth in a style somewhat similar to the classical paintings of Bali. The scroll would be unrolled as the narrator told the story. The tradition is believed to have come originally from south India.

Wayang golek puppet

Wayang orang and topeng

Wayang orang (often known as *wayang wong* in Java) is a form of drama performed by a human cast in fabulous costumes, acting out stories adapted principally from the *Ramayana*; today the form is in decline. More so than the puppet dramas, *wayang orang* has lost its audience to television and cinema, but is kept alive by a few troupes in Java and Bali. Performances or excerpts can be seen at several stages in and round Jakarta, Bandung, Yogyakarta, Solo and Semarang, and in Ubud on Bali, but these are a far cry from the performances of the early 20C, which attracted crowds of thousands and employed a cast of hundreds at the royal courts of central Java.

The various masked dance-dramas, *topeng*, remain popular on Bali: *topeng pajegan* is performed by a single artiste, who changes masks throughout the act, with different voices and traits for each character. Another very popular *topeng* is the *topeng panca*, performed by a troupe of five.

A form of *wayang orang* popularly known as *sendratari* was created in Bali in the 1960s. In *sendratari* (*seni-drama-tari* – 'art-drama-dance'), the actors mime to the accompaniment of gamelan and a narrator; usually the stories are taken from the *Ramayana* or *Mahabharata* (and performances may be advertised, rather misleadingly, as '*Ramayana* ballet'). *Sendratari* can be seen in Yogyakarta and Bali. With the cast sometimes numbering more than 100, these can be spectacular, colourful shows; most impressive visually are those shows performed at the open-air stage at Prambanan, near Yogyakarta.

Ketoprak

Ketoprak is a form of folk theatre still immensely popular on Java – especially in Yogyakarta. The genre comprises a vast repertoire of stories, including folk tales and legends, historical events, and adaptations of modern romances. Performances are always lively, with ridiculous clowns and riotous battles, accompanied by a gamelan orchestra. Visitors can usually find a performance in Yogyakarta, and sometimes in Jakarta and Bandung.

Gambuh

Considered to be Bali's oldest ritual drama, *gambuh* is now performed regularly at only one site – a temple in Batuan (see p 132). The stories of *gambuh* are based on the antics of the hero, Panji, in his pursuit of a beautiful princess. The costumes are magnificent, the choreography highly elaborate; the accompanying gamelan orchestra, unusually, incorporates long bamboo flutes known as *suling*. A performance is well worth seeing.

Calonarang and the Barong-Rangda drama

The *calonarang* is a rite of exorcism which traditionally was used by the Balinese to ward off epidemics and other misfortune; the performance incorporated the masked figures of Rangda and the Barong, two mythical figures which came to represent the forces of protection and destruction. Masks of these two beings are considered extremely powerful, and the actors who took on the roles for the ritual 'became' these powers. The final part of the ritual – a confrontation between Rangda and the Barong – ends dramatically with the entranced followers of the Barong turning their krises upon themselves.

In the 1930s, as a direct result of the interest shown in this ritual by anthropologists such as Gregory Bateson and Margaret Mead, and by foreign artists such as Walter Spies and Katharane Mershon, it was reworked into a commercial performance with greater appeal to foreign viewers: the length was shortened to one hour, the amount of dialogue was greatly reduced, and the dramatic aspects, especially of the final trance and suicide, were enhanced, to create what is now known as the 'Barong and kris dance'; performances are staged every week in Ubud.

Sanghyang and Kecak

The Balinese *sanghyang*, originally performed – like the *calonarang* – during an epidemic outbreak or natural disaster, is a ritual to invoke the evil spirits responsible for the pestilence to become benevolent. Traditionally, there were many forms of *sanghyang*, but the two versions most frequently performed were known as *sanghyang dedari* and *sanghyang jaran*.

In the former, two young girls are put into trance in the *pura dalem* (the village temple associated with death rites) and in this state 'become' celestial nymphs; they are carried in procession round the village and then dance, still entranced, to the accompaniment of alternating choruses of men (*cak*) and women (*kidung*); after the dance, the nymphs sprinkle holy water which has the power to cleanse the village of the malevolent spirits. In the *sanghyang jaran*, one or more male dancers in a state of trance ride wooden hobby-horses across red-hot coconut embers, to the accompaniment of the *cak* chorus.

With modern medicine and improved health practices, the epidemics which once swept across Bali – particularly at the end of the rainy season – have ceased, but the *sanghyang* has been revived as a tourist performance. The *sanghyang dedari* – popularly known as the 'angel dance' or 'trance dance' – and the *sanghyang jaran*, usually called the 'fire dance' or 'horse dance', are both performed several times each week in Ubud and in Bona, a village southwest of Gianyar, where the touristic reworking of the *sanghyang* was first effected.

The *kecak* dance-drama was created solely for tourists – in large part by Walter Spies, who was inspired by the **cak** chorus which accompanied the *sanghyang*. Spies helped to choreograph a drama – a scene from the *Ramayana* in which Rama's army of monkeys is sent to rescue his wife, Sita, from the clutches of the demon, Rawana – and replaced the gamelan with a vocal chorus repeating a rhythmic '*cak*'. In 1931, he increased the size of the chorus to 50 men and boys, and seated them in concentric circles round the stage for dramatic effect. Although this form quickly lost favour with the Balinese, foreign visitors were greatly impressed and the drama has become extremely popular among today's tourists. It is often performed in combination with the *sanghyang dedari* and *sanghyang jaran*.

Legong

The original Balinese *legong* was a court dance performed by two young women, and is believed to have been derived from the *sanghyang dedari* form. The choreography is extremely precise and the dancers' movements exceedingly delicate and refined. The best *legong* dancers would train for years to attain the absolute perfection required for the kraton performances.

The '*legong* dance' performed today for tourists is somewhat different, being a revue of several different Balinese dance forms, of which one part may be based on the traditional *legong*. This format was created in the early 1950s specifically for a troupe of dancers from Peliatan who toured Europe and the USA. The same program was adopted in the 1960s by the *Bali Beach Hotel* at Sanur (now the *Grand Bali Beach*) to entertain foreign tourists, and today this has been largely standardised for all '*legong* dance' performances.

Gamelan

Gamelan is the general name given to the dominant, traditional music form on Java, Bali and Lombok. A gamelan orchestra consists primarily of percussion instruments: tuned gongs, traditionally of bronze, xylophones with bronze or wooden bars, drums, beaten by hand, and wooden blocks. Other commonly found instruments include two-stringed, lute-like instruments played with bows. In west Java, the *angklung* is a common addition – an instrument with four bamboo tubes of different lengths, suspended in a frame and struck like a xylophone.

Each gamelan set is uniquely tuned and decorated, such that an instrument in one gamelan set is not interchangeable with a similar one from another. Each set is given a name, usually relating to their particular character. Old sets, such as those found in the Javanese *keraton* of Yogyakarta, Solo and Cirebon, are considered to possess supernatural powers and are held in great esteem. Gamelan tuning scales and musical styles vary from region to region in Java, and sometimes from town to town; the diversity is huge. The visitor will be able to hear gamelan at *wayang* performances and at most forms of dance and drama; several hotels, especially in Bandung, Yogyakarta and Bali, have short daily performances for guests.

1. *Terraced rice fields near Candi Kesiman Tengah in east Java (p 375)*

2. *Detail of finely carved stone panels in the porch of Candi Mendut in central Java (p 320)*

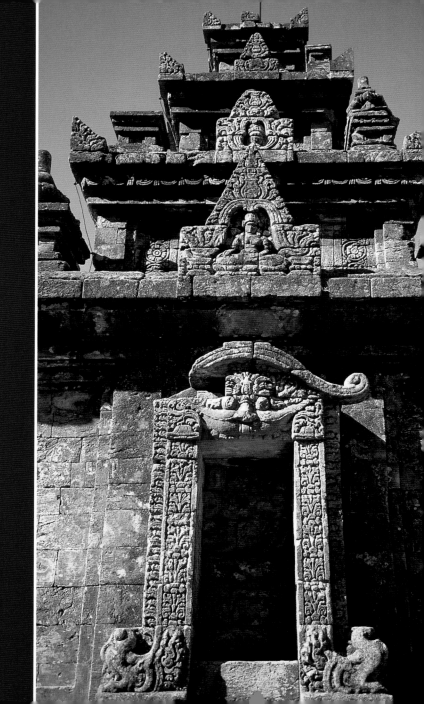

3. *Doorway of one of the Godong Songo temples in central Java (p 283)*

4. *Ijen crater in east Java (p 401)*

5. *A monument at Candi Loro Jonggrang in central Java (p 326)*

6. *The minaret of Mesjid Agung at Demak in central Java (p 289)*

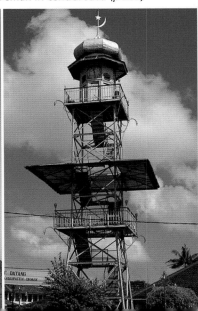

7. *Gunung Sumbing in central Java, viewed from Wonosobo (p 271)*

8. *Candi Jabung in east Java (p 398)*

9. *Terraced rice fields on the way to Candi Selogriyo in central Java (p 280)*

10. *The doorway of Candi Bangkal in east Java (p 378)*

11. *Gunung Merapi in central Java (p 336)*

12. *A temple at Gedong Songo in central Java (p 283)*

13. *Detail of Candi Shiva, Loro Jonggrang, central Java (p 327)*

14. *Tea estate south of Bandung, west Java (p 248)*

15. *Candi Borobudur in central Java, showing the corner where the 'hidden foot' is exposed (p 314)*

16. *Gopura Agung, the gateway at Taman Sari in Yogyakarta, central Java (p 308)*

17. *Candi Sari in central Java (p 326)*

18. *Statue of a kneeling dvarapala at Candi Gambar Wetan, east Java (p 362)*

19. *Temples on the Dieng plateau: Candi Srikandi in the foreground with Candi Puntadewa behind (p 276)*

20. The kori agung *gateway of a temple in central Bali*
21. *A* Heliconia *plant, widely grown in Bali*

22. *Typical Balinese multi-tiered merus and a shrine in a temple compound*
23. *A fishing boat at Negara in southwest Bali (p 174)*
24. *Wood carving at Pura Maospahit Gerenceng, Denpasar, Bali (p 105)*
25. *A gateway in the Bali Provincial Museum in Denpasar, Bali (p 103)*
26. *Rice fields north of Tirta Gangga in east Bali (p 155)*

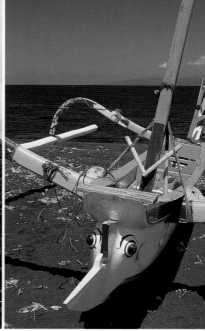

27. *The kori agung of a temple in south Bali*

28. *A jukung fishing boat at Kusamba in south Bali (p 149)*

29. *The water garden at Telaga Tista in east Bali (p 158)*

30. *A relief at Pura Meduwe Karang in north Bali (p 165)*

31. A floating fishing platform or bagan *near Lembar in southwest Lombok* (p 425)

32. A traditional rice barn in Lombok

33. A tomb of one of the Selaparang kings in east Lombok (p 418)

Further reading

Prehistory and history

Abeyasekere, Susan, *Jakarta: a History* (Oxford University Press, Singapore, 1987). An interesting social history of Indonesia's capital.

Bellwood, Peter, *Prehistory of the Indo-Malaysian Archipelago* (Academic Press, Sydney, 1985). A thorough introduction to the region's prehistory.

Blussé, Leonard, *Strange Company: Chinese Settlers, Mestizo Women and the Dutch in VOC Batavia* (Foris Publications, Dordrecht, 1986). A detailed account of the capital in the VOC period.

Lubis, Mochtar, *Indonesia: Land under the Rainbow* (Oxford University Press, Singapore, 1990). Indonesian history from an Indonesian scholar's viewpoint.

Ricklefs, M.C., *A History of Modern Indonesia since c 1300* (2nd ed., Macmillan, London, 1993). The most useful general reference work to the archipelago's history, with a strong emphasis on Java.

Van der Kraan, Alfons, *Lombok: Conquest, Colonisation and Underdevelopment, 1870–1940* (Heinemann, Singapore, 1980). A complex account of Dutch and Balinese roles in Lombok.

Arts and Architecture

Bernet Kempers, A.J., *Ancient Indonesian Art* (C.P.J. Van der Peet, Amsterdam, 1959). Informative, though slightly dated, introduction to early Indonesian sculpture and architecture.

Dumarçay, Jacques, *Temples of Java* (Oxford University Press, Singapore, 1986). A useful, if slightly presumptuous, introduction to Hindu-Buddhist architecture on Java.

Fischer, Joseph (ed.), *Modern Indonesian Art: Three Generations of Tradition and Change, 1945–90* (Panita Pameran KIAS, Jakarta, 1990). Exhibition catalogue with essays about some of Indonesia's most prominent artists.

Fontein, Jan, *The Sculpture of Indonesia* (National Gallery of Art, Washington, 1990). Finely illustrated exhibition catalogue with informative essays.

Gillow, John, *Traditional Indonesian Textiles* (Thames & Hudson, London, 1992). Discussion of textile types and patterns, with fine illustrations.

Hitchcock, Michael, *Indonesian Textiles* (British Museum Press, London, 1991). A general introduction to the archipelago's huge variety of textiles, materials and techniques.

Holt, Claire, *Art in Indonesia: Continuities and Change* (Cornell University Press, Ithaca, 1967). Once the definitive text on Indonesian arts, and still highly relevant.

Jessup, Helen, *Court Arts of Indonesia* (The Asia Society Galleries, New York, 1990). Lavishly illustrated with an informative text.

Kumar, Ann, and McGlynn, John, *Illuminations: the Writing Traditions of Indonesia* (The Lontar Foundation, Jakarta, 1996). Sumptuously produced guide to one of Indonesia's least-known arts.

Wright, Astri, *Soul, Spirit and Mountain: Preoccupations of Contemporary Indonesian Painters* (Oxford University Press, Singapore, 1994). A thorough discussion of modern painters in Indonesia.

Natural history

Allen, G.R., and Steene, R., *Indo-Pacific Coral Reef Field Guide* (Tropical Reef Research, Singapore, 1994). An excellent illustrated guide to Indonesia's reef life.

Coates, Brian J. and Bishop, K. David, A Guide to the Birds of Wallacea (Dove Publications, Alderley, Queensland, 1997). An excellent guide to the birds of Lombok as well as to those in the rest of Nusa Tenggara, sulawesi and the Moluccas.

Kuiter, Rudie, *Tropical Reef-fishes of the Western Pacific-Indonesia and Adjacent Waters* (Gramedia, Jakarta, 1992). Fine colour photos of most fish a diver is likely to see on Indonesian reefs.

MacKinnon, John, and Phillipps, Karen, *A Field Guide to the Birds of Borneo, Sumatra, Java and Bali* (Oxford University Press, Oxford, 1993). The definitive bird-watcher's guide to the islands.

Mason, Victor, and Jarvis, Frank, *Birds of Bali* (Periplus Editions, Singapore, 1989). Charmingly illustrated layman's guide to some of Bali's most common birds.

Veevers-Carter, W., *Land Mammals of Indonesia* (Intermasa, Jakarta, 1979). A thorough, illustrated survey, with full lists of English, Latin and Indonesian names.

Bali

Bernet Kempers, A.J., *Monumental Bali* (new edition, Van Goor Zonen, The Hague, 1990). A comprehensive, though rather dated, study of Balinese antiquities.

Brinkgreve, Francine, *Offerings: the Ritual Art of Bali* (Select Books, Singapore, 1992). Colourful, clearly explained guide to Balinese festival offerings, with fine photos.

Covarrubias, Miguel, *Island of Bali* (Alfred A. Knopf, New York, 1937). A romantic, but nevertheless highly informative and still relevant account of Bali, written by the Mexican artist.

Djelantik, A.A.M., *Balinese Paintings* (2nd ed., Oxford University Press, Singapore, 1990). A valuable survey of Balinese painting and styles.

Eiseman, Fred, Bali: Sekala and Niskala vols I & II (Periplus Editions, 1990). Essays on many aspects of Balinese society and arts, originally written in the 1980s; some are outdated but most are still highly relevant.

Eiseman, Fred and Margaret, *Flowers of Bali* (Periplus Editions, Singapore, 1988). A slim, attractively illustrated guide to some of the most commonly seen flowers on Bali.

Hauser-Schäublin, Brigitta, et al, *Balinese Textiles* (British Museum Press, London, 1991). An examination of the island's textile traditions.

Hitchcock, Michael and Norris, Lucy, *Bali: the Imaginary Museum* (Oxford University Press, Oxford, 1996). Marvellous photographs of 1930s Bali by Walter Spies and Beryl de Zoete with modern commentary.

Hobart, Angela; Ramseyer, Urs; and Albert Leeman, *The Peoples of Bali* (Blackwells, Oxford, 1996). Up-to-date, informative anthropological survey of the Balinese.

Koke, Louise G., *Our Hotel in Bali* (January Books, Wellington, 1987). An amusing autobiography by Kuta's first hotel operator.

Mabbett, Hugh, *In Praise of Kuta* (January Books, Wellington, 1987). Musings on Bali's best-known beach resort.

Mathews, Anna, *Night of Purnama* (Oxford University Press, Kuala Lumpur, 1983). Interesting autobiographical account of Gunung Agung's eruption on Bali in 1963.

Rhodius, Hans and Darling, John, *Walter Spies and Balinese Art* (Oxford University Press, Singapore, 1980). A biography of the German artist who came to Bali in 1927.

Warren, William, *Balinese Gardens* (Thames & Hudson, London, 1995). Magnificent illustrations of some of Bali's most delightful gardens.

General

Legge, J.D., *Sukarno: a Political Biography* (Allen & Unwin, Sydney, 1972). An excellent account of the turbulent Sukarno years.

Lindsay, Timothy, *The Romance of K'tut Tantri* (Oxford University Press, Singapore, 1997). An engaging attempt to separate fact from myth regarding K'tut Tantri.

Lubis, Mochtar, *Twilight in Jakarta* (Hutchinson, London, 1963). A vivid description of life in Sukarno's Jakarta of the 1950s.

Lueras, Leonard and Lorca, *Surfing Indonesia* (Periplus Editions, Singapore, 1997). Superbly illustrated surfer's guide to Indonesia.

Pane, Armijn, trans. McGlynn, John, *Shackles* (Lontar Foundation, Jakarta, 1989). Novel by a Sumatran writer, first published in 1940.

Ramage, Douglas, *Politics in Indonesia: Democracy, Islam and the Ideology of Tolerance* (Routledge, London, 1996). Detailed analysis of contemporary political discourse.

Schwarz, Adam, *A Nation in Waiting: Indonesia in the 1990s* (Westview Press, Boulder, 1994). An extremely well-informed survey of Indonesian politics in the Suharto era, emphasising the cronyism and corruption.

Tantri, K'tut, *Revolt in Paradise* (Heinemann, London, 1960). Self-promoting but nevertheless intriguing autobiography of an extraordinary character.

Toer, Pramoedya Ananta, *This Earth of Mankind, Child of all Nations, Footsteps* and *House of Glass*; translated by Max Lane (Penguin, Ringwood, 1979). Known collectively as the Buru tetralogy; Indonesia's best-known writer's best-known works, composed orally to entertain fellow prisoners while a political detainee on Buru, and only written down later.

Toer, Pramoedya Ananta, *The Fugitive* (Heinemann, Hong Kong, 1975). Pramoedya's first novel, written while a prisoner of the Dutch colonial authorities; the quintessential Javanese novel.

Van der Post, Laurens, *The Admiral's Baby* (John Murray, London, 1996). Autobiography set in the post-Second World War years, during the British occupation of Indonesia.

Denpasar and the southern resorts

Highlights. The southern part of Bali contains the capital, **Denpasar** (see p 101) – a busy, commercial centre of little charm, but with a few interesting sights – and several large **beach resorts** which cater to Bali's vast sea-and-sand tourism industry. The great majority of visitors to the island stay in one or other of the resort areas here for at least part of their trip, taking advantage of the pleasant beaches, the wide range of international food, the lively nightlife and the substantial shopping opportunities.

Each resort area has a distinct character. **Sanur** (see p 105) on the east coast near Denpasar, is a relaxed, generally mid-priced resort with a few large four- or five-star hotels and many smaller, comfortable but simple hotels and guest-houses. The public beach is nothing special, but Sanur's gentle pace and atmosphere make it popular with families, and with foreign expatriates who have made it their home.

In contrast, the sprawl of **Seminyak**, **Legian** and **Kuta** (see pp 110–114) is noisy and hectic, with constant traffic jams and a raucous nightlife. Kuta beach is magnificent – long, broad and sandy – and in high season can be very busy. The ubiquitous street vendors and masseuses are not permitted too far onto the beach, so you can have a degree of privacy, if desired. The narrow lanes behind the beach road are crammed with cheap lodgings, while the better hotels are mostly along the sea front. There are seemingly endless cafés, restaurants, pubs, warung, bars and shops here, and it is doubtless true that some visitors to Bali never step out of Kuta.

South of the airport is **Jimbaran Bay** (see p 114), a quiet and beautiful beach with several high-quality hotels. This is a charming spot, with many beachside fish restaurants; even if you don't stay here, a visit is recommended.

On the east side of the Bukit Peninsula is the very expensive tourist enclave of **Nusa Dua** (see p 116), an immense fenced compound containing a cluster of five-star hotels in magnificent gardens. Nusa Dua is virtually self-sufficient in services, with the tourist never needing to stray from the complex. If you want a few very comfortable days in a peaceful environment, sitting by the hotel pool with a book and a cocktail, then this might be the place to stay; otherwise it is really too far from anywhere else to be convenient, and does not – except in the most superficial of ways – give you an experience of Bali and the Balinese.

The **Tanjung peninsula** to the north of Nusa Dua has a string of mediocre, mid-priced hotels interspersed with a few excellent ones, but is even more isolated; however, it is good for water sports.

The **Bukit Peninsula** (see p 117), the dry, barren limestone region at the southern tip of Bali, is home to one of the island's best known temples, Pura Luhur Uluwatu, and has some of the island's best surf breaks.

Accommodation

The range of accommodation in south Bali is vast, with several hundred hotels, guest-houses, *losmen* and *penginapan* to choose from. Some of the world's finest hotels are found in this little corner of the island, but there is something to suit every budget, from $500 per night to less then $5.

If money is no object, book straight in at the marvellous *Oberoi* at the far north end of Legian beach, or nearby at the *Legian*; or perhaps, if you fancy a round of golf, at the wonderful *Amanusa* near Nusa Dua, which lies away from the sea. Otherwise, consult the lists of suggested hotels below; while far from comprehensive, they should provide a sampling of reliable, clean and comfortable places. In the peak tourism seasons – Christmas and New Year, and July–August – advance bookings are highly recommended.

Odalan dates for a selection of temples

Pura Agung Jagatnatha, Denpasar: festival on Purnama Kedasa (full moon of the 10th lunar month; Mar/Apr).

Pura Maospahit Gerenceng, Denpasar: festival on Purnama Jiyestha (full moon of the 11th lunar month; Apr/May).

Pura Sakenan, Pulau Serangan: festival on Saturday of Kuningan (week 12) and Sunday of Langkir (week 13): 12–13.8.00, 10–11.3.01, 6–7.10.01, 4–5.5.02, 30.11–1.12.02, 28–29.6.03, 24–25.1.04.

Pura Ulun Siwi, Jimbaran: festival starts on Friday of Dunggulan (week 11): 4.8.00, 2.3.01, 28.9.01, 26.4.02, 22.11.02, 20.6.03, 16.1.04.

Pura Luhur Uluwatu, Pecatu: festival starts on Tuesday of Medangsia (week 14): 22.8.00, 20.3.01, 16.10.01, 14.5.02, 10.12.02, 8.7.03, 3.2.04.

DENPASAR
• • • • • • • • • • • •

A very busy city which can barely cope with the amount of traffic passing through, Denpasar is the island's administrative capital and public transport hub. There is little reason to stay here since there is such a good choice of hotels in the nearby resorts, but it is worth visiting on day trips for its museums, a few interesting temples, and its lively markets.

Practical information

 Transport
Flights

For information on Ngurah Rai International Airport, the main gateway to Bali, see p 108.

Airline offices

Some airlines have offices in Kuta, Nusa Dua and Sanur; these are also listed here for convenience.

Bouraq Komplek Sudirman Agung, Jl. Sudirman, Denpasar, ☎ 241397

Garuda Jl. Melati 61, Denpasar, ☎ 225245; 24hr: 227788, 227824/5. Natour Kuta Beach, Kuta, ☎ 751179. Sheraton Nusa Indah, Nusa Dua, ☎ 771864. Hotel Sanur Aerowisata, Sanur, ☎ 289135. The Grand Bali Beach, Sanur, ☎ 288243. Hotel Bali Imperial, Seminyak, ☎ 730681.

Mandala Komplek Sudirman Agung, Jl.

Sudirman, Denpasar, ☎ 242933.
Merpati Jl. Melati 51, Denpasar,
☎ 235358.

City transport

Metered **taxis** are easy to flag down in
Denpasar and are the most comfortable
way to get around; check that the driver
resets the meter when you start.
Minibuses swarm along the main streets,
linking the various bemo terminals. They
are (inconsistently) colour-coded according to route, but it is not always easy to
find the correct one; it can be simpler, and
much more comfortable, to charter an
empty one and pay a bit extra. *Dokar*, the
pony-drawn carts, are a slow alternative,
but not much fun on busy streets. For **car**
or **motorcycle rentals**, there is a much
better choice in Kuta.

Inter-town transport

There are several **minibus terminals**,
each serving different destinations. For
routes to the south—the resort areas—
they leave from **Terminal Tegalsari**
(Tegal) on Jl. Imam Bonjol. For destinations to the east—Gianyar, Padangbai
and Amlapura—and to Ubud, they
depart from **Terminal Batubulan** on
the northeast edge of the city. Those to
western Bali depart from **Terminal
Ubung**, northwest of the city centre.

Inter-island transport

Tickets for **long-distance buses** to Java
or Sumatra can be bought from many
agents at the north end of Jl.
Diponegoro. Most of the buses depart
from **Terminal Ubung. Train tickets**
for Java can be bought from the
Perumka office just off Jl. Diponegoro.
The agent for *Pelni* **passenger ships** is
Diponegoro Travel at Jl. Diponegoro
165; four ships currently call at Benoa
harbour on their way to Nusa Tenggara,
Sulawesi and Irian Jaya.

 ## Accommodation

The vast range of hotels and
guest-houses in the nearby
resorts of Sanur, Kuta and Nusa Dua

make Denpasar's accommodation look
decidedly poor value, but for visitors who
prefer or need to stay in the town, there
are a few possibilities. The ☎ code is
0361; advance booking is not usually
necessary.

✰✰✰✰/✰✰✰ *Natour Bali* (☎ 225681; fax
235347) Jl. Veteran 3. Colonial-era
hotel with very variable rooms; those on
the east side of Jl. Veteran are the nicest.
✰✰ *Puri Agung Pemecutan*
(☎ 423491) Jl. Thamrin 2. Rather
gloomy rooms in the compound of
the old Pemecutan palace; very close
to the city centre.
✰ *Dua Bersaudara* (☎ 484704) Gg.
VII/5, Jl. Imam Bonjol. Just south of the
Tegal bemo terminal; good value for
small budgets.
✰ *Hotel Adi Yasa* (☎ 222679) Jl.
Nakula 23B. Basic, clean rooms round a
garden courtyard; friendly staff.
✰ *Nakula Inn* (☎ 226446) Jl. Nakula 4.
Clean, simple and friendly.

 ## Restaurants

For Western food, Denpasar
cannot compete with the vast
choice in the southern resorts. For local
food, try *Warung Wardani* at Jl.
Yudistira 2—a good value, simple
eatery; or *Warung Jawa Kinanthi*, on
the west side of Jl. Imam Bonjol, just
north of the Jl. Gunung Lawu junction,
which does excellent dishes at rock-bottom prices. Many fast-food restaurants
can be found in the shopping centres on
Jl. Teuku Umar, Jl. Dewi Sartika and Jl.
Sudirman, south of the city centre.

 ## Information and maps

Denpasar's **city tourist office**
(Dinas Pariwisata) on the corner of Jl. Surapati and Jl. Kaliasem can
provide a useful calendar of events,
including temple festivals, and public
transport information. The **provincial
tourist office** is on Jl. Parman in the
Niti Mandala area of Renon. The

Gramedia bookshop in Duta Plaza on Jl. Dewi Sartika, and Toko Gunung Agung in Libi Plaza on Jl. Teuku Umar have a selection of maps and English-language books, including the very good *Bali* map published by Periplus.

 Money, post and telecoms
Bank Lippo on Jl. Thamrin is usually efficient. The central **post office** is on Jl. Raya Puputan in Renon, and has a *post restante* service. Next door is the main 24-hour **telecoms office**, with a full range of facilities.

Consulates
The **Australian consulate** (☎ 235092) is at Jl. Moh. Yamin 4, Renon; in emergency it can assist citizens of Canada, New Zealand, and Britain. The **US consular agent** (☎ 233605) is on the west side of Jl. Hayam Wuruk, a few metres north of the traffic circle junction with Jl. Hang Tuah and Jl. Raya Puputan.

Exploring Denpasar

The **Bali Provincial Museum** (Museum Bali; open Sun, Tues–Thur 07.00–14.00; Fri 07.00–11.00; Sat 07.00–12.30; closed Mon and public holidays; entry charge) on Jl. Mayor Wisnu is the town's most important museum, with a small but interesting collection of ethnographic exhibits housed in pavilions built in various Balinese regional styles. The museum dates from the 1930s and its grounds are laid out in the form of walled courtyards connected by ornate gateways, in the style of a royal palace.

The **archaeological pavilion**, the first on the right, houses stone tools and axeheads, bronze bracelets and small statuettes. Of special note are the turtle-shaped sarcophagus and a couple of bronze drums. In the adjacent courtyard to the north is the **Buleleng pavilion**, which contains textiles and weaving tools. This pavilion was originally built for a Dutch colonial exposition which was held in Java in 1914.

Next is the long **Karangasem pavilion**, where ceremonial items are displayed; note the fine *tikas*, one of carved wood, the other painted on paper, depicting the Pawukon-cycle calendar. The doors and shutters of the pavilion are beautifully carved; on the verandah are many stone sculptures. The **Tabanan pavilion**, in the far northeast compound, has a collection of masks and costumes.

Immediately north of the Museum Bali is the **Pura Agung Jagatnatha**, a temple founded in the 1950s and dominated by a magnificent, high *padmasan*a dedicated to Sang Hyang Widhi Wasa, the supreme god of Balinese Hinduism, who is depicted in gold relief on the back support of the throne. The temple's *odalan* takes place on Purnama Kedasa (see box on p 101). On Hari Raya Saraswati, the last day of the Pawukon 30-week cycle (the Saturday of Watugunung week) is a festival dedicated to Saraswati, the goddess of learning and consort of Brahma; books should not be read on this day, but students have traditionally gathered at Pura Agung Jagatnatha in the early morning to make offerings.

On the west side of Jl. Mayor Wisnu is the **Alun-alun Puputan**, a grassy square with a large bronze statue on the north side depicting a group of Balinese at the infamous *puputan*—the fight to the end—of the raja's court on 20 September 1906.

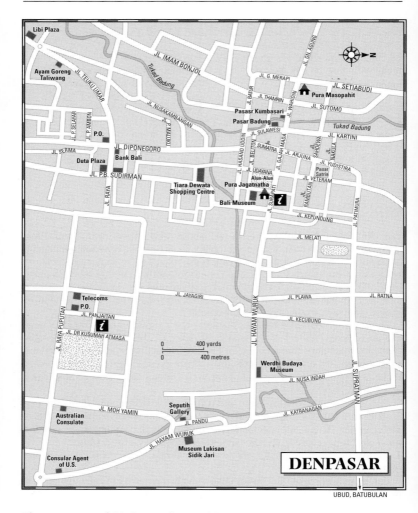

UBUD, BATUBULAN

The puputan of 20 September 1906

Dressed in ceremonial white and armed with lances and krises, the raja and his retinue marched from the palace—which at that time stood on the north side of the square—straight towards the Dutch forces. As the Balinese rushed forward, the Dutch opened fire; the raja was one of the first to fall. A frenzied, suicidal bloodbath followed, with the raja's entourage killing themselves and each other, while apparently hurling their valuables contemptuously at the Dutch; the death toll is estimated at more than one thousand. A second puputan against the Dutch followed later that day, led by the raja from the Pemecutan palace nearby.

A four-faced **image of Shiva** known as *catuhmuka* stands at the intersection at the northwest corner of the square, as guardian of the four directions.

Pura Maospahit Gerenceng, on the west side of Jl. Sutomo, is a temple of great but unknown age, badly damaged in the powerful earthquake of January 1917 but partially restored subsequently. Of particular note are the repaired reliefs on the brick gateway between the outer and middle courtyards, depicting a *garuda* on the south side and a monstrous guardian on the north. The gate into the furthest courtyard has very finely carved wooden doors. The central structure in the inner courtyard is Candi Raras Maospahit, a square brick shrine with a pair of terracotta guardian figures flanking the doorway.

The *pura* is entered along Gang III – a footpath off the west side of Jl. Sutomo along the south wall of the *pura*. Visitors can rent a sash at the entrance; a donation is required. The temple's *odalan* is held on Purnama Jiyestha (see box on p 101).

On Jl. Gajah Mada nearby are the markets of **Pasar Kumbasari** and **Pasar Badung**. The former, on the west bank of the Tukad Badung, sells a wide range of fabrics and clothing and arts and crafts. Pasar Badung, on the east bank a few metres south along Jl. Pulau Sulawesi, is a cavernous, three-storey, dimly lit market, selling everything from freshly butchered meat and pungent spices to flowers for temple offerings and brightly coloured batik.

North of the city centre, the **Pasar Satriya** at the corner of Jl. Abimanyu and Jl. Veteran has an art market on the top floor. The **bird market** (*pasar burung*) on the east side of Jl. Veteran, c 50m further north, sells fish, monkeys, rabbits and guinea pigs, as well as birds.

To the northeast, on Jl. Ratna, is **Pura Maospahit Tonja**, an old temple notable mainly for its ancient black stone altar or stool known as the *batu hitam* ('black stone').

East of the city centre, in the sprawling grounds of the government-run Taman Werdi Budaya Cultural Centre, is the **Werdi Budaya Museum** (open daily 08.00–16.00; closed on public holidays), a fairly good art museum with a wide selection of Balinese woodcarving and painting, ranging in date from the 1920s to the present day. Well-known artists represented include I Gusti Nyoman Lempad, Rudolf Bonnet, Willem Hofker, I Gusti Ngurah Gede Pemecutan, Arie Smit, Made Wianta, Kay It, and Nyoman Gunarsa.

Southeast of the city centre on Jl. Hayam Wuruk is the **Museum Lukisan Sidik Jari**, the private art museum of I Gusti Ngurah Gede Pemecutan, which houses dozens of the artist's own works dating from the 1960s to the present, mostly in his characteristic pointillist style. The collection is poorly displayed, but is worth a visit for those who like his work.

Nearby at Jl. Pandu 42 is the **Seputih Gallery**, the studio of artist Made Wianta (b. 1949), whose abstract work has established his international reputation; visitors are welcome, but should phone in advance (☎ 233613).

SANUR, PULAU SERANGAN AND BENOA HARBOUR

The beach at **Sanur**, c 7km southeast of Denpasar, was the landing site for the Dutch invasion force in 1906, and later – in 1942 – for the Japanese. In the 1930s this quiet village, then populated predominantly by farmers and a few fishermen, began to receive a trickle of foreign artists. In the vanguard were Adrien-Jean Le Mayeur de Merprès, a Belgian painter whose house here is now a museum; two Dutch brothers, Rolf and Hans Neuhaus, who opened an art gallery and aquarium; and an American couple, Katharane and Jack Mershon, dancer/choreographer and photographer respectively. Tourists came from Denpasar on day trips till the 1950s, when the first hotels were constructed at the beach. Today Sanur remains a very easy-going, surprisingly quiet resort, its sky-line dominated by the *Grand Bali Beach*, a monstrous hotel built with Japanese war reparation funds in the 1960s.

Though parts of the beach have been disfigured by thoughtless development too close to the water's edge, many of the beachfront lodgings have lush gardens flanking the shore. Swimming is safe at high tide in the shallow lagoon offshore, planted with sea-grass and protected from the waves which break on the fringing reef beyond.

Practical information

Transport

Green **minibuses** stream up and down Jl. Danau Tamblingan, the main street of Sanur which runs parallel to—but inland from—the coast; just signal for one to stop, climb in, and pay the fare when you jump out at your destination. Scheduled *Perama* **shuttle buses** to the airport, Kuta, Ubud and other destinations run from beside the entrance of the *Grand Bali Beach hotel* on Jl. Hang Tuah; they should be booked one day in advance.

Car and **motorcycle rentals** can be found at several places along Jl. Danau Tamblingan. *Hertz* at the Grand Bali Beach arcade rents cars by the day or week; as everywhere, prices are nego-tiable and depend on demand and season. **Public boats** to Nusa Lembongan leave in the morning from the beach outside *Hotel Ananda* at the end of Jl. Hang Tuah; at other times you can charter a whole boat. *Island Explorer Cruises* at Jl. Sekar Waru 14/D (☎ 289856) runs sail-ing cruises on a private yacht which can carry 24 passengers. *Sea Trek* (see p 24) runs wonderful scheduled cruises and group charters on traditional schooners from Bali through the islands of Nusa Tenggara and Sulawesi.

Accommodation

A few places are recommended below, though Sanur has almost a hundred places to choose from. The ☎ code is 0361. Advance booking is advised for July to August and December to January.

☆☆☆☆☆ *Bali Hyatt* (☎ 281234; fax 287693; e-mail: bhyatt@dps.mega.net.id) Jl. Danau Tamblingan. Large hotel with pleasant rooms in beautiful surround-ings; wide range of sports facilities; effi-cient staff.

☆☆☆☆☆ *Grand Bali Beach* (☎ 288511; fax 287917) Jl. Hang Tuah. Sprawling grounds with a long beach front; pleas-ant standard rooms, and some cottages scattered in the garden round a magnifi-cent fig tree. Room 327 has been pre-served as it was left after a fire devastated the hotel in 1993; daily offerings are pre-sented to the gods within.

☆☆☆☆☆ *Tandjung Sari* (☎ 288441; fax 287930) Jl. Danau Tamblingan 41. Tasteful rooms, but overpriced compared to others; most rooms have sunken bath, open-air shower; widespread use of attractive antiqued furniture and statu-ary; small pool and beach-side bar.

☆☆☆☆/☆☆☆☆ *Hotel Sanur Aerowisata* (☎ 288011/288980; fax 287566;

e-mail: sanurbch@dps.mega.net.id) Jl. Danau Tamblingan. Large hotel in mature gardens with large pool beside the beach; very good food and attractive decor.

☆☆☆☆ *La Taverna Bali* (☎ 288497; fax 287126) Jl. Danau Tamblingan. Beautiful rooms, though the standard ones are rather small. Attractive pool, restaurant near the small artificial beach; competent staff; pleasant gardens.

☆☆☆☆ *Puri Kelapa Garden Cottages* (☎ 286135; fax 287417) Jl. Danau Segara Ayu 1. Fine, peaceful gardens and pleasant pool. The rooms are better value than the cottages.

☆☆☆ *Hotel Gazebo* (☎ 288212/ 289256; fax 288300) Jl. Danau Tamblingan 35. Reasonable-value rooms with pleasant gardens.

☆☆☆ *Hotel Irama* (☎ 289060/286121 fax 288300) Jl. Danau Tamblingan 37. Very similar to Hotel Gazebo next door, under same ownership.

☆☆ *Laghawa Beach Inn* (☎ 288494/ 287919; fax 289353) Jl. Danau Tamblingan. A typical mid-priced Sanur hotel close to the beach with clean rooms, attractive gardens and swimming pool.

☆☆/☆ *Ananda Hotel* (☎ 288327) Jl. Hang Tuah 43. Good value, spacious rooms across the road from a grubby stretch of beach.

☆☆/☆ *Watering Hole* (☎ 288289) Jl. Hang Tuah 37. Clean rooms round a small courtyard garden; friendly people and average food.

☆ *Yulia Homestay* (☎ 288089) Jl. Danau Tamblingan 38. Very quiet location, clean rooms and friendly owners. They have another, less attractive branch at Jl. Danau Tamblingan 57.

 ## Restaurants and cafés

A stroll along Jl. Danau Tamblingan, especially at the north end, will take the visitor past scores of cafés and restaurants. Further south, *Warung Choice & Bakery* and the adjacent *Café Batujimbar* are both recommended. For nice views over the water (and the eroded beach) try *Terazza Martini* at the end of Jl. Kesuma Sari. *Trattoria da Marco* (open evenings only), off Jl. Cemara, has fine Italian food; the Italian restaurant at *La Taverna Bali* is also very good.

 ## Money, post and telecoms

There are many money changers along Jl. Danau Tamblingan, offering much better rates than the hotels. Sanur's main **post office** is on Jl. Danau Buyan, 350m west of the main bypass. The more convenient Karya **postal agent** is on Jl. Danau Tamblingan just south of *Café Batujimbar*. There is a *wartel* on the corner of Jl. Danau Toba and Jl. Danau Segara Ayu; others lie along Jl. Danau Tamblingan.

Travel agents

The efficient *Vayatour* (☎ 285555), on the east side of Jl. Bypass, is recommended for flight bookings. Pacto in the Grand Bali Beach can arrange local tours.

 ## Water sports and leisure activities

The Grand Bali Beach has a nine-hole golf course and a ten-pin bowling alley which non-residents may use for a fee.

The *Baruna* water sports office in the hotel's garden can arrange diving and other water sports. Several other dive operators can be found in Sanur, including *Indonesian Cactus Divers* at Jl. Bypass Ngurah Rai 15 (☎ 462063; fax 462164), which offers PADI courses. *Hotel Sanur Aerowisata* runs early morning bicycle tours round Sanur (☎ 288011). Paintball fans can play soldiers at Bali Splat Mas at Jl. Danau Tamblingan 118 (☎ 289073).

The small **Museum Le Mayeur** (open most mornings) on the sea front near the *Grand Bali Beach* is the former home of Belgian artist Adrien-Jean Le Mayeur de Merprès (1880–1958), who moved to Bali in 1932. He settled in Sanur three years later and married a famous local dancer, Ni Polok, who modelled for him in a huge number of his paintings. Le Mayeur returned to Belgium shortly before his death, suffering ill health, but his widow lived on in the house until her death in 1985. It now belongs to the government and houses a poorly maintained collection of his work, which is suffering greatly from the damp salt air. Le Mayeur's work is increasingly popular among international collectors: in May 1998, a large oil-painting by him sold at auction in Singapore for US$370,000.

On the sea-front footpath near the museum is Sanur's beach market, selling arts and crafts and cheap beach clothes.

Of considerable historical significance is **Pura Blanjong**, a temple at the south end of Sanur which houses an inscribed 10C cylindrical stone pillar, **Prasasti Blanjong**, discovered in 1932. It has been only partially deciphered, but appears to have been written in 914 on the order of a King Shri Kesari, and refers to a military campaign against Suwal in the Moluccas, and Gurun (which may be Nusa Penida, according to one source). The inscription is difficult to see as the pillar is usually wrapped in cloth.

Among the more interesting galleries and shops in Sanur are *Darga Galeri* and the adjoining *Foto Galeri Klick*, on Jl. Danau Tamblingan, which sometimes have unusual art work. A few metres south are the *Kika bookshop* (beside *Café Batujimbar*) and *Sari Bumi*, which sells fine ceramics. Along the same street are numerous shops selling all sorts of tourist souvenirs, textiles from around the archipelago, wood carvings, basketry and other crafts; starting prices are high, so determined bargaining is advised.

Pulau Serangan

On this small island, lying just offshore to the south of Sanur, is **Pura Sakenan**, an old temple on the northwest side of the island, which contains a high stone *prasada*. One of Bali's biggest *odalan* festivals is held here on the last day of Kuningan and the first day of Langkir, the 12th and 13th weeks of the 210-day Pawukon-cycle calendar (see box on p 101). Nearby is **Pura Susunan Wadon**, which has another *prasada* decorated with rather worn reliefs.

Transport

At high tide, boats ferry passengers from a mangrove-lined inlet south of Suwung, on the mainland a short distance east of Benoa harbour. A chartered boat is absurdly expensive, so try to join a public boat taking villagers back to the island. At low tide you can walk across the mud flats, but be prepared to get muddy.

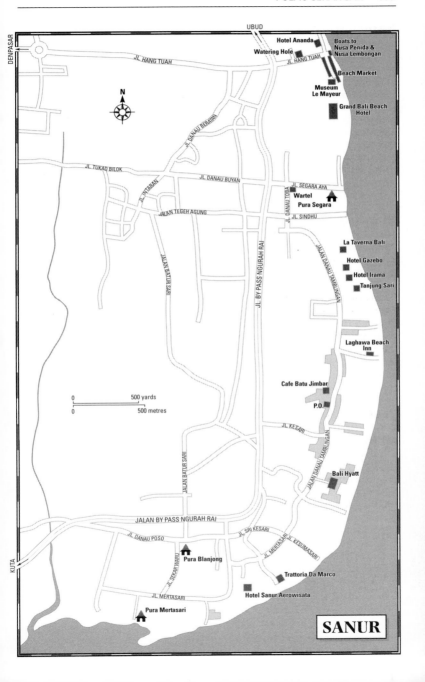

UBUD

DENPASAR

JL. HANG TUAH

Hotel Ananda
Watering Hole
JL. HANG TUAH

Boats to
Nusa Penida &
Nusa Lembongan

Beach Market

Museum
Le Mayeur

Grand Bali Beach
Hotel

JL. DANAU BERATAN

N

JL. TUKAD BILOK

JL. DANAU BUYAN

JL. SEGARA AYA

JL. INTABAN

JALAN TEGEH AGUNG

JL. DANAU TOBA

Wartel
Pura Segara

JL. SINDHU

JALAN BATUR SARI

La Taverna Bali

Hotel Gazebo

Hotel Irama

Tanjung Sari

JALAN DANAU TAMBLINGAN

JL. BY PASS NGURAH RAI

Laghawa Beach
Inn

0   500 yards
0   500 metres

Cafe Batu Jimbar

P.O.

JL. KESARI

JALAN DANAU TAMBINGAN

Bali Hyatt

JALAN BATUR SARI

JALAN BY PASS NGURAH RAI

JL. DANAU POSO

JL. SRI KESARI

JL. MERTASARI   JL. KESUMASARI

Pura Blanjong

JL. SEKAR WARU

Trattoria Da Marco

KUTA

JL. MERTASARI

Hotel Sanur Aerowisata

Pura Mertasari

SANUR

Benoa harbour

West of Suwung, the main highway continues west past the turning to Benoa harbour. Built on reclaimed land at the end of a causeway, Benoa is the main harbour in south Bali, used by *Pelni* passenger ships and the occasional cruise ship. There are daily dining-and-snorkelling cruises from here to Nusa Lembongan (see p 150), and on occasion it is possible to charter yachts here for cruises round the island or eastward through the Nusa Tenggara archipelago. The Mabua Express catamaran to Lombok (2.5 hours) departs from Benoa in the morning, returning in the afternoon; tickets can be bought from agents in all the main beach resort areas.

Beyond the harbour, the highway skirts the mangroves of Benoa Bay and approaches Kuta.

SEMINYAK, LEGIAN AND KUTA

The liveliest, noisiest and most crowded resort area in Bali, this urban sprawl, stretching from Seminyak in the north to Ngurah Rai Airport in the south, is culturally the most un-Balinese part of the island, with a huge number of migrant workers, but paradoxically for many foreign visitors is the quintessential Bali. This is where the real action is – the pubs and bars, the nightclubs, the restaurants, the surf, the bungee jumps, the irritatingly persistent street vendors, and of course the fabulous Kuta beach – a magnificent broad stretch of sand curving gently along the coast almost as far as the eye can see.

By contrast, to the north of Seminyak is **Berewa**, a small, isolated village with a cluster of hotels beside the very quiet and beautiful grey sand beach; for peace and quiet and fine views along the coast, this can hardly be bettered.

Practical information

Transport
Flights

The main gateway to Bali is Denpasar's Ngurah Rai International Airport, which is actually in Tuban, c 4km south of Kuta. It's an important hub for domestic flights, and also well served by international carriers; many of them have offices in Wisti Sabha, the building across the car park from the international departures terminal. (See p 14 for international airline offices.)

Arriving at Ngurah Rai Airport

If your documents are in order, immigration and customs procedures are usually fairly efficient. Note that you must be able to show a ticket out of Indonesia upon request. Corrupt officials here can be bloody-minded about this, as it's an easy way for them to get rich fast. Usually it is not good enough to explain that you will be leaving by ship (to Singapore, for example), or are planning to purchase a ticket within the country. You can expect to be taken aside and coaxed into paying a bribe of a few dollars.

Outside the international terminal are money changers, a hotel booking office, a snack bar, doughnut shop, and the taxi counter. If arriving in the evening in high season (July–Aug,

Dec–Jan) without a confirmed hotel room, you are strongly advised to arrange something at the booking office here, if only for the first night. Taxis to the required destination are paid in advance at the taxi counter.

On departure, travellers boarding international flights must pay a service tax; for domestic flights, this is usually included in the ticket price.

Services at the domestic terminal include money changers, a taxi counter, *Toyota Rent a Car* (☎ 755003), and even a helicopter charter company.

Taxis

Taxis are the most comfortable means of transport round Kuta and southern Bali; check that the driver resets the meter at the start of the journey.

Bemo

These minibuses ply the streets of Kuta all day long, following fixed routes. Tourists are frequently overcharged, and occasionally fall victim to pickpockets, but bemo remain the cheapest way to get around.

Tourist shuttle buses

Perama, which has an office near the south end of Jl. Legian, operates small scheduled buses from Kuta to the main tourist destinations on Bali, including Ubud, Candidasa, Sanur, Lovina and Padangbai. More expensive than public buses, but more comfortable and running to a timetable, these are recommended. They must usually be booked a day in advance. Other companies offering similar services are *Nomad* and *Simpatik*.

Car, motorcycle and bicycle rentals

Kuta is generally the cheapest place to rent a car, as for most of the year supply exceeds demand. *Toyota Rent a Car* (☎ 751282/753458), with an office on Jl. Raya Tuban between Kuta and the airport, rents well-maintained sedans and Kijangs (from $35 per day, but negotiable), and will deliver a vehicle to

your hotel in any of the southern resorts. Considerably cheaper are the small Suzuki jeeps found along Jl. Legian and round the corner along the southern axis of Jl. Pantai Kuta. They are extremely easy to drive, though back-seat passengers have an uncomfortable ride and poor views; they are also remarkably robust and simple—if not terribly powerful—and provided you drive sensibly, serious problems are unlikely. Check the vehicle throughly before renting; damage discovered later may be charged to you.

Prices are negotiable, but expect to pay $15–25 per day, depending on the vehicle's age and condition, and current demand. For weekly or fortnightly rentals, the daily rate is reduced considerably, especially if business is slow. You will be expected to leave your passport with the owner; make sure they provide the documents you will need if stopped by the police (which happens on a regular basis, in the hope that the tourist has infringed some rule and can be coaxed into paying a bribe). You must also have an international driving permit and your national driving licence.

Small motorcycles, up to 125cc, can also be rented in Kuta for a few dollars per day; you will need an international driving permit valid for motorcycles. Wearing a helmet is obligatory, and you would be completely mad to ignore the rule; nevertheless, people do, and people die. Bicycles are available and extremely cheap, but are really not much fun in the heat and heavy traffic; maintenance is usually poor.

Accommodation

With more than 400 places to choose from, it is not hard to find a room to suit your taste and budget. Listed below are a few recommendations; but if none appeal, it is extremely simple to wander round on your own to view others. The ☎ code is 0361. Advance booking is strongly recommended in July, August, December and January.

⭐⭐⭐⭐⭐ *Legian* (☎ 730622; fax 730623; e-mail: legian@idola.net.id) Jl. Laksmana, Seminyak. Very striking modern design, with beautiful rooms. Not for people of very conservative taste.

⭐⭐⭐⭐⭐ *Oberoi* (☎ 730361; fax 730791; e-mail: obrblres@indosat. net.id) Jl. Laksmana, Seminyak. Without doubt one of the most wonderful hotels in Bali; exquisitely designed in all respects.

⭐⭐⭐⭐⭐ *Hotel Imperial Bali* (☎ 730730; fax 730545) Jl. Dhyana Pura, Seminyak. A huge luxury hotel, with elegant rooms.

⭐⭐⭐⭐/⭐⭐⭐⭐ *Hotel Intan Legian* (☎ 751770; fax 751891). Excellent location very close to the beach in the heart of Legian.

⭐⭐⭐⭐/⭐⭐⭐⭐ *Natour Kuta Beach* (☎ 751361; fax 751362) Jl. Pantai Kuta 1. Unexceptional but pleasant rooms close to central Kuta. Some bungalows close to the beach. Large pool.

⭐⭐⭐⭐⭐/⭐⭐⭐⭐ *Vila Lumbung* (☎ 730204, fax 731106) Jl. Raya Petitenget, Petitenget. Attractive two-storey cottages with a rice-barn architectural theme; elegant furnishings; free-form pool.

⭐⭐⭐⭐ *Poppies* (☎ 751059; fax 752364) Jl. Popies I. Charming bungalows in a mature, tranquil garden in the heart of Kuta, a short walk from the beach; attentive staff, attractive pool, with excellent restaurant opposite. Also has four ⭐⭐⭐ bungalows in a separate, equally pretty garden.

⭐⭐⭐⭐/⭐⭐⭐ *Hotel Legong Keraton* (☎ 730280; fax 730285) Berewa Beach. The best of the lodgings at Berewa, on the coast northwest of Seminyak; very pleasant cottages in a spacious garden beside the beach.

⭐⭐⭐ *Bakungsari Cottages* (☎ 751868/754660; fax 752704) off Jl. Bakung Sari. Good value, typical mid-priced, small hotel in central location.

⭐⭐ *Un's Hotel* (☎ 757409; fax 758414) Jl. Benesari 16. Central Kuta location on quiet lane. Tasteful room furnishings and spacious verandah overlooking garden; open-air bathroom. Recommended.

⭐ *Raja Gardens* (☎/fax 730494) Jl. Dhyana Pura, Seminyak. A variety of pleasant rooms in quiet grounds near the beach.

⭐ *Three Brothers Inn* (☎ 751566; fax 756082.) off Jl. Legian. Lovely garden with pool; pleasant range of rooms, and good location near restaurants and the sea.

Restaurants and cafés

There are scores of cafés, bars, restaurants and *warung* of all styles and sizes. The great majority serve reasonable, but rarely exceptional food. The following are recommended as a starting point.

La Lucciola (☎ 261047), Jl. Laksmana, Seminyak, beside Pura Petitenget, serves excellent Italian food in a magnificent, breezy beach-side location. *Tj's* on Jl. Popies I, Kuta, has tasty Tex-Mex food in a relaxed, plant-filled setting. The *Kopi Pot* on Jl. Legian in central Kuta does good cakes and coffees as well as full meals. *Poppies Restaurant* on Jl. Popies I and *Un's Paradise Restaurant* round the corner serve generally high-quality food in very pleasant surroundings. *Warung Kopi* on Jl. Legian in central Legian does a good Indian buffet on Wednesday evenings. *Warisan* on Jl. Krobokan, north of the Jl. Laksamana turn-off to the Oberoi, is a charming art gallery-garden restaurant serving delicious international cuisine.

Information and maps

The *tourist information centre* on Jl. Bakung Sari has limited information but can answer basic inquiries. Maps of Bali published by Periplus and Nelles can be found in many souvenir shops in Kuta, and in the book section of the Matahari department store in Kuta Square.

Money, post and telecoms

There are dozens of **money changers** in Kuta who can change cash and travellers' cheques; rates vary considerably, so if changing a large sum it pays to shop around. *BCA* on Jl. Imam Bonjol offers good rates for credit cards. The **postal agent** on Jl. Melasti and *Ida postal agent* on Jl. Legian opposite Jl. Popies II provide key postal services. *Wartel Kambodiana* in Kuta Square is open 24 hours; another 24-hour *wartel* is on the south side of Jl. Popies II.

Kuta's history

In February 1597 the first Dutch ships to reach Bali—Cornelis de Houtman's expedition—landed briefly at Kuta. From the 17C–19C it became Bali's most important and highly lucrative slave market, controlled by the local rulers who shipped slaves from the islands of Nusa Tenggara; it was also a place of exile for lepers and Balinese criminals expelled from their villages elsewhere on the island.

Mads Lange, a flamboyant Danish trader, arrived in Kuta in 1839, after retreating from Lombok in the face of political disputes. He stayed in Kuta for 18 years, becoming a key mediator in peace talks between the Dutch and Balinese rajas in July 1849.

As at Sanur, it was the arrival of foreigners in the early 20C which ultimately transformed the miserably poor fishing village on Kuta beach into a booming resort. Among the first were Louise Garrett and Bob Koke, American artists who arrived in the mid-1930s and built beach bungalows for guests on the site of the present-day *Natour Kuta Beach* hotel. Another visitor in the 1930s was the extraordinary Glaswegian, Muriel Walker (1898–1997), who took the name K'tut Tantri. An early business partner of Garrett and Koke, with whom she soon fell into dispute, she ran a hotel of her own in Kuta for a while, then moved to Java during the Japanese occupation. After the Second World War she became 'Surabaya Sue', initially a radio propagandist for the nationalist forces fighting the Dutch, and later a speech writer for Sukarno (or so she claimed); she left Indonesia in 1947.

After Indonesian independence Kuta continued to receive a steady trickle of tourists, boosted from the late 1960s by growing numbers of Western hippies drawn by the wonderful Kuta sunsets and readily available marijuana and magic mushrooms; local villagers provided cheap and simple guest rooms and quickly learnt to adapt local dishes to Western tastes.

The subsequent tourist boom of the early 1970s attracted the attention of Jakartan investors who elbowed their way into the local economy; land prices soared, and hotels and guest-houses sprang up in a frenzy of uncontrolled development. The number of lodgings shot up from c 60 in 1973 to nearly 450 by 1994.

Kuta today is brash, highly commercial and undoubtedly successful in attracting the tourist hordes. There are scores of hotels, guest-houses and *losmen* catering to every budget; dozens of restaurants, cafés and bars offer food from all corners of the world. Everything you might desire on a holiday can be found here—from sun cream to helicopter rides, from a massage on the beach to a cottage with your own private plunge pool.

Kuta is also ugly, suffers from near-constant traffic jams, and for many Balinese has become a dreaded evil, a corruptor of Balinese culture and tradition. Others—from Bali and other islands, especially Java—are more curious and come to gawp at the topless Western women on the beach, or to search for jobs. Michel Picard, a sociologist well acquainted with Kuta, notes that it attracts 'a type of young Indonesians called "Kuta cowboys", with Western mannerisms and Australian accents, composed of failed artists, gigolos, pimps, traffickers of all sorts, or more generally, scammers ever in search of a new ploy.'

So while Kuta is a tropical paradise to some visitors, others find it a cesspit bursting at the seams with all the worst aspects of mass tourism. It can be a shopper's heaven or an excuse for an endless pub crawl, or it can be a depressing, tacky urban mess full of rude, desperate hawkers. It can be truly awful, or really tremendous fun.

Apart from the beach and the surf breaks, bungee-jumping and shopping, there is little to do in Kuta itself. The only site of any historical significance is the visually unimpressive **tomb of Mads Lange**, the Danish trader who died here in 1856. It lies on the south side of Kuta, just off the main bypass.

Swimmers should beware of the strong currents just offshore. Lifeguards patrol the part of the beach marked by red-and-yellow flags; swim elsewhere at your peril. There are several **bungee-jumping** towers in Kuta, including the *Bali Bungy Co* on Jl. Pura Puseh, just east of Jl. Legian; *A.J. Hackett Bungy* near the beach beside the *Double Six Club* in Legian; and the *Adrenalin Park* just south of Jl. Benesari. The latter also has a climbing wall and a gravity-defying 'human slingshot'. The Waterbom Park on Jl. Kartika Plaza in Tuban has waterslides and swimming pools, and is an excellent place to take children.

There are several popular surf breaks just off Kuta beach, and further north along the coast at **Petitenget** and **Canggu**. You can watch surfers at play from the beach near the Oberoi, from Kuta beach itself, or from the beach in front of the Hotel Patra Jasa Bali in Tuban.

JIMBARAN BAY

Jimbaran is a lively fishing village with several very good restaurants on the beach and a colourful fishing fleet moored offshore. Behind the lovely sand beach are a few excellent, expensive hotels. In the centre of Jimbaran village is Pura Ulun Siwi, an old temple whose *odalan* falls on the Friday of Dunggulan, the eleventh week in the 30-week *pawukon*-cycle calendar (see box on p 101).

Practical information

Transport

To stay here, you are advised to have your own transport or rely on **taxis**, as public transport south of Jimbaran village is infrequent. *Toyota Rent a Car* (☎ 0361 701747) has an office on the bypass near Jimbaran, and will deliver the vehicle to your hotel; an alternative is to rent a Suzuki jeep in Kuta (see p 111).

Accommodation

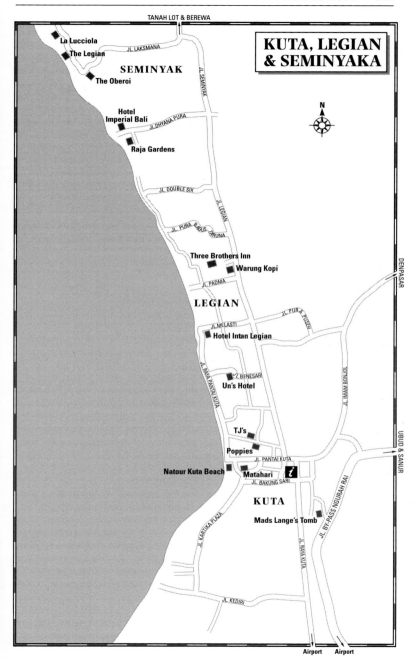

TANAH LOT & BEREWA

La Lucciola
The Legian

SEMINYAK

JL. LAKSMANA

JL. SEMINYAK

The Oberoi

Hotel
Imperial Bali

JL. DHYANA PURA

Raja Gardens

JL. DOUBLE SIX

JL. LEGIAN

JL. PURA BAGUS TARUNA

Three Brothers Inn

Warung Kopi

JL. PADMA

LEGIAN

JL. PURA PUSEH

JL. MELASTI

Hotel Intan Legian

JL. RAYA PANTAI KUTA

JL. BENESARI

Un's Hotel

TJ's

Poppies

JL. PANTAI KUTA

Natour Kuta Beach

Matahari

JL. BAKUNG SARI

KUTA

Mads Lange's Tomb

JL. KARTIKA PLAZA

JL. RAYA KUTA

JL. BY-PASS NGURAH RAI

JL. IMAM BONJOL

DENPASAR

UBUD & SANUR

JL. KEDIRI

Airport   Airport

KUTA, LEGIAN & SEMINYAKA

N

The ☎ code is 0361. Advance booking is advised.

☆☆☆☆☆ *Bali Inter-continental Resort* (☎ 701888; fax 701777). Enormous, luxurious hotel with remarkably little character.

☆☆☆☆☆ *Four Seasons Resort* (☎ 701010; fax 701020). Rather isolated on the south side of Jimbaran Bay. Exquisite villas, each with private plunge pool; excellent restaurants, sports facilities and white sand beach.

☆☆☆☆☆ *Keraton Bali* (☎ 701961; fax 701991). Pleasant, not exceptional rooms in two-storey blocks in a lush garden.

☆☆☆☆☆ *Pansea Bali* (☎ 701605; fax 701320). Magnificent cottages with elegant yet restrained furnishings. Pool, water sports and excellent food; friendly staff. Highly recommended.

☆☆☆☆☆ *Ritz-Carlton* (☎ 702222; fax 701555). A huge modern hotel, very luxurious but too impersonal for some.

NUSA DUA AND TANJUNG BENOA

On the far east side of the Bukit Peninsula is the five-star tourist enclave of Nusa Dua. To the north is a narrow peninsula, dotted with hotels, which ends at Tanjung Benoa.

Practical information

Accommodation

The five-star hotels all lie in beautiful gardens and offer similar facilities. The ☎ code is 0361. Advance booking is suggested in the high seasons (Jul–Aug, Dec–Jan).

Recommended is *Nusa Dua Beach* (☎ 771210; fax 771229; e-mail: ndbh-net@indosat.net.id). Other hotels here include *Bali Hilton International* (☎ 771102; fax 771199); *Hotel Putri Bali* (☎ 771020; fax 771139); *Grand Hyatt Bali* (☎ 771234; fax 772038; e-mail: gh-bali ☎ 2076747@ mcimail.com); *Meliá Bali* (☎ 771510; fax 771360; e-mail: meliabali@ denpasar.wasantara. net.id); *Sheraton Laguna* (☎ 771327; fax 772326); and *Sheraton Nusa Indah* (☎ 771906; fax 771908).

Along Jl. Pratama Tanjung Benoa, the road north from Nusa Dua to Tanjung

Benoa, are several more hotels, including the ☆☆☆☆☆ *Meliá Benoa* (☎ 771714; fax 771713; e-mail: meli-abenoa@denpasar.wasantara.net.id). Recommended is the beautifully designed ☆☆☆☆☆/☆☆☆☆ *Novotel Benoa Bali* (☎ 772239; fax 772237; e-mail: novobenoa@denpasar.wasantara.net.id) c 4km north of Nusa Dua, with several swimming pools and many activities for guests, including cooking, dancing and diving classes.

Restaurants

Staying in Nusa Dua, you are encouraged to eat in the generally excellent but expensive hotel restaurants. An alternative is the Galeria, a shopping mall in the centre of the enclave, which has several restaurants serving German, Italian and Japanese cuisine, as well as seafood and steaks.

History

The luxurious hotel enclave of Nusa Dua resulted from a 1971 masterplan for the development of tourism in Bali. This envisaged, over-optimistically, that by 1985 Bali would receive more than 700,000 tourists who would stay an average of four nights in luxury hotels. It was believed by the French consultants who were the plan's makers that Balinese culture and society would need protection from the influences of these foreign tourists, who in turn would want to stay in considerable comfort, near the airport, near the sea and within reasonable distance of the most attractive parts of southern Bali—notably the region round Ubud.

The fenced enclave concept was proposed as the solution to all these needs: the tourists would have a minimal impact on Balinese culture outside the enclave walls, but at the same time, by judicious use of architecture and careful landscaping, the tourist would be content in thinking this was a truly typical Balinese environment. Furthermore, the Indonesian government favoured the idea of a project which would generate hard currency to improve the country's balance of payments.

Progress was slow at first: land was bought from local villagers at less than the market value; they sued without success. The majority of jobs were promised to the locals, but in fact perhaps only 25 per cent have gone to them. The first hotel, *Nusa Dua Beach*, was finally begun in 1980 and was completed three years later as a showcase hotel. Others followed: by 1990 five hotels were operating, and in 1991 three more were opened. Initial low occupancy rates gradually picked up, and today the Nusa Dua concept is seen by the Indonesian government as a success story to be emulated elsewhere in the archipelago.

THE BUKIT PENINSULA

This barren limestone plateau at the southern tip of Bali has a few five-star hotels and one or two sights of interest, but is mostly visited by surfers searching for Bali's best breaks.

Accommodation

Several very expensive hotels are found on the peninsula. The ☎ code is 0361. The best of them all is the sublime ☆☆☆☆☆ *Amanusa* (☎ 771267; fax 771266), with magnificently luxurious villas beside a golf course, a short distance south of the Nusa Dua enclave; the pool suites (from $725) are recommended. Advance booking in high season is essential: repeat guests book months in advance and have priority.

The road south across the peninsula from Jimbaran comes to an intersection after c 5km. To the west (right) is **Pantai Balangan**, a popular surfing beach. The main road continues towards Uluwatu, and in Pecatu, c 4km further on, a lane to the right is signed to another surfing beach, **Padang-Padang**.

Pura Luhur Uluwatu, c 5.5km further, is spectacularly located on the cliff edge at the end of a narrow point. Built of hard coral, the temple's gateways are carved with elegant reliefs. Both the split gate leading into the middle court, and the arched gate into the inner court, are flanked by Ganesha figures; the latter gate is surmounted by fine *kala* faces.

Pura Luhur Uluwatu is considered to be one of the island's *sad kahyangan*, or 'sanctuaries of the world', a group of especially sacred ancient temples. Local legend tells of its building in the 11C and its renovation in the mid-16C by

Danghyang Nirartha, the Javanese Shaivite-Buddhist priest credited with reintroducing Shaivite Hinduism and Mahayana Buddhism to Bali, who later achieved his conscious death here. The present gateways are more recent—probably 17C–18C. The temple's odalan falls on the Tuesday of Medangsia, the 14th week in the Pawukon-cycle calendar (see box on p 101).

At the parking lot are several *warung* selling food and souvenirs. A path along the cliff edge presents a magnificent view of the temple. A lane to the north, a few metres before the parking lot, leads along the cliff top c 3km to a cluster of *warung*, where a path leads down through a narrow gorge to the very popular surfing beach, **Pantai Suluban**. The lane is only accessible to pedestrians and motorcycles; *ojek* wait for fares at the junction near the Uluwatu parking lot. The cliff top is a wonderful place to watch the surfers; drinks and simple food are available.

Ubud and vicinity

Highlights. The region round Ubud is the production centre for most of Bali's **arts and crafts**, and offers the visitor a vast array of paintings, wood carvings, jewellery, stone sculpture and much else; the **Museum Neka** (see p 124) and the **Agung Rai Museum of Art** (see p 130) in Ubud have the finest collections of Balinese painting in Indonesia. In the surrounding valleys are most of Bali's important sites of antiquity, including the **royal 'tombs' of Gunung Kawi** (see p 137), the cave of **Gua Gajah** (see p 134), and the rock-cut *candi* of **Tegallinggah** (see p 133). In Mengwi, to the southwest, is **Pura Taman Ayun** (see p 141), one of the loveliest of all the island's temples.

Accommodation

Ubud and the surrounding villages offer a vast choice of accommodation for every budget, and make an excellent base from which to explore central Bali.

Away from Ubud there are a few rather fine lodgings, such as the *Blue Yogi* at Pujung Kelod, northeast of Ubud; such places are detailed in the text below.

Odalan dates for a selection of temples

Pura Taman Pule, Mas: festival starts on Saturday of Kuningan (week 12): 10.3.01, 6.10.01, 4.5.02, 30.11.02, 28.6.03, 24.1.04.

Pura Puseh Batuan, Batuan: festival starts on Saturday of Wariga (week 7): 3.2.01, 1.9.01, 30.3.02, 26.10.02, 24.5.03, 20.12.03, 17.7.04.

Pura Desa Batuan, Batuan: festival starts on Saturday of Wariga (week 7): 3.2.01, 1.9.01, 30.3.02, 26.10.02, 24.5.03, 20.12.03, 17.7.04.

Pura Pusering Jagat, Pejeng: festival starts on Tuesday of Medangsia (week 14): 22.8.00, 20.3.01, 16.10.01, 14.5.02, 10.12.02, 8.7.03, 3.2.04.

Pura Penataran Sasih, Pejeng: festival on Purnama Kesanga (full moon of the ninth lunar month; Feb/Mar).
Pura Agung Gunung Raung, Taro: festival starts on Wednesday of Ugu (week 26): 15.11.00, 13.6.01, 9.1.02, 7.8.02, 5.3.03, 1.10.03, 28.4.04.
Pura Bukit Sari, Sangeh: festival starts on Wednesday of Julungwangi (week 9): 19.7.00, 14.2.01, 12.9.01, 10.4.02, 6.11.02, 4.6.03, 31.12.03, 28.7.04.
Pura Taman Ayun, Mengwi: festival starts on Tuesday of Medangsia (week 14): 22.8.00, 20.3.01, 16.10.01, 14.5.02, 10.12.02, 8.7.03, 3.2.04.
Pura Sadha, Kapal: festival starts on Saturday of Kuningan (week 12): 12.8.00, 10.3.01, 6.10.01, 4.5.02, 30.11.02, 28.6.03, 24.1.04.

Practical information

Transport
Public minibuses

Most public buses leave from the market on Jl. Raya Ubud, or round the corner in Jl. Wanara Wana. They depart when full or when the driver is tired of waiting, and are generally slow and uncomfortable. If you're in the mood, however, they can be interesting and even fun. The main routes are south to Batubulan (for Denpasar, the southern resorts and west Bali), and east to Gianyar (for east Bali); for routes to the north, check at the tourist information office, as services are infrequent.

Shuttle buses

Perama on Jl. Hanoman and *Nomad* on Jl. Raya Ubud run scheduled shuttle buses to Sanur, the airport, Kuta, Kintamani, Lovina, Candidasa, Padangbai and further afield. These are particularly useful for single travellers, being much cheaper than taxis, and faster, more comfortable though more costly than public minibuses. Tickets should be bought one day in advance from one of the many outlets in Ubud, and passengers can usually be picked up from their hotels.

Cars with driver

You cannot walk within 50m of the Jl. Ubud Raya–Jl. Wanara Wana junction without being asked: 'Transport?' Private taxis – usually minivans – gather here each morning in search of customers. Negotiate a price in advance, explaining very precisely where you want to go. Staff at the nearby tourist information office can suggest appropriate rates. If you're taking the vehicle for a day trip, check whether fuel and the driver's lunch are included or extra. If you find one driver particularly agreeable, it may be worth booking him for several days and negotiating a lower price.

Car rentals

There are usually numerous Suzuki jeeps for rent along Jl. Wanara Wana. Prices depend on demand, month, length of rental and your bargaining skill, but are usually c $20–40 per day. Read the section on private rentals (see p 26) before setting out.

Motorcycles and bicycles

Small, clutchless motorcycles and a few larger machines can be rented on Jl. Wanara Wana; an international driving permit valid for motorcycles is required. Many places rent bicycles, but the hills round Ubud are not ideal for cycling in the heat. They are very useful, however, if you choose to stay on the outskirts of Ubud yet wish to visit the centre frequently.

Flight reconfirmation

There are no airline offices in Ubud, and travel agents often charge absurd fees to reconfirm flights and are not always reliable; it is generally safer—and cheaper—to call the airline yourself from a *wartel*.

Accommodation

In and around Ubud there are several hundred hotels, guesthouses and *losmen*, providing the best choice of accommodation anywhere in Indonesia. Booking is recommended in high season (Jul–Aug, Dec–Jan); at other times, a glut of empty rooms encourages heavy discounting. For all but the very cheapest places (which probably cannot afford to drop their prices) and the most expensive (which remain popular all year round), expect to obtain a reduction of 15–60 per cent on the published rate, with breakfast and tax thrown in for free; staying two nights or more boosts your bargaining position considerably.

With such a huge choice, it can be difficult to know where to start looking. Hotels on main roads like Jl. Wanara Wana in the heart of Ubud are generally more expensive than their equivalent in the neighbouring villages. However, along almost every narrow lane and alley in central Ubud are simple guest-houses with rooms in small leafy family compounds for $5–8; they tend to be similar to each other and few are listed here, though they are very easy to find. To the west of Ubud is a steadily growing number of small, simple two-storey cottages—especially on the Penestana–Campuhan ridge—many of them offering wonderful views and complete tranquillity. Some, however, are booked out for months or years by expatriate traders, writers and artists. In Kedewatan, to the northwest, are some of the most wonderful hotels in the country, where you can spend $500 per night if you wish, for the utmost comfort, service and privacy. Those listed below can all be recommended. The ☎ code is 0361.

Central Ubud

The bustling heart of Ubud, among the restaurants, bars, shops and galleries, with all services close by.

✰✰✰/✰✰✰ *Ubud Village Hotel* (☎ 975571/974701/974704; fax 975069) Jl. Wanara Wana. Very central location with pool.

✰✰✰ *Ubud Inn* (☎ 975071; fax 975188) Jl. Wanara Wana. A slightly better than standard mid-priced hotel in central Ubud; has a pool.

✰✰✰/✰✰ *Cendana Cottages* (☎/fax 96243) Jl. Wanara Wana. Central Ubud location with pool; rooms in two-storey blocks.

✰✰ *Adi Cottages* (☎ 976127; fax 975231) Jl. Wanara Wana. Has a very small pool in a rather pleasant garden setting.

✰✰ *Artini 2* (☎ 975689; fax 975348) Jl. Hanoman. Clean rooms in a beautiful, mature garden with pool; some rooms rather dark; no off-road parking.

✰✰ *Kubuku* (☎ 975345/974742; fax 975120) Jl. Wanara Wana. Five rooms in a charming, shady grove surrounded by rice fields.

✰ *Praety Homestay* Jl. Sukma. Tiny, simple *losmen* with good rooms; friendly family and outstanding breakfast.

✰ *Siti Homestay* (☎ 975599) *banjar* Kalah, *desa* Peliatan. South of the main road through Peliatan. Plain, cheap, clean rooms in friendly compound.

West of Ubud: Campuhan, Penestanan and Sayan

A tranquil, hilly landscape of trees and rice fields, with magnificent views, and away from the frantic pace of central Ubud.

✰✰✰/✰✰✰ *Bali Ubud Cottages* (☎ 975058; fax 286971) Penestanan.

Thatched, large airy rooms round a pool; attractive garden.

☆☆☆☆/☆☆☆ *Taman Bebek* (☎ 975385; fax 976532; e-mail: tribwana@dps. mega.net.id) Sayan. Amid lush gardens, the fine villas have an air of slightly decaying elegance; the pool can be used by all guests if the presidential suite is unoccupied. 5.5km from Ubud centre.

☆☆☆ *Djagra's Inn* (☎/fax 974343) *banjar* Baung, Sayan. Four rooms only; the two upstairs have fine views across the Ayung valley. No pool, no restaurant, but a charming hideaway. 6.5km from Ubud centre.

☆☆ *Sayan Terrace* (☎ 974384; fax 975384) Sayan. Once magnificent views up the Ayung valley, now partially spoilt by construction of the Four Seasons Sayan hotel below; pleasant, though rather tired, rooms. 5.5km from Ubud centre.

☆ *Jagi Bungalows* Penestanan Kelod, 50m west of *Melati Cottages*. Four simple cottages, each with two bedrooms and balcony or verandah in extremely peaceful, individual gardens; small kitchen; access to a nearby pool.

☆ *Londo Bungalows* (☎ 976548) Campuhan. Six comfortable but simply furnished houses with kitchens on the Campuhan ridge to the west of the road; fine views over rice fields; very peaceful.

☆☆/☆ *Santra Putra* (☎ 977321) Campuhan. Spacious houses on the Campuhan ridge, with large windows and good views, run by two young artist brothers. Houses can sleep four at extra cost.

☆☆/☆ *Gerebig Bungalows* (☎ 974582; fax 975120) Penestanan Kelod. Variety of charming thatched one- and two-storey cottages overlooking rice fields; delightful location and friendly family.

☆ *Sadri Homestay* Campuhan. Two pleasant, simple cottages at the top of the Campuhan steps in a small secluded garden; fine views.

Northwest of Ubud: Sangginan, Kedewatan and Payangan

Most of the following have spectacular views over deep river gorges in very peaceful locations.

☆☆☆☆☆ *Amandari* (☎ 975333; fax 975335) Kedewatan. Perhaps the finest of the three Aman hotels on Bali; exquisite furnishings, excellent service, total privacy, marvellous views, and private pool with some suites; c 4km from Ubud centre.

☆☆☆☆☆ *Kupu Kupu Barong* (☎ 975478; fax 975079) Kedewatan. A magnificent hotel in a stunningly beautiful setting, providing some of the finest accommodation in Bali; 4.5km from Ubud centre.

☆☆☆☆☆ *Pita Maha* (☎ 974330; fax 974329) Sangginan. A beautiful small hotel overlooking the Wos Barat river; spa, fine pool, and expensive terrace restaurant.

☆☆☆☆☆ *The Chedi* (☎ 975963; fax 975968; e-mail: chediubud@ghmhotels.com) Melinggih Kelod, Payangan. Striking, highly imaginative, somewhat stark architecture, not to everyone's taste. Small rooms for the price; restaurant food and views are excellent; unusual pool; c 7km from Ubud centre.

☆☆☆☆/☆☆☆ *Ulun Ubud Cottages* (☎ 975024/975762; fax 975524) Sangginan. Comfortable rooms overlooking the Wos Barat river; the best views are from the twin-bed rooms; small pool.

☆☆☆ *Klub Kokos* (☎ 081 139 6218 (mobile); fax 974731) Bangkiang Sidem. Excellent value, beautifully designed cottages in the middle of nowhere, a 30-minute hike from Ubud or c 7km circuitous drive; the Balinese-Australian hosts invest profits in the local community.

☆☆ *Wisata Cottages* (☎ 975713; fax 975017) Sangginan. Good-value rooms overlooking the Wos river; small pool.

Restaurants, cafés and bars

Ubud has dozens of cafés and restaurants. Some are truly excellent; others, with well-established names, are now resting on their laurels and have become mediocre and overpriced. A few have achieved wonderful effects with location and decor, only to be let down by the food itself. Those listed here are only a tiny fraction of what is available.

Bali Buddha, Jl. Jembawan. A cosy bagelry with excellent fare; totting up the bill, however, can take forever.

Beggar's Bush, Campuhan, beside the Wos river bridge. Very pleasant bar and restaurant with convivial atmosphere.

Café Lotus, Jl. Raya Ubud. The original of a chain throughout southern Bali; located beside a lotus pond, behind which stands the façade of Pura Taman Saraswati; the service and rather over-priced food are variable.

Casa Luna, Jl. Raya Ubud. Especially good for vegetable juices, coffees, cakes and bread-based meals, but staff can be dreadfully elusive at busy times.

Exiles Café, Pengosekan. Small café with garden opposite Kokokan Club; a fine place for a beer, but serving unexceptional food.

Jazz Café, Jl.Sukma. Live jazz in the evenings.

Kagemusha, Pengosekan. A reputable Japanese restaurant, popular with visiting Japanese.

Kokokan Club, Pengosekan. Makes a very good attempt at producing authentic Thai food, in rather grand surroundings.

Kubuku, Jl. Wanara Wana. Extremely laid-back café offering tasty, cheap Indian-influenced food, served on veran-dahs overlooking rice fields.

Kupu Kupu Barong, Kedewatan (☎ 975478). The restaurant terrace has a sublime view over the Ayung gorge; the international cuisine has been variable in the past, but is now much improved; expensive.

Mendra's Café, Jl. Wanara Wana. Has a popular upstairs balcony overlooking the street; good for an evening beer or *brem*; unexceptional food.

Momoya, Jl. Suweta. A fine little café

that serves a tasty version of Japanese food. Recommended.

Sai Sai Bar, Jl. Wanara Wana. Popular evening watering hole with live music.

The Chedi, Payangan (☎ 975963). Serves excellent, expensive international cuisine in a beautiful setting.

The Village Café, Jl. Sukma. Offers an eclectic menu of tasty, very cheap food.

Tutmak, Jl. Dewi Sita. Excellent organic salads, pasta, coffees and fresh juices.

Information and maps

The **Ubud Tourist Information office** on Jl. Raya Ubud offers advice on accommoda-tion, transport, dance performances and festivals. For special occasions, such as important cremations, staff prepare use-ful pamphlets advising on appropriate behaviour and dress. A noticeboard here has occasional news of art, cookery, dance or language courses; personal messages can be left for friends. Free list-ings magazines, such as Bali Plus and Bali Kini, are often available from the counter.

Pondok Pekak, on the east side of Ubud's football pitch, is a friendly information and book exchange, with a library hold-ing many books about Bali.

The *Ubud Surroundings* map in the 'Travel Treasure Maps' series is invalu-able for visitors staying awhile in the Ubud area; its sketched maps are accu-rate and informative, showing footpaths and minor roads, and a huge number of Ubud's shops, hotels and restaurants. The *Bali Pathfinder* map, by local resi-dent Silvio Santosa, has detailed insets of central Ubud. The *Bali* map by Periplus includes a plan of the greater Ubud area. All these are usually avail-able in Ubud's bookshops.

Bookshops

Ary's Bookshop on Jl. Raya Ubud, near Ary's Warung, stocks maps, numerous books on Bali and Indonesia, and for-eign newspapers and magazines. *Adi*

Bookshop, on the corner of Jl. Hanoman and Jl. Raya Ubud, sells the Jakarta Post and second-hand paperbacks. *Ubud Bookshop*, on Jl. Raya Ubud, has a small selection of books about Indonesia. The *Ganesha Bookshop* nearby sells maps, guide books and second-hand paperbacks.

Money, post and telecoms

Useful **banks** on Jl. Raya Ubud include *BCA*, *Bank Lippo* and *Bank Duta* (all open Mon–Fri 08.00–15.00; all take M and V for a fee). *BNI* on Jl. Wanara Wana accepts travellers' cheques and cash. There are many private money changers, open for longer hours than the banks; exchange rates vary from place to place. The **post office** is on Jl. Jembawan. A 24-hour **telecoms office** is at the east end of Jl. Cok Putra Sudarsana. Other *wartel* are on Jl. Raya Ubud and Jl. Wanara Wana. E-mail services are available at *Pondok Pekak* (pondok@denpasar.wasantara.net.id), beside the football pitch on Jl. Wanara Wana, and at the *Nomad* wartel on Jl. Raya Ubud (nomad@denpasar.wasantara.net.id).

Performing arts and cultural events
Dance

There are several dances performed for tourists each evening at various stages in and around Ubud. These have been choreographed to maximise enjoyment for the foreign visitor who is unable to understand the language and whose attention span is short. The choice on offer most evenings includes legong—the court dance; an episode from the *Mahabharata* or *Ramayana*; the *barong* and *kris* dance; and an amalgamated version of *Kecak*, *Sanghyang Jaran* and *Sanghyang Dedari* (commonly known as the monkey, fire and trance dance). All the dances are purely commercial in nature, but no less entertaining for that. Transport (for those venues outside Ubud) and tickets are available from the tourist information office on Jl. Raya Ubud, which can provide a full schedule and recommend particular troupes. Most performances start between 18.30 and 20.00.

Gambuh

Sadly, the ancient court drama of *gambuh* is largely ignored by visitors. A dedicated troupe, attired magnificently and accompanied by a unique gamelan orchestra of unwieldy bamboo flutes, bells, drums and gongs, performs excerpts twice monthly (on the 1st and 15th of the month) at Pura Desa Batuan, just west of the Batuan intersection.

Shadow puppets

A *wayang kulit* performance can usually be seen once or twice a week; the tourist information office can provide details.

Ubud activities

Several mornings each week, the *Bali Bird Club* organises **bird walks –** delightful hikes through the country side round Ubud. There's a good chance of seeing 20 or more bird species, including several Indonesian endemics, but you certainly don't need to be a birdwatcher to enjoy the walks: they're a great opportunity to explore the local landscape. Contact the *Beggar's Bush* restaurant beside the bridge in Campuhan (☎ 975009). Victor Mason, the bird club's founder and owner of the restaurant, is the author of *Bali Bird Walks*, available locally, detailing numerous walks in the vicinity.

Several companies run **half-day rafting trips** along the very scenic Ayung river to the west of Ubud, among them *Bali Adventure Rafting* (☎ 721480), *Sobek* (☎ 287059) and *Ayung River Rafting* (☎ 238759/239440).

Various types of **massage** and **therapeutic baths** are available from *Ubud Sari Health Resort* at Jl. Kajeng 35,

Ubud (☎ 974393). Some hotels, including *Bali Spirit* (☎ 974013) in Nyuh Kuning and *Pita Maha* (☎ 974330) in Sanggingan, have in-house spa facilities open to non-residents.

Shopping
Along Jl. Raya Ubud and Jl. Wanara Wana are scores of shops selling paintings, wood carvings, bamboo wind chimes, jewellery, antiques, clothing and souvenirs. At first glance, there appears to be an astounding variety on offer; it quickly becomes apparent, however, that a great many paintings and wood carvings are amazingly similar, with the same designs and images continually repeated. Of note is the *Argasoka Textile Gallery* near the south end of Jl. Wanara Wana, which sells extremely intricate, beautiful silk batik by a couple of Yogyakarta-based artists. Prices are high, but the quality is excellent: these pieces take a long time to create. Kubuku, near the monkey forest, has a good selection of bamboo wind chimes. Stalls in the municipal market on Jl. Raya Ubud offer a wide choice of sarongs and sashes—the dress required for entering a temple anywhere in Bali.

Art galleries
Ubud—like Yogyakarta in Java—has a very large population of artists and would-be artists attempting to make a living from the tourist trade. While the quality of their work ranges from extremely good to very poor, there are a few galleries with regular exhibitions of local and foreign artists which are worth visiting.

Blue Moon. Two outstanding galleries run by Rachael Barrett, a long-time Bali resident—*Studio Blue Moon* on the corner of Jl. Raya Ubud and Jl. Sri Wedari, and the larger *Blue Moon Gallery* in *banjar* Kutuh Kaja, c 1km north of Jl. Raya Ubud along Jl. Tirta Tawar—display some of the most exciting and original art to be found in Ubud; prices are reasonable. The exhibitions by Indonesian and foreign artists change monthly and provide a most refreshing change from the often rather stale work shown in so many other Ubud galleries. *Munut Gallery*, Jl. Raya Ubud. A very large selection of Balinese art; somewhat repetitive, and with many versions and variations of well-known works. *Neka Gallery*, Jl. Raya Ubud. Similar in theme to the Munut Gallery, but usually with several works by long-established, highly regarded Balinese artists. *Seniwati Gallery of Art by Women*, Jl. Sri Wedari 2/B. A gallery run by women to promote women artists working in Bali; both a permanent collection and a selection for sale.

Exploring Ubud

Museum Neka
This privately owned museum (open daily 09.00–17.00) on Jl. Campuhan, c 2km northwest of the town centre, has the finest collection of Balinese paintings in Indonesia, with all the main styles well represented. The museum was opened in the mid-1970s by a savvy local dealer, Suteja Neka, and has steadily expanded. The art works are clearly labelled in English.

Gallery I contains various styles of traditional Balinese paintings, beginning with the classical style, usually depicting scenes from the Hindu-Buddhist epics such as the *Ramayana* and *Mahabharata*. The largely two-dimensional figures are similar in profile to the shadow puppets of the *wayang kulit* tradition, but the faces in the paintings are generally depicted in three-quarters view. The 'Ubud' style of painting which evolved in the 1930s is well represented in the gallery, together with the sombre, action-packed canvases of the 'Batuan' style, made famous by artists such as Ida Bagus Made Wija (1912–92), a high-caste brahmin born in Batuan, who became one of Bali's best-known artists; and I Wayan Bendi (b. 1950), also of Batuan.

Gallery II contains several works by Arie Smit (b. 1916), the Dutch artist who moved to Bali in 1956 and whose work gave rise to the 'Young Artists' style of painting in Penestanan, where he supplied enthusiastic boys with oil paints and canvas and encouraged them to paint. Bright colours and simple figures predominate. Paintings by contemporary Balinese artists are also shown here.

Gallery III houses black-and-white photos of Balinese scenes taken by Louise Garrett Koke, the young American choreographer who arrived with her future husband, Bob Koke, in the 1930s, and opened the first hotel in Kuta.

Gallery IV contains pen-and-ink drawings by I Gusti Nyoman Lempad (1862?–1978), the multi-talented architect, dancer and woodcarver.

Gallery V is hung with works by contemporary Indonesian artists.

The lower floor of **Gallery VI** houses works by well-established Indonesian artists, including several by Affandi (1907?–90), Hendra Gunawan (1918–83), Popo Iskandar (b. 1927) and Widayat (b. 1919?). Upstairs are paintings by foreign artists who worked in Bali, among them the Moscow-born German, Walter Spies (1895–1942), who died when a ship taking German civilian internees to Sri Lanka was sunk by a Japanese plane in January 1942; the Dutchmen W.O.J. Nieuwenkamp (1874–1950), Rudolf Bonnet (1885–1978), Willem Gerard Hofker (1902–81) and Han Snel (b. 1925); the Mexican painter and caricaturist, Miguel Covarrubias (1904–57); the Swiss, Theo Meier (1908–82), who lived in Bali from 1936–61; the Cantonese-born Singaporean, Lee Man Fong (1913–82); the Australian artist and writer, Donald Friend (1915–89); and the Manila-born Catalan, Antonio Maria Blanco (b. 1927), who still lives in Ubud.

Campuhan ridge

Even if you don't stay in this part of Ubud, it's well worth travelling c 1km west of the town centre and climbing the steps almost opposite the *Hotel Tjampuhan*, which lead onto the beautiful Campuhan ridge between the Wos and Agung rivers. The views here, overlooking rice fields and irrigation channels, are wonderful; some of the best of Ubud's 'rustic' accommodation is found in the vicinity. Close to the bridge in Campuhan is the **home of Blanco**, the flamboyant, theatrical painter who well understands the concept of self-promotion. Open to the public (for a fee), his studio is carefully arranged in the manner of an eccentric artist, its walls decorated with his erotic and whimsical paintings and sketches. He settled in Campuhan in the 1950s and has firmly established himself as one of Ubud's 'characters'. Either Blanco himself—complete with beret—or his Balinese wife is usually on hand to welcome visitors and ultimately to encourage them to buy his works. He's a warm, friendly character, always ready for a lively discussion on any subject.

Pura Gunung Lebah

This small temple, visible on the north side of the Campuhan bridge, is the starting point for a very pleasant walk north to Bangkiang Sidem and beyond.

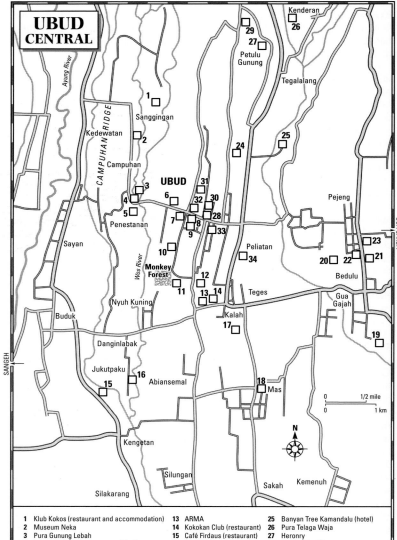

UBUD CENTRAL

1   Klub Kokos (restaurant and accommodation)
2   Museum Neka
3   Pura Gunung Lebah
4   Beggar's Bush (restaurant and bar)
5   Antonio Blanco's home
6   Museum Puri Lukisan
7   Tourist information centre
8   Market
9   Tutmak (restaurant)
10 Mendra's Café (restaurant)
11 Kubuku (restaurant and accommodation)
12 Kagemusha (restaurant)
13 ARMA
14 Kokokan Club (restaurant)
15 Café Firdaus (restaurant)
16 Candi Tebing Jukutpaku
17 Museum Rudana
18 Pura Taman Pule
19 Yeh Pulu
20 Candi Tebing Kalebutan
21 Museum Purbakala
22 Pura Kebo Edan
23 Pura Penetaran Sasih
24 Blue Moon Gallery
25 Banyan Tree Kamandalu (hotel)
26 Pura Telaga Waja
27 Heronry
28 Studio Blue Moon
29 Pura Desa Junjungan
30 Seniwati Gallery
31 Momoya (restaurant)
32 Puri Saren Agung (palace and hotel)
33 Bali Buddha (restaurant)
34 Pura Puseh Peliatan

The pura stands at the confluence of the Wos Barat and Wos Timur rivers and is said to date from the 8C.

A path follows the east flank of the *pura* and continues north along the ridge between the two rivers. Refreshment is available at **Klub Kokos**, a café with fine accommodation in Bangkiang Sidem, reached after a c 30-minute walk.

Museum Puri Lukisan

Between Campuhan and the centre of Ubud on Jl. Raya Ubud is Museum Puri Lukisan (open daily 08.00–16.00), an art museum with a smaller, less comprehensive collection than Museum Neka, but nevertheless well worth a look if time permits. It was opened in 1956 by the late prince of Ubud, Cokorda Gede Agung Sukawati, and the Dutch artist, Rudolf Bonnet, both of whom had been key figures in the local 'Pita Maha' arts guild of the late 1930s. The collection is especially strong on works in the 'Young Artists' style inspired by Arie Smit.

Pura Taman Kemude Saraswati

On the west corner of the junction of Jl. Ubud Raya and Jl. Kajeng, set back behind a pretty lotus pond where the **Café Lotus** is situated, is this small water temple, dedicated to Dewi Saraswati, the goddess of wisdom and learning. The temple was commissioned in the 1950s by the prince of Ubud, and the work was carried out under the direction of I Gusti Nyoman Lempad. Some of the sculpture is particularly fine, and well worth a look.

Pura Desa Ubud

A few metres further east is Pura Desa Ubud, beside which is a stage used during important festivals, and also regularly for dance performances for tourists.

Puri Saren Agung

On the north side of Jl. Raya Ubud, opposite the municipal market, is the palace of Ubud's royal family. Parts of it are open to the public, and rooms are available for ☆☆☆ rent (☎ 975057; fax 975137), although you risk being constantly disturbed by visitors. The palace was largely razed by the earthquake of 21 January 1917, but was subsequently rebuilt with the help of Lempad, who built the magnificent arched gateway on the east side of the main courtyard, in front of which dance performances are now held for tourists.

The monkey forest

At the south end of Jl. Wanara Wana is a small shady grove (open daily, small fee), the home to large numbers of long-tailed macaques who have grown fat and bold on snacks from visitors. Despite the monkeys, rather than because of them, it's a pleasant place to wander. A flight of steps to the right descends through the tangled roots of a colossal banyan tree to a small carp pool and water temple. On the southern edge of the forest is the small Pura Dalem of *banjar* Padang Tegal. A track continues south from the forest to Nyuh Kuning, past numerous shops selling all sorts of wood carvings.

Candi Tebing Jukutpaku

From Nyuh Kuning, take the main road west from the south end of the village, across the bridge over the Wos river to banjar Danginlabak. A few metres west of

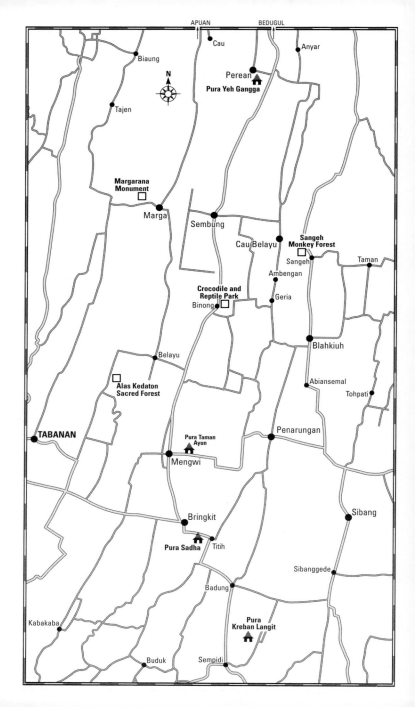

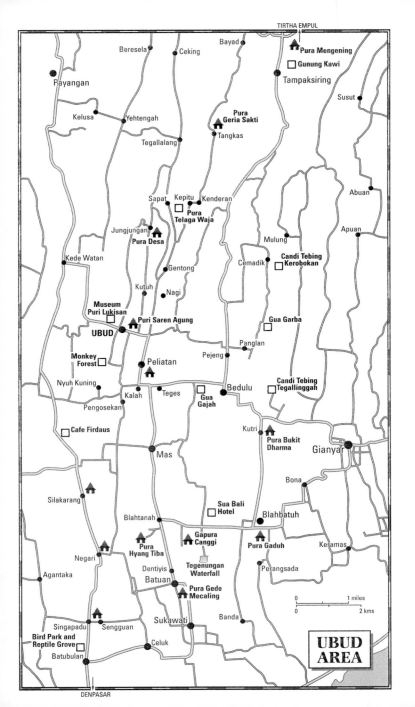

TIRTHA EMPUL

Bayad

Pura Mengening

Beresela   Ceking

Gunung Kawi

Payangan   Tampaksiring

Susut

Kelusa   Yehtengah

Pura
Geria Sakti

Tegallalang   Tangkas

Abuan

Sapat   Kepitu   Kenderan

Apuan

Pura
Telaga Waja

Jungjungan   Mulung

Pura Desa

Candi Tebing
Kerobokan

Kede Watan   Cemadik

Gentong

Kutuh   Nagi

Museum
Puri Lukisan

Puri Saren Agung   Gua Garba

UBUD   Panglan

Monkey
Forest   Peliatan   Pejeng

Nyuh Kuning   Candi Tebing
Tegallinggah

Kalah   Teges   Gua   Bedulu
Gajah

Pengosekan

Cafe Firdaus   Kutri

Pura Bukit
Dharma

Gianyar

Mas

Bona

Silakarang

Sua Bali
Hotel   Blahbatuh

Blahtanah

Gapura
Canggi   Pura Gaduh   Keramas

Negari   Pura
Hyang Tiba

Tegenungan   Perangsada
Waterfall

Agantaka   Dentiyis

Batuan

Pura Gede
Mecaling

Sukawati   Banda

Singapadu   Sengguan   0   1 miles

Bird Park and   0   2 kms
Reptile Grove

Batubulan   Celuk

UBUD
AREA

DENPASAR

the *balai banjar*, take the road south c 1km to the centre of *banjar* Jukutpaku in *desa* Singakerta. Here a sign to the east indicates a path to Candi Tebing, a small rock-cut *candi* carved into the cliff on the west bank of the Wos river; it's an easy walk of a few minutes from the road. Flanking the central niche which contains the *candi* are two empty rectangular alcoves which were probably used by hermits. The site probably dates from the 11C, but this is uncertain.

Agung Rai Museum of Art

A modern museum (open daily 09.00–18.00) on the northeast edge of Pengosekan, Agung Rai Museum of Art (ARMA; Museum Seni Lukisan Agung Rai) houses a huge, somewhat overwhelming collection of art. There are dozens of paintings in the classical Balinese style, and most subsequent local styles are well represented. Works by many of Java's most important artists are also displayed, together with examples by foreign artists in Bali. The museum can be entered from Jl. Hanoman or round the corner beside the **Kokokan Club**.

Museum Rudana

In *banjar* Teges, south of Peliatan on the main road towards Mas, Museum Rudana (open daily 09.00–17.00) is housed in a grandiose three-storey building overlooking rice fields. The large collection emphasises works by less well-known, up-and-coming artists, although there is a good selection of works by well-established artists from Java and Bali. The top floor consists mostly of traditional Balinese paintings, in the classical 'Kamasan' style, and the 'Ubud' and 'Batuan' styles.

South of Ubud: Singapadu, Mas and Batuan

Heading south from Ubud towards Denpasar and the southern resorts, the independent traveller has a choice of three main routes. The busiest, and so usually slowest, is the eastern road via Mas and Sukawati; the quietest is the middle route through Pengosekan; and the most scenic is the western road through Negari and Singapadu. Both the west and east roads have several places of interest. There are frequent public minibuses on the main road to Mas and Batuan, passing through Peliatan; for the western route, although there is direct transport to Singapadu, more frequently you must take a minibus to the junction at Kedewatan, on the northwestern side of Ubud, and then change onto any of the frequent southbound buses.

The western route

The main road west out of Ubud joins the Singapadu road at Kedewatan, where you should turn south through Sayan. After c 5km, you pass a junction beside a petrol station on the east side which leads back to Nyuh Kuning, on the south side of Ubud. (This is an alternative route out of Ubud, but necessitates passing through busy streets.) The pleasant **Café Firdaus** is beside the road c 1km further south, and c 2km beyond that is a cluster of temples in *banjar* **Silakarang**, with a couple of finely decorated kori agung.

In the **Pura Puseh Negari**, c 2km further south in **Negari**, are two more very ornate *kori agung*; another is to be seen at **Pura Desa Adat Kebon** in *banjar* Sengguan, on the corner at a road junction c 2.5km further on.

The **Bird Park and Reptile Grove** (Taman Burung dan Rimba Reptil; open daily 09.00–18.00), c 700m further south and signed to the west of the road, is an excellent place to bring children, though entry tickets are relatively expensive. The bird collection includes numerous macaws, cockatoos, parrots and lories; the magnificent Bali starling; cassowaries and hornbills; various birds of paradise from New Guinea; and an amazing singing and talking mynah. The reptile grove contains cobras, pythons (including the extremely rare Boelen's python, *Morelia boeleni*, from Irian Jaya, and an enormous 8m-long reticulated python), frogs, monitors, iguanas, Komodo dragons, and much else.

Just beyond the bird and reptile parks, the road joins the main Denpasar–Gianyar road on the north side of Batubulan.

The eastern route

Take Jl. Cok Putra Sudarsana east from Ubud town centre and turn south at the T-junction just beyond the telecoms office. The road runs through the centre of **Peliatan**, where there are dozens of shops selling small, colourful wooden mobiles, past the *Agung Rai Gallery*, which usually has a reasonable selection of paintings by Balinese artists on display and for sale, and past the intricately carved cluster of temples of **Pura Desa Gede Peliatan** and **Pura Puseh Peliatan** to the east of the road. Of note are the finely decorated *kori agung* of the *pura puseh*, the restored *bale agung*, and the *gedung penyimpanan*, an unusually tall brick depository containing the temple's precious relics.

In the centre of *banjar* Kalah, c 200m beyond, the road turns east towards Bedulu; after 350m, turn south once more on the road to Mas, passing Museum Rudana (see above) on the west side after c 650m.

Pura Taman Pule, c 1.5km further south on the east side in **Mas**, behind the playing field, is believed to be the site of the hermitage of the 16C Javanese sage, Danghyang Nirartha, from whom Bali's brahmana trace their ancestry; it is usually kept locked but is well worth visiting during its *odalan* (see box on p 118), when brahmins from all over Bali bring offerings. The intricately carved *kori agung* is guarded by a pair of elephants. In the square in front of the temple is a venerable *waringin* tree, round which are several small shrines; north of that is the very tall, straight-trunked *pule* tree.

Mas itself is an important woodcarving centre, and home to numerous galleries selling a vast array of carved wooden ornaments. South of Mas, the road comes to a major junction in *banjar* **Blahtanah**, marked by a hideous statue known as the *Brahma Lelare*.

A few metres south of the junction, a lane turns off west towards **Pura Hyang Tiba**, of interest to archaeologists because of an ancient chronogram found here. This lane divides after 160m: take the left fork and follow it 550m to the temple's east gate, where the pictorial chronogram can be seen, depicting 'moon, eye, bow-and-arrow, elephant', which dates it to 1336. The symbols are carved in two panels on the north side of the base of the southern elephant statue which guards the gateway. The lane continues to the rear courtyard, where there are some magnificent Ficus trees. A short stroll beyond the trees takes you down a flight of steps to open rice fields for a fine view, marred only by electricity pylons.

Continuing south, you reach **Batuan**, famous for the 'Batuan' style of painting—dark, busy canvases crowded with scores of people. One of the foremost exponents of this style is I Wayan Bendi (b. 1950), whose gallery, named after him, lies on the west side of the road and contains dozens of paintings in the style; artists to look out for include I Made Budi (b. 1932), I Wayan Taweng (b. 1925; father of I Wayan Bendi) and two of the earliest practitioners of the style—Ida Bagus Made Wija (1912–92) and Ida Bagus Made Togog (1913–89)—all from Batuan.

The *Dewata Bali* gallery, 100m further south in *banjar* **Dentiyis**, is another reputable outlet selling this style of paintings, run by descendants of two brothers, I Ngendon and I Patera, who are considered the founders of the 'Batuan' style.

At the intersection in the centre of Batuan, the road to the west leads after 200m to **Pura Puseh Batuan** and the adjacent **Pura Desa Batuan**, where performances of *gambuh* can be seen twice monthly (see p 123). These temples were largely restored in the late 1980s and early 1990s, having suffered severe damage in the earthquake of 1917. Of note are the large guardians facing west, flanking the road. The temples' *odalan* is held on the Saturday of Wariga week (see box on p 118).

South from the Batuan intersection, a lane leads after c 680m to the ruins of **Pura Gede Mecaling**, a long-abandoned temple of which there is now nothing to be seen save a couple of sculptures, including one of a long-tongued witch. It lies on the east side, just south of a tennis court. According to local myth, the site was the palace of Jero Gede Mecaling, an evil ogre who was eventually driven across the Badung Strait to Nusa Penida.

From the Batuan intersection, the main road heads east, then quickly turns south once more towards Sukawati, where there is a large craft market which seems to be on every tour itinerary. Of greater interest are the town's temples, especially **Pura Kawitan Dalem**, along a lane to the east, c 300m north of the market, past Pura Penataran Agung.

In Sukawati, a lane to the east behind the municipal market leads after c 4km to Pantai Saba and the ✫✫✫✫✫/✫✫✫✫ *Hotel Saba Bai* (☎ 0361 297070; fax 297171), a rather isolated but very pleasant hotel with elegant villas, beside the beach southeast of *desa* Saba.

Beyond Sukawati the main road turns west to **Celuk**, where dozens of goldsmiths and silversmiths line the road for c 2.5km. The manufacture of jewellery is now a huge cottage industry in the village, employing hundreds of local residents.

At Batubulan the main road turns south once more towards Denpasar.

Southeast of Ubud: Blahbatuh and Gianyar

At the junction in Blahtanah marked by the ugly *Brahma Lelare* statue, the main road to Gianyar, served by *bemo* from the Batubalan terminal in Denpasar, turns east off the Mas–Sukawati road. A short distance to the east along here, a lane to the south leads to Pura Canggi, notable for its **Gapura Canggi**, a gateway standing between the first and second courtyards of the *pura*. It is thought to date from the 14C or earlier, and was restored in the 1980s, with wooden doors placed in the opening. Prior to the 1917 earthquake, there were three such gateways; this was the only one to survive.

Back on the main road, at an intersection 850m further east, a lane to the south leads after c 1.5km to the **Tegenungan waterfall**, overlooked by the *Waterfall Restaurant*, which serves reasonable food and offers a view of the bungee jump (which, for bungee-jumpers, is the most scenic of the four in Bali).

To the north at the same main road intersection is ✩✩✩ *Sua Bali* (☎ 0361 941050; fax 941035), which has comfortable accommodation in a lovely garden. All guests at Sua Bali make a small donation to village funds, and in return may be invited to the community's meetings and festivals. Courses are offered in Indonesian language, cookery, Balinese craft-making and performing arts. Guests and villagers are actively encouraged to meet one another to discuss their different backgrounds, and an attempt has been made to ensure that the village benefits from the presence of the guest-house by employing local staff and using local craftsmen in the construction of the cottages; it's a worthy effort towards socially responsible tourism.

At the intersection in Blahbatuh, c 1.5km further east, the main road swings north. The lane to the east leads after 400m to **Pura Gaduh**, of note for the large stone head which lies in a shrine in the southeast corner of the east courtyard; it represents the giant, Kebo Iwo, who is said to have lived in the first half of the 14C. On the east side of the road in *banjar* **Kutri**, c 3km north of Blahbatuh, is **Pura Bukit Dharma**. At the right side of the rear courtyard, a long flight of moss-covered steps climbs through the roots of a giant banyan and assorted other trees to **Pura Durga Kutri** (Pura Kedarman), a simple pavilion containing a statue of Durga as the buffalo-demon slayer. The statue may be a portrait of Queen Gunapriyadharmapatni, consort of King Udayana in the early 11C.

Just north of Kutri, the main road turns east once more, past a livestock market (*pasar hewan*). A lane to the north, c 300m east of that corner, is unclearly signed to **Candi Tebing Tegallinggah**, an interesting complex of rock-cut *candi* and niches on the west bank of the Pekarisan river. Follow the lane a few metres, then turn left into another for 700m to a T-junction, where the *candi* is clearly signed to the right. A paved path leads down steps to the site beside the river, which here runs through a steep-sided, narrow gorge.

Near the south end of the site are two adjacent rock-cut *candi*, set back in a flat court, and flanked by six niches. In front of them are the collapsed remains of an old gateway to the court. A few metres further south is another gateway, still standing, with steps climbing up behind. South of that is the unfinished roof of what was presumably intended to have been a cloister. To the north of the two main rock-cut *candi* are several series of long rock-cut niches.

The site probably dates from the 11C; it was rediscovered in the 1950s and excavated by the government archaeological service. Take care as the ground can be extremely slippery, with some rocks coated in green slime; the drop into the ravine is precipitous and unguarded, but it's a delightful, somewhat mysterious place.

The main road continues east c 2km to **Gianyar**, the capital of Gianyar regency. It's a small, busy town, and an important weaving centre, though there are few sites of specific interest for the tourist. On the west side of the town along the main road are several weaving factories, including *Togog* on Jl. Astina Utara, and *Bakti* and *Cili* round the corner on Jl. Ciung Wenara; they produce good-quality *endek* (weft-ikat) cotton, silk and synthetic fabrics on semi-mechanised, fly-shuttle shaft-looms. Visitors are welcome to watch the various processes.

At the *bale banjar* in the town centre is a daily food market specialising in spit-roasted suckling pig (*babi guling*), for which Gianyar is justly famous. Directly opposite, on the south side of the street, is **Pura Dalem Teges**, notable for its amusing statues of men in European clothes and top hats, with dogs between their legs.

On the east side of the town centre is **Puri Agung Gianyar**, one of the best preserved of all Bali's royal palaces. Largely reconstructed after the 1917 earthquake, it is still occupied by the royal family and not open to the public, but some of the courtyards and pavilions can be glimpsed from the gates.

From Gianyar, the most direct route back to Ubud is via Bedulu and Peliatan.

Pura Dalem Teges statue

East of Ubud: Gua Gajah and Pejeng

Take Jl. Cok Putra Sudarsana east from Ubud and turn south through Peliatan, where the main road turns east. From the corner in Peliatan, continue east c 2km to **Gua Gajah**, the site of an extensive temple complex to the south of the road. Regular minibuses from central Ubud run along this route to Gua Gajah and continue east to the main junction in Pejeng.

Beyond the car park and scores of souvenir stalls, a path descends to a flat courtyard containing a few pavilions, bathing pools, a small *pura* and the cave itself, Gua Gajah ('elephant cave'). The pools at the centre were only rediscovered in the 1950s, despite the cave aleady being known to local villagers.

Above the cave mouth has been carved a monstrous face—most probably an image of Rangda, the witch—which may have been misinterpreted by early visitors, who thought it to be an elephant. A large piece of the face had fallen to the ground, making interpretation difficult; it was only replaced in the 1950s. Inside the cave entrance, a passage runs c 9m into the rock face, to a junction with a cross-passage which extends c 13m. The passage walls contain 15 niches; one at the east end of the cross-passage contains a set of three small stone *linga* on a pedestal.

The age and purpose of the cave remain unknown, though a late-11C date is generally suggested, and the cave may have been a Buddhist hermit sanctuary. Sculpted in the elaborate decoration surrounding the face of Rangda can be seen various animals and anthropomorphic figures.

The two **bathing pools** in the centre of the site, fed by seven fountains, were found buried under loose earth during excavations in 1954. When Nieuwenkamp visited the site in the mid-1920s, he found that the upper parts of seven figures with spouts had been placed in front of the cave mouth; during the excavations in the 1950s, the lower parts of the statues were found *in situ*, carved from the bedrock.

In a small pavilion to the left of the cave entrance are **three statues**: Ganesha in the centre; Hariti, the child-eating ogress who later became a Buddhist goddess of fertililty, on the right with several of her children; and an ogre on the left. Stutterheim dated the Hariti statue to c 1000.

A path to the south descends to a small bridge; just beyond, on the left beside the water, is a rock slab decorated with what appears to be the multi-tiered roof of a *stupa*, evidently once part of a much larger relief which has collapsed.

On the main road 300m east of Gua Gajah, a lane to the south leads to **Yeh Pulu**, where a series of reliefs have been carved in a 25m-long rock face. Stutterheim dated them to the 14C–15C, but other archaeologists have suggested the 10C–13C as more likely. Visited in the 1920s by Nieuwenkamp and by Van Erp, the archaeologist responsible for much of the renovation work at Borobudur, the reliefs have yet to be explained. From the road head, it's an easy 5-minute walk on a paved path through rice fields.

> ### The reliefs of Yeh Pulu
> The sequence of reliefs starts with what may be a representation of Krishna, with his right arm raised. Next comes a scene showing a man carrying a pole with two pots, following a woman towards a house; the door to the house is partially open, revealing a standing woman. A long diagonal groove is cut in the rock face above the scene, and above that can be seen a man hunting a wild boar, carved in a very simple style and probably more recent than the main reliefs. Beyond the house, a man stands with an axe or hoe slung across his shoulder, facing a kneeling woman in a cave, with three monkeys playing at her feet. To the right is a kneeling, anthropomorphic creature with a square hole in its belly, and an attendant standing by.
>
> In the floor here is the image of a man lying in the grip of an elephant's trunk, which is wrapped round his waist; the man's legs are missing.
>
> The next scene shows a man on horseback, another standing in an aggressive pose with a spear-like weapon, and a third armed with a sickle-like weapon, who is fighting a bear; a fourth man is attacking the bear from behind.
>
> Further to the right, two men carry off a couple of bears (or pigs?), hanging from a pole. Beyond them, a woman clings to a horse's tail, perhaps to speed up her pace or to slow the horse and rider. In front of the horse is a statue of Ganesha, seated in an alcove. Finally you reach a hermit's meditation niche and, opposite, a small bathing pool.

At the intersection in Bedulu, just beyond the turning to Yeh Pulu, the road to the north leads to **Pejeng** and, after c 500m, the **Museum Purbakala** (Gedung Arca; open daily 08.00–13.00) on the east side. (If travelling by *bemo*, get off at the main junction in Pejeng; the minibuses turn off south, and the sights described here all lie within a few hundred metres' walk to the north.) This small museum is notable for its collection of prehistoric stone sarcophagi, among some carved with turtle-like figures or with anthropomorphic heads. Many have been found in Bali, but few have been discovered undamaged. They are thought to have been used for the burial of important people; some have been found containing a flexed skeleton, while others were apparently used for the secondary burial of bones. A few have been found to contain funeral gifts, such as bracelets and beads, and bronze items.

A few metres north of the museum, in the rice fields on the west side of the road, is a small pavilion, known as **Pelinggih Arjuna Metapa**, which contains five statues. The main one is Arjuna, standing with a spout at his chest; flanking him are the two clowns, Twalen and Merdah, his assistants. Arjuna's face was stolen sometime in the late 1920s or 1930s. The other figures are a celestial nymph, now headless, but also with a water spout; and a damaged *kala* face.

Just to the north of the Arjuna statues, in **Pura Kebo Edan**, is a large stone statue c 4m high, known as the 'Pejeng giant'. Dated to the 13C–14C, it depicts a giant with snakes coiled round its legs, standing on a prostrate human figure. The giant is remarkable for its very large penis, usually wrapped modestly in a *poleng* cloth. In adjacent pavilions are several other statues and stone fragments.

A few metres further north is **Pura Pusering Jagat**, which also contains several pavilions housing curious stone antiquities; most are difficult to view properly. At the rear southeast corner a large cylindrical stone vessel can be seen. It is thought to have once held holy water; the exterior is intricately carved. A small pavilion in front of it contains the stone representations of a phallus and vulva. The former once had three balls just behind the glans; one has broken off.

The track running west from Pura Pusering Jagat leads to a small water pool, beyond which a path along the ridges of rice fields descends to the Kalebutan river, c 150m ahead. It crosses the river on a natural rock arch to the west bank, and at a well-defined fork the left branch leads to the water's edge. **Candi Tebing Kalebutan**, a rock-cut *candi* high on the wall of the east bank, is clearly visible from here, though out of reach; it is believed to date from the 14C. A few metres upstream, the river emerges from the high-roofed tunnel above which the path crossed the river; downstream is a flat grassy area surrounded by rock-cut niches. The *candi* was rediscovered in the mid-1920s, but quickly became overgrown and vanished once more. It was eventually found again in the 1950s, but by the early 1970s was again hidden. Today it is regularly cleared of encroaching vegetation.

In **Pura Penataran Sasih**, a few metres further north on the east side of the road, is the famous **'Pejeng Moon'**, a huge bronze kettledrum nearly 2m high. Today it is difficult to view properly, as it is situated high up in a pavilion in the temple courtyard. Nieuwenkamp visited it in 1908 and made very accurate drawings which show its mantle to be decorated with eight faces and geometric patterns; its origin is unknown, but the drum has been in this temple for several hundred years. Elsewhere in the temple are pavilions housing a number of stone antiquities.

Pejeng Moon

Just north of Pura Penataran Sasih, a lane to the right leads to *banjar* Panglan. To find the site of **Gua Garba**, follow this lane 1km to a T-junction; turn north (left) there, and after c 650m you will find a footpath to the east (right), descending through a small split gate to the west bank of the Pekarisan river. In the cliff are three rock-cut niches, known as Gua Garba, and believed to be hermits' meditation caves. South of the niches is the remains of an old gateway, behind which a flight of very steep, slippery steps climbs up the hillside.

At a road junction 300m further north, take the right fork c 2.5km to *banjar* Cemadik. Here, opposite the *bale banjar* on the west side, a track leads due east before turning north. After a few hundred metres, the path branches, with the right fork descending between two coconut palms to the west bank of the Pakerisan river. Looking north from the bank, you can see **Candi Tebing Kerobokan** in the cliff at the confluence of the Pakerisan and Kerobokan rivers. Standing 6m high, the rock-cut *candi* probably dates from the late-11C or 12C, and is flanked by two niches. To reach the *candi* itself, you must swim or wade across the Pakerisan; the view is good enough from the near bank, however. This charming spot is used by locals for bathing, so to avoid any embarrassment (mostly yours), ensure that your approach can be heard.

North of Ubud

The following suggested itinerary links up the main sites and a few minor ones in the area to the north of Ubud. It is intended for those returning to Ubud in the evening, not continuing further north to Kintamani or Gunung Batur, though this can be easily done. To follow this route in its entirety is impossible if you are relying on public transport; if you wish to see all the sites described, you are strongly advised to charter a vehicle. However, the major site of Gunung Kawi and those nearby in Tampaksiring are accessible from Ubud without difficulty— take a *bemo* to Bedulu, and change there for Tampaksiring.

Take Jl. Cok Putra Sudarsana east out of the centre of Ubud and turn north at the T-junction by the telecoms office. After c 3.5km, take a lane to the east (right) signed to *desa* Kenderan and follow it 1.6km to an intersection in the centre of *banjar* **Kepitu**, where the main road turns 90° to the east. At this point, a path to the west beside the *bale banjar* leads past Pura Telaga Waja to **Telaga Waja** itself, a sacred bathing pools complex in a beautiful setting. Just above the pools is a small terrace surrounded by several rock-cut meditation niches, partially collapsed and covered in moss. Casual visitors may not enter the pools area, but the view from the path is clear. From the northern pool, which is surrounded by three meditation niches, water is fed into the lower, larger pool; from there it emerges through spouts into the outer washing area.

From Kepitu, continue on the road past Kenderan, through a landscape of rice fields and coconut palms. After c 2km, in the centre of *banjar* Tangkas, you pass a beautiful *waringin* tree, and beyond that you reach **Pura Geria Sakti**, on the right side. A flight of steps leads up to the very picturesque *pura*, where the main shrine stands in front of a massive tangle of entwined trees. The *padmasana* at the northeast corner stands upon a moss-covered image of the cosmic turtle. This is one of the loveliest settings of any Balinese *pura*.

The royal 'tombs' of Gunung Kawi

The road north continues to Bayad, where you should turn east (right) for **Gunung Kawi** at Tampaksiring. After c 2km this road reaches an intersection; Tampaksiring lies to the south (right), c 500m, where the royal tombs are clearly signed to the east.

Flights of steps descend from the road, past numerous souvenir stalls to a cutting in the bedrock, and beyond that, an archway. To the left, just inside the arch, are four rock-cut *candi* in a row of east-facing alcoves, known as the **Queens'** or **concubines' tombs**, though in fact they are not tombs but more likely acted as temporary dwellings for the spirits of the deceased. To the north and south of the courtyard are large niches (the northern one has collapsed). From the Queens' tombs, a path leads east across the Pakerisan river to the five rock-cut *candi* known as the **royal tombs**, a bathing pool, a modern *pura* and a complex of ancient **rock-cut cloisters**.

Three of the *candi* at the royal tombs still bear inscriptions, visible above the fake stone-carved doors. However, only the northern one can be understood, and is thought to refer to Anak Wungshu (r. c 1050–77).

Southeast of the royal tombs is an extensive **complex of cloisters and niches** hewn from the bedrock, which provided meditation sites for hermits and presumably were occupied by the religious people who maintained the main *candi*. To the south of this group, c 80m away across rice terraces, is a series of cloisters with numerous roofed niches, similar to those found at Candi Tebing Tegallingah (see above); beyond these is a further courtyard surrounded by rock-cut niches.

The so-called **'tenth tomb'** is rarely visited, but is easy to reach. Return through the archway to the cutting on the entrance path, and just beyond this turn left across rice fields, along a path to an archway cut in the bedrock. Beyond it, worn steps descend to a modern concrete path which leads to many more niches and cloisters, and the 'tenth tomb'—another rock-cut *candi*. The path continues through another rock archway, from where it is a rough scramble to yet more cloisters.

The site of Gunung Kawi was well known to local villagers long before the Dutch

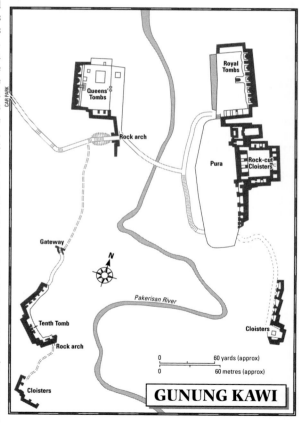

GUNUNG KAWI

Resident, H.T. Damsté, publicised the site in 1920. Soon after this, the inde-fatigable Nieuwenkamp discovered the 'tenth tomb', and in the 1940s Krijgsman started restoration work on some of the cloisters.

At the main road intersection 500m north of the Gunung Kawi site, turn east (right); after 150m, a track to the right leads to a car park for visitors to **Pura Mengening**, and a path behind descends to Prasada Mengening, past a small spring and bathing pool which are on the left just before the *pura*. The ruined *prasada* was revealed after excavations in the 1980s, and was reconstructed in the 1990s. It looks far more like small *candi* found in Central Java than any other structure in Bali. The rest of the *pura* is of little interest.

The bathing pools of **Tirtha Empul** lie c 500m further east along the main road, amid a mass of souvenir stalls and *warung*. In the centre of the complex, which probably dates from the 10C, is a large walled pool called **Taman Suci**, built round a natural spring. Water bubbles gently from beneath the pool, which is thick with ferns, slimy weed and fish. From here, the water flows through spouts on the south side into a smaller pool inhabited by large carp, and from there into a public bathing pool; this too is thick with slime, but that's of no concern to the young lads who splash contentedly. Above the pools to the west is a palace built by Sukarno in the 1950s.

Beyond Tirtha Empul, the road continues north to Penelokan (see p 161), on the rim of the Batur caldera.

Return west c 700m to the intersection, and continue straight over c 3km to another crossroads. Turn right here towards Sebatu, passing **Pura Gunung Kawi Sebatu** after c 250m. This is a charming water temple with a large carp pool and surrounded by lush gardens. To the front left are some public bathing pools; east of these is a sacred spring which visitors cannot enter. Behind the split gate, turn left to the main inner pool of crystal-clear water, stocked with carp.

The road east continues c 400m to **Sebatu**, a village of woodcarvers with several large workshops and a number of substantial temples. It is possible to follow the road north through the centre of Sebatu, then take the lane northwest from beside the **Pura Jaba Kuta**, notable for the massive fig tree which stands over it. After c 1km the lane joins the main Ubud–Batur caldera road. To the north (right) here, the road climbs through several woodcarving centres, including **Jasan**, and eventu-ally reaches the rim of the Batur caldera; the road is rough, however, and cannot be recommended. To the south, the road descends directly to Ubud.

Turn north here, and after c 50m take a lane to the west (left) to *desa* Taro. The lane descends steeply to the valley floor and climbs equally steeply up the other side, passing through bamboo groves, and arriving at the ancient village of **Taro** after c 5.5km.

A dirt track runs straight through the centre of the village (vehicles must detour to the left) to **Pura Agung Gunung Raung**, a temple with several fine pavilions and stone sculptures. It is notable for the fact that *kaja*, the direction of the Gods, which for almost all temples in this part of Bali is north towards the mountains, is in fact west towards Gunung Raung in East Java.

The foundation of Taro

Local myth contends that Taro was founded by Markandeya, the Javanese sage who, while meditating on Gunung Raung, was told by the gods to form a community at a certain forest in Bali (believed to be Alas Puakan, a sacred forest c 450m north of Taro). He and his disciples set to work, but many died from illness and attacks by wild beasts. Markandeya went back to Gunung Raung to seek the Gods' advice, then returned a second time, this time successfully, and founded the settlement of Taro.

Of note in the temple is a magnificent long pavilion with an atap roof, similar to those found in Bali Aga villages in east Bali (see p 152).

On the southeast side of the village, a lane runs east c 1km to the starting point for **elephant rides** through the surrounding countryside. On display here are several **albino cattle**, considered sacred, for which Taro is famous throughout Bali.

Return from Taro to the main Ubud–Batur road, and turn south through *banjar* Pujung Kaja, back towards Ubud. Along much of this road can be found seemingly endless woodcarving workshops, most of them churning out very similar items. *Yogi Biru*, in *banjar* **Pujung Kelod**, c 2km south, is a fine place to stop for refreshment, with excellent cakes. The friendly café also has a couple of charming ☆ rooms overlooking the rice fields (☎/fax 0361 901368); advance booking is advised, but a stay here is highly recommended.

Further south, the road runs alongside a magnificent valley of terraced rice fields, and after c 3km passes the *Kampung Café* in *banjar* **Ceking**—another beautifully situated café.

Tegallalang, c 2km beyond, is another important woodcarving centre, and the road through the *banjar* of Sapat and Gentong is lined with endless galleries.

A turning to the west, c 1.5km south of Gentong, leads to *banjar* **Petulu Gunung**, an important **roosting and nesting sanctuary** for several bird species, including c 6000 cattle egrets, a few little egrets, Javan pond herons, night herons, and a population of intermediate egrets. The village, c 1.5km from the main road, is best visited in the early evening (17.00–18.00), when the birds return to their roosts in the surrounding trees.

A remarkable story associates these birds with Indonesian politics: in November 1965, a week after the assassination of Indonesia's top generals in what was claimed to be a communist coup attempt in Jakarta (see p 66), the first birds began to arrive in the trees, just as the *banjar* was celebrating the rededication of a renovated temple. In subsequent weeks, as Java and Bali were thrown into paroxysms of violence following the coup attempt, thousands more birds arrived, and have roosted here ever since. Local villagers believe the birds to be the souls of those people slaughtered in Bali in those blood-soaked weeks.

Back on the main road, c 500m further south in *banjar* **Nagi**, the luxurious and elegantly furnished ☆☆☆☆☆ *Banyan Tree Kamandalu* (☎ 0361 975825/ 975835; fax 975851) lies to the east. Its more expensive rooms have private gardens or plunge pools and overlook the Petanu river. The junction with Jl. Cok Putra Sudarsana—the main street into Ubud—lies c 1.5km beyond.

As an alternative to backtracking from the heron sanctuary, follow the lane onward through Petulu Gunung, past rice fields to a T-junction. Turn south (left) here into **Junjungan**, passing the **Pura Desa** after 200m. The split gate here is flanked by two very tall, straight-trunked *pule* trees. At a junction by the *bale banjar* just beyond, Jl. Suweta turns off west (right) to arrive in the centre of Ubud beside the Puri Saren Agung; the direct road, Jl. Tirta Tawar, runs through Kutuh and past the ***Blue Moon*** art gallery before reaching the main street in Ubud.

West of Ubud

The route suggested here is not possible on public transport—although Sangeh can be reached by minibus from Denpasar—and is best achieved by chartering a car for the day.

The sacred **monkey forest** at **Sangeh** is best visited before 09.00 (or shortly before sunset), to avoid the tourist coaches; from Ubud, the most direct route winds along narrow lanes through Tohpati and Taman to Sangeh. The small forest, 500m north of the Sangeh junction, is a nature reserve (*cagar alam*) notable for its magnificent nutmeg trees, and home to scores of bold long-tailed macaques; hold on tight to your belongings. The temple in the heart of the forest, **Pura Bukit Sari**, is closed to visitors, except during its *odalan* (see box on p 119). However, clearly visible through the split gate is a fine *garuda* carved from bricks of stone; behind is a moss-covered *kori agung* leading into the main courtyard, which contains a fine nine-tiered *meru*.

The road north from the Sangeh nature reserve leads after 750m to ✩✩/✩ ***Taman Arum*** (☎ 0361 264601), where there are pleasant cottages in an attractive garden setting.

South from Sangeh, the road comes to Blahkiuh after c 3km, where there is a huge *waringin* tree growing beside the road. Opposite the tree, a lane to the west descends very steeply to the river, climbs the far bank, and turns north through Geria and Ambengan to Cau Belayu; here a turning to the west (left) leads to Sembung, on the main Mengwi–Bedugul road. Turn north here for the unusual temple of **Pura Yeh Gangga**, which lies to the west in Perean, c 5.5km to the north.

The *pura* contains a unique *meru* with a stone body, decorated with a fake door and a fine *kala* face. An inscribed stone found in the temple grounds bears a date equivalent to 1334. The site was substantially renovated in the 1950s. Today, the temple is usually closed to casual visitors, but it is possible to see the meru from the roadside.

South of Sembung, the road descends through *banjar* **Binong**, where the **Indonesia Jaya Crocodile and Reptile Park** (Taman Buaya dan Reptil; open daily 09.00–18.00) is situated, and on to **Mengwi**, the former capital of the old kingdom of Mengwi, which is now of interest chiefly for the fine state temple of **Pura Taman Ayun** on the east side of the village.

The temple dates from the mid-18C, but was considerably enlarged in the 1930s. The entire site is enclosed by a water-filled outer moat; at the southwest corner of the middle courtyard is a high kulkul tower which visitors are permitted to climb for a view over the compounds. Beyond, a flight of steps leads up to the *kori agung* which leads into the inner courtyard, which in turn is surrounded by an inner moat. Within this moat are numerous multi-tiered *meru*, some of them dedicated to the mountains of Bali—Agung, Batukaru and Batur.

Outside the outer moat at the southwest corner are a small museum and restaurant.

The direct road back to Ubud runs east from Pura Taman Ayun, via Penarungan, but a couple of minor sites can be seen southeast of Mengwi.

Pura Sadha, just south of the main Denpasar–Tabanan road in **Kapal**, is notable for its magnificent eleven-tiered brick *prasada*, and the several dozen miniature *padmasana* which lie to the south side. The temple probably dates from the late 17C or early 18C, but most of the present structures were rebuilt in the mid-20C, having been almost completely destroyed by the 1917 earthquake and subsequent general neglect by the local community. Only the split gate which separates the road from the first courtyard pre-dates the earthquake. Outside the temple is a huge *Ficus* tree.

One other site, only worth a visit during its *odalan*, when the adjoining cave is open, is **Pura Kreban Langit**, a small temple on the east bank of a tributary of the Badung river; the cavern contains several very unusual, moss-covered stone statues. To find it, follow the main Tabanan–Denpasar road south from Pura Sadha to Sempidi. At a corner where the main road turns sharply south, continue due east on a minor lane, which soon bends north. After c 1.5km, the *pura* is signed along a track to the west, beside the *bale banjar* of *banjar* Pekandelam.

From here, roads head northeast back to Ubud.

East Bali: Bangli, Klungkung and Karangasem

Highlights include the **Pura Kehen** (see p 143) in Bangli and the huge **Pura Besakih** (see p 144) complex on the slopes of Gunung Agung; the finely painted ceilings of **Taman Gili** (see p 147) in the centre of Semarapura; and the traditional village of **Tenganan Pegeringsingan** (see p 152). The island of **Nusa Lembongan** (see p 151) is popular with surfers; divers should head for **Tulamben** (see p 157), where a wreck just offshore is a haven for scores of fish species. The magnificent rice terraces round **Tirta Gangga** (see p 155) and **Sideman** (see p 159) offer some of the finest views in Bali.

Accommodation

There is a wealth of good lodgings in east Bali, including the coastal areas of Teluk Amuk, Candidasa, Bunutan and Tulamben. Inland, Tirta Gangga and Sideman both have excellent guesthouses.

Odalan dates for a selection of temples

Pura Kehen, Bangli: festival starts on Wednesday of Sinta (week 1): 13.12.00, 11.7.01, 6.2.02, 4.9.02, 2.4.03, 29.10.03, 26.5.04.
Pura Agung Kentel Gumi, near Gianyar: festival starts on Thursday of

Dunggulan (week 11): 3.8.00, 1.3.01, 27.9.01, 25.4.02, 21.11.02, 19.6.03, 15.1.04.
Pura Dasar Gelgel, Gelgel: festival starts on Monday of Kuningan (week 12): 7.8.00, 5.3.01, 1.10.01, 29.4.02, 25.11.02, 23.6.03, 19.1.04.
Pura Gua Lawah, near Padangbai: festival starts on Tuesday of Medangsia (week 14): 22.8.00, 20.3.01, 16.10.01, 14.5.02, 10.12.02, 8.7.03, 3.2.04.
Pura Lempuyang Luhur, near Tirta Gangga: festival starts on Thursday of Dunggulan (week 11): 3.8.00, 1.3.01, 27.9.01, 25.4.02, 21.11.02, 19.6.03, 15.1.04.
Pura Dalem Penataran Ped, Nusa Penida: festival starts on Wednesday of Kelawu (week 28): 29.11.00, 27.6.01, 23.1.02, 21.8.02, 19.3.03, 15.10.03, 12.5.04.

BANGLI AND VICINITY

Follow the main road east from Gianyar (see p 133), and after c 2.5km turn north onto the Bangli road. On the right side after 1km, you pass **Pura Dalem Sidan**, a temple with marvellous reliefs of demonic guardians.

   Bangli, c 9km further north, is a rather somnolent town with only basic accommodation. Pura Besakih (see below), Bali's most important temple, is within easy reach by private vehicle, but apart from that, it is easy enough to see Bangli's sights within a day and move on.

Practical information

Transport
Bemo from the **Terminal Loka Shrana** in the centre of Bangli run south to Gianyar and Denpasar, and north to Penelokan and Kintamani. For eastern destinations, you must usually take a bemo to the junction of the main Gianyar–Semarapura road and change there; at present there is no regular *bemo* service east to Rendang (for Candi Tebing Tembuku or Pura Besakih).

Accommodation and services
The best of the lodgings is the *Bangli Inn* (☆; ☎ 0366 91419) on the corner of Jl. Majapahit and Jl. Rambutan, with clean rooms and friendly staff. The **tourist office** (Dinas Pariwisata) is on Jl. Ngurah Rai; a 24-hour *wartel* is 150m further north. The **post office** lies c 200m west of the town's main intersection. *BNI* on Jl. Nusantara can change money. **Pasar Senggol** has a lively evening food market.

The most significant temple in Bangli is **Pura Kehen**, 1.5km north of the town's main intersection. The former state temple of the old Bangli kingdom, Pura Kehen dates back perhaps to the 9C, according to Sanskrit copper-plate inscriptions discovered locally, and was originally a shrine to Brahma. Three parallel stairways flanked by guardian statues climb from the road past five narrow terraces to the temple's gates. Of special note are the enormous *Ficus* tree at the back right of the first main courtyard, and the numerous multi-tiered *meru* to various deities in the innermost court. The temple's *odalan* is one the largest and most colourful in Bali, and well worth attending if your visit coincides (see box on p 142).

Candi Tebing Tembuku, a small rock-cut *candi* hidden deep in the countryside to the east of Bangli, is awkward to reach and mainly of interest to specialists; nevertheless, the scenery along the way is very pleasant—with a fine view of Gunung Agung to the north.

To reach the *candi*, take Jl. Erlangga c 3km east from Bangli to the intersection where Tambahan is signed to the south (right), and turn along here to *banjar* Tambahan Tengah, a further 2.5km; the footpath to the *candi* begins opposite the primary school (Sekolah Dasar Negeri). For a small tip, local children will guide you happily on the 15-minute walk. The *candi*, rediscovered in 1963, is cut into the soft cliff wall on the west side of the Cai river's thickly vegetated ravine.

From the Tambahan crossroads, the main Bangli–Rendang road winds east c 6km through a magnificently lush landscape to join the main Semarapura–Penelokan road.

Pura Besakih

Travelling north along the Semarapura – Penelokan road, the east turn to Pura Besakih is clearly signed in Menanga, c 2km north of Rendang; the temple complex is a further 5.5km.

Pura Besakih, 900m above sea level, is the most important and most extensive temple complex in Bali, attracting a steady stream of Balinese pilgrims, as well as coaches of foreign and Indonesian tourists. A visit to the complex can be a disappointment for visitors, however, as the temples are generally closed to non-Balinese and can only be viewed from the outside. Nevertheless, if you take a guide and are properly dressed, you may sometimes be permitted inside the temple compounds. Singlets or any scruffy clothes, even with a sarong and sash, may not be good enough; this is a place where Balinese disdain for tourists' uncouth ways is given full rein, though such a fuss is not usually made with the farthest-flung temples. If you are travelling independently by private transport, you may also be told to sign in at an office opposite the car park; this is a ploy to solicit a donation and, despite the huge sums written in the book, you are perfectly within your rights to politely refuse, especially if you have already just paid at the toll-booth down the road.

The temples

There are 22 temples at Besakih, most of them clustered tightly round **Pura Penataran Agung**, the largest and most important of them all. Looming over the site to the northeast is the frequently cloud-covered summit of **Gunung Agung** (3142m). It is uncertain when the first temples or shrines were built here, but the site is probably of proto-historic origin; local tradition claims the founder was a Hindu Javanese sage, Markandeya, who arrived in the late 8C.

Pura Penataran Agung honours Shiva and is the symbolic centre of the complex. This forms a trinity with **Pura Kiduling Kreteg** to the east, dedicated to Brahma, and **Pura Batu Madeg** to the northwest, associated with Vishnu. A secondary grouping of five temples is also significant; it includes the above three, with the addition of **Pura Gelap**, to the northeast behind Pura Penataran Agung, and **Pura Ulun Kulkul**, which lies on the west side of the approach avenue. This five-temple grouping represents the cardinal points and the centre, and it is at these five that the most important and elaborate rituals occur.

It is suggested that visitors limit their attentions to these temples, with perhaps a walk for the energetic to the isolated **Pura Pengubengan**, c 2km to the northeast and far from the crowds. Commerce has taken over the temples' approach—an avenue lined with souvenir stalls, vendors selling food and drink, and innumerable 'guides'.

Ceremonies
Besakih experiences scores of festivals, ceremonies and rituals each year; there is one or more every week. Some of the most important are listed below. In addition, there is a decennial festival, **Panca Wali Krama** (the next is in 2009), and the most significant of all, **Eka Dasa Rudra**, which takes place—at least in theory—at the turn of the Hindu century (last held in March 1979).

Pura Penataran Agung
Bhatara Turun Kabeh, the great annual festival for all the gods, involving all the public temples at Besakih, held on Purnama Kedasa (usually in April).
Bhatara Tiga Sakti, to honour the Hindu Trinity, identified by the magnificent triple-throne *padmasana* on the second terrace of Pura Penataran Agung; held on Purnama Kapat (usually in October).

Pura Batu Madeg
Aci Panaung Bayu; held on Purnama Kelima (usually in November)
Odalan Wuku; held on Monday of Tulu in the Pawukon cycle (19.6.00, 15.1.01, 13.8.01, 11.2.02).

Pura Kiduling Kreteg
Aci Penyeheb Brahma; held on Purnama Kenam (usually in December).

Pura Gelap
Aci Pengenteg Jagat; held on Purnama Karo (usually in August).
Odalan Wuku; held on Monday of Wariga in the Pawukon cycle (3.7.00, 29.1.01, 27.8.01, 25.3.02, 21.10.02, 19.5.03, 15.12.03, 12.7.04).

Pura Ulun Kulkul
Aci Petahuan; held on Tilem Kepitu (usually in January or February).
Aci Sarintaluh; held on Tilem Kewulu (usually in February or March).

Eka Dasa Rudra
Intended to pacify Evil, Eka Dasa Rudra is Bali's most elaborate religious ceremony. After the turmoil which had swept through Indonesia in the 1940s and 1950s – the Second World War, the subsequent anti-colonial war against the Dutch, and finally the guerrilla battles of the young republic, together with the heavy exploitation of timber, sulphur and rock from Gunung Agung, the sacred abode of the Hindu gods and ancestral deities – it was felt by some Balinese high priests that the ceremony was necessary to cleanse the island. Preparations began in late 1962, and the date of the main ceremony, the *taur*, was set for 8 March 1963. In February, though,

disaster struck: Gunung Agung erupted, initially with loud rumblings, later with huge clouds of ash, and finally with lava flows. Initially this was interpreted as a good omen, but as the activity increased, some priests began to argue that the date had been wrongly chosen – to suit political rather than religious considerations – and the gods were showing their displeasure.

The government in Jakarta considered it was too late to cancel the ceremony, and it duly went ahead, with President Sukarno in attendance, before a backdrop of ash clouds billowing from the volcano. Nine days later, Gunung Agung exploded in a tumult of lava flows and poisonous, superheated gas clouds, killing perhaps as many as 2000 people, leaving many thousands more homeless, and engulfing huge swathes of agricultural land in east Bali; many roads were destroyed and settlements were cut off.

When calm had returned to the mountain, it was decided that the ceremony should be held again, on a more auspicious date – 28 March 1979, which coincided with the last day of the Hindu Shaka year 1900.

It passed off smoothly, with more than 200,000 people and 24 high priests attending the main ceremony. Among the rituals required was the slaughter of as many species of creature as could be found on Bali; more than 80 were sacrificed, among them scorpions, centipedes, leopard cats, crocodiles, eagles, pigs, chickens, buffaloes, bats, turtles and rats. Ceremonies continued for a further 42 days, during which period the whole population of Bali was encouraged to come to Besakih.

Onward from Besakih

If heading north by car to Penelokan (see p 161), there is no need to return to the main Semarapura–Penelokan road at Menanga; instead, take the quiet lane west from Besakih, which follows a delightful roller-coaster route c 3.5km to join the main road further north. Eastbound travellers can return south to Rendang, and there turn east along the beautiful road through Muncan and Selat (see below).

The Gianyar–Semarapura road

East of the Bangli turn-off, the road crosses a large river bridge and swings south. A short way beyond, on the outside of another sharp bend to the south, is a cluster of temples, among them **Pura Agung Kentel Gumi**, with numerous multitiered merus and a fine *kori agung*. This is the site of a large and important odalan (see box on p 142).

At a junction c 3km further is the **Museum of Classical Balinese Painting** (Museum Seni Lukis Klasik Bali; open Tues–Sun 09.00–17.00), the private collection of locally-born artist, Nyoman Gunarsa (b. 1944), housed in a hideous three-storey concrete building. On the first floor are many classical-style paintings, mostly illustrating scenes from the *Ramayana* and *Mahabharata* epics. Some of the oldest paintings here are claimed to date from the 18C, but the collection includes modern works in the Kamasan style by well-known artist I Nyoman Mandra (b. 1946) and others; sculptures and magnificent antique wooden doorways are also displayed. On the top floor are paintings by Nyoman Gunarsa himself, many of them hung in his characteristic, hand-made, broad wooden decorated frames. The museum collection is huge, almost to the point of being overwhelming.

The turning to the west beside the museum leads after c 2.5km to **Tihingan**, a small village renowned for its manufacture of gamelan gongs; several signs along the main street indicate the location of workshops. Visitors are welcome, though there is not much to see. A great many of the gamelan instruments now used by musicians performing for tourist groups in Bali originate and are repaired here.

SEMARAPURA

The capital of Klungkung regency, Semarapura is a small, often congested town, with a few sights well worth stopping for, among them the remarkable paintings in the pavilions of Taman Gili.

Practical information

Transport

There are frequent **buses** and **bemo** to east and west along the main road; less frequent services operate north through Rendang to Pura Besakih or Penelokan. The **main terminal** is south of the town centre on Jl. Puputan.

Accommodation and services

☆ *Hotel Loji Ramayana* (☎ 0366 21044), on the east side of the town, has adequate rooms in the grounds of an old palace; it has a pleasant setting and friendly staff. The **post office** is west of Taman Gili on the main road. A **wartel** is on the southeast corner of the main junction, opposite Taman Gili. **Banks**, the main market, and shops selling 'antiques' can be found in the main street, Jl. Diponegoro, east of Taman Gili.

Beside the town's main intersection stands a **monument** commemorating the *puputan* of the royal court of Klungkung against the Dutch on 28 April 1908, launched in response to the Dutch government's attempt to suppress opium smuggling (not to abolish opium usage, but to control the highly lucrative trade). As at Denpasar nearly 18 months earlier (see p 104), the Dewa Agung of Klungkung, Bali's senior king, and his family's entire entourage, totalling more than 200 people, performed a ritualised suicide in front of the Dutch cannon.

Opposite the monument is **Taman Gili**, a small water garden which is virtually all that remains of the old Puri Semarapura, the royal palace built in 1710 which was destroyed by the Dutch assault. The remaining highlights are the magnificent **Kori Agung** – the decorated gateway on the east side, which somehow survived – and two pavilions with finely painted ceilings. The ceiling in the **Bale Kerta Gosa** (Hall of Justice), in the northeast corner of the compound, depicts scenes from the Bima Swarga, a Balinese adaptation of part of the Indian Mahabharata epic. In the narrative, the heroic Bima journeys into the underworld to rescue the lost souls of his parents (in the process battling demons) and then delivers them to heaven.

The detail of the paintings is hard to see, but the overall impression is delightful. Time has faded them, despite a partial restoration in the 1980s led by I Nyoman

Mandra, one of the foremost classical-style artists of his generation. Most of the panels seen today date from an earlier renovation in 1960, which in turn replaced versions from the 1930s and a reconstruction after the immensely destructive earthquake of 1917.

In the centre of the compound is the **Bale Kambang**, a rectangular pavilion surrounded by a lily-filled moat, which was the royal court's guardroom; the present building dates from the 1940s, though its smaller predecessor did survive the Dutch attack in 1908. The ceiling, supported by slender pillars, is decorated with painted panels depicting scenes from the tale of *Pan Brayut*, about a poor couple who were blessed with 18 children; and stories of *Sutasoma*, a wise and saintly ruler who dealt with his enemies through selfless acts of passive resistance.

On the west side of the palace compound is the **Museum Daerah Semara Jaya** (open daily), with a rather dull collection of historic artefacts. Of greatest interest are some old black-and-white photographs from the early 20C; Dutch readers can peruse copies of Dutch-language newspapers from the period of the puputan in April 1908.

Pura Taman Sari, the most interesting temple in Semarapura, lies northeast of the main intersection. Follow Jl. Gajah Mada north from the *puputan* monument and turn east after a short way along Jl. Gunung Semeru; the temple lies at the east end of this street.

In the far northeast corner is an eleven-tiered *meru* with grey stone walls, standing on a turtle and surrounded by a moat. Wrapped round it is a wonderful serpent, its head and tail meeting by the door. Flanking the moat are stone guardians; on the south side is a nine-tiered *meru*.

Outside the temple are a couple of warung serving snacks and drinks; it's a fine spot to relax awhile.

Kamasan and Gelgel

In the small village of **Kamasan**, c 2km south of Semarapura, are the studios of numerous artists who paint in the classical style found on the ceilings of the Kerta Gosa and Bale Kambang. To reach the village centre, follow Jl. Puputan south c 2km, and then turn east. Artists of repute include I Nyoman Mandra, I Nyoman Tresna, and I Nyoman Kondra; many more painters, and some ceramicists, are found along Jl. Kresna, which runs north-south along the west side of the village. Visitors to the studios are very welcome: the artists depend largely on passing tourists for the survival of their trade.

A few hundred metres south of Kamasan is **Gelgel**, which for 300 years prior to 1710 was home to the royal court of the Dalems, the royal dynasty which then moved to Klungkung. Today it is a quiet village, notable for its sizeable Muslim community and Bali's oldest mosque, and for two important temples—**Pura Penataran Jero Agung** and **Pura Dasar Gelgel**. Both are visually unremarkable, and are best visited during their *odalan*. Ceremonies at the latter are especially colourful; its *odalan* falls on the Monday of Kuningan week (see box on p 143).

East from Semarapura: the coast road

Travellers have a choice of two main routes to Amlapura. The most usual is the coast road via Gua Lawah and the popular resort of Candidasa; equally scenic, but with fewer specific sights, is the road inland through Sideman and Iseh. Visitors planning a circuit of the area are recommended to take the coast road eastbound and the inland road westbound.

At **Kusamba**, where the road comes to within a few hundred metres of the sea, you can find boats going to Nusa Penida (see below), though for foreign visitors the service from Padangbai (see below) is generally more convenient, as there is accommodation nearby to facilitate an early-morning start. Schedules from Kusamba are rather vague, but public boats usually leave in the morning (07.00–08.00) from near the fish market (*pasar ikan*), and again at about 13.00–14.00. At any time you can charter a tiny *jukung*—scores of which are usually drawn up on the coarse black sand beach—but the sea can be rough, and these small boats are easily swamped. A short walk west along the beach from the fish market brings you to a salt-producing area, which in the dry season provides a small income to supplement the local fishing trade.

To find the fish market, turn off the main road just east of the 'Denpasar 46.8km' marker. Arrive soon after 08.00 to watch the fleet arriving back with the night's catch.

The cave temple of **Gua Lawah**, 2.2km further east, is the roost for thousands of **cave fruit bats**, which cover every inch of the cavern ceiling; the row of meru in the entrance is thickly coated with pungent guano. The bats are mainly nectar- and pollen-feeders, emerging from the cave at dusk to feed on the mangroves fringing Benoa Bay; in turn, the bats are important pollinators of some of the mangrove species there. The temple's *odalan* falls on Tuesday of Medangsia week and is well attended (see box on p 142).

PADANGBAI

At a junction c 6km east of Gua Lawah a lane turns south to Padangbai, a small fishing village which serves as the port for vehicle ferries to **Lombok** and for small motor boats to **Nusa Penida**. It's a very relaxed place which only shows signs of urgency when a ferry arrives or departs. There is little reason to stay here except to catch a ferry, but there are a couple of pleasant white sand beaches nearby, and numerous *warung* on the waterfront serve freshly caught fish; accommodation is generally very simple.

Practical information

Transport
Jeep, motorcycle and **bicycle rentals** are available from shops and agents in Padangbai, though prices are generally higher than Kuta.
Public bemo run west to Denpasar and east to Amlapura.
Shuttle buses. Perama runs scheduled services to Kuta, Sanur, Candidasa, Ubud and Lovina, as well as to Senggigi and the Gilis in Lombok; tickets should be purchased a day in advance.

Boats to Nusa Penida and Nusa Lembongan
Public boats to Nusa Penida (45–60 minutes) depart in the morning when full, usually between 07.00–08.30. Go to the office early, sign on, and then wait until there are enough passengers for the

boat to depart. A private charter can be made at any time to either Nusa Penida or Nusa Lembongan.

Vehicle ferries to Lombok depart every two hours round the clock to Lembar (c 4 hours), though night-time services are sometimes cancelled. The *Kencana Express* is a more comfortable and faster passenger ferry.

Accommodation and services

The most upmarket hotel is the ☆☆/☆ *Hotel Puri Rai*, on the waterfront road east of the Nusa Penida boat office. The ☆ *Topi Inn* at the far east end of the same road has a nice balcony, but the rooms are very poky and the food can be awful; other simple hotels and *penginapan* can be found nearby. Set back from the beach is the ☆ *Pantai Ayu* (☎ 0363 41396), with clean rooms and friendly staff. There are numerous *warung* overlooking the harbour and on the lane which climbs out of the village on the west side. Several shops and agencies offer diving trips; there are *wartel*, money changers, and a postal agent in the village.

Apart from waiting for a ferry, there is little to do in Padangbai except visit the couple of charming **beaches** in easy walking distance from the port. The quietest is the very small white sand beach to the east. Follow the path to the left just beyond the *Topi Inn*, climb over the headland and descend on the far side. Drinks are available from a small *warung*, and snorkelling just off the beach can be quite productive: there is little coral, but plenty of fish.

West of the port is **Pantai Biastugal**, a larger, more popular beach, but with fewer fish. Follow the asphalt lane uphill to the west of the port and turn off left along a path just beyond the Warung Megibung.

NUSA PENIDA AND NUSA LEMBONGAN

For visitors, these two islands off Bali's southeast coast are of interest primarily for surfing and diving. The west shore of Lembongan is a popular surfers' haunt from May to October, while the channel between the two islands, and points round Nusa Penida's coastline, provide some excellent dive sites for experienced divers. Note that currents can be strong and that Nusa Penida is not recommended for novice divers.

Nusa Penida is a craggy limestone island, barren and dry, where farmers survive by growing cassava and a few fruits; the sea provides fish and income from seaweed farming. Nusa Lembongan, with just two small villages, receives more rainfall and is considerably greener. On the islands themselves, there is little for the casual visitor to do except explore the quiet byways.

Practical information

Transport
Boats to Nusa Penida

Daily services depart from Padangbai and Kusamba to Sampalan; the former is more efficiently organised.
Day-trip cruises. Several travel companies on Bali operate day trips to the islands for snorkelling, swimming and a buffet lunch:
Bali Hai Cruises (☎ 0361 720331): huge catamaran from Benoa harbour to Nusa Lembongan, mooring at a buoy off

Jungut Batu or taking clients to the Bali Hai Beach Club on Lembongan's southwest beach.

Lembongan Express (☎ 0811 393387): 20m-long motor launch with outriggers, from Sanur to Nusa Lembongan; cheapest of the day-trip options.

Quicksilver (☎ 0361 771997): a large catamaran from Beluga Marine at Tanjung Benoa to a mooring off Toyahpakeh on Nusa Penida.

Wakalouka (☎ 0361 723629/ 722077): 23m-long, twin-hulled sailing yacht, from Benoa harbour to Nusa Lembongan's Waka Nusa Resort.

Boats to Nusa Lembongan

The most regular service is the 1–2-hour crossing from Sanur; boats depart at about 08.00 from the ticket booth in front of the Ananda Hotel on Jl. Hang Tuah.

Accommodation and services

There is pleasant, simple accommodation on Nusa Lembongan, mostly at Jungut Batu on the northwest coast, close to the main surf breaks; on Nusa Penida, you are limited to basic *penginapan*.

NUSA PENIDA The simple but friendly ✯ *Losmen Made* in Sampalan is the only accommodation which can be recommended.

NUSA LEMBONGAN In Jungut Batu, ✯ *Bungalo Nusa Lembongan* has charming, colourful two-storey cottages which sleep three, and is run by very friendly staff. Alternatives nearby include ✯ *Bungalo Agung* and ✯ *Mainski*, a few metres further south. At the southwest end of the island, beyond *desa* Lembongan, is the rather dull ✯ *Bungalo Tanjung Sanghyang*; the *Bali Hai Beach Club* (for customers of Bali Hai Cruises only); and the very comfortable ✯✯✯✯/✯✯✯✯ *Waka Nusa Resort* (☎/fax 0361 722077/ 261130).

In Jungut Batu, the *Warung Ketut* behind Bungalo Nusa Lembongan is recommended for meals.

Exploring Nusa Lembongan

Jungut Batu's economy is based on tourism, fishing and seaweed farming; wherever you walk on the village fringe you find seaweed drying in the sun. There is little to see in the village, but you can take an easy walk round the island, heading first south to *desa* Lembongan and the pleasant beach on the southwest coast. Of note in Lembongan is an old wooden Ferris wheel, a block west from the market, and the strange underground house (*rumah tanah bawah*) – just a series of dank, claustrophobic passages, built, according to local myth, by one man with a spoon.

South of Lembongan, the main road descends to the coast; here it turns northeast to the bridge which crosses the shallow strait to **Nusa Ceningan**, the narrow island between Nusa Lembongan and Nusa Penida. Eventually the road leads back up the east coast of Nusa Lembongan, here fringed with mangrove, to Jungut Batu.

Exploring Nusa Penida

The easiest way to travel round the island is to charter a motorcycle with its owner in Sampalan, and spend a couple of days riding along the near-empty lanes, past small fishing hamlets. Sampalan itself is of little interest, but has the only decent accommodation and a *wartel*. **Gua Karangsari**, southeast of Sampalan, is a large cave inhabited by bats, an endemic crab species, and whip scorpions; locals will guide you through for a fee, to an opening at the far end, from which there are quite good views. Also worth a look are **Pura Batu Kuning**, on the east coast south of Suana; and **Pura Dalem Penataran Ped**, on the north coast at Ped. The latter is Nusa Penida's most important temple, dedicated to the demon, Jero Gede Mecaling, and though visually unimpressive, it is worth visiting on its *odalan*, when a great number of Balinese come over from the mainland (see box on p 143).

TELUK AMUK

Scattered along the coast of this broad bay to the east of Padangbai are several quiet beach-front hotels and the popular resort village of Candidasa. While much of the beach has been severely eroded by careless development, this can be a good base from which to explore the eastern tip of Bali.

Accommodation

The ☎ code is 0363.

☆☆☆☆☆ *Amankila* (☎ 41333; fax 41555) near Manggis, c 6km east of the Padangbai junction. One of Bali's three fabulous Aman resorts, with the usual impeccable service and style. Of special note is the magnificent swimming pool overlooking the ocean.

☆☆☆☆☆/☆☆☆☆ *The Serai* (☎ 41011; fax 41015; e-mail: serai-1@idola.net.id) c 1.5km further east. Slightly scruffy,

but generally good value with a large and lovely pool and garden; the rather small rooms are furnished with a simple elegance. Recommended.

☆☆☆ *Nirwana Cottages* (☎ 41136; fax 41543) c 2.5km further east. Pleasant cottages in a mature, leafy garden with a decent pool; good value.

☆☆☆/☆☆ *Hotel Rama* (☎ 41974) 300m further east. Good rooms, swimming pool and friendly service.

Tenganan Pegeringsingan

A lane to the north off the main road c 1km west of Candidasa climbs up to this unusual village, renowned as the source of wonderful **double-ikat fabric** known as *geringsing*.

History

The village is believed to be ancient, and the c 300 inhabitants, popularly known as Bali Aga, consider themselves to be among the original inhabitants of Bali—from the region of Bedulu in Gianyar, and before that from Java. In ceremonial processions, villagers carry pieces of old timber which they believe to be relics from a boat on which the original migrants were shipwrecked while crossing from Java.

A popular account of their origins tells how they were granted the comparatively large area of land they now own by the king of Bedulu, as a reward for finding his favourite horse. Though it was dead, the grateful king promised them land covering the area in which the decomposed horse flesh could be smelt. The village elder who accompanied the king's representative in measuring this area cannily carried a piece of rotting horse flesh in his pocket, thus greatly increasing the area of land awarded. The remnants of the horse are believed to be scattered round the village area as megaliths.

The question of the villagers' origin has been further researched by a geneticist, Breguet, who took blood samples from the majority of the villagers in the 1970s. He found that 18 of them possessed a special form of enzyme which is characteristic of Indians, but extremely rare elsewhere, indicating a possible migration from the subcontinent. Support for this comes from the very rare double-ikat cloth woven in the village; such fabric is also made in Orissa and Andhra Pradesh. Furthermore, for the Bali Aga of Tenganan, the most important deity is Indra, who they believe created the first people of Tenganan; this again suggests the possibility that they may be Vedic immigrants from ancient India.

The intricate *geringsing* fabrics play an extremely important part in rituals throughout Bali and are both very difficult and time-consuming to make; it can take six years just to make one particularly valuable shade of red dye. The indigo dyeing, on the other hand, is considered straightforward enough to be left to the villagers of Bugbug nearby.

The most sacred cloths are woven on a continuous-warp loom, which produces a tube of fabric that may be offered as clothing to deities and ancestral spirits. These cloths are believed to hold magical properties which protect the holder from illness; they can also be used to destroy an enemy or rival.

In some nearby villages—Bugbug, Timbrah, Asak and Bungaya—whose inhabitants are also considered to be Bali Aga, the sacred cloths are entwined round thrones on which statues of deities are carried to be ritually cleansed in the sea. Once the tubular cloth has been cut, it is considered fit only for humans.

Clothes made from the fabric are worn by the villagers at all public and private rituals, and the cloth is used by Balinese in tooth-filing ceremonies, at weddings and cremations, and in the ritual cutting of the first hair of children. Those cloths that have become impure through use in a cremation ceremony, or have been bleached in the sun or otherwise damaged, are sold to tourists visiting the village.

Tenganan is exceptionally neat and tidy, laid out along three parallel cobbled streets; it is also very wealthy, largely as a result of tourism, but also because Tenganan is fortunate in owning the largest traditionally-managed forest in Bali—covering more than 370ha—which provides a large proportion of the village's building needs. The main avenue, on the west side, leads up to the fine community hall, the *wantilan*. Visitors are welcome to look around the village for a small entry fee, but must be gone by dusk; the people are friendly but reserved, and despite the continual throngs of tourists, this remains a remarkably pleasant place to visit.

To the east is *banjar* Pande, where the overflow of inhabitants dwell, together with those who no longer abide by the constant rituals in Tenganan itself.

CANDIDASA

The resort of Candidasa has spread westward over the years as new hotels have been developed, and now reaches as far as the junction to Tenganan Pegeringsingan. The beach here is now almost non-existent, despite the construction of hideous concrete groynes, built in a futile attempt to slow erosion. Nevertheless, there are some very pleasant lodgings here, and all the services required of a small tourist resort. Candidasa remains a laid-back village which rarely seems very busy, despite the traffic rushing through all day long.

Across the road from the lily-filled lagoon is **Pura Candi Dasa**, cut into the cliff face and dedicated to Shiva and Hariti; it is said to date from the 12C. On the narrow neck of land between lagoon and sea is an ashram, which welcomes visitors of all religious denominations seeking a quiet, contemplative sojourn; excellent vegetarian food is served.

Practical information

Transport
There are frequent **bemo** passing through in both directions. *Perama* can arrange **shuttle buses** to other key tourist destinations in Bali; the office is on the west side of the village, a few metres east of the Lotus Seaview restaurant. **Car, motorcycle** and **bicycle rentals** can be arranged at travel agents on the main road.

Accommodation
With a choice of nearly 50 lodgings, Candidasa is rarely full, even at Christmas and New Year; almost every hotel will agree to a discount of anything up to 40 per cent, depending on your length of stay and negotiating skills. East of the village, where the main road swings north, quiet lanes lead to several more beachfront lodgings; most are disappointing, and rather far from the village centre without your own transport. The ☎ code is 0363.
☆☆☆☆ *Hotel Taman Air* (☎ 41540; fax 41164). Pleasant, if unexciting, bungalows surrounded by very beautiful water

gardens, with attractive wooden verandahs and a tiny swimming pool; very peaceful and private. Recommended.
☆☆☆ *Kubu Bali* (☎ 41532; fax 41531). A very lovely setting in an amphitheatre-like hollow in the hillside; the fine views from the top compensate for the many steps up to the higher rooms; two pools, including one near the top. Highly recommended. Food at the roadside restaurant is unreliable, however.
☆☆/☆ *Penginapan Kelapa Mas* (☎/fax 41947). Very reasonable bungalows with open-air bathrooms in a lush garden; good value for low budgets.
☆ *Sindhu Brata* (☎ 41825) beside the lagoon. Clean and pleasant rooms in a large grassy compound behind the beach. Recommended.

Services
The postal agents, banks and money changers can all be found in the village centre, together with numerous warung and restaurants; travel agents can arrange diving tours.

East of Candidasa

The road winds past Bukit Gumang before descending to a broad flood plain and, after c 5km, the village of **Bugbug**, a Bali Aga village to the north of the road. A few hundred metres beyond, a lane to the northwest climbs through several more Bali Aga villages—**Timbrah**, **Asak** and **Bungaya**. All are far less traditional than Tenganan Pegeringsingan, but retain certain rituals which identify them as Bali Aga. In the first two you can see striking *bale banjar* beside the road; at the unusual walled village of Bungaya, stop for a look round the market square on the northwest side before turning east towards Amlapura along a gently descending lane; at a T-junction after 1.7km turn right, and continue a further 1.3km to rejoin the main coast road in Subagan.

AMLAPURA

A rather dull and quiet town, Amlapura has little of interest for the casual visitor. The **Puri Agung**, one of three palaces close together on Jl. Sultan Agung—the only one open to the public—is of slight interest.

Practical information

Transport
There are regular ***bemo*** and **buses** west from Amlapura to Semarapura, Gianyar and Denpasar, and far less frequent services to Tirta Gangga and Culik. To explore this area thoroughly, you need your own vehicle.

Services
There is no reason to stay in Amlapura when there is such a good choice at **Tirta Gangga** to the northwest, or Candidasa on the coast to the southwest. Amlapura does, however, have banks, a post office, *wartel*, market, petrol and several simple *warung*.

Taman Ujung and the coast road

The road through Ujung, c 3km southeast of the market in Amlapura, passes the old water gardens of Taman Ujung, largely destroyed by the 1963 eruption of Gunung Agung, but now undergoing redevelopment. The garden was created c 1919 for the raja of Karangasem, but little of the original now remains, except the whitewashed pillars of a large pavilion.

Beyond the gardens, the road winds through very dry but extremely picturesque scenery round the eastern tip of Bali, skirting the summits of **Gunung Seraya**. Rough and potholed in places, it makes for a slow journey, best by motorcycle. Across stone-terraced fields, planted with cassava, maize, sweet potato and dry rice, you get wonderful ocean views; the farmers here, constantly fighting against drought, try to insure against total crop failure by growing two starch crops simultaneously.

The coast road eventually reaches Bunutan and the growing number of lodgings found along this stretch of coast (see below).

TIRTA GANGGA

The main road to Bali's north coast climbs gently northwards from Amlapura, passing after c 4.6km a turning signed to the ☆☆ *Cabe Bali Inn* (☎/fax 0363 22045), an overpriced, rather unimaginative group of bungalows. The final stretch of road before Tirta Gangga climbs through beautiful rice terraces, best viewed from the top. Tirta Gangga in fact consists of little more than the delightful

Tirta Gangga water gardens (Taman Tirta Gangga; small entry fee), on the west side of the road above a huge array of rice terraces. The pools are open to the public for swimming.

Practical information

Accommodation

Close to the water gardens are several simple lodgings, many of them offering fine views. The ☎ code is 0363.

☆☆ *Tirta Ayu Homestay* (☎ 21697) located within the water gardens complex; overpriced.

☆☆ *Puri Sawah* (☎ 21847) 80m beyond the water gardens; only two rooms, both very pleasant, though better views upstairs; a beautifully situated restaurant. Recommended.

☆ *Kusumajaya Inn* (☎ 21250) 150m beyond the water gardens, high on the hillside up a long flight of steps; the staff used to be more pleasant and the rooms better maintained.

☆ *Prima Bamboos Homestay* (☎ 21316; fax 21044) c 750m beyond the water gardens; clean, simple airy rooms with excellent views from the verandahs. Recommended.

☆ *Geria Semallung Homestay* (fax 21044) in *banjar* Tanah Lengis, *desa* Ababi, c 2km beyond the water gardens; simple, spacious and light bungalows; magnificent views in a very peaceful location; vegetarian food. Highly recommended.

Sights near Tirta Gangga

High on the slopes of Gunung Agung to the northwest of Tirta Gangga is the **war memorial of Tanah Aron**, from which there is one of the finest panoramic views in Bali, encompassing the coast from Lombok to Nusa Penida and Nusa Lembongan, with Gunung Agung looming large to the north.

The simplest route to the monument is to turn south from Tirta Gangga as far as *banjar* Padangkerta where, at a sharp left-hand bend, a side road goes off to the right. Follow this northwest 2km and then turn left towards the centre of Budakeling. After 100m, a lane to the right marks the start of a 7.5km climb up the mountain slopes to the memorial.

The monument was erected to commemorate those who fought for independence against the Dutch, and is decorated with eight reliefs depicting scenes from the struggle; atop the memorial is a statue of an Indonesian soldier clutching the national flag and a revolver.

One of Bali's most important temples, **Pura Lempuyang Luhur**, also lies close to Tirta Gangga. Take the Culik road 5.6km beyond the water gardens and turn off right along a potholed lane. After c 5km is the car park, where there are numerous *warung* selling snacks and drinks. From here, a very long series of steps climbs to the hilltop temple. It is visually unremarkable, though the views are excellent, and is best visited during its *odalan*, held on the Thursday of Dunggulan (see box on p 143). The main shrine is dedicated to Ratu Gede Meduwe Gumi, the great lord who owns the realm.

Beyond the car park, the asphalt road continues c 3km to the road head at a television relay station, from where there are excellent views on a clear day; in the mist it is extremely eerie, with steep, fluted ridges appearing unexpectedly from the gloom.

CULIK AND TULAMBEN

The road north from Tirta Gangga to Culik is one of the most scenic stretches in Bali, offering supremely beautiful vistas of rice terraces dotted with coconut palms and small thatched, bamboo *bale*. In Culik, c 6km beyond the Pura Lempuyang Luhur turn-off, a road turns off right to Amed (see below) and the coastal road round the Gunung Seraya massif.

Beyond Culik the main road descends to the coast, crossing after 6km an old lava flow from the 1963 eruption—now just a broad river bed filled with huge boulders; on a clear day there are fine views of Gunung Agung. After a further c 2km, you reach the first of a string of hotels and bungalows centred round the village of **Tulamben**, very popular among divers who come to visit the wreck of an American army cargo ship which lies just 30m offshore, 3m below the surface.

The wreck of the *Liberty*

The *Liberty* was torpedoed in the Lombok Strait by a Japanese submarine on 11 January 1942 while en route from Australia to the Philippines. Two destroyers lashed the ship between them in an attempt to reach Singaraja's port, but after taking on too much water it was beached at Tulamben. Quickly stripped of its cargo and anything that could be removed, its rusting hulk remained on the beach till Gunung Agung erupted in March 1963; the earthquakes which accompanied the eruption pushed the ship off the beach, at the same time splitting the hull into sections.

Today it is easy to reach: you can just paddle out from the shore, and even snorkellers can have a great time. Its lowest part lies c 30m down, and the hull has become a haven for hundreds of species of very tame fish. It's best to visit in the early morning or late afternoon, before and after the day trippers. Dives, equipment hire and courses can be arranged through the nearby Mimpi Resort or Indonesian Cactus Divers at the Emerald Tulamben Beach Hotel.

Practical information

Accommodation

Lodgings here cater primarily to European diving groups; there is little beach to speak of. The ☎ code is 0363.
☆☆☆☆☆/☆☆☆☆ *Emerald Tulamben Beach Hotel* (☎ 22490). The largest hotel in the area; pleasant rooms, though the size of the hotel makes it rather impersonal.
☆☆☆☆☆/☆☆☆☆ *Mimpi Tulamben Resort* (☎/fax 21642; fax 21939). The cheapest rooms are cramped, dark and overpriced; the more expensive rooms are delightful—the best in the Tulamben area.

☆ *Bali Sorga Bungalo*. Nothing special, but reasonable rooms and a pleasant restaurant close to the beach.
☆ *Bali Koral Bungalows*. Small white bungalows with thatched roofs; rather cramped, but adequate.
☆ *Ganda Mayu Bungalows*. Somewhat run-down, but probably the cheapest accommodation in Tulamben.
☆ *Puri Madha Beach Bungalows*. Plain, clean rooms with bathroom, fan and tiled floors; unexciting but practical. The *Liberty* wreck lies directly offshore.

The coast road continues northwest from Tulamben through rather dull scenery, though traffic is light and progress can be quick. There is little to see before Tejakula (see p 165).

AMED AND BUNUTAN

In Culik, c 10km south of Tulamben, the side road leads to **Amed** and **Bunutan**, where there are several pleasant, though very isolated hotels. There is little to do in this area except laze and relax, and even as a base from which to make day trips it is rather inconvenient as much of the road surface remains very poor and there is little public transport; without your own vehicle you are largely dependent on overpriced *ojek*.

Practical information

Accommodation
Pasih Luwung Resort I and II
(✮✮✮✮/✮✮✮; ☎ 0361 431273; fax 0363 21044). Two adjacent, almost identical bungalow groups under the same ownership; tasteful white brick bungalows with thatched roofs and air-con; beautiful gardens and decent pool.
Aiona (✮✮). A funky place with two extremely basic rooms; rather charming but overpriced.
✮✮/✮ *Good Karma*. Simple, pleasant rooms with the best situation of all Bunutan's accommodation on a decent beach; but rather overpriced, and let down by very indifferent service.
✮ *Pondok Vienna Beach*. Pleasant, basic cottages beside a good stretch of beach.

SIDEMAN AND VICINITY

The inland route west from Amlapura or Tirta Gangga to Rendang is highly recommended for those with their own transport, especially those who have already travelled the main coastal road. The easiest route from Amlapura is to take the main road north towards Tirta Gangga, turning off at Subagan onto the Bebandem road. This climbs steadily through *banjar* **Abian Soan**, where very simple, rustic rooms are available at ✮ *Homestay Lila*, on the east side of the road c 2.5km before Bebandem.

In *banjar* **Pande Sari**, a few metres northeast of the centre of Bebandem on the Budakeling road, you can hear the hammering of blacksmiths; visitors are welcome to enter the workshops. Silversmiths also work in the village, producing delicate jewellery.

Heading west from Bebandem, a turn to the north after 2.4km marks the route to the water garden of **Telaga Tista**, 1.7km further. The artificial lake contains an island with several shrines, linked to the shore by a causeway; the situation is charming, with a fine view to the south over rice fields. It dates from the beginning of the 20C, another of the gardens built by the raja of Karangasem.

Beyond the water gardens, the main road winds westward c 8.5km through *salak* orchards to a junction in *banjar* **Wates Tengah** where ✮✮ *Pondok Bukit Putung* (☎ 0366 23039) is signed to the left, a further 900m. This hotel has drab, overpriced rooms, but the restaurant terrace has a marvellous view over the south coast, so a stop for a drink or snack is recommended. Nusa Penida, Teluk Amuk, and part of Lombok are clearly visible.

Near Duda, c 3km further west, a road to the south (left) turns off towards Iseh, **Sideman**, and eventually Semarapura. The first half of this is a magnificent drive, descending beside rice terraces and past a boulder-strewn river course, through countryside dotted with coconut palms and bananas. There is also some wonderful accommodation along here, if you can think of a reason for staying overnight.

Practical information

Accommodation in Sideman

The ☎ code is 0366.

✩✩✩✩/✩✩✩ *Patal Homestay* (☎ 23005; fax 23007) 2km north of Sideman. Four rooms scattered across a hillside; the highest room has a magnificent view of Gunung Agung and is huge and airy; highly recommended.

✩✩✩✩/✩✩✩ *Subak Tabola Inn* (☎/fax 23015). Signed to the west in the centre of Sideman, it lies 2.3km from the main

road along a scenic track through rice fields. A magnificent garden setting with a pool. Rooms of very variable size, with broad verandahs; the smallest are poor value. Extremely isolated.

✩✩✩/✩✩ *Sideman Homestay* (☎ 23009; fax 23015) 250m further south on the main road in Sideman, under same ownership as the Subak Tabola Inn; four rooms reached up a flight of steps from the road. Very pleasant staff.

In the centre of Sideman are two weaving outlets producing beautiful *endek* fabrics: Bali Busana Ayu, 50m south of the turning to the Subak Tabola Inn, and Pelangi, a further 50m south.

The scenery from Sideman to Semarapura is not so exciting; travellers are advised to return north to Duda, and continue west along the Rendang road.

From the junction at Duda, continue west 1.5km to a turning to the north in *desa* Selat which leads to **Pura Pasar Agung**, an important temple high on the southern slopes of Gunung Agung. The lane climbs steeply uphill for 9.5km through Sebudi and Sogra. Both settlements were wiped out in the 1963 eruption, but have subsequently been re-established. A writer who witnessed the eruption described a search party finding a Pompeii-like scene at Sogra, with bodies perfectly preserved under a thin coating of volcanic ash, evidently overcome in an instant by poisonous gas. The higher you climb, the more desolate becomes the scenery, with old lava flows still clearly visible beneath a thin dressing of grass.

The temple also was destroyed in the eruption, but was rebuilt in time for the Eka Dasa Rudra festival in 1979. Nearly 300 steps climb up to the temple gates from the parking lot. In the innermost court are several multi-tiered *meru*, *padmasana*, and a *padma tiga* in the far northeast corner; the views to the south are tremendous.

Continuing west, the main road passes through amazing amphitheatres of rice terraces, with fine views of Gunung Agung to the north. West of Muncan the route skirts a beautiful river gorge, which it then crosses to double back along the far bank, before turning west once more to Rendang and the main Semarapura–Penelokan road. Turn south for Semarapura and Denpasar; or north for Pura Besakih and Penelokan.

North Bali: Batur, Bratan and the coast

Highlights of the region include the magnificent **Batur caldera** and **volcano** (see p 163), and the beautiful lakes of **Bratan**, **Buyan** and **Tamblingan** (see p 167) to the west. On the north coast are some of Bali's most interesting temples, decorated with amusing reliefs.

Practical information

Transport

There are frequent public *bemo* along the north coast road, passing through Singaraja and Lovina. To the east, beyond Tejakula, transport becomes less frequent. Inland, regular services run along the road from Kubutambahan to Kintamani and Penelokan, although you will usually need to charter a vehicle to explore the caldera of Gunung Batur. Trying to do this in Penelokan can be an unpleasant business, because of persistent pressure from rude and aggressive touts. If at all possible, charter your vehicle for the day elsewhere, and pass through Penelokan as quickly as you can.

Regular transport is also available on the main road between Singaraja and Lake Bratan. Visitors bound for Munduk may face a wait, but there are services from the Pancasari transport terminal near Lake Buyan.

Accommodation

Accommodation is available at Penelokan and Kintamani along the rim of the Batur caldera, and on the caldera floor at Toya Bungkah and Kedisan. Along the coast, by far the largest choice is found at Lovina, but rooms can also be found to the east at Air Sanih, and in Singaraja itself. Round the western lakes, there are several hotels and losmen at Bedugul and Pancasari; those who want complete peace and quiet should try Munduk or Gesing.

Odalan dates for a selection of temples

Pura Ulun Danu Batur, Kintamani: festival on Purnama Kedasa (full moon of the tenth lunar month; March/April).

Pura Ulun Danu Batur, Songan: festival on Purnama Kapat (full moon of the fourth lunar month; September/October).

Pura Ulun Danu Bratan, Danau Bratan: festival starts on Tuesday of Julungwangi (week 9): 18.7.00, 13.2.01, 11.9.01, 9.4.02, 5.11.02, 3.6.03, 30.12.03, 27.7.04.

THE BATUR CALDERA
. . . .

Coming from the south, you have a choice of five main routes, all running roughly parallel along separate ridges. The westernmost road, which can be ollowed from Kedewatan, just west of Ubud, provides some of the finest scenery and is the most straightforward approach from the Ubud area, emerging on the caldera rim a short distance east of Kintamani.

Immediately east of this is the Jasan road, which is very rough and potholed in sections, and cannot be recommended. Further to the east is the road from Tampaksiring, which is smooth but scenically uninspiring, as too is the main road from Bangli. The easternmost approach through Rendang, which bypasses Pura Besakih, is very beautiful in its upper section.

There are two possible approaches from the north coast: the main road from Kubutambahan, or the steep winding lane which climbs from the coast road just west of Tejakula. Both are fine routes, but the latter is quieter.

The caldera rim

Frequently chilly and wet or shrouded in mist, the caldera rim can be a miserable place. However, when the sun shines and the skies are clear, it offers the finest view in Bali – across to Lake Batur and the sheer face of Gunung Abang to the east, with the cratered slopes of Gunung Batur in front.

Penelokan, the junction town from where a steep lane descends to the caldera floor, is notorious for its aggressive – and sometimes abusive – hawkers, and is not a place to linger. It does have several large, overpriced restaurants serving generally dull food and catering primarily to coachloads of tourists, but the independent traveller seeking sustenance with a view is advised to head for the smaller cafés further west along the rim, where there is less hustling.

Gunung Abang (2153m), the highest point on the caldera rim, is an easy target for keen hikers, though views along the way are limited by thick vegetation. Immediately south of Penelokan, turn east onto the Suter road, which follows the caldera edge through pine forest for c 4km before turning south at a sharp bend. At this corner, a track continues east along the rim, leading past several small temples, and steadily deteriorating into a narrow footpath before reaching the summit. Take plenty of water and snacks, and allow 1.5 – 3 hours for the walk to the top, with half that for the return; it is not recommended in the rainy season, as the path becomes very slippery.

West of Penelokan, the road passes numerous *warung* and cafés with fine views across the caldera. After 1.7km, the road to Jasan descends to the south; 2.7km further the Kedewatan road turns off south.

Pura Ulun Danu Batur, the area's most important temple, lies c 600m further northwest along the caldera rim. As with so many temples in Bali, the complex is visually unimpressive despite its size, only really coming alive during festivals, when it attracts large crowds; the *odalan* lasts eleven days (see box on p 160).

The temple was originally located in the village of Batur on the caldera floor, below its present position on the rim. Both village and temple were largely destroyed by Gunung Batur's eruption in 1926, and were subsequently relocated to the rim during the late 1920s and early 1930s. Of the dozens of shrines in the temple compound, the most important is the eleven-tiered *meru* dedicated to the goddess of the caldera lake waters, Dewi Ulun Danu. She is linked in this shrine to the god of Gunung Agung. The nine-tiered *meru* to the left is for Ratu Gede

Meduwe Gumi, the great lord of the realm, who is associated with Pura Lempuyang Luhur, near Tirta Gangga in east Bali. The nine-tiered *meru* to the right is dedicated to Bhatara Gede Gunung Agung, the supreme deity of Gunung Agung and Pura Besakih.

There is basic accommodation in Kintamani, the best of which is the very simple ✿ **Losmen Miranda**. From here you can arrange a guide for the walk down into the caldera and ascent of Gunung Batur.

On the northwest side of the caldera rim is **Gunung Penulisan** (1745m), on the summit of which stands **Pura Tegeh Koripan** (Pura Puncak Penulisan), an ancient temple complex built on a series of ascending terraces in very tranquil surroundings. It's a simple walk up a long flight of steps from the main road. The topmost temple, **Pura Panarajon**, contains several dated stone statues, probably portrait statues, from the 11C–14C.

The caldera floor

The steep lane down from Penelokan descends in a series of hairpin bends to a T-junction on the crater floor after c 3.5km. To the right, the road passes through the small settlements of **Kedisan** and, 4km further, **Buahan**, both of which have simple *losmen* and *penginapan*. At the road head beyond in Abang are several *warung*; from here a footpath continues along the lake shore to Trunyan.

Trunyan

This is a culturally curious village, inhabited by Bali Aga people, which is famous in Bali for the disposal of its dead by decomposition in the open air, rather than burial or cremation. In the village temple is a 4m-high stone statue known as Bhatara Da Tonta (or Dewa Ratu Gede Pancering Jagat; 'the god who is the centre of the world'), which may be the image referred to in 10C copperplate inscriptions about Trunyan.

A visit to Trunyan is not advised, however: you will not be able to view the statue, and the attitude of the villagers to tourists – perhaps not surprisingly, since most visitors simply wish to gawp at the decaying bones of the villagers' dead relatives – is not especially friendly; extortion and persistent hassling for money are frequent.

Toya Bungkah

The left turn at the T-junction on the crater floor leads across a rough lava field to Toya Bungkah, passing after c 2km the overgrown remains of old houses and temples destroyed in Gunung Batur's eruptions.

The inhabitants of the caldera are poor: the climate is harsh, and agriculture is limited by the extensive lava fields. As a result, there is a sense of desperation in their dealings with wealthy outsiders, which results in persistent hustling to take up services offered, whether it be a room for the night or a guide for the walk up Gunung Batur; be prepared, but be polite.

Toya Bungkah, with more than a dozen hotels and *losmen*, has the best choice of accommodation in the caldera, though visitors will be constantly hassled until they have chosen their lodging for the night. The setting is pleasant, nevertheless, though the ugly hot springs complex now dominates the village. Recommended is ☆ *Arlina's* (☎ 0366 51165), which has clean, simple rooms.

Gunung Batur

This active volcano (1717m) is fairly easily climbed from either Toya Bungkah or from the north side. There are several craters on the volcano, aligned roughly along a north–south axis; the highest is accessible and offers fine views. In the dry season, there are usually a couple of small stalls set up on the summit with soft drinks, hot drinks and a few snacks sold at high prices.

Hotel staff and others will try hard to convince you a guide is needed for the ascent. In fact, this is not necessary unless you wish to climb in the dark to be at the summit for sunrise. You may, however, want a guide for companionship; if so, ensure that both parties know precisely what the fee includes and where the guide will take you, negotiate a reasonable price of a few dollars—not the huge sums of $30 or more which are initially suggested—and pay only when the trip has been completed to your satisfaction. Regrettably, guides here have earned themselves a reputation for overcharging and not delivering what they promise. Clearly though, it only takes a few behaving like this to tar all with the same brush; competent, friendly and fair guides undoubtedly exist.

The path from Toya Bungkah starts just south of the ticket office on the Kedisan road, and repeatedly splits and rejoins; follow any of the tracks uphill to the west and you cannot go very wrong. The highest crater has a few steaming vents, but most volcanic activity is currently found to the southwest of the summit, in the smaller, more recent craters. Batur last erupted in August 1994, spewing out large volumes of ash and dust; since then it has been fairly quiet, but climbers should be aware that this is very much an active volcano.

Beyond Toya Bungkah, the road continues anticlockwise round Gunung Batur, for much of the way crossing a chaotic landscape of lava blocks interspersed with small flat patches of land, on which farmers eke out a living growing cassava, onions and a few other vegetables.

In Songan, 3.5km from Toya Bungkah, the road comes to a T-junction. To the right, the lane leads after 1.5km to **Pura Ulun Danu Batur** at the northern tip of the lake. Dedicated to the lake goddess, Dewi Ulun Danu, for whom animal sacrifices in the lake are made every ten years, the temple is of significance because the lake is believed to feed the natural springs in eastern Bali which irrigate the all-important rice fields.

Just behind the temple, a steep, rocky path climbs up a cleft in the caldera wall to the rim, from where a path continues northeast to the main north coast road at Lupak.

Beyond Songan, a narrow asphalt road continues round Gunung Batur, passing after 1.7km a turn to the left to **Serongga**, from where you can climb to Batur's summit in c 1 hour. Even on this approach you are likely to encounter hustlers who demand money for right of access to either the road or the volcano, or both. For the next c 14km, the road meanders across the barren landscape of old lava fields, finally emerging on the caldera exit road just 250m below Penelokan.

The north coast

Beyond Penulisan, where the main road finally leaves the caldera rim and turns northwest, there is a choice of routes down to the coast. Westbound travellers can stay on the main road to Kubutambahan, c 37km; those heading east should turn off right onto the Tejakula road, c 7km beyond Pura Puncak Penulisan—a wonderful winding lane with fine views.

Much of the north coast is of little of interest to the casual visitor, but the stretch between Tejakula in the east and Seririt in the west contains plenty to see, including several ornate temples and the north coast's main beach resort area at Lovina.

SINGARAJA

Bali's second city after Denpasar, Singaraja has little to recommend it, but it is a useful service centre, and has a couple of minor points of interest. Few visitors stay in the town, as Lovina's dozens of resorts lie just a few kilometres to the west.

Practical information

Transport

A major transport hub for north Bali, Singaraja has three **bus stations**: **Terminal Banyuasri**, on the west side of town, serves the northwest coast from Lovina to Gilimanuk; **Terminal Penarukan**, on the east side, serves the northeast coast as far as Amlapura; and **Terminal Sukasada** serves Bedugul and points south to Denpasar. Bemo and dokar operate within the city.

Accommodation and services

If you need to stay here, the ☆☆/☆ *Hotel Wijaya* (☎ 0362 21915; fax 25817) on Jl. Sudirman is recommended. The **post office** and a 24-hour *wartel* are on Jl. Imam Bonjol. The **tourist office** is at Jl. Veteran 23. Traveller's cheques, cash and credit cards can be used at *BCA* in the city centre, and at other banks.

Those visitors with an academic interest in the subject should visit the **Gedong Kirtya**, a government-run library of traditional manuscripts made from leaves of the lontar palm, *Borassus sundaicus*, on Jl. Veteran. Since the library's foundation in the 1920s by the Dutch Resident, L.J.J. Caron, the collection has grown to several thousand, gathered from all over Bali and Lombok; a few are usually on display. The life span of a lontar text is limited by the climate to c 50 years, so skilled staff are continually making new manuscripts and meticulously copying old ones. Visitors are welcome to have a quick look round, and will usually be able to see a few ancient copper-plate inscriptions also stored here.

Immediately behind the library is a small **weaving factory** that produces silk and cotton *endek* cloth.

Pura Jagatnatha on Jl. Ngurah Rai is the largest temple in the city. Consecrated in the early 1990s, the temple is closed except during festivals, but its detailed carving can be seen from the street.

East of Singaraja

The first site of interest along the main coast road east from Singaraja is **Pura Beji** in **Sangsit**, 250m north off the main road. This extremely ornate *subak* temple is decorated with marvellous reliefs and a magnificent *kori agung*. The original temple here was built in the 15C on the site of a well. The lane beyond the temple down to the sea, where a number of fishing boats are usually to be seen.

Further east along the main road, c 600m, you reach a turn to the south to Jagaraga. On the east side along here after 4km is the **Pura Dalem Jagaraga**, well-known for its reliefs of cars, aeroplanes and other modern objects on the front wall's exterior; note on the right the Dutchmen being carjacked by gangsters.

☆☆☆/☆☆/☆ *Berdikari Cottages* (☎ 0362 25195), on the coast road 300m east of the Jagaraga turning, offers rather dull lodging. Further east the road comes to Kubutambahan and the turning south to the Batur caldera (see above).

Pura Meduwe Karang, on the coast road 500m east of the Batur turning, is another north coast temple with wonderful reliefs, including—on the north wall—the much-photographed figure riding a bicycle, said to represent W.O.J. Nieuwenkamp (1874–1950),

Pura Meduwe Karang relief

the Dutch artist who was one of the first Europeans to explore Bali thoroughly, during his visits in 1904, 1906–07, 1918, 1925 and 1937.

At Air Sanih, c 5km further east, are several hotels and bungalows, including the reasonable ☆☆ *Puri Sanih Bungalows*, which has bungalows facing the beach and an attractive swimming pool of natural spring water.

Tejakula, further east again, is of mild interest for its whitewashed baths in the village centre, just south of the main road, which originally were used for bathing horses but are now the communal public baths.

Beyond Tejakula, there is little of note until Tulamben (see p 157). As you travel further east, the terrain becomes drier and the vegetation more sparse, with increased numbers of lontar and coconut palms, and plots of cassava.

LOVINA
• • • • • • • •

The main beach resort area of the north coast, Lovina is really nothing very special. Nevertheless, it has the best range of accommodation in north Bali and is a convenient base from which to explore the coast and the lakes near Bedugul. The black sand beach is less inviting than the broad swathe of white sand at Kuta, but is much quieter and remains a focal point of the local fishing community. Dolphin-watching has been promoted by local travel agents as a tourist attraction, but a trip is often a disappointment and cannot be recommended unreservedly. Several companies run diving courses from Lovina.

As at Kuta, development here has been largely unplanned, with the result that the heart of Lovina, round the village of Kalibukbuk especially, is a chaotic mess of cramped, rather run-down *losmen* and cafés. At the east and west extremities of the tourist strip, lodgings tend to be newer and better maintained, more spacious and more expensive.

Practical information

Transport

Frequent *bemo* leave from the Banyuasri terminal in Singaraja, and will stop on request anywhere along the stretch of road through Lovina. Coming from other parts of Bali, you may need to change vehicles in Singaraja. *Perama* **shuttle buses** operate between Lovina and other key tourist destinations, including Ubud, Kuta, Sanur and Candidasa; they should be booked one day in advance. Small **jeeps**, **motorcycles** and **bicycles** can be rented from several agents in Lovina.

Accommodation

Coming from Singaraja's Banyuasri terminal, the first accommodation appears after c 2.5km; you pass the last c 8km further on. With c 100 hotels, *losmen* and *penginapan* to choose from, Lovina for most of the year experiences a severe glut of rooms; prices are always negotiable, with discounts of 25–40 per cent often obtainable—depending of course on your length of stay and bargaining skills. Below are a few recommendations. The ☎ code is 0362.
✪✪✪ *Sol Lovina* (☎ 41775; fax 41659; e-mail: sollovina@singaraja.wasantara. net.id). Good value, smart and colourful

rooms close to the sea.
✪✪✪/✪✪ *Hotel Baruna* (☎ 41745). Decent bungalows and rooms; pool and beach-front bar; diving trips can be arranged.
✪✪ *Hotel Banyualit* (☎ 41789; fax 41563). Cottages in a shady garden with pool, a short walk from the beach.
✪✪/✪ *Hotel Kalibukbuk* (☎ 41701). Beach-front location with good rooms.
✪✪/✪ *Rambutan Cottages* (☎ 41388; fax 41057). Very pleasant rooms in a mature garden, with a good restaurant and pool.
✪ *Hotel Pantai Bahagia* (☎ 41017). Simple, clean, cheap rooms on a beach-front location; often poor food.

Services

Along the main road in Kalibukbuk, at the heart of the Lovina beach strip, are numerous postal agents, money changers, travel agents, dive operators, restaurants and bars, a petrol station, and the *Perama* shuttle bus office. *Spice Dive* (☎ 41305/41509; fax 41171; e-mail: spicedive@denpasar. wasantara.net.id) offers reputable PADI-certified diving courses, and organises dives at Tulamben and Amed (see p 158) and Pulau Menjangan (see p 175).

Around Lovina

Apart from the beach there are few attractions in the immediate vicinity of Lovina. One place well worth visiting, however, is the charming **hot springs** bathing complex near **Banjar**, a few kilometres to the west.

From the clearly signed junction on the coast road, turn south to the market in Banjar's centre. Just beyond, the springs are signed to the left, 1km further. Avoid weekends and holidays, when the pools can be crowded; at other times this is a delightfully refreshing place in which to relax amidst beautiful plants. Above the main pool is a smaller, hotter pool; below to the left is the soaping pool. The restaurant overlooking the gardens is let down by the rather morose staff.

In Seririt, 4km further west along the coast road, is the turning to Munduk (see below) and the extremely scenic, north-south cross-island route (see p 173) to Medewi beach or Antosari. Further west, the coast road passes the main north coast port at Celukan Bawang and eventually reaches Pemuteran and Labuhan Lalang, from where boats run to Pulau Menjangan, the site of some of Bali's best coral reefs (see p 175).

Bedugul and the western lakes

Approaching the Bedugul area from Singaraja, the main road climbs steadily through very lush scenery, past the **Gitgit waterfall**, to the rim of an ancient caldera. Just beyond the turning to Munduk (see below), it descends steeply down the thickly-wooded caldera wall, where a colony of macaques waits greedily for titbits from passers-by.

To the west of the road on the caldera floor is the ☆☆☆ *Hotel Bali Danau Buyan* (☎ 0362 21351/23739; fax 21388), with pleasant, spacious, four-person self-catering bungalows in gardens; there is no lake access.

Beside the Terminal Pancasari, 300m further south, a lane to the west follows the south shore of Lake Buyan for c 2.7km to the road head, from where you can walk further west, past the end of the lake to Lake Tamblingan. It is definitely possible—but an uncomfortable scramble—to make your way first to **Pura Dalem Tamblingan** on the south shore of Lake Tamblingan, and from there, clockwise round the lake to Pura Gubug (see below) on the southwest shore, from where a good track leads up to the Munduk road. The terrain is awkward, however, and you should take a compass or a guide if you don't wish to risk spending several hours lost in the woods.

The ☆☆☆☆☆/☆☆☆☆ *Bali Handara Kosaido Country Club* (☎ 0632 22646; fax 23048), c 1km south of the Pancasari terminal, has a magnificently situated 18-hole golf course open to the public for a fee.

Further south, the road reaches the west shore of **Lake Bratan**, famous for the immensely picturesque *meru* of **Pura Ulun Danu Bratan**. The much-photographed eleven-tiered and three-tiered meru appear as separate islands when the lake's water level is high. The larger one is dedicated to Vishnu and the lake goddess, Dewi Ulun Danu; the smaller to Shiva. The seven-tiered *meru* on shore is dedicated to Brahma. The complex, built by the ruler of Mengwi, is said to date from the mid-17C. Unusually, it also has a Buddhist *stupa*, the **Candi Kuning**, with small Buddha images seated in niches.

The colourful market of **Candi Kuning**, 1200m beyond the temple, is usually stocked with a large variety of fresh fruit, vegetables and flowers. Try bargaining here and you risk being ignored: stall-holders are used to visitors paying silly prices and prefer a more malleable type of customer.

Just beyond the market, a lane to the west leads after 800m to Bali's Botanical Gardens, passing en route several rather gloomy but cheap *penginapan*. The extensive gardens, established in 1959, sprawl across more than 120ha and are richly endowed with plants and birds. They are best visited on a weekday at opening time (07.00) to benefit from the coolest hours of the day; at weekends, parts of the gardens can be noisy and busy, and by mid-morning it is too hot to enjoy the walking.

South of the gardens, the road climbs once more out of the old Bratan caldera, past several overpriced and dilapidated hotels. Birders wishing to visit the Botanical Gardens early should consider staying in the vicinity however; recommended for its views—though not for its rather shabby and overpriced bungalows—is ✩✩✩/✩✩ *Hotel Bukit Permai* (☎ 0368 21443).

The **Taman Rekreasi** (recreation park) and *Hotel Bedugul*, c 700m further on, are popular with Balinese at weekends; boats can be hired on Lake Bratan from here, and a path starts from here to the summit of Gunung Catur (Gunung Mangu; 2096m), where there is a small temple, **Pura Puncak Mangu**, in very picturesque surroundings. Allow 2–3 hours for the ascent, and half that for the return; take tough shoes, plenty of water and snacks, as the path is relentlessly uphill, steep and slippery in places.

Beyond the Hotel Bedugul, the road starts descending southward to Pacung and Luwus, and eventually to Mengwi (see p 141).

Munduk and vicinity

One of the loveliest parts of Bali is the hilly region to the west of Lake Tamblingan. To reach it, turn west off the main Singaraja–Bedugul road just to the north of the Bratan caldera. The quiet road follows the caldera rim above Lake Buyan and Lake Tamblingan, with occasional views of the lakes through the trees. After 8km, a lane to the left descends for c 2.5km to Pura Gubug, on the southwest shore of Lake Tamblingan. It's a charming, peaceful location: the dilapidated eleven-tiered and nine-tiered *meru* have ferns and wild grasses sprouting from their roofs, and on the lake are small bamboo fishing platforms. On the south shore can be seen Pura Dalem Tamblingan, which can be reached on foot.

On the Munduk road 4.5km further is a footpath to the right which descends to the **Munduk waterfall**, a popular swimming spot for local children. Continue 1.4km further to reach the wonderful ✩✩✩ *Puri Lumbung Cottages* (☎/fax 0362 92810/92514). Cottages constructed in the form of rice barns offer fine views across rice terraces; the food is authentically Balinese; and the staff can arrange all sorts of hikes, drives and visits to coffee and clove plantations or subak irrigation systems.

On the edge of Munduk village, c 700m further, are three simple ✩✩ bungalows—*Meme Soeroeng, Mekel Ragi* and *Guru Ratna*—also managed by Puri Lumbung Cottages; in the village itself are several old Dutch colonial buildings, now rather run-down.

At a junction c 2km beyond the village, a lane to the left leads after 3.8km to the ✩ *Gesing Inn*, a very simple guest-house with a couple of rooms, which rarely receives visitors because of its isolated but undeniably charming position. Up the hill 700m beyond the guest-house is a magnificent fig tree with an immense root system in which children can hide. The lane beyond continues 2.5km to an unremarkable temple at the road head, from where there are quite extensive views in the dry season.

Beyond Munduk the road descends through Banyuatis, and eventually reaches Mayong on the cross-island road between Seririt and Antosari.

West Bali: Tabanan, Jembrana and Pulau Menjangan

The undoubted **highlight** of western Bali is the magnificent **coral reef** round **Pulau Menjangan** (see p 175), which offers the finest diving and snorkelling in Bali. Inland, the **Pura Luhur Batukaru** (see p 172) has one of the island's most charming temple locations, high on Gunung Batukaru.

Practical information

Transport
Except on the main coastal road, public transport is infrequent and slow, and the visitor with a full schedule is advised to charter a vehicle and driver, or to rent a car in Ubud or one of the southern resorts. Large **buses** operate between Denpasar and the western port of Gilimanuk, passing through Tabanan and Negara; however, most sites of interest lie off the main road, and often you must charter an *ojek* at the main road junction.

Accommodation
Accommodation can be found in isolated spots along the south coast, including Yeh Gangga, Tibubiyu and Balian. On the north coast, Pemuteran has several excellent lodgings. Penebel, not far from Pura Luhur Batukaru, has pleasant rooms.

Odalan dates for a selection of temples
Pura Penataran Tanah Lot: festival starts on Wednesday of Langkir (week 13): 16.8.00, 14.3.01, 10.10.01, 8.5.02, 4.12.02, 2.7.03, 28.1.04.
Pura Alas Kedaton: festival starts on Tuesday of Medangsia (week 14): 22.8.00, 20.3.01, 16.10.01, 14.5.02, 10.12.02, 8.7.03, 3.2.04.
Pura Luhur Batukaru: festival starts on Thursday of Dunggulan (week 11): 3.8.00, 1.3.01, 27.9.01, 25.4.02, 21.11.02, 19.6.03, 15.1.04.
Pura Luhur Rambut Siwi, Jembrana: festival starts on Wednesday of Prangbakat (week 24): 30.5.01, 26.12.01, 24.7.02, 19.02.03, 17.9.03, 14.4.04.

Tanah Lot

One of Bali's most over-hyped tourist attractions, **Pura Penataran Tanah Lot** can be seen on dozens of postcards and tourist brochures, and in virtually every photographic book about Bali. The diminutive temple, perched on a low stack a few metres offshore, is undeniably picturesque, but as so often happens in situations like this, the reality is a huge anticlimax. Nevertheless, tour groups flock here by the score for the sunset each evening, arriving a few minutes before, and departing soon after, leaving just enough time to down an overpriced drink.

To the Balinese, however, the temple is one of the island's most sacred; local folklore believes it to have been founded in the mid-16C by the Javanese Shaivite-Buddhist sage, Danghyang Nirartha, who is also associated in myth with Pura Luhur Uluwatu (see p 117) and Pura Rambut Siwi (see below). It is best visited at the time of its *odalan* (see box above). This festival is one of the best to observe in Bali because of its coastal location, but visitors must be properly dressed with sarong and sash; singlets and shorts are totally inappropriate.

It's a short walk from the car park at the large souvenir market to the sea, where a dozen or more *warung* serve food and expensive drinks on the raised terrace overlooking the beach and temple. At the back of the beach opposite the temple is a small cave inhabited by grey-and-black-striped sea snakes, *Laticauda colubrina*, which, for a fee, visitors can see; although their venom is toxic they are slow to anger, though their human guardians imply that these sacred snakes (*ular suci*) are extremely dangerous.

You can walk along the cliffs in both directions for good views of the temple. A short distance to the east is the Nirwana golf course; to the west the path passes several small headlands, on each of which sit small, unremarkable temples. From one of these – Pura Galuh – there are good views of Tanah Lot and of the coastline to the west; the most interesting is **Pura Batu Bolong**, which lies across a narrow rock arch.

Practical information

Accommodation
There is little reason to stay overnight at Tanah Lot as it is so close to the resorts of southern Bali. However, it does enable you to explore the area at first light, when there are no other visitors. The ☎ code is 0361. Recommended are the ☆☆/☆ *Dewi Sinta Cottages* (☎ 812933) beside the market in the centre of Tanah Lot. Next door is the more expensive ☆☆☆ *Mutiara Tanah Lot* (☎ 812939). An alternative is the luxurious ☆☆☆☆☆ *Le Méridien* (☎ 243691; fax 812398), part of the controversial Nirwana Bali Resort just outside Tanah Lot, with an 18-hole, Greg Norman-designed golf course.

Tabanan

Tabanan is an important service centre, market and transport hub for the local population, but offers little of specific interest for the casual visitor. The exception is the small *subak* **museum** in the Mandala Mathika Subak complex off Jl.

Gatot Subroto. The office is primarily an advisory and training centre for *subak* officials from across Bali, but in the basement is a small but interesting collection of fish traps and tools used in rice cultivation, and an explanation of the *subak* irrigation system, which for many generations has sustained Bali's rice production. In the grounds can be seen a replica of a traditional Tabanan house, a rice barn, a small *subak* temple, and irrigation channels forming part of the local *subak*, one of more than 300 in Tabanan regency alone.

To find the museum, turn north along Jl. Ngurah Rai, then west along Jl. Gatot Subroto. Just before the Taliwang Bersaudara restaurant on the left, a lane doubles back up the hill to the complex.

A few kilometres northeast of Tabanan, on the Margarana road, is the protected holy forest of **Alas Kedaton**, home to several troupes of macaques and a seasonal roost of **large flying foxes**, *Pteropus vampyrus*. Amid the trees is **Pura Kedaton**, believed to have been built in the 11C by a Javanese Hindu priest, Mpu Kuturan.

The forest, clearly signed c 600m east of the road, is very popular with coach tours, and the parking lot is surrounded by souvenir stalls and *warung* selling food and drink. It's best to come in the early morning before the tourist hordes.

North of Alas Kedaton is the **Margarana monument** (Monumen Nasional Taman Pujaan Bangsa Margarana), dedicated to the 1372 soldiers who died fighting the Dutch in Bali from 1945 to 1950, and more specifically, the nearly 100 men who died here on 20 November 1946 in one of the major battles of the war. Among the dead was Ngurah Rai, hero of the Balinese resistance forces. The text of a letter he wrote, refusing to surrender to the Dutch, is inscribed on the main monument.

Outside the memorial park is a plaque listing the dead, their birthplace and place of death. Inside, behind the large monument, are neat rows of simple *candi* representing the dead, among them Hindus, Muslims, Christians and a few Japanese who sided with the Balinese.

To find it, turn north from the forest; after c 1.5km the road swings to the east, reaching the intersection in Belayu after c 1km more. Turn north (left) here, and after c 5km the road turns west into the centre of Marga; continue c 600m beyond Marga to the monument, on the right.

From the centre of Marga, a road runs north c 12km to Apuan, where it swings west towards Jatiluwih and Pura Luhur Batukaru. (A side road continues north c 5km from this corner to join the main Mengwi–Bedugul road at Pacung, where you should turn north [left] for Bedugul and Lake Bratan, or south for Ubud. Just before reaching Pacung, the lane passes *Restoran Ume Luang*, in a marvellous setting surrounded by terraced rice fields, and providing a good excuse for a snack or drink.)

Continuing west from Apuan, you reach a junction at the small market of **Senganan** after c 2.5km. To the left is Penebel (see below), but travellers are advised to follow the beautiful route to the right towards Jatiluwih. This passes the well-situated *Restoran Soka Sari* after c 3.5km, and for the next 4km the narrow road winds through spectacular amphitheatres of terraced rice fields. At the next junction, c 7km beyond the restaurant, the road to the right leads after c 3km to **Wongaya Gede** (for Pura Luhur Batukaru); to the left, a very scenic lane descends to Penebel.

In Wongaya Gede, **Pura Luhur Batukaru** is signed to the north (right), but if time permits, first turn south c 1.5km for a quick look at the unusual syncretic architecture of the Catholic church of **St Martinus de Porus** in *banjar* Pengaggahan, *desa* Tengkudak. Note the *kulkul* in the northwest corner of the compound and the entrance in the form of a split gate, the finely carved wooden doors and the cement reliefs; the church serves a tiny Christian community of less than a dozen families.

Return north through Wongaya Gede and continue c 2.5km to the parking lot at Pura Luhur Batukaru.

Pura Luhur Batukaru

One of Bali's most important temples, Pura Luhur Batukaru (Batukau) is surrounded by mature trees and splendid shrubbery which thrive in the cool moist air. There has been a temple here on the southern slopes of Gunung Batukaru (2276m) since perhaps the 11C, and it has subsequently become the state temple of Tabanan. Its *odalan* attracts crowds from all over Bali (see box on p 169).

In the first courtyard, entered through a split gate, are two long, thatched pavilions; behind, steps lead to the inner court which contains many multi-tiered *meru* dedicated to Tabanan's deified rulers.

Steps down to the east side lead to a small lake with an island on which stand two shrines, one for the goddess of Lake Tamblingan, the other for the god of Gunung Batukaru; just north of the lake, a spring emerges through a water spout surrounded by moss-covered statues.

Penebel

The closest accommodation to Pura Batukaru is found in the small market town of Penebel. The most scenic route is via Wongaya Gede, where you should turn east towards Jatiluwih for c 3km before turning south along a beautiful lane, past many traditional rice barns built of timber and bamboo, raised on stilts and roofed with thatch of sugar-palm fibres.

After c 6km, this road arrives at the centre of Penebel, beside the market. Turn north (left) here for the very pleasant ☆☆ *Pondok Wisata Taman Sari* (☎ 0361 812898), clearly signed off to the east (right) after c 500m. Though perhaps a little overpriced, this is a delightful place to stay, run by a friendly family.

Just south of the market in Penebel, the main road runs past a magnificent fig tree, and c 3km beyond, a turning to the west (right) leads after a further c 2km to ☆☆☆☆ *Yeh Panes* (☎ 0361 262356), the only other accommodation in the area. Hot springs here feed outdoor whirlpool baths in a well-maintained garden. The rooms, however, are very overpriced, though hard-headed bargaining should reduce the price by up to 40 per cent.

Continuing south on the main road to Tabanan, you pass **Taman Kupu Kupu Bali** (Bali Butterfly Park) in *banjar* Sandan Lebah, *desa* Wanasari; Tabanan is a further c 7km.

Yeh Gangga

On the coast c 8km south of Tabanan along a potholed road is Yeh Gangga, a broad but unexceptional black sand beach. A few metres away is the friendly and very pleasant ☆☆☆/☆☆ *Penginapan Bali Wisata* (☎ 0361 261654; fax 812744), with good-sized bungalows, attractive gardens, a salt-water swimming pool, and fine views over rice terraces to the sea. Staff can arrange horse-riding from the next-door riding stables.

Kerambitan

In this village, c 5km east of Tabanan, are two palaces inhabited by descendants of the Tabanan ruling family. **Puri Anyar** is the more interesting, with well-maintained pavilions filled with heirlooms, and several guest rooms containing four-poster beds. The palace infrequently holds evenings of food and traditional dance for large tour groups, with a local dance troupe performing the *calonarang*.

Puri Agung, on the west side of the village, is rather less well-maintained, but also welcomes visitors and has rooms for let. Neither palace is really prepared for individual travellers, however, though accommodation can sometimes be provided.

Pasut and Tibubiyu

Opposite the Puri Agung in Kerambitan, a lane runs southwest through the villages of Tista and Yeh Malet to the beach at Pasut. On the left in the village of **Tibubiyu**, c 1.5km before the beach, is ☆☆ *Bungalo Beebees*, with attractive two-storey cottages shaped like rice barns. The staff are very friendly, and the small restaurant looks out over rice fields; it's a charming, isolated place to stay. The beach is a 20-minute walk away through the fields.

The southwest coast road

At Antosari, c 16km west of Tabanan along the main highway, a road turns off north towards Seririt on the north coast. There are no specific sights along here, but it's an extremely scenic road, well worth taking if you can think of a reason for doing so. After c 9.5km it passes *Café Belimbing*, from where there is a fine panorama over a huge swathe of terraced rice fields, and then winds onward through very picturesque countryside to the junction in Pupuan, a further 19km. Here you can continue to Seririt on the north coast, or turn west through Tista to rejoin the main south coastal highway at Pekutatan.

Beyond Antosari, the main road descends southwest past terraced rice fields to the sea, where it turns northwest along the coast. The ☆☆/☆ *Balian Beach Bungalows* (☎ 0361 813017), c 9.5km west of the Antosari junction, are a justifiably popular surfers' hang-out, situated in a shady garden dominated by coconut palms, close to a surf break at the mouth of the Balian river.

☆☆☆☆/☆☆☆ *Sacred River Retreat* (☎ 0361 732165; fax 730904), 400m further along the highway, is a centre for spiritual self-development, offering yoga and meditation, massage and vegetarian food; the setting is beautiful (though the nearby highway can be noisy), the rooms are tasteful, and anyone is welcome.

The road runs close to the sea for the next c 20km to Pekutatan, where a road turns inland to Pupuan (see above) and Seririt. This very scenic, cross-island route climbs steadily through intensively farmed countryside, with frequent glimpses of a deep valley and wooded hills to the west; small rubber plantations and clove bushes (identifiable by the distinctive reddening clove buds and the trees' rounded crowns) line the road higher up. After c 9km, the road passes through a bunut tree (*pohon bunut bolong*: 'the bunut tree with the hole'), whose extensive aerial roots flank the asphalt with little effort. The road comes to the market of **Tista** after a further c 8km, where the road divides; turn right for the direct route to Pupuan, and left for the longer route via Sepang. This is a remote – though very fertile and fairly well-off – part of Bali, where foreign visitors remain a curiosity and comparatively little English is spoken.

Further west from Pekutatan on the coastal highway, you come to **Medewi** after c 2.5km. There are several hotels here, but none can be recommended; Medewi is really best ignored.
 Pura Luhur Rambut Siwi, c 5.5km beyond, is notable in local folklore as the location of a hair of the 16C Javanese Hindu-Buddhist priest, Danghyang Nirartha, which is believed to be buried beneath the main three-tiered *meru* in the inner courtyard. Visually the temple is dull, though the caretaker-guide will spice up his spiel to earn a decent tip.

NEGARA AND VICINITY

Between Balian and Gilimanuk, Negara is the only place with any decent accommodation. The capital of Jembrana Regency, it's a busy little town which acts as the main service centre for western Bali. There is little of interest here for the tourist, however.

Practical information

Accommodation
The ☎ code is 0365.
☆☆/☆ *Hotel Prima Agung* (☎ 41876; fax 41743) at Jl. Ngurah Rai 111, and ☆☆/☆ *Hotel Wirapada* (☎ 41161) at Jl. Ngurah Rai 107, 200m apart, have similar rooms at similar prices, though the former is newer and has slightly better facilities. In *banjar* Batuagung, outside the town centre, are ☆ *Cahaya Matahari Bungalows* (☎ 40632),

signed to the north along Jl. Majapahit, off the main road at an intersection on the east side of town. The rooms are pleasant, but nothing special.

Services
Along Jl. Ngurah Rai to the west of the hotels are several **banks**, including *Bank Danamon* and *BCA*. A 24-hour **wartel** is on Jl. Sudirman, just west of the Jl. Ngurah Rai junction.

Palasari and Blimbingsari

The remarkable Christian churches in these two villages are worth a visit for their striking architecture. For route-finding reasons, travellers with their own vehicles will find it easier to visit Blimbingsari first. These two Christian enclaves were established in the late 1930s, as a result of the twin desires of the Dutch government to open up land in this formerly uncleared forest and to minimize the impact of Christian communities on Bali.

A Chinese evangelist named Tsang Kan Foek, sent from Singapore by the Christian and Missionary Alliance in 1929, had quickly found support among several Chinese families in Denpasar and by 1930 had a few Balinese followers. Despite initial objections by the Dutch government and local princes who felt their authority threatened, a small Christian community developed and a Catholic church was built in Mengwi. Social frictions grew as Christian converts refused to contribute to community festivals (which were mostly based upon Balinese Hindu traditions), and in 1939, the government made available some uncleared forest land in Jembrana in an effort to calm the situation. Blimbingsari was established in an area known previously as Alas Rangda, considered a place of evil. The settlement, predominantly Protestant but with a few Muslim families, was laid out in the shape of a huge cross; by April 1940, nearly 40 families had been settled. Soon after, the island's Catholics created a similar new settlement at Palasari.

To find the churches, ignore the turning signed north to 'Bendungan Palasari' c 15km west of Negara, and continue west along the highway c 3km to another turning to the north, signed to both Blimbingsari and Palasari. This route reaches the unusual **Protestant church** in Blimbingsari after c 5.5km; completed in 1981, it's an open-sided structure with a huge, three-tiered shingle roof supported by pillars and surmounted with a crucifix. In front is a somewhat baroque gateway.

The road east from here leads to the main Palasari road, where you should turn right towards the centre of Palasari; the huge **Catholic church**, built in the 1950s and renovated in the 1990s, is on the east side of the football pitch in the village centre. From here, follow the main Palasari road c 6km back to the coastal highway, rejoining it at the sign to 'Bendungan Palasari'.

West Bali National Park

Covering a huge swathe of western Bali, including the Gunung Prapat Agung peninsula and Pulau Menjangan, the park is best known for its Bali mynah breeding programme, which is endeavouring to boost the numbers of this extremely rare bird, Bali's only endemic species. Although the park was originally planned to cover nearly 80,000ha, only 19,000ha have actually been gazetted, with the rest awaiting the resolution of a dispute between the National Park authorities and Bali's provincial Forest Service.

The most visited part of the park is **Pulau Menjangan**, a small island which is surrounded by Bali's finest coral reefs. Boats to the dive sites depart from **Labuhan Lalang**, a small port c 13km northeast of Cekik. The boat charter costs c $25 for up to 10 people for a maximum of four hours (which includes 30 minutes travel each way); there are further charges for snorkelling equipment hire, car parking, an obligatory park guide, insurance and tax. It is best to set off early – soon after 08.00. The nearest accommodation is at Gilimanuk or – greatly preferable – at Pemuteran (see below).

On the Gunung Prapat Agung peninsula is the release site for Bali mynahs being re-introduced to the wild. Visitors are unlikely to see them, however, as people are kept away from the site to prevent disturbance.

> ### The Bali mynah
>
> The Bali mynah (*Leucopsar rothschildi*), also known as Rothschild's mynah or Bali starling, is a supremely beautiful, pure white bird with black wing and tail tips and bright blue skin around the eye. While many thousands are kept in captivity around the world—especially in the USA—the only wild ones are found in the National Park.
>
> The bird was first recorded in 1911, and even then was confined to the western tip of Bali. Since then, hunting for private collections and continual environmental degradation of its roosting and nesting habitat have steadily reduced numbers. In 1979, an estimated 200 birds remained, but the population crashed heavily in the 1980s, with a census in late 1990 finding only 13–18 birds. Since then, a major international conservation effort has been launched to try to save the bird in the wild, and numbers are believed to have recovered very slightly, but fluctuate greatly—somewhere between 30 and 60.

There are several walking trails in the park, including a path to the west side of the Prapat Agung peninsula; in the dry season especially, this can be a good place to see wildlife, including several deer species, crab-eating macaques and the occasional banteng. All hiking groups must be accompanied by a park guide.

For information about walks, consult staff at the park headquarters (open Mon–Thur 07.00–14.00; Fri 07.00–11.00; Sat 07.00–12.30) on the west side of the road at Cekik, c 13km west of the Blimbingsari turn-off. Note that there appears to be an element of corruption here, with some members of staff requesting unofficial donations to 'help save the Bali starling'; don't be fooled.

Gilimanuk

Of little interest except as the port for the ferries to Banyuwangi on the east Java coast, Gilimanuk does have a few basic *losmen* and *penginapan*—none of which can be recommended—and several restaurants; a *wartel* lies opposite the ferry terminal.

There is a small archaeological museum (*museum purbakala*) c 600m from the ferry terminal, but this appears to be almost permanently closed. On display are exhibits from a Bronze-Iron Age burial ground here; pottery from the site has been radiocarbon-dated to 195 BC–AD 450.

Ferries to Java officially depart every 15 minutes round the clock. The crossing itself takes 20–30 minutes, though loading and unloading can take at least as long as that; travellers with vehicles may face a longer wait on public holidays, and especially in the days before the Galungan festival and Nyepi, when Balinese flock home from Java.

Pemuteran

From the junction in Cekik, the road to the north coast runs inland across the neck of the Prapat Agung peninsula and past the National Park harbour at Labuhan Lalang. Much of the route is lined with plantations of a teak wood, *Manikara kauki*, very popular with Balinese woodcarvers. At Pemuteran, c 17km beyond Labuhan Lalang, there are three excellent lodgings, which make this the best base from which to visit Pulau Menjangan. Snorkelling on the reef offshore can be good; dive trips to the local reef or to Pulau Menjangan (see above) can be arranged through the highly regarded *Reef Seen Aquatics* (☎/fax 0362 92339) near *Taman Sari*.

Practical information

Accommodation
The ☎ code is 0362.
☆☆☆☆☆ *Matahari Beach Resort* (☎ 92312; fax 92313), c 1.5km east of Pondok Sari. Extreme luxury; a full range of water sports; very professional, friendly staff; and a shady black sand beach.

☆☆☆☆/☆☆☆ *Taman Sari* (☎ 92623; fax 0361 286297). Very elegant, beautifully furnished bungalows in a large garden beside the beach; safe sea swimming but no pool. Highly recommended.
☆☆ *Pondok Sari* (☎/fax 92337). Slightly shabbier, but with an equally lovely garden. Recommended.

The meru in a Balinese temple courtyard, always found with an odd number of tiers, up to a total of eleven

JAVA

JAKARTA

The urban sprawl of Greater Jakarta, stretching over almost 700 sq km and providing a home for more than ten million people from all corners of the archipelago, is undoubtedly a congested, humid, and at times immensely frustrating city. Lightly dismissed by some writers as dull and polluted, Jakarta nevertheless epitomises modern, urban Indonesia at its most frantic, exuberant and desperate. Despite the obvious discomforts, a stay in the city should not be passed over too readily, for this is the powerhouse of the nation, with the widest ethnic representation, the greatest variety of regional foods, the finest art collections, the best museums, the most sophisticated shops. Jakarta is the vast archipelago's nerve centre, attracting most of the nation's wealth and an endless flow of migrants; from the city issues a massively centralised and overly bureaucratic administration which can nevertheless reach the smallest village on the most far-flung island. Like all main cities in developing countries, Jakarta displays gigantic disparities – between traditional and modern, between poor and rich – which even the most myopic of newly arrived visitors cannot fail to notice.

Highlights include the fine collections in the **National Museum**, and the view from the top of the **National Monument**; the spectacular *pinisi* in the harbour at **Sunda Kelapa**; and the paintings in the **Fine Arts Hall** in Kota. **Taman Mini** and **Ragunan Zoo** are recommended, especially for children; and Jakarta is the best single source for most of the country's **crafts**. The islands of the **Seribu archipelago** offer excellent diving and snorkelling.

The city

Dominating the skyline of Jakarta's **business district** are scores of steel-framed, glass-clad, air-conditioned towers of office space, the favoured workplace for the comparatively affluent middle class, many of whom live in distant dormitory suburbs far to the south and west, where land is still affordable. These towers are the modern heart of the city – the immediately visible signs, together with expensive cars in the streets, and designer-label boutiques in the shopping malls, of the breakneck pace of economic growth which Jakarta experienced through the 1980s and much of the 1990s.

However, peer from these towers' upper storeys and far below can still be seen the banana leaves and terracotta roof tiles of an older Jakarta of traditional *kampung* neighbourhoods, pavement *warung*, *jamu* sellers and food pedlars.

North of the tower blocks is **Menteng**, a wealthy turn-of-the-century residential neighbourhood with tidy, leafy streets and large colonial-era houses skulking behind high walls and heavy gates. The home of former president Suharto is here, together with many foreign embassies and the city's best hotels, including the *Mandarin Oriental* and the *Grand Hyatt*. On the north edge of Menteng are mid-priced hotels and the generally dreadful, low-budget accommodation of the Jl. Jaksa area.

Beyond, you reach the vast grassy plain of **Lapangan Merdeka**, with the gold-tipped **National Monument** at its centre. On the square's east side is Gambir train station, the most useful station for departing Jakarta by rail. On all sides of the huge square are architectural relics of the Dutch colonial presence, among them the marvellous **National Museum** and the **Presidential Palace**. Nearby are the great white-domed **Istiqlal Mosque** and Lapangan Banteng, a smaller square flanked by colonial architecture.

The other main area of interest to visitors is **Kota**, c 5km further north, past the chaotic markets of Glodok, the city's **Chinatown**. Kota's **museums** and the magnificent **Bugis ships** moored in the harbour of Sunda Kelapa should not be missed.

Far from the sea in the southern suburbs is **Blok M**, one of the main shopping districts, with several large malls and department stores, while nearby **Kemang** is the place to go for chic restaurants, cafés and bars. **Ragunan Zoo**, much further south, is the best in Indonesia; and the sometimes underrated **Taman Mini** to the southeast is packed with cultural exhibits from across the archipelago.

Practical information

Flights
Soekarno-Hatta Airport,
c 26km northwest of central Jakarta, is the main arrival point for visitors to Java and is the principal hub for domestic flights round the archipelago. *Merpati*, however, operates a few services to Bandar Lampung (55 minutes) and Bandung (40 minutes) from the older Halim Perdana Kusuma Airport, c 13km southeast of the city centre.

Arriving at Soekarno-Hatta Airport
Officials at the Immigration desk may demand to see proof of onward passage from Indonesia – usually an air ticket. Without this to hand you may be taken aside and obliged to buy a full-fare ticket on the spot, or (preferable to both parties) provide a small financial 'gift' to the official. There are two terminals: one for domestic flights, the other for all international flights and Garuda's domestic routes. Shuttle buses run between the two but are infrequent, so take a taxi if in a hurry to catch a connecting flight. Both terminals have currency changers,

post and telecom services, information desks, left-luggage facilities, fast-food restaurants, snack bars and toilets. The only hotel nearby is the ✩✩✩✩ *Sheraton Bandara* (☎ 559 7777; fax 559 7700), which lies a short taxi ride away.

Transport between airport and city
By taxi

Outside both terminals are official taxi ranks. Avoid unauthorised taxis and check that the driver resets the meter at the start of the journey. In addition to the final meter reading, the passenger must pay three road tolls and an airport surcharge, which the driver will add to the total. A ride to central Jakarta, including tolls and surcharge, should cost US$5–8 and takes c 30–60 minutes. More comfortable and expensive than standard taxis are *Silver Bird* limousines (US$7–12) which can be ordered from a desk outside the arrivals hall of Terminal 2-D.
By bus

For a fixed fare, *Damri* air-conditioned buses run from both terminals to several city destinations, most central of which – and probably most useful to foreign visitors – is Gambir railway station on the east side of Lapangan Merdeka; from here, most city-centre hotels are a short taxi or *bajaj* ride away. Gambir is also the place for those wishing to jump on the first train out of Jakarta. Taxi drivers meeting the airport buses at Gambir are often unwilling to use their meters and demand high fares, so if your baggage permits, you may do better to walk a short way down the road and hail a passing cab, preferably a pale blue-coloured *Blue Bird*.

Other Damri bus destinations include Blok M (useful for south Jakarta), Jl. Angkasa in Kemayoran (for north Jakarta), and Rawamangun (in east Jakarta).

Car rentals

You are strongly advised not to drive yourself from the airport unless you are already familiar with Jakarta's traffic and streets. Hertz in Terminal 2 offers expensive chauffeured cars; much cheaper self-drive deals are available in the city.

Departures

Each of the two terminals is split into three sections. In general, Terminal 1-B is for *Merpati*, and 1-C is for *Bouraq, Mandala* and all other non-Garuda domestic flights. Terminal 2-D is for non-*Garuda* international flights, while 2-E and 2-F are for all *Garuda* flights. A tax is payable upon departure for international flights; for domestic routes, this is usually included in the ticket price.

Domestic airlines in Jakarta

Bouraq Jl. Angkasa 1–3, Kemayoran, ☎ 629 5364.
Garuda Hotel Indonesia, Jl. Thamrin, ☎ 230 0468 Wisma Dharmala Sakti, Jl. Sudirman, ☎ 251 2235/7 Garuda bldg, Jl. Medan Merdeka Selatan.
Mandala Jl. Garuda 76, Kemayoran, ☎ 424 6100 Jl. Veteran I/34, Gambir, ☎

381 1107 Hotel Kartika Chandra, Jl. Gatot Subroto.
Merpati Jl. Angkasa 2, Kemayoran, ☎ 654 8888 City check-in, Gambir train station, Jl. Medan Merdeka Timur (free bus to airport), ☎ 350 1433.

Trains

Most trains of use to visitors depart from **Gambir station** on the east side of Lapangan Merdeka. These include frequent daily services to Bogor and comfortable express trains to Bandung, Yogyakarta, Solo, Semarang and Surabaya, as well as many slow and crowded economy-class trains. One booking office here (open 07.30–19.00) handles the *Sembrani, Bima* and *Parahyangan* services; another deals with the *Argobromo, Argogede* and *Argolawu*. Tickets for all other trains are bought in the main part of the station at the relevant ticket windows, clearly signed. A separate reservations office takes booking requests for up to seven days before departure; advance booking is strongly recommended at any time, and is absolutely essential for public holidays. To avoid lengthy queues, it can be well worth buying tickets through travel agents for a small surcharge.

Useful train services from Gambir

Argogede to Bandung (2 hours 20 minutes), twice daily each way, morning and evening, executive and business.
Parahyangan to Bandung (3 hours), ten times daily each way from 05.00–20.30, executive and business.
Argobromo overnight to Pekalongan, Semarang and Surabaya (9 hours), executive only.
Bima overnight to Surabaya (12 hours), air-conditioning, reclining seats.
Sembrani overnight to Semarang & Surabaya (10 hours), air-conditioning, reclining seats.
Argolawu overnight to Cirebon,

Purwokerto, Yogya and Solo (7 hours), air-conditioning, reclining seats, executive only.
Cirebon Expres to Cirebon (3 hours), three or four times daily each way, executive and business.
Fajar Utama Yogya by day to Yogya (8 hours), executive and business with air-conditioning.
Senja Utama Yogya overnight to Yogya (8 hours), twice nightly, executive and business.
Senja Utama Solo overnight to Yogya & Solo (8 hours), executive, business and couchette (sleeper).

City buses

These are very cheap, but also usually crowded, sweaty and slow, and not much fun unless you have never experienced such things before. Finding your way round the network can be difficult since bus route maps do not exist, and the large variety of bus types makes travel confusing at first. Destinations are displayed on the front, so you need to be equipped with a good street map. The visitor information centre on Jl. Wahid Hasyim can advise on specific routes, particularly to well-frequented tourist sights. **Note:** thieves are constantly at work on the bus system, and distracted visitors who are concentrating on not getting lost can be relatively easy targets.

Inter-town buses

The bus stations for destinations outside Jakarta lie far from the city centre and it is easier to leave Jakarta by train if possible, even if going only as far as Bogor. There are three main bus stations: **Kalideres**, on the often congested Jl. Daan Mogot, 14km west of Lapangan Merdeka, which serves destinations to the west, including Serang, Merak and Labuan; **Pulogadung**, 10km east of Lapangan Merdeka on Jl. Perintis Kemerdekaan, which handles buses to north coast towns including Cirebon,

Pekalongan and Semarang, as well as services to Yogyakarta and beyond; and **Kampung Rambutan**, which lies beside the Jagorawi toll-road to Bogor, c 18km south of Lapangan Merdeka and offers buses to the south and southeast of Java. This is the best organised of the three, but all are somewhat grim places.

Pulogadung and Kampung Rambutan share services to certain destinations, so it is wise to check first with hotel staff or at the visitor information centre to avoid a time-wasting journey to the wrong terminal. The Pulogadung terminal is likely to be replaced in 2000 or soon after with a larger site at Pulogebang, 5km further east.

Ships

Several *Pelni* passenger ships stop at Jakarta's Tanjung Priok harbour on their circuits round the archipelago, most of them bound for ports in Sumatra or Kalimantan, or directly for Surabaya. Advance bookings are recommended, but beware that ships' schedules may occasionally change with little warning. Tickets can be bought at the *Pelni* offices at Jl. Gajah Mada 14 and at Jl. Angkasa 18. Good travel agents can make the arrangements for a reasonable surcharge, saving you time and effort.

Taxis

The most comfortable way to get around the city, taxis are usually easy to find except during a rainy rush hour. Take reading material to combat boredom in the traffic jams. It is always worth seeking out *Blue Bird Group* taxis (☎ 794 1234 or 798 1001), which include Gamya, Morante, Pusaka Nuri and Cakrawasih. They are usually clean and well-maintained, with accurate meters and polite drivers who know their way around. Beware especially of *President* taxis, painted either pale blue, in imitation of *Blue Bird*, or red-and-yellow; many Jakartans consider them unsafe to use. In any case, if you are bound for a rather obscure destination, particularly in residential suburbs, you may have to direct the driver once he leaves the main highway. Expect to round up the final meter reading to the next Rp500: drivers NEVER admit to having small change. Rogue drivers do exist, and lone foreign women have occasionally encountered problems. If you feel uneasy, terminate the journey at the earliest possible opportunity, or wait for the next suitable stop in the traffic, leave the fare on the seat and jump out.

Bajaj

These noxious orange three-wheelers are banned from some main thoroughfares but can be useful for nipping through quiet back streets. The price must be negotiated in advance; bajaj drivers in central Jakarta usually begin the bargaining process with ourageous demands, so be prepared to try several and negotiate firmly. Some also have only a very hazy idea of the street layout, particularly if they are outside their normal operating district, so carry a map and be prepared to help them find the way. They can be chartered by the hour, or even by the day.

Car rentals

Driving yourself in Jakarta is not recommended unless you are used to the driving style or planning to stay several weeks. International operators like *Budget* (☎ 568 6524) and *Hertz* (☎ 252 3333) will only rent cars with a driver, and this is expensive ($75 per day or more).

For self-drive rentals of several weeks or more, for a driving tour through Java or further afield, the best deals are from local rental companies. Recommended is *Toyota Rent a Car* at Gedung Toyota Astra Motor on Jl. Sudirman (☎ 573 5757), which has a good range of Toyota sedans and Kijangs. Monthly

rates start from c $700, but are open to negotiation. The price can be negotiated to include insurance, breakdown rescue and servicing, and *Toyota Rent a Car* has offices in Bandung, Surabaya and elsewhere, so may also allow the car to be dropped off at your destination. Before you set off, make sure you know exactly what is and what is not included in the price, and what to do in the event of breakdown or accident.

Hotels

If on a brief visit, you are advised to stay as close as possible to Lapangan Merdeka, the vast grassy plain with the National Monument at its centre, which lies at the heart of the city's sights. Jakarta has many high-quality hotels, aimed primarily at the business traveller. The area ☎ code is 021. Among the best are the *Shangri-La*, the *Gran Meliá* and the *Regent*, but most of the major international chains are represented here, including *Holiday Inn Crowne Plaza* (☎ 526 8833; fax 526 8832); *Jakarta Hilton* (☎ 570 3600; fax 573 3089); *Le Méridien* (☎ 251 3131; fax 571 1633); and *Borobudur Inter-Continental* (☎ 380 5555; fax 380 9595; e-mail: jakarta@interconti.com). Several good value, mid-priced hotels have been built recently; most of these are found around Kebon Sirih, Gondangdia and Menteng in central Jakarta. The low-budget guest-houses and hostels, which are mostly gathered round Jl. Jaksa, just south of Lapangan Merdeka, tend to be appalling.

Allow yourself an increased budget for Jakarta; hotel rates are significantly higher than elsewhere, and a pleasant room in which to escape the heat and smog of the city is a wise investment. Any hotel with a room rate of much less than $35 is generally dismal. However, there is usually a glut of empty hotel rooms in the city, and heavy discounting is almost always available if you ask; never expect to pay the published rate, which is often absurdly high. With persistence (or an impressive business card and a few white lies), your bargaining skills may win you a truly excellent deal. Even when booking in advance by e-mail, you can sometimes negotiate a very good rate.

Below are listed some of the better hotels. This is by no means a comprehensive list; the visitor information centre on Jl. Wahid Hasyim can advise on others if none of these satisfy. Jakarta's travel agents can also usually obtain discounted rates at the better hotels. Price categories listed are based on their official (and often unrealistic) prices; discounted rooms can be up to 60 per cent cheaper.

☆☆☆☆☆ *Hotel Aryaduta* (☎ 231 1234; fax 380 9900; e-mail: 2096395@ mci-mail.com) Jl. Prapatan 44–48. Very central location with an excellent Italian restaurant. Refurbished in 1997.

☆☆☆☆☆ *Grand Hyatt* (☎ 390 1234/310 7400; fax 334321) Jl. Thamrin. Extremely comfortable hotel with a large shopping mall below, in a very convenient location.

☆☆☆☆☆ *Gran Meliá* (☎ 526 8080; fax 526 8181; e-mail: granmel@indo.net.id) Jl. Rasuna Said. Futuristic design and eye-catching lobby; good rooms and excellent cuisine. Aimed at the business traveller.

☆☆☆☆☆ *Hotel Indonesia* (☎ 230 1008/390 6262; fax 230 1007/314 1508) Jl. Thamrin. The grande dame of Jakarta's hotels, opened in the early 1960s and now outclassed by newcomers despite recent refurbishment; has nostalgic appeal and excellent location.

☆☆☆☆☆ *Mandarin Oriental* (☎ 314 1307; fax 314 8680; e-mail: reserv@mojkt.co.id) Jl. Thamrin. For many years one of Jakarta's finest

hotels, but now facing more competition. Outstanding cuisine and high-quality furnishings.

☆☆☆☆☆ *The Regent* (☎ 252 3456; fax 252 4480) Jl. Rasuna Said. The top business traveller's hotel, with excellent facilities, in central business location.

☆☆☆☆☆ *Shangri-La* (☎ 570 7440; fax 570 3533; e-mail: sljktbc@rad.net.id) Kota BNI, off Jl. Sudirman. Opulently furnished hotel with very good food.

☆☆☆☆☆/☆☆☆☆ *Hotel Omni Batavia* (☎ 690 4118; fax 690 4092) Jl. Kali Besar Barat 46. One of the few hotels in Kota, but somewhat scruffy for a hotel which opened in 1995. Pleasant dining facilities.

☆☆☆☆/☆☆☆ *Hotel Bumi Johar* (☎ 314 5746; fax 314 5759) Jl. Johar 17–19. Clean and friendly with straightforward rooms. No pool. Opened March 1997.

☆☆☆☆/☆☆☆ *Hotel Cemara* (☎ 390 8215/314 9985; fax 324668/324417) Jl. Cemara 1. Reasonable-sized rooms and good value compared to others in same price bracket. No pool.

☆☆☆☆ *Paragon* (☎ 391 7070; fax 316 0715) Jl. Wahid Hasyim 29. Not as good value as the Cemara or Bumi Johar, but pleasant rooms and friendly staff in a good location.

☆☆☆ *Hotel Marcopolo* (☎ 230 1777/325409; fax 310 7138) Jl. Teuku Cik Ditiro 19. Despite its ugly appearance, this offers excellent value. Spacious, clean rooms with TV, mini-bar and pleasant bathrooms; decent pool.

☆☆☆ *Wisma Internasional Gondia* (☎ 390 9221/5672; fax 390 5673) Jl. Gondangdia Kecil 22. Good value, simple air-conditioned rooms in small garden on quiet lane. TV and phone; friendly and very relaxed.

☆☆☆/☆☆ *Hotel Alia Cikini* (☎ 392 4444/334589; fax 392 8640) Jl. Cikini Raya 32. One of the best low/mid-priced deals in Jakarta. Reasonable rooms, small pool.

Restaurants, cafés and bars

There is a colossal choice of eating establishments in Jakarta, ranging from restaurants with Michelin-rated chefs to simple pavement *warung* serving plain fried rice. You can find freshly cooked food almost everywhere, though it must be said that some does not look too appetising. However, unless you are a diehard *warung* enthusiast, Jakarta is not the best place for pavement eating: the roads are busy, the air is polluted and the heat is exhausting. Often a good venue for Indonesian dishes is the top floor (or sometimes basement) of a shopping mall, which is given over to a dozen or more stalls offering different dishes. There are numerous fast-food chain restaurants, including *A&W, Dunkin' Donuts, KFC, Häagen-Dazs, McDonald's* and *Sizzler*, as well as branches of *Planet Hollywood, Hard Rock Café*, and the *Fashion Café*. Below are a few recommended eateries, listed from north to south in the city, where you can get off the street and into cooler, more relaxing surroundings; in your wanderings you will stumble across dozens more.

Café Batavia Beautifully furnished but rather pricey bar and restaurant on Taman Fatahillah in Kota, near the Puppet Museum and old City Hall. Well worth a visit if sightseeing in the area.

Queen's A good-value Tandoori restaurant at Jl. Veteran I/6, near the Istiqlal mosque. A few doors down are two others, also justifiably popular: *Maharani* at 17 and *Sahara* at 23.

J.J.'s Jl. Tanah Abang II, west of Lapangan Merdeka and next to the Tanamur nightclub; good international food.

Ambiente An expensive Italian restaurant in *Hotel Aryaduta*, Jl. Prapatan, serving superb food; excellent service.

Hazara Jl. Wahid Hasyim, near *Hotel Arcadia*. A delightful Indian restaurant with a simple bar upstairs, complete with pool table and darts board.

Sarinah food court In the basement of the *Sarinah* department store, corner of Jl. Thamrin and Jl. Wahid Hasyim. Packed with office workers at lunchtime. Tasty, cheap food, but rather dimly lit environment.

Oasis Jl. Raden Saleh, Cikini. For *rijsttafel* in an old Dutch house and garden. Average food in a pleasant setting; a favourite for Jakartans with out-of-town guests.

Plaza Indonesia food court on the top floor of the eponymous shopping mall, with a wide range of Indonesian and Western food all day long. Adjoining the *Grand Hyatt*, Jl. Thamrin.

Spice Garden A top-class Sichuan restaurant in the *Mandarin Oriental*, Jl. Thamrin; very highly regarded, but not cheap.

Tokyo Joe An extremely good, expensive Japanese restaurant in the *Mandarin Oriental*, Jl. Thamrin, which Japanese visitors love.

Zigolini's An excellent but pricey Italian restaurant in the *Mandarin Oriental*, Jl. Thamrin.

B.A.T.S The popular *Bar At The Shangri-La*, Kota BNI, off Jl. Sudirman, has live jazz, terrific food and a funky atmosphere.

Empire Grille A revolving restaurant at the top of Menara Imperium, Jl. Rasuna Said, near the *Regent Hotel*. Marvellous views over the city at dusk.

Plaza de España A very relaxed Spanish restaurant at the *Holiday Inn Crowne Plaza* on Jl. Gatot Subroto, with tasty tapas and flamenco dancing; fun to visit with a group.

Plaza Senayan food court in Plaza Senayan. The best and most expensive food court in Jakarta, with especially good Japanese food.

Han Kuk Kwan Panin Bank Centre, Jl. Sudirman 1. Excellent Korean food, highly rated by Korean residents.

Koi Gallery Jl. Mahakam I/2, Blok M.

Reasonable food in an art-gallery setting.
Balemang Jl. Wijaya, east of Blok M.
Highly rated Italian and Asian food.
Nasi Kapau Jl. Melawai, Blok M. Not
cheap, but some of the very best spicy
Padang food in town, according to afi-
cionados.
Sushi Tengyoku Jl. Radio Dalam, south
of Blok M. A long way to go, but well
worth it for sushi lovers.
Café Granita Jl. Kemang, near
Kemchicks supermarket in south
Jakarta. Superb coffees and good food.
Twilight Café Jl. Kemang, near
McDonald's. Reliably good Indonesian
food and a very pleasant atmosphere.

Information and maps
Staff at the visitor information centre **(pelayanan
informasi pariwisata**; open Mon–Fri
08.30–16.30, Sat 08.30–14.00) in the
Teater Djakarta on Jl. Wahid Hasyim
can answer specific questions about
sights and transport; the main Jakarta
city tourism office is inconveniently
located at Jl. Kuningan Barat 2 near the
intersection of Jl. Gatot Subroto and Jl.
Rasuna Said, and is less used to answer-
ing casual inquiries. The excellent
Jakarta Citymap published by Falk to the
scale 1:15,000 is the best street map
and usually can be found in the city
bookshops. The *Jakarta* map by Nelles to
the scale 1:22,500 is more widely available outside Indonesia, but is not as
accurate. Locally published maps (scale
1:20,000) are nearly as good and
cheaper. Falk also publishes a superb
street atlas covering Greater Jakarta
and beyond, which is highly recommended if you plan to stay awhile.

Money
In central Jakarta, *Bank Duta*
(M, V) in Hotel Indonesia is
one of the few that does not charge
commission for credit-card transactions.
BII (M, V) has useful branches on Jl.

Thamrin in Plaza BII and Plaza
Indonesia. *Hongkong Bank* at the World
Trade Center on Jl. Sudirman has an
ATM which accepts Visa cards. *BCA* (M,
V) in Wisma BCA on Jl. Sudirman is effi-
cient. *American Express Bank* is in
Graha Aktiva on Jl. Rasuna Said, with
another branch at Jl. Melawai 7, Blok M.
Major credit cards are widely accepted in
hotels, restaurants and shops, but some
– especially travel agents – like to impose
a surcharge for credit-card purchases.

Post and telecoms
The central post office (open
daily 08.00–20.00) on the
corner of Jl. Lapangan Banteng Utara
and Jl. Gedung Kesenian has a poste
restante service (counter 55; address
mail to Poste Restante, Kantor Pos
Pusat, Pasar Baru 10710, Jakarta
Pusat). Stationery can be bought from
kiosks inside and from street vendors
outside on Jl. Pos. The philatelic office
(Kantor Filateli) is also on Jl. Pos.

Convenient **postal counters** are
also found in Sarinah (5th floor) and
in Plaza Indonesia (basement), both on
Jl. Thamrin. Kota's post office is on the
north side of Taman Fatahillah, next
to Café Batavia. In Menara Cakrawala
on the corner of Jl. Thamrin and Jl.
Wahid Hasyim is a **24-hour telecoms
office**, across from the visitor information office; another is at Gambir station.

Medical services
Highly regarded hospitals
(*rumah sakit*), with well-
trained staff and English widely spoken include *MMC* at Jl. Rasuna Said,
kav. 21, Kuningan (☎ 520 3435),
where a typical consultation will cost
upward of $80; and *Medistra* at Jl.
Gatot Subroto, kav. 59 (☎ 521 0200).
There are scores of pharmacies in the
city where most common medicines
can be purchased.

Travel agents and tours

Vayatour, with branches in Plaza Chase on Jl. Sudirman (☎ 570 4119), in Wisma Nusantara at Jl. Thamrin 59 (☎ 310 0720), and at Landmark Center I on Jl. Sudirman (☎ 520 9755), is usually efficient and fair value; staff can arrange flights, train and ship tickets, and discounted accommodation. Other reputable agents include *Pacto* (☎ 797 5874/9) and *Satriavi* (☎ 380 3944/5813). One agent specialising in development education tours is *Bina Swadaya Tours* (☎ 425 5354; fax 425 6540; e-mail: bst@cbn.net.id).

City sightseeing tours lasting 4–9 hours cost $20–50 per person and can be arranged by most agents. Full-day tours include lunch and can be a relaxing way to see several sights if time is short. One company to try is *Boca Pirento* (☎ 668 2029/30; fax 668 2035); it can also be worth asking at the visitor information centre on Jl. Wahid Hasyim for recommended tours.

Bookshops and libraries

Times Books in Plaza Indonesia on Jl. Thamrin has probably the best range of general English-language books and magazines. Sarinah, also on Jl. Thamrin, has a good selection of books about Indonesia. *Gramedia* on Jl. Melawai III at Blok M and the branches of *Gunung Agung* in Atrium Shopping Centre on Jl. Senen Raya, in Plaza Blok M at Blok M, and at Jl. Kwitang 38, have fewer books in English, but are among the best for Indonesian-language books and locally published provincial and district maps.

The **State Library** (Perpustakaan Negara) on Jl. Salemba Raya is open to the public for research purposes and houses a large collection about Indonesia. The **Australian Embassy** and **Erasmus Huis** (the Dutch cultural centre), both on Jl. Rasuna Said, as well as the **British Council** in the S. Widjoyo Centre on Jl. Sudirman, all have excellent libraries (☎ 719 1947) with books about Indonesia, together with newspapers, books and magazines from their respective countries. The **Indonesian Heritage Society** has an excellent library (☎ 719 1947) about Indonesian culture, but is usually open only to members.

Performing arts and cultural events

There is plenty for the arts enthusiast in the city, and most art exhibitions, concerts and stage performances are listed in the 'Where to go in Jakarta' column of the *Jakarta Post* or in the more comprehensive *What's On Jakarta Program*, a monthly listings magazine. Each year since 1994 there has been a two-month international arts festival, Festival Istiqlal, held from September to November, with events taking place in all the city's major arts venues.

Taman Ismail Marzuki (TIM; ☎ 334740; open Tues–Sat 09.00–21.00, Sun 07.00–21.00) at Jl. Cikini Raya 73 is the city's primary arts centre and home of the Jakarta Arts Council. Opened in 1969, the complex sprawls over 8ha and houses several theatres, art galleries, exhibition halls, a planetarium, a dance studio and an arts institute. Named after a local composer, Ismail Marzuki, TIM hosts a huge variety of events, including music, dance, theatre, films and poetry readings, as well as all kinds of art exhibitions including sculpture and photography, both foreign and local; the planetarium has some shows in English. Within the complex are several food outlets.

Gedung Kesenian Jakarta (Jakarta Arts Building; ☎ 380 8283), a neo-Classical Empire-style building on the corner of Jl. Pos and Jl. Gedung Kesenian, also has a wide-ranging programme, which usually includes ballet and dance, concerts and solo recitals. Once a month there is a *wayang orang* performance, usually an episode from the *Ramayana* or another classical tale. Built as a theatre—the Schouwburg—in 1821, it was used in 1945 for the first sitting of a preparatory independent Indonesian parliament. The monthly programme is usually available from the visitor information centre on Jl. Wahid Hasyim.

Wayang Orang 'Bharata' (☎ 421 4937). The same troupe which performs the *wayang orang* at Gedung Kesenian Jakarta performs most evenings at its own theatre on Jl. Pasar Senen, near the intersection with Jl. Kalilio and Jl. Gunung Sahari I. A visit is recommended. This classical theatre tradition is kept alive by the Bharata Foundation (Yayasan Bharata), whose office is at Jl. Kalilio 15.

There are numerous other venues which host occasional performances and exhibitions. The **Gedung Pameran Seni Rupa** (Art Exhibition House) at Jl. Medan Merdeka Timur 14, opposite Gambir station, is a government-run venue which has sporadically hosted art exhibitions since 1988. Short *wayang kulit* or *wayang golek* performances are staged on most Sunday mornings at the **Puppet Museum** at Jl. Pintu Besar Utara 27 in Kota and/or at the **National Museum on** Jl. Medan Merdeka Barat; check at the visitor information centre for the latest schedules. The **Goethe Institut** (☎ 850 9132) at Jl. Matraman Raya 23, the **British Council** (☎ 252 4115) in the S. Widjoyo Centre on Jl. Sudirman, and the **Centre Culturel Français** (☎ 390 8580) at Jl. Salemba Raya 25, all show occasional films in their respective languages; the **Australian Embassy** (☎ 522 7111) on Jl. Rasuna Said hosts art exhibitions. **Erasmus Huis** (☎ 525 2321/0571), the Dutch cultural centre, also on Jl. Rasuna Said, holds both art exhibitions and concerts, and hosts the **Indonesian Heritage Society** (☎ 548

1553), which has occasional seasons of weekly evening lectures in English on different aspects of Indonesian culture. The Indonesian-American Cultural Center on Jl Pramuka is also patron to regular events.

There are several galleries run by private foundations, including **Galeri Lontar** at Jl. Utan Kayu 68/H (☎ 856 7502, 857 1121) and Bentara Budaya, owned by the Kompas publishing group, which stage well-produced exhibitions. The Galeri Foto Jurnalistik Antara (closed Mon) on Jl. Antara, across the canal from Gedung Kesenian Jakarta, sometimes holds noteworthy photo exhibitions.

Sports facilities

Apart from a swimming pool or tennis court, which your hotel may provide, there are a few sports available to casual visitors. There are half a dozen golf courses in Jakarta open to the public. Most central are the **Senayan Golf Course** on Jl. Asia Afrika (☎ 571 0181) and the more expensive **Jakarta Golf Club** on Jl. Rawamangun Muka in east Jakarta (☎ 489 5107/2347). There are many others in the suburbs and nearby towns. Jet-skiing, mountain-biking, triking, paragliding and microlight-flying, swimming and golf are all available at the excellent **Lido Lakes** complex run by ☆☆☆☆/☆☆☆ *Hotel Aryaduta Lido* (☎ 0251 242020; fax 242017), c 80km south of Jakarta at Jl. Raya-Sukabumi Km21. There is a good ten-pin bowling alley in the **Megamal** at Pluit, north Jakarta, which was used for the 1997 Southeast Asian Games; and you can go ice-skating at **Mal Taman Anggrek**. At the *Strike Zone* in the **Senayan sports complex** off Jl. Sudirman you can practise baseball batting, while munching on (almost) genuine all-American hot dogs. White-water rafting trips on the **Citarik River** near Pelabuhanratu, 150km south of Jakarta, are run by *BJ's Rafting*, Jl. Duren Tiga 42/A in south Jakarta (☎ 794 5923). For the more sedate, there are usually a number of chess players hanging out for a challenging game from a passer-by along the pavement of Jl. Gedung Kesenian, near the central post office.

Shopping

Still one of the best shops for **Indonesian crafts** is *Sarinah*, on the corner of Jl. Thamrin and Jl. Wahid Hasyim, home of Jakarta's first escalator. Several floors are dedicated to batik, ikat, wooden carvings, *wayang*, and a score of other arts and crafts from across the archipelago. Prices are fixed, but fair. An equally good selection can be found at Blok M's *Pasaraya* department store. For **groceries** and other daily needs the supermarkets in the basement of Sarinah and in Plaza Indonesia are convenient.

You will need expert knowledge to buy genuine **antiques**, but a huge variety of interesting trinkets and dusty, ancient-looking bric-à-brac can be found in the Jl. Surabaya flea market in Menteng or in a few shops on Jl. Kebon Sirih Timur, off Jl. Wahid Hasyim. In both cases, bargain hard: initial asking prices are absurd.

Most of the better **art dealers** and **galleries** are in the affluent suburbs of south Jakarta. There are dozens in the city, but recommended as a starting point are *Duta Fine Arts Gallery* at Jl. Kemang Utara 55/A; *Oet's Gallery* at Jl. Palatehan I/19 at Blok M, with another branch, called *Ikawati Gallery*, at Jl. Kemang Utara 15; *Hadiprana Gallery* at Jl. Palatehan I/38; *Edwin's Gallery* at Jl. Kemang 21; and Galeri Teguh at Jl. Gaharu I/3, Cilandak Barat. Prices are not low. *The C-line Gallery* in south Jakarta has established a reputation for showing works of the best young artists.

Wooden furniture of variable quality is found along Jl. Ciputat Raya in south Jakarta, where several dealers have large warehouses and workshops repairing old pieces and producing replicas. They can arrange shipment and will search for specific pieces, but woodworm can be a problem and the wood does not always travel well to less humid climates.

Before leaving the city it is worth visiting some of the fashionable **shopping malls** which have appeared in recent years, even if only to gawp. *Plaza Indonesia*, beneath the Grand Hyatt, Jl. Thamrin, was for several years the home of Mammon in Jakarta, but has been eclipsed by *Plaza Senayan*, which has an astonishing number of very expensive international designer boutiques. *Megamal* in Pluit, north Jakarta, is a comparatively downmarket but huge shopping mall. Most Jakartans, however, still do their grocery shopping in humble local markets.

History

Sunda Kelapa to 1527 The coastal region round Jakarta has been settled by humans since prehistoric times, but clear evidence of a port here dates from the 12C, when a harbour called Sunda Kelapa served the inland Hindu-Buddhist kingdom of Pajajaran near present-day Bogor. Early as Muslim traders transferred their business to other ports, among them Sunda Kelapa and its western neighbour, Banten. In 1526 or 1527 Sunda Kelapa was seized from Pajajaran by Muslim forces from Demak in central Java, who renamed it Jayakarta; they took Banten at the same time.

Jayakarta, 1527–1619 For the next 90 years Jayakarta played a largely subordinate role to Banten, the dominant pepper-trading port in the archipelago. However, the first Dutch expedition to the East Indies, led by Cornelis de Houtman, reached Banten in 1596, signalling the start of Dutch interest in the islands which would eventually make Jayakarta the region's most important city.

For the next 20 years Jayakarta was caught up in a power struggle involving ever-shifting alliances between Dutch, Portuguese and English traders, the powerful state of Banten and the prince of Jayakarta, who was seeking to assert his independence from Banten. De Houtman's financially profitable voyage spawned a flood of private Dutch expeditions to the Indies and led to the establishment in March 1602 of the Amsterdam-based Vereenigde Oost-Indische Compagnie (VOC or 'United East India Company'). Formed by the merging of competing trading companies from across the Netherlands, and controlled by a powerful board of directors known as the Heeren XVII ('Seventeen Gentlemen'), the VOC was granted quasi-sovereign powers by the Dutch states-general to build fortresses and wage war throughout Asia to benefit Dutch trade. The Company, based initially in Ambon, established trading posts in Banten in 1603 and in Jayakarta in 1611, with a view to making the latter its permanent base.

This opportunity arose in late 1618 when Banten, with English support, moved to defeat Jayakarta and the Dutch. An English admiral, Thomas Dale, acting for Banten, sailed into Jayakarta's harbour where he attacked a small Dutch fleet under Jan Pieterszoon Coen. Coen, outnumbered, prudently withdrew to Ambon to fetch a larger fleet, and returned in May 1619. By this time the Bantenese had broken their alliance with Dale, who fled, and had driven off Jayakarta's ruler and occupied the town, leaving the VOC garrison marooned in its fortress. The Company, meanwhile, engaged alternately in drunken debauchery and prayer, and renamed the town Batavia, after the ancient Germanic kingdom which once existed between the Waal and the Rhine. Upon his return, Coen drove out the Bantenese, razed the town, and set about building Batavia as a new base for the VOC.

Batavia and the VOC, 1619–1799 For many years after 1619, Batavia remained largely cut off from its hinterland. By seizing the port, Coen had upset Sultan Agung, the ruler of the powerful central Javanese kingdom of Mataram, who had intended to control the harbour for himself. Faced with attacks from Agung's forces, the Dutch forbade Javanese to live within the city walls. In August 1628, Agung's army of 60 ships and 10,000 men reached the city, only to succumb to hunger and disease. After a siege lasting four months, the remnant withdrew, first executing the commanders who had failed them. A larger force in 1629 suffered the same fate, leaving Batavia free from any further threat from Mataram.

17C Batavia lay at the heart of a Dutch trading empire that stretched from Cape Town to Japan. It was clearly Dutch in character, with canals and architectural styles transplanted from Europe to such an extent that a visitor in the 1680s considered it an even finer town than Amsterdam. The land, however, was low-lying and flood-prone. The canals, unable to cope with the heavy rains, harboured typhoid and dysentery; fish-ponds, dug between the city and the sea from the late 1720s, provided the perfect breeding ground for mosquitoes, and malaria epidemics started sweeping through the city from 1733.

Ships began to shun the port. Captain James Cook, calling here in late 1770, saw most of his crew go down with sickness, with seven deaths. The city's wealthier residents moved inland in search of a more healthy location, spreading down Molenvliet (present-day Jl. Gajah Mada) to Weltevreden (Lapangan Banteng). The once fine merchant houses on the canals of Kota were deserted or became coach houses.

In the late 17C, the population numbered about 30,000, of whom half were slaves. The wealthiest Europeans owned 100 slaves or more, but the majority of slave-owners were in fact Chinese, who had been trading here since before the Dutch arrived. A new, clumsily implemented immigration policy led in 1740 to an anti-Chinese pogrom, which destroyed for good the previously friendly relationship between Dutch and Chinese in the city.

Batavia's decline dates from this point; its commercial strength was further undermined by smuggling rackets, corruption and mismanagement by VOC personnel, and growing competition from the English. Under the Treaty of Paris in 1784, which ended the Anglo-Dutch war in Europe, the VOC was forced to abandon its trade monopoly and allow English merchants into the archipelago. By the end of the 18C the VOC was bankrupt.

Dutch colonial rule, 1800–1942 The VOC was dissolved formally in 1800, but the Company's city had already crumbled. In 1795 the Netherlands fell to the French, and the new regime sent Marshal Daendels to be Governor-General (1808–11). He moved the seat of government to Weltevreden and tore down the old city walls. A century of growth under the Dutch, with a brief British interregnum (1811–16) under Thomas Stamford Raffles, restored Batavia's fortunes to the extent that by 1930 the population was more than 500,000.

The 19C saw the emergence of the orang Betawi, an ethnic grouping unique to Batavia, which evolved from the huge number of ethnically mixed marriages within the city among diverse groups from across the region. In the 17C and 18C the Dutch had brought slaves from the outer islands of the archipelago (especially Bali and south Sulawesi) and from Luzon, the Coromandel coast, Malabar, Bengal and Arakan, and encouraged other free settlers (Chinese, Moors from south India, Malays, Balinese, Ambonese and Japanese) to come to Batavia. With the abolition of slavery in 1812, the ex-slaves were free to settle in the city, and were gradually absorbed into the dozens of other groups until the separate ethnic identities were largely lost. The orang Betawi ('Batavia people') came to be characterised by their strong Islamic beliefs, their own language (unusually, a distinctive dialect of Malay in the midst of a region dominated by Sundanese), their own social ceremonies, dress, music, dances and oral traditions. The orang Betawi still exist, but are very much a minority in modern Jakarta, having been superseded by more recent waves of immigrants, especially in the post-Second World War period.

Jakarta after 1942 The Japanese occupied Batavia, and renamed it Jakarta, during the Second World War. After the Japanese surrender, Indonesian independence was proclaimed here by Sukarno and Hatta in August 1945, but in September forces of Lord Louis Mountbatten's British Southeast Asia Command arrived to secure the islands. For a while in 1946, Jakarta was a disputed enclave in a sea of republican territory: the surrounding rice lands were held by republicans, and the city itself was divided among them, the British and Dutch. The young republican government withdrew to Yogyakarta from mid-1947 to 1949, and the Dutch briefly ran Jakarta once more, until the final transfer of sovereignty in December 1949.

In the postwar period Jakarta has experienced immense population growth, from one million in 1948, to nearly 11 million today. Sukarno shifted the hub of the city from the colonial squares to the Jl. Thamrin-Jl. Sudirman axis, demanding that all buildings along Jl. Thamrin be at least five storeys high; this plan backfired, as most of the government departments which held land along Jl. Thamrin could not afford such extravagance. He envisaged a modern city of grandiose buildings and statues; slums were to be swept away and replaced with tower blocks. His dreams, however, were not affordable. By 1965, with inflation at absurd levels, mounting corruption, bureaucratic inefficiencies, and Sukarno's plans growing ever more ostentatious, Jakarta's infrastructure was crumbling once more.

On coming to power in 1965, Suharto appointed a retired marine general, Ali Sadikin, as mayor and subsequently governor of Jakarta (1966–77). Sadikin mounted a massive clean-up and refurbishment of the city, coupled with an authoritarian rule which got things working again but made life miserable for the poorest – the slum dwellers and becak drivers.

The tower blocks that Sukarno had wanted finally began to appear in the 1990s. However, the once ubiquitous becak all but vanished, perceived by the planners of the shiny modern metropolis to be an embarrassment of backward technology. Most of these tricycles were finally rounded up in the early 1990s and carried off to other Indonesian towns or dumped off the coast. But while more than a million people had once depended on them – directly or indirectly – for a living, little new employment was created in their place. Today, unless you have a car or can afford the taxi fare, a voyage round Jakarta's streets entails an uncomfortable, frustratingly slow ride on a crumbling bus, or else a deafening, exhaust-inhaling caper in a decrepit orange *bajaj*. The streets cannot cope with the volume of rush-hour traffic, so commuters spend hours every day in sluggish or stationary queues, or they go shopping till the traffic has cleared. It is easy to understand the appeal of the elegant, air-conditioned shopping malls; there's little possibility of most Jakartans affording what's on offer, but window-shopping is free and the air is chilled.

The riots of 1998 In early 1998, with the Indonesian economy in tatters, Jakarta's university students were in the vanguard of those calling for economic and political reform and for President Suharto's resignation. Their protests began as peaceful but vociferous campus demonstrations, but the killing in early May of four students by security forces on the Trisakti University campus in eastern Jakarta triggered a wave of public anger which ultimately brought about Suharto's downfall. Those Jakartans frustrated by the growing unemployment and economic hardship found a worthy cause in the student-led, anti-Suharto demonstrations. Increasingly the anti-government feeling was expressed in riots and the looting of shopping malls, among them Slipi Plaza, just off the Jl. Parman toll-road, which was burnt down.

The Chinese commercial district of Glodok, in the north of the city, was also a popular target, with many shops razed and their owners attacked – and in some horrific cases, raped, burned and murdered. Students, meanwhile, occupied the parliament at Senayan in central Jakarta and remained there till Suharto announced his resignation on 21 May.

Renewed rioting in November 1998 claimed at least 16 lives, as protesters demanding greater and faster political and economic reform clashed with security forces armed with tear gas and plastic bullets at the Atma Jaya University campus in the city centre. This time, the fighting spread along Jl. Sudirman in the central business district, the heart of the city's wealth.

The following week a vicious gang fight in north Jakarta between Muslims and Christians led to 11 churches being attacked, with seven destroyed or severely damaged; at least three people were hacked to death. By early 1999, calm had been restored to the city, although tensions still occasionally flared in certain neighbourhoods.

Exploring Jakarta

To visit Jakarta's sights in historically chronological order, you should start at Kota and Sunda Kelapa, the site of the earliest settlement, and move southwards to Lapangan Merdeka, Gambir and Menteng. However, for practical reasons, it is recommended that visitors start their exploration at Lapangan Merdeka and leave Kota for another day. Lapangan Merdeka is closer to most hotels, it provides easy terrain for walking or taking a *bajaj* between sights, and is close to a large number of restaurants and cafés (round Jl. Agus Salim and Jl. Wahid Hasyim) in which to rest tired feet or quench your thirst while adapting to the city's rhythms. The heat, pollution and traffic jams take their toll on the unsuspecting visitor, so do not try to see too much in one day.

Lapangan Merdeka

The **National Monument** (Monumen Nasional or Monas; open daily 08.30–17.00), an obelisk soaring more than 130m at the centre of Lapangan Merdeka, is a fitting place to start a city tour. Begun in 1961 to celebrate the 16th anniversary of the nation's independence, and opened to the public in the early 1970s, this marble-clad structure, topped with a flame of gilded bronze, offers a wonderful panorama across the city in all directions. Its design vaguely represents the Hindu symbol of the *linga*, the stylised phallus, which partially explains its ribald nickname, 'Sukarno's last erection'.

In the basement are 48 well-crafted dioramas, representing key moments in Indonesia's history from 3000 BC up to the 1969 'act of free choice' in West New Guinea. An elevator carries visitors to the viewing platform just below the top, where there is often a refreshing breeze.

Lapangan Merdeka (Freedom Square), the vast green square surrounding the monument, was used in the late 18C for grazing animals. This was forbidden after 1809, when Governor-General Daendels made it a military training ground known as the Champs de Mars. The historian Adolf Heuken narrates how a local butcher sought (in vain) to be made a member of the Raad van Indië (Council of

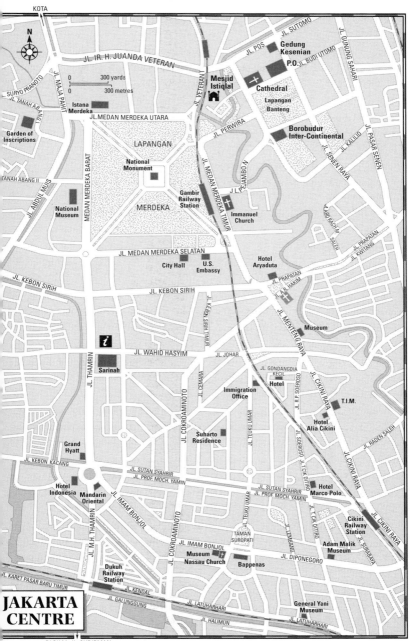

KOTA

N

JL. IR. H. JUANDA VETERAN

JL. SUTOMO

JL. POS

Gedung Kesenian

P.O.

JL. BUDI UTOMO

JL. GUNUNG SAHARI

0   300 yards
0   300 metres

SURYO PRIANOTO

JL. MAJA PAHIT

Mesjid Istiqlal

JL. VETERAN

Cathedral

Lapangan Banteng

JL. TANAH A.BANG I

Istana Merdeka

JL.MEDAN MERDEKA UTARA

JL. PERWIRA

Borobudur Inter-Continental

JL. KALLIO

JL. PASAR SENEN

JL. SENEN RAYA

Garden of Inscriptions

JL. ABDUL MUIS

LAPANGAN

MEDAN MERDEKA BARAT

National Monument

JL. P.CIAMBON N

JL. SENEN RAYA

TANAH ABANG II

National Museum

MERDEKA

Gambir Railway Station

JL. MEDAN MERDEKA TIMUR

Immanuel Church

K.ABU.RAGM.H. SALEH

JL. PRAPATAN

JL. KWITANG

JL. MEDAN MERDEKA SELATAN

City Hall

U.S. Embassy

Hotel Aryaduta

JL. PRAPATAN

JL. KEBON SIRIH

JL. KEBON SIRIH

JL. A.R. HAKIM

JL. MENTENG RAYA

Museum

JL. KEBON SIRIH HIBUS

i

JL. WAHID HASYIM

JL. JOHAR

JL. GONDANGDIA KECIL

JL. CIKINI RAYA

Hotel

Sarinah

JL. THAMRIN

JL. CEMARA

JL. COKROAMINOTO

Immigration Office

JL. R.P. SOEROSO

T.I.M.

JL. TEUKU UMAR

Suharto Residence

Hotel Alia Cikini

JL. SOEROSO

JL. TCIK DITIRO

JL. RADEN SALEH

Grand Hyatt

JL. KEBON KACANG

JL. SUTAN SYAHRIR

JL. PROF. MOCH. YAMIN

JL. SUTAN SYAHRIR

JL. PROF. MOCH. YAMIN

Hotel Marco Polo

JL. CIKINI RAYA

Hotel Indonesia

Mandarin Oriental

JL. IMAM BONJOL

JL. COKROAMINOTO

Cikini Railway Station

JL. SURABAYA

JL. M.H. THAMRIN

JL. TEUKU UMAR

TAMAN SUROPATI

JL. LEMBANG

Adam Malik Museum

JL. KARET PASAR BARU TIMUR

Dukuh Railway Station

JL. IMAM BONJOL

Museum

Nassau Church

Bappenas

JL. DIPONEGORO

JAKARTA CENTRE

JL. KENDAL

JL. GALUNGGUNG

JL. LATUHARHARI

JL. HALIMUN

General Yani Museum

JL. LATUHARHARI

BLOK M, JL. SUDIRMAN

the Indies), the colonial governing body which was exempt from such a ban, so that he might graze his cattle there.

After 1818 the square, renamed Koningsplein (King's Square), was built upon, but since independence most buildings have been cleared away. **Gambir Station** remains but has been raised on stilts, and several statues have been erected; the square is still undergoing alterations. To the north of Monas is a bronze **equestrian statue of Prince Diponegoro** (1785–1855), who led a five-year revolt against the Dutch in central Java before being tricked into captivity in 1830. The sculpture was donated to the nation by a former honorary consul in Italy. Nearby is a bronze **bust of Chairil Anwar** (1922–49), who, despite his short and wild life, is considered one of Indonesia's finest poets. A poem he wrote in 1943 entitled *Diponegoro* is inscribed on the plinth. West of Monas is a **bust of Mohammad Husni Thamrin** (1894–1941), a nationalist and member of the Volksraad (People's Council) who campaigned for Betawi estate workers' rights. Considered a potential troublemaker by the Dutch as they prepared for war with Japan, he was arrested in January 1941 for communicating with the Japanese. Already terminally ill, he died in custody five days later.

National Museum

West of the square is the National Museum (Museum Nasional or Museum Pusat; open Tues–Thur and Sun 08.30–14.30; Fri 08.30–11.30; Sat 08.30–13.30), which has the finest prehistoric, ethnographic, ceramic and Javanese Hindu-Buddhist art collections of any Indonesian museum. The first acquisitions were made by the Batavian Society for the Arts and Sciences, a colonial scientific institution founded in 1778 by J.C.M. Radermacher, a member of the Council of the Indies. He met an untimely death in 1783, killed by mutinous Chinese crew on his ship. The present Neo-classical building dates from the 1860s. In front stands a bronze elephant sculpture donated by King Chulalongkorn of Siam during his visit in 1871. (He took away with him several notable Hindu-Buddhist statues from temples in central Java and stone reliefs from Borobudur, now in the National Museum in Bangkok.)

There are **guided highlight tours** in English (Tues–Thur at 09.30, and the last Sunday of the month at 10.30), French (Wed at 09.30) and German (Thur at 10.00), usually given by knowledgeable expatriate volunteers; these tours are highly recommended.

In the **entrance hall** sit large andesite images of the Buddha from Borobudur and a *padrão*—a tall, inscribed stone of Portuguese origin, originally erected on the city's foreshore in 1522 (which at that time was just 450m north of today's Taman Fatahillah) to commemorate a friendship treaty between Portugal and the king of Sunda. The stone was unearthed on present-day Jl. Cengkeh during building work in 1918. In a room to the left can be seen the saddle and lance of Prince Diponegoro. The **inner courtyard** is filled with a great number of Hindu and Buddhist stone sculptures, relief panels and early inscriptions, mostly unprovenanced, collected by Dutch administrators from sites in central and east Java, Sumatra and Kalimantan. Most striking among them is the colossal 4.4m high, mid-14C statue of the demonic Buddhist deity, Bhairava, from Padang Roco in west Sumatra. This image, probably a portrayal of Adityavarman, the ruler of a local kingdom called Malayu, stands on a corpse which lies on a bed of skulls; in his hands he holds a sacrificial knife and a skull-bowl. Adityavarman espoused an esoteric doctrine which emphasised the redeeming effects of such rituals as dancing on cremation grounds and uttering diabolical laughter. Inscriptions from the period describe how devotees drank the blood of human victims from such skull-bowls.

Rooms on the courtyard's south side display fine **textiles**. At the west end is a magnificent collection of Chinese **ceramics**, including pieces from the Han dynasty (206 BC–AD 220), an extensive Ming collection, early examples from Vietnam and Thailand, and fine 17C–19C Japanese wares. In adjoining rooms are wooden scale models of traditional Indonesian houses, a noteworthy collection of early bronzes, mostly of Hindu deities, and some marvellous bronze **kettledrums**, bronze and brass *moko*, and prehistoric tools and weapons. Galleries along the north side of the courtyard house a large ethnographic collection. Upstairs is an air-conditioned **treasure room** with intricate gold kris scabbards, jewellery and betel-nut containers. Many of the gold artefacts come from a spectacular hoard unearthed in late 1990 and early 1991 in *desa* Wonoboyo near Prambanan in Central Java, which yielded many silver items and more than 32kg of gold objects. The trove has been dated palaeographically to the late 9C or early 10C from inscriptions found on some of the pieces.

Around Lapangan Merdeka

South of the National Museum, at the intersection of Jl. Thamrin and Jl. Medan Merdeka Selatan, is a dramatic polyester-resin **sculpture** of a chariot drawn by eight horses, entitled *Ardjuna Victorious*, made in 1987 by a Balinese sculptor, Nyoman Nuarta (b. 1951).

Northwest of the museum on Jl. Tanah Abang I is the rather strange, but historically interesting, **Garden of Inscriptions** (Museum Taman Prasasti; open Tues–Thur and Sun 09.00–15.00; Fri 09.00–14.30; Sat 09.00–12.30). Set into the walls at the entrance are numerous tombstones, mostly from the 17C and 18C, which were brought here from old churches and graveyards in Jakarta as these were demolished and their sites redeveloped. Most are from families of important Dutch merchants and government officials. For example, second from left outside the entrance is one dedicated to Pieter Janse van Hoorn (d. 1682) with 'HK No.26' etched heavily into it (denoting 'Hollandsche Kerk' or Dutch Church). He was a gunpowder manufacturer in Holland who later became a member of the Council of the Indies. He served briefly as ambassador to Peking (1666–68), and his son later became Governor-General in Batavia (1704–09). On the same stone can be read 'F. Tack', referring to François Tack, van Hoorn's son-in-law, who died in the Kartosuro *keraton* near Solo (see p 337) in 1686 while doing battle with the forces of Untung Suropati, the Balinese rebel leader.

The **cemetery** here is all that remains of a much larger 18C–19C graveyard, razed in the 1970s. Among the tombs is that of Olivia Raffles (1771–1814), wife of Thomas Stamford Raffles, the Lieutenant-Governor of Batavia (1811–15) and founder of Singapore (1819), who had her buried beside their close friend, John Leyden (d. 1811). The distinguished archaeologists J.L.A. Brandes (1857–1905) and Willem Stutterheim (1892–1942), who were responsible for many early archaeological discoveries in Java, are buried here, as is Major-General A.V. Michiels, Commander-in-Chief of the 1849 expedition to Bali, who died there of his battle wounds.

On the north side of Lapangan Merdeka is **Istana Merdeka** (Freedom Palace), the president's official residence. Built in the 1870s to replace the smaller Istana Negara (State Palace) which faces Jl.Veteran to the north, it was used originally for official receptions by Dutch governors-general, who named it Koningsplein Paleis. Later, commanders of the Japanese occupation army lived here, followed by Sukarno, who survived a 1960 assassination attempt here by a rebel air force pilot in a MiG fighter. Apparently there is still a bullet hole in one of the mirrors in the front hall, where today the president receives the credentials of foreign ambassadors.

Istana Negara, to the north, was built at the end of the 18C as a private country house. When the owner died in 1820 it was bought by the colonial government for use by the governor-general, until it became too small and Istana Merdeka was built. Next door is **Bina Graha**, a modern building where cabinet meetings are held; also nearby, on the corner of Jl. Juanda and Jl. Hayam Wuruk, is the former **Hôtel des Galeries** (1930), a now shabby but once striking Art Deco building similar to some in Bandung.

On the south side of the square, near the fortified American Embassy, is the present-day **City Hall** (Balai Kota), whose offices were moved here from Taman Fatahillah in 1925.

Opposite Gambir station on the corner of Jl. Pejambon is the Neo-classical **Immanuel Church** (Gereja Immanuel), a circular, domed building with portico extensions to east and west and surrounded by Palladian columns. Named Willemskerk on its completion in 1839, in honour of King Willem I of the Netherlands (r. 1813–40), it once held an exuberantly baroque pulpit, which was lost during the Japanese Occupation, when the church became a repository for the ashes of fallen Japanese. It was renamed Immanuel Church in 1948, and since then has belonged to the Protestant Church of West Indonesia.

East of the Ciliwung river on Jl. Pejambon are two buildings of interest. Just across the bridge is a white building now inscribed 'BP-7'. This was built in 1927 as the new meeting hall for the **Council of the Indies**. A short distance further on is the **Pancasila Building** (Gedung Pancasila), a single-storey structure in front of the Department of Foreign Affairs. Built c 1830 as the residence for commanders-in-chief of the colonial army, in 1918 this palace became the meeting hall of the People's Council, the part-elected, part-appointed 'parliament' which had very limited powers. Initially most members were Europeans, and even after reforms in the 1920s, Indonesians could only just claim a majority. During the Japanese Occupation the Committee for the Preparation of Independence met here to decide policy. The present name dates from 1 June 1945, when Sukarno delivered a speech here, *Lahirnya Pancasila* ('The birth of Pancasila'), in which he listed five concepts to be included in the state philosophy. The five which were finally incorporated into the Preamble of the 1945 Constitution—belief in God, humanitarianism, nationalism, democracy and social justice—did, in fact, vary somewhat from his speech.

Lapangan Banteng

The square at the north end of Jl. Pejambon, known today as **Lapangan Banteng**, was in the early 19C a military parade ground. At the centre is a remarkable bronze **sculpture**, *The Liberation of Irian Jaya*, by Edhi Sunarso, celebrating that territory's transfer from an interim United Nations administration to Indonesian sovereignty in May 1963. Depicting a muscular giant who has just torn apart the chains binding his arms and legs, it was based on a sketch by Sukarno and Henk Ngantung, Governor of Jakarta (1964–65) and respected artist, whose work can be seen in the Art Hall and Ceramic Museum (see below). Watch where you walk here: the area beneath the monument is used as an open toilet.

The Empire-style building on the east side of the square, now housing the **Department of Finance**, was begun in 1809 by Marshal Daendels, who intended it to be his new palace. But he was recalled by Napoleon in 1811 and it was left to his successor, Governor-General Jan Willem Janssens, to complete it; he put a temporary *atap* roof on the unfinished parts before it was finally completed in 1828.

The Neo-classical building at the north end of the palace was added 20 years later; this was the **High Court**, which after independence continued to be used as the supreme court, Mahkamah Agung, until the current, modern one was built near Istana Merdeka on Jl. Medan Merdeka Utara.

Across Jl. Budi Utomo is another neo-Classical building, once a 19C **Masonic lodge**, now a pharmacy. The Lodge, called *De Ster in het Oosten* ('The Star in the East'), was known locally as 'Satan's House' on account of its mysterious, secretive visitors. On the northwest side of the square is a neo-Gothic **Catholic cathedral** with notable spires, dating from a 1901 reconstruction on the site of an early 19C church. The architect's plans were based on a design by the assistant parish priest, A.P.M. Dijkmans.

West of Lapangan Banteng stands the city's most important mosque, **Mesjid Istiqlal** (Independence Mosque), which was completed in 1978. The largest in Indonesia, it is open to conservatively dressed visitors.

Sunda Kelapa and environs

Kota, the site of old Jayakarta, the 16C coastal settlement founded by Fatahillah, has several interesting sights, though none date from that early period. Go first to the small harbour of **Sunda Kelapa** (Pelabuhan Sunda Kelapa), where a long row of several dozen Bugis *pinisi*, the traditional wooden-hulled cargo ships from south Sulawesi, are always to be seen discharging or loading cement and timber; a constant stream of porters bowed under heavy loads picks its way nimbly along precarious gangplanks. Boatmen beside the wharf will row visitors round the harbour for a small, negotiable fee; go early or late in the day to avoid the hot sun.

South of the harbour gate, cross the evil-smelling Ciliwung river—here lined with rickety shacks of corrugated iron—and turn west on Jl. Pakin over the even more malodorous Kali Besar. On the northwest side of the bridge is the small **Uitkijk** (lookout or harbour-master's tower), built in 1839. It stands on the site of an earlier fort, the **Culemborg bastion**, dating from 1645, built by the VOC to control the seaward entrance to Batavia. Opposite the tower, on the south side of Jl. Pakin, can be seen **old VOC buildings**, now very dilapidated. These were part of a shipyard for the repair of small ships which could sail up the Kali Besar.

A lane to the north off Jl. Pakin leads to the **Maritime Museum** (Museum Bahari; open Tues–Thur and Sun 09.00–15.00; Fri 09.00–14.30; Sat 09.00–12.30), located inside some magnificent VOC warehouses once used for storing spices, coffee, tea and cloth. Known as **Westzijdsche Pakhuizen** ('Warehouses on the West Bank'), the original structures were built in the mid-17C but have

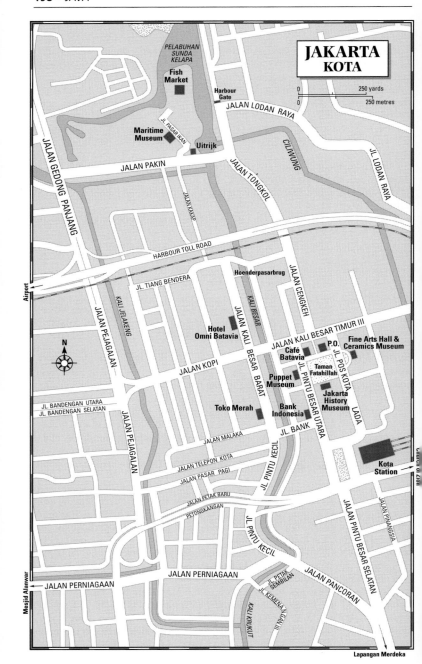

JAKARTA
KOTA

PELABUHAN
SUNDA
KELAPA

Fish
Market

Harbour
Gate

JALAN LODAN RAYA

0   250 yards
0   250 metres

Maritime
Museum

JL. PASAR IKAN

Uitrijk

JL. LODAN RAYA

JALAN PAKIN

JALAN TONGKOL

CILIWUNG

JALAN GEDONG PANJANG

JALAN KAKAP

HARBOUR TOLL ROAD

Airport

JL. TIANG BENDERA

Hoenderpasarbrug

JALAN CENGKEH

KALI JELAKENG

JALAN PEJAGALAN

KALI BESAR

Hotel
Omni Batavia

JALAN KALI BESAR BARAT

N

JALAN KALI BESAR TIMUR III

Fine Arts Hall &
Ceramics Museum

Café
Batavia

P.O.

JL. POS KOTA

JALAN KOPI

JL. PINTU BESAR UTARA

Puppet
Museum

Taman
Fatahillah

LADA

JL. BANDENGAN UTARA
JL. BANDENGAN SELATAN

Toko Merah

Bank
Indonesia

Jakarta
History
Museum

JALAN PEJAGALAN

JALAN MALAKA

JL. BANK

JALAN TELEPON KOTA

JL. PINTU KECIL

Kota
Station

Church of Zion

JALAN PASAR PAGI

JALAN PETAK BARU

PETONGKANGAN

JALAN PINTU BESAR SELATAN

JALAN PINANGSIA

Mesjid Alanwar

JALAN PERNIAGAAN

JL. PINTU KECIL

JALAN PERNIAGAAN

JL. PETAK
SEMBILAN

JL. KEMENANGAN III

JALAN PANCORAN

KALI KRUKUT

Lapangan Merdeka

been renovated many times. Their preservation is an ongoing problem as salt-water seepage threatens the foundations.

The museum collection comprises several fishing boats and scaled-down replicas from various parts of the archipelago, displays of fishing techniques and equipment, marine fauna and early maps.

Along the lane north of the museum is a **fish market** (*pasar ikan*) and ship's chandlers; to catch the lively market in full swing, you need to be here very early (04.00–05.00). A pungent, fishy smell hangs in the air all day, and the lanes are strewn with nets and buoys.

Back on Jl. Pakin, turn south along Jl. Kakap past the back of the old VOC ship-yards and beneath the toll-road bridge, to reach Jl. Kali Besar Barat on the west bank of the stinking canal. A few metres further south is the distinctive **Hoenderpasarbrug**, a renovated 17–18C Dutch drawbridge spanning the Kali Besar, which once separated the Chinese and Indian merchant quarters.

Further south along the west side of Jl. Kali Besar Barat are some fine old buildings, among them the old **Toko Merah** ('red shop'), a notable brick building built c 1730 as two separate houses.

History

Toko Merah's original owner was Gustaaf Willem Baron van Imhoff (1705–50; Governor-General 1743–50), a social reformer and member of the Council of the Indies who clashed frequently with Governor-General Adriaan Valckenier (Governor-General 1737–41), especially over the latter's handling of gangs of unemployed and illegal Chinese immigrants, who by 1740 were plundering the countryside outside the city walls. Valckenier's decision to arrest and deport them caused panic among the well-established Chinese community in the city, which believed that the VOC was going to take them too and throw them to the sharks offshore. In October, after some Europeans were killed by a Chinese gang, Valckenier imposed a curfew and ordered a search of Chinese houses for weapons. The search quickly grew out of control and unleashed a ferocious anti-Chinese sentiment in the rest of the population, which exploded into a brief but bloody slaughter of between 5000 and 10,000 Chinese throughout the city. Van Imhoff blamed Valckenier for the Chinese killings and consequential revolts elsewhere in Java. In December Valckenier arrested van Imhoff and sent him back to the Netherlands, only for the VOC's board of directors there to appoint him the next Governor-General and send him straight back to Batavia. Valckenier, meanwhile, was arrested in Cape Town on his way home, and brought back to Batavia, where he later died in prison.

In Toko Merah, van Imhoff set up a marine academy to improve the education of naval officers. On his death he was buried in the new Dutch Church on the site of the present-day Puppet Museum, where his tombstone can be seen. Toko Merah is now an office of P.T. Dharma Niaga.

Taman Fatahillah and environs

400m northeast from Toko Merah is **Taman Fatahillah**, an island of calm amidst heavy traffic. On the west side of this paved square is a large **bronze cannon**, known as Si Jagur, which was probably brought to Java by the Portuguese in the 16C. On the south side is the old **City Hall**, the third to be built on this site since 1620.

History

Finished in 1710, the City Hall housed upstairs a magistrates' court which sat three times a week, and the *Raad van Justitie* (Council of Justice), which was the highest court until the mid-19C. Prisoners were kept on the ground floor and in another building behind while awaiting trial or sentence. Beneath the hall were more dungeons, poorly ventilated and susceptible to flooding. Many cases never got to trial: in the mid-19C, typically 85 per cent of detainees died within four months, mostly from dysentery or typhus. Executions took place in the square each month, watched over by the judges from the balcony upstairs. While most of the condemned were hanged or guillotined, some suffered a hideous death by impalement, a process which could last several days. A European visitor in 1676 witnessed four beheadings, one hanging, six broken on the wheel, and eight whipped and branded. One infamous prisoner who passed through here was Prince Diponegoro, brought here from Magelang in 1830 after his five-year rebellion against the colonial powers, before being exiled to Sulawesi, where he died in 1855.

The City Hall has housed the **Jakarta History Museum** (Museum Sejarah Jakarta; open Tues–Sun 09.00–15.00) since 1974, but in recent years has been almost empty of exhibits. The interior of the building is worth a look nevertheless.

On the east side of the square is the **Fine Arts Hall and Ceramics Museum** (Balai Seni Rupa dan Museum Keramik; open Tues–Sun 09.00–15.00). This fine neo-Classical building, completed in 1870, replaced the City Hall as the home for the Council of Justice. Reopened as an arts museum in 1976, it contains a substantial ceramics collection donated to the nation in 1974 by Adam Malik, Indonesia's vice-president (1978–83) and prolific art collector. Nearly all the paintings here are also from his collection. They include works by many of Indonesia's most admired artists, among them Affandi, Basoeki Abdullah, Dede Eri Supria, Dullah, Hendra Gunawan, Nyoman Gunarsa, Popo Iskandar and Widayat. Classical Balinese art styles are also well represented.

This is the best permanent modern art collection in Jakarta open to the public, but sadly the building is terribly neglected, with mildewed walls and rising damp. In the courtyard is a bronze bust of S. Sudjojono, who with Affandi, Hendra Gunawan and Sudjana Kerton, is considered one of the fathers of modern Indonesian painting.

Across the busy Jl. Pintu Besar Utara on the west side of the square is the **Puppet Museum** (Museum Wayang; open Tues–Thur and Sun 09.00–15.00, Fri 09.00–14.30, Sat 09.00–12.30), built on the site of the old Reformed Church (1640–1732), Batavia's main church in the 17C.

History

Jan Pieterszoon Coen (1587–1629), the city's founder, was buried in a cemetery here, as were 18 governors-general after him. The church was replaced by a new Dutch Church (1736–1808), which then was damaged by an earthquake and subsequently demolished by Marshal Daendels; a godown was later erected on the site. The present façade dates from 1912, but the building behind was built in 1938. From 1939–73 it housed the Museum of Old

Batavia (which then moved to the City Hall), and in 1975 reopened as the Puppet Museum.

Upstairs is a huge array of traditional puppets—*wayang golek*, *wayang kulit* and *wayang kelitik*, some more than 180 years old. There are many unusual ones: *wayang kulit kancil*, depicting giraffe, deer, modern human beings and trees; a set of *wayang kulit wahyu* made in 1960 by a Catholic priest in Solo for performances at Christian festivals, with puppets depicting hell, Adam and Eve, St Peter and the Crucifixion of Christ; and a set of *wayang suluh* ('instructional puppets') made in the 1940s for an anti-Dutch propaganda campaign, which includes depictions of Sukarno and Willem Schermerhorn, the former Dutch Prime Minister who led the Dutch delegation in the independence negotiations at Linggajati in 1946–47. There are fine Chinese puppets, huge one-piece scenes from Cambodia, and others from India, Malaysia, Vietnam and Europe.

In a small court downstairs are old **gravestones** which once lay in the two old churches on this site. Most were transferred to the Garden of Inscriptions on Jl. Tanah Abang I, but a few remain here, including that of Governor-General van Imhoff.

For a rest and refreshment, step into the *Café Batavia* on the north side of Taman Fatahillah; the food is good, the decor wonderful, the prices high.

The alley leading north between the café and the post office holds a busy **market** which spills out into Jl. Kali Besar Timur III; look out for the snake-tonic vendor, who has been slitting his snakes here most mornings for many years.

Before leaving the Taman Fatahillah area, spare a quick look for the grandiose *Bank Indonesia* on the south corner of Jl. Pintu Besar Utara and Jl. Bank, which was built in 1909 as the Javasche Bank.

More notable is the **Church of Zion** (Gereja Sion) on Jl. Pangeran Jayakarta, a short way southeast of Kota station.

History

The oldest church in Jakarta, Gereja Sion was completed in 1695 but has been restored repeatedly, most recently in 1978. Inside is the original pulpit—a magnificent baroque structure dating from 1695—and some of the old ebony pews, copper chandeliers, the beautifully carved organ casing and elaborate chairs. Buried here is Governor-General Hendrik Zwaardecroon (1667–1728; Governor-General 1718–25), who donated his garden beside the graveyard to the church. His wish to be buried beside the common people was fulfilled, and he is the only governor-general still lying in his original burial site.

The church is connected historically with the *Mardijkers* or 'liberated ones'—mostly south Asians brought to Batavia as prisoners from former Portuguese trading posts in south and southeast Asia captured by the Dutch in the mid-17C. The richer ones among the prisoners, including the 'pure' Portuguese, settled within Batavia's walls. The poorest, however, were enslaved and could only buy their liberty by renouncing Catholicism and joining the Dutch Reformed Church; those that did became the *Mardijkers*. As their community expanded in this area—outside the city walls—they established a cemetery in 1655; they built a shed on the site in 1676 for catechism classes, and this was later replaced by the church. Despite there being no true

Portuguese here, the church became known by the Dutch as Portugeesche Buitenkerk ('Portuguese church outside the walls'), a name which lingers on today through its local appelation, Gereja Portugis.

Glodok and Jl. Gajah Mada

Glodok, the heart of Jakarta's present-day **Chinatown**, lies c 600m south of Kota station. This is a frantically busy, rather grubby shopping area of market stalls and shop-houses where all manner of Chinese foodstuffs and trinkets can be found; much of Glodok was razed during the riots of May 1998, when Jakarta's Chinese community found itself the scapegoat for the nation's political and economic troubles. On Jl. Petak Sembilan, which runs parallel to the murky water of Kali Besar, is one of the oldest surviving Chinese temples, **Klenteng Jin-de Yuan** ('Temple of Golden Virtue'). It dates from the mid-17C but has been renovated many times; numerous Buddhist—and a few Taoist—deities can be seen inside. Nearby, on Jl. Kemenangan III, is another Chinese temple, **Da-shi Miao**.

West of Glodok, along Jl. Perniagaan and then Jl. Pangeran Tubagus Angke, you will arrive after c 1700m at a small mosque, **Mesjid Alanwar** (Mesjid Angke), the most noteworthy of several old mosques in the neighbourhood west of Kota and Glodok. Built in 1761 by a Chinese for Balinese Muslims who then occupied the district, it has an unusual winged door and a two-storey tiled roof.

South of Glodok, the twin thoroughfares of Jl. Gajah Mada and Jl. Hayam Wuruk link Kota and Lapangan Merdeka, following the course of the old Molenvliet canal. About 1km south of Glodok, on the west side of Jl. Gajah Mada, is the **Museum of National Archives** (Museum Arsip Nasional), a beautiful Dutch mansion built in 1760 by Reinier de Klerk (1710–80). He arrived in Batavia as an ordinary seaman but climbed steadily through the ranks, becoming a member of the Council of the Indies and finally Governor-General (1777–80).

Menteng and Senen

At the centre of the traffic circle outside *Hotel Indonesia*, 1500m south of Lapangan Merdeka on Jl. Thamrin, stands a **bronze sculpture** from 1962, raised on high concrete pylons, entitled *Welcome* and depicting two walking figures, their arms raised in greeting. The artist, Edhi Sunarso, later sculpted *The Liberation of Irian Jaya* in Lapangan Banteng.

Southeast of the monument, near Taman Suropati, is the small, and these days rarely visited, **Museum of the Drafting of the Proclamation Text** (Museum Perumusan Naskah Proklamasi; open Tues–Sun 09.00–12.00) at Jl. Imam Bonjol 1.

History

Before the Second World War this was the British consul's residence. Later it belonged to Japanese vice-admiral Maeda Tadashi, who held remarkably progressive views on Indonesian nationalism. Early in 1945 he used Japanese naval funds to finance Mohammad Hatta and Sukarno on a speaking tour across the archipelago. In the early hours of 17 August 1945, Sukarno, Hatta and the Republic's first foreign minister, Subardjo, together with prominent youth leaders, gathered in Maeda's house to draw up the text for the Proclamation of Independence, while Maeda apparently retired upstairs to bed.

There is little to see here: some furniture, a marble replica of the text, bronze busts of the three authors, and photos of the committee members who approved the final draft. Sayuti Melik, a left-wing nationalist and later minister, typed up the final version, correcting Sukarno's spelling mistakes. His bust is displayed with the typewriter in the grandly named Proclamation Text Typing Room, a tiny cubbyhole beneath the stairs. The museum will delay you for 15 minutes at most.

Next to the museum is the former **Nassau Church** (1936), and beyond that stands a former **Masonic lodge** (c 1925), now the office of Bappenas, the national development planning board.

On the grassy traffic island in front of Bappenas are **three bronze statues** of Raden Adjeng Kartini (1879–1904; see p 296), a friendship gift from Japan. The quiet neighbourhood round Taman Suropati—the former Burgermeester Bisschopsplein—remains an affluent one: the large house (1939) on the north corner of Jl. Taman Suropati and Jl. Syamsu Rizal was once the city mayor's residence; many buildings are now occupied by foreign diplomats.

A further 500m southeast of Taman Suropati, on the west corner of Jl. Lembang and Jl. Latuharhari, is the **Museum of the Revolutionary Hero General A. Yani** (Sasmita Loka Pahlawan Revolusi Jenderal A. Yani; open Tues–Sun 09.00–14.00). This is the former home of Ahmad Yani, murdered here early in the morning of 1 October 1965 during the so-called PKI coup attempt (see p 66).

The house has been left largely unchanged since his death: the old television, the once-fashionable bar furniture, his pyjamas and Old Spice shaving cream remain in place. The weapons used to kill him are displayed, and on the wall hangs a picture, its frame pierced by a bullet fired during the assault; a plaque on the floor of the dining room marks the spot where he died. Of note are the painting and photo of General Nasution's five-year-old daughter, Irma, who was fatally wounded the same night at her father's house by assassins searching for him; she died five days later. Photos in a back room show the bodies of the generals being recovered from Lubang Buaya (see below) and reconstructed scenes from the events of that night. In the front garden is a statue of General Yani.

At Jl. Diponegoro 29, 750m to the northeast, is the **Adam Malik Museum** (Museum Adam Malik; open Tues–Sat 09.30–15.00; Sun 09.30–16.00), from 1965 the home of Adam Malik (1917–84), former foreign minister (1966–78) and vice-president (1978–83), who was an art lover and enthusiastic collector. The house, with marble floors and walls, exudes a whiff of ostentatious kitsch, but is crammed with collections of Chinese, Japanese and European ceramics, walking sticks, cameras, stamps, guns and kris, Chinese ivory, radios, medals, textiles and 8C Tang dynasty Chinese martavans.

This Aladdin's cave includes a room of 16C–20C East European icons collected during Malik's time as ambassador in Moscow (1960–64), including some by Fabergé. Also displayed is a tasteless North Korean vase, a gift from President Kim Il Sung in 1983.

A block further east is the Jl. Surabaya **antiques market**, where genuine antiques may be hard to find. Further east still, on Jl. Proklamasi across the railway line, is the **Monument to the Proclaimers of Indonesian Independence, Sukarno and Hatta** (Monumen Pahlawan Proklamator Kemerdekaan

R.I. Soekarno-Hatta). The monument, inaugurated by Suharto in August 1980, consists of bronze statues c 4.5m high of Sukarno and Hatta, with a model of the proclamation document itself. The two men stood before a small crowd here at 10.00 on 17 August 1945 while Sukarno read out the proclamation of Indonesia's independence, written, corrected, approved and typed with great haste just a few hours earlier. Nearby stands a 17m-tall white column with a lightning bolt at its top; this supposedly marks the spot where Sukarno stood.

Gathered around the small pond of **Situ Lembang**, 300m northeast of Taman Suropati, are drinks and satay vendors offering welcome refreshment.

The **residence of former president Suharto** stands on Jl. Cendana to the northwest; only the guards outside distinguish it from other houses in the street. Nearby, on the corner of Jl. Teuku Umar and Jl. Cut Nyak Dien, is a rather charming building dating from 1913, used originally by the Batavian Arts Society; today it is the head office of the Immigration Department.

On the east side of Jl. Menteng Raya, a short way to the northeast, is the **Museum of the 1945 Fight for Freedom** (Museum Gedung Joang '45; open Tues–Thur and Sun 09.00–15.00; Fri 09.00–14.30; Sat 09.00–12.30). Formerly a Dutch hotel, the building was used during the Japanese Occupation by Indonesian nationalist youth groups as a venue for political meetings. Exhibits include the cars used by Sukarno and Hatta after August 1945, but the documentary displays are of little interest to non-Indonesian readers.

On the traffic circle at the junction of Jl. Menteng Raya and Jl. Hakim stands a small **bronze sculpture**, *The Farmer*, by the Russian sculptor Matvei Manizer (1891–1966), which depicts a peasant guerrilla receiving a plate of rice from a woman. Sukarno, an admirer of Manizer's work, was given it for the nation during a visit to the USSR.

A few metres away, on the south side of Jl. Hakim, is the Anglican **All Saints Church**, built in 1829 but later extended. This rather squat building replaced an earlier bamboo chapel built by the London Missionary Society in 1822. There are some tombstones of note, including that of James Bowen, captain of the *Phoenix*, who died in 1812 after an attack on 'a Powerful Pirate at Sambasse' (Sambas, on the west Kalimantan coast). The church holds some services in English.

Northeast of the church, on Jl. Abdul Rachman Saleh, is the small and almost forgotten **Museum of the National Resurrection** (Museum Kebangkitan Nasional; open Tues–Thur and Sun 08.00–14.30; Fri 08.00–11.30; Sat 08.00–13.00), which gets so few visitors that it is frequently closed during official opening hours. This was where Budi Utomo, one of the first modern nationalist movements, was founded on 20 May 1908 by Dr Wahidin Sudiro Husodo (1852–1917), Dr Sutomo (1888–1938) and politicised students from Stovia (the school for the training of native doctors), which stood on this site. Their aim was to unite the various nationalist groups under one banner and promote Indonesians' awareness of democracy and their civil rights.

A block further east is **Pasar Senen**, a busy market area with shopping centres and a local bus station. On the corner of Jl. Stasiun Senen and Jl. Kramat Bunder is a **bronze sculpture**, *Monument to National Social Solidarity*, depicting seven comrades-in-arms.

Scattered across the city are several other noteworthy sights, but such is their location that perhaps only two or three may be seen in a day.

Museum Tekstil

The Textile Museum (Museum Tekstil; open Tues–Thur and Sun 09.00–15.00, Fri 09.00–14.30; Sat 09.00–12.30) at Jl. Tubun 4 in Tanah Abang has a small but interesting display of Indonesian textiles. The late 19C building, built by a French merchant, has large columns at front and back, between which sun screens were placed to keep out the sun. The façade now sports a more recent and slightly incongruous corrugated iron canopy.

The collection includes examples of batik from most of Java's main production centres as well as lesser-known regions, including unusual pieces from Serang and Indramayu in West Java; *batik tulis* from Tulungagung; and a fine *kain panjang* from Batang near Pekalongan. There is a wonderful battledress from Irian Jaya made of woven rattan threads; bark cloth from Sulawesi; and *songket* from Sumatra. Apart from some fine double-ikat *geringsing* from Bali, however, there are very few examples of eastern Indonesia's magnificent ikat tradition.

Military museums

Reached by bus or taxi, Jl. Gatot Subroto 14, on the south of the city, houses the large **Armed Forces Museum** (Museum ABRI 'Satriamandala'; open Tues–Sun 09.00–15.30), which has a huge number of dioramas telling the authorised story of the military from the start of the independence struggle to the 1970s. This is recommended viewing for those interested in Indonesian history and politics.

Apart from the dioramas showing battles against the Dutch in the 1940s and campaigns to put down secessionist rebellions across the archipelago in the late 1950s and early 1960s, there are rooms of weaponry and uniforms. The *konfrontasi* period is illustrated, while East Timor is briefly glossed over. In the grounds outside are heavy weapons, military vehicles and aircraft.

Within the same compound is **Museum Waspada Purbawisesa**, with two more floors of dioramas and some gory photos, most of them concerned with campaigns against the Tentera Islam Indonesia (Indonesian Islamic Army) which sought to establish an Islamic state in Indonesia through the 1950s and early 1960s. More recent illustrated episodes include the 1981 hijacking of a *Garuda* jet by Muslim extremists and the bombing of Borobudur in January 1985.

War cemeteries

750m east of Jl. Rasuna Said is the **Jakarta War Cemetery** and the adjacent Dutch Field of Honour, **Ereveld Menteng Pulo** (open daily 07.00–18.00). The former contains 1181 Commonwealth graves (including 715 British, 304 Indians and 96 Australians). Among them is Brigadier A.W.S. Mallaby, whose murder in Surabaya on 30 October 1945 triggered the bloody Battle of Surabaya (see p 385). In the Dutch cemetery are 4270 graves of civilian men, women and children and soldiers, who died in Japanese prison camps in Java, Kalimantan, Sulawesi and Sumatra. The cemeteries are immaculately maintained by the Commonwealth War Graves Commission and the Netherlands War Graves Foundation; staff on site can assist in the search for a particular name.

Klenteng Sentiong

One of Jakarta's most interesting Chinese temples, Klenteng Sentiong (Wan Kiap Si or Vihara Buddhayana), is found at Jl. Lautze 38 in Pasar Baru, 900m north of Lapangan Banteng.

History

The original house on this site was built in 1736 by Frederick Julius Coyett, a member of the Council of the Indies, who amassed a collection of Javanese Hindu statues from sites in central and east Java. Governor-General Jacob Mossel, a subsequent owner of the house, who had previously been Governor in Negapatnam (Nagappattinam) in India, may have added to the collection. Mossel died in 1761, and shortly afterwards the house was bought by a Chinese man who wanted the land in order to expand an adjacent Chinese cemetery.

Under Chinese ownership, the house was converted to a Buddhist temple, and over the years it has been altered and new buildings have been erected. The old Hindu statues can still be seen, among them images of Ganesha, Durga, and Nairrita, the guardian of the southwest, astride his demon mount.

Ancol

At Ancol on the north coast, 10km north of central Jakarta, is an enormous entertainment complex, **Taman Impian Jaya Ancol**, which can be reached by bus from Kota or Senen. The attractions include a large amusement park, **Dunia Fantasi** (Fantasy World; open Mon–Sat 14.00–21.00; Sun 10.00–21.00), offering fairground rides and other entertainments designed primarily for children. Nearby are **Gelanggang Renang**, a water park with slides and a wave machine; **Gelanggang Samudra**, an oceanarium with performing marine mammals; and **Seaworld** (open Sun–Fri 09.00–20.00; Sat 09.00–21.00), with an underwater viewing tunnel. The whole complex gets very crowded at weekends, but in midweek is quiet. There are dozens of food stalls, and an **art market** set up by a philanthropic art collector, Ciputra, to help struggling artists. At the northwest corner of the site is a marina from where boats depart for the nearby Thousand Islands archipelago (see p 208).

The road heading east along the sea front from Ancol leads to **Ereveld Ancol** (open daily 07.00–18.00), a Dutch war cemetery containing the remains of more than 2000 men and women who were executed or died during the Japanese Occupation; many have been transferred from cemeteries in Kalimantan, Sulawesi and Sumatra. Among those buried here are 130 officers and men of the Commonwealth, thought to have been victims of mass executions carried out by the Japanese in early 1942.

500m further east, reached along Jl. Pantai Sanur V, is **Klenteng Ancol** (Da-bo-gong Miao; temple to Da-bo-gong), a mainly Taoist Chinese temple which dates back to the mid-17C or earlier. Pork is forbidden at the temple site, despite the Chinese love for the meat, because it is also a sacred place for Muslims: in addition to the Chinese deities, there is a tomb of two Muslims in a room behind the main sanctuary. Little is known of their origin.

This temple, awkward to find, is probably only worth a visit if you are in the area and have not yet seen another Chinese temple in Jakarta. Much of the site has been rather garishly renovated in recent years.

Muara Angke

Birdwatchers can visit the 27-hectare nature reserve at **Muara Angke**, reached easily by taxi from the north side of Jl. Pantai Indah Utara II on the west bank of the Muara Angke river in north Jakarta. Remarkably, considering the site is now surrounded by ever-expanding housing estates, this is the best place in Java to see the indigenous Javan coucal. The best time to visit is from November to March, when migrant species add to the numbers. There is a viewing tower near the road, and a rather dilapidated boardwalk leading through mangroves.

South Jakarta

Should you be heading north from Blok M to Jl. Sudirman, look out for the huge **bronze sculpture**, *Youth*, at the junction of Jl. Sudirman and Jl. Sisinga-mangaraja. This celebrated statue, depicting a grimacing young man carrying a flaming plate, was donated to the nation by Pertamina, the once notoriously corrupt state-owned oil and gas company. It supposedly represents the determination of youth to develop the country, but to many observers it looks more like a waiter carrying a flambéed dish, and has become known as 'Hot-plate Harry' to expatriates in Jakarta.

20km to the southeast of the city centre, near the intersection of the Jagorawi toll-road and the outer ring road, is the immense **Taman Mini Indonesia Indah** ('Beautiful Indonesia-in-miniature Park', known as Taman Mini; open daily 08.00–17.00). The park, which sprawls over more than 100 hectares, was opened in the mid-1970s as a giant cultural museum of all things Indonesian, overseen by former President Suharto's late wife, Ibu Tien. Take a bus to Kampung Rambutan terminal, then a local bus to the park.

In the grounds are pavilions representing all of Indonesia's provinces, the major ethnic groups and religions. There are aviaries; museums dedicated to fauna, insects, philately, transport, sports, the military, handicrafts and traditional costumes; a cinema with a huge Imax screen showing an introductory film about the country; cactus and orchid gardens, and much more.

There are plenty of food stalls and a monorail to run visitors round the site. Despite its distant location, Taman Mini is well worth a visit – but not on weekends or public holidays, when it is packed, or on Mondays when several parts are closed.

To the northeast of Taman Mini, c 4km by road, is **Monumen Pancasila Sakti**, off Jl. Pondok Gede Raya. This site, better known as **Lubang Buaya** ('crocodile hole'), is where the bodies of six army generals and General Nasution's adjutant were tossed down a disused well on the night of 30–31 September 1965 (see p 66). In standard history texts, the Indonesia Communist Party (PKI) is blamed for the murders; the whole truth of what happened on that night remains uncertain.

In a rather tatty museum at the site are life-size models of the victims – subsequently declared national heroes – and photographs from the event. Their bodies were later buried with full honours at the Kalibata Heroes' Cemetery in south Jakarta.

Kebun Binatang Ragunan (Ragunan Zoo; open daily 09.00–18.00), at the south end of Jl. Warung Jati Barat, 15km south of the city centre, is one of Indonesia's better zoos. In the collection are many indigenous mammals, reptiles and birds, including the Komodo dragon.

The Java Sea

Off the coast is an archipelago of small islands and atolls, **Kepulauan Seribu** ('thousand islands'), some of them of historical interest, others now popular weekend resorts for Jakarta's wealthier residents. Among those closest inshore are **Onrust**, once an important VOC shipyard and fort, and nearby **Kahyangan**, **Kelor** and **Bidadari**, on each of which stand the remains of forts.

History

> Prior to the founding of Batavia in 1619, Dutch ships were already using Onrust as a repair dock. During the 17C, a fort and hospital were established on the island, which became essential to the defence of VOC shipping, particularly from French attack. By the late 18C there were perhaps 2000 people living here, most of them ships' carpenters. Captain Cook's *Endeavour* was repaired here in 1770, and Onrust remained a busy victualling station till the English razed it in 1800.

To the northwest of Onrust is **Pulau Rambut**, an important bird reserve and the only known breeding site round Java for the milky stork. Large colonies of darters, herons, egrets, bitterns and ibises, as well as other waders, kingfishers and ducks, roost on this 18-hectare island, as well as a colony of about 20,000 flying foxes. Unfortunately, the main feeding grounds for many of these birds are the dwindling mangroves and marshes beside the airport toll-road, which are steadily being drained and built on.

The best resort islands are much further out into the Java Sea, where the water is clear and there are nesting beaches for green and hawksbill turtles. The better resorts include *Resor Kul Kul Kotok* on **Kotok** and those on **Sepa**, **Pelangi** and **Putri**. All are catering primarily for well-off Jakartans, and generally are very comfortable, if somewhat overpriced (☆☆☆☆☆/☆☆☆), and they all offer substantial discounts from Sunday to Thursday. Boats depart from Ancol Marina; bookings are most conveniently made through travel agents in the city, though there are offices at the Marina itself. For diving, it is best to book direct through a diving centre; *Aquasport* (☎ 719 9045; fax 719 8974) or *Laut Dive Indo* (☎ 750 4963; fax 750 4969) are both recommended. Some of the best reefs for diving are found round **Kotok** and **Gosonglaga**; **Peniki** and **Papa Theo** have wrecks lying offshore. For snorkelling, Kotok is among the best.

Banten, Krakatau and the west coast

Highlights include the fortress ruins and historic mosque of Banten, once the busiest trading port in the archipelago; a boat ride to Krakatau (see p 218), the active island volcano in the Sunda Strait; and the magnificent Ujung Kulon National Park (see p 221), which provides Java's last remaining habitat for the Javan rhino. Don't expect to see this rare and elusive mammal: instead, visit the park for the fine coastal scenery, forested hiking trails and the chance to see nesting turtles, water monitors and herds of banteng and Timor deer.

Practical information

Travel advice
Jakarta to Banten Lama is c 90km via the Jakarta–Merak toll-road. Banten to Carita is 73km via Pandegelang, or 74km via Ciomas and Padarincang. The route is flat and rather dull from Jakarta to Serang, but from here the road to Labuan winds round the foot of two forest-covered volcanoes, Gunung Karang and Gunung Pulosari. Recommended for travellers with their own transport is the very scenic and quiet route from Serang to the coast via Ciomas. Note that traffic on the west coast is very heavy at weekends, when the entire area is best avoided.

Public transport
Frequent **buses** leave Jakarta's traffic-snarled Kalideres bus terminal to Serang, from where minibuses ply the road to Banten Lama. Buses to Pandegelang and Labuan leave Serang all day long. From Labuan, minibuses run north along the coast road to Carita's resorts and Anyar. **Trains** run to Serang and Banten from Jakarta's Tanah Abang station, but they have to go through Rangkasbitung to the south, and are very slow.

Private transport
Take the Jakarta–Merak toll-road west to the Banten Lama exit at Km 71.5. To avoid Serang town centre, turn right immediately after passing through the toll-gate and at the next T-junction turn right to pass under the main road. Follow this country lane north for 11km and then turn left to Banten Lama (not signed), past salt marshes and fishponds. After 6km, the road crosses the railway line and immediately ahead lie the ruins of the **Kaibon Palace**, the first visible sign of old **Banten**.

Accommodation
The coast between Labuan and Anyar has a huge number of hotels and resorts. Serang (see p 214) has the best accommodation near to the sights of old Banten, while Rangkasbitung (see p 215) makes a pleasant stop en route to Bogor.

BANTEN
• • • • • • • • •

History
The kingdom of Banten dates back to the 11C–12C, and possibly to the early 10C. A stone inscription, dated 932 and written in an old Malay script, mentions a kingdom known as Sunda that was based at Banten Girang, c 4km

south of present-day Serang. Until the 13C it was a vassal of Shrivijaya, the powerful Sumatran-based empire, but by the 15C it seems to have come under the suzerainty of Pajajaran, a Hindu-Buddhist kingdom based near present-day Bogor. Banten's territory comprised the Sunda Strait coast, a part of Java's north coast, and Gunung Pulosari. It was an important trading state even before the arrival in 1511 of Portuguese seeking spices; Chinese merchants had long been coming here, attracted by the high-quality pepper grown inland near Pandegelang and in southern Sumatra.

Banten's Hindu rulers, threatened by the expanding Muslim kingdom of Demak in central Java and recognising they were unlikely to receive protection from their suzerain, Pajajaran, which by the 16C was in terminal decline, sought a deal with the Portuguese, granting them unlimited access to pepper supplies in return for providing a naval defence for the port. Negotiations were concluded in 1522, but it took nearly five years for the Portuguese to sail home, obtain Dom João III's accord, and return. As they arrived offshore in late 1526 or early 1527, forces loyal to Demak under the command of Hasanudin seized Banten and prevented the Portuguese from landing. Hasanudin quickly took control of the lucrative pepper trade, granting limited access to the Portuguese, and in the mid-16C took advantage of the death of the sultan of Demak to end Banten's obligations as its vassal state. He probably moved the royal residence from Banten Girang to Banten port in the 1530s, though Banten Girang remained a country residence for Banten's Muslim rulers till at least the end of the 17C. By Hasanudin's death c 1570, Banten had become one of southeast Asia's largest cities and its power extended over most of west Java and a large part of southern Sumatra.

The arrival of the Dutch The first Dutch expedition to the East Indies, led by Cornelis de Houtman, reached Banten in June 1596, using maps stolen from the Portuguese by Dutchman Jan Huygen van Linschoten while in Portuguese employ. This was a tremendous blow to the Portuguese, who till then had held a monopoly on the valuable European spice trade. De Houtman's men were impressed by Banten's size, which compared favourably to that of Amsterdam, and by its population of traders from ports across the Indian Ocean and South China Sea.

The end of the 16C, however, signalled a decline in Banten's fortunes. Its ruler, Hasanudin's grandson, Maulana Muhamad, was killed in 1596 during an ill-planned military expedition against Palembang in Sumatra. He left no adult successor, and a power struggle followed.

The first English expedition arrived in 1602, under Sir James Lancaster, to find Banten on the verge of civil war over how to deal with the recently arrived Dutch traders. In 1601, the Dutch had crushed the Portuguese in a naval battle in the Bay of Banten, fought partly for control of the spice trade, but fuelled by their religious differences: the Dutch Calvinists resented the Portuguese Catholics' excellent relations with Banten. As the Bantenese squabbled among themselves, both Dutch and English took their business elsewhere: the Dutch to Jayakarta (Batavia), the English to Legundi, an island in the Sunda Strait.

After the seizure of Batavia by Jan Pieterszoon Coen in 1619, the VOC blockaded Banten in the hope of winning its trade. While Banten, in return, embargoed pepper exports to Batavia, it was unable to prevent many merchants from transferring their allegiance to Batavia. By the 1630s, with its economy greatly weakened, Banten was forced into a peace treaty with Batavia.

Recovery and growth In the mid-17C Banten became the main trading base for the English East India Company, which had given up on Legundi in 1628. The port's fortunes were boosted further in the 1660s, when the VOC in Batavia forced all Portuguese traders to leave Makassar, the main port of south Sulawesi. For 20 years the Portuguese there had operated a highly profitable trade with Manila, selling goods in return for Spanish silver coin. Banten took over this trade from 1663.

Banten's shrewd minister of foreign trade, a Chinese named Kaytsu, also set up a Bantenese trading company with its own fleet, captained by Europeans, which could compete directly with the various European Companies in the port. The city also benefitted from the decline of other ports in the region. By 1680 the English and Dutch trading posts had been joined by Danish, French, Portuguese, Indians and Chinese. Pepper stocks had recovered and Banten experienced a second boom period, only to end as the first had at the start of the 17C, over an internal power struggle, this time between Sultan Ageng and his son, Sultan Haji. It ended with Haji besieged in his own palace by his father, appealing to the Dutch in Batavia to rescue him. The VOC seized the opportunity to take control of Banten in 1682, expelling all foreigners and demanding a monopoly of the pepper trade. They tore down the city's fortifications and built Fort Speelwijk at the harbour entrance. For the next 120 years Banten was under VOC control.

In the colonial period after 1800, Banten fell into decline as the Dutch moved the local administration to Serang, and the harbour was allowed to silt up. Today, old Banten is a quiet fishing port.

Old Banten

Little remains today of the early-19C **Kaibon Palace** (Keraton Kaibon), built for Ratu Asyah, mother of the last sultan of Banten, except for a few split gates and partially rebuilt brick walls. Goats graze within the ruins, which are flanked to the west and south by a water-filled moat.

From the palace, cross the river to the north and immediately turn left. After 400m the road swings north beside the east wall of the **Surosowan Palace** (Keraton Surosowan). If the gates are locked, you can climb onto the wall near the east gate to see inside. The architect of this huge fortified palace was a renegade Dutchman, Hendrik Lucasz Cardeel, who had left Batavia, converted to Islam and won the patronage of Sultan Haji, the son of Sultan Ageng. Built in 1680, the fortress became Sultan Haji's refuge in 1682 when he came under attack from his furious father. A Dutch fleet from Batavia eventually rescued Haji, while his father fled inland. Ageng surrendered the following year, was imprisoned and died in Batavia in 1692.

Follow the road along the north side to the car park and food stalls; scores of souvenir stands flank the path beyond the car park, which leads to a scruffy museum, the old *alun-alun* and the mosque.

The small **archaeological museum** (Museum Situs Kepurbakalaan Banten Lama; open Tues–Sun 09.00–16.00; entry by donation) has a rather dull collection of items recovered from excavations in the Surosowan Palace and elsewhere in old Banten: large terracotta pots, coins, ceramics and tiles; of note is a damaged stone statue of Nandi, discovered during the digging of an irrigation channel, which strongly suggests the presence of a Hindu temple here prior to Banten's capture by the Islamic kingdom of Demak in 1527.

To the front left of the museum is a large, early-16C **bronze cannon** known as Ki Amuk. It bears Arabic inscriptions and is believed to have come from the Javanese kingdom of Demak. Across the path to the south of the cannon lies a low, flat-topped, **rectangular stone block** known as *Watu Gilang*, which was believed to possess divine power and was used as a throne by the sultans of Banten in times of crisis from the early 16C to late 17C.

To the west is the old *alun-alun*, and beyond that, the octagonal **minaret**, built c 1620. For a small donation to the caretaker, you can climb to the top for a good view over old Banten.

The venerable **Mesjid Agung** (Grand Mosque) is believed to date from the reigns of Hasanudin and his son, Maulana Yusuf in the mid-16C. Although rebuilt many times, the general structure appears to have remained the same: 17C travellers wrote of the unusual five-tiered roof, which it retains. Pilgrims come here throughout the year to visit the many important Muslim tombs in the surrounding cemeteries.

On the north side of the mosque is a small room containing the **tomb of**

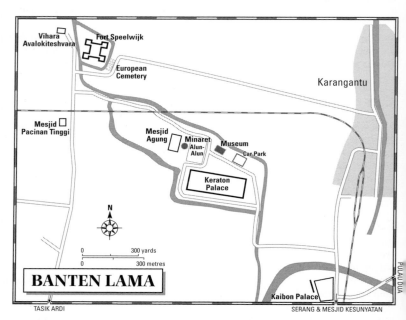

Hasanudin, who seized the city in 1527. Other important graves here belong to Maulana Muhamad, Hasanudin's grandson, who died at the siege of Palembang in 1596; Sultan Ageng Tirtayasa, who died in prison in Batavia in 1692; and his treacherous son, Sultan Haji (d. 1687), who had asked the Dutch to intervene against his father in 1682.

On the south side of the mosque is a two-storey building known as **Tiyamah**, dating probably from the 18C and containing more tombs and a small museum, which is usually open only on Sundays.

Walk or take a *becak* along the lane which heads northwest from the mosque across the railway line, and after c 250m, at the T-junction, turn north to reach the huge walls of **Fort Speelwijk** (Benteng Speelwijk), a Dutch fortress built c 1685 at what was then the harbour entrance. All that remains of the fort itself are the massive walls and some rooms in the northwest corner which may have been an armoury. Today water buffalo graze and young boys play inside the walls, and a building in the southwest corner is used as a stable.

Outside the east moat is a **European cemetery** with 18C and 19C tombstones. The coast now lies 1km further north, the result of the siltation which finally ended Banten's role as a port of any significance. From the east gate of the fort, a road runs east 1.5km to **Karangantu harbour** (Pelabuhan Karanganto), a small but busy modern port, filled with fishing boats.

Just to the northwest of the Speelwijk Fort is **Vihara Avalokiteshvara**, a Chinese Buddhist temple which, despite many renovations, probably dates from the early 18C. The principal images are the Goddess of Mercy (Kuan-im) and Avalokiteshvara.

Heading south from the temple, the road crosses the railway line after c 400m and just beyond is a whitewashed, two-storey minaret—all that remains of a mosque known as **Mesjid Pacinan Tinggi**. It perhaps was a mosque for the large Muslim Chinese community in Banten, but this is uncertain.

Continuing south a further 2.5km, you reach **Tasik Ardi**, a rectangular reservoir with an artificial island at its centre. The site, dating from the early 17C, is now used for recreation, with pedalos and food stalls; it was used originally as a place of relaxation for the sultan and royal court. From 1703 it was used as a reservoir for Banten's water supply, linked by canal to the Surosowan Palace. On the way here, you can see two old, rectangular **whitewashed buildings** in the rice fields, which were used as water purification reservoirs for Banten's drinking water supply.

Pulau Dua

Just northeast of old Banten is Pulau Dua, an important 30-hectare bird reserve noted especially for its colonial-nesting species: cormorants, herons, egrets, ibises and sometimes storks. Occasionally a colony of island flying foxes roosts here. Although in fact an island, it is now most easily reached on foot past fish-ponds; the 500m-wide channel which in the 1930s separated it from the Java shore has now completely silted up. There is a walking trail in the reserve, but care must be taken during the breeding season (mid-January to mid-July) not to disturb the birds. It may at times be closed to visitors.

To get there, take the lane east across the railway line from the Kaibon *keraton*; after c 5km, near a huge tree on the left, a path leads north c 1500m past fishponds to the mangroves. Beyond is a guard post and the official trail.

From the Kaibon Palace, the main road south to Serang passes after c 300m an unusual mosque, **Mesjid Kesunyatan**. Kesunyatan was an important Islamic centre from the mid-16C, possibly founded by Maulana Muhamad's religious teacher; the mosque, although renovated, retains an old three-tiered roof and a square-based minaret.

The **tomb of Maulana Yusuf**, 700m further south and across the railway line to the east, lies in a walled enclosure surrounded by rice fields. This is another popular pilgrimage spot for Javanese Muslims, but as with most important Muslim tombs in Java, it possesses little of visual appeal to the casual observer.

SERANG

Lying 7km south of Banten, Serang is of no special interest to the visitor, but has the best accommodation close to Banten.

Practical information

Transport

There are frequent **buses** to Jakarta, Cilegon and Labuan. Two slow, economy-class **trains** pass daily through Serang to Jakarta and Merak. **Car rentals** with driver are available from agencies on Jl. Yani just east of the *wartel*. This can be a pleasant way to explore the Banten area; rates are negotiable.

Hotels and services

✫✫ *Hotel Mahadria*, Jl. Kimas Jong 12, on the south side of the *alun-alun* behind the Perjuangan '45 monument, offers clean, friendly accommodation. A cheaper alternative is the string of shabby *penginapan* at the east end of Jl. Tirtayasa. The **tourist office** (Dinas Pariwisata) is at Jl. Maulana Hasanudin 148, but is of little help. There are **banks** and a **post office** in the town centre, and on Jl. Yani two blocks east of the monument is a 24-hour **wartel**.

To reach Labuan and the west-coast resorts, there is a choice of routes from Serang. Least attractive is that through **Cilegon**, passing the sprawling P.T. Krakatau Steel complex and the adjacent industrial zone. More scenic is the main road via **Pandegelang**, which skirts the two dormant volcanoes, Gunung Karang and Gunung Pulosari. Both routes are well served by public bus. The tidy little town of Pandegelang, 23km south of Serang, is the junction for **Rangkasbitung**, of interest to those heading for Bogor (see p 223) or wishing to visit the Baduy villages in the Kendeng hills (see p 216). A third route, more beautiful and less busy, is via **Ciomas** and **Padarincang**, but this trip can only be made by private transport. The route is described overleaf.

Leave Serang on the main Pandegelang road, which passes the archaeological site of **Banten Girang** after c 4km.

Excavated in the 1980s and 1990s, Banten Girang lies on the west bank of the Cibanten. There is little to see here, except for a man-made cave with three main chambers, which is considered locally to be the meditation site of Pucuk Umun, the last Hindu priest-king of Banten Girang. To the northwest is a brick pavilion containing two visually unremarkable tombs, said in local lore to belong to two brothers who were the first in Banten Girang to convert to Islam.

Continue south 4km further to a road signed right to Batu Kuwung. This lane ascends gently through terraced fields and villages for 13km to Ciomas. At the market here a right turn (unsigned) leads past the **Batu Kuwung hot springs**, where there is a grubby hot-water public bathing pool, and where private hot- and cold-water cubicles can be rented.

To the north of this road, though not visible from the road itself, is **Rawa Danau**, the only significant swamp forest left in Java. It lies on the floor of an ancient caldera, whose form can best be seen along the road from Ciomas. Home to the endangered **Javan leaf monkey** (*surili*), the **Siamese crocodile** and a rich avi-fauna which includes the endemic **black-banded barbet**, the swamp is officially a nature reserve (**Cagar Alam Rawa Danau**), but this nominal status counts for little: for the local population it provides valuable farming land, a rich hunting ground, and a ready supply of timber. Birdwatchers may find a visit rewarding.

The Batu Kuwung road eventually joins the main coast road c 30km beyond Ciomas. Carita lies 23km south along the coast (see p 218).

RANGKASBITUNG AND THE BADUY VILLAGES

Rangkasbitung, 24km east of Pandegelang, is a neat and pleasant town with a charming residential neighbourhood of quiet, tree-lined streets. This is the start-ing point for visits to the Baduy villages in the western Kendeng hills, and can be a useful stopping point on the beautiful but slow Pandegelang–Bogor route.

Practical information

Transport

Infrequent **buses** go to Pandegelang and Labuan, and along the slow, pot-holed, but very scenic road to Bogor. Economy-class **trains** run via Rangkasbitung between Jakarta and Merak. **Minibuses** to Leuwidmar, for the Baduy villages, depart from the cen-tral market.

Hotels and services

☆☆☆/☆☆ *Hotel Kharisma Jujuluk*, with adequate rooms and a huge swimming pool, is the best hotel, but lies outside the town centre on the Jakarta road. The cheaper, more basic ☆☆/☆ *Hotel Ksatria* on Jl. Ksatria is friendly and cen-tral. Nearby is the **tourist office** (Dinas Pariwisata) at Jl. Pahlawan 13, which can arrange a permit for a visit to the Baduy. **Banks** are located near the mar-ket and minibus terminal. There is a 24-hour *wartel* on Jl. Multatuli, off the north side of the *alun-alun*.

The Baduy

The Baduy are an extremely isolated community of around 6000 ethnic Sundanese who live in the Kendeng hills south of Rangkasbitung and west of Gunung Halimun. They call themselves *orang Kanekes* ('people of Kanekes'), and the name 'Baduy' may be a derogatory epithet originally given them by their Muslim neighbours, likening them to the Arabian bedouin.

Together with several other, smaller communities in Java, they are remarkable for their strict adherence to customary rules which govern many aspects of daily life. What makes the Baduy exceptional is the extreme isolation in which they live, and the degree to which their age-old rules – increasingly impractical in today's world – still dominate their lives.

The Baduy territory is divided into an inner core and an outer buffer zone. Entry by foreigners and non-Baduy Indonesians is strictly regulated: foreigners may not enter the inner territory, while Indonesian visitors may only stay three days.

The outer Baduy The outer territory comprises 40 or so villages, which subsist largely by dry-rice cultivation on the steep hillsides. The growing of irrigated rice is not allowed, nor is the keeping and eating of animals. Cash crops are forbidden, as is the concept of profit. Objects made from modern materials are also considered taboo. Homes traditionally are built completely from vegetation-based materials and without iron nails. The only metal permitted is for personal knives. Traditional *adat* clothes are worn every day: dark blue or black clothing, with a similar coloured head sash.

There are signs that some of these traditional taboos are slowly breaking down. Youths in the outer villages are increasingly seen with radios and plastic objects, and nails are now regularly used in construction.

The inner Baduy Covering one third of the total Baduy territory, and containing one seventh of the population, the inner domain has three major settlements – Cibeo, Cikartawana and Cikeusik – and is surrounded to north, east and west by the outer territory; to the south are thickly forested hills. The inner Baduy are considered spiritually superior to the outer population. If they break the traditions they can be expelled to the outer zone, and ultimately to the world outside. In Cikeusik, spiritually the most important of the three settlements, the inhabitants dress in clothes of woven rattan threads; the two other villages have adopted more comfortable cotton. All wear white head sashes.

The whole Baduy community is led by three *pu-un*, akin to priest-kings, who have political and religious powers and live in the three inner settlements. Several times each year they tour the outer villages to ensure that the occupants are complying with customary laws. Radios, TVs, rubber sandals and other taboo-breaking objects are confiscated.

Origins and beliefs The origins of the Baduy are not clear. Until recently, the dominant theory was that they were refugees from Pajajaran, the Hindu-Buddhist kingdom based near present-day Bogor, which fell into decline and was eventually taken over by Muslim forces in the late 16C. There is very little evidence to support this, however, and the Baduy themselves deny it. Without doubt their religious ideas predate the arrival of Islam in Sunda;

they may in fact be the remnant of a religious community which followed old Sundanese beliefs with additional Hindu-Buddhist traits. Such communities of mystics are known from old texts to have existed in isolated locations – on mountain tops or at river sources – in the 10C to 12C, and would have been consulted regularly by local princes.

The physical focus of Baduy religion, which they (and many Sundanese and Javanese) consider to be the original Sundanese religion, is a terraced sanctuary called Arca Domas in the inner domain. It consists of 13 ascending terraces, on some of which stand megaliths, placed in commemoration of the community's deified ancestors. Its annual cleansing is the responsibility of the *pu-un* of Cikeusik. Near the south end of the inner territory is another, similar, holy site of marginally less importance, called Sasaka Domas, which is maintained by the *pu-un* of Cibeo.

The Baduy and the world outside With formal education not permitted and modern medicine out of reach, sickness takes a heavy toll on the Baduy. Furthermore, their territory is constantly under threat of encroachment from outside, and food production within their lands is generally not enough for self-sufficiency, yet they are forbidden to seek work outside.

While other Indonesians respect them as a source of great wisdom concerning the original ways of their ancestors, and come seeking counsel, some Baduy who have themselves ventured out to Jakarta and elsewhere are increasingly aware that life outside the Baduy lands has its advantages. Islam too is finally making inroads in the outer villages closest to the roads, where motorcycles, mosques, and houses of brick and cement are starting to appear.

Visiting the Baduy Unless you speak good Indonesian and have a specific reason for visiting the Baduy, it is probably best not to go unless you take an interpreter, since no English is spoken. Information required for a visit is available from the tourist office in Rangkasbitung. For your hosts, it is advisable to take food supplies, such as dried fish and salt, instant noodles, sugar and tea, as well as plenty of *kretek* clove cigarettes.

LABUAN AND THE COAST

Southwest of Pandegelang the road skirts Gunung Pulosari to reach the sea at **Labuan**. On weekends and holidays the coastal strip between here and Anyar is packed with visitors from Jakarta, and the road can be very congested; in midweek it is almost empty. The beaches have suffered from the mining of coral and sand for the construction industry: degradation and severe erosion have resulted in places. Nevertheless, property developers continue to build huge condominiums and resorts, catering to the comparatively wealthy Jakarta market an easy three hours' drive away.

Practical information

Transport

A constant stream of minibuses plies the coast road between Labuan and Cilegon, from where inter-town buses go to Jakarta and other towns in West Java.

Hotels and services

There are dozens of places to stay along the 40km of coast between Labuan and Anyar, with more being built. Prices rise to absurd levels on Friday and Saturday nights, but midweek bargains are available. As good as anywhere are the two branches of ✰✰✰/✰✰ *Puri Retno*, 21km and 25km north of Labuan, or the cheaper cottages of ✰✰/✰ *Desiana*, 9km north of Labuan. There are **banks** and a supermarket in Labuan; the **post office** is 1km north of town on the Carita road, and a 24-hour **wartel** lies 1km out on the Pandegelang road.

At **Carita**, a still quiet and slow-paced fishing village 7km north of Labuan, brightly painted boats are moored in the river mouth. Beside the 10km stone, a shady lane heading inland marks the start of a pleasant one to two-hour walk to **Curug Gendang**, a small, pretty waterfall. The path, through degraded lowland forest, is clearly signed and offers quite good **birdwatching**, with several Javan endemics such as the white-breasted babbler, and more than 120 other species recorded here; the falls are best after sustained rain, but the path then becomes slippery.

At several points along the coast road the sea comes into view, fringed with coconut palms. **Karang Bolong**, c 17km north of Carita, is a popular but dull beach with a natural rock arch. It is packed at weekends when scores of *warung* set up in the huge coach park opposite, selling food and drink.

North of the turning inland to Batu Kuwung hot springs, the coast road passes more resorts and unsightly condominiums before reaching **Anyar Kidul**, 39km north of Labuan, where there is a 65m-high iron lighthouse. It was built in 1885 to replace one destroyed here two years earlier by the tidal waves unleashed during Krakatau's violent eruption (see below). For a small donation the caretaker allows visitors to climb to the top, from where the islands of the **Krakatau group** and Sebesi and Sebuku can be seen, together with Gunung Rajabasa on Sumatra.

At Anyar market, 5km further north, or at some of the resorts nearby, boats can be chartered to **Pulau Sangiang**, a forested island in the Sunda Strait with a pleasant sandy beach and coral reef, and the ruins of a Japanese gun emplacement from the Second World War. In the rainy season, however, the seas round the fringing coral reef can be too churned up for good snorkelling.

Anyar, an important port in the 19C, was the starting point of the Great Post Road (Groote Postweg) built by Marshal Daendels from 1808, primarily for strategic military reasons. It wound its way across Java for c 1000km to Panarukan, near Situbondo on East Java's north coast.

Krakatau Nature Reserve

Currently among the most active of Indonesia's volcanoes, in the 19C **Krakatau** produced one of the world's most powerful known eruptions, generating tsunamis which completely overwhelmed settlements along the coasts of southern Sumatra and west Java. A series of eruptions from its descendant, Anak Krakatau ('Krakatau's child') in February 1999, which could be heard and seen from the Java coast, show its continued wakefulness. If you should find it slumbering, a visit is highly recommended, but be sure to heed local advice; it has claimed many lives.

History

Some geologists believe that **ancient Krakatau** was a 2000m-high volcano, more than 10km in diameter, which destroyed itself in a massive eruption in the 5C or 6C. Three islands were left—volcanoes lying in the submerged caldera. These were built upon by new volcanic deposits ejected from the watery depths, and eventually merged to form **historic Krakatau**, an island measuring c 9km by 5km with three volcanoes. Seven eruptions were recorded between the 9C and 16C, but by the 19C the island was considered dormant. Captain James Cook, aboard the *Endeavour* on his first voyage, reported finding a village and cultivated fields when he stopped at Krakatau in January 1771. In February 1780, after his death in Hawaii during the third voyage, the *Resolution* and *Discovery* stopped there on the way back to England and reported Krakatau clad largely in forest. By the 1880s the islands were forested from shore to peak.

In May and June 1883 Krakatau showed signs of life once more, with eruptions from the northern volcano, Perbuatan, and booming explosions which could be heard in Anyar. On 26 August eruptions could be heard in Bogor and Jakarta, where volcanic ash fell. That evening a large tsunami hit Merak. At 02.00 on the morning of 27 August, a 1m-thick layer of hot ash and pumice fell on the *Berbice*, a ship lying 100km downwind. At 05.30 that morning, a 30km-high column of tephra was seen spewing from the volcano. Soon after, a huge tsunami smashed into Anyar, destroying the port and killing most of the inhabitants.

It was probably this same wave which hit the Sumatran coast, devastating coastal villages and beaching the government gunboat, Berouw. The sky turned black, even in Jakarta, and at 10.00 the greatest explosion occurred—equivalent to 100–150 megatons of TNT – which generated a tsunami with an advancing front up to seven storeys high. It swept through the Sunda Strait, destroying what remained of Merak, Anyar and more than 300 other settlements, and killing more than 36,000 people. The *Berouw* was carried nearly 3km inland and dumped 9m above sea level; her 28 crew perished.

The waves raced across the open ocean at more than 700km/h, stranding vessels in port at Auckland, New Zealand. In Freemantle, Australia, wool bales piled on the docks ready for loading were washed away by waves sweeping over them. The waves were still 1m high when they reached Sri Lanka, where one person drowned; 32 hours after the initial explosion, the waves reached Le Havre in the English Channel as 1cm-high swells.

The air wave created by the blast reached Krakatau's antipodes – Bogotá, Colombia – whereupon it bounced back, returning to Krakatau at 05.00 on 28 August; it then bounced back and forth for five more recorded passages over the earth's surface. The sounds of the eruption were the greatest ever recorded in terms of audible range, carrying south to Freemantle, north to Singapore and west to Rodriguez Island, 4600km away in the Indian Ocean.

Most of the tephra rained back down on the earth's surface as a mud rain, lasting 3–4 hours; the *Gouverneur-Generaal Loudon*, sailing from Jakarta to Teluk Betung on Sumatra, was covered with 150cm of mud in 10 minutes. However, some fine particles and aerosols from the eruption reached an altitude of 50km and diffused through the stratosphere, creating brilliant sunsets around the world for several years, especially in the northern hemisphere.

All that remained of Krakatau was half of Rakata, the southernmost of the island's three volcanoes, which now extended 1km further south and was covered in a 60m-thick carpet of debris. The rest of the island had been replaced by a submarine caldera up to 360m deep. Two outlying islands, Sertung and Panjang, also survived, both covered in a thick layer of ash and pumice. All plant and animal life was destroyed. By the morning of 28 August, the cataclysmic explosions, which had blown nearly 20 cu km of tephra into the sky in less than two days, had totally ceased. The sea was filled with huge fields of floating pumice, some of which washed up 18 months later in Micronesia, 6500km away, entangled in the huge buttress roots of large tree trunks. Vast amounts of pumice were still being found in the Indian Ocean in 1885.

The volcano grew quiet once more till 1927, when renewed activity in the submerged caldera produced several temporary islands, which were soon eroded away by wave action or destroyed by explosions. On 12 August 1930 the fourth in the series emerged, and this time continued to grow beyond the reach of the sea. Known as Anak Krakatau, today it has a diameter of c 2km and a height of c 270m, although small eruptions through the 1990s have constantly changed its height and shape. Its most recent victim was an American tourist, caught by renewed volcanic activity in June 1993.

Flora and fauna have been recolonising the islands ever since the 1883 eruption: a scientific expedition visiting Rakata in early 1884 found a tiny spider. Today at least 40 bird species have been noted, as well as several small reptiles. Trees on Rakata are now more than 35m high, and Sertung carries large stands of casuarinas; green turtles nest on some beaches.

Boats can be chartered from Labuan or from several resorts and travel agencies along the coast, including *Krakatau Ujungkulon Tour and Travel*, 8km north of Labuan, and *Black Rhino*, north of Km10. The journey takes c 4 hours each way. The cost of a charter is high ($120–240 per boat, depending on season and boat), so it is worth seeking out fellow travellers to share the costs; the travel agent can usually help with this. It is also important to agree before departure what the itinerary includes and what is provided in the price. Most include food, a landing on Anak Krakatau (if it is safe), and snorkelling. If you want to land on the other islands, negotiate this in advance. It is best to go between May and September; during the rainy season (November–March), when storms are more frequent and the sea can be dangerously rough, sensible boatmen will refuse to go; the others will demand a high price.

Despite the possible dangers, a visit to the islands 50km offshore from Carita can be very exciting if you have a sound boat and the weather is good. On the journey look out for dolphins, frigate birds, flying fish, the white-bellied sea eagle and Javan hawk-eagle. The first view of Anak Krakatau, as the boat rounds the northeast point of Rakata and passes beneath its immense cliff, is tremendous. Take very solid, heatproof footwear for walking on the volcano, plenty of sun protection and drinking water.

Ujung Kulon National Park

This magnificent park, designated a UNESCO World Heritage Site, is home to Indonesia's last surviving population of Javan, or **lesser one-horned rhinoceros**, *Rhinoceros sondaicus*, hunted since the 12C for its single horn of matted hair, which many Chinese believe holds aphrodisiac qualities. It is just possible that some survive in the Tenasserim Hills along the Thai-Burmese border or in remote parts of peninsular Thailand, but Ujung Kulon is the best place to see them—or at least their spoor, which is all the casual visitor can expect to see, since sightings of the 50 or so animals themselves are extremely rare indeed.

Largely covered with coastal forest, mangroves and lowland rainforest, Ujung Kulon was gazetted as a conservation area in 1958, and today comprises 760 sq km on Java's southwestern peninsula and several nearby islands. Leopard, banteng, muntjak, common wild boar, mouse deer, warthog, Javan leaf monkey and Javan gibbon inhabit the park, and its rivers are almost the last home for the **estuarine crocodile**, Java's largest reptile; **green**, **leatherback** and **hawksbill turtles** nest on the peninsula's beaches; and the large **water monitor**, a shy lizard which can grow to a length of 2.4m, can be seen here. Related to the larger and better-known Komodo dragon, the water monitor has been hunted relentlessly for its valuable hide and because of its appetite for domestic chickens. Visitors have a good chance of seeing—or hearing—the rhinoceros hornbill; other birds include ruddy kingfisher, great-billed heron, and an endemic: the black-banded barbet.

Hiking trails exist round much of the mainland peninsula and on the islands of Panaitan and Peucang; to explore it all will take at least a week, but a stay of at least three days is strongly advised. At the **Ciujungkulon feeding ground** on the peninsula opposite Pulau Peucang, and at **Cigenter feeding ground** nearer to Pulau Handeuleum, there is a good chance of seeing banteng and Timor deer, especially early in the morning. Along the trail between the two is the beautiful **Nyiur Bay**, a tranquil contrast to the rugged south coast. Both coasts are worth exploring; on the south is a meditation cave, **Sanghyang Sirah**.

Practical information

Permits
Park entry permits, insurance and **information** can be obtained from the park office (open Mon–Fri 08.00– 16.00), 1500m north of Labuan on the Carita road.

Transport
Package tours operate from Carita, Labuan and Jakarta, and are the easiest

but most expensive way to visit the park. Usually they involve taking a boat from Labuan or Carita to Pulau Handeuleum or Pulau Peucang, both within the park, where there is accommodation. **Boat charters** can also be arranged through the park office; these are expensive, so it is worth finding travelling companions. The cheapest option is to go by **road** (96km) from Labuan to the park headquarters at Taman Jaya via Cibaliung and Sumur. This is a scenic route, but the road is very poor indeed beyond Cibaliung. From Taman Jaya, **hiking trails** lead west along the peninsula; a guide can be hired from the park office there.

Accommodation and facilities

On Pulau Peucang there are comfortable ✩✩✩/✩✩ cottages, a restaurant and an information centre. Snorkelling is good here and off **Pulau Handeuleum**, where there is more basic ✩✩/✩ accommodation. Camping is permitted at the various guard posts, and there are a few, rather feeble, shelters along the coastal trails. On **Pulau Panaitan** there is no alternative but to camp. At **Taman Jaya** there is a ✩✩ lodge run by the national park, and cheaper ✩ private home-stays. If you are planning a hike of several days you should bring food supplies, sun protection, suitable footwear, and money for the obligatory guide and porters if required (c $5 per day).

Bogor, Puncak and Pelabuhanratu

Highlights include Bogor's fine **Botanical Gardens** (see p 224) and the excellent **Ethnobotany Museum** (see p 226); a drive through tea estates to the cool upper slopes of **Puncak** (see p 227) and the **Cibodas alpine gardens** (see p 228); and for the energetic, a hike to the summit and gently smoking crater of **Gunung Gede** (see p 229).

Practical information

Travel advice

Jakarta to Bogor, c 60km via the Jagorawi toll-road, is usually a fast but dull journey. On Saturdays and public holidays, however, traffic streaming out of Jakarta can crawl bumper to bumper almost the whole way to Cipanas. On Sunday afternoons the road between Ciawi and Cipanas becomes westbound only, as people flock back to Jakarta.

Public transport

From Jakarta, Bogor is best reached by train (1 hour); services leave regularly from Gambir Station. Frequent, fast buses depart from Kampung Rambutan bus terminal in southern Jakarta (c 90 minutes), but from central Jakarta it can take 40 minutes or more to reach the terminal itself. At Bogor's Baranang Siang bus terminal, take a lime-green no. 03 angkot to the town centre, or walk for about 20 minutes.

Accommodation

There is good accommodation in **Bogor**, on the upper slopes of **Puncak**, at **Selabintana** above Sukabumi, and at **Pelabuhanratu**. Simple guest-houses are available at the entrance to **Gede Pangrango National Park**.

BOGOR

One of the wettest places in Java, Bogor is nevertheless a pleasant town with several sites of interest, and is many visitors' first port of call after Jakarta. When not in cloud, **Gunung Salak** looms over the town to the south, and to the southeast are the tea-covered slopes of **Gunung Pangrango**. Just west of the town centre the Cisadane river has cut a deep cleft through bamboo and banana groves, with terracotta-tiled homes encroaching ever more precariously onto its steep banks. The fine view from Jl. Paledang across the Cisadane to Gunung Salak is worth seeking out, but the volcano's appearances are rare.

History

There is evidence that the area round Bogor was inhabited at least 1500 years ago. In hills c 15km west of the town two ancient stone inscriptions and a pictograph were discovered in the mid-19C. Written in Pallawa script, the inscriptions have been dated on epigraphic grounds to the mid-5C. One of them, originally found in the bed of the Ciaruteun river but now removed from the stream, refers to Purnavarman, ruler of a kingdom called Taruma; above the inscription are carved two human-shaped footprints, said in the inscription to be his. Another inscription found here refers to a pair of elephant-shaped footprints belonging to Purnavarman's elephant. Other inscriptions and pictographs associated with Purnavarman have been found at Tugu in north Jakarta, and at sites northeast of Bogor and much further west, so the precise location of this early kingdom is unclear.

By the 12C–14C, much of Sunda (western Java) was ruled by a Hindu-Buddhist state called Pajajaran, which was based near modern Bogor. This was finally conquered c 1579 by the powerful sultanate of Banten, bringing the demise of western Java's last significant Hindu-Buddhist state.

Modern Bogor has grown since the mid-18C round the site of a country house used by Dutch governors-general seeking a retreat from the heat of Batavia. They named it Buitenzorg ('without a care'). The present palace dates from the mid-19C, but its predecessor was used by Sir Thomas Stamford Raffles, Lieutenant-Governor of Java (1811–16), as his place of work and for entertaining. He visited Batavia only rarely.

Practical information

Transport

Tiny lime-green **minibuses** (*angkot*) follow fixed routes round the town. Useful for visitors are nos 03, 06 and 13, which operate between the bus station and central locations in the town, passing generally anticlockwise round the Botanical Gardens. The blue 05 angkot goes to Ciampea from the Merdeka sub-terminal on Jl. Merdeka. **Pony traps** (*delman*) operate in the town, but are not much fun in heavy traffic. Outside the Botanical Gardens' main entrance are private **taxis**—usually Kijangs—which can be chartered with a driver for excursions. The fare is negotiable in advance, and hotel staff can advise on appropriate prices for your destination. **Buses** depart from the Baranang Siang terminal on Jl. Pajajaran to Jakarta and all regencies in West Java, as well as a few places further afield. Note that some

Jakarta buses take the slow old road, not the fast Jagorawi toll-road, so check before boarding. There are frequent **trains** to Jakarta, and three daily to Sukabumi from the railway station on Jl. Raja Permas.

Hotels

The area ☎ code is 0251. Bogor's better hotels include the refurbished ☆☆☆ *Hotel Salak* (☎ 346938, fax 350800), centrally located at Jl Juanda 8, and the ☆☆☆/☆☆ *Mirah Sartika* (☎ 3122343) at Jl. Dewi Sartika 6/A. Slightly further out are the ☆☆☆/☆☆ *Hotel Pangrango* (☎ 328670; fax 314060) at Jl. Pangrango 23 and the nearby ☆☆☆/☆☆ *New Mirah Hotel* (☎ 328044; fax 329423) at Jl. Megamendung 2. For smaller budgets, the ☆☆ *Wisma Ramayana* (☎ 320364) at Jl. Ir.H. Juanda 54 is good value and very popular.

South of Bogor, at Jl. Raya Bogor-Sukabumi Km21, is the ☆☆☆☆/☆☆☆ *Hotel Aryaduta Lido* (☎ 242020; fax 242017), which offers jetskiing, golf, microlight-flying, mountain-biking, paragliding and swimming.

Information and services

Staff at the **tourist office** (Dinas Pariwisata) on the corner of Jl. Pemuda and Jl. Merak, north of the town centre, can sometimes arrange a visit to the Istana Bogor for groups, but it may take a few days to organise; an individual stands little chance, and would do best to book a visit through a travel agent or hotel in Bogor. *BirdLife International* (PO Box 310/Boo, Bogor 16003; ☎/fax 333234; e-mail: birdlife@server. indo.net.id) has a well-stocked ornithology library open to visiting birdwatchers. The PHPA office beside the gardens' main entrance can provide information about Indonesia's national parks.

Bank Bali (M, V) is at Jl. Kapten Muslihat 17/A. *BCA* (M, V) is at Jl. Juanda 28. The **post office** is also on Jl. Juanda.

An efficient 24-hour **telecoms office** is at Jl. Pengadilan 14. Smaller 24-hour *wartel* are found at the main entrance to the Botanical Gardens and on Jl. Malabar I.

Cafés

Opposite the post office on Jl. Juanda and close to the Botanical Gardens is *Jongko Ibu*, a friendly café serving consistently good Sundanese food. The simple *Salak Sunset Café* in the Alliance Française de Bogor at Jl. Paledang 38 has fine views of Gunung Salak on clear days.

Botanical Gardens

Bogor's Botanical Gardens (Kebun Raya; open daily 08.00–17.30) dominate the town's centre, acting as a giant traffic circle round which scores of little *angkot* swarm all day long. Entrance tickets can be bought at the main entrance on Jl. Juanda on the southwest side of the gardens, and visitors can hire guides from the information office here. Motor vehicles are allowed in except on Sundays, when the admission price drops and the gardens fill with throngs of picnickers. The best time to visit is midweek, early in the day: it rains in Bogor on two out of three days, usually in the afternoon.

History

The Botanical Gardens were established in 1817 by C.G.C. Reinwardt, a Dutch botanist, with assistants from London's Kew Gardens. Reinwardt and his successors slowly built up the collection into a world-class botanical garden. Under Johannes Elias Teysmann (1808–82), a plant systematist who came to Java as the chief gardener for the governor-general and later became chief curator, and Melchior Treub, a plant morphologist and physiologist who became director in 1880, aged 29, the garden became renowned for the scientific research carried out there.

The Dutch were especially keen to develop varieties of cash crops such as cinchona (for quinine), tea, coffee and cacao. Treub built new laboratories, including one at the alpine garden extension at Cibodas, and encouraged foreign scientists to do research here by opening the 'Foreigners' laboratory'. During the gardens' heyday (1880–1930) there were c 10,000 plant varieties under cultivation. Since independence, the garden's diversity has deteriorated considerably, largely through lack of funding; by 1991 the number of varieties had dropped to 3370. Recently, however, new investment has seen a slight increase.

Although the Bogor gardens remain the finest in Indonesia, their history is not blemish-free. In late 1894 the water hyacinth was introduced here. Under favourable conditions, this native of Brazil can spread ferociously quickly: a single plant can be a source of 3000 others within 50 days, and offspring from a single plant can cover 600 sq m in a year. Excess growth was dumped in the Ciliwung river which flows through the gardens, and the plant spread incredibly fast through Java. By 1931 Rawa Pening, the lake near Salatiga, was completely covered by it, and it has today become a curse of many of Java's reservoirs and waterways.

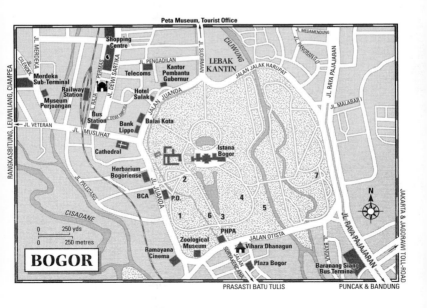

Wander at will through the Gardens or hire a guide at the entrance. Worth a special look are the **bamboo and rattan groves** (1) and the overgrown Christian **cemetery** (2) on the west side; and the **cenotaph** (3) beside the lake in memory of Olivia Raffles, the wife of Sir Stamford Raffles, who died at Buitenzorg in 1814: on it are inscribed the first lines of a love poem she had written to John Leyden, her Platonic lover and her husband's best friend. Also take a look at the colony of **large flying foxes**, *Pteropus vampyrus* (4), which roosts seasonally in a 150-year-old native kauri tree; the **water gardens** (5) and collection of succulents; and, if in bloom, the spectacular and bizarre **titan arums**, *Amorphophallus titanum* (6), from Sumatra.

The *Café Botanicus* (7) on the east side of the Gardens offers a fine view over lawns down to the river. The orchid house is usually closed to the public.

Other sights in Bogor

Outside the entrance to the Gardens is a lively **pavement market** along Jl. Otista, selling fruit and vegetables, flowers and pet rabbits. Just opposite, on the corner of Jl. Surya Kencana, is **Vihara Dhanagun**, a Chinese temple dating from at least the 18C, with flower stalls in front.

Close by on Jl. Juanda is the **Zoological Museum** (Museum Zoologi; open Sat–Wed 08.00–16.00, Thur–Fri 08.00–15.00), which has galleries of stuffed birds and mammals – including a Javan rhino – and the skeleton of a blue whale washed ashore in 1916 near Pameungpeuk on the south coast. Other displays include insects and amphibians. English descriptions are intermittent.

On the west side of the Gardens is the excellent **Ethnobotany Museum** (Museum Etnobotani Indonesia; open Mon–Thur 08.00–15.45; Fri 08.00–11.00) in the cavernous basement of the Herbarium Bogoriense; the entrance is on Jl. Kantor Batu. Run on a shoestring budget by a small, enthusiastic team, it houses an extensive collection of plant-related items from across the archipelago. Note under the stairs behind the ticket desk a heavy stone slab, in memory of R.H.C.C. Scheffer (Director of the Botanical Gardens 1868–80).

On display are fish and animal traps, baskets, household utensils, mats, children's toys and farming tools made from bamboo, pandanus, rattan, coconut, banana fibre, palmyra, gourds and other plants. There are hunting tools and weapons from several islands, and grass clothing from Irian Jaya and Kalimantan. Wooden ploughs and drums, mortars for pounding sago, plants which provide dyes and traditional medicines are all shown, together with exhibits from Bali, from Tanah Toraja in south Sulawesi, and from the Batak of Sumatra. The rattan display includes an incredible 53m-long vine. Unfortunately, most of the exhibit explanations are in Indonesian only.

While the majority of these items are no longer seen in Indonesian towns, many are still widely used in rural areas – especially in the outer islands – where plants like bamboo or rattan, or the sugar palm in Nusa Tenggara, remain immensely important.

Istana Bogor, the palace used by Sukarno and where much of his private art collection is hung, lies adjacent to the Gardens, behind broad lawns grazed by a herd of chital. This herd, now numbering several hundred, has grown from three pairs introduced at the beginning of the 19C.

The palace was strafed by an Air Force pilot in 1960 during an abortive coup attempt against Sukarno; and it was here that Sukarno was forced to sign the Supersemar (Surat Perintah Sebelas Maret) document on 11 March 1966, which gave Suharto full authority to put an end to student demonstrations in Jakarta and effectively marked the complete transfer of power from Sukarno to Suharto. The embittered Sukarno lived under de facto house arrest in the palace until his death in June 1970.

To the north of the Botanical Gardens, a short *becak* ride or walk along Jl. Sudirman, the **Peta Museum** (Monumen dan Museum Peta; open 09.00–14.00) houses a collection relating to the Indonesian nationalist movements of the 20C, among them the Pembela Tanah Air (PETA: 'Defenders of the Fatherland'), a volunteer youth army organised in 1943 by the Japanese, who wished to create a guerilla force to resist an Allied invasion. Among its officers was Sudirman, who was later to become a nationalist general of great repute. The museum, opened in 1996, is primarily of interest to historians.

The **Museum of the Struggle for Independence** (Museum Perjuangan; open 09.00–14.00; closed Fri), 800m northwest of the Gardens on Jl. Merdeka, opened in 1957 and has rather dull displays relating to the fight against the Dutch in the late 1940s. Weapons, newspapers, money and clothing from the period are displayed, together with dioramas of guerilla attacks. Near the entrance is a bust of Captain Muslihat, a local hero from the period.

A small-scale, but well-known **wayang golek workshop**, owned by 'Pak' Dase, can be found c 250m to the north of the Botanical Gardens in the Lebak Kantin neighbourhood. Descend the steps immediately west of the Ciliwung river on Jl. Jarak Harupat and head for the tight cluster of houses straight ahead; anyone here can lead you to his house, where someone will explain the manufacturing process. You will be gently encouraged to buy, but there is no obligation.

On the south side of Bogor on Jl. Batu Tulis, c 3km from the Ramayana movie theatre on Jl. Juanda, is a small shrine containing a large **inscribed stone** (*prasasti batu tulis*) dating from 1533. In front of it is another stone, bearing two footprints. The inscription states that it was made by Sura Wisesa, ruler of Pajajaran (1521–35) in memory of the foundation of the kingdom in 1333 by a certain Maharaja.

SOUTHEAST OF BOGOR

Puncak

Puncak ('summit') refers broadly to the area of high land round the 1800m-high pass on the main Bogor–Cianjur road. Frequently shrouded in mist, it is an immensely popular weekend retreat for Jakartans seeking cool, clean air and (sometimes) fine views, and many Jakarta-based companies have villas here for their employees' use. Wealthy individuals have second homes here, and there are scores of guest houses, hotels and hostels for everyone else. The whole Puncak area is best avoided at weekends, as the traffic jams and crowds can be overwhelming, but in midweek it is a pleasant, quiet spot, with heavily discounted accommodation available.

Practical information

Public transport

An endless stream of **buses** and **minibuses** climbs from Bogor all day long; on weekdays any Bandung-bound bus will go via Puncak.

Private transport

If driving from Bogor, it is best to take the toll-road loop to Ciawi, thereby avoiding a slow crawl along the old, more direct road. Drivers should watch out for crazy overtaking manoeuvres on the sharp, steep bends near the summit; buses are the worst culprits.

Beyond Ciawi the road begins its long ascent up to the **Puncak pass**. The *Bali International Youth Hostel* is on the left just before the 'Jakarta 78km' stone, c 7.5km from the Ciawi traffic lights. The *Pondok Pemuda Kopo International* is another hostel 2km further in Cisarua. Both offer good, cheap accommodation, but are far from the summit. In the vicinity are several all-night discos, favoured by the young rich of Jakarta and Arab visitors. At the 82km stone, **Taman Safari Indonesia** (Safari Park; open daily) lies to the right. A cross between an open zoo and funfair, the park is a good place to bring children; animals include the Sumatran tiger and rhino, Komodo dragon, orang-utan and several African mammals.

Beyond the park the road passes numerous restaurants, including the bizarre *DC-6 Aero-Restaurant* on the right and a huge ship on the left, before reaching the **tea plantations** of the Gunung Mas estate. The road through the plantations becomes steep and winding, and offers fine views across this smooth green carpet of neatly trimmed tea bushes. The **Gunung Mas factory**, to the right just before the 87km stone, is open to the public for interesting guided tours and a tasting of the tea at the café near the entrance.

Higher up the slopes of Puncak are several popular viewpoints well served by warung and restaurants. The top of the pass is reached just beyond the large *Rindu Alam restaurant*.

Cibodas and Gede Pangrango National Park

At the 8km stone in **Cimacan**, c 7km beyond the Puncak pass, a lane to the south climbs steadily for 4km to the Cibodas Alpine Gardens and the entrance to Gede Pangrango National Park. The entire route is lined with colourful plant nurseries, which at weekends attract buyers from Jakarta. Just below the gardens' entrance are scores of roadside *warung* and souvenir stalls; silent and empty in midweek, they do a brisk trade at weekends.

Th **Cibodas Alpine Gardens** (Kebun Raya Cibodas; open daily 08.00–17.30) were laid out over 100ha in the 1830s on the northern slopes of the Gunung Gede-Gunung Pangrango volcano at an altitude of 1425m. The Dutch believed a high-altitude research station was necessary to promote economically important crops such as tea, coffee and cinchona. The latter, from which quinine was extracted, was brought to Java from the Andes in 1854; 70 plants survived the journey and were planted here before being transplanted to the slopes of Gunung Malabar, south of Bandung. By the start of the Second World War, 90 per cent of the world's quinine came from the Malabar estates. Today, with synthetic alternatives available, the old cinchona estates have been planted with tea.

The Gardens, of little importance today, are far less visited than the more accessible Botanical Gardens in Bogor, and offer pleasant walks and good birdwatching.

Gede Pangrango National Park is one of Indonesia's most visited and best managed parks, with the status of a UNESCO Biosphere Reserve. There are waterfalls and a rich avifauna, but the main attraction is the trail to the summit of **Gunung Gede** (2958m) and the view over the somnolent crater's fumaroles. It last erupted in 1957, briefly ejecting ash to an altitude of 3km.

Part of Gunung Gede became the Dutch East Indies' first conservation area in 1889. Today covering c 15,000ha, the National Park is covered mostly in everwet forest and experiences high rainfall; hikers should expect rain at any time. More than one third of **Java's 590 wild orchid** species grow here, and most of **Java's endemic birds** can be found, including the brown-throated barbet, chestnut-bellied partridge, Javan scops owl and Javan hawk-eagle. Mammals known to inhabit the park – but hard to find – include leopard, Javan gibbon, Javan leaf monkey (*surili*), ebony leaf monkey (*lutung*), muntjak, and the infamous stink badger, which if disturbed can emit such an appalling, nauseating stench from its anal glands that humans may vomit or even faint.

The trail to the summit of Gunung Gede and back can be done in one (long) day, but if you wish to climb Gunung Pangrango too, an overnight camp is necessary.

Practical information

Permits
These must be obtained from the Park office near the road head before entering the Park. If you wish to start the ascent early, obtain the permit the previous day (before 16.00). In the rainy season (Dec–Jan) the park trails are sometimes closed to prevent injury and to limit erosion.

Accommodation
☆ *Freddy's Homestay*, set back from the road c 400m below the road head in Cibodas, is rather poky and damp, but is popular with birdwatchers and back-packers; the owner is very money-conscious, but a logbook here provides information on the latest bird and mammal sightings. Preferable for comfort and setting is the delightful, if rather tired, ☆☆ *guest-house* within the Cibodas Alpine Gardens, which must be booked in advance at the Botanical Gardens office in Bogor. A third option is the ☆ *Pondok Pemuda Cibodas* (youth hostel) near the Park office, which has simple but clean dormitories and rooms; in midweek, you may be the only guest here. Smarter hotels can be found on the main road in and near Cipanas.

The Cibodas trail

The most used path to Gunung Gede's summit, this route passes a series of water-falls and hot springs and is a generally easy climb; a section near the top is permanently roped to assist walkers. There is an excellent guidebook to the first part of the trail, *Cibodas to Cibeureum* by Keith Harris (1994), which should be available from the Park office, and a simple trail map is given to climbers. Fast walkers can reach the summit in 4 hours, but it is best to allow 5–6. To ascend and descend this route in one day, start at sunrise.

For most of the way the trail leads through shady forest. At Kandang Badak, a very messy campsite, the path divides: the right fork leads to Gunung Pangrango, the left to Gunung Gede. The latter is more interesting; the former is higher but lacking good views. Round Gunung Gede's summit you can often see the endemic volcano swiftlet.

The Gunung Putri trail

This is an alternative – and perhaps preferable – route of ascent (c 3–4 hours to the Alun-alun Suryakencana; 1 hour more to Gunung Gede's summit). Far less used, it also enables you to walk a horseshoe, rather than retrace your steps. It is recommended to ascend by this route and descend on the Cibodas trail.

To reach the Gunung Putri gate at an early hour, arrange a minibus or motor-cycle charter the night before at Cibodas: a driver on the Cimacan–Cibodas route or a local lad with a motorcycle will usually oblige. Take the Bogor–Cianjur road further east through Cipanas, beyond the Istana Cipanas (see below) to the **Simpang Raya market**, where an asphalt lane leads south (right) to the trail's starting point.

The path starts climbing beside terraced fields of onions and garlic and then enters woodland for most of the way before emerging onto a flat, grassy meadow at 2635m – the floor of an old crater known as the **Alun-alun Suryakencana**. A profusion of Javan edelweiss grows here, though large old specimens – which could reach a height of 8m – are now very rare, having suffered at the hands of collectors. From the north end of the meadow, on a clear day, you can see the north coast of Java.

The path follows the old crater floor southwest past a small pool to the south side of Gunung Gede's new summit cone where, at a junction, it turns steeply up to the wooded peak. The main crater path continues to the west end of the meadow, where it descends steeply south to Selabintana; from this point Gunung Salak can be seen on a cloudless day. On the summit of Gunung Gumuruh – the high point on the outer rim of the old crater – is a strange grave-like site which local legend claims to be the burial site of Siliwangi, ruler of Pajajaran (1482–1521).

In Cipanas on the main Bogor–Cianjur road, the **Istana Cipanas** (Cipanas Palace), to the south of the road, is a fine villa which was used by Sukarno as a summer retreat in the 1950s and 1960s. In the grounds are some hot springs from which Cipanas ('hot river') gets its name; the villa is not open to visitors.

WEST OF BOGOR

Inscribed stones and waterfalls

Most easily found with the help of a guide, these sites are perhaps best visited by taxi from Bogor, with a driver who knows their locations. The Bogor–Leuwiliang road is narrow and often extremely congested; a very early start is advised. The stones are of special interest to archaeologists, since they bear the second oldest Sanskritic inscriptions known in Indonesia (the oldest are from Kalimantan); to the layman, however, they may be of little interest.

Near the village of **Ciampea**, c 20km northwest of Bogor, can be seen two of the **mid-5C inscriptions** associated with Purnavarman, the ruler of Taruma. Take the main Bogor–Leuwiliang road west from the town centre and after c 15km turn off north to Ciampea (signed). Follow this lane c 6km through Ciampea market, and turn off left shortly before it crosses a steel girder bridge. After a further 3km, a track to the right at a sharp left-hand bend signals the route to the inscribed stones. Follow the track over a bridge and through rice fields to the primary school (*sekolah dasar*) on the left side. Here a locked shelter contains a boulder bearing what is known as the 'Kebon Kopi inscription' ('Coffee gardens inscription'), discovered in the mid-19C in what was then a coffee plantation, and incised with a pair of elephant-shaped footprints. The ancient inscription attributes them to Purnavarman's elephant.

A few metres further, a path to the right leads down towards the river bank, where there is another inscribed rock, which was found in the river bed in the mid-19C but moved to the bank in the 1980s. This has a pair of human-shaped footprints and a four-line text, known as the 'Ciaruteun inscription', describing the prints as those of Purnavarman. A third boulder, lying in the river bed a short distance away, bears a pictograph of swirling designs. Local children can usually be found to show the way.

On the northern slopes of **Gunung Salak**, 11km southwest of Bogor, are numerous high waterfalls, hot springs, fumaroles and bubbling mud pools. Most easily accessible from Bogor is **Curug Luhur**, a 40m-high waterfall near desa Gunung Malang. More distant are **Curug Seribu**, c 100m high, and the nearby **Curug Cigamea**, both at Gunung Salak Endah, a recreation area on the northwest slopes of Gunung Salak. While none of these are truly outstanding (except after the heaviest of rain), the lanes to them pass through beautiful hill scenery and small, rather isolated villages which make this an enjoyable excursion.

SOUTH OF BOGOR

Gunung Halimun National Park

This magnificent swathe of mountainous rainforest receives few visitors, largely because it is hard to reach, and as yet there are few facilities for guests. Nevertheless, visitors interested in natural history, who are prepared to travel rough and with a flexible timetable, will find the effort well worthwhile; plan for a visit of 2–3 days at least.

Gunung Halimun is home to several endangered mammals and endemic birds, contains many waterfalls, and co-exists with several tea estates and a clove plantation in its midst. Covering c 40,000 hectares, it is most easily accessible in the (relatively) dry season (June–September), when the rough roads are at their best, but expect rain all year round.

The park is an important refuge for the endangered **Javan gibbon**, the **Javan leaf monkey** (*surili*), and the beautiful **ebony leaf monkey** (*lutung*), all endemic to Java. More common, but very hard to see, are long-tailed macaques which feed on the forest floor, barking deer and the occasional wild pig. More than 120 bird species are known from the park, among them endemics such as the tiny pygmy tit.

Guides from Nirmala tea estate in the heart of the park can take you to the **Cihanjawar** and **Piit falls**. People in *desa* Mekarjaya can show you several other waterfalls. The mountain peaks are thickly forested; ascents to the summits of Gunung Halimun and Gunung Kendeng are very demanding and are not rewarded with fine views.

Practical information

Travel advice

The easiest access is from **Parungkuda** on the Bogor–Cibadak road, at a turn-off 500m south of the 'Bandung 118km' stone; the National Park is signed 29km from here. Park headquarters is at **Kalapanunggal**, c 22km along this road, before you reach the eastern Park boundary, where a permit must be obtained. The all-weather road continues to Cipeuteuy, and eventually to Nirmala tea estate, but there is little—if any—public transport beyond Cipeuteuy. If you have the time, it makes a pleasant walk of about a day; otherwise hope for a lift from a passing estate truck.

Accommodation

At present, only camping is available, and visitors need to bring all their own equipment. There are several approved sites, but in reality, you can camp almost anywhere if you are self-sufficient. With knowledge of Indonesian, a visitor can sometimes rent a room in a house; park officials may offer you a room, or at least help you to find one.

Gede Pangrango National Park: southern approaches

Continuing south from Bogor, the main road reaches **Cibadak**, where it turns east towards Sukabumi and the small hill resort of Selabintana. In **Cisaat**, at the 98.7km post, a lane to the north climbs for c 10km to **Situgunung**, a small lake in an outlying fragment of Gede Pangrango National Park. A path here leads to a waterfall which becomes an impressive torrent in the rainy season.

From Cisaat, continue east c 4km to **Sukabumi**, where the road to **Selabintana** is clearly signed to the left. Near the road head on the southern slopes of Gunung Gede are several hotels, the best of which is the charming ☆☆☆☆/☆☆☆ *Hotel Selabintana* (☎ 0266 223204; fax 221501). A road to the left, 1km before the hotel, winds for 6km through tea plantations to the Selabintana park gate and office, from where there is a steep, little-used path to the summit of Gunung Gede. The Cibeureum waterfall, the highest in the park, lies a pleasant 2.5km walk from the park gate, near to which are several warung selling food and drink.

PELABUHANRATU AND THE SOUTH COAST

From Cibadak a road runs c 50km southwest to Pelabuhanratu, a small fishing port, near to which are many hotels and a few reasonable surfing beaches popular with weekend visitors from Jakarta and Bandung. It is possible to swim here, but watch out for rip currents in the vicinity; to avoid nasty lacerations on the sharp reefs, surfers should wear protective clothing. The road winds through small villages and beautiful countryside of terraced rice fields and rubber plantations. Pelabuhanratu itself is of little interest, although the early morning fish market can be worth a look: large sharks, lobsters and swordfish are sometimes on display.

Practical information

Transport
Regular **buses** run from Bogor, Cibadak and Sukabumi, and small **mikrolet** run along the coast road to Cisolok and beyond.

Accommodation
In the town itself are several basic peng-inapan and a couple of hotels. Better places are found along the coast road towards Cisolok. The best are often full at weekends, but offer cheaper midweek rates. The area code is 0268.
☆☆☆☆/☆☆☆ *Pondok Dewata* (☎ 41022;

fax 41532) on the edge of town. Overpriced, but reasonable rooms; swimming pool. Keep an eye on your valuables.
☆☆☆☆/☆☆☆ *Samudra Beach Hotel* (☎ 41200) 6km west of Pelabuhanratu. A slightly faded old-timer on a good beach; pool and tennis courts.
☆☆☆ *Mustika Ratu* (☎ 41233). 8km west of Pelabuhanratu. Mid-priced, with clean but unexceptional rooms.
☆☆☆ *Pondok Kencana* (☎ 41465; fax 41466) just beyond Mustika Ratu. Comfortable bungalows and a pool.

Recommended.

☆☆☆/☆☆ *Pantai Mutiara* (☎ 41330) 12km west of Pelabuhanratu. Pleasant, mid-priced bungalows, a pool and beach access.

☆☆ *Ocean Queen Hotel* (☎ 021 769 6059) 2.5km west of Cisolok, this has excellent self-catering bungalows and a pool on a stark but beautiful black sand beach. The best of the lot, it is always full at weekends. Bookings only through the Jakarta office—and rarely available.

Services

BCA on Jl. Siliwangi can change foreign currency and travellers' cheques; a *warparpostel* for postal and telecoms facilities is on the right beyond the petrol station.

Round Pelabuhanratu

Gua Lelai, a well-known bat cave, lies c 4km from the town. The two million **wrinkle-lipped free-tailed bats** which live here support a valuable guano industry; at dusk these insectivorous bats stream out to feed, each consuming perhaps five grammes of insects per night, and so accounting for a staggering ten tonnes eaten by the colony daily.

In **Cisolok**, 15km west of Pelabuhanratu, a road to the north leads after 2km to **hot springs**, where small geysers spout from the river bed. The water is believed locally to have curative powers.

Beyond Cisolok the road winds c 47km through fine coastal scenery to **Bayah**. At the junction here, the road to the left continues along the coast, through a landscape of rice fields, which descend in terraces to the sea, and leads eventually to the very shabby town of Malingping (37km) and the small fishing settlement of Muara Binuangeum.

The road to the right in Bayah leads through **Cikotok**, where there is a gold mine, to one of west Java's most remote sites of antiquity, **Candi Cibedug**. Public transport runs from Bayah as far as **Cipulus**, c 25km. From here take an *ojek* on a very rough road to **Citorek**, and from there it is a walk of c 2–3 hours to the *candi*. A guide is needed from Citorek. The site is heavily overgrown with trees, but the large candi itself consists of a series of pyramidal stone-walled terraces. Its date is unknown, but the site is assumed to be of proto-historic origin. To get there and back in one day, start extremely early.

The Citorek valley is home to the **Kasepuhan people** who, like the Baduy to the northwest (see p 216), live by a code of ancient customary law, which has only permitted them to cultivate irrigated rice and use agricultural tools since the early 20C. It is possible that the stone terraces of Candi Cibedug once played a role similar to the sacred ancestral worship sites of the Baduy.

From Pelabuhanratu, a turning 4.5km east of town leads southward through Jampangkulon and Surade to **Ujung Genteng** (c 80km), a cape covered with wild sugar palms. Several important breeding beaches for **green** and **hawksbill turtles** lie nearby; the turtles nest throughout the year, but are most numerous from August to November. Accommodation is available in a simple *losmen* belonging to 'Pak' Majid, whose wife cooks very good food. There is quite good snorkelling offshore from here—many fish can be seen, but not coral; and a few surfers occasionally reach the cape. Mosquitoes are a nuisance, so come prepared.

Bandung

With a population of about 2.2 million, Bandung is the third largest city in Java after Jakarta and Surabaya, but it has a noticeably more relaxed atmosphere. In part this is because all but the immediate downtown area is surprisingly well endowed with parks and areas of greenery; partly it is because the steep slopes of the sprawling northern suburbs simply do not permit the kind of population density found in the coastal cities. And while downtown Bandung is as congested, grimy and noisy as any large Indonesian city, it lies 700m above sea level, so it rarely gets as hot or humid as Jakarta or Surabaya. Another compensation is the array of architectural delights; considerable numbers of Art Deco buildings from the 1930s remain, and while some are in terminal decline, others have been lovingly renovated and given a new lease of life.

As the provincial capital of West Java, Bandung is an important centre for higher education and the arts; it has a great variety of restaurants and cafés, a couple of Indonesia's best hotels, several museums and adventurous art galleries that feature up-and-coming Indonesian artists; and is flanked to north and south by magnificent volcanic landscapes which make for excellent excursions.

Practical information

Getting there

Frequent buses run to Bandung from all main towns in West Java, and from many places further east. From Jakarta, the train is preferable, being more comfortable and usually faster. There are direct flights from Jakarta, Palembang, Semarang, Surabaya, Yogyakarta and Singapore.

Private transport

From Jakarta to Bandung several routes are possible for travellers with private vehicles. The main road via Purwakarta is the worst, with the stretch between Purwakarta and Cimahi being frequently slow, dangerous and heavily polluted by truck exhausts. Better alternatives are via Subang (c 2.5–3 hours) or via the Puncak pass, which is slower (c 3.5–4 hours) but offers fine views.

A fourth variation via Purwakarta and Wanayasa, to Ciater and Lembang (which can include the craters of Gunung Tangkuban Perahu en route; see below) is recommended. On the south side of Purwakarta, turn left at the junction signed to Wanayasa; this quiet road climbs through charming countryside and, just beyond a small lake at Wanayasa, turns left (signed to Subang) past terraced rice fields and tea plantations to the small settlement of Sagalaherang, and finally reaches the Subang–Lembang road. Lembang lies 23km south from here, beyond the turning to Gunung Tangkuban Perahu.

Inter-city transport
Trains

The excellent *Parahyangan* service (3 hours) runs non-stop to Jakarta more than ten times daily between 05.00 and 20.30; the smart *Argogede* is even faster, with one early morning and one afternoon service. There are two overnight trains to Yogyakarta and Surabaya: the *Turangga* (c 11 hours), and the *Mutiara Selatan* (12.5 hours). The *Pajajaran* is a daytime train to Solo via Yogyakarta (c 8 hours). An alternative is the slower, daytime *Badra Surya* to Surabaya via Yogyakarta and Solo (c 14 hours). There are also very slow local trains.

Buses

Most westbound buses (to Jakarta, Bogor, Rangkasbitung, Labuan, Merak etc.) depart from the **Leuwipanjang terminal** on Jl. Leuwipanjang, which runs between the inner ring road and Jl. Soekarno Hatta, just west of Jl. Kopo. Buses to Ciwidey and local towns south of Bandung depart from the **Abdul Muis terminal** on Jl. Pungkur, 700m south of the *alun-alun*. Most eastbound and inter-province buses (to Sumedang, Garut, Pangandaran, Yogyakarta, Surabaya and Madiun etc.) depart from the **Cicaheum terminal** east of the city centre along Jl. Yani. To get to the latter can take 40 minutes or more on a bad day, so check first that you need to go there: the tourist office or hotel staff can advise.

Flights

From **Husein Sastranegara Airport**, c 4km from the city centre and best reached by taxi, *Merpati* has direct flights to Jakarta's Halim Airport, Palembang, Semarang, Surabaya and Singapore, and *Bouraq* flies to Yogyakarta.

Airline offices

Bouraq at Jl. Naripan 44 (☎ 022 436436); *Garuda* at the Hotel Preanger Aerowista; *Mandala* at Jl. Halimun 15 (☎ 022 303868); Merpati on Jl. *Asia Afrika* opposite the Savoy Homann (☎ 022 441226).

Local transport
Taxis

Taxis are metered and plentiful—except when it's raining—and are the most comfortable way to get around. *Angkot* operate on fixed routes, are very numerous and cheap, and generally more useful than the city buses; tall foreigners will find them a squeeze. Useful routes include Stasiun Hall–Dago, Stasiun Hall–Lembang, Stasiun Hall–Ciumbuleuit, Abdul

Muis–Dago and Abdul Muis–Cicaheum. Hotel staff can usually advise for specific trips and fares. Becak can be found in the residential parts of Bandung and are pleasant to use on the quieter streets, or early on weekends.

City buses

Buses are often uncomfortably full and slow, but cheap; beware of pickpockets. Useful routes include Cibeureum–Cicaheum, which runs east via Jl. Kebon Jati, Jl. Lembong and Jl. Yani to the Cicaheum terminal, and west via Jl. Asia Afrika and Jl. Sudirman.

Car rentals

Both *Toyota Rent a Car* at Jl. Asia Afrika 123 (☎ 022 434009/ 434333) and the more expensive *Avis* agent at the Hotel Preanger Aerowista (☎ 022 431631/430682) have Kijangs and sedans for rent, with driver or for self-drive, at daily, weekly or monthly rates. There are also several local companies, including *Tara* at the Sheraton (☎ 022 250 0303).

 ## Hotels

Bandung has dozens of hotels to suit all budgets and tastes. The best are extremely good, but many mid-priced hotels tend to be very ordinary and poor value. Discounts of up to 40 per cent are widely available. The telephone code for Bandung is 022.

✭✭✭✭✭ *Chedi* (☎ 230333; fax 230633; e-mail: chedibdg@idola.net.id) Jl. Ranca Bentang 56–58. Modern hotel high above the town centre in the clean air of Ciumbuleuit. Beautifully furnished with impeccable taste; fine views; highly recommended.

✭✭✭✭✭ *Hotel Preanger Aerowista* (☎ 431631/430682; fax 430034; e-mail: preanger@indo.net.id) Jl. Asia Afrika 81. An architecturally striking building; pleasant rooms and good-quality service in a central downtown location.

✭✭✭✭✭ *Hyatt Regency* (☎ 421 1234; fax 420 4090) Jl. Sumatera 51. Luxury hotel

with all the usual facilities; opened 1997.
✩✩✩✩✩ *Savoy Homann* (☎ 432244/
430083; fax 436187) Jl. Asia Afrika 112.
Charming Art Deco building, partially
renovated in mid-1990s, with large
rooms. Very central and highly recommended; good coffee shop.
✩✩✩✩✩/✩✩✩✩ *Hotel Horison*
(☎ 305462; fax 305614), Jl. Pelajar
Pejuang '45 no. 121. A poor location
on the busy ring road, but has good
rooms, bungalows, tennis courts, and a
huge swimming pool.
✩✩✩✩✩/✩✩✩✩ *Hotel Panghegar*
(☎ 432286/432287/432296) Jl.
Merdeka 2. Notable for its revolving
roof-top restaurant, central location
and comfortable rooms.
✩✩✩✩✩/✩✩✩✩ *Sheraton Bandung*
(☎ 250 0303; fax 250 0301) Jl. Juanda
390. Above the town in Dago; very comfortable, with typical Sheraton facilities.
✩✩✩✩ *Hotel Papandayan* (☎ 210799;
fax 310988) Jl. Gatot Subroto 83.
Modern hotel with pleasant rooms, a
good pool and tennis courts, and an
open-air coffee shop.
✩✩✩/✩✩ *Arjuna Plaza* (☎ 231328; fax
234742) Jl. Ciumbuleuit 152. One of
the best mid-priced hotels; reasonable
rooms, friendly staff and a choice of
swimming pools.
✩✩✩/✩✩ Patradissa (☎ 420 6680) Jl. H.
Moh. Iskat. Adequate rooms in a useful
location, a convenient 5-minute walk
from the train station.
✩✩ *Hotel Braga* (☎ 420 4685) Jl. Braga
8. The old Hotel Wilhelmina, now a bit
run-down, but in a good central location; good value.
✩✩/✩ *Hotel Surabaya* (☎ 436791) Jl.
Kebonjati 71–75. Has cheap rooms in a
once-charming, but now rather shabby
building; a hint of faded colonial grandeur.
✩ *Losmen Moritz* (☎ 420 5788/7495)
Jl. Belakang Pasar. Among the best for
small budgets; very simple but spotless
rooms and shared bathrooms, close to
the train station.

 ## Restaurants, cafés and bars

Bandung offers a great variety
of cuisines, from subtle Thai dishes to
bland American fast food; there are
relaxed garden restaurants and lively
European-style bars, aromatic pastry
shops and warung offering simple food.
Jl. Braga is especially notable for its
bakery-cafés, but don't expect anything
too imaginative.
Babakan Siliwangi Jl. Siliwangi; a large
open-air restaurant serving reasonable
Sundanese food in raised pavilions;
attracts large groups at weekends, and is
not a place for quiet contemplation.
Braga Permai Jl. Braga 58. One of many
similar bakery-cafés on Jl. Braga (others
include Canary, French Bakery and
Sumber Hidangan).
Braga Pub and Restaurant Jl. Braga 19;
serves a limited choice of Indian and
Western food.
Café Venezia Jl. Sukajadi; has reasonable
food in a very pleasant garden setting.
Dago Tea House Jl. Bukit Dago Utara, at
Dago. Nothing special about the food,
but a fine location with good views.
Glosis Jl. Gunung Agung in
Ciumbuleuit; good European food served
indoors or out.
Hotel Panghegar Jl. Merdeka; expensive,
excellent food in the revolving roof-top
restaurant; has fine night-time views
across the city.
North Sea Jl. Braga 82; European-style pub
with Western food; a good place for a beer.
Restoran Tizi Jl. Kidang Pananjung off
Jl. Juanda; a pleasant outdoor setting,
sometimes accompanied by annoying
muzak; steaks and predominantly
Western food.
Royal Siam Jl. Braga, just south of the
railway crossing. Has very good, rather
expensive Thai food served in a pleasant
atmosphere.
Tenda Biru Jl. Braga 17. Good, cheap
Sundanese food; open 24 hours.
Recommended.

Yoghurt Cisangkuy Jl. Cisangkuy 66; near the Geology Museum, serves unusual flavoured yoghurts, juices and simple food in a garden; extremely popular with local students; recommended.

Information and maps
Staff at the small **tourist information centre** at the northeast corner of the *alun-alun* can advise on public transport within and from the city. The city's **main tourist office** (Dinas Pariwisata; closed Sat/Sun) is at Jl. Yani 277, c 2km from the junction with Jl. Asia Afrika, on the northeast corner of Jl. Bengawan. There is also a **tourist information counter** on the south platform of the train station. *Gramedia* on Jl. Merdeka and Gunung Agung in Plaza Bandung Indah sell books in English and maps; recommended is the *Bandung/West Java* travel map by Periplus Editions. Copies of old topographic maps from the 1940s, covering most of Indonesia (scale 1:50,000), can be bought at the Geological Museum, together with geological maps. The **Volcanological Survey of Indonesia**, behind the Geological Museum, has a small library with information – mostly in Indonesian – about the country's volcanoes. The libraries of both the **Dutch Cultural Centre** (open Mon–Fri 09.00–16.00, Sat 09.00–12.00) at Jl. Diponegoro 25 and the **Goethe Institut** (open Mon–Fri 09.00–12.00, 14.30–17.00) at Jl. Martadinata 48 have several English-, Dutch- and German-language books about Indonesia.

Money
Useful banks include *BCA* (M, V) and BII (M, V), both on Jl. Asia Afrika close to the Hotel Preanger Aerowista; *Bank Bali* (M, V) on Jl. Merdeka; and the very efficient *Citibank* (M, V), on Jl. Juanda. *HongKong Bank* at Jl. Asia Afrika 141 has a 24-hour ATM which accepts most Visa cards. *Bank Panin*, opposite the HongKong Bank, takes Amex.

Post and telecoms
The **main post office** is on Jl. Asia Afrika. There is a 24-hour **telecoms office** on Jl. Lembong immediately east of the Hotel Panghegar, and there are numerous *wartel* throughout the city, including one opposite the Savoy Homann.

Travel agents
Generally reliable, with competitive prices, are *Pacto* at the Savoy Homann, *Satriavi* in the Hotel Preanger Aerowista, and *Vayatour* at the Hotel Panghegar.

Consulates
The **Dutch Consulate** is at Jl. Diponegoro 25 (☎ 431419), the **French** at Jl. Purnawarman 32 (☎ 445864).

Performing arts
The *Gedung Kesenian Rumentang Siang*, at Jl. Baranang Siang 1 (☎ 433562), has night-long *wayang golek* performances on alternate Saturdays, and on other nights has drama, dance and other live shows.

Art galleries and crafts
Studio R.66 at Jl. Martadinata 66 has regular, well-regarded exhibitions of contemporary art. *Galeri Bandung* at Jl. Siliwangi 16 and *Galeri Soemardja* at Jl. Ganesha 10 are both also worth checking.

‘Pak’ *Ruhiyat's wayang golek workshop* is hidden away off Jl. Pangarang, south of the Savoy Homann; turn off along a steeply descending alley called Jl. Pangarang Bawah III (a local guide will probably befriend you in hope of a commission). *Wayang golek* and other traditional crafts can also be found at *Cupu Manik*, a private house at Jl. Haji

Akbar 10; and at *Sarinah*, the department store on Jl. Braga.

Shopping

On Jl. Dalem Kaum, to the west of the *alun-alun*, are numerous supermarkets, fast-food restaurants, clothes and music shops; this is one of Bandung's liveliest shopping districts. Of note too, is Jl.

Cihampelas, known to tourists as **'Jeans Street'** and famous for its clothing stores with fantastic, amusing neon-lit façades. Besides jeans, the shops sell good value T-shirts, belts, bags etc. *Plaza Bandung* Indah on Jl. Merdeka is a modern, air-conditioned shopping centre, a popular late-afternoon gathering place.

History

Sometime in the distant past, perhaps 8–10,000 years ago, debris from an eruption of Gunung Tankuban Perahu blocked the westward flow of the Citarum river near present-day Padalarang, damming the valley and creating an enormous lake – Danau Bandung – which covered 130 sq km. Eventually, 6–7000 years ago, the river found another exit to the southwest, and eroded a small gorge which led it back to its old course near present-day Rajamandala. The lake drained away, leaving an immensely fertile plain which attracted farmers, despite its tendency to flood on occasion.

The Hindu-Buddhist kingdom of Pajajaran possibly controlled the Bandung basin from the 14C, but if so it left little evidence. Until the arrival of Daendels' Great Post Road in 1810 there was little of note in the area; modern Bandung was essentially a Dutch creation. By 1830 this once-insignificant stop on the Great Post Road was becoming an important, if modest, service centre for the first European planters, who found the favourable climate and fertile soil of the surrounding countryside excellent for growing coffee and tea. The railway from Batavia reached Bandung in 1884, bringing a rush of new planters. By the end of the 19C there were more than 150 large estates in the region, growing tea, coffee, rubber and cacao; by the mid-1920s, more than 1000 plantations had been established, and 25,000 Europeans had settled in Bandung and the surrounding Parahyangan (Priangan) highlands. The city became the weekend gathering place for the estate owners.

The 1920s and 1930s were the city's colonial heyday, when it became a fashionable shopping and cultural centre for Java's resident Europeans; it was the intellectual centre of the Dutch East Indies, attracting some of the most avant-garde architects and creative town planners, among them C.P. Wolff Schoemaker, Henri Maclaine Pont, A.F. Aalbers, Thomas Karsten and J. Gerber. Almost 8 per cent of Bandung's population was European or Indo-European, and large, spacious residential districts were developed which incorporated parks and gardens, a legacy modern Bandung has been fortunate to keep.

In 1927, the young Sukarno, having completed his engineering studies at the Bandung Technical College, founded the Partai Nasional Indonesia (PNI), the first major political party with an ethnically Indonesian membership, which sought to achieve independence for Indonesia through non-cooperation. By the end of 1929 the PNI had around 10,000 members throughout Java and south Sumatra, but Sukarno was arrested and stood trial in 1930.

He was sentenced to four years in Sukamiskin prison (which stood on the present-day Jl. ABC), but was released in December 1931 on the orders of Governor-General de Graeff.

During the Second World War, Bandung was controlled by the Japanese, whose military headquarters at the southwest end of Jl. Sultan Agung still stands. In October 1945 the Japanese turned the city over to the British; when it became clear to the Republicans in March 1946 that the city was to be given back to the Dutch, they razed part of the southern suburbs in protest, turning them into a 'sea of fire' (lautan api). A large memorial to this stands across the ring road from the West Java Provincial Museum.

Exploring Bandung

Downtown Bandung is most easily explored on foot. The European quarter, rather more spread out, is best visited by *becak*. The higher suburbs are served by an endless flow of minibuses.

The city centre

A convenient starting point is the *Hotel Preanger Aerowista* on the busy Jl. Asia Afrika (the old Great Post Road). The main building, with its fine Art Deco details, was designed in 1926 by C.P. Wolff Schoemaker, opened in 1928 and finally completed the following year. Renovations in the late 1980s have made this one of Bandung's best hotels.

From there head a few metres west along Jl. Asia Afrika to the wonderful curved façade and classic Art Deco tower of the *Savoy Homann*, designed by A.F. Aalbers in 1939. The hotel dates back to the 1880s: the oldest part can be seen from the garden restaurant inside. Numerous original or replica details remain: stained-glass panels, ornate ceilings and mouldings. Even if you are not staying here, it is worth taking a look inside.

Continue west to **Gedung Merdeka**, on the corner of Jl. Asia Afrika and Jl. Braga. The western part of this building, formerly the Concordia club, was built in the late 19C, but was altered by Wolff Schoemaker in 1921. The eastern, curved part was added by Aalbers in 1940; this now houses the **Museum of the Asian-African Conference** (Museum Konperensi Asia Afrika; open Mon–Fri 08.00–16.00).

History

Held in April 1955, the Conference, better known as the Bandung Conference, marked the arrival on the world stage of the Non-aligned Movement. Sukarno succeeded, in the conference's final communiqué, in winning the delegates' endorsement of Indonesia's claim over West New Guinea, which he sought to take from the Dutch. The list of conference delegates read like a roll-call of future prominent Asian politicians, among them Sihanouk and Son Sann from Cambodia; Raul Manglapus, Carlos P. Romulo and Macapagal from the Philippines; Burma's U Nu; Zhou Enlai, Nasser, Nehru (with his daughter, Indira Gandhi) and Pham Van Dong. The photos on display show the intense excitement and optimism of the period. Among the exhibits is a report into the crash on 11 April of the *Kashmir Princess*, an

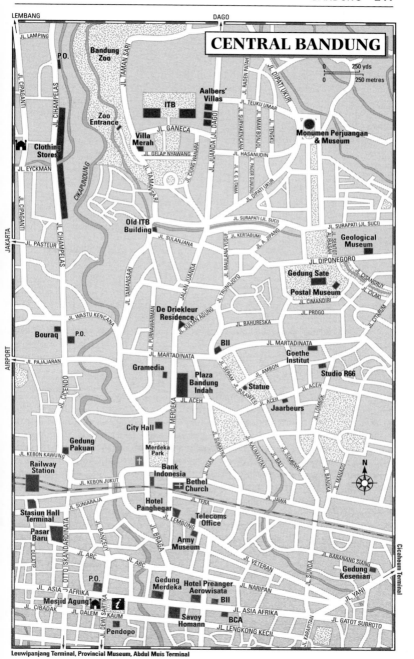

CENTRAL BANDUNG

LEMBANG

DAGO

JL. LAMPING

P.O.

Bandung Zoo

JL. CHAMPELAS

JL. TAMAN SARI

ITB

Aalbers' Villas

JL. RADEN PATAH

JL. DIPATIUKUR

250 yds

250 metres

JL. CIPAGANTI

Zoo Entrance

JL. GANECA

Villa Merah

JL. GELAP NYAWANG

JL. TEUKU UMAR

JL. IMAM BONJOL

JL. SURYAKENCANA

JL. TENGKU

Monumen Perjuangan & Museum

Clothing Stores

JL. EYCKMAN

JL. CHAMPELAS

CIKAPUNDUNG

JL. CUNG WARARA

JL. JUANDA (JL. DAGO)

JL. R. G. UTAMA

JL. HASANUDIN

JL. PAGER GUNUNG

JL. DIPATI UKUR

JAKARTA

JL. CIPAGANTI

JL. PASTEUR

JL. TAMAN SR RI

Old ITB Building

JL. SULANJANA

JL. TAMANSARI

JALAN JUANDA

JL. MAULANG YUSUF

JL. KERTABUMI

JL. A. JIPANG

JL. SURAPATI (JL. SUCI)

JL. SURAPATI (JL. SUCI)

JL. SENTOT ALIBASAH

Geological Museum

JL. DIPONEGORO

JL. CISANGKUY

Gedung Sate

Postal Museum

JL. CILAKI

JL. CIMANDIRI

JL. LITARUM

JL. PROGO

JL. WASTU KENCANA

P.O.

De Driekleur Residence

JL. PURNAWARMAN

JL. SULTAN AGUNG

JL. TRUNOJOYO

JL. BAHURESKA

Bouraq

JL. PAJAJARAN

JL. CICENDO

JL. MARTADINATA

BII

JL. MARTADINATA

Goethe Institut

Studio R66

AIRPORT

Gramedia

Plaza Bandung Indah

JL. ACEH

JL. MERDEKA

JL. SERAM

JL. SULAWESI

JL. AMBON

Statue

JL. ACEH

JL. LOMBOK

Jaarbeurs

City Hall

Gedung Pakuan

JL. KEBON KAWUNG

Merdeka Park

Bank Indonesia

JL. KEBON JUKUT

Bethel Church

JL. NIAS

JL. SUMATRA

JL. KALIMANTAN

JL. BALI

JL. SURABAYA

JL. MADO

JL. BANGKA

N

Railway Station

JL. SUNIARAJA

JL. TERA

JL. JAWA

Stasiun Hall Terminal

Hotel Pangehar

JL. LEMBONG

Telecoms Office

JL. BRAGA

Cicaheum Terminal

Pasar Baru

JL. OTTO ISKANDARDINATA

JL. ABC

JL. BANCEUY

Army Museum

JL. ABC

JL. VETERAN

JL. BARANANG SIANG

JL. SUNDA

Gedung Kesenian

P.O.

Gedung Merdeka

Hotel Preanger Aerowisata

JL. NARIPAN

JL. ASIA AFRIKA

JL. YANI

JL. AFRIKA

JL. ASIA

Mesjid Agung

JL. DEWI SARTIKA

JL. DALEM KAUM

BII

Savoy Homann

BCA

JL. ASIA AFRIKA

JL. GATOT SUBROTO

JL. CIBADAK

Pendopo

JL. LENGKONG KECIL

JL. KARAPITAN

Leuwipanjang Terminal, Provincial Museum, Abdul Muis Terminal aircraft carrying some of the Chinese delegation; a bomb was blamed.

The museum was opened by Suharto on 24 April 1980, the 25th anniversary of the conference.

Further west is the *alun-alun*, flanked on the south side by the recently rebuilt 19C *pendopo*, the former residence of the Indonesian regent. He was the local ruler whose home was moved here by the Dutch when the Great Post Road reached this point in 1810, so they could better keep an eye on him. The Dutch Assistant Resident lived on the north side of the square.

The city's main mosque, **Mesjid Agung**, lies on the west side; the steel-clad minaret dates from its renovation in 1970. Running west from the southwest corner of the alun-alun is Jl. Dalem Kaum, a hectic and extremely noisy shopping district. The central **post office**, on the corner of Jl. Banceuy and Jl. Asia Afrika, dates from 1927.

On Jl. Otista, northwest of the *alun-alun*, is **Pasar Baru** – a pungent, very busy and rather ramshackle market surrounded by decaying shop-houses. In the morning, the lanes are crowded with shoppers jostling to reach stalls and shops selling foodstuffs, ironmongery and much else.

Jl. Braga, running north from the Gedung Merdeka, was a fashionable shopping street in the early 20C, and is worth a wander today. On the west side is the old **Majestic Cinema**, one of Wolff Shoemaker's many projects in the city; on the east side is the former Hotel Wilhelmina (now the *Hotel Braga*), the *Sarinah* department store and, on the corner of Jl. Naripan, the distinctive Art Deco façade of the *Bank Jabar* building, formerly the office of the First Dutch Indies Investment Bank. This was another of Aalbers' designs (1935–36), but remained unfinished; it should have been extended from the high blank wall now facing south. North of the Jl. Naripan junction are Jl. Braga's bakery-cafés, offering the chance to rest.

The **Museum Mandala Wangsit Siliwangi** (Army Museum; open Mon–Sat 08.00–14.30) on Jl. Lembong, was built in 1950 as the staff quarters for the army's West Java 'Siliwangi' division. Its collection includes weapons, rather amateurish war paintings depicting the independence struggle, gruesome photos of atrocities from the war against the guerrillas of Darul Islam (1948–62), and others relating to the plot by the notorious Dutch Captain Raymond 'Turk' Westerling to assassinate cabinet ministers of the newly independent government in 1950. Westerling, whose reign of terror in south Sulawesi in 1947 had caused several thousand Indonesian deaths, seized key locations in Bandung in January 1950, including the Siliwangi division's staff quarters (the site of this museum), but was persuaded to withdraw by the Dutch garrison commander, who was still in the city. Westerling's forces retreated to Jakarta but were repulsed from there too, disrupting his assassination plans; he fled the country the following month.

Further north along Jl. Braga is the provincial branch of *Bank Indonesia*, formerly the Javasche Bank, designed by E.H.G.H. Cuypers in 1918. The **Bethel Church** on the corner of Jl. Perintis Kemerdekaan and Jl. Braga, dating from 1925, and the **Church of St Peter** (Gereja Santo Petrus) on the corner of Jl. Jawa and Jl. Merdeka, built in 1922, are both the work of Wolff Schoemaker.

On the north side of Merdeka Park, past the large statue of a white rhino, is the old **Gemeentehuis** (City Hall), built 1929–35 and designed by E.H. de Roo. The original building can now only be seen from the south: newer, higher structures have been built round it.

On the east side of Jl. Merdeka is the former **School van der Ursuline**, also designed by Cuypers, with a distinctive two-tier roof; today it is a computer management institute.

West from the City Hall, a road leads over the Cikapundung river through a quiet residential neighbourhood to **Gedung Pakuan**, the provincial governor's official residence on Jl. Otista. Built in the 1860s, this was formerly the home of the Dutch Resident.

Just north of the City Hall is **Plaza Bandung Indah**, a modern, air-conditioned shopping centre with fast-food, clothing stores and bookshops. Two blocks further north is the old **'De Driekleur' residence** on the corner of Jl. Juanda and Jl. Sultan Agung. Built in 1937 by Aalbers, this was once an extremely fine Art Deco building; now a bank's office and sadly neglected, it is barely worth a second glance.

The old European quarter

Starting from the Plaza Bandung Indah, head east along Jl. Aceh. On the north side of the street between Jl. Sumatra and Jl. Sulawesi is the headquarters of the army's West Java 'Siliwangi' Division. On the east side of Jl. Kalimantan, opposite, is the former **Palace of the Commandant**, designed in 1918 by C.P. Wolff Schoemaker and his brother, R.L.A. Schoemaker, and still used by the military.

The small, wooded **traffic park** (*taman lalu lintas*) on the west side of Jl. Kalimantan is a children's playground, with miniature roads and road signs, and a small railway.

Further east along Jl. Aceh is the former **Jaarbeurs** building on the south side, used by the Dutch as a hall for trade fairs and now a military teaching college. Designed by Wolff Schoemaker in 1920, it is notable today for the somewhat prudish covering—since independence—of the statues' formerly naked genitalia.

Turn north along Jl. Sulawesi, past **Taman Maluku** on the east side. At the northwest corner of the park is a **statue of Pastor J. Verbraak** (1835–1918), a Dutch military priest who was caught up in the Aceh War (1873–1903).

The **Postal Museum** (Museum Pos dan Giro; open Mon–Thur 08.00–13.00; Fri 08.00–10.00; Sat 08.00–11.30; Sun 09.00–15.00) at the north end of Jl. Cisanggarung has a small collection of exhibits concerned with the history of the Indonesian postal service and philately; it is of interest to specialists.

The **Geological Museum** (Museum Geologi; open Mon–Thur 09.00–15.00; Fri 09.00–11.00, 13.00–15.00; Sat–Sun 09.00–13.00) nearby on Jl. Diponegoro, was opened in 1929 as the Geological Laboratory. The collection includes fossils, skeletons and minerals; exhibits on volcanoes, earthquakes, and oil production; and some fine pieces of petrified wood. Everything is dust-covered, and there are few labels in English.

To the west on Jl. Diponegoro, set back from the road, is **Gedung Sate** ('satay building' – named after the satay skewer-like roof spire), built in 1920 by J. Gerber. It is flanked by two architecturally similar wings: that to the east was built at the same time; the west wing was built in the 1970s, but successfully blends with the original design. Gedung Sate was formerly the office of the colonial government's technical services department and now houses the provincial governor's office.

North of Gedung Sate, a broad avenue leads to the huge concrete **Monumen Perjuangan** (monument and museum of the struggle for independence), completed in 1997. Outside, long panels show in relief vainglorious scenes from Indonesian history, with the inclusion of Bandung landmarks such as the *Savoy Homann* and Gedung Merdeka. Inside are exhibits relating to the fight for independence.

The northern suburbs
On the west side of Jl. Juanda, just a few metres north of the junction with Jl. Ganeca, are three unusual houses in a row, nos 111, 113 and 115, designed by Aalbers in 1937.

Turn west along Jl. Ganeca to the **Bandung Institute of Technology** (Institut Teknologi Bandung; ITB), one of Indonesia's most important centres of higher education. Of architectural note here are two remarkable halls with magnificent sweeping, multi-tiered roofs, designed by Henri Maclaine Pont in 1920 as the Technische Hoogeschool (Technical College), the forerunner of ITB.

At the west end of Jl. Ganeca is **Bandung Zoo** (*kebun binatang*; open daily), which has animal enclosures scattered through shady grounds. The animals displayed include leopard cat and tiger, orang-utan, gibbon, Javan leaf monkey, sun bear, and the rare Bawean deer.

On the corner of Jl. Taman Sari and Jl. Gelap Nyawang, opposite the zoo entrance, is **Villa Merah** ('Red Villa'), designed by R.L.A. Schoemaker in 1922 and built with bricks shipped from the Netherlands.

Further south on Jl. Taman Sari, at the junction with Jl. Sulanjana, is a fine **mansion** on the east side; this was the original site of Bandung's technical college prior to 1920, and is now the residence of ITB's rector.

Outlying sights
There are a few places on the city margins which cannot be visited easily in conjunction with others; nevertheless, they should not be neglected.

The **West Java Provincial Museum** (Museum Negeri Propinsi Jawa Barat 'Sri Baduga'; open Tues–Sun 08.00–16.00) is difficult to reach because of frequent traffic congestion, but worth the effort. It lies on the south side of Jl. Lingkar Selatan (the southern inner ring road), at the junction with Jl. Otista and Jl. Pelindung Hewan.

The museum houses a small, interesting collection of archaeological and cultural exhibits relating to West Java. There are photographs of a number of minor archaeological sites, including the terraced pyramidal site of Candi Cibedug near Bayah (see p 234). **Prehistoric exhibits** include the petrified skull of a prehistoric buffalo and chopping tools, axe heads, pottery and jewellery. In an inner courtyard are rather crude replicas of several early stone inscriptions and Hindu images found in the province. An ethnographic collection upstairs includes a model of a Baduy village and a life-size replica house. Also of note are a selection of traditional **farming and fishing implements** and a huge ceremonial carriage from a palace in Cirebon. On the top floor are musical instruments, implements of the traditional Sundanese debus performance, *wayang kulit, wayang* *golek* and *wayang cepak*, masks, batik and some magnificent carved wooden wall panels from Cirebon.

A **Dutch war cemetery**, Ereveld Pandu (Pandu Field of Honour), containing almost 4000 graves, lies adjacent to the Pandu public cemetery off the west side of Jl. Pasir Kali, most easily reached by taxi. Buried here are soldiers who died at Ciater and Subang, to the north of Bandung, while fighting the Japanese; and the remains of soldiers and civilians transferred from cemeteries in south Sumatra, Bangka and south Sulawesi. The site is carefully maintained by the Netherlands War Graves Foundation.

Thomas Karsten (1884–1945), the architect responsible for so many fine early 20C buildings, is buried in another Dutch cemetery, **Ereveld Leuwigajah**, c 3km south of Cimahi on the west side of Bandung. Interned by the Japanese, he died in the camp hospital in April 1945. The cemetery contains more than 5000 graves, many of them transferred from sites in east Kalimantan, Sumatra and Bangka. To find it, turn south along Jl. Gatot Subroto from the traffic lights in the centre of Cimahi.

Villa Isola, one of Bandung's finest Art Deco buildings, is on the west side of Jl. Setiabudi, 6km north of Bandung, just below the Ledeng minibus terminal. Built to C.P. Wolff Schoemaker's design in 1932 for a wealthy Italian, it is now a teacher training college. Visitors may enter the grounds, but not the building.

Fighting rams (*adu domba*) can be seen on alternate Sundays at a ring off Jl. Setiabudi near the Ledeng terminal. Take Jl. Sersan Bajuri opposite the terminal and turn left after c 400m to find the action. The animals do not fight to the death, blood is rarely spilt, and the atmosphere is exciting.

Around Bandung

Bandung makes an excellent base for exploring the beautiful countryside of the Parahyangan highlands which flank the city to the north and south. These volcanic hills present the visitor with smoking sulphurous craters and steaming vents, eerie lakes and numerous hot springs. It is an area with great hiking opportunities, and has the added advantage of a relatively cool climate.

The excursion north to **Lembang** and **Gunung Tangkuban Perahu** (see p 246) takes you to the rim of Java's most accessible active volcano. The beautiful **Cisangkuy** and **upper Citarum valleys** (see p 248) to the south offer panoramic views across some of West Java's most striking cultivated landscapes of rice and tea. The **Ciwidey valley** (see p 251) to the southeast is the location of the magnificent milky crater lake of Kawah Putih. To the northeast, the trip to **Sumedang** and **Gunung Tampomas** (see p 251) combines a visit to an historically important museum with the opportunity to climb a long-extinct volcano. On the edge of Bandung, within easy reach of the city centre, the **Cimahi Falls** and **Situ Lembang** (see p 253) are sites of considerable natural beauty.

LEMBANG AND GUNUNG TANGKUBAN PERAHU

A pleasant day excursion can be made to the cool highland market town of Lembang, continuing to the craters of Gunung Tangkuban Perahu. On the return from Lembang, you can choose between the bus and an easy, generally downhill walk from the Maribaya hot springs through a wooded gorge to Juanda Park, and from there down to the *Dago Tea House*.

Practical information

Public transport
Minibuses to Lembang depart from the Stasiun Hall terminal beside Bandung's train station. These can also be picked up along Jl. Sukajadi or Jl. Setiabudi. From Lembang, any transport bound for Ciater or Subang will pass the turn-off to the volcano, though from here you may have to walk up at least part of the entry road, c 4km, if traffic is light. To reach Maribaya, charter a **pony trap** from Lembang or take a minibus.

Private transport
Take Jl. Sukajadi and Jl. Setiabudi north past the Villa Isola and the Ledeng minibus terminal. This road climbs eventually to Lembang; at the main intersection in Lembang, turn left towards Subang and continue 9.5km to the turning on the left signposted to Gunung Tangkuban Perahu.

Lembang

From the Ledeng terminal the road winds upward, passing the Bosscha Observatory after 6km and, on the southern edge of Lembang, the ✿✿✿/✿✿ *Grand Hotel Lembang* (☎ 022 278 6671; fax 278 6829). This is a comfortable colonial-era hotel dating from the 1920s, with spacious—if somewhat threadbare—old suites and a less interesting modern wing; it can be very cool at night here. Just beyond the Grand Hotel Lembang is a **vegetable market** on the left; at weekends the small town is filled with shoppers from Bandung seeking out fresh produce at low prices.

The road turns sharply right c 500m beyond the hotel, and just beyond, Jl. Jayagiri turns uphill to the left, signposted to Taman Junghuhn. A lane to the right off Jl. Jayagiri after c 500m leads to a small wooded park with the **grave of Franz Wilhelm Junghuhn** (1809–64). The grave lies in what, at the time of his death, was about to become a large cinchona plantation. The gates may be locked, but you can walk round to the left beside the adjacent houses and enter through a back entrance.

Franz Wilhelm Junghuhn
Junghuhn, a German naturalist from Mansfeld, arrived in Batavia in 1835 as an officer in the Dutch Indies army. With admirable foresight, his commander permitted him to study full-time the region's natural history, and Junghuhn worked his way methodically through Java and Sumatra, record-

ing and publishing his findings. His best-known book, published in 1853, was for many years the key text on Java's natural history. In the 1850s he pioneered the development of cinchona plantations in Java for the extraction of quinine, first at the Cibodas Alpine Gardens near Gunung Gede, and later at Gunung Malabar to the south of Bandung.

At the main intersection in Lembang the main road turns left (north), climbing up the southern slopes of Gunung Tangkuban Perahu, past terraced fields of vegetables, then through a pine forest where a left turn is signed to the volcano.

Gunung Tangkuban Perahu

The entry lane climbs for c 4km to the car park on the rim of **Kawah Ratu**, the largest of Gunung Tangkuban Perahu's three main craters. The last major eruption was in 1967, but there has been a small amount of seismic activity since late 1992, and visitors are advised not to descend within the craters. A clear but uneven path leads anticlockwise round the edge of Kawah Ratu, past a mass of souvenir and food stalls; wear sturdy shoes. This is an easy stroll with good views into the crater, which has a small lake and several active fumaroles. The path leads past gnarled shrubs and stunted trees to the saddle separating Kawah Ratu from the less active **Kawah Upas** behind. A third crater, **Kawah Domas**, can be reached by a 20-minute walk through woods from beside the information centre in the car park. From this crater it is possible to continue along another path which brings you out lower down on the lane leading back to the main Lembang–Subang road, negating the need to walk back up to the top car park.

Ciater hot springs

North of the Gunung Tangkuban Perahu turning, the Subang road descends across slopes covered in a green carpet of tea bushes to Ciater (7km). Here, a right turn leads after 600m to ✰✰✰✰/✰✰✰ *Sari Ater Hot Spring Resort* (☎ 0264 470891/2; fax 470890). Nearby are dozens of cheap *penginapan*, but there is little reason to stay in Ciater; Indonesians are attracted simply by the cool climate. The resort's hot-water swimming pool is open to non-residents for a fee, but the resort itself is rather soulless.

Maribaya hot springs and the Cikapundung gorge

Back at the crossroads in Lembang, turn east (left if coming from the volcano) and after 5.5km you will reach the Maribaya hot springs and a path to a waterfall on the right side. The waterfall, **Curug Ciomas** (or Curug Omas), is a 15-minute walk from the Maribaya car park.

Maribaya is also the starting point for a delightful, easy walk down to Juanda Park (Taman Juanda) through the Cikapundung gorge (1.5–2 hours; c 7km). After passing through the gorge, the path emerges into the shady park where at the road head there is a cliff containing an old Dutch casemate (*gua Belanda*) dating from the Second World War. Follow the road past food and drink stalls, and fork right down a dirt path to some old Japanese-built munitions stores (*gua Jepang*); young boys with torches will eagerly guide you inside for a small tip, but there is little to see. The path continues to the Taman Juanda car park, from where you can take a minibus or walk further down to Dago and the *Tea House* for a well-earned rest.

THE CISANGKUY AND UPPER CITARUM VALLEYS

Although time-consuming if you rely on public transport, this otherwise excellent excursion takes in some of West Java's finest mountain scenery, passing tea estates, hot springs, and smoking solfataras. Because of the poor state of some of the roads and the general paucity of public transport, it is best done in two days, with a stop either at Pangalengan or at the Mess Malabar in the Malabar tea estate near Pintu.

Practical information

Public transport
Buses to Pangalengan run from Bandung's Abdul Muis terminal on Jl. Pungkur. From Pangalengan, minibuses run to Pasir Malang, Pintu and Santosa. From Santosa, minibuses run north through Pacet to Ciparay and (infrequently) south to Arjuna.

Private transport
Leave the Padaleunyi toll-road, which skirts the south side of Bandung, at the Jl. Moha Toha exit, and turn south along a very congested road through Dayeuhkolot and Banjaran; progress along here can be slow. In Banjaran, c 1.2km beyond a sharp right-hand bend, turn off left onto the Pangalengan road. From here the traffic eases and the road starts climbing.

Gunung Malabar

The western slopes of Gunung Malabar were once covered with tea and cinchona plantations. Some tea estates still remain near Pangalengan, but most have long been abandoned. The derelict remains of one are found along a lane to the east, 5.5km south of Banjaran. The lane—Jl. Gunung Puntang—climbs through terraced rice fields and small hamlets for 9km to a barrier (small fee), and beyond enters a pine forest with dense undergrowth, ending at a parking lot with warung and a campsite. Several trails lead into the forest here, and it is apparently possible to hike to the summit of Gunung Malabar, though a guide is needed (but difficult to find: ask at the entry barrier).

Close to the car park are more than a dozen ruined, heavily overgrown bungalows which once housed the tea estate managers; some name plates—mostly Chinese and Dutch—are still attached to the buildings.

Near here was the site of **Radio Malabar**, a radio link with the Netherlands set up in 1923, with what, at that time, was the world's most powerful transmitter. Nothing remains now of this ambitious project, which entailed stringing antennae across a deep ravine on the mountain.

Pangalengan

Back on the main road, continue south 17km to Pangalengan, passing more tea plantations. This small market town is itself of little interest, but has reasonable guest-houses for visitors wishing to explore the area.

Practical information

Accommodation
On the main street, 100m to the left at the T-junction, is ✩✩/✩ *Puri Pangalengan* (☎ 022 597 9292), a clean, simple hotel.

The ✩✩/✩ *Citere Guest House* (☎ 022 597 9423) is 3km further on beyond the town, in a very pleasant rural setting with fine views from some of the rooms.

At the Pangalengan T-junction, the left branch passes through the town and on to Pintu. The right branch turns sharp left immediately and then runs past the grassy banks of **Situ Cileunca** and **Situ Cipanunjang**, two small, interconnected reservoirs which are used for boating and fishing. The road is very rough as far as Pulosari but improves beyond the lakes.

At the junction in Pasir Malang, 9.5km from Pangalengan, turn left to Pintu (the road to the right here leads eventually to the south coast, but is extremely rough in places).

The Bosscha memorial and Mess Malabar
The Pintu road offers magnificent views over extensive tea plantations, and after 7km reaches another junction.

To the left here, 100m away, is the **grave and memorial of Karel Albert Rudolf Bosscha** (1865–1928), who pioneered the development of tea plantations round Gunung Malabar in the 1890s. The memorial lies in a pretty flower garden, shaded by trees. The village of **Pintu** lies 1km further.

To the right at the Bosscha memorial junction, the road leads after 1300m to Bosscha's old Malabar tea estate (where the gateposts still stand, dated 1896) and his former residence, which is now *Mess Malabar*, a rather charming ✩✩ guest-house (☎ 022 597 9401; advance bookings only).

Bosscha's home was damaged in the Second World War but has been rebuilt in a sympathetic style. The guest rooms are in a modern annex and are overpriced, but the setting is enchanting; good meals are available, and staff can provide bicycles for rent or arrange a visit to the nearby **tea factory**. Tour buses sometimes pass through, stopping briefly for lunch.

Cibolang hot springs and Gunung Windu

From the Malabar estate, return towards Pintu, but instead of entering the main street, turn sharp right and follow the road 5km, passing a tea factory, to **Cibolang hot springs** (Air Panas Cibolang); the hot-water pools are set back 1.3km from the main road along a very rough track. Their situation, at the foot of the wooded flank of **Gunung Windu**, makes them some of the most attractive in the region, but their isolated location means they are usually almost deserted; foreign visitors will quickly attract curious onlookers.

From the back of the swimming pool complex a path climbs up the southwestern slopes of the volcano, and after c 20–30 minutes reaches some half-dozen fumaroles of sulphurous gas amidst yellow sulphur rock. There is apparently a more extensive crater higher up.

The road beyond the hot springs passes another tea factory to **Santosa**, a tiny tea estate workers' hamlet. Turn right here to reach the spectacular crater of Gunung Papandayan, or turn left to descend the lovely Citarum valley to Pacet and back to Bandung.

Gunung Papandayan: the western approach

Harder to reach than the eastern approach from Garut (see p 257) because the road is very poor, this route does have the advantage of allowing you to drive right to the crater rim. Note that there is no public transport to the top.

From Santosa take the winding road south towards Arjuna, turning off east at **Cileuleuy** after c 14km. Without your own vehicle, it is easiest to charter an *ojek* in Santosa (or Cileuleuy); the climb to the road head is c 12km.

Kawah Mas ('golden crater') presents a chaotic sight of bright yellow sulphur rock, steaming, hissing fumaroles and very friable lava. You can wander at will, but the clouds of choking sulphurous smoke should be avoided: they will burn your throat, your eyes will water and you will quickly be gasping for breath. Take care at every step.

The Citarum valley

Take the Pacet road north from Santosa; beyond Kertasari (4km) the route is very rough, but then for several kilometres the beautiful Citarum valley presents spectacular vistas of terraced rice fields cascading down the hill sides, best viewed under the late afternoon sun (or, less practically, very early in the morning). Lower down, the road passes an old quinine estate at **Arjasari**, where archaeologists have mapped an extensive network of proto-historic raised earth mounds, embankments and ditches several kilometres in length; their function is unknown. To the casual eye there is little to see; the earthworks are buried in thick undergrowth or beneath plantations.

The road continues through Pacet and arrives eventually at **Ciparay**, 34km from Santosa. From here it is a slow haul through heavy traffic back to Bandung.

THE CIWIDEY VALLEY

An easy trip south of Bandung takes in some fine highland scenery and visits the volcanic crater lake of Kawah Putih, invigorating hot springs and a small lake in the heart of a tea plantation.

Practical information

Public transport

Buses run from Bandung's Abdul Muis terminal to Soreang, and from there to Ciwidey and Rancabali.

Private transport

Leave the Padaleunyi toll-road south of Bandung at the Kopo exit and turn south, taking the right fork towards Soreang after 9km. Ciwidey is c 12km beyond Soreang, and Rancabali a further 16km. The road south from Bandung can be congested through Katapang, but beyond Soreang the route starts climbing and traffic is lighter.

Kawah Putih and Gunung Patuha

A turning to the east, 11km south of Ciwidey, leads to **Kawah Putih** ('white crater'), a magnificent volcanic crater lake of milky turquoise water, often shrouded in mist. The entry road winds for 5.5km through forest to a car park; the lake is a short walk beyond – part of the **Gunung Tilu nature reserve**. In the past, sulphur was mined here in small quantities; the old shafts can be seen to the right as you approach the lake edge. An easy trail leads round the lake, and it is possible to climb up to the summit and upper crater of **Gunung Patuha** (2434m) in c 1 hour; take the path to the right up the narrow ridge between the car park and lake.

Cimanggu and Ciwalini hot springs

Back on the main road, continue south past the **Cimanggu hot springs** and swimming pool (c 1km) to the cleaner, and much more pleasant **Ciwalini hot-water swimming pool** (Kawasan Agrowisata Ciwalini), in a peaceful setting 1km further on, surrounded by tea bushes.

Beyond Ciwalini, the road descends through tea estates to **Rancabali** and **Situ Patengan** (3km), a small lake with food stalls, surrounded by trees and more tea bushes; it can be quite busy at weekends.

SUMEDANG AND GUNUNG TAMPOMAS

Just possible to do as a very long day trip, this is better done in two separate visits, or with an overnight stay in Cimalaka's simple accommodation. Sumedang's small but interesting museum is well worth a look; an ascent of Gunung Tampomas (1684m) is for those who like a stiff climb rewarded with fine views.

Practical information

Public transport

Buses to Sumedang depart from Bandung's Cicaheum terminal. From Sumedang, any Cirebon-bound bus will pass Cimalaka, the starting point for Gunung Tampomas.

Private transport

Take the Padaleunyi toll-road south of Bandung to its eastern end and continue straight on along the Sumedang road. Avoid leaving Bandung along the very slow and congested Jl. Yani, even though this is shorter and avoids the toll.

The road from Cileunyi to Sumedang follows the route of Marshal Daendels' Great Post Road, a winding route that climbs steadily for c 8km to Tanjung Sari, and consequently suffers from continual traffic jams. From there it descends gently through dense forest to Sumedang. Beside the road, just east of the 'Bandung 34km' stone, is a **monument** depicting Daendels and the local ruler, Kusumahadinata (Kornel), shaking hands at a meeting in 1810.

History

As Regent of Sumedang, Kornel was under obligation to provide labourers to build the stretch of the post road through his territory. This he did, but the severe engineering difficulties they encountered through this rough terrain proved too much for their simple tools, and Kornel authorised them to stop work. Daendels came to negotiate and was received politely but coldly by the suspicious Kornel, who, if we are to believe the monument, never took his hand off his kris. Daendels, recognising the possibility of an uprising, provided the equipment and labour needed from his own forces.

Sumedang

The main sight of Sumedang is the **Museum Prabu Geusan Ulun** (open Tues–Sun 08.00–12.00), which lies to the right opposite the town's *alun-alun*. Named after Sumedang's ruler of the late 16C, Geusan Ulun, who sheltered fugitives fleeing the sultanate of Banten's attack on Pajajaran, the museum comprises five buildings tucked away inside the local government office complex.

The first building is the former residence of the Regent, with a fine verandah at the back. Exhibits include old costumes; weapons, including 16C cannons from Banten, left behind by Maulana Yusuf's forces during the sultanate's expansion across western Java; and a bed, reputed to be Kornel's. Immediately behind is the Regent's family residence; exhibits here include kitchen utensils, handwritten copies of the Koran and old money. An adjacent building has some magnificent heirlooms, including a pair of fine gold ceremonial crowns, gold belts and other decorative ornaments; there is a magnificent collection of kris, including that said to be worn by Kornel at his meeting with Daendels. Other buildings contain a gamelan collection donated by the former mayor of Jakarta, Ali Sadikin, who was born in Sumedang, and old *wayang golek* and *wayang kulit*.

A short walk from the museum is the rather dull grave of Cut Nyak Dien, a national heroine from Aceh, who with her husband was involved in the Aceh wars against the Dutch in the late 19C and early 20C. Kornel is buried in another graveyard nearby.

Gunung Tampomas

From Sumedang continue on the Cirebon road c 7km to **Cimalaka**, then a further 2km to *Tampomas Baru*, a restaurant on the south side of the road. Almost directly opposite is a track where the walk begins to Gunung Tampomas, a Holocene-epoch, long-extinct volcano. The restaurant owner can find a guide, which is recommended, though not essential. The path passes through thick forest before reaching an open, grassy summit with fine views. Allow 3–4 hours for the climb, and an hour less for the descent.

There is simple accommodation beside the restaurant for those who want to start the climb early or return late.

THE CIMAHI FALLS AND SITU LEMBANG

In this excursion to areas of natural beauty northwest of Bandung the route passes a fine viewing point on the way to several waterfalls and a charming, isolated lake. The waterfalls can be busy at weekends. Allow a long half-day, or a full day if walking to all the sites.

Practical information

Public transport

Take a **minibus** from downtown Bandung to Lembang, and from there another to Cisarua (c 8km); the turning to Cisarua lies 500m below the Grand Hotel Lembang, and it can be easier to find transport by waiting at this junction. The Cimahi falls are all within easy walking distance of Cisarua market. A rough lane to the north in Cisarua leads to the small lake, Situ Lembang; there is no public transport, so either walk the 7km each way, or charter an *ojek* in Cisarua. The Cihanjuang viewpoint is a walk of c 3km from Cisarua market, along asphalt roads; an *ojek* would take 5 minutes.

Private transport

Take the Cisarua road from Lembang c 6km, and then turn south; the Cihanjuang viewpoint is off to the west (right) after c 2km. Return to the Cisarua road and continue west 1.3km to the village centre; park near the gate to the Cimahi falls. For Situ Lembang, continue through Cisarua c 400m to the rough lane on the right and follow this to the lake.

The Cihanjuang viewpoint

One of the finest panoramas in the Bandung area is from a bluff overlooking the Cimahi gorge, above the village of Cihanjuang. On a clear, sunny morning the view across the Bandung basin to the southwest is magnificent. To the northwest are the slopes of Gunung Burangrang.

Cimahi falls

Close to the village of **Cisarua** are three fine waterfalls (Curug Cimahi) on the Cimahi river. The lowest is reached through a gate in the centre of the village; steps descend steeply from the road.

To reach the middle waterfall, walk 300m east of the village to where a path leads uphill from the road, beside a small bridge. The walk takes 15–20 minutes and involves fording the river.

The path to the highest and least visited waterfall starts from a point on the road c 60m east of the previous path, and climbs through fields to emerge above the middle fall. The path is indistinct in places, but it is difficult to get lost. Take some water and snacks.

Situ Lembang

This beautiful small reservoir is a 1.5–2 hour walk from Cisarua, so if walking both ways allow c 4–5 hours for the round trip. It is easier to take an *ojek* from Cisarua market at least one way. The track is rough in places, but the walk is very pleasant, passing through a pine plantation and then into montane vegetation; the reservoir was built by the Dutch in the 1930s to provide Lembang with drinking water.

In midweek, when there are few other people around, this can be a good birdwatching site. The huge crater in which Situ Lembang lies is part of an ancient volcano which once dwarfed Gunung Tangkuban Perahu.

Cipanas, Tasikmalaya and Pangandaran

Highlights. This area of western Java is one of tremendous natural beauty, a landscape dominated by volcanoes; important historical sites are few. The small **Candi Cangkuang** (see p 255) near Leles, the spectacular crater of **Gunung Papandayan** (see p 256), and the alluring lake at **Kawah Telaga Bodas** (see p 257) are all very worthwhile destinations. There are dozens of opportunities for hikers: **Curug Citiis** and **Gunung Guntur** (see p 256) near Cipanas, **Gunung Cikuray** (see p 257) near Garut, and **Gunung Galunggung** (see p 260) near Tasikmalaya are some of the best. **Pangandaran** (see p 261), on the south coast, is a slow-paced, relaxed beach resort, and the starting point for a highly recommended boat trip through the mangrove waterways of **Segara Anakan** (see p 263).

Practical information

Travel advice

Bandung to Garut is c 65km (or c 80km via the faster Padaleunyi toll-road); detour to Candi Cangkuang, 3km each way; detour to Cipanas, 2km each way. Garut to Kampung Naga is 25km, Kampung Naga to Tasikmalaya, 32km, and Tasikmalaya to Pangandaran via Banjar, c 110km.

Public transport

Buses run frequently from Bandung's Cicaheum terminal to Garut and Tasikmalaya. For Candi Cangkuang, stop in Leles opposite the mosque, at the junction signed to Stasiun Karangsari, and take a dokar from here. For Cipanas, alight at the clearly signed junction 9km further south and wait for a **minibus** up to the village (or walk 2km).

Private transport

For a quick exit from Bandung, take the toll-road to Cileunyi from the Jl. Pasteur toll-gate, and follow the main road straight to Garut. A recommended detour turns off south towards Majalaya just before Cicalengka. Follow this c 5km, then turn left and follow a winding lane 19km through hills to rejoin the main road at Kadungora. This may not save time, but is much more scenic.

Accommodation

A good choice is available at Cipanas, Garut, Tasikmalaya and Pangandaran.

Candi Cangkuang and Situ Cangkuang

The main road from Cileunyi to Nagreg is often busy and slow. In Leles, c 4km beyond Kadungora, turn east opposite the Mesjid Agung to **Candi Cangkuang** (3km), lying on the far shore of a small lake, **Situ Cangkuang**. Visitors are encouraged to take a raft across the water (although there is a path through rice fields a few hundred metres back along the road).

Today this is the only Hindu *candi* still standing in West Java, and much of it has been rebuilt. The small structure stands on a low hill, shaded by trees, and has been vaguely dated to 7C–10C; it has few decorative details, but an opening on the east side contains a damaged image of Shiva. Beside the *candi* is the 17C tomb of a certain Arif Muhammad, a soldier of the Mataram kingdom who, legend has it, raised a family here.

At the foot of the hill is **Kampung Pulo**, a tiny hamlet of brightly painted houses with a small prayer hall at the west end. This is one of a very few remaining settlements in West Java still practising a very old form of *adat*, the customary law which controls certain aspects of daily life. The *adat* here is believed locally to have been handed down from Arif Muhammad and his descendants: among the rules is a tradition forbidding four-legged livestock in the hamlet, and the striking of gongs; the laws are not explained, nor are they questioned. This somewhat mystical place is a popular pilgrimage site with local Javanese.

The path beyond the prayer hall leads to a couple more graves, one of them said to belong to a local holy man.

Cipanas

Accommodation

There are a couple of very good hotels, and several rather unexciting ones, grouped closely together. Most rooms have private baths fed by the hot springs. Recommended is ☆☆/☆☆

Kampung Sumber Alam (☎ 0262 21027/28000; fax 22569), the best hotel here, with attractive rooms built over fish-ponds, and a swimming pool. A reasonable alternative is ☆☆ *Cipanas Indah* (☎ 0262 81736).

The Cipanas turn-off is 9km beyond Leles. A rather dreary resort village which has grown up round some hot springs, it only really comes alive at weekends. Nevertheless, Cipanas is a good base from which to explore the numerous volcanoes in the vicinity; for accommodation it is preferable to Garut, although the latter has banks and many more shops.

Curug Citiis and Gunung Guntur

The closest excursion to Cipanas is the walk to the cascades of **Curug Citiis** (c 2–3 hours, although this can be made shorter by driving or taking an *ojek* most of the way). A guide is recommended, though not really needed unless you wish to continue to a second waterfall and then up to the summit of **Gunung Guntur** (2249m), the volcano that looms over Cipanas to the northwest. To the top and back is a long day's hike, so a dawn start is advised; your hotel can usually arrange a guide.

Gunung Papandayan and Kawah Kamojang

The easiest approach to Gunung Papandayan's spectacular crater is from Cisurupan, south of Cipanas. On the way the route passes the turning to Kawah Kamojang, an area of intense geothermal activity on the west side of Gunung Guntur.

Using public transport, take a minibus from Cipanas to Cisurupan, and then an *ojek* at the junction signed to Gunung Papandayan. The Kamojang area is harder to reach: with luck you will find an *ojek* or a minibus at the junction in Samarang, but it can be easier to charter a vehicle from Cipanas for a day or half-day to visit both sites.

Head first for **Gunung Papandayan**, as there is more walking involved and it is preferable to avoid the midday heat. Take the road to Samarang (c 9km) and continue past the Kawah Kamojang turn-off a further 7.5km to the junction with the main Garut–Cikajang road. Turn south to Cisurupan (6.5km) and bear right at a left-hand bend, signposted to Gunung Papandayan. From here it is a 9km climb to the car park, and from there a 20–30-minute walk to the crater.

Gunung Papandayan (2665m) erupted most recently in 1923, but its last major eruption was in 1772, when the northeast flank collapsed, destroying 40 villages. The view across the crater from the highest side is tremendous: a yellow-stained Gehenna of sulphurous fumaroles and bubbling mud; on a clear day the almost perfect cone of Gunung Ciremai can be seen on the northeast horizon.

Back in Samarang, turn off west; the road climbs steadily, with a fine view to the south of Gunung Cikuray across the Cimanuk valley. After 14km, the **Kamojang crater complex** (Wana Wisata Kawah Kamojang) is clearly signed to the right. Beyond the toll-gate is a bubbling mud pool, **Kawah Manuk**, on the left; just beyond is another small pool, **Kawah Brecek**. From the car park at the road head it is a short, easy walk to the main geysers and bubbling, steaming fumaroles where the caretaker will entertain visitors with a few tricks. There is a pleasant circular walk through forest, past various other sites of geothermal activity.

Garut

Hotels and services

There are several simple losmen in town, but the nicest places are on the outskirts. ☆☆/☆ *Sarimbit Guest House* (☎ 0262 21033), on the main road in Tarogong, has reasonable rooms and friendly staff. The modern ☆☆☆/☆☆ *Hotel Ngamplang* (☎ 0262 21480/24702), 4km south of Garut, is very clean and in a fine setting, but isolated and characterless. For money, *BCA* (M, V) is at the top end of Jl. Ciledug. *Bank Lippo* and the **post office** are on Jl. Yani, the main thoroughfare and shopping area.

There is little reason to stay here, although it is a useful public transport hub. The accommodation is generally better in Cipanas, 5km north.

Kawah Telaga Bodas

This is a beautiful, very isolated, volcanic crater lake high on the northern flank of the Gunung Galunggung massif, 25km from Garut. Though hard to reach, it is one of the finest camping or picnic sites in West Java, with several good walks in the vicinity.

Follow Jl. Yani east out of Garut c 11km to Wanaraja, where a lane to the right, indistinctly signed, leads steadily uphill 14km to the lake. An *ojek* can be chartered at the junction. The track is very rough and rocky in places, especially on the lower section, and is not accessible by sedan; a small jeep can do it without much difficulty. The route climbs along ridges with magnificent panoramas, and then through forest. At the top of the pass, a narrow track to the right climbs briefly to the crater rim and then descends gently to the lake shore after 800m. The beautiful milky-green lake is best seen on a clear day; look carefully and you can see small gas bubbles rising from the lake bed. Looming over the water is Gunung Masigit.

The road beyond the pass descends steeply, and quickly deteriorates to a single-file footpath; after a 20-minute walk, you reach **Cipanas Telaga Bodas**, a tiny hamlet in the forest with some tremendously rustic hot springs, a small mosque and some *warung*. This footpath leads eventually down to the road head on the east side of Gunung Galunggung, and thence to Cisayong, Indihiang and Tasikmalaya.

Kampung Naga

The road south from Garut climbs across the lower slopes of Gunung Cikuray into the extremely beautiful **Ciwulan river valley**, which it follows down to the unusual village of **Kampung Naga**. Traffic can be slow along this winding road, but the terraced rice fields present a fine spectacle. A car park on the left just beyond the 'Bandung 88km' stone marks the village, reached down a long flight of concrete steps.

One of less than half a dozen communities left in Sunda whose way of life follows an extraordinarily rigid *adat*, Kampung Naga attracts a steady stream of tourists. Its situation on the bank of the Ciwulan river is glorious, but unless you enjoy poking your nose uninvited into other people's homes, a visit here may be a somewhat uncomfortable experience: tourists are politely tolerated, but not openly encouraged.

The village *adat* prescribes all houses to be made from natural materials. The walls are of timber and painted, plaited bamboo, and the thatched roofs of sugar-palm fronds. At the back of the village is a small mosque, and beside it the *balai kampung*, the village meeting hall. Behind these, and higher, is the *rumah adat*, an unpainted building surrounded by a bamboo wicker fence; this is the village elders' meeting chamber, the most important structure in the village, used for adat ceremonies. According to the *kepala adat*, the elder responsible for implementing the traditional law, Kampung Naga has existed in this manner for at least 800 years.

There are neither vehicles nor electricity here, and farming is done entirely with hand-powered tools. A few souvenir stalls have been set up for tourists.

TASIKMALAYA

Practical information

Transport

Eastbound **trains** include the overnight *Turangga* and *Mutiara Selatan* to Yogyakarta, Solo and Surabaya. The daytime *Pajajaran* goes as far as Solo. Westbound trains to Bandung include the *Turangga*, the *Mutiara Selatan*, and the *Mataram*. There are several economy-class trains in both directions. **Buses** to most West Java towns depart from the main bus terminal on Jl. Juanda (Jl. By-pass) on the southwest side of town. Angkot to Indihiang can be picked up on Jl. Martadinata. Bemo to other destinations depart from various locations; hotel staff can advise for specific routes.

Accommodation

The nicest hotels are found along Jl. Martadinata on the northwest side of the town. Simple, cheap *losmen* can be found on Jl. Tarumanagara, which runs south from the train station. The phone code is 0265.

☆☆/☆ *Hotel Abadi* (☎ 333789) Jl. Empang 58. One of the best low-budget hotels in town; clean and well-run.

☆☆☆/☆☆ *Hotel Kencana* (Jl. Yudanegara 17. Right in the town centre, but near the principal mosque.

☆☆☆/☆☆ *Hotel Mahkota Graha* (☎ 332282) Jl. Martadinata 45. Popular with foreign tour groups, and within walking distance of the town centre.

☆☆/☆ *Hotel Mandalawangi*
(☎ 331347/332920) Jl. Martadinata
177. A pleasant hotel in a garden setting 2km northwest of the town centre.

☆☆☆/☆☆ *Hotel Ramayana* Jl. Martadinata
333. Overpriced and dull, but does have a
swimming pool.

☆☆ ☆ *Hotel Widuri* (☎ 334342) Jl.
Martadinata 51. A friendly, simple hotel
with clean, cheap, unexciting rooms.

Food

Rumah Makan Eot, on the west side of
Jl. Sukardjo, serves good local food.
Nearby, *Cahaya* has European food and
is rather more upmarket. On the northeast outskirts is *Ponyo*, one of a west
Java chain, with average food in a pleasant setting. In the town centre are
dozens of warung.

Services

Banks, including *BII* (M, V) and *Bank
Bali* (M, V) are clustered at the west end
of Jl. Yudanegara. The **post office** is at
Jl. Otista 6. Nearby is the **tourist office**
(Dinas Pariwisata) at Jl. Otista 2. There
are 24-hour *wartel* on Jl. Yudanegara
and just east of the *alun-alun* at Jl.
Merdeka 23.

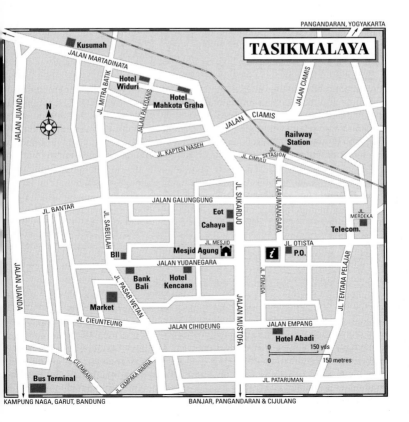

This lively market town is a pleasant place to break a journey. With several decent hotels, a thriving crafts industry and the nearby crater of Gunung Galunggung to visit, it merits an overnight stay.

Kawah Galunggung

A large, deep volcanic crater lake northwest of Tasikmalaya, Kawah Galunggung requires a rather arduous walk up a steep, sandy slope; the view, on a clear day, is well worth the effort. Take an *angkot* from Tasikmalaya to Indihiang, and from there an *ojek*.

In Indihiang, c 5km north of Tasikmalaya, turn west beside the **Bank Rakyat Indonesia**; *ojek* usually wait at the junction. Follow this rough road c 15km to some hot springs (*air panas*) and a swimming pool. These are not terribly exciting, but a footpath from the back of the complex leads to the crater (c 3km). Allow 1–1.5 hours to the rim and take a hat, plenty of drinking water, and sun cream: it can be a mercilessly hot climb, with little shade.

Visitors with their own transport or coming by *ojek* can drive c 2km past the hot springs entrance gate, bypassing it to the left. From the parking area beyond, it's a hard 30–40-minute climb through volcanic sand up to the crater's east rim. A steep path leads down inside the rim to the lake.

Gunung Galunggung (2168m) exploded at dawn on 5 April 1982, after almost 63 years of silence. The first eruption was followed by a further series of minor and major ones, and caused the evacuation of 35,000 people from the eastern slopes. 94,000 hectares of agricultural land were covered with thick ash and debris, and the estimated cost of the damage was c US$100 million. Fresh water became scarce in the area for many months, as the volcanic ash filled all water courses. The eruption series finally ended in early 1983.

Situ Lengkong and Astana Gede Kawali

These minor historical sites lie to the northeast of Tasikmalaya. Situ Lengkong is a small lake with an island on which lie several graves, said to be of kings from the 7C Galuh kingdom which once controlled a large part of Sunda. At Kawali, further east, is a shady grove containing several unusual inscribed stones of unknown origin, possibly from the Galuh era. Take a *bemo* from Rajapolah to Panjalu, and another to Kawali.

In **Rajapolah**, c 8km north of Indihiang, are many shops that sell handicrafts made from bamboo, rattan and pandanus leaf. To reach Situ Lengkong, take the lane east from Rajapolah to Cihaurbeuti, and at a T-junction after c 1km, turn north towards to Panumbangan (18km). At the Cikijing/Kawali junction, turn right towards Kawali, and after 500m the road will reach Situ Lengkong, on the edge of Panjalu. Small boats carry visitors to the thickly wooded island where the graves lie.

At the *alun-alun* in **Panjalu**, c 400m beyond the car park, note at the southeast corner an unusual structure called **Bumi Alit**, where the heirlooms of the kings of the Panjalu (Galuh) kingdom are stored. It is usually kept locked, but ask around nearby and someone will eventually find the caretaker.

Continue east through Panjalu towards Kawali, passing the turn to some pleasant waterfalls, **Curug Tujuh Cibolang**. It's a very pretty route from Panjalu to the main Kawali–Cikijing road. Turn south (right) to the *alun-alun* in Kawali; the **Astana Gede Kawali** lies c 1km southwest of the *alun-alun* along narrow lanes. Anyone in the village can direct you.

This is an enchanting site containing several inscribed stones under small shelters. Fantastic trees draped in huge epiphytes and lianas shade the site, which also contains several Muslim graves. Outside the entry gate, follow the track 200m further, past a tree roost used by flying foxes, to what appears to be an old bathing place in a dark grove on the left.

Karang Kamulyan

From Tasikmalaya, the main road to the east passes through Ciamis to Banjar. The strange site of Karang Kamulyan (Cagar Budaya Bojong Galuh Karang Kamulyan) lies 17km east of Ciamis to the south of the road. Somewhat similar to Astana Gede Kawali, but busier and with less to see, Karang Kamulyan is said to be the site of the capital of the Galuh kingdom (?7C–10C). The 'ruins' are mostly just neat piles of river rocks, recently re-laid, lying amid bamboo groves at the confluence of the Citanduy and Cimuntur rivers.

PANGANDARAN

A rather scruffy fishing village which has become a surprisingly popular, if unsophisticated, beach resort, Pangandaran is one of the most accessible points on Java's south coast, and also one of the safest places to swim, though the beach is not especially attractive.

There are direct buses from Tasikmalaya and Ciamis; from most other towns you must change in Banjar. By train, alight in Banjar and finish the journey by bus.

The road from Banjar winds through a densely wooded landscape for much of the c 65km to Pangandaran. Shortly before the coast, it passes **Gua Donan**, a roadside cave used as a roost by insectivorous bats. (Until 1982, visitors could take one home as a souvenir.)

The centre of Pangandaran lies on a narrow isthmus joining the mainland to a forested peninsula. There is a tourist fee to pay when you first enter, and you will be given a street plan; keep the ticket as proof of payment for subsequent days.

Practical information

Hotels

There are dozens of places to choose from, to suit all budgets. However, many are overpriced and dull. Those recommended are listed below. The phone code is 0265.

☆☆ *Adam's Homestay* (☎/fax 639164) Jl. Pamugaran (west beach). Small and friendly, with tastefully furnished rooms and self-catering bungalows, a swimming pool and tasty but limited range of food. Highly recommended.

✷ *Delta Gecko* at Cikembulan, 4km west of Pangandaran. Very popular low-budget dormitory and bungalow accommodation near a quiet beach; bicycles available; vegetarian food.

✷ *Losmen Kalapa Nunggal* at Cikembulan, 4km west of Pangandaran. A very good value, low-budget *losmen* run by a friendly couple. Highly recommended.

✰✰✰✰/✰✰✰/✰✰ *Sunrise Beach Hotel* (☎ 639220/1) Jl. Kidang Pananjung 175. The best of the large hotels; good rooms and pool.

✰✰✰/✰✰ *Surya Pesona* (☎ 639428) Jl. Pamugaran (west beach). A large, comfortable resort hotel with pool.

Food and services

Along Jl. Pamugaran and Jl. Bulak Laut especially, there are numerous restaurants serving Western food, with plenty of fresh fish dishes. Along the west beach front further south are scores of *warung* selling cheap Indonesian food. Other simple cafés lie along Jl. Kidang Pananjung, the main street that runs north–south through the village centre.

Bank Rakyat Indonesia has branches on Jl. Kidang Pananjung and near the bus terminal; they change cash and most travellers' cheques (but not Visa cheques). Some shops and travel agents will give cash advances for Mastercard or Visa, but charge large commissions. The **post office** and 24-hour **telecoms office** are on Jl. Kidang Pananjung; and there are many **travel agents**, all offering similar tours to the Green Canyon, jungle walks and countryside tours, and which can also arrange onward transport to certain destinations, including Yogyakarta via the Kalipucang–Cilacap boat. Many outlets rent **bicycles**, often in poor condition; a few rent **motorcycles**.

Around Pangandaran

There are few specific sights in Pangandaran; local life revolves round the fishing fleets which come and go regularly. The east beach is the main fishing beach; brightly-painted boats with outriggers are usually drawn up on the sand, with larger boats moored offshore. This is the heart of the village.

Much of the large peninsula south of Pangandaran village is a nature reserve (*cagar alam*) to which access is controlled. When it is open to the public, banteng hybrids (banteng crossed with domesticated Bali cattle), macaques, and several bird species, including hornbills and the black-banded barbet, can usually be seen or heard.

The northern part of the reserve, however, is the **Pangandaran Nature Tourism Park** (Taman Wisata Alam Pangandaran), a buffer zone permanently open to visitors which contains some old Japanese bunkers, quite large caves, and some pleasant trails and beaches; you will see macaques and usually mouse deer here.

The **Green Canyon**, c 26km west of Pangandaran, is a charming if small river canyon leading to a waterfall; the water, flanked by forest, does appear remarkably green. This is Pangandaran's chief attraction, so it is best to go very early in the morning to beat the crowds; avoid weekends completely. Travel agents in the village can arrange a trip, or you can make your own way there by minibus, through Parigi and Cijulang. Guests staying at *Delta Gecko* can take paddleboats to the canyon (as opposed to the usual motorboats).

Segara Anakan

A wonderful boat trip is possible from **Kalipucang**, c 17km northeast of Pangandaran, through Segara Anakan, a large mangrove-fringed lagoon, to **Cilacap**. Boats usually depart from Kalipucang up to five times daily (between 07.00 and 15.00; but note that the timetable varies frequently). The boat passes down the Citanduy river to the lagoon, then takes the narrow passage between the mainland and **Nusa Kambangan**, a slender island which houses three high-security prisons for political detainees; today most of it is a nature reserve.

The mangrove forests of **Segara Anakan** are the most extensive remaining in Java, and support at least **85 bird species**, including the endangered milky stork, which roosts here but is not known to breed, Javan kingfisher, racket-tailed treepie and lesser adjutant. There have been sightings here of the Javan coucal, a very rare Javan endemic.

The boat calls at several villages along the way before arriving, c 4 hours later, at the small jetty in Lomanis (Pelabuhan Penyeberangan Cilacap), 5km north of Cilacap town centre.

Travel advice Note that if you are driving east from Pangandaran, there is no need to take the main road through Banjar and Majenang to Wangon; instead, turn east across the Citanduy river on the north side of Kalipucang and follow flat country roads through Pamuan, Sidareja and Jeruklegi. This is half the distance.

CILACAP

Of little interest except as a transit point for those taking the Kalipucang–Cilacap boat, Cilacap does have reasonable accommodation and the massive ruins of a 19C coastal fortress. Sir Francis Drake anchored here in 1580 during his global circumnavigation, attracted by the distant outline of Gunung Slamet. The port today is an important petrochemicals centre.

Practical information

Transport

Boats to and from Kalipucang dock at the small Lomanis jetty, c 5km north of the town centre. Usually, up to five boats depart daily between 07.00 and 15.00; the delightful trip through mangrove forest and narrow waterways takes c 4 hours. The **bus station** is c 4km north of the town centre on Jl. Gatot Subroto; take a *becak* to reach it.

Hotels and services

The best hotel near the town centre is the expensive and very comfortable ✪✪✪✪/✪✪✪ *Hotel Wijayakusuma* (☎ 0282 34871; fax 31150) at Jl. Yani 12/A, with swimming pools. The **tourist office** (Dinas Pariwisata) at Jl. Yani 8, a 24-hour **telecoms office** and the **post office** are all nearby. *Bank Lippo* (M, V) is further north on Jl. Yani.

Tucked away behind large oil storage tanks on the south side of Cilacap, 2km from the *Hotel Wijayakusuma*, is a ruined **Dutch fortress** (*benteng pendem*) built in the 1860s. Only the stone parts of this once huge fort, which covered 16.5ha, still remain: the ramparts, casemates, and munitions stores. Surrounding it is a flooded moat.

The caves of Karangbolong

On the coast c 50km east of Cilacap is a large limestone massif riddled with caverns and narrow passages. Several are home to **edible-nest swiftlets**, whose nests, made from their saliva, have been highly sought after since the 17C or even earlier. In the 18C–19C, the annual harvest weighed three or four tonnes, comprising perhaps 400,000 nests. This highly lucrative collection continues today, though the harvest has fallen to less than 100kg per year. Most noteworthy is **Gua Petruk**, a very beautiful cavern open to visitors; a guide can be found at the entrance. **Gua Jatijajar**, c 7km north, has been rather spoiled by the addition of concrete statues and graffiti. Well-equipped cavers can explore **Gua Barat**, which has more than 7km of passages, and **Gua Macan**, which contains Java's largest known chamber; contact *Finspac* (see p 39) for more information.

To reach the caves, take the main road east from Cilacap towards Kebumen, and turn off south just beyond Tambak. There is frequent public transport along the highway, and the bus conductors know the road to the caves.

Cirebon and vicinity

Cirebon stands beside the busy north coast highway, along which traffic thunders night and day, and is far from the principal tourist route through Java. As a result, relatively few visitors to the island make the special effort to go there, but it is nevertheless a pleasant port, with several sites of interest within the city and nearby.

Practical information

Transport
There are frequent **buses** between Cirebon and Bandung, Jakarta, Tasikmalaya and many north coast towns. The **bus station** is on Jl. By-pass, 2km south of the city. The most useful **train service** to/from Jakarta is the *Cirebon Expres* (c 3 hours). Other services passing through Cirebon include the daytime *Fajar Utama Yogya* between Jakarta and Yogyakarta (c 5 hours); the overnight *Argolawu* between Jakarta and Solo; and the *Sembrani* and *Argobromo* (both overnight) between Jakarta and Surabaya. One *Pelni* **ship** calls at Cirebon on its route to/from Kalimantan. Within the city, the ubiquitous *becak* provide a cheap and efficient service.

Hotels

The published tariffs of the more expensive hotels are absurdly high and usually negotiable; expect to get discounts of 30–50 per cent. The phone code is 0231.
☆☆☆☆ *Hotel Bentani* (☎ 203246; fax 207527) Jl. Siliwangi 69. A new hotel with rather small, overpriced, but pleasant rooms; very good Japanese restaurant.
☆☆☆☆ *Hotel Penta* (☎ 203328; fax 204491) Jl. Syarief Abdurachman 159. In the heart of town; the rooms are adequate but nothing special.
☆☆☆☆ *Hotel Prima* (☎ 205411/ 205475; fax 205407) Jl. Siliwangi 107. One of Cirebon's smartest hotels, with clean, comfortable rooms, small swimming pool and good range of facilities.
☆☆☆/☆☆ *Hotel Sidodadi* (☎ 202305/ 208693; fax 204821) Jl. Siliwangi 72–74. reasonable rooms on the north side of the city centre; top-floor rooms are usually heavily discounted.
☆☆/☆ *Hotel Asia* (☎ 202183) Jl. Kalibaru Selatan. Friendly, low-budget hotel with simple rooms round a small garden court.

Food and services

Maksim on Jl. Syarief Abdurachman is a popular Chinese-run seafood restaurant. The *Mal Cirebon* contains a *Hero* supermarket and numerous fast-food restaurants, including *KFC*, *McDonald's*, *Dunkin' Donuts* and *Pizza Hut*. The *Jatibarung* café on the corner of Jl. Karanggetas and Jl. Kalibaru Selatan does excellent, very cheap and tasty food. *La Palma*, a bakery on the south side of the City Hall, has a good choice in the mornings.

Banks. For money, *BCA* on Jl. Karanggetas exchanges US$ cash and some brands of traveller's cheque. For other money needs try the cluster of banks on Jl. Yos Sudarso, including *BCA*, *Bank Danamon*, *Bank Lippo* and *BNI*.

The **post office** and a 24-hour **wartel** are also on Jl. Yos Sudarso. A reasonably efficient **travel agent** is Nenggala Grage at Jl. Pasuketan 41. Cirebon is extremely well supplied with **cinemas**; almost everywhere you look in the city centre are multiplex theatres, with lurid posters advertising the current attractions.

History

The growth of Cirebon is traditionally associated with Sunan Gunung Jati (d. c 1570), one of the nine Muslim *wali*, holy men who are credited with bringing Islam to Java. However, it seems likely that Islam had already reached the port in the mid-to-late 15C, when the Muslim kingdom of Demak took control of the region. Gunung Jati is believed to have been born near the town of Lhokseumawe in northern Sumatra, but when the Portuguese arrived there in the 1520s he departed on a pilgrimage to Mecca. On his return he settled in Demak, married the sultan's sister, and may have been involved in Demak's attack on Banten in the 1520s, though most sources credit his son, Hasanudin, with the conquest. In the 1550s, Gunung Jati moved to Cirebon and founded a separate dynasty, and the city was established as an important north coast port.

Exploring Cirebon

The most interesting of Cirebon's old royal palaces is the **Keraton Kesepuhan**, part of which is open daily to visitors (08.00–17.00), together with two small museum buildings. it is claimed that a palace was first built here in the mid-15C, but the present buildings date from a major renovation in the early 20C. Of note

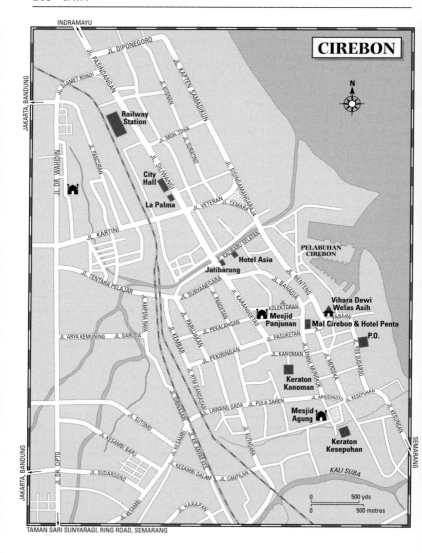

in the reception hall are the European furnishings—chandeliers, tiles, furniture and paintings—and Chinese porcelain. The museum collection includes a wonderful 16C–17C carriage, a curious sedan chair used in royal circumcision ceremonies, Portuguese-era coats of mail, and old weapons.

On the west side of the square in front of the *keraton* is **Mesjid Agung**, the principal mosque. From here, Jl. Lemah Wungkuk runs northwards, filled for much of its length with a busy **street market**. Near its northern end, Jl. Kanoman leads west to **Keraton Kanoman** (open daily 08.00–17.00). This palace dates from the same period as the Keraton Kesepuhan, but there is little to see except the *gedung pusaka*—a small, dusty collection of heirlooms which includes two more fine old carriages. The other Cirebon *keratons* are closed to the public.

Worth a brief look is the **Mesjid Panjunan** on the corner of Jl. Kolektoran and Jl. Panjunan, which has an old, two-tiered shingle roof and a shingle-clad minaret.

A short walk to the southeast is the **Vihara Dewi Welas Asih** (Goddess of Mercy Temple) at Jl. Kantor 2, just east of the Jl. Banteng junction. This Chinese temple, one of the most interesting on Java, contains several hundred painted panels and a principal shrine dedicated to the Goddess of Mercy. In an eastern courtyard is a rusting anchor, attributed by local tradition to the fleet of Zheng He, the Chinese envoy from the 15C Ming court, but in fact almost certainly from a more recent VOC ship. (Exactly the same story is told at Gedung Batu, a Chinese shrine in Semarang—see p 291.)

Across the street are the elegant **1920s offices** of *BAT Indonesia*, one of the country's largest cigarette manufacturers. In the harbour (Pelabuhan Cirebon), a short walk to the east, a dozen or so Bugis *pinisi*, the elegant wooden-hulled ships which trade throughout the archipelago, can usually be found; ask the guards at the gate for permission to enter.

To the north on Jl. Siliwangi is the remarkable Art Deco **city hall** (*balai kota*), designed in 1927 by a Dutch architect, J.J. Jiskoot, and decorated with amusing lobster ornamentation (Cirebon is known as *kota udang*—'shrimp' or 'lobster' city).

To the southwest of the city centre, beside the busy ring road, is **Taman Sari Sunyaragi**, a curious royal pleasure garden begun at the turn of the 18C and completed in 1741. It contained bathing pools for the sultan and his wives, but was largely destroyed during the Java War (1825–30). In the 1850s the sultan of the Keraton Kesepuhan had it rebuilt to Chinese design; today it comprises an extremely odd jumble of narrow pathways and cement grottoes.

Sights near Cirebon

The small village of **Trusmi**, west of Cirebon, has several factories that produce some of the finest Cirebon-style **batik**. Take the Bandung road c 7km from Cirebon to **Plered**, where 'Batik Trusmi' is signed to the north at a busy junction with traffic lights. The Cirebon–Plered road is often congested, so allow plenty of time for the journey; public transport is very frequent.

To the northwest of Cirebon, along the Indramayu road, is the **Astana Gunung Jati**, a graveyard containing the tomb of Sunan Gunung Jati. It lies on the west side of the road, across from other tombs on a small hillock on the east side, overlooking the sea. **Indramayu**, further north, is another important batik-producing centre.

Linggarjati

South of Cirebon, off the main Kuningan road, is the small village of Linggarjati, where on 15 November 1946 the Dutch signed the first, short-lived diplomatic agreement with the Republic of Indonesia. The hotel where the signing took place is now a small museum, **Gedung Perundingan Linggarjati** (Linggarjati Conference Building).

Take the Kuningan road 19km south from the Cirebon bypass, and shortly beyond Cilimus turn off right to Linggarjati. On public transport, you must change at the Cilimus terminal. The museum is on the left after 2.5km, beyond the Hotel Linggarjati.

History

The ill-fated Linggarjati Agreement, initialled on 15 November 1946 by the Indonesian nationalist delegation and one led by the former Dutch prime minister, Willem Schermerhorn, recognised the Republic of Indonesia as the de facto authority in Sumatra, Java and Madura. The agreement resulted from a year of negotiations initiated by the British, who were anxious for a settlement to be reached before they withdrew their troops from Java and Sumatra in December. The two signatories also agreed to co-operate in the creation by 1 January 1949 of a federal United States of Indonesia, in which the Republic would be one of the states, while the Dutch would remain in control of others within the union. The federation would be headed symbolically by the Dutch Queen.

Although the Agreement was finally signed in March 1947, it was destined to be short-lived. The two sides were immensely distrustful of each other, and both faced strong political opposition at home to the treaty, because of the concessions made. In July 1947 the Agreement was effectively tossed aside as the Dutch began their 'police actions' in Java.

Gunung Ciremai

The highest mountain in West Java, Gunung Ciremai (3078m) is one of the most handsome of Java's volcanoes and is a challenging climb. A long ascent can be made from Linggarjati, where there is a choice of reasonable accommodation, including the ☆☆ *Hotel Linggarjati* (☎ 0262 6185); staff can help arrange a guide. An overnight stay on the mountain is required, unless you wish to walk through the night, so camping equipment and food must be brought.

Ciremai last erupted in 1951, but remains active. It's a c 8-hour walk to the summit, and the descent takes c 4–5 hours. Allow 2–3 hours more if you wish to descend to the smoking crater. On a clear day there is a magnificent view in every direction from the narrow rim.

Cipari

At the archaeological park at Cipari (Taman Purkabala Cipari), to the southwest of Kuningan, is a **prehistoric burial site** which has been under excavation since the mid-1970s. The small site museum has some remarkable stone tools and body ornaments.

To get there, take the Cikijang road south out of Kuningan and turn right to Cigugur after c 2km. In Cigugur, note the **ancient fish-ponds**, believed locally to have been built by Muslim missionaries in the 16C, and now stocked with large carp-like fish. The fish are considered sacred, and are fed generously. Turn right to the archaeological site c 1km beyond Cigugur.

Baturaden, Wonosobo and Dieng

Highlights. Without doubt the highlight of the area is the **Dieng plateau** (see p 273), a magnificent landscape of cultivated, terraced hillsides encircling a plain pockmarked with craters of bubbling mud and sulphurous lakes. Scattered across the marshy plain are early Hindu temples, and on its fringes are small villages, framed by distant volcanoes.

Practical information

Travel advice

Wangon to Purwokerto is 31km via either Ajibarang or Jatilawang and Rawalo. Purwokerto to Banyumas is c 20km, Banyumas to Wonosobo c 80km, Wonosobo to Dieng 26km.

Public transport

Travelling between West and Central Java, at some stage you will almost certainly find yourself in Cilacap or passing through Wangon (unless you take the busy north coast road). From Cilacap there are buses to Purwokerto via Rawalo, and to Wonosobo via Banyumas. From Wangon, there are frequent departures in every direction, with buses passing through all day long; the bus station lies to the north of the main junction. Minibuses to Baturaden depart frequently from Purwokerto. From Wonosobo, regular minibuses take the main road to Dieng.

Private transport

Between Wangon and Purwokerto (for Baturaden) there is a choice of routes. On a very clear day that via Ajibarang is recommended, as it offers a fine view of Gunung Slamet; otherwise take the Jatilawang route, as the road beside the Serayu river is interesting and traffic is usually lighter. This is also the best route if heading directly for Banyumas, Wonosobo and Dieng.

Accommodation

Accommodation is available in Purwokerto and the rather more pleasant hill resort of Baturaden. Wonosobo, at the foot of the Dieng plateau, is the usual base from which to visit Dieng and has several reasonable hotels, but there are simple guest-houses on the plateau itself which are definitely worth considering if you can survive with few comforts.

Wangon

Wangon is little more than a traffic-snarled junction on one of the two main roads which pass between West and Central Java; a steady flow of vehicles passes through, day and night. It is, however, a useful place to stop for food; recommended is the *Jaya Putra*, a simple but popular café a few metres west of the central intersection, on the south side of the road.

The road from Wangon to Ajibarang passes through desa Cikakak, where an asphalt lane to the west, 4.5km north of the Wangon crossroads, leads 1.5km past pollarded trees and small hamlets to a small mosque, **Mesjid Saka Tunggul**. This is said to date from 1522, but the present structure, though older than most Javanese mosques, was clearly rebuilt more recently. It is notable for its elaborately carved (though garishly painted) central pillar which supports the roof; there is also some finely carved Arabic calligraphy. In mid-1998, a local holy man had a vision that valuable artefacts lay buried nearby; after three weeks of digging, his followers unearthed two gold statues of the Buddha and other objects. Just past the mosque, to the left, is the grave of a Muslim mission-ary, Mbah Tulih, who is regarded locally as the mosque's founder.

Purwokerto

There is little reason to stop in Purwokerto, but should you need to, the ✿✿/✿ *Hotel Borobudur* (☎ 0281 35341/37747) at Jl. Yosodarmo 32 can be recom-mended; the rooms are large and clean, the staff friendly, and it's five minutes by becak from the train station. The bus station, however, is far away on the south side of town, on Jl. Gerilya (Jl. By-pass).

The nearby **Museum Bank Rakyat Indonesia**, on the corner of Jl. Sudirman and Jl. Wiryaatmaja, displays samples of money from the Majapahit kingdom, the Dutch East Indies, Portuguese Timor, the Japanese occupation, and the numerous local currencies used in the late 1940s, as well as old money boxes, photos from the colonial era, dioramas and old banking machinery. In the grounds is a late-19C building which housed the original savings bank.

Baturaden

A hill resort on the southern flank of Gunung Slamet, Baturaden is a popular weekend getaway but is almost deserted in midweek. It's a rather cramped little village, with dozens of losmen, villas and hotels squashed together, few of them making full use of what could be very fine views. Nevertheless, it offers good walking opportunities, waterfalls and hot springs.

Hotels
The best by far is the large, but thought-fully designed ✿✿✿✿/✿✿✿ *Queen Garden Hotel* (☎ 0281 38388/39688), 4.5km east of Baturaden centre, with swim-ming pool and tennis courts; many rooms have excellent views. Also recom-mended are the ✿✿✿/✿✿ *Rosenda hotel and cottages* (☎ 0281 32570), closer to Baturaden itself. In the village are dozens of villas and losmen with similar facilities, wildly overpriced for what they offer. The very simple ✿ *Wisma Kartika Asri*, near the top of the village but at the bottom of the price scale, has a few basic rooms with pleasant balconies.

Kawasan Wisata Baturaden, on the northwest side of the village, is a recre-ation area with swimming pool and waterslide, botanical gardens and a small zoo. Footpaths lead through the forest behind to a couple of hot-water springs. The one known as **Pancuran Tujuh** (or Pancuran Pitu: 'seven spouts') lies in a pretty location with good views (2.5km on foot; c 6km by road).

At **Telaga Sunyi**, c 3km east of Baturaden on the lane to the *Queen Garden Hotel*, footpaths climb high above a small stream-filled ravine through pleas-ant woods.

Gua Lawah is an unusual lava cave on the eastern flank of Gunung Slamet, which has some magnificent stalactites. Take the lane northeast from Baturaden towards Pancuran Tujuh; at the junction in the forest where the track to the hot springs turns off left, keep straight on for the cave. Except at weekends, you will need to charter a vehicle for this route, or take public transport via Purbalingga and Bobotsari.

Gunung Slamet

The second highest mountain in Java at 3418m, Gunung Slamet is also one of the island's most active volcanoes and a popular climb. It erupts gently most years, and in August 1996 emitted fireballs and clouds of white ash. The forested slopes are home to the rare, endemic **Javan gibbon** and **ebony leaf monkey**, and many bird species. The mountain also has some of Java's heaviest rainfall (7000–8000mm per year), so be prepared for rain if planning an ascent.

There are three main routes to the barren cinder cones at the summit: a western approach; the climb from Baturaden; and the ascent from Banbangan on the east side, which is the only one currently allowed. A guide is needed on each route. To reach **Banbangan**, take a bus from Purwokerto to Purbalingga, and then to Bobotsari. Trucks run from there to **Penjangan**, from where it is a c 1-hour walk to Banbangan, where guides can be hired. Climbers camping on the mountain overnight must obtain a permit from the *Pasanggrahan Perhutani Serang* (Serang Forestry Office) nearby. Slamet can be climbed in a very long, tiring day (c 8 hours up, and 4 hours down), but it is best to take two days.

From Purwokerto, the main eastbound roads follow the Serayu river upstream to Wonosobo. In **Banyumas**, the **Museum Wayang Sendang Mas** has a small, dusty collection of *wayang kulit* and *wayang golek*, very simply displayed; visitors are rare, but enthusiastically received. To find it, turn west off the main road opposite the *Bank Rakyat Indonesia*, and after a few metres turn north at a small monument; the museum is beside the old *pendopo*.

Northeast of Banyumas, the main road reaches **Kelampok**, where dozens of shops selling rather gaudy ceramics line the road.

In Banjarnegara, a very scenic minor road turns off north to the Dieng plateau (see below), but for travellers on public transport, it is easier to take the main route via Wonosobo. On a clear day, the last stretch into Wonosobo offers excellent views of Gunung Sumbing and Gunung Sundoro (Sindoro).

WONOSOBO

Wonosobo is a pleasant, hilly town surrounded by fine scenery. Many tourists use it as a base from which to visit Dieng (though it is greatly preferable to stay overnight in Dieng, if you can tolerate the simple accommodation), so there are plenty of hotels and restaurants. At the north end is the picturesque *alun-alun*, flanked by huge fig trees.

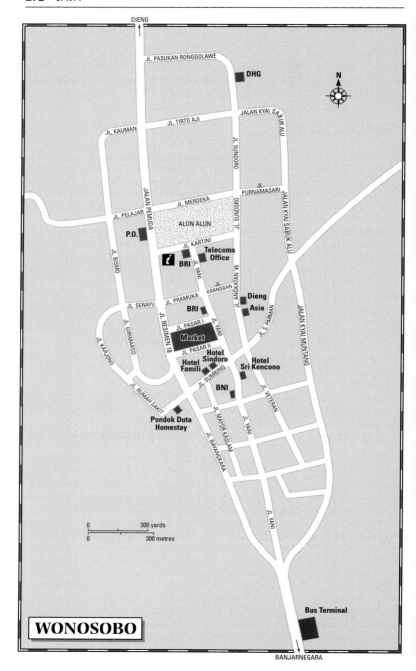

DIENG

JL. PASUKAN RONGGOLAWE

DHG

N

JALAN KYAI SABUK ALU

JL. TIRTO AJI

JL. KAUMAN

JL. SUNDORO

JL. PURNAMASARI

JALAN KYAI SABIK ALU

JL. MERDEKA

JL. PELAJAR

ALUN ALUN

JL. SUNDORO

JALAN PEMUDA

P.O.

JL. KARTINI

BRI

Telecoms Office

JL. BISMO

JL. YANI

JL. KRANGGAN

JL. SERAYU

JL. PRAMUKA

BRI

Dieng

JL. ANGKATAN '45

Asia

JALAN KYAI MUNTANG

JL. GIRIMARGO

JL. RESIMEN 18

JL. PASAR I

Market

JL. S. PARMAN

JL. KARJONO

JL. PASAR II

Hotel Sindoro

Hotel Famili

Hotel Sri Kencono

JL. RUMAH SAKIT

JL. SUMBING

BNI

JL. VETERAN

Pondok Duta Homestay

JL. MAYOR KASIAM

JL. YANI

JL. BANANGKARA

JL. YANI

0   300 yards

0   300 metres

Bus Terminal

WONOSOBO

BANJARNEGARA

Practical information

Transport

The main **bus terminal** is 1.3km south of the Jl. Sumbing–Jl. Yani junction. Local **buses** to Dieng leave from Jl. Resimen 18 on the west side of the market. Dokar can be found on Jl. Pasar II for short journeys round town.

Hotels

☆☆ *Hotel Sri Kencono* (☎ 0286 21522) on Jl. Yani is one of the best, and quite central. ☆☆ *Hotel Surya Asia* (☎ 0286 22992; fax 23598), further south on Jl. Yani, is also better than average. Recommended for low budgets is the cheerful ☆ *Pondok Duta Homestay* at Jl. Rumah Sakit 3.

Food and services

The *DHG* restaurant on Jl. Pasukan Ronggolawe has good food in pleasant surroundings; sit on the upper balcony. The *Asia* on Jl. Angkatan '45 is an unjustifiably popular, overpriced tourist restaurant; better is the nearby *Dieng* restaurant. There are also plenty of streetside *warung*.

For **money**, BNI is on Jl. Yani near the Sri Kencono; *BRI* is at the north end of Jl. Yani, beside the *alun-alun*. The **post office** is on the west side of the *alun-alun*, and a 24-hour **telecoms office** is on Jl. Yani almost opposite the BRI. A **tourist information office** (Dinas Pariwisata) is nearby at Jl. Kartini 3.

From Wonosobo to Dieng

The main road from Wonosobo up to the Dieng plateau, steep and winding in the upper part, climbs along the Serayu valley. A pleasant detour to Telaga Menjer, a circular crater lake, is recommended for those with private transport, or for those who have time to wait for a minibus to the lake or who want to walk.

Telaga Menjer

Turn left off the main road in **Garung**, c 8km north of Wonosobo. The lane climbs steeply for 3.5km to the lake, past a small hydroelectric power station fed by the lake. Public transport is intermittent.

For the best views, climb clockwise round the crater rim past terraced fields of tobacco, cassava, pepper, bananas and cabbage until you emerge above the pine trees. Another path leads to the water's edge, where boats can be chartered.

An extremely picturesque lane continues northeast from the lake through hilly, cultivated countryside and small hamlets, rejoining the main Wonosobo–Dieng road after 6km at **Kejajar**. There is no public transport, but it makes a very fine walk, luggage permitting. In Kejajar, catch another minibus to Dieng.

The main road reaches the edge of the Dieng plateau 10km beyond Kejajar, at Dieng Wetan. This final stretch is frequently shrouded in cloud, and becomes progressively steeper.

THE DIENG PLATEAU

The hills surrounding the Dieng plateau receive more than 7000mm of rain per year; the plateau itself gets half that. Expect rain or damp cloud here at any time, and bring warm clothes for chilly evenings.

The plateau, c 2100m above sea level, is an area of intense volcanic and geo-thermal activity, and is **potentially extremely dangerous**. Poisonous subterranean gases seeping to the surface have killed people on numerous occasions, most recently in 1992. The worst event in recent history happened in early 1979, when an earthquake struck the area in the middle of the night, followed immediately by a gas eruption from the Sinila crater on the northwest side of the plateau. People living in the vicinity fled west along the track towards Batur, but were trapped by poisonous gas escaping through fractures in the ground. Almost 150 people died, and many more were injured.

In January 1993, very hot (93°C) mud suddenly began spurting 2–15m high from a new 5m-diameter vent near the main group of temples on the marshy plain; after a few weeks it stopped.

To live in such an unpredictable, often damp and chilly, world requires a considerable degree of stoicism: the plateau dwellers are undoubtedly resilient and hard-working. The horticulture-based economy relies on volcanic activity to provide the deep, fertile soils, but at the same time this volcanicity can be a curse, an undiscerning destroyer.

Despite the dangers, the plateau itself is densely populated; to get away from human activity, you must climb into the northern hills—Gunung Butak Petarangan, Gunung Ngaglik and Gunung Perahu—inhabited by the ebony leaf monkey and Javan gibbon.

Practical information

Transport

To get to most of the sites you must walk or hitchhike, although there are infrequent minibuses along the Pekasiran road, which passes close to some of the small lakes and active craters. All the temples are in easy walking distance. Frequent minibuses depart to Wonosobo; fewer take the Batur road.

Hotels and food

Only very basic accommodation is available on the plateau. ☆ *Bu Jono* and ☆ *Losmen Homestay* are adjacent *losmen* in **Dieng Wetan**, at the junction with the Wonosobo road; ☆ *Losmen Asri*, with a simple upstairs balcony overlooking the plateau, lies a short walk south. All have similar facilities and prices. ☆☆/☆ *Hotel Gunung Mas*, to the west on the main street, has marginally better, but overpriced rooms (substantial discounts given). It is easiest to eat at the losmen; *Bu Jono* and *Losmen Homestay* are the most reliable. There are also several very simple *warung* in the village.

Scattered across the plateau are eight small Hindu temples and other minor structures dating back to the 8C. They represent just a fraction of the dozens, perhaps hundreds, of structures which are believed to have once stood on the plateau.

History

The dating of the Shaivite temples at Dieng is of necessity rather vague, and must be based largely on architectural and epigraphic evidence, as very few dated inscriptions have been found. The oldest inscription discovered in the vicinity represents the Pallava script of the mid-7C; the latest is an inscribed rock dated to 1210. More than a dozen other inscriptions have been dated palaeographically to the start of the 9C. Thus it appears the plateau was occupied, probably continuously, for more than five centuries.

Architecturally, the Dieng temples show remarkable variety, but scholars generally agree that Candi Arjuna, Semar, Srikandi, Gatotkaca and Dvaravati are the earliest, dating from the first third of the 8C, while Puntadewa, Sembadra and Bima date from the middle half of the same century. Some, like Gatotkaca, were probably altered over time as taste and need dictated.

The religious site was probably chosen for its proximity to volcanic activity and curative sulphur springs, as with Gedong Songo (see p 283) later on. Very little is known of the Sanjaya kings who built the Dieng temples; they shared power in Central Java with the Buddhist Shailendra dynasty in the early 8C–early 9C, before absorbing the latter.

The reason for Dieng's decline is unknown. Possibly it was a result of volcanic activity; perhaps an epidemic decimated the population. Nevertheless, reports from the early 19C indicate there were several hundred ruined structures on the plain, which at that time was covered in thick forest and swamp. Almost all have now vanished, their masonry lost beneath volcanic ash falls or taken by villagers to build homes.

The Arjuna temple group and Candi Gatotkaca

The most noteworthy of Dieng's temples is the group of five that stands on the marshy floor of the plateau in front of **Dieng Wetan**. At the north end is **Candi Arjuna**, which opens to the west through a projecting porch framed by a *kala-*

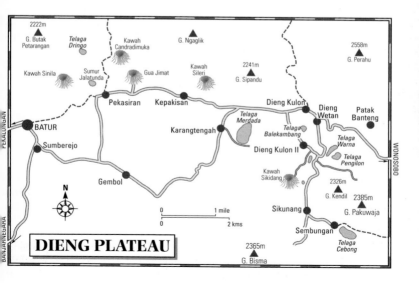

DIENG PLATEAU

makara decorative element; almost certainly it once contained a linga and yoni, for beneath the north-facing false window is a *makara*-shaped spout, usually associated with the outflow of lustral water poured over the linga.

Directly opposite, facing Candi Arjuna, is the smaller **Candi Semar** (Sumar), which would have housed an image of Nandi, Shiva's bull mount. The doorway possesses a fine kala-makara ornamentation.

Beyond Candi Arjuna and old foundations is **Candi Srikandi**, which bears damaged bas-reliefs in three false windows. On the north side is Vishnu, recognisable by the cakra in his raised right hand; on the east is Shiva; and Brahma is on the south. Much of the roof has disappeared.

Candi Puntadewa, the next in line, is unusual in having two flights of steps up to the cella. The porch of **Candi Sembadra** displays a carved *kala* face.

The path continues to **Candi Gatotkaca**, raised slightly above the plateau floor and overlooking a small lake, **Telaga Balekambang**. This small, simple west-facing *candi* contains a yoni. Brick slabs discovered outside the south wall during excavations in 1979 indicate the former presence of other structures.

Across the road from the *candi* is a small statuary store (*gedung koleksi arca*) containing dozens of Hindu statues and stone carvings recovered from the plateau area. There are many images of Durga, Ganesha, Shiva and Nandi, kala faces and gargoyles, and *yoni* and *linga*. Notable is an unusual statue of Nandi seated cross-legged in an anthropomorphic posture, with Shiva mounted on its shoulders.

Candi Bima and the Sikidang crater

The road south from Candi Gatotkaca passes through a small hamlet, **Dieng Kulon II**, and c 900m from the *candi* reaches **Candi Bima**, at the junction of the Kawah Sikidang road. The *candi* roof is remarkable: five of probably seven storeys remain, each divided into arched niches or false windows somewhat characteristic of Indian temples in Orissa, and containing human-shaped stone heads. Being the tallest *candi* still standing, it was named in the 19C after Bima, the tallest of the heroes in the Ramayana epic. Above the east-projecting porch is a *kala* face.

The road southwest from here leads after 900m to **Kawah Sikidang**, a very active area of bubbling mud and boiling water craters where steam and sulphurous gases leak from hissing fissures and gurgling vents. In March 1992, a sudden poisonous gas emission 200m west of Sikidang killed three people. Take great care where you walk.

Telaga Warna and Gua Semar

Southeast of Candi Bima, the road passes the entrance to **Telaga Warna** ('coloured lake'). The lake water is a brilliant blue-green, the precise shade depending on the light at any given time. A smell of sulphur comes from the surface, but paddling ducks seem unconcerned. A path leads clockwise round the lake, past **Kawah Sikendang** at the north corner, which is just a small patch of shore displaying signs of recent volcanic activity; the water here is gently bubbling. On the east side, a path can be found climbing steeply through bushes up the side of the crater wall to a narrow ridge, from where there is a marvellous view southwest across the lake, and also northeast to the village of **Patak Banteng**, surrounded by terraced hillsides. On a (rare) clear day there is also an excellent view of Gunung Sundoro to the southeast.

Skirting Telaga Warna in an anticlockwise direction brings you to **Telaga Pengilon**, a duller-coloured lake. Between the two lakes is a narrow wooded peninsula containing three small caves, **Gua Jaran**, **Gua Sumur** and **Gua Semar**. The latter, now fenced off, is a popular meditation cave, used by both Suharto and Sukarno; in 1974 Suharto and the Australian prime minister, Gough Whitlam, reputedly ventured inside for private discussions.

From Telaga Warna the road runs 1km north to the junction beside Bu Jono. 150m from here, along the Wonosobo road, a path to the north leads to a bathing place with ancient stone water spouts, known as **Bhima Lukar**.

Gunung Pakuwaja and Telaga Cebong

100m west of the entrance to Telaga Warna, a road turns south towards **Sembungan**, a large village on the shore of **Telaga Cebong**. Just 150m along this road, a lane turns off left and climbs for 1.5km to a roadhead at the foot of **Gunung Pakuwaja**, where there are a couple of capped geothermal wells. From the roadhead, it's an easy climb along farmers' paths up the cultivated, terraced slopes of Gunung Pakuwaja to the summit (2385m); the views are excellent.

The Sembungan road continues south through *desa* **Sikunang**, then past several geothermal wells before descending steeply to the lake shore and Sembungan village (c 4km). A pleasant hiking track continues east beyond the lake shore and eventually descends to the main Wonosobo–Dieng road, from where it is easy to catch a minibus back to Dieng.

Candi Dvaravati and the Pekasiran road

From the Wonosobo road junction in Dieng Wetan, the main street runs west through **Dieng Kulon** (400m), where an asphalt lane leads north through the village to **Candi Dvaravati**. Broad steps lead up to the *candi* past terraced vegetable plots. It's a simple structure with little decoration, but has a fine aspect overlooking the central plateau.

The main road forks c 1.5km further west: left to **Telaga Merdada**—a pretty, circular crater lake (1.8km) and Batur (10km); and right to **Pekasiran**. Stay on the Pekasiran road and continue west 1.5km to a roadside memorial listing the disasters caused by volcanic activity on the plateau. The worst of those mentioned was a landslide in 1957 to the north of *desa* Kepakisan, which killed 450. Earthquakes, poisonous gas clouds, volcanic eruptions and landslides have all taken their toll, and there have been plenty more since 1986, when this memorial was erected.

The road north at this junction leads after 500m to **Kawah Sileri**, a crater lake of extremely hot water from which billow clouds of steam and sulphurous gas. In 1944 Kawah Sileri erupted, killing 117 and injuring 250. Blocks thrown out by the explosion landed on *desa* Bitingan, 1km away, where 11 died. Another eruption from the crater in 1964 killed a further 114.

Continue west through *desa* Kepakisan. A footpath to the north, 2.5km west of the village, leads to Gua Jimat, a large, but unspectacular hole in the ground c 250m from the road, which occasionally vents poisonous gas.

In *desa* **Pekasiran**, 900m further west, a rocky track to the north climbs to **Kawah Candradimuka**, clearly signed at the main road junction. As you approach, you will see clouds of steam and sulphur gas rising from the crater vicinity. A path leads down to the bubbling mud and boiling water in a spectacular narrow ravine from which water spurts high in the air; approach with care.

Continue further up the same track for c 15 minutes, then turn off left onto another path; where this crosses water pipes, turn uphill and follow the pipes to **Telaga Dringo**, a greatly shrunken crater lake sitting in a broad crater. Young boys can sometimes be found fishing here, though there can't be many fish left; most of the water is pumped out for irrigation.

200m west of the Kawah Candradimuka junction the main road turns south and quickly deteriorates as it descends through cabbage fields for 2.5km to the main Dieng–Batur road. A minor track continues west past some concrete steps on the north side which lead up to **Sumur Jalatunda**. This is a very deep, sheer-sided crater lake, overgrown with vegetation, and certainly impressive.

To find **Kawah Sinila**, the cause of the 1979 disaster, descend the concrete steps from Sumur Jalatunda, cross the little bridge to the west, and just before passing the gopura gateposts a few metres further, branch right and follow a narrow footpath up through the terraced fields of cabbages, onions and tobacco. After c 10 minutes, turn left at an intersection (the path to the right here descends to a bamboo bridge) and climb for a few minutes up to the small, somewhat eerie crater lake.

The main track from Sumur Jalatunda continues west c 3km to Batur, from where there are infrequent minibuses back to Dieng through Sumberejo and Gembol.

Magelang, Ambarawa and Gedong Songo

Highlights. An area often ignored by visitors in their haste to reach Semarang, Yogyakarta or Solo, this pocket of Central Java does in fact have some glorious volcanic scenery and at **Gedong Songo** (see p 283), the most lovely setting of any *candi* in Java. If you can, take the path also to **Candi Selogriyo** (see p 280). Steam train enthusiasts especially should visit the Ambarawa **railway museum** (see p 282) for a ride on the cog-railway. **Kopeng** (see p 281) is a rather charming highland market town, with superb views.

Practical information

Public transport
Heading east or south from Dieng, you must return first to Wonosobo, from where there are regular **buses** over the Kledung Pass to Temanggung, Magelang, Ambarawa and Yogyakarta.

Private transport
With your own vehicle, a recommended route east from Dieng is via the scenic lane between Gunung Butak and Gunung Sundoro to Ngadirejo; there turn south past the turn-off to Candi Pringapus to reach the main road at Parakan.

Accommodation
Accommodation can be found at Magelang, Kopeng and Bandungan. There are also hotels in Ambarawa and Salatiga, but Bandungan is preferable to the former, and Kopeng is more fun than the latter.

Via the Kledung pass

The main road between Wonosobo and Parakan is smooth and busy, the gradient gentle; on a clear day there are excellent views of Gunung Sundoro and Gunung Sumbing, both of which are most easily climbed from the pass.

For **Gunung Sumbing** (3371m), stop at the entrance posts to *desa* Garung, shortly before the top of the pass, from where it is a 1-hour walk to the village. To get an early start, you should stay with the village headman (*kepala desa*), who can also find a guide. The climb begins through vegetable gardens just behind the village and takes c 7–8 hours to the summit, and 4–5 hours back. The summit is a jagged crater rim, with fumaroles smoking gently on the crater floor. Take plenty of water, strong boots, sun protection and a flashlight; a pre-dawn start is advised.

The ascent of **Gunung Sundoro** (3136m) starts from Kledung itself, and is rather easier, though takes just as long.

At the top of the pass is **Rumah Makan Dieng Kledung Pass**, with a wide choice of food and drinks. The road beyond descends through tobacco fields to Parakan, from where minibuses run north towards Candi Pringapus (c 7km) and Ngadirejo.

Via Ngadirejo

Turn east off the Dieng–Wonosobo road c 2km south of Kejajar, along a lane signed to **Argo Wisata Kebun Teh Tambi**. The lane climbs steadily for c 5km through the tea plantation and vegetable gardens before descending again very steeply; there are fine views of **Gunung Sundoro** and **Gunung Butak** (2136m). Volcano climbers could almost certainly find an easy path up Gunung Butak from this road.

After descending 4.5km, you reach a sharp right turning – the quickest way to Ngadirejo – passing through the pines of **Jumprit forest**; within the forest is a sacred spring from which water is drawn for the annual Wesak ceremony at Borobudur (see p 314). The road passes through Jumprit and tobacco fields to Ngadirejo.

Turn south here towards Parakan, and after 1.2km you will pass a cobbled lane to the west, beside a branch of **Bank Rakyat Indonesia**, which leads to Candi Pringapus (1.6km).

Candi Pringapus

This small Shaivite temple, dating probably from the mid-9C–early 10C, is one of several small Hindu temples built at this time in the former frontier lands which had marked the previous separation of Hindu and Buddhist influence.

The west-facing porch is surrounded by a *kala-makara* ornamentation, and inside is a statue of Nandi; the exterior walls are decorated with bas-reliefs of apsaras and vines. The *candi* was largely rebuilt in 1932, though its roof remains incomplete. In the temple enclosure are fragments of carved stone, including some fine *kala* faces, which remained from the renovation or were brought here from other local sites.

In the vicinity was the site of the now-vanished Candi Perot, where two almost identical inscriptions, dated to 850–51, were discovered. They list the king, the dignitaries, village elders and witnesses who took part in a ceremony called *manusuk sima*, a ritual by which the king freed a piece of agricultural land from taxes or from its original use so that its yield could instead be used for religious purposes—usually the construction of a temple in his name.

If you follow the track uphill c 50m beyond the *candi* and turn right along a narrow irrigation stream, you will find another stone statue of Nandi lying beside a small concrete reservoir; Candi Perot was probably nearby.

Before leaving, sign the visitors' book and leave a small donation for the caretaker.

Candi Selogriyo

A small Shaivite temple on the minor road between Windusari and Bandongan, to the northwest of Magelang, Candi Selogriyo can be reached by public transport from Temanggung, but more easily from Magelang. The approach walk through an amphitheatre of rice terraces is one of the loveliest to any temple in Java.

To reach it from Temanggung, travel south on a quiet lane to **Tembarak** (6km) and then to **Windusari**, a further 10km. Turn right towards Bandongan at a T-junction in Windusari, and stop at **Kembang Kuning**. At a sharp left-hand bend here, an asphalt track leads steeply up to the right; this is the way to the *candi*.

If coming from Magelang, go west to **Bandongan** (4km) and then turn north to Kembang Kuning, 6km further.

Walk from the main road up to the road head in the village, and ask some children to show you the path. It's a walk of 40–60 minutes, gently uphill through glorious scenery. The *candi* itself, built in the 9C, has little decoration and is in poor repair. Flanking the east-facing doorway are niches containing damaged high reliefs of Nandishvara and Mahakala, which may perhaps have been added at a later date. Old photos show them with their heads intact; the vandalism occurred sometime before 1978. In niches on the exterior walls are images of Agastya, Ganesha and Durga, all damaged. Although the *candi* was completed structurally, the sculptor's work remains unfinished.

MAGELANG

A pleasant if unexciting junction town on the busy Semarang–Yogyakarta highway, Magelang does offer reasonable accommodation and can be a useful base for a night or two.

Practical information

Transport

The main **bus station**, Terminal Tidar, is on Jl. Sukarno-Hatta. **Becak** operate in the town centre.

Hotels

The ☎ code is 0293.
☆☆☆/☆☆ *Hotel Puri Asri* (☎ 65115/64114) Jl. Cempaka 9, off Jl. Diponegoro; pleasant cottages and rooms overlooking the Progo River; swimming pool. Recommended.
☆☆ *Hotel Borobudur Indah* (☎ 64502/65081) 4km north of Magelang on the main road. Good for avoiding the town centre.
☆☆/☆ *Hotel Bayeman* Jl. Tentara Pelajar 45. Clean and friendly; recommended.
☆☆/☆ *Hotel Citi* (☎ 63347/8) Jl. Daha 23. Pleasant setting and good value.
☆ *Hotel Lokasari* Jl Katamso, off Jl. Tentara Pelajar. Cheap, clean and simple.

Services

For **money**, *BII* is on Jl. Yani; *BCA* is on the corner of Jl. Alun-Alun Utara and Jl. Yani. The **post office** is at the southeast corner of the *alun-alun*, close to the shopping centres.

The tiny **Museum Pangeran Diponegoro**, tucked away in the office complex of Central Java's deputy governor, was formerly the 19C Dutch Resident's house and is the place where Diponegoro was arrested in March 1930 during negotiations with the Dutch. There is little to see, but the view of Gunung Sumbing is good.

The **Museum Sudirman** at Jl. Ade Irma Suryani C-7 is the house where General Sudirman died of tuberculosis in 1950. It would not be a lie to call the museum astoundingly dull.

Without doubt the most exciting thing to do in Magelang is **rafting** on the Progo river, which can be arranged at the *Hotel Puri Asri*.

Kopeng

A tiny hill resort at 1500m altitude on the Magelang–Salatiga road, Kopeng is a delightful, relaxed village with some decent accommodation, friendly people and excellent scenery. On the road up from Magelang the peaks of Gunung Merbabu, Telomoyo and Andong can all be seen; Telomoyo is a long-dead Holocene-epoch volcano disfigured by modern telecoms masts.

The ☆☆/☆ *Hotel Griya Loka Indah*, at the west end of the village, is recommended, offering fine views of Gunung Telomoyo to the north. Uphill to the south of the road is the large ☆☆/☆ *Hotel Kopeng*, an old Dutch-built complex with a large, chilly swimming pool and rather dingy rooms. Behind it are colourful flower nurseries. A lively roadside market selling fresh produce operates in the mornings on the main road.

A walking track climbs to **Hutan Wisata Umbul Songo**, a wooded hill above the village with a waterfall and springs; ponies can be hired for the ride up. The summit of **Gunung Telomoyo** (1893m) can be reached by road; it is best to charter an *ojek* in the village.

Looming over Kopeng to the south is **Gunung Merbabu** (3142m), dormant for the past 300 years, which can be climbed from the village; your hotel can organise a guide. The round trip takes a full day, requiring a very early start. From the summit there is a magnificent view of **Gunung Merapi** to the south, which is truly spectacular if the latter is erupting: orange-glowing lava flows can be seen at night, and huge lava rocks bounce down the ash-covered slopes during the day. If Merapi is very active, it is well worth camping—with a pair of binoculars—on Merbabu to watch.

Ambarawa

Easily reached from Magelang, Salatiga or Semarang, Ambarawa is the starting point for an enjoyable ride on a rack-railway, which unfortunately is absurdly difficult (or expensive) for individuals to organise alone, and a visit to the temples of Gedong Songo. There is accommodation in Ambarawa, but the choice and location at **Bandungan**, a hill resort above the town, is greatly preferable (see below).

At a junction marked by an army tank monument in the centre of Ambarawa, turn south along Jl. Pemuda to the **Railway Museum** (Museum Kereta Api), on the right side after 500m. This is the old Ambarawa train station which used to serve the Semarang–Magelang route until the line closed in the 1970s. It is now used only for tourist rides on the delightful **rack-railway** (*rel bergigi*) to Bedono (c 20km round trip). In sidings beside the station's platforms are more than 20 old steam locomotives of European origin, dating back to the 1890s. One of them (no. 19) was built for the Hedjaz railway which ran through Syria, Palestine and Jordan; the locomotive was diverted to Java after the destruction of the Hedjaz line in 1918 by T.E. Lawrence of Arabia.

Because the train only operates when there is a group booked, the best chance for an individual visitor is on a Sunday morning, when there is most likely to be a group of local tourists. In midweek, you are more reliant on a (comparatively rare) foreign tour-group booking. Individuals are advised to phone the station (☎ 0298 91035) several days before their planned visit to see if they can be added to a group already booked; their itinerary should be as flexible as possible. An alternative is to put your own group together and share the charter cost; the train will then leave at a time you choose. Depending on the exchange rate it can cost anywhere between $90 and $170 to charter.

Opposite the army tank monument at the Jl. Pemuda junction is a small, dull military museum, **Museum Isdiman**, of little interest except to the most enthusiastic of military historians. Isdiman was a local hero in the fight for independence.

Jl. Pemuda continues past the railway museum and winds round Rawa Pening to Salatiga.

BANDUNGAN AND GEDONG SONGO

The temples of Gedong Songo, above the hill resort of Bandungan, have the finest aspect of all Java's *candi*, with a view encompassing seven volcanoes on a clear day.

From Ambarawa, take the signed road north to **Bandungan** (7km), 400m east of the army tank monument. At the main junction in Bandungan, turn left for Gedong Songo and most of Bandungan's better accommodation.

Hotels

There is a large choice here, though many hotels are rather shabby or overpriced. The following are recommended. The ☎ code is 0298.

☆☆☆/☆☆ *Hotel Nugraha Wisata* (☎ 91501). The most comfortable hotel in Bandungan, with smart, clean rooms and pool.

☆☆/☆ *Hotel Rawa Pening* (☎ 91134). Split into two parts: the cheaper rooms are in the eastern section; better rooms and the pool are a few metres further west along the main street. The restaurant food can be appalling.

☆☆ *Hotel Kusuma Madya* (☎ 91136/91503). Comfortable rooms, but few have views.

☆ *Wana Wisata Inn* (☎ 91120). Along a side lane to the north. Adequate but dull rooms; a low-budget standby.

The heart of Bandungan is the **main junction**, where market stalls are piled high with fruit, vegetables and flowers, and *warung* serve food all day. There is little else to do here except visit the temples of Gedong Songo. Both Bandungan and the temples can be extremely busy on Sundays and public holidays, and are then best avoided.

Take the road left at the junction by the market, pass the hotels and turn right up a steep lane to the entrance gates of Gedong Songo, c 2km further.

On a clear day it is worth getting to the temples of **Gedong Songo** as the site opens (open daily 06.15–17.15); to the south can be seen Gunung Merbabu, with the lower Gunung Telomoyo in front and Gunung Andong to the right; Gunung Merapi is just visible behind Merbabu.

History

The Shaivite temples of Gedong Songo date from 730–80, except perhaps for the first one encountered on the path, which is possibly from the early 9C. Built on the southern flank of Gunung Ungaran, their location was probably chosen for the hot sulphurous springs in the vicinity. The main shrine of each cluster was dedicated to Shiva, often with a subsidiary shrine to Nandi placed opposite.

The temples had long been forgotten when they were rediscovered in the mid-18C. The first two temple groups were repaired in the 1920s and 1930s, the others in the 1970s and 1980s.

Through the gates, follow the looping path anticlockwise past the temples. The first, restored in 1928–29, is almost bare of decoration except for false windows framed by *kala-makara* motifs. Inside is a *yoni*.

The second *candi*, higher up, has the *kala* motif round niches on the exterior walls; it is empty inside. Opposite the west-facing entrance is the base of a smaller temple which faced east.

The path climbs through tobacco fields to the third main group, a cluster of three small temples. Two of them face each other, and are clearly related. The largest, dedicated to Shiva, has its full complement of statues in the exterior niches. Flanking the entrance are the two *dvarapalas*: Nandishvara to the north with a water pot in the left hand, and Mahakala to the south with a club in the right hand. Durga is on the north side, Ganesha on the east, and Agastya on the south; the interior is empty. The smaller *candi* opposite would have been dedicated to Nandi, the mount of Shiva.

Beyond this cluster, the path drops into a narrow ravine where sulphurous gas bubbles up from water pools, and hot water flows from beneath rocks; the air is heavy with the smell of sulphur. The fourth group, up the other side, was once a cluster of at least nine structures; only one has been restored, but the *kala-makara* ornamentation is damaged and all the niches are empty except for a badly weathered figure, Agastya, in the south one.

A few metres uphill to the northeast of the cluster are two small sites in total ruin. The fifth main group, further south, has the best aspect of all. Seven volcanoes can be seen on a clear day: the Merbabu group, with Sumbing and Sundoro visible further west, and Gunung Lawu just in sight to the east.

In this temple group, only one of an original six *candi* has been fully restored. Its east niche contains a statue of Ganesha; the others are empty.

From here the path descends back to the entrance gate to complete the circuit.

Candi Ngempon Pringapus (Candi Muncul)

Of interest mainly to specialists—or those who enjoy exploring just for the sake of it—the Candi Muncul site consists of the damaged remains of five or six small *candi*, partly dismantled, in a charming riverside setting.

Just south of the **Karangjati** market on the main Salatiga–Semarang highway (and c 1.5km south of where the Bandungan road joins that highway) turn off east along a lane for 1.6km to a turn-off right called Jl. Kertanegara. Follow this c 750m through *desa* Ngempon to a factory on the right, and here take a narrow lane to the left, which becomes a stony track after c 60m. After a further c 50m, this track forks; take the slightly higher path to the right across a tiny brook and follow it for c 150m down through very pretty rice terraces to a footbridge over the Buyaran river. The *candi* site is clearly visible a few metres downstream on the same bank.

Rediscovered and excavated in 1952–53, the temples appear very small, and probably date from the 9C. Of the original six, five bases have been partially reassembled, together with the upper roof sections of three of them, and incomplete walls of four. The statues discovered here—several images of Ganesha, Shiva and Durga—have been removed to the Museum Ronggowarsito in Semarang.

During excavations, a bronze pipe was found sticking out of the ground in one of the six small structures. This was the top part of a pipe which ran down to the lid of a buried reliquary casket, found in situ. Originally it would have been joined at the top to a now vanished *yoni* in the cella of the *candi*. Holy lustral water, collected in the well of the *yoni*, would have run through the pipe and over the corporeal matter in the funerary urn beneath.

The north coast: Pekalongan, Semarang and Kudus

It must be said that much of the north coast is scenically rather dull, usually very hot and humid, and—except in east Java—is lacking in sites of cultural interest. Such sites do exist, but are few and far between; most of them—mosques or tombs of holy men—are relics of the expansion of Islam in the 15C and 16C. While these are of interest to the specialist or the pilgrim, they are not generally high on the agenda of most foreign tourists; accordingly, comparatively few travel this route. It is an area for those who already know other parts of Java intimately and are looking for something new.

Public transport
There are very frequent bus services all along the north coast, and the Jakarta–Surabaya train line passes through Pekalongan and Semarang.

PEKALONGAN

Renowned in the late 19C and early 20C for its marvellous handmade batik, and today reliant on fishing and factory-produced batik, the coastal town of Pekalongan lies c 100km west of Semarang and 130km east of Cirebon. There is little reason to come here except to purchase batik, but it makes a pleasant stop if you must travel along the coast road, which is not scenic and usually very busy.

The most interesting, but least practical, approach to Pekalongan is from Batur on the edge of the Dieng plateau (see p 273), which requires at least one change of bus en route.

Practical information

Transport
The **bus terminal** is on the Semarang road, 150m east of the Jl. Wahidin junction. There are frequent buses in both directions along the coast, and **minibuses** south to Kedungwuni. From the **train station** on Jl. Gajah Mada there are numerous trains west to Jakarta and east to Semarang and beyond. Useful services to Jakarta include the *Fajar Utama* (daytime; c 6 hours); *Senja Utama* (overnight; c 6 hours); and the more expensive *Argobromo* (overnight; 4 hours 10 minutes). These trains also have eastbound services to Semarang.

Hotels
The ☎ code is 0285.

☆☆/☆☆/☆ *Hotel Nirwana* (☎ 22446) Jl. Dr Wahidin 11. The best hotel in town, but overpriced for what it offers.

☆☆/☆ *Hotel Hayam Wuruk* (☎ 22823) Jl. Hayam Wuruk 152. Pleasant rooms and friendly staff in a very central location; recommended.

☆☆/☆ *Hotel Istana* (☎ 23581) Jl. Gajah Mada 23–25. Clean, adequate rooms.

Food and services

Rumah Makan Puas, a café on Jl. Surabaya, has simple but tasty dishes. *Es Teler* 77 on Jl. Dr Cipto has very average food in a better-than-average setting.

For **money**, *BNI*, *BII* and *BCA* are all on Jl. Imam Bonjol. The **post office** is at the north end of Jl. Diponegoro.

History

Pekalongan's recent history is inextricably linked to batik. From the early 19C, the town became one of the first important production centres of batik cap, the batik made by applying the pattern of wax to cloth using rectangular cast-metal plates. This proved much faster, and hence cheaper than the traditional batik canting or batik tulis, by which the pattern was drawn with a pen-sized bamboo stick attached to a copper vessel containing the hot wax. Arab merchants would come to Pekalongan and pay Javanese and Indo-European women to make batik, which they would then purchase and sell on, especially to the Banten area, where there was no local batik industry.

By the mid-19C the industry had become a major employer for the town, sometimes with detrimental effect. In the 1840s, vast areas of land were planted with indigo to provide a key dye. Over time, this so depleted soil nutrients as to cause a series of bad rice harvests several years after indigo planting was cut back.

By the late 19C, Pekalongan's cap industry was totally controlled by Chinese and Arab traders. The canting, run by Indo-European women, began to disappear in the 1920s, unable to compete on cost. The cap industry continues, still dominated by the Chinese, who manufacture, and the Arabs, who trade. A handful of canting producers still exist, producing magnificent, very expensive batik.

Apart from the numerous **batik shops** clustered along Jl. Hayam Wuruk west of the *Hotel Hayam Wuruk*, there are a few buildings of historic interest round the shady square at the north end of Jl. Diponegoro. At the southwest corner is the former Dutch Resident's house; opposite is the City Hall (Balai Kota). At the north end are the Dutch Reformed Church, built in the mid-19C, and the former Colonial Club; to the southeast, behind the City Hall, are the remains of an 18C fort built by the VOC and now used as the local prison.

Across the bridge southeast of the square is a small and unremarkable Chinese temple, **Po An Thian**, on Jl. Blimbing. On Jl. Sultan Agung, running south from the bridge, is **Pasar Banjarsari**, a lively market which usually has a quite good range of batik, as well as fresh produce. The quiet residential neighbourhood to the east is the traditional Arab quarter; there are batik dealers here, but they are renowned for driving a hard bargain. One to visit is *Tobal* on the north side of Jl. Teratai.

To the south across Jl. Dr Cipto is the *alun-alun*, with the **Mesjid Al Jami** on the west side.

The sugar mill at **Sragi**, c 10km southwest of Pekalongan, has more than 20 narrow gauge steam locomotives working on its extensive network of tracks, and is of special interest to enthusiasts because of the large variety of locomotives used in the mill yards. During the harvesting season (May to September) you can expect to see a dozen or more at work on most days.

At **Weleri** on the road between Semarang and Pekalongan, a turn-off south leads to **Curug Sewu**, a spectacular waterfall on the north flank of Gunung Perahu.

SEMARANG

The capital of Central Java, Semarang (population c 1.5 million) is an important commercial city, with one of the north coast's few deep-water ports. The old warehouse quarter in front of Tawang train station is now run-down but interesting to wander in; here is found the striking Protestant church. To the south is Chinatown, a lively and interesting neighbourhood with Jl. Pekojan at its heart. Simpang Lima, the huge traffic circle further south, has the city's main shopping malls; the Tugu Muda traffic circle to the west is surrounded by historic buildings. The hilly southern suburb of Candi Baru is an alternative place to stay, though too far to be totally practical if you wish to see the city sights.

Practical information

Transport
The main **bus station**, Terminal Terboyo, is c 4km east of the city centre on the usually very congested Kudus road. There are frequent buses to most north coast towns, and inland to Ambarawa, Magelang, Yogyakarta and Solo.

The Tawang **train station** is more central, but many of the overnight services, both to Jakarta and eastbound to Surabaya, either pass through Semarang in the middle of the night or reach their destination extremely early in the morning (01.00–04.00). Among the more useful services are *Fajar Utama* (daytime; c 7 hours) to Jakarta; *Jayabaya* (overnight) to Jakarta; and *Argobromo* (overnight; 5 hours 45 minutes) to Jakarta.

The domestic **airlines** have flights to and from Semarang's Ahmad Yani Airport, and all have offices in town. Direct destinations include Denpasar (1 hour 50 minutes), Jakarta (55 minutes) and Surabaya (1 hour). *Garuda* (☎ 413217) is at the Hotel Graha Santika.

Bouraq (☎ 543065) is at Jl. Gajah *Mada* 61/D. Merpati (☎ 517137) is at Jl. Gajah Mada 17. *Mandala* (☎ 444737) is at Bangkong Plaza B-7 off Jl. Mataram. Several *Pelni* **passenger ships** pass through Semarang on their regular circuits round the islands. The office is on the corner of Jl. Mpu Tantular and Jl. Kutilang. For getting round the city it is simplest to use the many *becak* and **taxis**.

Hotels
As in most towns, Semarang's better hotels usually offer large discounts on their published tariffs. An alternative to the city is to stay in the hills at Candi Baru, a residential suburb south of the city centre. Note, however, that it is awkward to get around there without your own transport. The phone code is 024.

☆☆☆☆☆/☆☆☆☆ *Hotel Graha Santika* (☎ 413115/413121; fax 413113) Jl. Pandanaran 116-120. One of Semarang's best hotels, with very comfortable rooms and professional staff; recommended.

☆☆☆☆☆/☆☆☆☆ *Hotel Patra Jasa*
(☎ 314441; fax 314448) Jl.
Sisingamangaraja, Candi Baru, c 5km
from Simpang Lima. Very good
rooms, pool, tennis courts and nine-
hole golf course.

☆☆☆☆/☆☆☆ *Hotel Metro* (☎ 547371) Jl.
Agus Salim 2–4. Despite its hideous
façade, the rooms are good value and it
has a very central location.

☆☆☆/☆☆ *Hotel Candi Baru* (☎ 315272)
Jl. Rinjani, off Jl. Parman at Candi Baru,
c 4km from Simpang Lima. A magnificent, if slightly run-down, building dating from the 1920s.

☆☆☆/☆☆ *Hotel Quirin* (☎ 547063) Jl.
Gajah Mada 44–52. Decent, clean rooms;
one of the better mid-priced hotels.

☆☆☆/☆☆ *Hotel Natour Dibya Puri* (☎
547821–3) Jl. Pemuda 11. This once-
splendid colonial hotel has fallen on
hard times; rooms are generally quite
good value, but vary widely.

☆☆/☆ *Hotel Nendra Yati* (☎ 544202) Jl.
Gang Pinggir 68. Reasonable rooms in
the heart of Chinatown.

☆ *Hotel Oewa Asia* (☎ 542547) Jl.
Sugiono. Basic but clean rooms in a
low-budget hotel close to the town centre; friendly staff.

Food and services

Toko Oen on Jl. Pemuda, sister
restaurant to the much better
one in Malang, is an old-fashioned place
with old waiters and reasonable but
overpriced food; you pay for the decor
and atmosphere of faded grandeur.
Mbok Berek at Jl. A Yani 170 has excellent fried chicken. There are scores of
streetside ***warung*** round Pasar Johar
and the old market district, offering
cheap, simple dishes. American fast food
can be found on Jl. Pemuda and in *Mal
Ciputra*, the large shopping mall at
Simpang Lima.

For **money**, *BCA* (M, V) is on Jl.
Pemuda. *Bank Duta* (M, V) is on the
north side of Mal Ciputra. *Gunung
Agung* in Mal Ciputra sells local maps
and a small selection of books in
English. *Matahari* department store is at
Simpang Lima. *Gramedia* on Jl.
Pandanaran sells the *Jakarta Post* and
maps. There is a 24-hour ***wartel*** on Jl.
Suprapto, not far from the post office.
Haryono is a generally reliable travel
agent at Jl. Pandanaran 37
(☎ 444000).

History

A commercial trading port for centuries, Semarang was visited by Chinese
and Indian traders from at least the 15C. The Dutch VOC maintained a trading post here in the 17C, and in 1708 moved its coastal headquarters here
from Jepara. In 1741 the VOC fort came under seige from Chinese fleeing the
Dutch-incited slaughter of ethnic Chinese in Batavia. They were joined by
Pakubuwono II of Kartosuro who, despite being advised to the contrary,
believed he could gain more by supporting the Chinese rather than the Dutch.
In November, however, with 20,000 Javanese and 3500 Chinese laying siege,
Dutch relief forces arrived; the Chinese in the area were massacred, and
Pakubuwono was forced to beg Dutch forgiveness before ultimately with-
drawing from the anti-VOC war.

200 years later, Semarang was once again caught up in war. The battle of
Semarang, from 14–19 October 1945, caused the deaths of around 2000
Indonesians and 500 Japanese. Having formally surrendered to the Allies and
allowed the Republicans to take over the city, the Japanese found themselves
under Allied orders to retake the city and hold it till the forces of the British
Southeast Asia Command arrived. On 14 October they began this operation;

the Republicans retaliated by murdering between 100 and 300 Japanese, and the fighting intensified. The British troops, most of them Indians, finally arrived on 19 October to find that the Japanese had almost regained full control, but with high casualties on both sides.

Exploring Semarang

To get a feel for Semarang's commercial history, take a stroll round some of the quiet streets between Jl. Suprapto and Jl. Tawang. Here lie semi-derelict warehouses and decrepit shipping offices, together with the domed Protestant church, **Gereja Immanuel** (Gereja Blenduk), built for Pastor Fredericus Martannus during his mission to Semarang (1894–95) by two Dutch architects, W. Westmaas and H.P.A. de Wilde, on the site of a late-18C church.

Turn south beside the post office (built 1906–07) towards the covered market, **Pasar Johar**. The streets in the vicinity are the main shopping area in the city. **Mesjid Agung**, in the Kauman district immediately to the south, dates from the late 19C, when its predecessor burnt down.

To the east, Jl. Pekojan is at the heart of Semarang's **Chinatown** and is well worth a wander. On the north bank of the river, turn west along Gang Lombok, past a simple café called *Lunpia Semarang*, to **Tay Kak Sie**, an interesting Chinese temple with many Buddhist, Confucian and Taoist shrines. This venerable joss-house has been here at least since the 18C.

South of Chinatown, along Jl. Dahlan or Jl. Gajah Mada, you come to **Simpang Lima**, a huge grassy square used for fairs and political rallies, around which traffic circulates all day long. On its north and east sides are two of Semarang's main shopping plazas, Mal Ciputra and Plaza Simpang Lima. On the west side is Mesjid Baitturahman, the city's largest mosque.

To the west, Jl. Pandanaran leads to another traffic circle, Simpang Tugu, with the unremarkable **Tugu Muda** (Youth Monument) at its centre. This commemorates the young Republican fighters who died in the battle of Surabaya in October 1945.

On the northeast side of Simpang Tugu is a notable building with twin towers, known today as **Lawang Sewu**. Built in 1902 by Dutch architects J.F. Klinkhamer and B.J. Ouëndag as offices for the Dutch Indies Railway Company, it is now very run-down and badly in need of refurbishment.

On the northwest side of Simpang Tugu is the **provincial governor's residence**, built originally for the Dutch Governor of the Northeast Coast, Nicolaas Hartingh (governor, 1754–61). Across Jl. Sugiyopranoto from there is the Museum Perjuangan Mandala Bhakti, a small military museum (open Tues–Fri 09.00–13.00), and across Jl. Sutomo from there is a Catholic church dating from 1937.

Museum Ronggowarsito, the east Java provincial museum on Jl. Abdulrachman Saleh, c 3km west of the Simpang Tugu traffic circle (open daily 08.00–13.00; closed on public holidays), has a wide-ranging collection, which includes fossils and prehistoric artifacts, drum heads from bronze kettledrums and a complete *moko*, a Hindu-Buddhist section with small bronze figurines, stone inscriptions and statuary (including many stone images from Candi

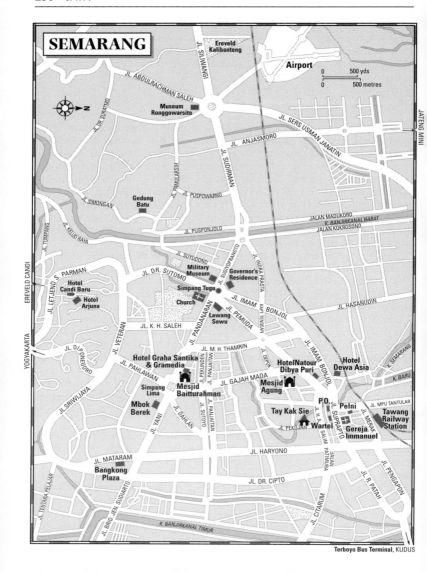

Ngempon Pringapus; see p 284), and sections on Islam and colonial history. Dioramas depict historical events, including the battle of Semarang in 1945; and there is a small ethnographic collection with implements used in fishing and farming, blacksmithery and woodcarving; beautiful krises and textiles, *wayang* of many sorts and musical instruments.

Jl. Siliwangi, the main road west from the museum traffic circle, leads after 550m to **Ereveld Kalibanteng**, a Dutch war cemetery with more than 3000 graves in neat rows. Most of the dead were women and children who died in Japanese prison camps at Ambarawa and elsewhere. Near the far end of the central avenue is a notable bronze statue of an emaciated child carrying work tools. At the back of the cemetery, up a few steps, is another sculpture showing women and a child embracing in solidarity.

East of Museum Ronggowarsito, a road runs north c 2km to **Jateng Mini** ('Central Java in Miniature', also known as Puri Maerokoco; open daily 08.00–20.00) where pavilions representing the different regencies (*kabupaten*) in the province display their crafts.

An important Chinese shrine, **Gedung Batu** (or Gua Sam Poo), southeast of the Museum Ronggowarsito on Jl. Simongang, attracts a steady stream of Chinese visitors who come to pay their respects at a shrine to Sam Poo Kong, better known as **Zheng He** (1371–1435), a Chinese envoy from the Ming dynasty court.

Legend has it that Zheng He, a Muslim eunuch from landlocked Yunnan, pursued a successful military career in north China before being sent in 1405, by the Yongle emperor, to establish trade links and friendship agreements with states in southeast Asia. His first expedition, comprising c 27,000 men and more than 300 ships, was followed by subsequent ones to the Philippines, Java, Sumatra, Malaysia and Thailand, Bengal and Sri Lanka, and perhaps as far as the Swahili coast of east Africa. He came twice to Java in the early 15C; this shrine commemorates his second visit, in 1416.

The entrance is protected by two guardian figures; at the rear is a tiny, incense-filled grotto flanked by dragons, containing his altar. Further to the left is a pavilion containing a ship's anchor, which folklore claims to be from his ship, but in fact is from a VOC ship. In the temple complex are many other, less interesting shrines.

East of Semarang

East of the city centre on the main Kudus road, c 3km from Semarang's post office, is **Museum Jamu Nyonya Meneer**, a museum run by one of the largest *jamu* (herbal medicine) manufacturers in Indonesia.

South of Semarang

Off the south side of Jl. Parman in Candi Baru, near the Hotel Candi Baru, a road passes through the small Taman Jenderal Sudirman to **Ereveld Candi**, a Dutch war cemetery containing more than 1000 graves. Most are of servicemen who died in Central Java; others were moved after independence from cemeteries in Sulawesi and Sumatra. Like Ereveld Kalibanteng near the city, this is immaculately maintained by the Netherlands War Graves Foundation.

A place definitely not to be recommended is **Semarang's zoo** (Taman Margasatwa dan Kebun Binatang Tinjo Moyo), a shockingly bad drive-in zoo where the animals are kept in dismal conditions. Animal rights activists should have a look. Take the main Salatiga road south from **Candi Baru** and turn west along a narrow lane, Jl. Karangrejo, immediately north of the bridge over the toll-road. The zoo entrance is 2km away.

Further south, 4.7km beyond the toll-road underpass, is the Jamu Jago factory on the west side, with the **Museum Jamu Jago**, a small museum promoting jamu.

Demak

The main road east from Semarang reaches the *alun-alun* in Demak after c 26km.

History

The early history of Demak is unclear, but for a period of 50 or so years in the 16C it rose to a position of considerable prominence in Java before fading just as quickly. At that time it was a coastal port, but silting since then means it now lies 13km from the sea.

Demak was probably founded in the late 15C by a Chinese Muslim, perhaps called Cek Ko-po. His grandson or son, called Trenggana, campaigned relentlessly to expand Demak's influence through Java. Kediri, the last Hindu-Buddhist state in east Java, was taken by Trenggana in 1527. Forces loyal to him took Tuban, Banten and Sunda Kelapa (Jakarta) the same year. Madiun was conquered in 1529–30, followed by Surabaya and Pasuruan in the 1530s. Gunung Penanggungan, the holy Hindu mountain south of Surabaya, was taken in 1543, followed by Malang in 1545. In 1546, however, Trenggana was murdered during an expedition against Panarukan.

With his death, Demak's power rapidly dwindled. Trenggana's successor, known in court chronicles as Sultan Prawata (r. c 1546–61), did not continue the expeditions, and a period of confusion and then decline followed. It is doubtful if even under Trenggana Demak's 'empire' had been anything more than a loose federation of small states; any centralised control was probably minimal. Inevitably, Demak was in turn conquered in 1588 by the state of Mataram, based near present-day Yogyakarta.

Demak today is a small market town, its main attraction being **Mesjid Agung** on the west side of the *alun-alun*. This is considered one of Java's oldest mosques, perhaps the oldest – probably from the early 16C – and one of the most important pilgrimage sites for Javanese Muslims. The three-tiered roof represents the *meru*, the mythical cosmic mountain of the Hindu world, and the old wooden pillars which support the *pendopo* are said to have been brought from the pre-Islamic state of Majapahit, near present-day Mojokerto.

In the mosque compound are graves claimed to be of Raden Patah, regarded as the first sultan of Demak, and Trenggana. In fact it is difficult to know who Raden Patah was; he may have been Cek Ko-po himself, or his son, or someone else completely. The court chronicles, in an effort to establish a direct historic link between Hindu-Buddhist Majapahit's decline and Islamic Demak's ascendancy, paint him as the offspring of a union between the last Majapahit king and a Chinese princess; these same chronicles date Majapahit's fall to 1478–79. In fact, if Majapahit did fall in those years, it almost certainly was not to Demak (which at that stage may not have existed) but to another Hindu-Buddhist dynasty or break-away branch of its own dynasty which moved the capital to Kediri. Any direct link between Majapahit and Demak is extremely tenuous, but this inconsistency is irrelevant to the present-day pilgrims who flock to the mosque.

The road north from the *alun-alun* crosses a bridge after c 750m, where the Purwodadi road turns off right past the **grave of Sunan Kalijogo**, one of the *wali songo*, the nine men believed to have introduced Islam into Java. He is cred-ited with helping the Mataram dynasty establish itself as the pre-eminent power in Java in the late 16C; the tomb is a popular place of pilgrimage.

There is little reason to take the Purwodadi road further unless heading for Solo or Madiun. However, 20km east of Purwodadi on the Blora road, a turn-off south in the centre of Wirosari leads to the rather bizarre **Bledug Kuwu**, a further 6km. Here, a broad expanse of mud pools gently erupts at irregular intervals. It is diffi-cult to get a clear view, even from the viewing tower and platforms provided. It is apparently safe to walk quite close to the pools, but care should be taken.

KUDUS
• • • • • • • •

A small town 25km northeast of Demak, Kudus is known throughout Java for its al-Manar mosque and the manufacture of *kretek* (clove) cigarettes. There is little else here for the casual visitor.

Practical information

Transport
The **bus terminal** is on the south side of town. There are no trains or flights to Kudus.

Hotels
The choice of accommodation in Kudus is rather dismal. The ☎ code is 0291.
✮✮✮/✮✮ *Hotel Kudus Asri Jaya* (☎ 38449). The town's best hotel, but far out to the south, and opposite a large electricity transformer station.

✮✮/✮ *Hotel Air Mancur* (☎ 32514) Jl. Pemuda 70. Simple, reasonable rooms in central location.
✮✮/✮ *Notosari Permai* (☎ 37227) Jl. Kepodang 12. Rather gloomy, but ade-quate rooms.

Services
For **money**, *BCA* and *BNI* are on Jl. Yani. A 24-hour *wartel* is further south. The **post office** is on Jl. Sudirman.

History
While Demak's power was growing in the early 16C, Kudus was emerging as an Islamic holy city and place of learning associated with Sunan Kudus, another of the *wali songo*. Tradition has it that he was the fifth *imam* at the Mesjid Agung in Demak, and played a key role in the campaign against Kediri in 1527, before moving to Kudus. The town's name derives from the Arabic al-Quds (Jerusalem).

The **Mesjid al-Manar**, on Jl. Menara on the west side of the town, provides the main interest. Attributed to Sunan Kudus, whose grave lies at the back of the compound, it has been dated by an inscription over the mihrab to 1549. While the main body of the mosque has been rebuilt in the 20C, it is surrounded by much earlier brick split gateways and a remarkable *menara* (minaret) at the front; more brick structures are within the modern mosque itself. They bear a remarkable similarity to the style seen at Hindu *candi* in Trowulan (the site of the pre-Islamic state of Majapahit; see p 379) and elsewhere.

On Jl. Sunan Kudus a few metres east of the mosque is a small Chinese temple, opposite which a narrow alley leads to the very minor ruins of **Langgar Bubar**, a small brick structure inscribed with floral motifs, which probably dates from the same era as Mesjid al-Manar.

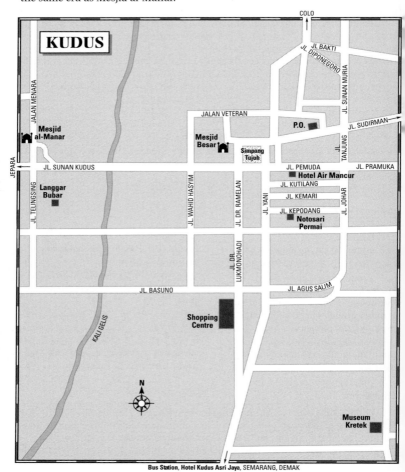

KUDUS

On the south side of Kudus is the **Museum Kretek** (open Sat–Thur), which provides a brief history of the clove cigarette industry in Java. It has an illustrated biography of Niti Semito, the eccentric entrepreneur who helped develop the *kretek* concept into a huge, multi-million-dollar industry, and it explains the various qualities of cloves and the traditional and modern manufacturing processes.

Colo

Above Kudus on the southern flank of Gunung Muria is the 16C **tomb of Sunan Muria**, another of the *wali songo*. Take the road to Colo, c 18km, from where pilgrims must climb a long stone stairway through terraced fields to the tomb. The scenery and views are excellent; the grave site is of only limited interest to the casual visitor.

Jepara

On the coast 35km northwest of Kudus and reached by bus from Kudus and Semarang, Jepara is a small port famous for its wooden furniture industry. The main road is lined with dozens of workshops, especially in *desa* **Tahunan**, c 4km before Jepara, where the roadside is piled high with chairs, tables, cupboards and window frames or blocked by container trucks waiting to be loaded.

Hotels

The nicest hotel is the ☆☆/☆ *Hotel Ratu Shima* (☎ 0291 91406) at Jl. Sutomo 13–15, which has pleasant, good-value rooms.

History

Jepara first comes to historians' attention in the early 16C. In 1513 its ruler, Yunus, with his brother-in-law Trenggana, the ruler of Demak, led a force of 100 ships and 5000 men from Jepara and Palembang against Portuguese Malacca, but was defeated. Jepara's heyday came during the reign of Ratu Kalinyamat in the second half of the 16C. In 1551 and again in 1574 Jepara besieged Portuguese Malacca, both times unsuccessfully.

In the early 17C, both the Dutch VOC and the English East India Company set up trading posts here, by which time the port had come under Mataram's control.

Relations between the VOC and Javanese at Jepara were poor. Dutchmen were said to have relieved themselves against the Jepara mosque, and in 1618 the Gujerati who governed Jepara for Mataram attacked the VOC trading post, killing three Dutchmen and taking others prisoner. In November 1618 the Dutch responded, burning all the ships in the harbour and much of the town. In May 1619 Jan Pieterszoon Coen, on his way to Batavia, paused here to burn the port once more, as well as the English trading post. For much of the 17C Jepara was the main north coast port for the VOC, until its headquarters was moved to Semarang in 1708.

The **Museum R.A. Kartini** (open Mon–Fri 07.00–16.00; Sat, Sun, hols 09.00–17.00) is next door to the tourist office (Dinas Pariwisata) on the north side of the *alun-alun*. Kartini's father, the Regent of Jepara, was a progressive thinker who permitted her to attend the European lower school here at a time when most Javanese officials found the idea of female education irrelevant. She went on to become a very well-known promoter of women's rights before her death in 1904 at the age of 24. The museum has furniture from their home in Jepara, and photos.

Across the bridge on the north side of the *alun-alun*, take the first road on the left, Jl. Pahlawan, up the hill 400m past the popular *Pondok Rasa* restaurant to the heroes' cemetery (*taman makam pahlawan*). Just beyond it lie low stone ramparts – all that remain of a 17C **VOC fortress**, now largely overgrown and grazed by goats.

In **Mantingan**, south of Jepara off the main Kudus road, is the **grave of Ratu Kalinyamat**, Queen of Jepara in the late 16C, when Jepara's power was at its zenith. Some of the original sculpted stone medallions from a mosque built here in 1559 have been preserved in the walls of a new mosque built in the 1920s; remarkable designs on some depict animals composed entirely of floral components – an apparently traditional Javanese technique which fitted perfectly the requirements of Islamic art in avoiding the representation of animals and humans.

On the coast 45km northeast of Jepara is the site of a 16C **Portuguese fort** (*benteng Portugis*). However, very little remains, the road is bad and the scenery is unspectacular; this excursion is not advised.

Pakis Baru and Trangkil sugar mills

On the east side of Gunung Muria are two privately owned sugar mills (*pabrik gula*) which still use steam locomotives to shuttle sugar cane from field to mill. **Trangkil** lies c 12km north of Pati on the Tayu road and is home to the last steam locomotive built in the UK (excluding later replicas and locos built for tourist purposes) – a small saddle-tank locomotive built by the Hunslet Engine Company of Leeds in 1971. Enthusiasts wishing to see the working steam trains should visit during the harvesting months (June–October) at 13.00 when the locos leave the mill to collect the sugar cane; the loaded trains return in the late afternoon.

The **Pakis Baru** mill is on the main road further north, c 4km southwest of Tayu, and has a couple of Java's oldest working locomotives – built in Germany in 1899 and 1900.

Visitors are welcome to look round both mills.

Karimunjawa National Marine Park

Most of the smaller islands of the Karimunjawa archipelago, which lies c 85km offshore from Jepara, belong to the National Park. In the dry season the archipelago is a magnificent place, with clear seas, sandy beaches, extensive coral reefs and mangrove forest. Avoid visiting in the rainy season, when the choppy sea and cloudy skies can make life miserable.

A drawback is the cost and time involved in getting from Pulau Karimunjawa, the main island where the Jepara boat docks, to the peripheral islands. The accommodation is also very limited; Indonesians tend to come here just for the weekend, or even on a long day-trip. This is a place to bring camping equipment, a good supply of food and water, and plenty of books to read. It is possible to charter a boat to drop you at one of the small islands, camp out for a few nights, and then be picked up again. Charter costs are shared if you can find travelling companions.

Getting there

Boats depart from Pantai Jepara, just outside Jepara town, to Pulau Karimunjawa two or three times weekly (usually Tues, Fri and Sun, but liable to change); the crossing takes 5–6 hours and costs c $6–8.

Accommodation

There are now several simple ☆☆/☆ *losmen* and *penginapan* on some of the islands, especially Pulau Karimunjawa and Pulau Tengah. However, there is nothing remotely sophisticated.

Yogyakarta

One of the most visitor-friendly cities in Java, Yogyakarta is well endowed with sites of interest, including the most important royal court still flourishing in Java. It also makes an excellent base from which to visit central Java's finest ancient temples, climb (or perhaps just view) the magnificent Gunung Merapi, and explore the craggy coastline of the Indian Ocean.

People who have known the city a long time complain of growing traffic jams and pollution, and while they have a point, Yogya nevertheless remains one of the easiest and most enjoyable cities to explore.

Cultural **highlights** include the historic **Keraton** and the **Museum Sono Budoyo**. Arts lovers should be sure to experience at least a *wayang kulit* or gamelan performance, or the dramatic *Ramayana* ballet at Prambanan, and visit some of the many galleries; especially recommended are the **Museum Affandi**, the **Museum Wayang Kekayon** and the small **Brahma Tirta Sari batik** studio. The village of Kota Gede (see p 311) is also well worth a visit.

Practical information

Transport
Flights

Cities served by direct routes to/from Yogya include Bandung, Denpasar, Jakarta, Medan, Padang, Palembang and Surabaya. **Adisucipto Airport** is c 10km east of the city centre on Jl. Solo. All the domestic airlines have offices in Yogya: *Bouraq* at Jl. Mentri Supeno 58; *Garuda* at Jl. Mangkubumi 52; *Mandala* at the Hotel Meliá Purosani on Jl. Suryotomo; *Merpati* at Jl. Diponegoro 31.

Trains

Useful services from Yogya include the *Fajar Utama Yogya* daytime train to Jakarta (c 8 hours) and the *Bima, Senja Utama Yogya* and *Senja Utama Solo* overnight trains which leave Yogya from the early evening onwards, to arrive in Jakarta very early the following morning. Only the *Senja Utama Solo* has couchettes. The eastbound *Bima* and *Mutiara Selatan* are overnight services to Surabaya, arriving in the early morning. Advance bookings can be made at the station, or through travel agents for a small commission. There are regular economy services to Solo.

Buses

The main station for inter-town buses is **Terminal Umbulharjo** on Jl. Veteran, southeast of the city centre. For some popular destinations, including Malang, Semarang, Surabaya and Bandung, it can be simpler to book a comfortable air-conditioned bus through an agent on Jl. Sosrowijayan or Jl. Prawirotaman, who will then ensure you are picked up from their office. Jakarta-bound travellers are advised to take the **train**, since buses terminate at Pulogadung, 10km from the city centre in east Jakarta.

Taxis

Yogya's taxis are all metered, usually well maintained, and the most comfortable way to get round town. In contrast to Jakarta, the drivers are generally polite and friendly.

Becak

The ubiquitous *becak* drivers can be maddening with their persistent sales patter, but they are fun on the quieter roads and go slowly enough for you to see the passing scenery. They will frequently try to take you shopping (for a commission) and will charge considerably more to go north (generally uphill) than south (mainly downhill). Bargain the fare to a realistic level, but don't be

uncompromisingly mean: supply exceeds demand, and drivers desperately need the income.

Andong

These four-wheeled pony traps are slow and uncomfortable, but nevertheless enjoyable. They can usually be found at the north end of Jl. Malioboro.

Rentals

Car, motorcycle and bicycle rentals are easy to find in Yogya, and well worthwhile for the independence they give you. *Bali Car Rental Service* on Jl. Airport, just in front of Adisucipto Airport, has self-drive jeeps and Kijangs at competitive rates. There are several rental outlets along Jl. Pasar Kembang/Jl. Jlagren near the railway station, including *Fortuna* at Jl. Jlagren 20, which has a range of motorcycles and can provide Suzuki jeeps. Others can be found on Jl. Prawirotaman. For a small group, it can be best to rent a minibus with driver from a travel agent: negotiate a deal which takes you exactly where you want.

 ## Hotels

Yogya has a huge number of hotels, guest houses and simple *losmen*, catering to all budgets. The most expensive hotels tend to be along Jl. Solo, the main road running east from the city towards the airport; scores of mid-priced guest houses can be found south of the *keraton* on Jl. Prawirotaman and parallel streets; and several dozen very cheap and basic *losmen* and *penginapan* can be found near the train station in the alleys off Jl. Sosrowijayan and Jl. Pasar Kembang. Travellers wanting sublime luxury with no expense spared should try ✶✶✶✶✶ *Amanjiwo* (☎ 0293 88333; fax 88355; e-mail: amanjiwo@idola. net.id) at Borobudur (see p 312) c 30mins from Yogya. A selection of the better hotels in the city is listed here; if none satisfy you, the tourist office on Jl. Malioboro can recommend others, or it is easy to find many more on your own by wandering in the above-mentioned neighbourhoods. At the more expensive hotels, you can often negotiate a discount of up to 50 per cent, as there is a glut of rooms. The ☎ code is 0274.

✫✫✫✫✫ *Sheraton Mustika* (☎ 511588; fax 511589) Jl. Adisucipto. Opened mid-1997, c 9km east of the city centre. Very comfortable rooms, a good buffet and exceptional pool.

✫✫✫✫✫/✫✫✫✫ *Hotel Acacia* (☎ 566222) Jl. Adisucipto 38. Threadbare carpets and generally in need of refurbishment, but a good-sized pool.

✫✫✫✫✫/✫✫✫✫ *Hyatt Regency* (☎ 869566; fax 869577; e-mail: hry@idola.net.id) Jl. Palagan Tentara Pelajar. On the northwest side of the city, offering standard Hyatt facilities. Opened late 1997.

✫✫✫✫✫/✫✫✫✫ *Meliá Purosani* (☎ 589521/589523) Jl. Suryotomo 31. Very comfortable hotel in the heart of the city; attractive swimming pool and garden; food has been disappointing in the past.

✫✫✫✫ *Hotel Phoenix* (☎ 566617) Jl. Sudirman 9–11. Renovated and extended 1930s building of considerable charm. Pleasant, but rather small rooms; tiny pool.

✫✫✫✫ *Natour Garuda* (☎ 512114) Jl. Malioboro 60. The old Grand Hotel, dating from 1911. Extended and modernised, and rather overpriced, but in an excellent, central location.

✫✫✫✫ *Hotel Puri Artha* (☎ 563288) Jl. Cendrawasih 9. Very pleasant rooms in a quiet location east of the city centre. Recommended.

✫✫✫/✫✫ *Peti Mas* (☎ 61938/60163) Jl. Dagen 27. Clean rooms in a slightly cramped compound with pool; friendly staff. An excellent location, but the call to prayer at a nearby mosque can be loud.

✫✫✫/✫✫ *Batik Palace Cottage*

(☎ 561828/561823) off Jl. Dagen. Rooms and cottages in central location near Jl. Malioboro; swimming pool and small garden.

✫✫ *Wisma Gadjah II* (☎ 372037) Jl. Gerilya (Jl. Prawirotaman II). A beautiful old house with a few simple rooms and restaurant. Recommended.

✫✫/✫ *Rose* (☎ 377991/380011) Jl. Prawirotaman 22–28. Very good value, simple, clean rooms; large swimming pool; friendly staff. Often has European tour groups. Similar accommodation close by at Galunggung and Duta guest-houses.

✫✫/✫ *Bladok* (☎ 560452) Jl. Sosrowijayan 76. Good value, spotlessly clean, very basic rooms in a central location, with attractive little verandah café; often full.

Restaurants, cafés and bars

An immense variety of food and drink is available, from excellent five-star hotel restaurants to the hundreds of roadside warung which are set up at night. In the main tourist neighbourhoods, Jl. Prawirotaman and Jl. Sosrowijayan, almost every other building is a restaurant, though the fare can be bland and repetitive. A few recommendations are listed below.

Lotus Garden Café and Lotus Breeze, under the same management, on Jl. Gerilya (Jl. Prawirotaman II), have extensive menus and pleasant decor.

Hanoman's Forest, Jl. Prawirotaman, has nightly 2-hour shows of *wayang golek*, *wayang kulit* or dance, very popular with tour groups; the food is average.

Going Bananas, a craft shop at the east end of Jl. Prawirotaman, has a very short menu but tasty food.

Pesta Perak, Jl. Tentara Rakyat Mataram, has a good buffet of Javanese food.

Legian Garden Restaurant, overlooking Jl. Malioboro, has a pleasant atmos-

phere and reasonable food.
Hotel Aquila Prambanan, Jl. Solo, has an excellent Javanese buffet in the evening; a good place to try authentic local dishes in very comfortable surroundings.

Information and maps

The **tourist information centre** at Jl. Malioboro 16 (open Mon–Fri 07.30–19.00, Sat 09.00–14.00) can provide a simple street map, general information about Yogya and the surrounding area, and an up-to-date timetable for gamelan, *wayang* and dance performances in the city. The tourist police share the office. **Bookshops** sell the *Yogyakarta/Central Java* map by Periplus, which has a reasonable street plan and map of the area surrounding Yogya.

Banks and money

There are numerous banks along Jl. Solo and Jl. Mangkubumi, and moneychangers round Jl. Prawirotaman and Jl. Sosrowijayan. *BCA* (M, V), with branches at Jl. Mangkubumi and Jl. Sudirman, offers an efficient service. Major credit cards are increasingly widely accepted at hotels and travel agents, but don't rely on them when purchasing goods or food.

Post and telecoms

The central **post office** is on Jl. Senopati opposite the Museum Benteng; a small one is on Jl. Sosrowijayan. Numerous **wartel** can be found in the city, many of them open 24 hours.

Medical services

One of Yogya's best **hospitals** is the *Bethesda* on Jl. Sudirman (Jl. Solo), where the staff speak good English and the quality of service and care is generally excellent.

Travel agents and tours

Many agents on Jl. Sosrowijayan, in the north of the city, and Jl. Prawirotaman, south of the *keraton*, offer local tours to Borobudur, Prambanan, Gunung Merapi, the Dieng plateau and further afield. They can also arrange bus, train and air tickets. Recommended for flight bookings is *Pacto* in the Hotel Natour Garuda on Jl. Malioboro. Domestic air tickets are sometimes (but not always) available more cheaply from the airlines themselves, as some offer discounts on early-morning or late-night services.

Bookshops and libraries

Maps and English-language publications are available at branches of *Gramedia* on Jl. Sudirman and in Mal Malioboro on Jl. Malioboro; and at branches of *Gunung Agung* at the Galeria on Jl. Sudirman and Exim Plaza on Jl. Adisucipto. *Gadjah Mada University Press* has a shop at its office on the university campus, off the west side of Jl. Kaliurang; its catalogue carries a range of academic books about Indonesia, many in English. **Karta Pustaka** (Dutch-Indonesian cultural centre) at Jl. Suroto 5 (☎ 586227) has a small library of predominantly Dutch- and English-language books about Indonesia.

Performing arts

Yogya has the widest variety of easily accessible performing arts of any Javanese city, including gamelan and *wayang kulit*, *wayang golek*, *wayang wong*, and traditional dance. There is a performance of one or more of these every day of the week, somewhere in the city. The tourist office or your hotel can provide the current programme. Classical Javanese dance. Rehearsals by royal court dancers are held within the *keraton* compound, usually on Sunday mornings. The **Mardawa Budaya School** stages dance excerpts at the *Dalem Pujokusuman* stage just off Jl Katamso (usually on Mon, Wed and Fri evenings).

Gamelan

Rehearsals can be heard twice-weekly within the *keraton* (usually Mon and Wed mornings); this is one of the best settings in which to experience it. Occasional performances can be seen at the *Istana Pakualaman* on Jl Sultan Agung, the *Hotel Ambarrukmo Palace* on Jl. Solo, and the *Hotel Natour Garuda* on Jl. Malioboro.

Wayang golek

Regular performances are held at the *Nitour Travel office* on Jl. Dahlan, and at the **Agastya Art Foundation**, off Jl. Prapanca to the southwest of the *keraton*.

Wayang kulit

An all-night, 8-hour performance with a full gamelan orchestra is held on one (usually the second) Saturday night each month in the pavilion on the south *alun-alun*. The **Agastya Art Foundation** also organises excerpt performances for tourists several afternoons each week.

Wayang wong

Outside the rainy season, excerpts of *Ramayana* tales in the form of 'sendratari' (seni-drama-tari: art-drama-dance) are performed on the outdoor stage at Prambanan, east of Yogya; the setting is spectacular. Regular Ramayana ballet performances are also held at the Purawisata stage on Jl Katamso in the city.

Fine arts and galleries

There are hundreds—perhaps thousands—of 'artists' in Yogya, trying to make a living from the tourist trade. Most, in fact, are young entrepreneurs selling cheap batik pictures churned out in large workshops; themes tend to be similar and quality low, but they make fine, light, easily transportable

souvenirs. However, there are also many excellent artists here too, some with well-established national and international reputations. Some of the best exhibition galleries and individual artists are listed below.

Amri Gallery Jl. Gampingan 6, northwest of the keraton. Amri Yahya's batik modern art and oil paintings are now extremely expensive, but his reputation is high.

Ardiyanto Gallery on Jl. Magelang, 400m south of the ring road intersection. A beautiful house filled with very beautiful objects. Top-quality pieces at high prices.

Bentara Budaya Jl. Suroto off Jl. Sudirman. Exhibition venue with irregular shows, often of painting or photography. One of Yogya's best general art galleries.

Brahma Tirta Sari at Banguntapan near Kota Gede. Exceptional batik fine art by a Javanese-American partnership, Agus Ismoyo and Nia Fliam. Their fine art works on silk rank among the very best, as savvy museum curators in Australia and elsewhere are realising. Take Jl. Karanglo east from the centre of Kota Gede and continue straight across the ring road; the small studio is on the right side.

Cemeti Jl. Ngadisuryan 7/A. The most adventurous contemporary art venue in Yogya, run by a Javanese-Dutch partnership, with regular exhibitions by Indonesian and foreign artists, encompassing all art media.

Tulus Warsito Jl. Jogokariyan 69/B off Jl. Parangtritis. Another batik artist of international repute, Tulus Warsito also paints with acrylics.

 ## Shopping

The pavements of Jl. Malioboro are filled for much of the day, but especially in the evening, with endless stalls selling arts and crafts, clothing, leather work, jewellery and much else. These are aimed squarely at the tourist market, both local and foreign; hard bargaining is required. Several of Jl. Malioboro's shops sell local batik fabric, but for a wide choice of **batik paintings** visit the workshops round Jl. Tirtodipuran, where there are also several galleries selling 'antiques' of uncertain age. Batik sellers also loiter round the Taman Sari water palace, many with tall stories to tell regarding special sales and discounts; caveat emptor! **Pasar Beringharjo** on Jl. Yani is a lively market selling fresh produce.

Kota Gede, southeast of the city centre, is home to dozens of artisans making silver jewellery and ornaments. The large factories, such as those at the east end of Jl. Ngeksigondo and along Jl. Kemasan, offer good-quality but uno-

riginal pieces. Strongly recommended for his very high quality and original pieces is **Priyo Salim** (☎ 376601), whose home is along an alley off the north side of Jl. Karanglo, a few metres east of the Kota Gede market square; he will make anything to order, however fantastical the design.

Note At many shops—especially the silver workshops—if you arrive by *becak*, taxi or tour bus, your driver will almost certainly expect to receive a commission from the shop, which will then be added discreetly to your bill. To avoid this, it is preferable either to pay off the driver at a neutral location and then walk a short way to the shop which interests you; or make it quite clear to the shop staff from the start that you came by your own design and were not brought speculatively by a driver.

History

From the 8C–10C this part of Central Java – known as Mataram – between the Progo and Opak rivers and Gunung Merapi, was ruled by a succession of Indianised rulers who were responsible for building the magnificent temples at Borobudur and Prambanan. They suddenly – and inexplicably – shifted their capital to East Java c 928, and for more than six centuries Mataram remained relatively deserted. At the end of the 16C, according to Javanese legends, the area was revived by a new Islamic power based at Kota Gede, the small village on the southeastern outskirts of modern Yogyakarta. This dynasty, perhaps founded by Panembahan Senopati (r. c 1584–1601), has ruled this part of Central Java to the present day.

Mataram reached its zenith under Senopati's grandson, Agung (r. 1613–45), who succeeded in establishing his sovereignty over most of east and central Java. From 1614 he moved his court c 5km south of Kota Gede to Karta. Having wrested control of Surabaya in 1625 – his last major conquest in east Java – he turned his attention to the VOC, which had seized Batavia in 1619. Agung sent expeditions there in 1628 and 1629; both were disastrous. For the next 12 years he campaigned relentlessly in central and east Java. In 1641 he was granted the title of sultan from Islamic authorities in Mecca, and in 1645 began construction of a large burial site at Imogiri, south of Karta. By his death the same year, he was overlord of all central and east Java and Madura.

His son and successor, Amangkurat I (r. 1646–77), lost everything. In 1647 he moved to a new court at Plered, just northeast of Karta, but his rule was little more than a tyranny that alienated potential allies. Eventually, in 1675, rebellion broke out against the regime; in 1677 the Plered court was sacked by Madurese forces led by Trunojoyo, who looted the treasury and then withdrew to Kediri. Amangkurat I fled, and died a month later, having passed his holy regalia to his son, Amangkurat II (r. 1677–1703), who was left with no royal court, no treasury, no army, nor kingdom.

He made an alliance with the VOC in 1677, and together they forged a string of victories which led to Amangkurat II establishing a new court at Kartosuro in 1680, near present-day Solo, c 50km east of Plered. Once safely established in his court, Amangkurat II began to ignore VOC demands and sheltered Untung Suropati, a Balinese wanted by the VOC for the murder of 20 European troops. A VOC force led by Captain François Tack arrived in February 1686 to arrest Suropati, but was routed by the combined forces of Suropati and Amangkurat II; Tack's body was found with 20 stab wounds.

Amangkurat II's kingdom was falling apart, however. After Tack's death, Suropati departed to east Java to build up a power base there, and Amangkurat II died in 1703, to be succeeded by his son, Amangkurat III (r. 1703–08). In 1704 the VOC, convinced that he lacked the support of the Javanese, recognised his uncle, Pakubuwono I (r. 1704–19), as ruler instead, and so began the First Javanese War of Succession (1704–08). Fierce fighting ensued, involving both would-be rulers as well as Suropati (supporting Amangkurat III), the VOC, and Madurese forces (supporting Pakubuwono). Suropati was killed in 1706 and Amangkurat III made peace with the VOC in 1708, whereupon he was exiled to Sri Lanka and later died there.

Pakubuwono I died in 1719 and was succeeded by his son, Amangkurat IV (r. 1719–26); family feuding led to the Second Javanese War of Succession (1719–23) and again the VOC was involved, this time in support of Amangkurat IV. With VOC help he triumphed, but on his death in 1726 he was succeeded by his 16-year-old son, Pakubuwono II (r. 1726–49).

By this stage, consecutive rulers of the Kartosuro court had built up huge financial debts to the VOC, which maintained a garrison at the court's expense. VOC support was not cheap, but the rulers were in a quandary: only the VOC could provide the military support they needed, but at the same time it was impoverishing the court, and the heavy taxes were alienating the population. Pakubuwono II was required to make huge payments every year, and eventually these began to cause unrest among his subjects. Court intrigues increased, and growing anger in the countryside coincided with huge problems for the VOC in Batavia, which was facing growing epidemics and large economic losses.

An anti-Chinese pogrom in Batavia in 1740 was followed by Chinese-led uprisings against the VOC in other Javanese towns. Pakubuwono II seized this opportunity to break with the VOC, and attacked its Kartosuro garrison, whose inhabitants were either killed or converted to Islam. However, the VOC soon re-established control and Pakubuwono II made peace once more, only to find both himself and the VOC the targets of a general uprising. Only with Madurese and VOC support did Pakubuwono II keep his throne.

In 1743, he abandoned the Kartosuro court and moved 12km east to present-day Surakarta (Solo). Still troubled by rebellions, he offered a hereditary appanage of land and provisions for 3000 households to anyone who would put them down. Mangkubumi, one of Pakubuwono II's brothers, who had rebelled against the court in 1741 but had subsequently returned to the fold, took up the challenge and succeeded. When Pakubuwono II, on Dutch advice, failed to pay up, Mangkubumi rebelled once more, setting himself up at Yogya in a parallel court; in May 1746 the Third Javanese War of Succession (1746–57) began.

Once again, VOC intervention was required. In 1754, the Dutch Governor of the Northeast Coast, Nicolaas Hartingh, began negotiations with Mangkubumi, ending with the Treaty of Giyanti in 1755, by which the VOC recognised Mangkubumi as Sultan Hamengkubuwono I, the ruler of half of central Java, based at Yogyakarta, while Pakubuwono III, who had succeeded his father, Pakubuwono II, in 1749, remained in control of Surakarta. Mas Said, another key rebel who had originally fought for Mangkubumi but subsequently split from him, found himself up against the combined forces of Surakarta, Yogyakarta and the VOC, and was forced to negotiate a peace. In 1757 he swore allegiance to all three and in return received a hereditary appanage from Surakarta of 4000 households, and became Mangkunegoro I (r. 1757–95), with his own princely domain under Surakarta. In 1774, Surakarta and Yogyakarta agreed to a permanent partition of power and agreed land settlements.

Peace of sorts followed for the next c 40 years, but in 1812, for the first – and only – time, the court of Yogykarta was plundered by a European power. It was not the Dutch, however, but British under Thomas Stamford Raffles, who ransacked the court.

As a result of the Napoleonic wars in Europe, the Dutch ruler, William V, fled to England in 1795 and instructed Dutch possessions to surrender themselves to the British, to keep them out of French hands. Raffles arrived in Batavia in 1811, and after encountering hostility from Hamengkubuwono II, plundered the Yogyakarta court the following year. The British remained on Java until 1816, when it was returned to Dutch.

There followed a period of growing discontent, and in 1825 the Java War began, with Yogyakarta at its heart. Diponegoro (1785–1855), eldest son of Sultan Hamengkubuwono III (r. 1810–11, 1812–14) launched an uprising against the Dutch at Tegalrejo—now a suburb in northwest Yogyakarta— which spread rapidly through central and east Java. Despite initial victories, by 1828 Diponegoro's rebels were faltering. Defections from his ranks forced him into negotiations with the Dutch in March 1830, when he was promptly arrested. The rebellion was over having claimed more than 200,000 Javanese lives.

Yogyakarta remained at peace for the next 100 years, the period of Dutch colonial rule. Japanese forces occupied the city from 1942–45, during which time Sultan Hamengkubuwono IX (1939–88) stubbornly refused to honour Japanese requests for labourers. His concern for his people and his later support for the Republican government won him huge respect after independence was finally won in 1949. During the years of revolution against the Dutch (January 1946–December 1948, and July–December 1949), the Republican government temporarily moved to Yogyakarta.

Exploring Yogyakarta

Sites of interest are spread throughout the city. Nevertheless, it is an easy place to get around, with *becak* and taxis almost always readily found.

Museum Sono Budoyo

Beside the northern *alun-alun* is the Museum Sono Budoyo (open Tues–Thur 08.00–13.30; Fri 08.00–11.15; Sat–Sun 08.00–12.00), which has an excellent collection of cultural exhibits from Java and Bali. The building, designed by Thomas Karsten in the traditional Javanese *pendopo* style, was completed in 1935.

In the front hall are sets of gamelan from palaces in Yogya and Cirebon. In other rooms are displayed early bronze *moko* and the drumhead of a bronze kettle drum; a fine 10C–12C bronze head, partially covered with gold leaf fragments; numerous small bronze figurines; fine examples of batik, including rare ceremonial dodot, and displays illustrating different styles and methods of batik manufacture; *wayang kulit* and *wayang kelitik*, including puppets of Prince Diponegoro and General de Koch, the Dutch general who arrested him (see p 281); *wayang golek*; and fine masks (*topeng*), including some magnificent, terrifying ones from Bali. There are beautiful carved wooden doors from Kudus; krises, spears and silverware. In the courtyards outside are many stone sculptures, mostly from Hindu-Buddhist sites in Central Java.

On the west side of the *alun-alun* is the **Mesjid Ageng**, dating from the late 18C, and behind that is the Kauman district, a rather picturesque neighbourhood of narrow alleys which traditionally was the centre of Islamic learning in the city. The mosque's caretaker is usually around to show visitors inside the mosque, which is one of Java's most interesting. The roof is supported by massive *jati* hardwood pillars from the Wanagama forest, the floor is of Italian marble, and the chandeliers and verandah tiles are Dutch.

The Keraton

The northern *alun-alun*, a grassy square at the north end of the *keraton* complex, is the site of Yogya's major fairs and important court festivals. Both this and the southern *alun-alun* contain a pair of venerable banyan trees. South of the square is the **Keraton Ngayogyakarta Hadiningrat** (open Sun–Thur 08.30– 13.00; Fri–Sat 08.30–11.00), which visitors enter from the west side, along Jl. Rotowijayan. Guided tours are available, although the guide's command of English may be limited. It is worth passing through the complex with the guide, then wandering back alone at will.

The *keraton* was designed by Prince Mangkubumi in 1755–56 after the Treaty of Giyanti (1755), by which the VOC acknowledged him as Sultan Hamengkubuwono I of Yogya; construction took almost 40 years, and little has been added since.

At the centre of the first courtyard entered is a *pendopo* pavilion, where the sultan would sentence criminals. Passing south through the gateway into the next courtyard, you will find two pavilions; the larger one, **Bangsal Sri Manganti**, to the right, is used for gamelan and dance performances.

Continuing south into the next courtyard, you come to a fine, octagonal music

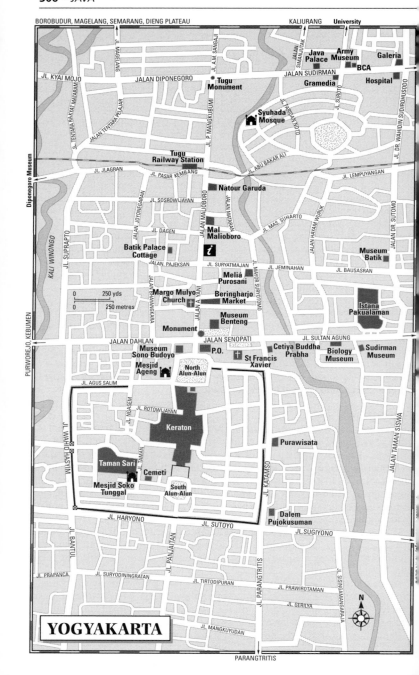

BOROBUDUR, MAGELANG, SEMARANG, DIENG PLATEAU

KALIURANG   University

JL. MAGELANG

JL. A.M. SANGAJI

JL. KYAI MOJO

JALAN DIPONEGORO

Java Palace

Army Museum

Galeria

JALAN SUDIRMAN

BCA

Tugu Monument

Gramedia

Hospital

JL. SURYOTO

JL. TENTARA RAKYAT MATARAM

JALAN TENTARA PELAJAR

JL. P. MANGKUBUMI

JL. PIARANTO

JL. DR. WAHIDIN SUDIROHUSODO

Syuhada Mosque

Diponegoro Museum

Tugu Railway Station

JL. JLAGRAN

JL. PASAR KEMBANG

JL. ABU BAKAR ALI

JL. LEMPUYANGAN

KALI WINONGO

JL. SUPRAPTO

JL. JOYONEGARAN

JL. SOSROWIJAYAN

Natour Garuda

JALAN MALIOBORO

JALAN MATARAM

JALAN HAYAM WURUK

JL. MAS SUHARTO

JL. DR. SUTOMO

JL. DAGEN

Mal Malioboro

Batik Palace Cottage

JALAN PAJEKSAN

𝑖

JL. SURYATMAJAN

JL. JEMINAHAN

Museum Batik

JL. BAUSASRAN

Meliá Purosani

Margo Mulyo Church

JALAN BHAYANGKARA

JALAN A. YANI

JL. MAYOR SURYOTOMO

Beringharjo Market

Istana Pakualaman

0   250 yds
0   250 metres

Museum Benteng

Monument

JALAN SENOPATI

JL. SULTAN AGUNG

PURWOREJO, KEBUMEN

JALAN DAHLAN

Museum Sono Budoyo

P.O.

St Francis Xavier

Cetiya Buddha Prabha

Biology Museum

Sudirman Museum

Mesjid Ageng

North Alun-Alun

JL. AGUS SALIM

JL. WAHID HASYIM

JL. NGASEM

JL. ROTOWIJAYAN

JL. TAMAN

Keraton

Purawisata

JALAN TAMAN SISWA

Taman Sari

Cemeti

Mesjid Soko Tunggal

South Alun-Alun

JL. KATAMSO

Dalem Pujokusuman

JL. HARYONO

JL. SUTOYO

JL. SUGIYONO

JL. BANTUL

JL. PANJAITAN

JL. PARANGTRITIS

JL. SISINGAMANGARAJA

JL. PRAPANCA

JL. SURYODININGRATAN

JL. TIRTODIPURAN

JL. PRAWIROTAMAN

JL. GERILYA

N

YOGYAKARTA

JL. MANGKUYUDAN

PARANGTRITIS

pavilion decorated with stained glass. The most striking structure here is the magnificent central throne hall, **Bangsal Kencono**, on the right side.

Take a look at the **Bangsal Manis**, the banquet hall on the south side of the Bangsal Kencono, then pass east through the arch into the old royal stable yard, where there are two large drums flanking the gateway opposite. North of the stable yard is a smaller courtyard which houses a display of glassware and cutlery belonging to the *keraton*. South of the stables is the **Museum Sri Sultan Hamengku Buwono IX**, which contains personal effects of the sultan, who died in 1988.

Back in the main courtyard beside the banquet hall, you can pass south into another, largely empty, courtyard. To the south of it is a bridge, the Jembatan Gantung, over a dry watercourse which was once part of the hydraulic system which sustained the Water Castle to the west. Further south again, you eventually reach the southern *alun-alun*, but it is more interesting to retrace your steps.

On Jl. Rotowijayan, near the *keraton* entrance, is the **Museum Kareta Karaton**, housing a collection of royal carriages, most rather dusty and tatty.

Keraton festivals

The most colourful is the **Garebeg Maulud** celebration, which occurs on the last day of what in pre-Islamic Java was a six-day annual harvest festival called Sekaten. With considerable pragmatism, this has been incorporated into the Islamic calendar so that **Garebeg Maulud** now coincides with the anniversary of the prophet Muhammad's birthday (12 Mulud in the Islamic calendar; from 2000–2004 this festival advances by 11 or 12 days each year, from mid-June to late April).

The ceremony involves a procession of *keraton* guards and court retainers marching from the *keraton* to the Mesjid Ageng. Following them are *gunungan* – mountain-like offerings of rice cakes decorated with hot peppers, eggs and green beans, which are blessed at the mosque and then broken into fragments to be used as sacred amulets by the thousands of spectators. That evening, an all-night *wayang kulit* performance is held at the *keraton*, to which the public are welcome. This is an opportunity to watch *wayang kulit*, with a full gamelan orchestra, in a truly traditional atmosphere.

Other important and visually dramatic festivals are the **Garebeg Puasa**, which celebrates the end of Ramadan (during 2000–2004 this advances from early January to early November); and **Garebeg Besar**, which occurs on the Islamic festival of Idul Adha (during 2000–2004 this advances from mid-March to late January), which celebrates the submission of Abraham to Allah, and is marked by the sacrifice of animals.

Taman Sari

At the west end of Jl. Rotowijayan, turn south along Jl. Ngasem to the large **Ngasem market** (Pasar Ngasem), which is well worth a wander for market lovers. The area to the south of the market was in the second half of the 18C a large pleasure palace and garden for the royal court, known as **Taman Sari** ('fragrant garden'). It was begun by Hamengkubuwono I in 1758 and completed in 1769, but was abandoned shortly after his death in 1792. Parts of it, now in ruins, can still be seen, but much of the area is now occupied with modern houses.

The main part of the Taman Sari complex is reached off the west side of Jl. Taman Sari. Beyond the ticket kiosk, you enter a courtyard containing two bathing pools, now empty, which would have been used by concubines and princesses, while the sultan looked on from his tower on the south side; he had his own private bathing pool.

Passing to the west, you reach an immense, decorated gateway, **Gopura Agung**. North from here are steps that descend into a long tunnel which once passed beneath an artificial lake; the tunnel has been restored, but the lake site has now been built over. You emerge from the tunnel near the remains of a large, two-storey mansion which lay at the heart of the complex; from its ruins there are good views across the market to the north. A tunnel to the west leads to the remarkable **Sumur Gumuling**, a circular two-storey structure, originally partly underwater; its original use remains unclear, but it may perhaps have been a mosque or a meditation chamber.

South from the Gopura Agung, along alleys in the crowded *kampung*, you come to the remains of the sultan's sleeping quarters, which are still used for meditation.

Jl. Ahmad Yani and Jl. Malioboro

At the main intersection just north of the northern *alun-alun* lies the **Central Post Office** (built 1909). On the southwest corner is the **Bank Negara Indonesia 1946** (built 1923), and to the north, opposite that, is the former colonial **Society Club** (built 1912), now known as Gedung Senisono and used as an exhibition hall. A monument on the northeast corner of the intersection commemorates the Republicans' surprise attack on the city on 1 March 1949, when they succeeded in holding it for six hours.

Behind the statue stands **Museum Benteng** (open Tues–Thur 08.30–13.30; Fri 08.30–11.00; Sat–Sun 08.30–12.00) in the old Fort Vredenberg, built by the VOC from 1756. Today it is a history museum depicting 19C and 20C Indonesian history in photographs and dioramas.

Across Jl. Yani from the fort is the government guest-house, built in 1823 as the **Dutch Resident's house**. North of the old fort is **Pasar Beringharjo**, the main market in central Yogya.

Further north on Jl. Malioboro is the regional legislature building, which contains in its grounds an evocative life-size **sculpture of General Sudirman** (see overleaf) by Hendra Gunawan (1918–83). The general is depicted wearing an oversized greatcoat.

East Yogyakarta

Close to the junction of Jl. Katamso and Jl. Senopati, a short distance east of the Museum Benteng, is an interesting **Chinese temple**, Cetiya Buddha Prabha, decorated with fine painted panels and protected by noteworthy guardians.

Further to the east is the rather dingy **Biology Museum** (open daily, mornings only) at Jl. Sultan Agung 22. The collection comprises many stuffed birds and mammals, including wild boar, gibbons and Komodo dragons. It is somewhat neglected, but rummage in the dusty corners and you may happen upon something strange—for instance, the photo of a human corpse recovered from the body of a 6m-long python in central Sulawesi in April 1979.

Nearby at Jl. Bintaran Wetan 3 is the **Sasmita Loka Panglima Besar Jenderal Sudirman** (open Sat–Thur 08.00–15.00), a museum dedicated to General Sudirman (1916–50) who led the Republican armed forces in the revolution against the Dutch. This building was his residence while he was based in Yogya prior to December 1948. For seven months he and his men travelled through Central and East Java, until they arrived back in the city in July 1949 after the Dutch withdrawal.

On display are his personal effects and dioramas illustrating his guerilla journey. For much of his life he suffered poor health, including tuberculosis, as a result of which he had a lung removed in 1948, and had to be carried frequently in a sedan chair.

Nearby, on the north side of Jl. Sultan Agung, is the **Istana Pakualaman**, a palace complex used by descendants of the brother of Sultan Hamengkubuwono II. It dates from 1812–13, when the newly arrived British under Thomas Stamford Raffles deposed Hamengkubuwono II for his refusal to co-operate with them. His brother, Notokusumo, curried favour with the British by supporting their ousting of Hamengkubuwono, and as a reward was granted an independent, inheritable appanage of 4000 households, a cavalry corps, and the name Pakualam I (r. 1812–29). His descendants have lived here since then.

To the north off Jl. Sultan Agung, along Jl. Suryopranoto and then Jl. Dr. Sutomo, is the **Museum Batik Yogyakarta** (open Mon–Sat 09.00–16.00), a private museum with an interesting, if rather poorly displayed, collection of early 20C batik from different parts of Java. There are pieces from some of the best known early Chinese batik houses, together with explanations of batik techniques, and scores of cap, the patterned copper plates used in the batik cap process.

Continuing east along Jl. Sultan Agung, you pass the **Semaki Heroes Cemetery** (Taman Makam Pahlawan) on the south side. Among those buried here are General Sudirman and two victims of the September 1965 coup attempt – Katamso and Sugiyono – who were murdered in Yogya that same night. The cemetery is entered from the west, on Jl. Soga.

Just across the Gajah Wong river to the east you will come to the **Gembira Loka Zoo** (Kebun Binatang Gembira Loka; open daily 08.00–17.30), on the corner of Jl. Kusumanegara and Jl. Kebun Raya. It has a pleasant riverside aspect, but some animals—particularly the orang-utans—live in a deplorable state. There is a good selection of Indonesia's native fauna, including Komodo dragons, the charming anoa from Sulawesi, binturong, civet cats, tapirs and banteng, and many bird species, including the rhinoceros hornbill, crested serpent-eagle and booted eagle. Avoid weekends in particular if stone-throwing at animals and prodding with sticks upsets you.

Where Jl. Kusumanegara reaches the eastern ring road, a lane called Jl. Raya Wonocatur continues straight across to reach an old 19C bathing pool, **Gua Situs Siluman**, on the south side after a few hundred metres. There is little to see at this minor site, of interest to specialists only, except some damaged Garuda statues and the remains of old walls.

Continuing south along the ring road, the excellent **Museum Wayang Kekayon** (open Tues–Sun 08.00–15.00) is to be found to the east at the next intersection. This is a private museum with a wonderful collection of puppets displayed in a series of rooms round a modern *pendopo*. There are sets of *wayang kulit*, *wayang kelitik*, and *wayang golek*, illustrating tales from the *wayang purwa*, *wayang wahyu* and *wayang kancil* traditions; most have an English explanation. Costumes and masks from *wayang wong* are displayed, with an especially notable set of dark wood *topeng* from Madura. This is the most informative puppet museum in Indonesia and is highly recommended, even for those with only a passing interest in the subject.

North Yogyakarta

At the centre of the busy Jl. Mangkubumi-Jl. Sudirman intersection is the **Tugu monument**, a rather dull column originally built to mark the founding of Yogyakarta in 1755; the current one is a replacement from 1889, and provides a useful landmark.

To the east from there is the **Army Museum** (Museum Pusat TNI–AD 'Dharma Wiratama'; open 08.00–13.00, closed Fri), on the corner of Jl. Sudirman and Jl. Cik Ditiro; the site is the former headquarters of the Republican Java Command, used during the struggle for independence when Yogya was the de facto capital.

It houses a large collection of military memorabilia from the post-1945 era, including photos and maps of the many campaigns across the archipelago; weaponry and uniforms; and examples of the very primitive medical equipment used during the war. More recent episodes in military history—Operasi Trikora in West New Guinea in 1961, and the failed coup attempt in September 1965— are also illustrated.

Further east along Jl. Solo, a road to the north a short way east of the Exim Plaza leads to the **Museum Seni Lukis Kontemporer Nyoman Gunarsa**, a museum of contemporary Indonesian art owned by the well-known artist Nyoman Gunarsa. Only a few of his own works are shown, however, and the general quality of display is poor; the museum is in need of refurbishment.

The **Museum Affandi** (open Tues–Sun 09.00–15.00, Mon 09.00–13.00) further east on the north side of Jl. Solo, by contrast has a wonderful collection of oil paintings by Affandi (?1907–90). Considered one of the greatest of modern Indonesian artists, Affandi was born in Cirebon but lived here till his death at an uncertain age. Somewhat eccentric, and increasingly long-sighted as he got older, the jovial and charming Affandi has probably the highest international profile of any 20C Indonesian artist. As he told Astri Wright, the art historian '"No-one knows when my real birthday is, so we celebrate it whenever I feel like it!" This feeling generally arose three or four times a year.'

His grave and that of his wife, Maryati, who died in 1991, lie together in the garden between the two main galleries. His flamboyantly painted car is parked in the grounds.

Further east still, you pass the stark **Hotel Ambarrukmo Palace**, built with Japanese war reparation funds. In the grounds are parts of a mid-19C royal rest house: a fine *pendopo* pavilion called Pendopo Agung Ambarrukmo, with a royal residence, the *dalem*, behind, and an octagonal two-storey *bale kambang* now used as one of the hotel's restaurants.

On the east side of the ring road (Jl. Janti) which runs south off Jl. Solo, is the **Air Force Museum** (Museum TNI–Angkatan Udara 'Dirgantara Mandala'), in a hangar within the military airport complex. Among the large collection of aircraft from Indonesian aviation history are the remains of a Dakota fuselage, shot down by Dutch pilots on 29 April 1947 while flying from Singapore to Yogya with three top officers of the fledgling Indonesian air force and a cargo of medical supplies.

Far to the north on the ring road is the **Monumen Yogya Kembali** ('Return to Yogya Monument') which commemorates the return of the Republican government to Yogyakarta on 6 July 1949 after the Dutch withdrawal the previous month. The architecturally striking monument houses a museum and dioramas, and on the balustrade are 40 reliefs depicting Indonesian history from the proclamation of independence in August 1945 to the formal transfer of sovereignty in December 1949. Historians may find it of interest.

Tucked away in a quiet neighbourhood to the west of the Tugu monument is the **Diponegoro Museum** (Museum Monumen Pangeran Diponegoro 'Sasana Wiratama'; open daily 08.00–12.00), off the west side of Jl. Cokroaminoto. It contains a very small collection of artefacts—shields, spears and krises with beautiful scabbards dating from the Java War (1825–30), when Diponegoro's base here was razed by the Dutch. Caught unawares, he supposedly escaped through a hole which can still be seen in the west boundary wall.

South Yogyakarta

Due south from the southern *alun-alun* along Jl. Panjaitan is a two-storey **pavilion**, used by former sultans as a deer-hunting tower. Deer would be driven from the forest towards the tower, which in the 19C was surrounded by the sultan's private game reserve, for him and his retinue to hunt at their leisure.

To the southeast of the *keraton* is **Kota Gede**, the former capital of the Mataram kingdom in the 16C. Despite the expansion of Yogya's suburbs, Kota Gede remains a quiet village of narrow alleys, silver workshops and large mansions which once belonged to Arab, Dutch and Chinese merchants; at its heart is an important royal cemetery where many of Mataram's rulers were buried.

Take a bus or taxi east along Jl. Sugiyono from the southeast corner of the *keraton* wall and at the end turn south to the market in the centre of Kota Gede. South from the market a narrow lane leads to the royal graveyard (open Mon–Thur 09.00–11.00; Fri 13.00–15.00), where visitors may hire the traditional Javanese dress which must be worn to enter.

At the front entrance are two very large banyan trees; the older one is said to have been planted by Sunan Kalijogo, one of the *wali songo* (see p 293), who was buried at Demak. The graves include those of Senopati (r. c 1584–1601) and Sultan Hamengkubuwono II (r. 1792–1810, 1811–12 and 1826–28).

At the cemetery is a bathing complex with a couple of fish-ponds, and beyond are a few remnants of the later Mataram palace. A small building in the square contains a massive, glossy rock, Watu Gilang, and three balls, Watu Canteng, said to date from the time of Senopati.

Turn west from the market to return to Yogya through the centre of Kota Gede, past many fine old buildings and silver workshops.

Around Yogyakarta

With its huge range of hotels, restaurants and services, Yogyakarta is an ideal base from which to explore the magnificent temples of **Candi Borobudur and vicinity** (see below) to the northwest. The **temples of Kalasan, Prambanan and Klaten** (see p 324) to the east are mostly smaller and less well-known, but the soaring spires of the Loro Jonggrang complex should not be missed. A trip to **Imogiri and the south coast** (see p 333) takes the visitor away from temples to the rugged cliffs of Java's southern shore and the royal tombs of the Mataram kings. North of Yogyakarta are **Gunung Merapi and Kaliurang** (see p 336), the former one of Java's most dangerous, yet visually impressive volcanoes, and the latter an easily accessible hill resort that offers an escape from the hot, humid lowlands.

CANDI BOROBUDUR AND VICINITY

This makes a full day excursion to the northwest of Yogyakarta, with visits to Indonesia's best-known historical site, Borobudur, and other nearby temples. One of Java's finest art museums lies en route, and there are three minor temple groups which can also be included in the tour.

Practical information

Travel advice

Borobudur is an extremely popular site among both foreign and local tourists, and tour buses start arriving from 07.30; by 08.30 it can be crowded and noisy. To contemplate this splendid monument in relative peace and quiet, ideally you should sleep in Borobudur village the previous night and be at the gate soon after its 06.00 opening. Another possibility is to go in the late afternoon, but you run the risk of running out of time.

The route description in this section assumes that you will be visiting Borobudur first.

Public transport

There are regular buses to Borobudur from Yogyakarta. Beware that in the past this route has been a popular haunt of pickpockets.

Private transport

A great advantage in renting a vehicle in Yogyakarta is the freedom it gives you to explore the quiet country lanes and reach the smaller, lesser-known temples and ruins in the area, such as Gunung Wukir, Candi Ngawen and the Candi Sengi group. These are all minor sites, but are well worth finding, if only because the journey takes you deep into the countryside.

To reach Borobudur from Yogykarta, take the main road, Jl. Magelang, north from the city centre, through Muntilan, to the clearly signed turning to the left.

Accommodation

Within walking distance of Borobudur are several simple guest-houses and *losmen*.

☆☆/☆ *Pondok Tinggal* (☎ 0293

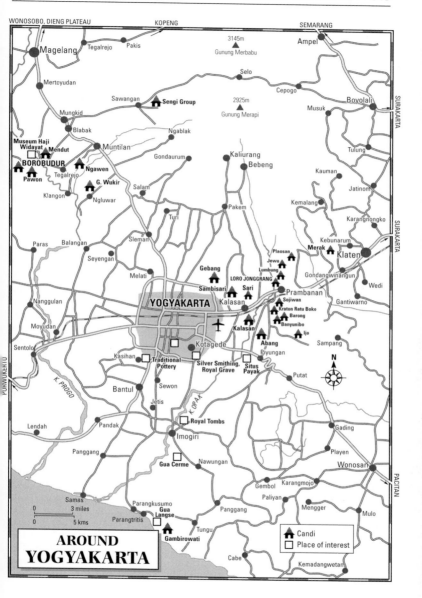

AROUND
YOGYAKARTA

88145/88245) has a pleasant atmosphere and airy rooms decorated with bamboo. ☆ *Lotus Guest House* , a few metres from the entry gate, is friendly and offers very spartan, cheap rooms. ☆☆☆ *Hotel Manohara* (☎ 0293 88131/88266), within the monument grounds, has smart rooms but is not especially good value, although admission to Borobudur is included in the price. A five-minute drive from Borobudur is the fabulous ☆☆☆☆☆ *Amanjiwo* (☎ 0293 88333; fax 88355; e-mail: amanjiwo@idola.net.id), with architecturally striking, supremely luxurious suites, some with private plunge pools. This is one of the most magnificent places to stay on Java.

Candi Borobudur

This magnificent monument is deservedly Java's most famous tourist attraction. Visitors with a particular interest in Java's Hindu-Buddhist sites will need a long half-day to really enjoy the beauty and atmosphere of this wonderful place. Borobudur is open daily 06.00–17.30, and the entry fee includes a guided tour.

History

Archaeologists believe that a pre-Buddhist structure, comprising a series of three stone terraces, was built on the site of Borobudur, probably in the second half of the 8C by Hindus. When the Buddhist Shailendras took over the site, c 760–80, building resumed on top of the original three terraces.

At some point the monument must have partially collapsed or the foundations subsided, necessitating the construction of a broader base which hid a sequence of reliefs carved round the original base (see below). It was probably completed c 860.

After the departure of the Shailendras in the mid-10C, Borobudur was not immediately forgotten. Chinese ceramics and coins from the 11C–15C have been found here, and it is likely that pilgrims continued to visit the decaying monument in this period, probably in diminishing numbers until the site was indeed abandoned by the faithful and became overgrown. It appears never to have been completely forgotten, but became a popular viewpoint and lookout over the surrounding countryside, with parts of the monument always remaining visible.

It is not a solid stone structure; the core is a natural but asymmetrical hill upon which earth was mounded to improve the symmetry, and the mantle of andesite-basalt stones on which the monument is built were placed upon that.

In the modern era, Borobudur first attracted attention once more in the early 19C, when Thomas Stamford Raffles (Lieutenant-Governor of Java 1811–16) organised a survey of Java's ancient monuments. In 1814 the undergrowth was cut back to reveal the extent of the ruins, and Raffles instructed a Dutch engineer, H.C. Cornelius, to draw up a plan of the site and make drawings, some of which survive today. Further excavations were made in the 1830s and 1840s, clearing the galleries of soil built up over the centuries. In 1844 a tea house was opened at the summit, where the damaged stupa revealed an incomplete Buddha image. By the 1850s, superstitious Javanese were once again coming to the monument to pay homage.

However, the site began to deteriorate rapidly as the clearance of vegetation and soil exposed it once more to the ravages of rain and wind. At the start of the 20C, as official concern about the monument's condition grew, a Dutch engineer named Theodore van Erp was appointed to preserve the site, and undertook a partial restoration (1907–11). He began by excavating the plateau round the site, and unearthed numerous Buddha heads, gargoyles, lion statues and carved panels. Ultimately he found so many pieces that an attempt was made at an extensive restoration, starting in 1908. Many of the stupas on the round terraces had been looted by treasure seekers, but some revealed old coins and small bronze Buddha images.

Despite van Erp's efforts, water penetration continued to damage the foundations, but it wasn't till the 1950s that the newly independent Indonesian government began to consider further repairs, by which time Borobudur was in a critical condition. Full-scale restoration finally began in 1973. This massive task, involving the removal of more than one million stones, their cleaning and replacement, together with the installation of a vital water drainage system, took a decade. In 1985, two years after its completion, nine of the *stupas* on the round terraces were damaged by bombs blamed on Muslim extremists; the damage was relatively minor.

Borobudur is approached along an avenue from the east side. The monument comprises a broad terrace at the base, with a series of four rectilinear galleries above, leading eventually up to three round terraces and the large *stupa* at the summit.

Before climbing on to the first terrace, walk to the southeast corner, where four panels of the so-called 'hidden foot' lie exposed.

The hidden foot. During the construction of Borobudur, 160 panels round the base of the monument were carved with reliefs illustrating the 'Sutra of cause and effect', a discourse by the Buddha on the effects – either punishment or rewards – resulting from certain human actions, known in Sanskrit as the *Karmavibhanga*. Soon after – or even during – their carving, the monument began to collapse and a broad terrace was constructed round the entire structure to secure the foundations; as a result, the reliefs were completely buried.

Rediscovered by a Dutchman named IJzerman in 1885, the carved panels were uncovered and photographed in sections in 1890–91, before being hidden once more. During the Second World War, a curious Japanese, Furuzawa, made an exploratory dig at the southeast corner and found them again by chance; his excavation was left exposed after the war. During the UNESCO-assisted restoration in 1973–83, four panels in this corner were left uncovered, together with part of a fifth on which the reliefs had never been completed or had been partially erased. These are the only ones visible today.

The message of the few exposed panels is not clear; others, now hidden, include scenes of murderers impaled on huge thorns, and bird hunters stabbed by dagger-shaped leaves falling from trees.

The broad terrace. From the wide terrace created by the extension, the reliefs on the outside of the first balustrade are visible—illustrations of anthropomorphic celestial beings, demonic guardians, floral motifs and wishing trees. On the parapet above them are the remains of 104 niches containing seated images of the Buddha; parts of the parapet and some of the niches and images are now missing.

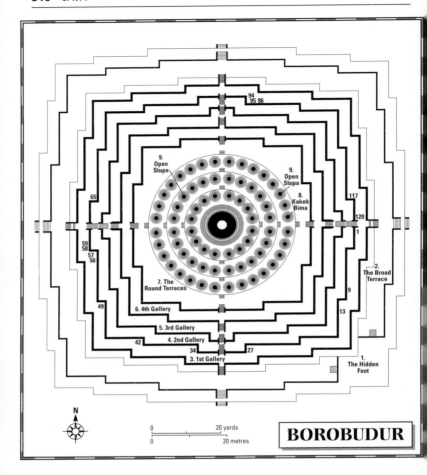

9.
Open
Stupa

9.
Open
Stupa

8.
Kakek
Bima

7. The
Round Terraces

6. 4th Gallery

5. 3rd Gallery

4. 2nd Gallery

3. 1st Gallery

2.
The Broad
Terrace

1.
The Hidden
Foot

94
95 96

65

117

120
1

9

13

59
58
57
56

49

42

34

27

N

0   20 yards

0   20 metres

BOROBUDUR

The first gallery. From the open terrace, steps lead up into the first gallery. Here are four series of reliefs, comprising two tiers on each gallery wall. Both tiers on the outer wall depict scenes from the *Jataka* or *Jatakamala* narratives, concerning acts of self-sacrifice by the Buddha in his earlier incarnations, prior to his rebirth on Earth.

The lower series on the inner wall illustrates some of the *Avadana* stories—tales of heroic deeds similar in nature to the *Jataka*, except that the central character is not the Buddha.

The upper series on the inner wall depicts a version of the life story of Shakyamuni, the historical Buddha, according to a text called the *Lalitavistara*, or one similar. The narrative runs clockwise from the east stairway in 120 panels, starting with the Buddha announcing in the palace of the Gods that he has decided to be reborn on Earth; it concludes with the Buddha's first sermon after his Enlightenment, in the deer park at Sarnath. On the parapet above are another 104 niches containing seated Buddha images.

For the casual visitor, this is probably the most rewarding of the four galleries to explore. Below are listed several of the most interesting panels, located on the adjacent plan.

Highlights of the Lalitavistara reliefs

1 The Bodhisattva, soon to become Shakyamuni, sits in the Heaven of Contentment, flanked by celestial beings and drummers.

9 Queen Maya (depicted with the high triangular headpiece) is surrounded by attendants, having just been chosen as the future Buddha's mother.

13 The Buddha enters the womb of Queen Maya in the form of an elephant calf (depicted at top left).

27 Queen Maya takes a carriage to Lumphini Park to give birth to the Buddha.

34 Prince Shakyamuni and King Suddhodana go with their large retinue to the temple.

42 Shakyamuni, having agreed to marry Gopa, gives her a ring.

49 To win over his bride's father, Shakyamuni must prove his worth. This panel shows him in an archery contest, where he shoots an arrow through seven trees.

56 In the first of Shakyamuni's four encounters which motivate him to search for enlightenment, he sees an old man (shown at far left).

57 In the second encounter, he sees a sick man (depicted at far left).

58 In the third encounter, he sees a corpse (at far left) surrounded by grieving relatives.

59 In the fourth encounter he sees a monk, whose calmness—in striking contrast to the pain and sorrow of the three others—motivates Shakyamuni to follow his example.

65 Shakyamuni flees from his princely life with the help of the gods who support the hooves of his horse, Kanthaka, in their hands (at left) so as not to arouse the guards.

94 Shakyamuni, by touching the ground with his right hand, calls on the earth goddess to bear witness to his previous sacrifices and good deeds, in response to the demon Mara's attempts to prevent him achieving enlightenment. The earth goddess, clutching a vase, rises beside Shakyamuni's right hand. Mara is riding an elephant to the left of her.

95 Mara's daughters dance seductively before Shakyamuni in an attempt to prevent his enlightenment.

96 Shakyamuni achieves enlightenment.

117 The Buddha once again meets his five disciples, who at first keep their distance.

120 The Buddha preaches his first sermon to the disciples in the deer park at Sarnath.

The second gallery. There are two series of reliefs in the second gallery, one on each wall. Those on the outer wall are more *Jataka* and *Avadana* stories; on the inner wall are a series of 128 panels taken from the *Gandavyuha*—the concluding part of a collection of texts called the *Avatamsakasutra*—which describes the pilgrimage of a youth named Sudhana who visited a series of teachers to learn how to become a bodhisattva. The *Gandavyuha*, the most important of the texts illustrated on Borobudur, is continued in the reliefs of the third and fourth galleries. There are 88 more niches containing seated Buddha images on the parapet above the panels.

The third gallery. Starting once again from the east gate, the narrative of the *Gandavyuha* continues, first in a series of 88 panels on the inner wall, then in 88 more on the outer. Many of the latter are damaged, and several are in the wrong place because at the time of Van Erp's restoration the narrative had not yet been identified. It is now known that they illustrate Sudhana's visit to the realm of Maitreya, the Buddha of the Future. The parapet above contains 72 Buddha images in niches.

The fourth gallery. The Sudhana story continues on the outer wall of this gallery. On the north side of the monument, he finally passes on to the realm of the bodhisattva Samantabhadra, where he remains for the rest of this series and for the final sequence of reliefs on the inner wall. On the parapet above the fourth gallery are 64 Buddha images in niches, all seated in *vitarka mudra*, a gesture of discourse or teaching.

The round terraces. The next stage comprises stepped, round terraces containing diminishing numbers of hollow stone *stupas*, which each house a Buddha image displaying the *dharmacakra mudra*, the most common teaching gesture.

On the lowest terrace, the *stupa* immediately north of the east stairway contains an image known as Kakek Bima, which is believed to grant magical powers to those who can reach in and touch it. On both the lowest and middle terraces a *stupa* has been left open, so that the images of the Buddha can be seen more clearly. The *stupas* on both the lower terraces are built from a stone lattice with diagonal windows, with a square *harmika* above. Those on the top terrace have square windows with an octagonal *harmika*. The reason for these variations remains unknown.

At the very apex is another *stupa*, solid in appearance. During restoration, an unfinished Buddha image was found inside a hollow chamber here; it now sits in the nearby museum courtyard.

Borobudur's iconography. The meaning of Borobudur has puzzled many scholars and produced dozens of theories. The general view today is that it was a multivalent monument—one with numerous meanings and associations. It was evidently a pilgrimage route, where Buddhist pilgrims would have been led repeatedly round the monument in a clockwise direction, slowly ascending through the galleries past the numerous sequences of reliefs, to the summit—a total distance of several kilometres. They would have progressed from the educational reliefs of the hidden foot, to the *Jataka* and *Avadana* stories of earlier incarnations, to the life of the Buddha himself, and then to the series concerning Sudhana's quest for the wisdom to become a bodhisattva.

There are (or were originally) 432 Buddha images displayed on the five parapets of the galleries. The 368 Buddha images on the lower four parapets are multiple representations—92 of each—of the four Jinas or directional Buddhas described in a mandala known as the *Vajradhatu*, which was popular in Java in the 8C–9C. On the east side are images of Aksobhya making *bhumisparsha mudra*; Ratnasambhava displaying *varada mudra* is on the south; Amitabha in *dhyana mudra* is on the west; and Amoghasiddhi making *abhaya mudra* is on the north.

The 72 images on the round terraces have been identified as representations of Vairocana, the Supreme Buddha and fifth Jina, who is traditionally depicted with the four Jinas above. The 64 images on the highest parapet probably also represent an aspect of Vairocana.

The **museum** to the north of the monument has many photographs of Borobudur taken before and during the restoration in 1973–83, which give an indication of just how immense the task was. There are also illustrations, with descriptions, of many of the carved panels. In the museum courtyard is the unfinished Buddha image making *bhumisparsha mudra*, which was found within the summit *stupa*. Outside the museum are thousands of pieces of stone, left from the restoration.

An **audio-visual show** run by the *Hotel Manohara*, northeast of the monument, illustrates some of the highlights of Borobudur, as well as nearby Candi Mendut.

From Borobudur, take the main road east towards Candi Pawon and Candi Mendut.

Candi Pawon

This small temple, lying on a straight-line axis between Borobudur and Candi Mendut, but rather closer to Mendut, has attracted several theories as to its purpose. One often expounded view, for which there is no real evidence, supposes it to have been a point on a pilgrimage route which linked the three. Another suggests it was the funerary temple of Indra, the Buddhist Shailendra king who is credited with building the version of Candi Mendut that stands today; again, there is no evidence.

The present structure was not the first on the site. During the temple's (somewhat inaccurate) restoration at the turn of the 20C, an earlier earthen terrace faced with brick was discovered. It is probable that, together with Borobudur and Mendut, it was originally a Hindu construction, which was later altered.

The *candi* faces west, and its exterior walls, pierced by pairs of unusually small windows, carry large reliefs of *kinnara* figures with wishing trees and money pots. It seems likely that the present structure was a temple to Kuvera, the god of riches, and dates from the first quarter of the 9C.

Close to Pawon on the west bank of the Progo river is a site known as Candi Banon or Candi Bajong, where beautiful statues of Shiva, Vishnu and Brahma were discovered. They are now in the National Museum in Jakarta; the temple, however, if indeed there ever was one there, is no longer visible.

From Candi Pawon, cross the Progo river to the triangular intersection where the **Museum Haji Widayat** (open Tues–Sun 09.00–16.00) can be found. This excellent museum of contemporary art, opened in 1994, is one of the finest in Indonesia. Owned by Haji Widayat (b. 1919), himself an artist of considerable international repute, it houses many of his own very distinctive works, and those of other Indonesians, among them Bagong Kussudiardja, Ivan Sagito and Nindityo. A visit is highly recommended.

From the museum, take the Magelang road 1km to Candi Mendut, on the left side soon after crossing the Elo river bridge.

Candi Mendut

Mendut is a Buddhist temple thought to date from c 800, during the reign of the Shailendra king, Indra (r. c 782–812). It was rediscovered in the 1830s, having been largely buried by earth or volcanic ash. During restoration (1897–1908), the remains of an earlier brick sanctuary, possibly Hindu in nature, were discovered within the present structure. Van Erp, who took over the restoration in 1908, was unable to complete it as major parts of the roof and porch were missing, having been either removed by villagers for building, or possibly carried away by a powerful volcanic eruption from Gunung Merapi. The temple is unusual in facing northwest; the reason for this remains unknown.

Inside the **cella** are three very fine stone statues. Facing the entrance is an image of the historical Buddha, Shakyamuni Gautama, making *dharmacakra mudra*. To his right is the bodhisattva Avalokiteshvara, seated in the *lalitasana* posture with the right leg pendant; to Shakyamuni's left is the bodhisattva Vajrapani.

On the **inner walls of the porch** are finely carved stone panels. That on the northeast wall depicts Hariti, the child-eating ogress who was converted to Buddhism by Shakyamuni and became a Buddhist goddess of fertility; she is shown here surrounded by children. On the southwest wall is her male counterpart, Atavaka. Above each panel are reliefs depicting four kneeling, heavenly beings; in the adjacent alcoves are panels depicting wishing trees.

On the **exterior walls of the candi body** are huge, somewhat damaged, reliefs. At the centre of the rear wall is a four-armed standing figure, probably Avalokiteshvara; the figures at the centre of the two side walls possibly depict an eight-armed form of the goddess Cunda (on the northeast wall) and Prajnaparamita, the goddess of transcendental wisdom (on the southwest), or perhaps both are versions of Cunda or the goddess Tara. Flanking each of these large panels is a pair of narrower panels which, together with a pair of reliefs flanking the porch entrance, probably once comprised a group of eight bodhisattvas. Some are now almost indistinguishable.

The Tantri panels of Candi Mendut

Outside the porch and flanking the open terrace which surrounds the main temple body, is a series of 31 panels, some of which bear reliefs illustrating recognisable scenes from Tantri texts; some are wonderfully preserved and well worth viewing.

Moving clockwise round the temple body from the porch, the ninth panel reached depicts the tale of the jackal and the bull, in which a jackal follows a bull for years, hoping his testicles will fall off and give him a tasty variation to his usual diet.

The next panel tells the tale of the goat who fools a tiger. Here a tiger, on the left, is shown tied to a monkey, with a goat on the right. In the story, a tiger meets a goat which claims to eat tigers. The frightened tiger flees and is found by the monkey who, on hearing its story, explains it is not true. The tiger, however, will only dare to return if tied to the monkey; this is what happens.

The 24th panel, on the southwest side, shows a cat on the right with three mice on the left. In the story, the cat has grown too old to hunt mice, so in order not to starve he tricks them by saying he has become an ascetic and no longer eats flesh. The mice come daily to pay homage, and for a while he picks off the tail-ender each time without the others noticing. As their numbers diminish, they eventually realise what is happening.

Two panels further along is a scene showing a monkey on a crocodile's back. The crocodile's wife wants a monkey's heart for dinner. Her husband lures the monkey on to his back with the promise of plentiful fruit on the far bank. Halfway across, he tries to drown the monkey, but the monkey convinces him that monkeys hang their hearts in trees and if the crocodile puts him ashore he will fetch his; the crocodile believes him, and he escapes.

The last but one panel shows a rather indistinct two-headed bird, one head hanging down to the left. The story is of the bird Bherunda, which has one stomach and two quarrelling heads. One wishes to drink nectar without sharing it; the other, in revenge, eats poisonous fruit which kills the bird. In the relief, one head appears to have already died.

On the **wings of the stairway** are more reliefs depicting Tantri texts. Some on the northeast wing are particularly clear. At far left, on the second-from-bottom row, is the story of the brahmin and the grateful crab, showing the brahmin sitting beneath a parasol on the left with a crab, in the bottom right, holding (unclearly) the head of a dead bird and a dead snake in its claws. In this well-known story, a crow and a snake plot to kill the brahmin, but the crab, who had earlier been rescued by him, kills them before the snake can strike. (Another version has the snake biting the brahmin, who succumbs to the poison; the crab seizes the crow and holds it hostage while the snake sucks the poison from the brahmin; once this is done and the brahmin revives, the crab kills both snake and crow.)

The central panel on the bottom row of the same wing shows two scenes from another popular tale about a turtle and two geese. The top part shows two birds carrying a stick in their claws, from which a turtle is hanging by its mouth; below are some hunters with bows and arrows. In the lower part, a group of men cluster round the turtle on the ground. In the story, the turtle lives in a lake where he makes friends with two geese. When a drought threatens his life, the geese offer to fly him to another lake, warning him not to open his mouth en route. In mid-journey, however, they fly over a group of men who are surprised to see the strange threesome. The turtle cannot resist the temptation to show off, opens his mouth to speak, and falls to the ground, where the men grab him for dinner.

The walls of the **temple base** itself are decorated with panels which alternately contain geometric, stylised floral motifs, and floral motifs with a male figure at centre, which may represent a *yaksa* or possibly a heavenly being.

Adjacent to the temple is a modern *vihara* where a small Buddhist community is based.

From Candi Mendut, take the main road 5km northeast to join the Yogya–Magelang highway.

Detour to the Candi Sengi group

Suggested only for those with a special interest in early temples, or for those with their own transport, this is an easy and very picturesque detour. By public minibus, take the Selo road from Blabak as far as Sawangan, from where the temples are a short walk.

From Mendut, on reaching the Yogya–Magelang highway, turn north towards Magelang, and after c 1700m turn off right in Blabak along Jl. Sawangan, signed indistinctly to 'Komplek Candi Sengi'. After c 11km you reach an intersection in Sawangan; here the extremely scenic left-hand fork (the main road) winds up to the village of **Selo** on the col between **Gunung Merapi** (2911m) and **Gunung Merbabu** (3145m), from where both volcanoes can be climbed. The accommodation in Selo is extremely basic and not recommended. Though guides are not needed for either ascent, Merapi is most easily climbed with a group tour arranged through an agent in Yogya. Guides can also be hired in Selo itself. For Merapi, allow three to five hours for the ascent and half that to descend. Merbabu takes an hour more in each direction: the walking is easier but the distance longer.

For the three temples of the Candi Sengi group, take the middle road in Sawangan. After 300m this crosses a girder bridge, and 200m further on **Candi Asu** can be seen on the left side of the road. It is difficult to enter as the enclosure is usually locked, but most of it can be seen from the road.

A short walk from there is the small **Candi Pendem**. To find it, follow the road from Candi Asu c 50m back towards the bridge, then follow a narrow brook along the tree line up the slope and the *candi* will come into sight after c 100m. It lies below present ground level, so is difficult to see until you are almost on top of it. Only the base and a part of the temple body remain, but it clearly indicates how easy it is for *candi* sites to be completely engulfed in volcanic deposits, to vanish for decades or centuries.

To find the third site, **Candi Lumbung**, cross the road bridge back towards Sawangan and after a few metres turn into the field on the left, following a footpath towards the river which has just been crossed on the bridge. The *candi* lies partly below ground level close to the river bank. The roof is missing, but this is the best preserved of the three.

This Hindu temple group has been dated to the second half of the 9C. Local farmers will be happy to guide you for a small tip, but are not really needed; nevertheless, few visitors come to these sites, so an outsider quickly attracts a small entourage.

Return to the Yogya–Magelang highway and turn south, past the Borobudur turning to Muntilan, c 7km.

Candi Ngawen

On the south side of Muntilan, c 250m north of the large girder bridge, turn off west a few metres south of the ***Tape Ketan Muntilan Fastfood*** restaurant and follow the asphalt lane c 1.5km to an intersection. Here, turn left on to a rough village road for a further 1.5km; this is only suitable for a jeep or motorcycle.

The site of Candi Ngawen, on the right side, comprises a row of five largely ruined temples, almost certainly dedicated to the five Jinas, and is believed to date in its present form from c 824. They all face east, and traditionally have been numbered I to V from north to south; only Temple II is now in good repair, having been partially reconstructed in 1927 by P.J. Perquin. Of note are the gargoyles, in the form of lions rampant, sculpted in the round at three of the four corners of the temple base. On the inward- and outward-facing pediments of the entrance portico, and above the entrance of the main temple body, are *kala* reliefs; inside the cella is a headless image of the Buddha making *varada mudra*, which probably represents Ratnasambhava (Samkusumitaraja), the Jina of the south.

Temple IV contains another headless Buddha image, which appears to be Amitabha, the Jina of the west, in *dhyana mudra*.

While Temples II and IV are cruciform in shape, I, III and V are square. This has led archaeologists to suppose that the two groups are from different periods. One suggestion is that I, III and V were the originals, dedicated to the Hindu Trinity – Shiva, Vishnu and Brahma – with the extra two added to convert the complex to a Buddhist sanctuary dedicated to the five Jinas in the early 9C; others disagree.

Piled at the front of the compound is a jumble of stones from the site, many with carvings on. A small water-filled moat surrounds the five *candi*.

Return to the main road in Muntilan and turn south, over the bridge.

Candi Ngawen

Candi Gunung Wukir (Candi Canggal)

Turn west off the main Yogya–Magelang road beside the 21km stone, 500m south of a large Chinese cemetery on the west side. Follow the lane c 2km to white gate posts on the right side, signed 'Jl. ke Desa Tirta'. Turn in here and after 100m fork left; after 200m more you reach *desa* Canggal, where the site caretaker *(juru kunci)* lives. Canggal is a charming village with friendly inhabitants; someone here will guide you past the fish-ponds and fruit trees on the 10-minute stroll to the *candi* up the hill on the far side of the stream.

The Hindu site consists of foundations only, but the setting is delightful. The ruin of the main sanctuary contains a large *yoni*; in front of it are three smaller sanctuaries, the central one containing a statue of Nandi. Other pieces of statuary lie in the vicinity.

A stone inscription known as the Canggal Charter, dated 732, was discovered near the entrance to the courtyard here in 1879. Written in Sanskrit language in Pallava characters, it tells of the erection of a *linga* on a hill by King Sanjaya. A missing part of the inscribed slab was found in 1937 at the site of the excavated sanctuary, seeming to confirm the highly probable assumption that the inscription does refer to this particular temple.

Visitors will be asked to sign the guest book; a small donation is appropriate.

Return to the Magelang–Yogya highway and turn south to Yogyakarta, c 20km.

TEMPLES OF KALASAN, PRAMBANAN & KLATEN

Detailed below are more than 20 temple sites which dot the flat plain to the northeast of Yogyakarta. To see them all in one day may just be possible, but is certainly not desirable; it would be an exhausting and visually overwhelming experience. For a one-day visit, it is advisable to select a few of the most interesting; recommended are Sambisari, Kalasan, Sari, Loro Jonggrang, Sewu, Ratu Boko and Merak. If you have the time and interest, it is well worthwhile spending another day visiting some of the less frequented sites, ideally with a day in between, doing something totally different.

Practical information

Travel advice
Many of the temples are found close to the main Yogyakarta–Solo highway. The main exceptions, necessitating a considerable detour, are Gebang, Plaosan, Ratu Boko, Banyunibo, Barong, Ijo and Merak.
Transport
There are very frequent **buses** along the main highway, which can drop you outside the temples that lie beside the road, or at the closest junction for those that are set back a short distance. To reach some, such as Sambisari, Plaosan and

Ratu Boko, you will need to take a *becak* from the junction, or walk 1–2km; details are given with each temple listed below. With your own car, motorcycle or bicycle, you of course have far greater flexibility, and many more sites can be visited in one day.

Accommodation
There are a few rather dull hotels and *losmen* near the Loro Jonggrang temple group, but visitors are strongly advised to stay in Yogyakarta.

Candi Gebang

A small, mid- to late-8C Shaivite temple to the northeast of Yogyakarta, Candi Gebang is not easily reached by public transport. To find it, turn north off Jl. Solo, 150m east of the *Hotel Ambarrukmo Palace*. After nearly 3km this lane crosses the ring road, becoming Jl. Nusa Indah. Follow this for 1.8km, then turn right into desa Gebang, following the signs through the village to the *candi*, 1km further.

The *candi*, reconstructed in the 1930s, opens to the east and contains a *yoni*. Flanking the entrance are two niches, the north one containing a headless, armless figure, probably Nandishvara; the head was stolen c 1989. The image in the south niche has been stolen in the period since the reconstruction. A statue of Ganesha is seated in a niche on the west side of the *candi* body; those on the south and north are empty, but once held statues of Agastya and Durga.

The *candi* came to light in 1936 when villagers, removing stones for building materials, uncovered the Ganesha statue. Further digging revealed the ruined temple, which was subsequently restored.

Candi Sambisari

Take Jl. Solo (the main highway) east past the airport to the 10.2km post, where a lane to the north is signed clearly to the *candi*, 2km further.

The Shaivite temple lies several metres below the present ground level, raised on a low man-made platform of volcanic tuff. Probably built in the early to mid-9C, it was later completely buried in volcanic ash from Gunung Merapi, which helped to preserve it in a remarkably good state; a farmer working in his field rediscovered it in 1966.

In the walled courtyard are three low stone platforms facing east, with the main *candi* behind them opening to the west. The three small platforms were subsidiary shrines, perhaps roofed with wood. Inside the main temple are a very large *yoni* and *linga*, the latter nearly 1m high. The magnificent *yoni* is decorated with a *naga* head.

The doorway of the main temple body is flanked by carved stone *makaras* and surmounted by a lintel carved with a fine *kala* face. As at Candi Gebang, niches beside the doorway once would have contained images of Nandishvara and Mahakala. An image of Durga slaying Mahishasura, the buffalo demon, is found on the north side; the dwarf-like figure kneeling on the buffalo's head is the defeated demon emerging from the buffalo corpse. Ganesha is in a niche on the east side, and Agastya on the south; all the niches are decorated with *kala-makara* motifs.

On the floor of the inner enclosure, surrounding the main cella, are 12 round or square raised stone slabs on the ground, believed to be the foundation stones for wooden posts which once supported a timber roof over the whole structure; buried beneath eight of them were found reliquary caskets.

The site was largely excavated in the 1960s, although the high water table in the vicinity has prevented a full exploration of the foundations; it is thought to be built atop a series of rectangular terraces.

Candi Kalasan

Further east along the main highway, Candi Kalasan lies on the south side near the 14.1km post. A temple was perhaps first built here in 778, but the present large structure is thought to be the third on the site, and probably dates from the early or mid-9C.

An inscription usually associated with the original temple describes its founding and dedication to the goddess Tara as a merit-making act by the ruler, Rakai Panangkaran, who freed a village called Kalasa from taxes so its yield could instead be used to support the temple. Many scholars have associated the Kalasa in the text with Candi Kalasan, though there is no other evidence.

The *candi* comprises three subsidiary cellas round a larger central one, which is reached through a fifth chamber on the east side, and now contains only a large throne; the discovery here of a footrest suggests the original icon was a very large Buddha image seated in *pralambapadasana*, perhaps similar to, but much larger than, the principal image at Candi Mendut.

The temple was partially excavated and restored in the late 1920s and the 1940s, and some of its wonderful ornamentation has survived intact, notably the *kala* head carved above the door of the south cella. Surrounding the *candi* were the remains of 52 *stupas*, beneath and between which were found more than 80 caskets containing ashes and funerary objects.

Candi Sari

Just 450m northeast of Candi Kalasan, on the north side of the main highway, is a lane leading to Candi Sari, 300m further.

This is a magnificent two-storey structure dating from the 9C, which once had three rooms on each floor; the wooden floor of the upper storey is now missing, but the slots for the joists are clear to see.

The entrance, in the middle of the east side, is surrounded by a fine *kala-makara* ornamentation; beneath the *makaras* are a pair of kneeling elephants. Short passages lead off the central room into side rooms to left and right. The south one contains the remains of a plinth, and there was also once a wooden staircase to the upper storey from here. Inside the rooms, niches decorated with the *kala-makara* motif probably once held small statues.

The outside walls are decorated with reliefs depicting bodhisattvas and the goddess Tara. The roof is unusual in comprising nine *stupas*, three above each room.

Candi Loro Jonggrang

The most magnificent of all the temples in this area, the Loro Jonggrang complex is the one to visit if you have time for only one site; after Borobudur, it is the most visually striking of all Java's sites of antiquity. The towering *candi* can be seen on the north side of the road, c 2km northeast of Candi Sari.

History

Epigraphical evidence from inscriptions indicates that the Loro Jonggrang group may date from c 856; one suggestion is that it may have been built by the Hindu ruler Rakai Pikatan and his Buddhist consort Pramodavardhani, daughter of a Shailendra king, to symbolise the unity between the Shaivite Sanjaya rulers and the Buddhist Shailendra dynasty.

Although never truly 'lost', the temple group was reduced to a huge, heavily overgrown pile of stones, whose modern rediscovery began in the 1730s when a Dutchman, C.A. Lons, found and sketched the site and sent a report to the Dutch Indies government. IJzerman began clearing the site in 1885, and in the early 20C van Erp began excavating. A systematic reconstruction was begun in 1918 by P.J. Perquin, who spent eight years slowly piecing together the stones of the Shiva temple, and subsequently by van Romondt in the 1930s. Work was curtailed by the Japanese occupation in 1942, and Candi Shiva's reconstruction was not completed till 1953. Since then, all the other main structures have been rebuilt.

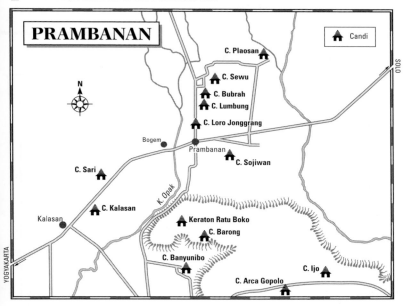

The Loro Jonggrang monuments

The central compound of the complex comprises three elegant temples dedicated to Brahma, Shiva and Vishnu, with three smaller ones in a row opposite, dedicated to their mounts – Hamsa (Angsa; a goose), Nandi (a bull) and Garuda (a mythical bird) respectively. These all stand on a raised terrace surrounded by a wall with four gates, outside which are the remains of 224 small sanctuaries.

Candi Shiva The largest of all the structures in the Loro Jonggrang complex, Candi Shiva towers nearly 50m high. On each side a stairway ascends to a narrow gallery which surrounds the temple body. The parapet of the gallery is decorated with a series of carved panels depicting episodes from a Javanese version of the Indian *Ramayana* epic, which starts from the east stairway and runs clockwise round the gallery and back to the east stairs; the narrative continues on Candi Brahma.

Above the gallery, the stairways lead up to four cellas within the temple body. The most important is that on the east side, containing a statue of Shiva, which some scholars have suggested may be a portrait statue of Rakai Pikatan; the entrance is flanked by niches containing large images of Nandishvara and Mahakala. In the south cella is Agastya; in the west is Ganesha; and in the north cella is an eight-armed image of Durga, slayer of the buffalo-demon, Mahishasura, which is portrayed as a dwarf-like creature standing on the buffalo's head.

Archaeologists excavating the foundations at the end of the 19C found an urn buried nearly six metres below the main cella floor, containing earth mixed with charcoal and ashes, together with coins, copper fragments, agates, beads, and gold and silver foil; most remarkable were 12 pieces of gold leaf (seven of them

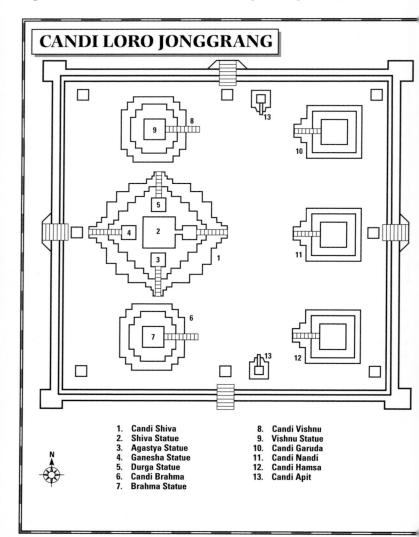

CANDI LORO JONGGRANG

1.	Candi Shiva	8.	Candi Vishnu
2.	Shiva Statue	9.	Vishnu Statue
3.	Agastya Statue	10.	Candi Garuda
4.	Ganesha Statue	11.	Candi Nandi
5.	Durga Statue	12.	Candi Hamsa
6.	Candi Brahma	13.	Candi Apit
7.	Brahma Statue		

N

inscribed, others cut into shapes recognisable as turtle, snake, lotus, an egg and an altar). Beneath the urn was an inscribed gold plate.

Candi Brahma To the south of Candi Shiva, the Brahma temple contains a single cella which houses a four-faced statue of Brahma. On the balustrade of the gallery below the cella entrance is the series of *Ramayana* reliefs which continues the narrative from Candi Shiva; the sequence runs clockwise round the temple body.

Candi Vishnu North of the Shiva temple, Candi Vishnu contains a four-armed statue of Vishnu. Reliefs on the balustrade depict episodes from the *Krishnayana*, which tells of the exploits of Krishna, the eighth incarnation of Vishnu and a popular hero of the *Mahabharata* story.

Buried deep beneath the cella floor was an earthenware pot containing a bronze box. Its contents included silver leaves depicting turtles, a *chakra* (the disc – one of Vishnu's attributes) and a *vajra* (thunderbolt); a gold lotus; a silver cross; agates; and fragments of gold and silver leaf.

The three subsidiary temples on the east side of the terrace share a similar design. Of note are the carved panels round each base, similar to those on the main temples, which depict birds, wishing trees, animals and *kinnaras*; separating the panels are carved lions. The cella of **Candi Nandi** contains a fine image of Shiva's bull mount, Nandi, flanked by the moon god Chandra on a seven-horse chariot, and the sun god Surya on another drawn by ten horses. During excavations, archaeologists discovered a well-preserved human skeleton buried in a 6m-deep pit beneath **Candi Garuda**, which has led some scholars to suggest the possibility of human sacrifice.

Beside the north and south gates of the enclosure wall are two rather narrow structures known as *candi apit* ('squeezed candi'), both now empty, their purpose unknown. Round the enclosure boundary are eight small shrines covering the foundation markers demarcating consecrated ground; a ninth marker is buried beside the eastern staircase of the Shiva temple.

Of the ruined shrines outside the enclosure wall, a couple have been reconstructed: one at the northeast corner and another on the east side. It is possible that not all the 224 structures were completed: in the 1930s van Romondt only found the remains of 172, and built replica foundations of the missing 52.

Candi Lumbung and Candi Sewu

In easy walking distance to the north of the Loro Jonggrang complex, the partially reconstructed **Candi Lumbung** comprises a central sanctuary surrounded by 16 smaller structures. The main temple opens to the east, and its walls contain small niches which once held statues.

A short distance north lies the ruin of Candi Bubrah, and beyond that you reach **Candi Sewu**.

The name Candi Sewu ('thousand temples') refers to the 240 small shrines in four concentric rows round the main temple sanctuary. The temple today consists of a large central cella joined by a surrounding gallery to four smaller rooms at the cardinal points. It has undergone several alterations in the past, and its original plan is thought to have been simpler.

In 1962 an inscription dated 792, written in old Malay, was found in one of the small shrines on the southwest side of the central sanctuary. It provided evidence that the temple was substantially altered at that time, having been built originally in 782 by the Shailendra ruler, Rakai Panangkaran (the builder of Candi Kalasan).

Almost all the subsidiary temples are today incomplete, though many reliefs remain on the exterior walls. Of note are the magnificent kneeling *dvarapalas*, the squat guardian figures carved in the round.

To the east of Candi Sewu are the remains of Candi Asu, which probably dates from the same time as Candi Sewu.

Guardian at Candi Sewu

Candi Plaosan

This cluster of temples, c 2km northeast of Candi Sewu, is spread to north and south of the road and has been undergoing restoration since the mid-1980s. Despite its Buddhist nature, the complex was built probably in the mid-9C with assistance from Rakai Pikatan, the Hindu ruler who built Loro Jonggrang. Short inscriptions found on the subsidiary shrines indicate that local dignitaries followed his example in providing funds. It thus confirms the belief that Hinduism and Buddhism then existed in Central Java in peaceful coexistence.

Plaosan Lor, to the north, comprises a pair of two-storeyed, west-facing sanctuaries, similar in plan to Candi Sari and surrounded by a combination of 58 subsidiary shrines and 116 *stupas* arranged in three concentric rows. A few metres further north is a third sanctuary. The two central structures each contain a porch, from which one enters into three rooms linked by short passages; these contain stone images of bodhisattvas, which originally would have flanked a central Buddha image, probably of bronze. The exterior walls are carved with reliefs of divinities, and carvings inside may be portraits of donors who funded the temple.

Plaosan Kidul, south of the road, is a small west-facing *candi* with little decoration.

Candi Sojiwan

This Buddhist temple, currently undergoing reconstruction, lies c 1km south off the main Yogya–Solo highway a short distance east of the Loro Jonggrang complex. It dates from the mid-9C, and is worth a visit, partly to appreciate the immensely complex work involved in a restoration such as this, and in part for its stone panels carved with Tantri themes which, however, are now very badly weathered.

If you move clockwise round the sanctuary from the west-facing porch, the second panel on the north side shows the tale of the crocodile and monkey, familiar from Candi Mendut (see p 320). The next one shows a lion leaping to attack a bull, and refers to a story in which lion and bull are best friends until the lion's jealous minister – a jackal – succeeds in pitting them against each other. Many of the others are now difficult to read: the fourth panel on the east side is the story of the brahmin and grateful crab, also seen on Candi Mendut; the fourth on the south side – another found also on Mendut – refers to the tale of the jackal and bull.

Keraton Ratu Boko

In the centre of Prambanan, opposite the Loro Jonggrang complex on the main highway, a road turns off south towards Wonosari. Follow this nearly 2km to a steep lane on the left which climbs up the hillside to the site of Keraton Ratu Boko.

From the parking lot, a path leads up to a partially restored stone gateway, split on two levels. Looking back west from here, you have a magnificent view over the Loro Jonggrang temples to Gunung Merapi. The role of the gateway is not known; local tradition believes it to be the entrance to a royal palace.

To the left inside the gateway is an artificial mound known as Candi Pembakaran ('site of burning'), regarded as a cremation site, though there is no evidence for this.

A path at the far southeast corner of the flat plateau behind the gateway leads southeast to a site known as the *pendopo*, a large walled enclosure with openings on the north, west and south sides. Inside is a raised stone-faced platform on which a wooden roof was probably once erected. To the south and east of the enclosure are other, larger raised platforms; further east is a series of artificial pools, accessed through two stone gateways decorated with magnificent *kala* heads; yet more platforms lie beyond.

A path to the north of the *pendopo* enclosure leads to two man-made meditation chambers. To the left of the first one, a flight of stone steps climbs a few metres to a large rectangular pool and the second chamber.

The whole site remains somewhat enigmatic, though excavations continue in the hope of finding explanations. Both Buddhist and Shaivite antiquities have been found here, and it seems probable that the site dates from the late 8C or early 9C.

Candi Banyunibo and Candi Barong

From the Keraton Ratu Boko take the Wonosari road 1km further south, and turn left at the sign to **Candi Banyunibo**. This small but beautifully restored Buddhist sanctuary lies a few metres to the south of the lane.

To reach Candi Barong, continue east along the lane and turn left at the end. At the end of this spur, walk c 10 minutes up a steep concrete slope and follow a path to the top of the plateau.

Candi Barong, its reconstruction virtually complete after a decade of work, comprises two small sanctuaries on a stone terrace, which itself lies above a much broader terrace. It appears that the original plan called for three sanctuaries to be built, but only two were completed; they are decorated with *kala-makara* motifs.

Behind Candi Barong a path leads north 200m to the site known as Candi Dawungsari, which is simply a jumble of hundreds of stone blocks.

Arca Gopolo and Candi Ijo

A few hundred metres further south along the Prambanan–Wonosari road, take a left (east) turn towards Candi Ijo. The road soon starts climbing and after c 1.5km passes a rough track on the right signed to '**Arca Gopolo**'. Follow this track 250m to a cluster of houses where a path leads down the slope to the left to a shady bathing place. In the trees here is a group of very large stone statues *(arca)*. Some of them are headless Buddha images, but the main figure is a marvellous 3m-high statue of Agastya.

Because women sometimes bathe here, male visitors should try to let their presence be known in advance of their arrival, to avoid embarrassing either party; usually a young boy from the hamlet can be found to act as guide for a small tip.

Back on the road, continue uphill to **Candi Ijo**. The first evidence of the site is an extensive area of piled stone blocks on the left – a storage site for the blocks during the ongoing restoration; the *candi* itself is just beyond.

Candi Ijo, a Shaivite sanctuary dating probably from the mid-9C, opens to the west and is decorated with fine reliefs, including a magnificent *kala* face above the doorway. Inside are a very large *yoni* and *linga*. Two notable statues have been found here: one of Vishnu in his fourth incarnation as Narasimha, depicted tearing open the chest of the demon-king Hiranyakashipu, who was about to kill his own son because he worshipped Vishnu; and one of Vishnu in his incarnation as Trivikrama, the dwarf who paced out the universe in three giant strides. Unfortunately, neither are now in situ.

Candi Abang

Almost 4km further south along the Prambanan–Wonosari road, a lane turns off right (west), signed to Candi Abang. Along here 1.2km, a well-worn path on the right (north) side of the road leads to the summit of a low hill and the *candi*. Candi Abang is in fact a huge mound covered by earth and grass; a few piles of stone blocks lie nearby, and a hole dug into the mound's north side has revealed bricks. The reason for coming is the very fine 360-degree view from the grassy summit.

Candi Merak

Back on the main Yogyakarta–Solo highway at Prambanan, turn east towards Klaten. After c 9km, immediately beyond the Gondang sugar factory (Pabrik Gula Gondang) on the left side—which houses a **Sugar Museum**—turn left and follow the lane c 2km to a T-junction. Turn right here, and after 250m turn left at a junction beside a beautiful *waringin* tree. Follow this lane c 3km to a junction marked by a small tower and turn right there. Almost immediately–after 130m–turn off left once more, passing beneath a metal bar. The *candi* is on the right after a further 750m.

Despite the difficulty in reaching it, Candi Merak is well worth a visit. If the site is locked, ask nearby for the key holder *(juru kunci)*, who lives very close by and is happy to receive visitors.

A 9C Shaivite sanctuary, Merak has not been fully restored, but instead lies in partially rebuilt sections, scattered across the compound: the main part of the base; the temple body; the roof of the porch; and the main roof sections. All are virtually complete, but the keystones which would have told archaeologists how the various sections fitted together have not been found, and as a result the reconstruction cannot be completed.

A niche on the west side of the temple body contains an image of Ganesha; Durga as slayer of the buffalo-demon is on the north side. The wings of the staircase are decorated with fine reliefs of *yaksas* armed with clubs and daggers. In the compound is a damaged *yoni* which was originally inside the temple cella.

Archaeologists excavating the site discovered a narrow bronze pipe which originally connected the *yoni* spout in the cella to a reliquary casket buried beneath the cella floor, indicating that the lustral water which collected in the well of the *yoni* was then piped down to the funerary casket to provide a material link between the symbolic and physical remains of the individual for whom the temple was built.

IMOGIRI AND THE SOUTH COAST

A pleasant full-day drive passes the royal tombs of Imogiri to the rugged south coast cliffs near Parangtritis.

Practical information

Travel advice

The route suggested below follows back roads which are poorly served by public transport. Visitors are strongly advised to hire a vehicle for the day. The main sites, however, can be easily reached by bus along less interesting main roads.

Accommodation

The only place worth staying along this route is the highly recommended ☆☆☆☆/☆☆☆ *Queen of the South* (☎ 0274 367196), magnificently located on the cliff-top overlooking the beach at Parangtritis; otherwise, stay in Yogyakarta.

From the ring road on the east side of Yogyakarta, take the Wonosari road southeast past the Museum Wayang Kekayon. On the south side of the road, c 60m west of the 'Yogya 12km' stone, a lane leads to the 9C remains of a stone bathing pool known as **Situs Payak**. Today lying c 5m below ground level, it comprises a small rectangular bathing place with a surrounding wall of volcanic tuff.

Beyond Payak, the main road climbs up a steep escarpment from which there are excellent views back across the plain, and 12km from the ring road you should turn right on a quiet road signed to **Dlingo**. This forks after 200m; take the right fork, which climbs along a narrow ridge past a television transmission mast. At a second fork, after 6km, turn right towards Imogiri; at a third fork, 500m beyond, turn right again. The route winds through shady forest, and after a further 10km a lane doubling back to the right winds along an adjacent ridge to reach the side entrance of the **royal tombs of Imogiri** *(makam raja-raja* or *makam suci)*. Entering here, instead of the main entrance further on, avoids a climb up a long flight of steps. Otherwise continue 1.6km to the main road in **Imogiri**, where the main entrance lies to the right.

The Imogiri cemetery complex (open Mon 10.00–13.00, Fri 13.30–16.00) comprises a series of walled courtyards built in tiers on the hillside, each containing a number of royal tombs of the Mataram dynasty kings. Most important, and lying at the highest point, is that of Sultan Agung (r. 1613–46). The latest addition is Sultan Hamengkubuwono IX (1939–88), who is buried in the courtyard closest to the tombs' side entrance.

Pilgrims flock to the tombs, and in particular to that of Sultan Agung. Visitors who wish to enter his tomb are required to wear traditional court dress, which is provided at the complex. Foreigners are welcome; a small donation should be given to the keeper of the tomb inside the dim, candle-lit chamber.

From the tombs' side entrance, follow the main road down to Imogiri village. At the T-junction here, the tombs' main entrance lies c 600m to the right. Turn left here for the coast, and after c 1km, at a large triangular junction, keep left (straight on) and follow the main road round to the left 250m further on. This is the Panggang road, which follows a very scenic route over a ridge of hills.

After c 5km it crosses a large steel girder bridge, and just beyond is a turn-off right which climbs steadily through tobacco fields for 3.5km to **Gua Cerme**, a long river-filled cavern. A guide will provide a lamp; visitors must expect to get wet.

The Panggang road continues south through a very barren and dry limestone landscape – the Gunung Kidul area – which is one of the poorest in Java. Of note are the laboriously built, dry limestone-faced terraces on which farmers struggle to grow their crops. There has been a major transmigration programme to encourage people to move away from the area and relieve the pressure on those who remain, and large stands of teak forest have been planted; life remains desperately hard, however.

At the T-junction in Panggang, 11km further, turn right to Parangtritis, or left to the quiet, grey sand beaches of **Baron** and **Krakal**, further east along the coast.

Heading west along the Parangtritis road, look out for the natural spring known as **Ngeleng**, on the left side near the 'Yogya: 37km; Parangtritis: 9km' stone, in a shady grove of magnificent trees. The road eventually descends very steeply into Parangtritis, passing the left turn to the *Queen of the South* hotel, which lies 800m away. The same track is signed to a small meditation cave in a magical location at the foot of the cliffs, called **Gua Langse**, and a pair of mid-15C stone-faced terraces known as **Candi Gambirowati** (Dataran Tinggi Gambirowati), which are decorated with carved panels.

For the adventurous and agile visitor, a descent down the cliff face to Gua

Langse is exciting, though it is potentially **very dangerous** and this writer will not be held responsible for any injury, loss or inconvenience sustained by any person attempting it! Follow the rough track past a huge concrete emplacement which dates back to the Second World War; the path gradually narrows, and c 15 minutes walk beyond the emplacement you reach a cluster of houses, where there is a visitors' book to sign and a small donation will be requested. The path continues to the cliff edge, where a series of bamboo ladders lead down the sheer cliff face to the rocky shore. This is not for the faint-hearted, but in fact is not as difficult as it looks; local women climb down with babies strapped to their backs, and men descend with huge bundles of belongings on their heads.

The cave at the base, with small meditation cells, is unremarkable, but visitors will be offered refreshing, sweet tea by the caretaker, an elderly lady who has been here since the late 1960s. Along the shore outside the cave, waves crash tirelessly against immense boulders. In the late afternoon sunshine, this does seem a truly magical place. The climb back up is wearying, and it's advisable to then call at the *Queen of the South* for a refreshing beer.

The grey sand beach at **Parangtritis** is popular among local Javanese, but is not especially attractive; the food stalls offer delicious fresh fish and you can take rides in a pony trap along the beach, but the sea is not considered safe for swimming. In the low hills behind the beach are several tombs of Muslim holy men, visited occasionally by pilgrims.

A short distance west of Parangtritis a lane turns off left to **Parangkusumo**, where there is a shrine which is said to mark the entrance to the chthonic kingdom of Ratu Kidul, the legendary goddess of the southern ocean known and feared by all Javanese.

The Ratu Kidul legend

According to the Yogyakarta version of the Ratu Kidul legend, she is said to be of human origin – a princess of the early Hindu kingdom of Pajajaran – and to reside in an underwater palace, where she rules over a kingdom structured in the same way as the Mataram kingdom of the 16C. With two female chief ministers, named Nyai Roro Kidul and Nyai Riau Kidul, and a spirit army, she protects 'Mataram' (modern Yogya and Solo), whose sultans are considered to be her human spouses. If angered, Ratu Kidul can be malevolent, so she must be appeased with regular rituals. Her clothing is said to be of green silk; human visitors wearing green to the beach are said to be at risk of drowning.

Once a year a ceremony called *labuhan alit* is held on the anniversary of the sultan's coronation. A delegation of *keraton* officials takes offerings to Gunung Merapi, Gunung Lawu and Parangkusumo, which is regarded as the entrance to her underwater palace. Here the founder of Mataram, Senopati (1575–1601), first met Ratu Kidul and they fell in love. The ceremony is said to date back to Senopati's time, but may be even older. Today it is seen as an expression of the continuing marital relationship between sultan and goddess, connecting him to the unlimited natural power of the sea. His hair cuttings and fingernail clippings are buried at Parangkusumo each year, and his used clothes, with some new ones, are given to the ocean. Once the offerings have been made, young boys fish out the wet clothing, now believed to possess supernatural powers, and sell it.

The road which continues through Parangkusumo runs past a spectacular land-scape of sand dunes. Return from Parangkusumo to the main road and turn left for Yogyakarta, c 28km.

GUNUNG MERAPI AND KALIURANG

An easy half-day trip exploring the southern slopes of Gunung Merapi, this is best done during a weekday.

Transport
Regular minibuses run to Kaliurang from the terminal in Yogyakarta on Jl. Simantunjak, off Jl. Sudirman.

Accommodation
There are plenty of rooms in Kaliurang, but quality is generally poor and prices are high; Yogyakarta is greatly preferable.

Kaliurang

The Kaliurang road north from Yogya climbs steadily for c 25km to this rather shabby hill resort. You could stop on the way at *Pusat Rehabilitasi Yakkum* (open Mon–Fri 08.00–16.00, Sat 08.00–12.00), on the east side near the 13.5km marker. This is a non-governmental organisation which trains physically disabled people in various crafts in the hope that they can then support themselves finan-cially; the shop sells their work – wood and leather crafts and toys.

Kaliurang is very quiet in midweek and outside school holidays, and the air is pleasantly cool. There are several walks in the vicinity, though an eruption in late 1994 closed off a swimming pool just above the village and a path higher up the mountain slopes to the observatory at Plawangan. At the time of writing, it was not known whether these may be reopened. On the west side of the village is a viewpoint overlooking an earlier lava flow.

Gunung Merapi

Looming above Kaliurang is the magnificent, but immensely destructive, volcano Gunung Merapi (2911m), which has erupted continually through much of the 1990s and caused many deaths, most disastrously in October 1994, when super-heated, invisible gases known as *nuées ardentes* tore through two villages and burnt 500ha of forest near Kaliurang. As the volcano's eruptions continued, more than 6000 people were evacuated, and the following month several vil-lages were destroyed by pyroclastic flows; by December there were more than 60 dead. In July 1998 similar numbers were again evacuated as the volcano once more showed signs of erupting.

An ascent is possible from Kaliurang when the volcano is calm, though the easier climb is from **Selo** on the north side on the col between Merapi and Merbabu, its higher, but long-dormant neighbour. A hike up the lower slopes to a fine viewpoint can be most easily arranged at ☆ *Vogels Hostel* (☎ 0274 895 208), a drab and basic guest-house in the village; for this, an overnight stay in Kaliurang is needed.

For the latest information on Merapi's volcanic activity, contact the office of the **Merapi Volcano Observatory** at Jl. Cendana 15, Yogyakarta (☎ 0274 514180, 514192).

Bebeng viewpoint

Descend from Kaliurang to the 'Yogya: 22km' stone and take an east turn here, signed to **Kaliadem**. This passes a pleasant restaurant, *Kalikuning*, on the left, from which there are fine views of Merapi on a clear day. Continue to a T-junction and turn left, uphill, to the excellent viewpoint at Bebeng. If Merapi is erupting at the time, you can watch volcanic boulders bouncing down the dusty, ash-covered slopes near the summit.

Return to the main Kaliurang–Yogya road and descend to Pakem. For an excellent lunch, turn east at the junction here and follow the road 2km to *Moro Lejar*, a fresh-fish restaurant with small bamboo pavilions over the fish-filled ponds. There are delightful views over the rice fields, and excellent food; on a Sunday, avoid the normal lunch hours as it is often very busy.

Surakarta (Solo) and vicinity

Highlights. Compared with Yogyakarta, Surakarta, commonly known as Solo, has fewer attractions, but its two *keraton* are well worth a visit. To the east is the remarkable 15C Candi Sukuh (p 343), one of the strangest temples in Java. Hikers will enjoy an ascent of Gunung Lawu (p 345), a 3265m-high, Holocene-epoch volcano, which can be climbed in a long day.

Accommodation

Accommodation is easily found in Surakarta. Tawangmangu and Sarangan, on the slopes of Gunung Lawu to the east, are pleasant, if unexciting, hill towns popular with Javanese seeking to escape the heat of the lowlands; both have numerous hotels, and can be useful bases from which to visit Candi Sukuh and Candi Ceto, or to climb Gunung Lawu.

Keraton Kartosuro

Today, almost nothing remains of the Keraton Kartosuro except the massive red brick walls which once surrounded the palace. To find it, take the main Yogykarta–solo road east through Prambanan and Klaten to the junction in Kartosuro (Kartasura), and turn east towards Solo. At the traffic lights immediately east of Pasar Kartosuro, turn south. Follow this road 300m to a T-junction, turn left there and after c 70m turn right, continuing south once more for 300m. The high brick wall of the old *keraton* can be seen on the right side, but continue round to the entrance on the south side. Much of the old palace compound is now filled with banana groves and a Muslim cemetery planted with frangipani trees.

History

In 1677, after the sacking by Madurese forces of the Mataram dynasty's palace at Plered near Yogyakarta (see p 302), the young Amangkurat II (r. 1677–1703) set up a new court at Kartosuro. This was where François Tack (see p 303) met his death in 1686, tricked by Amangkurat and the Balinese rebel, Untung Suropati, whose combined armies routed Tack's small VOC contingent.

Amangkurat pleaded his innocence, which no VOC official believed, but it was more prudent at the time for the VOC to make its peace with Kartosuro, faced as it was with numerous other threatened revolts. The *keraton* thus remained the home of the shaky, VOC-backed royal court till 1743, when Pakubuwono II (r. 1726–49) abandoned it to establish the new keraton in Solo.

In July 1741, Pakubuwono temporarily broke with the VOC and killed some of Kartosuro's VOC garrison to support an anti-VOC uprising which was sweeping across Java. However, by early 1742 the rebellion appeared to be faltering and Pakubuwono begged for Dutch forgiveness. For this betrayal, the rebels turned on him too, and seized Kartosuro in June. Only in December did the VOC and their Madurese allies, led by Cakraningrat IV, retake the *keraton* and expel the rebels. The VOC handed the throne back to the chastened Pakubuwono, but he abandoned the court in 1743 and moved to Surakarta.

SURAKARTA (SOLO)

East from Kartosuro, the main road runs straight to the heart of Solo—a busy town which, like Yogyakarta, is a centre for the arts and home to two royal palaces. Smaller and with fewer attractions than Yogya, it nevertheless is a pleasant place to stay for a night or two, and the visitor should at least visit the two palaces, some of the markets and the town's museum before moving on.

Practical information

Transport
Trains

Westbound services from Stasiun Solo Balapan, on Jl. Monginsidi on the north side of the city, include the very comfortable *Argolawu* to Jakarta (c 7 hours), the Bima, and the Senja Utama Solo (c 8 hours), which is the only service with couchettes. The *Mutiara Selatan* runs overnight to Bandung. Eastbound, the *Bima* and the *Mutiara Selatan* run overnight to Surabaya.

Buses

The main bus station, **Terminal Tirtonadi**, lies just north of the train station, and is most easily reached from the city centre by *becak* or taxi. There are regular services to most towns in Central Java and to major cities in East and West Java.

Flights

There are as yet few flights from Adisumarmo Airport, c 12km northwest of the city centre, although Merpati and Silk Air share a service to Singapore. The nearest major airport is at Yogyakarta, which is used by all domestic airlines.

Airline offices

Airlines maintain offices in Solo, mainly to sell flights out of Yogyakarta. *Bouraq* is at Jl. Gajah Mada 86. *Garuda* is in Wisma

Lippo, on the corner of Jl. Kartini and Jl. Slamet Riyadi.

Hotels

Solo has plenty of expensive and low-budget hotels, but a dearth of decent mid-priced rooms. Many hotels lie west of the city centre, along Jl. Slamet Riyadi. The ☎ code is 0271.

☆☆☆☆☆/☆☆☆☆ *Hotel Sahid Kusuma* (☎ 46356/45512; fax 44788) Jl. Sugiyopranoto 20, opposite Jl. Imam Bonjol. Extremely comfortable hotel with pleasant rooms in a central location.

☆☆☆☆☆/☆☆☆☆ *Hotel Sahid Raya Solo* (☎ 44144; fax 44133) Jl. Gajah Mada 82. One of Solo's best hotels, with very good rooms and a decent swimming pool.

☆☆☆☆☆ *Hotel Agas* (☎ 720746; fax 720747) on the corner of Jl. Muwardi and Jl. Sultan Hasanudin. Very comfortable, though unimaginative in design.

☆☆☆☆/☆☆☆ *Novotel Solo* (☎ 724555; fax 724666; e-mail: nov_solo @slo.mega.net.id), Jl. Slamet Riyadi 272. Opened 1997; stark exterior with comfortable rooms and pool.

☆☆☆☆/☆☆☆ *Riyadi Palace* (☎ 717181; fax 721552) Jl. Slamet Riyadi 335. Rather far from the city centre, but a good hotel.

☆☆☆☆/☆☆☆/☆☆ *Hotel Dana* (☎ 711976; fax 713880) Jl. Slamet Riyadi 286. A range of rooms to suit most budgets.

☆☆☆/☆☆ *Griyadi Sahid Kusuma* (☎ 54122; fax 632680) Jl. Sugiyopranoto 8. Very good-value rooms with free access to facilities at the nearby Hotel Sahid Kusuma; highly recommended.

☆☆ *Hotel Arini* (☎ 721559/716525) Jl. Slamet Riyadi 361. Good value, quiet and secure, but rather lifeless.

☆☆ *Ramayana Guest House* Jl. Wahidin 22. A friendly, simple and good-value guest-house with a pleasant courtyard; recommended.

☆☆/☆ *Putri Ayu* (☎ 711812/722939) Jl. Slamet Riyadi 331. Reasonable value, but rather far from the city centre.

☆ *Happy Homestay* off Jl. Honggowongso, southwest of the city centre. Very basic rooms, owned by a friendly family who can arrange bicycle tours to see the manufacture of batik, wayang, gamelan etc.

Information, food & services

The **tourist office** (Dinas Pariwisata) is behind the Museum Radya Pustaka on the south side of Jl. Slamet Riyadi; its helpful staff can advise on performances of dance, gamelan, *wayang* etc.

Adem Ayem at Jl. Slamet Riyadi 342 and *Pringgodani* on Jl. Sutan Syahrir serve good Javanese food. For cheap, standard Indonesian dishes try the cafés on Jl. Dahlan, including Warung Baru. In the evenings, the extremely popular pavement **warung** along Jl. Teuku Umar offer local dishes such as *nasi liwet* and *nasi gudeg*. For American fast food, visit *Swensens* and *KFC* on the north side of Jl. Slamet Riyadi.

The main **post office** is on Jl. Sudirman. *Bank Duta* on Jl. Slamet Riyadi can change cash and travellers' cheques. There is a 24-hour **telecoms office** on Jl. Mayor Kusmanto, near the post office.

Shopping

The market stalls of **Pasar Triwindu**, off the east side of Jl. Diponegoro, have interesting arts and crafts and bric-à-brac; note the scores of batik cap stamps. There are many batik clothing outlets in Solo, among the best known of which is *Batik Keris* on Jl. Yos Sudarso. The huge, two-storey *Pasar Klewer* has an enormous range of fabrics and is reputedly the biggest textile market in Java. *Pasar Gede* is a lively, colourful fruit and vegetable market, best visited in the early morning; the market building was designed in the 1920s by the Dutch architect Thomas Karsten, and is notable for its natural lighting.

Purwosari Plaza, on the corner of Jl. Perintis Kemerdekaan and Jl. Slamet Riyadi, is a modern shopping centre with a supermarket.

The *Jakarta Post* is available from a tiny newsagent's kiosk on the west side of Jl. Diponegor.

History

Surakarta's past is inextricably tied to that of Yogyakarta (see p 302). As the result of a family squabble in 1746 between Pakubuwono II, the ruler of the Surakarta *keraton*, and his brother, Pangeran Mangkubumi, based at Yogya, two parallel 'royal' courts competed for legitimacy. The problem was only partially resolved by the Treaty of Giyanti in 1755, negotiated by the VOC, which formally recognised both: Yogya, ruled by Sultan Hamengkubuwono I (Mangkubumi), and Surakarta, ruled by Pakubuwono III; the kingdom was partitioned between the two courts.

Mas Said, a rebellious nephew of Pakubuwono II who had previously caused trouble for both the Surakarta court and subsequently for Mangkubumi, now found himself isolated against both courts and the VOC; he negotiated a peace in 1757, in return for which he received a hereditary apanage from the Surakarta court, established his own palace, Pura Mangkunegaran, northwest of the Surakarta *keraton*, and took the name Pangeran Adipati Mangkunegara I (r. 1757–95).

Finally in 1774, both the major courts of Yogyakarta and Surakarta negotiated a permanent partition of land and power. Both Surakarta's palaces and dynasties survive today.

Exploring Solo

The more interesting of Solo's two palaces is the **Pura Mangkunegaran** (open Mon–Sat 09.00–14.00, Sun 09.00–13.00), entered from Jl. Ronggowarsito. A guide will accompany you round the palace, which is still used by family members – though the prince and his family live in Jakarta.

In the front *pendopo agung* are four gamelan sets, one of which is played to accompany a traditional dance practice on Wednesday mornings (10.00–12.00), and again on Saturdays (without the dance). Behind the *pendopo* is the *peringgitan*, a raised platform where *wayang kulit* is performed. Beyond that is the *dalem* – the living quarters – where the collection of family heirlooms is displayed. It includes gold jewellery, krises, spears, *wayang*, porcelain and glassware; of note are the traditional chastity plates and sheath, and the rare *wayang beber*.

The much larger **Keraton Kasunanan**, historically the more important palace but today rather less interesting, lies at the south end of Jl. Sudirman (open Mon–Thur 08.30–14.00, Sun 08.30–15.00). The royal court moved here from Kartosuro in 1745, at which time the banyan trees seen on the *alun-alun* were planted. On the south side of the *alun-alun* you pass through the *pagelaran*, the large pavilion which is separated from the *keraton* proper by a road and gateways. This is where traditionally the ruler granted an audience to visitors. South of the *pagelaran* you reach the main northern entrance

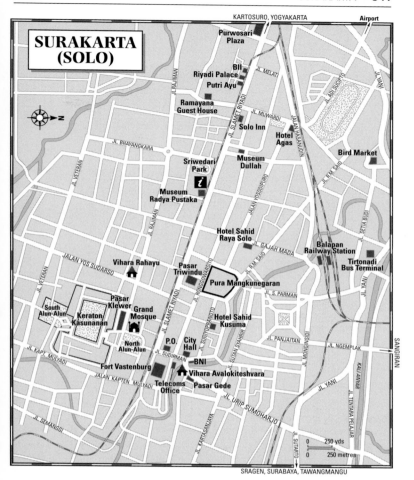

SURAKARTA (SOLO)

KARTOSURO, YOGYAKARTA — Airport

Purwosari Plaza

BII
Riyadi Palace
Putri Ayu

JL. MELATI

JL. RAJIMAN

JL. SLAMET RIYADI

JL. MUWARDI

Ramayana Guest House

Solo Inn

JALAN HASANUDIN

JL. ADI SUCIPTO

JL. YANI

Hotel Agas

JL. BHAYANGKARA

Sriwedari Park

Museum Dullah

JL. YOSODIPURO

Bird Market

JL. RM. SAID

JL. VETERAN

JL. RAJIMAN

Museum Radya Pustaka

JL. SETIA BUDI

Hotel Sahid Raya Solo

JL. GAJAH MADA

Balapan Railway Station

JALAN YOS SUDARSO

JL. RM. SAID

Tirtonadi Bus Terminal

Vihara Rahayu

Pasar Triwindu

JL. RINGGOWARSITO

Pura Mangkunegaran

JL. S. PARMAN

JL. VETERAN

Pasar Klewer

Grand Mosque

JL. SLAMET RIYADI

JL. YANI

South Alun-Alun

Keraton Kasunanan

Hotel Sahid Kusuma

JL. SUGIOPRANOTO

North Alun-Alun

P.O.

City Hall

JL. PANJAITAN

JL. NGEMPLAK

JL. KAPT. MULYADI

JL. SUDIRMAN

BNI

JL. SUTAN SYAHRIR

JL. URIP SUMOHARJO

DISINGUNGUN

SANGIRAN

Fort Vastenburg

JALAN KAPTEN MULYADI

Telecoms Office

Vihara Avalokiteshvara

Pasar Gede

JL. YANI

KALI ANYAR

JL. TENTARA PELAJAR

JL. SEMANGGI

JL. KARTASANJAYA

JL. SUTARTO

250 yds
250 metres

JL. ADI SUCIPTO

SRAGEN, SURABAYA, TAWANGMANGU

to the *keraton*, known as the *kori kemandungan*. Visitors must walk round to the east side to enter the shady, sandy courtyard, which contains a fine octagonal tower on its north wall. This is where the sunan or ruler of the *keraton* is said to commune once a year with Ratu Kidul, the goddess of the southern ocean (p 335).

On the west side of the courtyard is a marble-floored *pendopo*, and behind that is the *dalem*, or living quarters. A fire in 1985 devastated much of this part of the *keraton*.

Within the complex is a museum displaying the royal heirlooms, including krises, small Buddhist statuettes, gamelan, *topeng* and *wayang kulit*, carriages and palanquins. More royal carriages can be seen in garages on the north side of Jl. Sasonomulyo, just west of the *kori kemandungan*.

On Jl. Slamet Riyadi, the **Museum Radya Pustaka** (open Tues–Thur and Sun 08.00–13.00, Fri–Sat 08.00–11.00) has a small collection of artefacts, including various *wayang* forms from around Java and Bali, krises, spears, pottery, porcelain, glass and gamelan. Note the delightful old clock from the *keraton*. In the rear courtyard are stone sculptures and fragments.

West of the city centre, on Jl. Dr Cipto Mangunkusumo, is the Museum Dullah (open daily 08.00–12.00), a private art collection built up by the respected artist Dullah (1919–96), which contains many of his works and those of other artists.

Other sites worth a look include the remains of **Fort Vastenburg**, a now very neglected mid-18C VOC fort, its south and north walls covered with weeds and shrubs. It stands northeast of the Keraton Kasunanan along the north side of Jl. Slamet Riyadi.

Two Chinese temples are worth a look: the **Vihara Avalokiteshvara**, beside Pasar Gede on the south side of Jl. Martadinata, and the **Vihara Rahayu**, on Jl. Yos Sudarso just south of the Jl. Rajiman junction.

The fine *Bank Indonesia* building north of the main post office on Jl. Sudirman was formerly the Javasche Bank.

SIGHTS AROUND SOLO

A few places round Solo are worth a day or half-day trip, among them the important archaeological site of Sangiran, where early humanoid skulls were discovered; this is primarily of interest to the palaeontologist rather than the layman. On the lower western slopes of Gunung Lawu, to the east of Solo, are two rather remote 15C temples, Candi Sukuh and Candi Ceto, which receive a steady trickle of visitors. Further east is the hill town of Tawangmangu, a transit point for those climbing Gunung Lawu, one of Java's most easily reachable peaks; beyond is the small lakeside village of Sarangan, with a fine hotel for relaxing after the climb.

Sangiran

By private transport, take Jl. Sugiyono north from Solo c 14km towards Purwodadi, and turn off right at the clearly signed Sangiran junction c 500m north of the 'Semarang 114km' stone. After 3.5km, the Sangiran site is signed to the right. Buses run from Jl. Yani in Solo to the Sangiran junction, from where you can either walk or take an *ojek*.

The small **Sangiran Prehistoric Site Museum** (Museum Situs Prasejarah Sangiran) houses a collection of fossils found in the vicinity, including the (replica) fragments of a skull of *Pithecanthropus erectus*, a hominid dated to the Middle Pleistocene epoch (130,000–700,000 BP). Other fossils are from Palaeolithic stegodon, hippopotamus and long-extinct buffalo skeletons.

Fragments of the first *P. erectus*, comprising a skull cap and a tooth, were found by Eugène Dubois in 1891 at Trinil, a site east of Sangiran but also on the Solo river plain. In 1937 near Sangiran, one of G.H.R. von Koenigswald's local collectors found a second *P. erectus* skull cap, but smashed it into 30 pieces to try to increase his finder's fees. Once recovered, it was found to be similar, but not identical, to Dubois's find. In 1938, von Koenigswald's collectors found heavily weathered fragments of a third skull; skeletal remains of more than 30 *P. erectus* have now been found here.

P. erectus (today usually known as *Homo erectus*) was shorter than modern man, with a small brain which indicates a comparatively low intelligence level. His limbs were similar to those of modern man, but he had beetle brows, a sloping forehead and powerful jaws equipped with large teeth. Various forms of *H. erectus*, considered to be a single but variable species, have been found in Africa and other sites in Asia.

Other fossils in the museum include bones and three huge tusks from the Pleistocene-epoch stegodon, a type of elephant with tusks so close together that the trunk could not fit between.

Candi Sukuh and Candi Ceto

These two temples can be visited in a day-trip from Solo, or en route to Tawangmangu, Gunung Lawu and Madiun.

Take the main road east from Solo, through Karanganyar to **Karangpandan**, where a road to the left c 800m beyond the bus station is clearly signed to Candi Sukuh and Candi Ceto. Take this road c 5km to a fork, where Sukuh lies to the right, 1.7km further, and Ceto to the left. By bus from Solo, change at Karangpandan and take an *ojek* from there.

This mysterious site of **Candi Sukuh** (open daily 06.15–17.15) looks more like an ancient temple of pre-Columbian origin than a Javanese Shaivite construction. It comprises three ascending, west-facing terraces, entered through gateways, on the highest level of which is a truncated **stone pyramid**, its flat top accessed by a stairway through the west side. At the foot of the staircase are three turtle-shaped altars. At front left of the pyramid is an unusual stone ensemble: a large relief showing the divine teacher, Bhatara Guru, and Bima (both forms of Shiva) standing within an arch formed by pair of mythical, horned beasts; and a stone water channel atop a series of panels, each carved with a scene from a popular story known as the *Sudamala*. The channel indicates that holy water from a nearby mountain spring may have played an important role in the temple rituals.

More of the carved panels have been lined up along the north side of the compound, and at least one has been dated, by its chronogram, to the mid-15C. Other dates found on the terraces range from 1416 to 1459.

Dotted round the compound are more oddities: a square-shaped stone shrine on the west side of the main temple, opening to the west and covered in two tiers of reliefs; several sculptures of winged bird-men – some bearing inscriptions – on the terrace in front; a well-known relief on three panels, south of the main temple, showing an elephant-figure in a blacksmith's shop, which despite much scholarly research has not yet been clearly explained; and a figure, on the south of the small square shrine, notable for its large, erect phallus. In the gateway of the lowest terrace are carved symbols representing female and male genitalia.

The temple, which together with Candi Ceto (see below) is the most recent of Java's known sites of antiquity, appears to blend imagery from the Shaivite linga cult – so common to Hindu Java – with pre-Hindu terraced sanctuaries and the worship of megaliths.

Sukuh was rediscovered in 1815 during the cataloguing by Thomas Stamford Raffles of Java's sites of antiquity. Several studies were made of the site in the 19C, and in 1917 a restoration was attempted by the government; the most recent reconstruction was in the 1980s. Although a large, inscribed *linga* was discovered at the site, the purpose and meaning of Candi Sukuh remain unknown.

From Candi Sukuh, you can walk c 1.8km (30 minutes) to the remains of Candi Planggatan, a minor site reached by descending south along the narrow lane from Candi Sukuh, past the small statuary store (rumah arca Sukuh). The lane bridges a small stream and ascends across steeply terraced hill slopes planted with vegetables to an intersection. Here turn sharp left, and in the nearby village turn right to the *candi*. All that remains is a raised terrace, heavily overgrown with trees and grass, and half a dozen damaged reliefs which lie near the southwest corner of the terrace.

From Candi Sukuh, return to the **Candi Ceto** fork and turn right. The temple is a further 9.5km, clearly signed, through tea estates, the final 2km of road climbs extremely steeply. From Ngrolok, minibuses run to Kadibekao, and you can take a taxi from there.

Built in the second half of the 15C, Candi Ceto originally comprised 14 ascending terraces on a hillside, of which only the higher eight, separated by gateways, are of significance today. Parts of the site, including a large gateway and several pavilions, were built in the mid-1970s in an unsatisfactory attempt to recreate its original appearance; some statuary is also recent.

Of greatest interest here are the **stone pavements** on one of the lower terraces. One part is shaped to symbolise human genitalia; behind this is the form of a turtle on the back of a bat. On the triangular paving beside the phallus, carvings of several creatures can be identified; their meaning is unknown. On the highest terrace is a truncated pyramid-like structure, somewhat similar to Candi Sukuh.

Outside the enclosure, you can walk c 80m up the wooded slope behind to a small **bathing place** with more statues of recent origin. In the 1970s this was a popular meditation site, and a small wooden shrine remains here, though visitors are now few.

TAWANGMANGU, GUNUNG LAWU & SARANGAN

Continue east along the main Solo–Tawangmangu road c 11km to the bottom of Tawangmangu, where the market and minibus terminal are to be found.

Tawangmangu

Tawangmangu has a dozen or more hotels and guest-houses, but there is little to do here except visit a cave—Gua Maria—or the more interesting waterfall, Grojogan Sewu, which lies 1km to the left, signed off the main road. The area round the waterfall gets very crowded and litter-strewn on Sundays. However, the town does provide a pleasant break from the heat of the Solo plain, and is a useful transit point for eastbound travellers who have just visited Candi Sukuh.

Hotels and food

Recommended are *Hotel Pondok Garuda*, on the left 500m north of the minibus terminal; and *Hotel Komajaya Komaratih* (☎ 0271 97125; fax 97205), on the right 1.2km further up the road. There are many other guest-houses and *losmen* higher up. Eat at the *rumah makan Sapto Argo*, whose local specialities include whole cooked rabbit and rabbit satay; it lies 400m south of the Hotel Komajaya Komaratih, on the same side.

Beyond Tawangmangu, the road continues to climb for c 5km up the west flank of Gunung Lawu, past a string of villages and intensively farmed vegetable plots, until it crosses a bridge marking the boundary with East Java. In the tiny village of **Cemoro Sewu**, c 500m beyond the boundary, a clear path to the left climbs to the summit of Gunung Lawu (3265m).

Gunung Lawu

One of the easiest and most interesting volcanoes to climb in Java, Gunung Lawu is a relatively popular pilgrimage site because of the many old stone-terraced ruins near its summit. It's a long day hike along a clear path, and climbers should start at or shortly before sunrise, taking plenty of water, sun protection and good walking shoes.

The path climbs initially through pine forest before entering the remnant of some ever-wet forest. Above 3000m the vegetation is stunted and the views are good. Allow 6–8 hours for the ascent, and half that for the descent, with 1–2 hours to explore the summit area.

The stone terraces possibly predate the arrival of Hinduism in Java, but it is more likely that they date from the mid-15C and were used by worshippers who resisted the expansion of Islam across Java. At the Javanese New Year a huge number of pilgrims climb the mountain to perform traditional rituals at the sites.

Sarangan

From Cemoro Sewu the road climbs briefly, then descends extremely steeply into Sarangan, 5km further east and almost 1300m above sea level. The village surrounds a small lake, **Telaga Pasir Sarangan**, and there are several waterfalls in the vicinity.

The only reason to come here really is to stay at the ✭✭✭/✭✭/✭ *Hotel Sarangan* (☎ 0351 98022; fax 98203), a colonial relic near the top of the hill, with fine views over the lake. This is a charming place to stay, especially after a hard hike up Gunung Lawu; the rooms are large, airy, and fairly well maintained.

Beyond Sarangan, the main road descends, past the smaller Lake Wahyu, to Madiun (see p 348).

Pacitan and Madiun

Highlights include the caves and coastal scenery round Pacitan (see p 347), and the charming Lake Ngebel to the southeast of Madiun (see p 349).

Practical information

Public transport
There are regular, though rather infrequent **bus** services on the main roads between Solo, Pacitan and Madiun. To reach some of the sites mentioned below, travellers should alight at the nearest main road junction and wait for minibuses that take the side roads.

Accommodation
A good selection of hotels can be found in Pacitan and Madiun.

The road from Solo to Pacitan
The main road south from Solo (Surakarta) runs through rather dull scenery as far as **Wonogiri**, where the road divides. Of interest to steam engine enthusiasts is the **Tasik Madu sugar mill**, c 1km east of the road on the north side of Sukoharjo, where you can usually find narrow gauge steam locomotives at work in the mill's yards from June to September. Heading for Pacitan from here, it is possible to pass either side of the Gajah Mungkur reservoir; the main road is the shorter east route via **Baturetno**, but the west route – straight on through Wonogiri – is more scenic.

South of Wonogiri, the road climbs over a low ridge and then descends close to the reservoir shore, passing a recreation park with a swimming pool and boats for hire.

The road passes through Wuryanto and Eromoko to **Pracimantoro**, where a road turns off left beside the bus station, signed to Giribelah; this is the road for Pacitan. At the next main intersection, go straight over for Pacitan (clearly signed), passing through a parched, semi-barren landscape of terraced fields, littered with limestone outcrops. 15km beyond the intersection you reach a turn signed left to a cave, **Gua Manis Sari**, and 120m further a track to right leads after 1.6km to the more impressive **Gua (Guwo) Tabuhan**.

At the cave parking lot vendors sell polished stones of various sorts from the Pacitan district. In the cave's front chamber are large stalactites which can be struck to make a sound like gamelan. An ensemble of players will play tunes on the stalactites for a fee ($5–6); the deeper recesses of the cave are used for meditation.

Beyond the cave, c 1km, past houses advertising agate (*batu akik*) and other gemstones for sale, you reach the main Baturetno–Pacitan road. Pacitan lies 32km to the right; in Donorejo, 3km to the left, are several gemstone dealers.

Heading for Pacitan, you come after 3.5km to **Punung**, where a lane to the west (right) beside the market leads to several caves, including the spectacular Gua Gong.

Excursion to Gua Gong

Follow the very scenic lane c 6.5km, past Gua Putri, to Gua Gong; the final stretch of road is cobbled. The cave entrance is to the left along a rough path of sharp limestone rocks, a 10–15-minute walk from the road. The cave itself is quite large, with some extremely beautiful stalactite formations. It's the best one open to the public in the area; the extensive system of Luweng Jaran nearby, with more than 26km of passages, is open only to official expeditions.

From Punung, continue south on a winding road through very beautiful wooded scenery for c 16.5km to a road to the west (right), near the 'Pacitan 12km' stone, signed to Kalak and Watu Karung.

Excursion to Watu Karung and Pantai Pasir Putih

This delightful winding lane, potholed in parts, meanders c 13.5km through small villages to the coast at **Watu Karung**, a small cove with a fishing fleet. If visiting on a morning excursion from Pacitan, come early to meet the fleet returning from a night at sea; the fresh catch is sold at the simple concrete shelter.

The road continues over the steep ridge immediately beyond, and in the next village a signed lane to the left leads to the pretty **Pantai Pasir Putih** ('White Sand Beach'), flanked by low, wave-cut cliffs; it is a popular haunt of local rod fishermen. Swimming is possible (though there may perhaps be rip tides on occasion), but you may not get much privacy in front of the village; it's better to walk to a quieter spot.

The road beyond continues to **Kalak**, where there is another large cave, but is passable only by motorcycle, not by car; it becomes very steep and rough c 5km before Kalak.

Back on the main Pacitan road, the coast soon appears, with wonderful views over Pacitan Bay. The road descends to sea level, passing a large **monument** with statues of General Sudirman and Slamet Riyadi, which commemorates the independence struggle.

Just beyond a large girder bridge, a lane to the right leads to the seaside and the very relaxed and friendly ☆ *Happy Bay Beach Bungalows* (☎ 0357 81474). This is the best place to stay in the Pacitan area; booking is recommended.

On the main road, 100m further on, is a rather bizarre tomb on the left side of the road, with an epitaph written in secret code.

PACITAN
· · · · · · · · · ·

The beautiful bay at Pacitan has clean sand and reasonably safe swimming, but there is no shade. There is little else to come to Pacitan for, so it makes sense to stay at the beach bungalows if possible. Alternative accommodation is available in the town itself, 1.5km further, along the main street, Jl. Yani, which runs parallel to—but a short distance north of—the main bayside road. To reach it, take the first road left beyond the mysterious tomb.

Practical information

Transport

Buses to Ponorogo and Madiun, Wonogiri and Solo leave regularly from the bus terminal south of the town centre. For local transport to nearby caves and Watu Karung, alight at the relevant junction and wait for local minibuses.

Hotels and services

Recommended is *Hotel Bali Asri* (☎ 0357 81170/81345) at the west end of Jl. Yani. The *Hotel Pacitan*, further east on Jl. Yani, is adequate and cheaper, and also near a cluster of pavement *warung* which open in the evening. *Rumah makan Srikandi* on Jl. Yani has average food in very clean surroundings.
BNI on Jl. Sudirman at the east end of town can change **money**; there is a 24-hour *wartel* on Jl. Yani just east of the Srikandi restaurant.

The road from Pacitan to Madium

This very scenic road climbs imperceptibly alongside the Grindulu river for the first 34km to Tegalombo. In the dry season, the river bed is almost dry and is busy with rock breakers, gravel extractors and gem seekers; in the rainy season it can be a raging torrent, especially in the narrows of the upper reaches. The route is narrow and winding, and drivers should be alert for speeding buses.

Beyond Tegalombo, the road climbs over the watershed, out of the Grindulu valley, and quickly joins a tributary of the Madiun river for the descent to SLAHUNG. From there the road widens, straightens, and is less interesting. The final approach to Madiun passes large fields of sugar cane.

MADIUN
. . . .

Madiun itself has few attractions; it does, however, have plenty of reasonable hotels, and can provide a useful base for several excursions—west to Gunung Lawu, north to the archaeology museum at Trinil, and east to the tranquil Lake Ngebel.

Practical information

Transport

Buses leave from Terminal Purboyo, behind the huge sugar factory on the north side of town. The **train station** is off Jl. Pahlawan, 900m north of the Hotel Merdeka. Useful services include the overnight *Bima* to Jakarta and the east-bound *Argopuro* morning service. The majority of other, fast trains pass through Madiun in the middle of the night: the *Bima* to Surabaya at 03.00, the *Mutiara* to Surabaya at 02.00, etc. Becak provide the easiest way round town.

Hotels

Madiun has a good selection of hotels. The phone code is 0351.
☆☆☆/☆☆ *Hotel Merdeka* (☎ 62547/ 63635–7; fax 62572) Jl. Pahlawan 42. Madiun's best hotel, with a very good pool.
☆☆ *Hotel Kartika Abadi* (☎ 57372/

52081) Jl. Pahlawan 54, on the corner of Jl. Pahlawan and Jl. Semeru; pleasant hotel, with all air-conditioned rooms.
☆☆/☆ *Hotel Mataram* (☎ 63602) Jl. Sutomo 2. Small rooms, but only a few metres from the train station.
☆ *Hotel Pondok Indah* Jl. Merapi 10, off Jl. Pahlawan. The best-value cheap rooms in town, but can be rather noisy if busy.
☆ *Hotel Tejo* (☎ 62020) Jl. Sutomo 61,

on the corner with Jl. Sumbawa. Adequate, cheap rooms.

Services
The **post office** is on Jl. Pahlawan, just south of the railway crossing. For **money**, try *BCA* on Jl. Sudirman, just east of the Jl. Sutomo junction; or *BNI* on Jl. Sutomo, very close by. A 24-hour *wartel* is on Jl. Pahlawan.

Excursions from Madiun

To the west are Gunung Lawu and the hill resorts of Sarangan and Tawang-mangu (see p 344). Southeast of Madiun on the west flank of Gunung Liman is Telaga Ngebel, a lovely crater lake which makes an excellent picnic spot. Northwest of Madiun, past the Purwodadi sugar mill where you can still find steam locomotives in use, is the village of Trinil, with a small, rather dull archae-ological museum, probably of interest only to the specialist. A longer excursion is possible to the sustainably managed Cepu forest, on the Cepu–Blora road (see below).

Telaga Ngebel
Hugely more charming than the over-developed lake at Sarangan, Ngebel can be busy at weekends, when crowds of young people ride their motorbikes round the lane which hugs the lake shore, but in midweek it is extremely peaceful and a fine place for hiking and a picnic.

Take the Ponorogo road south from Madiun and turn off east (left) at *desa* Mlilar, just south of the 'Ponorogo 8km; Madiun 20km' stone; the junction is not clearly signed. The road climbs and winds for 16km to the lake shore, which lies at 734m and is surrounded by low wooded hills.

There is simple accommodation available at the tiny hamlet on the east shore, and several *warung* provide food.

Museum Trinil
Take Jl. Urip Sumoharjo west from Madiun, and after c 11km take the right fork north towards Ngawi, past the large Purwodadi sugar mill where a few steam locomotives are still used to haul sugar cane from the fields. Your best chance to see them working is in the morning during the harvesting season (June–October). At the intersection on the south edge of Ngawi, turn left along the Solo road. After c 10km, the museum is signed to the right (north), 3km from the main highway in *desa* Trinil.

The tiny museum (open Tues–Sun 08.00–15.30) has only one display room, which contains a large fossilised stegodon tusk and many other animal fossils, including a prehistoric rhinoceros skull.

Cepu forest
Northwest of **Cepu**, itself c 40km north of Ngawi, is a large teak forest managed

by Perhutani, the state-owned body within the Department of Forestry which has the dual aims of making a profit and benefiting social welfare. To this end, the timber is cut manually by teams of lumberjacks following an 80-year cycle of felling and replanting, and oxen are used to drag the sawn logs to the loading points. Until a few years ago, the logs were hauled from the forest by steam locomotives along a c 100km network of tracks. Today, the extraction is usually done by road, unless the way is too waterlogged or the cutting area too remote; at such times, the old locomotives are fired up and taken out.

The *Perhutani* office on Jl. Sorogo in Cepu can arrange day-trips for groups of 15 or more people to take a logging train into the forest to be loaded with timber in the traditional way. This is a wonderful experience – a rare opportunity to see a working steam railway and to hear the lumberjacks singing Javanese work songs. The cost includes full board at the comfortable Perhutani guest-house.

Perhutani staff can usually direct individual travellers to the current work sites; the forest flanks the main Cepu–Blora road to the north of Sambong. The ☆☆/☆ *Hotel Miranda* in Cepu has decent rooms.

Rejosari sugar mill

The sugar cane country round Madiun is popular among steam railway enthusiasts during the harvesting season (June–October). Working locomotives can usually be found at the Rejosari mill at **Gorang Gareng**, southwest of Madiun. Just west of the Gorang Gareng intersection is the mill's loading yard where visitors are welcome to watch operations. Much of the work bringing cane in from the surrounding fields is now done at night.

Kediri, Tulungagung and Blitar

Highlights in this area include the beautiful reliefs at **Candi Tegowangi** and **Candi Surowono** near Pare (see p 353), the large temple complex at Panataran near Blitar (see p 359), and the smaller **Candi Sawentar** (see p 362). Also well worth a look are the two huge **Ganesha** statues at Boro and Karangkates (see p 359).

Practical information

Travel advice

The main western approach to this area, from Madiun, is via the fast, flat Nganjuk road that skirts the north side of Gunung Wilis to Kediri; side roads branch off to some minor *candi* and the spectacular Sedudo waterfall. The southern route, via Trenggalek to Tulungagung, is more scenic, but longer and slower.

Continuing east, the northern route from Kediri to Malang via Pare passes near two important *candi*, Tegowangi and Surowono, before winding through a forested landscape to Pujon and the sprawling hill resort of Batu. From there, a steep, congested road descends to Malang.

The southern route, via the Tulungagung–Blitar road to the south of the Gunung Kelud massif, passes close to many minor *candi* and the important temples of Panataran.

Accommodation

Accommodation is available on the highway near Nganjuk; high on the north flank of Gunung Wilis, near Sawahan; in Kediri, Tulungagung and Blitar; and at Pare, Songgoriti, Batu and Selekta on the Kediri–Malang road.

The Nganjuk road

The 51km from Madiun to Nganjuk are fast but dull. Just west of Nganjuk, the **Nirwana** (☎ 0358 21430/21222) beside the highway offers good food and clean accommodation. In Nganjuk itself a main road turns off northeast to Kertosono, Jombang and Surabaya, but is not recommended, being flat and tedious.

Southeast of Nganjuk, a road to the right beside the 'Kediri 26km' stone leads after 250m to **Candi Lor**, a very ruined *candi* on a raised terrace, now heavily overgrown and with tree roots entwined picturesquely round the surviving brickwork. On the west side of the *candi*, which probably dates from the 14C–15C, are some stone fragments and part of an unidentified statue. If the site is locked, locals will point you in the direction of the caretaker (*juru kunci*), who lives in the village along the lane opposite.

Candi Ngetos and the Sedudo waterfall

Back on the main highway, you reach a small traffic circle beside the 'Kediri 25km' stone; turn right here for Candi Ngetos and the Sedudo waterfall. At a T-junction after 4km, turn left, and at a fork 2.5km further, the falls are c 20km to the right; the *candi* lies 3km to the left.

On the right side of the road in *desa* Ngetos, the large, 10m-high red-brick **Candi Ngetos** has been partially restored, but remains incomplete. You can climb up the west side to the empty cella, which now has no roof. Round the top of the wall is a frieze of floral motifs. It probably dates from the late 14C or early 15C; at some stage there was a smaller *candi* standing adjacent, within the same enclosure wall.

The site is kept locked, but the caretaker lives nearby and will readily open the gate; a small donation is appropriate.

The waterfall road climbs steadily through beautiful scenery, through the small market of Sawahan (11km). If travelling on public transport, you must take an *ojek* from here, as the buses go no higher.

A road to the right, c 800m beyond the Sawahan market, leads to ☆☆/☆ **Hotel Wisata Karya**, a slightly shabby hotel in a lovely setting. Some of the rooms – not the best ones, alas – have a fine view from their verandahs towards the summits of **Gunung Wilis** (2563m), an ancient Holocene-epoch volcano, and the Sedudo waterfall is just visible.

Sadly neglected, with fish swimming in the murky swimming pool, the hotel is a charming place to stay if you want total seclusion and don't expect too much from the food; the friendly staff have few visitors except at weekends.

The approach to the waterfall is winding and steep, passing terraced rice fields and small hamlets; cloves drying beside the road emit a sickly-sweet aroma. The road ends at the waterfall itself, beyond *desa* Ngliman.

The **Sedudo waterfall** (Air terjun Sedudo) plunges c 100m over a cliff to a small artificial bathing pool at its base. Although the volume is small, the spectacle is wonderful. Despite its isolation, the site can be busy on Sundays; in midweek you may be the only visitor. *Warung* sell snacks and drinks.

There are several other waterfalls in the vicinity, including another nearby of similar height, but Sedudo is the most accessible.

KEDIRI

From the traffic circle on the Nganjuk–Kediri highway, continue southeast to the town centre. Kediri has little to recommend itself to the visitor, but it is a convenient overnight stop for travellers on the road between Madiun and Malang or Blitar, and a useful base from which to visit the temple sites around Pare, the marvellous Catholic church at Pohsarang, the meditation caves of Gua Selomangleng, and the steam locomotives at work in the Merican sugar mill.

Practical information

Transport
The **trains** that pass through Kediri are generally slow and cannot be recommended; the **buses** are far quicker. The main bus station, **Terminal Tamanan**, is west of the Brantas river, along Jl. Agus Salim and Jl. Semeru from the new bridge. Travel round the town centre by becak.

Hotels and services
☆☆☆/☆☆ *Hotel Merdeka* (☎ 0345 81262/83443; fax. 81263) at Jl. Basuki Rachmat 4 is the best hotel. Further south on the same street is the very pleasant ☆☆/☆ *Hotel Penataran*. ☆ *Hotel Prima* on Jl. Yos Sudarso, close to the old bridge, is cheap, simple and friendly.

BCA (M,V) is on Jl. Brawijaya; *BII* and a 24-hour *wartel* are on Jl. Hayam Wuruk. The post office is on the corner of Jl. Sungkono and Jl. Diponegoro.

Sights near Kediri

Of the few places of interest round Kediri, the nearest are **Gua Selomangleng** and the adjacent **Museum Airlangga**, c 3km from the town centre. Take Jl. Veteran west from near the old bridge, and continue west along Jl. Mas Trip.

The museum has a large collection of Hindu-Buddhist statuary and carved stone reliefs, but this writer has never found it open. Gua Selomangleng, a few metres beyond the museum, comprises two small artificial caves, each with an inner chamber, and decorated with a relief of the Buddha and other images. It possibly dates from the later 10C.

In *desa* Pohsarang, to the southwest of Kediri, is a most unusual **Catholic church**, designed in 1936 by Henri Maclaine Pont at the request of a group of Roman Catholics in the village.

Its highly unorthodox design, using what Maclaine Pont called 'A-yokes' to support the four roof beams, was complemented by the magnificent **brick carving** round the altar, which is itself hewn from a slab of stone. Of special note is the splendid font made from a huge clam shell, beside the altar. The original church had no walls; these were added later.

The church is flanked by two **grottoes**: from the Lourdes grotto on the west side a series of 14 carved reliefs set into the churchyard wall, representing the Stations of the Cross, lead to the grotto of the Holy Sepulchre on the east. Note also the fine bell tower constructed of river rocks.

On the north side are walled terraces descending to a large outside altar. Maclaine Pont built a grass-covered **amphitheatre** to the east of this, with seating for more than a thousand people, in which to perform mystery plays. These quickly became immensely popular; the very first performance, of Joseph in Egypt, boasted a pharaoh's palace, an Egyptian temple, the house of Potiphar, Abraham's tent, and a Nile barge suspended from cables, which crossed back and forth with passengers throughout the performance.

To find the church, take the main road west from the Tamanan bus station to Semen, where there is a left turn signed to Pohsarang. The church is through the village on the right side, 5km from the Tamanan terminal.

On the northern outskirts of Kediri is the **Merican sugar mill** (Pabrik Gula Merican) where small steam locomotives are found operating during the cane harvesting season (June–October). These narrow gauge locos are fuelled by bagasse, the residue from sugar cane crushing, which sends out bright Roman candles of sparks – a remarkable sight in the dark. Visitors to the mill usually must pay an entry fee. To find it, take the main Nganjuk road north c 2km from the old bridge to *desa* Merican; the mill is to the east.

The antiquities of Pare

The temples near Pare can be visited on a day trip from Kediri, or en route between Kediri and Malang; if you are dependent on public transport, the former is preferable. Buses run to Pare from Kediri in the west, Jombang in the north, and from Malang in the east, and you can take a *becak* easily from there to the temples.

Take Jl. Yani northeast out of Kediri. At an intersection just beyond the 'Pare 17km' stone, a sharp left turn leads after 2.5km to the site of the **Arca Totok Kerot**, an extremely large, still partially buried, *dvarapala* statue which was discovered beneath volcanic ash in the late 1970s. The exposed part is in excellent condition.

Continue on the main road towards Pare, and at an intersection c 2km before the town, turn left on to the Papar road. After c 3km, **Candi Tegowangi** is indicated to the right, 1.2km further on.

Seemingly never completed, the base of Candi Tegowangi probably dates from the late 14C and is decorated with wonderful reliefs depicting scenes from the Sudamala legend, which also appears on reliefs at Candi Sukuh near Solo (see p 343). There is no trace of any infrastructure on the base, but it remains unclear whether this is because it was never completed, or because it was never meant to be more than a just a raised platform. To the southeast is a smaller structure, also decorated with reliefs.

Continue to Pare and take the main Pare-Jombang road to the north, turning off right to **Candi Surowono** along Jl. Wahid Hasyim. The *candi* is in *desa* Canggu, a further 2.5km. If it is locked, the caretaker can be found along the first road to the right beyond the *candi*, in a house a short way along on the left side.

The reliefs of Candi Surowono

Like Tegowangi, Candi Surowono consists of a stone foot and a base, decorated with fine reliefs, but is probably slightly earlier, dating from the mid-14C. A damaged statue of Agastya found here indicates that it was a Shaivite construction. The foot has small, separate, carved panels, some of which depict floppy-eared animals, while others have been identified as scenes from Tantri tales; the base above has scenes from several popular narratives, among them the story of *Shri Tanjung*, about a woman killed for her apparent infidelities.

Notable among the Tantri reliefs on the foot is one on the north side clearly showing a snake and a frog, with food piled on a dish between them; it illustrates the tale of a snake who tries to win a frog's confidence by posing as a creature of great virtue.

On the south side, near the east corner, is a pair of adjacent panels, each showing a bird standing; they depict the tale of the heron, fish and crab. In the first (east) panel, the bird, wearing a small turban, looks at three fish in the water; in the second, the bird has a crab claw wrapped round its neck. In the story, a heron poses as an ascetic at a fish pond. The fish find it weeping one day, and ask what is wrong (east panel). The heron replies that fishermen are coming to catch the fish and it is grieving for them. They agree to be flown by him one by one to a new pond, but he swallows them en route. The crab, last to be rescued, spots fish bones on the ground, realises the truth, and squeezes the heron to death with its pincer (west panel).

Further west on the south side is the tale of the crocodile and bull, showing a crocodile emerging from the water on the right and a bull on the left, standing facing the water. The bull helps the crocodile get back in the water when it ventures too far onto the land; once back in the water, however, the crocodile forgets its debt and holds the bull captive till it is rescued by another animal (usually a monkey), who tricks the crocodile back on to the land.

The Pare–Malang road

From Pare the main road continues east to Kandangan, where you should keep right for Malang, and then starts climbing across the forested lower slopes of Gunung Argowayang. At the 'Pujon 15km' stone, a right turn leads after c 3.5km to **Danau Selorejo**, a pleasant lake with warung serving freshly caught fish. To the southwest of the lake lies **Gunung Kelut** (1731m), an active volcano which last erupted in 1990, killing 32 and causing 50,000 to be evacuated; an eruption in 1919 killed more than 5000, while another in 1586 caused lahars which may have killed as many as 10,000. It also boasts Indonesia's oldest historically recorded eruption – in AD 1000.

East of Danau Selorejo, the road winds round the northern slopes of Gunung Kawi-Butak (2651m), a long-dead Holocene-epoch volcano, to Pujon. Soon after, a right turn leads to **Coban Rondo**, a spectacularly high waterfall which attracts crowds from Malang at weekends.

Beyond the waterfall turning, the route descends to **Songgoriti**, a weekend hill resort catering mainly to Surabayans, off to the left of the main road. In the heart of the resort, amidst hotels and sulphur baths, is the tiny **Candi Songgoriti**, a partially ruined Shaivite temple dating from the 9C–10C, which lies beside some bubbling sulphurous springs.

In **Batu**, further east, the main road is lined with expensive hotels, which receive an influx of visitors each weekend from Malang and Surabaya. Although renowned for its apple orchards, Batu is not an especially pleasant place, and traffic is heavy. On the west side of Batu, a road leads north c 6km to Selekta (Selecta), past colourful plant nurseries and more hotels and villas.

Selekta, like Songgoriti and Batu, is overwhelmed with visitors at weekends; at its heart is a hot spring with a swimming pool (pemandian panas), a market and scores of warung. Beyond Selekta a narrow road winds north through magnificent mountain scenery to Pacet (see p 375). This road is highly recommended for its fine views; it is also the starting point for a climb up Gunung Welirang (3156m).

Beyond Batu, it is usually a slow crawl down to Malang (see p 364).

TULUNGAGUNG

Tulungagung, 31km south of Kediri, is itself of no special interest, but to the southeast are several minor *candi* and ancient meditation caves which may be of interest to visitors. Difficult to reach on public transport, they are best seen by chartering a vehicle for a day through your hotel.

Practical information

Transport
The main **bus station** is on Jl. Yos Sudarso on the southwest side of town. **Becak** operate round the town centre.

Hotels and services
The best hotel is ✩✩✩/✩✩ *Hotel Narita* (☎ 0355 21608/21718; fax 22869) at Jl. Agus Salim 87, north of the *alun-alun*. *Hotel Gajah Mas* (☎ 0355 21996) on Jl. Kartini, on the southwest side of the *alun-alun*, is mid-priced, clean and friendly.

The **post office** is on the west side of the *alun-alun*. BCA is on Jl. Diponegoro, south of the *alun-alun*; nearby, on the corner of Jl. Diponegoro and Jl. Yani Timur, is a **telecoms office**.

Minor sights near Tulungagung

Take the Pantai Popoh road south from the main intersection with traffic lights. After c 5km, an indistinctly signed turning in *desa* Boyolangu leads west (right) to **Candi Boyolangu** (= Candi Gayatri). Follow the dirt road c 600m to the *candi*. This Buddhist site, dating from the second half of the 14C, comprises two west-facing brick bases which would originally have had a wooden super-structure; the further one bears a large, very damaged statue, probably of Prajñaparamita. The *candi* has been identified by some historians as a shrine commemorating Queen Gayatri (= Rajapatni; d. 1350), the consort of Majapahit's founder, King Kertarajasa, for whom a memorial ceremony was held in 1362.

Just 250m further south on the Pantai Popoh road, a turn to the east (left) is signed to Candi Sanggrahan. At an intersection 2.5km along here, the late 10C, man-made meditation caves called **Gua Selomangleng** are signed to the south (right) along a dirt road. After 500m, a footpath leads straight ahead to the caves. (Visitors must register in the last house on the left before the path begins; a small donation is appropriate.)

The footpath runs straight for c 300m, crossing a stream bed; it then forks left to the cave, again dipping across a watercourse, and heading for the large black rock outcrop up to the left. If you reach a Muslim cemetery on your left, you have missed the fork.

The left-hand cave contains reliefs depicting scenes from the *Arjunavivaha*, but stinks of guano; above the cave, a very large, heavily weathered *kala* face has been carved in the rock. There are excellent views from the slope above the caves.

Return north to the intersection, and continue straight over for 120m to a right turn along a dirt lane signed to Candi Sanggrahan (Candi Cungkup). At a small intersection 400m along here, turn north once more (left) to the *candi*. Candi Sanggrahan comprises a very broad brick base on which are found some small, headless Buddha images. The collapsed *candi* body was built of stone.

Return to the Sanggrahan–Gua Selomangleng intersection and turn east (left). At a T-junction after 600m, turn south (right) towards **Candi Dadi**, and fol-low the road c 850m to the house of the site caretaker (*juru kunci*), which is the second house on the right just after the road swings sharply to the left.

Candi Dadi is the remains of a large stupa built on a hill top behind the houses. It's an easy walk, c 40 minutes–1 hour, with excellent views. Avoid the midday heat, which makes the walk exhausting. The archaeologist Willem Stutterheim (1892–1942) theorised that the *candi* was a hermit's meditation site, but modern scholars think this unlikely.

Continue past Candi Dadi c 1.4km to a T-junction and turn north (left). Follow this lane 900m to the next T-junction, on a bend; turn right (straight ahead) and after 150m you will reach the parking lot for **Gua Pasir**, another man-made meditation site.

Behind the parking area are many damaged statues and pedestals. To the left, 80m away across a grassy flat area, are several large boulders carved with much eroded reliefs; still identifiable are an elephant and a monkey, and two anthropomorphic figures. The cave itself lies up the slope behind—a

5–10-minute scramble—up a steep path, part of the way up a worn rock stair-way. Several reliefs depicting the *Arjunavivaha*, probably dating from the 14C, decorate the cave, but sadly are heavily covered with modern graffiti. Stutterheim believed the cave to be the hermitage of Rajapatni, the grand-mother of King Hayam Wuruk (r. 1350–89) of Majapahit.

There is a marvellous view west from here, over the completely flat plain dominated by coconut palms.

Beyond the parking lot you reach an asphalt road after c 650m; turn left to reach the main Tulungagung–Blitar road, or turn right to visit another minor site, **Candi Ngampel**, 8km further south.

For Candi Ngampel (Candi Ampel), follow the sealed road 8km to a sharp left-hand bend in *desa* Ngampel. Turn off right here, and after 80m turn left on to a narrower dirt track to the *candi*, 150m further. Little remains of the early-15C brick temple, now covered in tree roots. On the west side are two small, kneeling *dvarapalas* beneath a simple shelter, with a *yoni* in front.

The Tulungagung–Blitar road

The main road running east 35km to Blitar is flat and fast. At a point 150m west of the 'Blitar 26km' stone, a road south leads to **Candi Mirigambar** (Candi Gambar; c 7km), a late-14C *candi*.

Follow the road south c 2km to a T-junction; turn west (right) and after 100m turn south once more to *desa* Mirigambar, 2.7km. Turn west (right) opposite the village headman's office (*kantor kepala desa*), and at a very minor intersection after 300m turn left to the *candi*, 100m further, flanked by two *beringin* trees.

Round the *candi* base are panels bearing damaged, but still quite distinct reliefs; flanking the stairs up to the foot are guardian figures.

The *candi* is associated with an inscribed copper plate found nearby which was issued by King Vikramavardhana (r. 1389–1429), the nephew and successor to Hayam Wuruk, who ruled in the western part of the Majapahit kingdom.

The main road continues east along the Brantas valley through Ngunut and Rejotangan. Immediately before the bridge over the Brantas, a right turn leads to the ruined site of **Candi Simping** (Candi Sumberjati). Follow the side road c 2.5km, then turn left; the *candi* is 500m further, on the left side.

All that remains of the temple, which was probably built to commemorate King Kertarajasa, the founder of Majapahit (r. 1293–1309), is the rebuilt out-line of the structure's base; hundreds of stones are piled up round the central structure, awaiting reconstruction. Of note are four matching *kala* faces which once stood above the doorway and side wall niches. A magnificent 2m-high relief of a four-armed deity, possibly a portrait statue of Kertarajasa, was found here; it is now in the National Museum in Jakarta. The caretaker's house is 100m before the *candi*, on the same side.

Directly after crossing the Brantas river, turn left to see the wonderful **Arca**

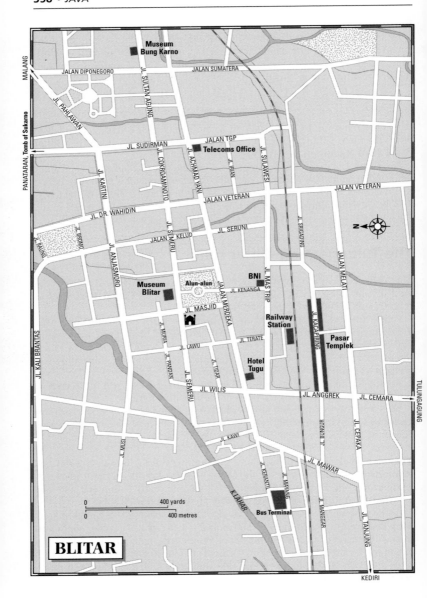

MALANG

PANATARAN, Tomb of Sukarno

Museum
Bung Karno

JALAN DIPONEGORO

JALAN SUMATERA

JL. SULTAN AGUNG

JL. PAHLAWAN

JL. SUDIRMAN

JALAN TGP

Telecoms Office

JL. IRIAN

JL. SULAWESI

JL. COKROAMINOTO

JL. ACHMAD YANI

JL. KARTINI

JALAN VETERAN

JALAN VETERAN

JL. DR. WAHIDIN

JL. SEMERU

JL. SERUNI

JL. BROMO

JALAN SEMERU

JL. KELUD

JL. SRIGADING

JALAN MELATI

JL. ANJASMORO

Museum
Blitar

Alun-alun

JALAN MERDEKA

BNI

JL. MAS TRIP

JL. KENANGA

Railway
Station

JL. KAPAL PRING

Pasar
Templek

JL. MASJID

JL. MURA

JL. LAWU

JL. TERATE

JL. PANDAN

Hotel
Tugu

JL. TIDAR

JL. SEMERU

JL. WILIS

JL. ANGGREK

JL. CEMARA

TULUNGAGUNG

JL. KALI BRANTAS

JL. KAWI

JL. CEPAKA

JL. MUSI

JL. TANJUNG

JL. PANGGANG

JL. MAWAR

JL. KEBANTIL

KLI MAHAR

JL. MAYANG

Bus Terminal

JL. MANGGAR

0   400 yards
0   400 metres

BLITAR

KEDIRI

Ganesha Boro (statue of Ganesha of Boro), on the right after 50m. One of the finest and largest (1.7m high) Ganesha statues in Java, it is actually not from Boro but from Kademangan across the river, and has a chronogram which dates it to 1219–60 (the chronogram can represent any one of four dates in this period, so cannot be more precise). On its reverse is carved a *kala* face.

BLITAR

Famous as the birthplace and burial site of Sukarno, modern Indonesia's first president, Blitar is close to several interesting temples and is a useful base for exploration, with good hotels.

Practical information

Transport
Train services through Blitar include the Mutiara Selatan to and from Bandung, and the Matarmaja between Malang and Jakarta. In general, **buses** are more frequent and faster. There are **becak** and **dokar** for journeys in town.

Hotels and services
Blitar's finest hotel is ✿✿✿✿ *Hotel Tugu* (☎ 0342 81766/81687; fax 81763),

completely renovated in 1996–97, and now very comfortable. *Hotel Saptra Mandala* (☎ 0342 81810) at Jl. Slamet Riyadi 31 has good mid-priced and cheap rooms.

For **money**, *BNI* is at the corner of Jl. Mas Trip and Jl. Kenanga; *BCA* and *Bank Danamon* are on Jl. Merdeka. A 24-hour **telecoms office** is at the junction of Jl. Sudirman and Jl. Yani.

On the north side of the *alun-alun*, the small **Museum Blitar** houses a collection of statuary and carved stone, mostly from Panataran (see below). The **tomb of Sukarno** (*makam* Bung Karno) lies c 2km north of town on the Panataran road; it's a popular pilgrimage place for Javanese, but of no great interest to foreign visitors. The house where he grew up, at Jl. Sultan Agung 59, is now the very dull **Museum Bung Karno**, with family photos and furniture. Market aficionados will enjoy a wander through **Pasar Templek**, which sprawls along Jl. Kacapiring, off Jl. Anggrek to the south of the railway line, selling everything from fresh fruit to birds and motorcycle spare parts.

In the early morning, you can find caged birds hanging outside shops along the west end of Jl. Merdeka, their owners gently spraying them with water; when the traffic noise dies down, the air is filled with birdsong.

Candi Panataran

The most extensive temple complex in East Java, and undoubtedly one of the finest, Panataran (open daily 07.00–17.00) lies c 10km north of Sukarno's tomb. The structures here were built during a period of at least 250 years; dates found here range from 1197 to 1454.

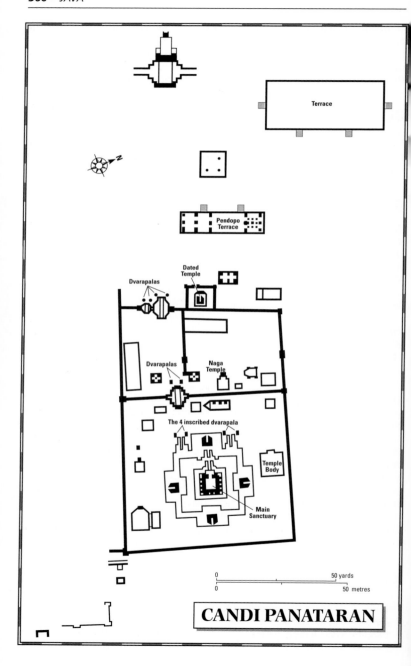

Terrace

Pendopo Terrace

Dvarapalas

Dated Temple

Dvarapalas

Naga Temple

The 4 inscribed dvarapala

Temple Body

Main Sanctuary

0   50 yards
0   50 metres

CANDI PANATARAN

You enter from the southwest side into the westernmost of three courtyards. In the middle of the west courtyard is a rectangular stone platform with two staircases on its west side. Known as the **pendopo terrace**, it dates from 1375; its function is unknown. On the terrace walls are a series of narrative reliefs, partially weathered, which include episodes from the tale of *Shri Tanjung* (as at Candi Surowono; see p 354), and from the tale of *Bubhuksa and Gagang Aking* (about two brothers, one Buddhist, the other Hindu, who compete to be more virtuous).

At the northwest corner of the courtyard is a larger **terrace**, undecorated except for *nagas* which are carved round the base, entwined at the corners. At the four staircases, dvarapalas can be seen standing on the *naga* bodies.

Guarding the entrance to the middle courtyard are four stone kneeling *dvarapalas*. North of them is the so-called **dated temple**, an exquisite structure with a date equivalent to 1369 carved above the west-facing doorway. Fine *kala* faces stare down from above the doorway and empty niches; the roof is similar in style to that of Candi Kidal (see p 368). Inside is a damaged Ganesha statue.

At the back of the middle courtyard is the Naga temple, named on account of the naga which is carved in loops round the walls of the now roofless, square structure. It probably dates from the late 14C. Nine anthropomorphic statues are sculpted in high relief on the walls and corners of the temple body, their feet pointing to the left as if walking round the temple, each with an arm raised to support the body of the *naga*.

In the eastern courtyard is the **main sanctuary**, dating from 1374 and comprising three storeys or terraces. It is believed to have been the favourite sanctuary of Hayam Wuruk, the great ruler of Majapahit. Flanking each of the two stairways which lead up on to the first terrace is a pair of bulging-eyed *dvarapala* statues, standing on a cushion of skulls, each with a snake over the shoulder and a club in hand; these are dated 1347. The reverse side of each *dvarapala* is carved with a scene from an animal tale. The northernmost one shows a man carrying a stick over his shoulder, from which hangs a turtle; ahead walks a deer, looking back at the man. It may refer to a story about small animals which free each other: a deer, a turtle, and in some versions a mouse, a crow and doves, are caught at different times by a hunter, only to be rescued by the others. Here it appears the deer is luring the hunter; in one version it feigns death, the hunter drops the turtle to capture the deer, and the turtle escapes.

The adjacent *dvarapala* carries a scene from the crocodile and bull story (seen at Candi Surowono), showing the bull carrying the crocodile back to the water. The tales on the two southern *dvarapalas* are less clear.

The walls of the first terrace are decorated with fine narrative reliefs from the *Ramayana* epic, alternating with medallions that depict birds. The reliefs on the second terrace are from the *Krishnayana*; those on the third depict Garudas and winged *nagas*.

On the north side of the main sanctuary is the partially reconstructed **temple body**, which originally would have sat above the third terrace. It had niches which probably would once have contained images of Shiva, Brahma, and Vishnu; the mounts of the latter two – Hamsa and Garuda – can be seen below the respective niches. No trace of the roof remains, and it is possible that it was built of timber and palm fibre, like the modern Balinese *meru*. Certainly, the Panataran complex, with its multiple courtyards, and with the main temple tucked into the rearmost one, can be seen as a precursor of today's Balinese temples.

Southeast of the east courtyard, a path leads to a small **bathing pool**, its inner wall decorated above the water line with fine reliefs of animals.

Candi Gambar Wetan

This is a very minor site, awkward to reach (impossible on public transport except an *ojek*) but described for its interesting location—in a pretty garden in the middle of a coffee estate.

From Candi Panataran, go back 600m towards Blitar, and turn left at the signed junction, past magnificent trees with vast aerial roots, to another left turn after c 4km. This dirt lane arrives at a triple-fork junction; take the left-hand lane, which soon crosses a dam wall. At a T-junction on the far side, turn right, passing a checkpoint into a coffee plantation; explain your destination to the guard. Take the first track right, 100m beyond the barrier, through the coffee estate to the *candi*, on the right after 1.7km.

There is little to see except a kneeling *dvarapala*, still partly buried at the foot of a stairway, and another at the top, behind which is the remains of a small *candi* base. Nearby are damaged statues and other stones from the site.

The Blitar–Malang road

The most important of several temple sites along the road is **Candi Sawentar**, 2km south of the main road from a turning just east of the SMA school in Garum, c 10km from Blitar. The early-13C *candi* is on the right, just beyond a very prominent beringin tree.

Steps on the west side lead on to the *candi* foot. Inside the cella is a *yoni*; above the narrow doorway is a very damaged *kala* face. Flanking the doorway are two small niches, with others on the three side walls, each surmounted by a *kala* face; the roof has been partially rebuilt. The roof vault was closed with a slab of stone carved with a relief depicting Vishnu mounted on a horse; it is assumed to have been a Vishnuite temple.

Further east on the main highway, a road turns off north in Talun to **Candi Kotes** and **Candi Wringin Branjang**, passing after a few metres a checkpoint with a metal barrier. The sites are only worth a visit if you have your own transport.

At an intersection after 4km, Candi Kotes is signed to the left, 1.2km, and Candi Wringin Branjang to the right. Candi Kotes is a very minor site, comprising little more than two raised platforms with small pedestals.

The more interesting Candi Wringin Branjang, currently being excavated, shows clearly how easily a temple could be covered with volcanic ash and mud. From the intersection, head east 300m, then turn north 1.2km. At this point, where the main road turns sharp right, continue straight ahead on a rougher lane for c 2.5km to a fork. Take the left fork and continue 2km to a football field on the right. Turn left opposite, passing straight through *desa* Sukomulyo and through a gate opening into a sugar cane plantation on the far side. Follow this track for c 2km to the *candi* itself, on a gently sloping hillside covered in pine trees. The first structure reached is a small stone, roofed sanctuary; up the hill behind are structures discovered in 1996. In the lower one, a *dvarapala* has been partially unearthed (with the intention of removing it to a protected place); the upper site appears to be an altar or shrine.

Just east of Wlingi on the main highway, a lane to the north is signed to **Candi Plumbangan**. Turn along here and after c 1.5km turn left; in *desa* Plumbangan,

800m further, take an earth road to the left where the asphalt road turns sharp right. The *candi* – in fact a stone gateway – is 200m along here, surrounded by several *yoni*, a fine Nandi and other statue fragments; it dates from 1390. Of note is a very large stela beneath a canopy.

Further east on the Blitar–Malang road, a very sharp turn doubling back to the left (just a few metres before the Taman Wisata Karangkates on the right) leads 700m through a set of open metal gates to a small enclosure containing a marvellous huge **statue of Ganesha** – the **Arca Ganesha Karangkates**, standing on a cushion of skulls and holding an axe in one hand. On a clear day there is a good view of Gunung Kawi-Butak from here.

Malang and the Bromo-Semeru massif

Highlights. **Malang** is one of the most pleasant towns in east Java, and is an excellent base from which to explore surrounding sights. To the east are the important temples of **Candi Jago** (see p 367) and **Candi Kidal** (see p 368), beyond which a lane climbs up to the west rim of the marvellous **Tengger caldera** (see p 368). Northwest of Malang is **Candi Singosari** (see p 369), with its well-known colossal guardian statues. **Gunung Bromo** (see p 370) is the most popular tourist attraction in east Java, and is definitely worth exploring. On the south coast is the beautiful, isolated white sand beach of **Pantai Ngliyep** (see p 372), a place for complete relaxation. For the mountain climber or hiker, a walk in the **Semeru massif** (see p 373), perhaps to the summit of Java's highest volcano, is highly recommended.

Practical information

Travel advice
For several of the routes out of Malang, it is recommended that travellers charter a vehicle for the day. Almost all the places described are reachable on public transport, but it can be time-consuming and frustrating. A charter is suggested particularly for Pantai Ngliyep, the road to Ngadas, and the Nongkojajar–Wonokitri route. See below for rental details.

Accommodation
Malang has a wide range to suit most tastes and budgets. Elsewhere, there are very simple rooms at Wonokitri, Wonokerto, Cemoro Lawang and Ranupane, all round the Tengger caldera, and at Pantai Ngliyep. More comfortable hotels can be found at Tosari and Sukapura, on different approaches to the Tengger caldera, but both are poorly located.

MALANG

A busy but spacious town on the upper reaches of the Brantas river, with attractive neighbourhoods and a wealth of interesting sights nearby, Malang is an enjoyable place to stay. Ringed by volcanoes, the fertile valley is a major source of sugar cane; in the highlands to east and west are Java's main apple orchards.

Practical information

Transport

There are three main **bus terminals**, all of them far from the city centre: **Arjosari**, c 7km north of the centre, off Jl. Yani, is mainly for buses to Surabaya, Jakarta and routes along the north coast; **Gadang**, c 5km south of the centre, is for buses to the south; and **Landungsari**, c 7km west, is for buses along the Kediri road. Check with your hotel staff to avoid a wasted journey to the wrong terminal. From the **railway station** on Jl. Trunojoyo, to the east of Taman Tugu, the *Matarmaja* is a slow overnight service to Jakarta (18 hours); the *Rengganis* is a daytime service to Banyuwangi. *Becak* and **taxis** operate in town; *mikrolet* link the main bus stations as well as following other routes, their routes indicated by initials ('A–T' is Arjosari to Tidar; 'A–G' is Arjosari to Gadang, etc.).

Among the **airlines**, only *Merpati* flies from Malang—direct to Jakarta—but Surabaya's airport is in easy reach. For **car rentals**, try *Alfaria Romeo Rent-a-car* at Jl. Kawi 23, opposite the Jl. Tangkuban Perahu junction, or travel agents (see below), or ask at the tourist office or your hotel. To drive to the floor of the Tengger caldera, a 4WD vehicle is essential. These are available at Ngadas, Wonokitri and Cemoro Lawang, but prices are high so it is advisable to try to share the charter with others.

Airline and shipping offices

Bouraq at Jl. Bandung 1, on the corner with Jl. Besar Ijen; *Garuda* inside *Bank Lippo* on the east side of the *alun-alun*; and *Merpati* in Hotel Kartika Prince on Jl. Suprapto, all have flights out of Surabaya. *Mandala* shares an office with the shipping company, *Pelni*, on Jl. Sugiyopranoto. Note that flights out of Surabaya can be substantially cheaper if bought from travel agents, rather than direct from the airline.

Accommodation

There are plenty of good hotels in Malang, which makes it an excellent base for a few days. The ☎ code is 0341.

☆☆☆☆/☆☆☆☆/☆☆☆ *Hotel Graha Cakra* (☎ 324989; fax. 367856) Jl. Cerme 16. A charming building with pleasant rooms and attentive staff.

☆☆☆☆☆/☆☆☆☆ *Hotel Tugu* (☎ 363891; fax. 362747) Jl. Tugu. Very central and beautifully decorated.

☆☆☆/☆☆ *Hotel Kartika Kusuma* (☎ 350520) Jl. Kahuripan 12. Very reasonable rooms.

☆☆ *Splendid Inn* (☎ 366860; fax. 363618) next door to Hotel Tugu; good-value, mid-priced hotel in central location.

☆☆ *Enny's Guest House* (☎ 551369; fax. 552801) Jl. Taman Wilis (= Jl. Gading) just off Jl. Wilis. Friendly and relaxed with spotless rooms, including unusual bamboo suites in a private roof garden.

Hotel Helios (☎ 362741) Jl. Pattimura. Pleasant, simple mid-priced and low-budget rooms.

Restaurants

Toko 'Oen', operating on the same site on Jl. Basuki Rachmat since the late 1920s, has become an institution of sorts, especially among Dutch visitors. Its popularity lies largely in the preserved decor and furnishings: the food is good, but not exceptionally so. *Rumah Makan Cahyaningrat* at Jl. Soekarno-Hatta 18 has excellent Javanese food in a pleasant setting; if a tour group is in town, there may be a gamelan performance. *Und Corner* is a small bakery and coffee shop attached to Hotel Tugu on Jl. Kahuripan. Adjacent is *Restoran Melati*, also part of the hotel. Both are very good.

Information and services

There is a **tourist information office** at Jl. Semeru 4, and a smaller information booth across Jl. Mojopahit from the Pelni office. *Gramedia*, next door to Toko 'Oen' has maps, postcards, newspapers, including the *Jakarta Post*, and a reasonable selection of English-language books.

The **post office** is on the south side of the *alun-alun*. For **money**, *BCA* (M, V) is on the corner of Jl. Basuki Rachmat and Jl. Kahuripan. *BII* is nearby on Jl. Basuki Rachmat. There is a 24-hour **telecoms office** on Jl. Basuki Rachmat. *Pasopati Tours and Travel*, an efficient, reliable travel agent at Jl. Basuki Rachmat 11, and *Haryono Travel* at Jl. Semeru 16/A, can arrange hotel discounts, flights, car rentals and airport transport.

A pleasant half-day can be spent in Malang, though there are few specific sights. The **old colonial residential district** to the west of Jl. Basuki Rachmat is distinguished by large Dutch bungalows and broad, tree-lined avenues. Here, on Jl. Besar Ijen is the **Museum Brawijaya** (open daily 09.00–14.00), a military museum with a rather ordinary collection of weaponry, uniforms, paintings, old black-and-white photographs of Malang, and newspaper cuttings. In front are a bust of Sudirman and old military vehicles.

The **bird market** off Jl. Mojopahit, and the nearby flower market are always busy and worth a stroll; fish and the occasional monkey are also sold here. Part of Jl. Mojopahit, between the Brantas river bridge and the bird market, is full of stalls selling **secondhand books**. The dimly lit basement of the central **Pasar Besar** is one of Malang's most interesting markets. The caretaker at the nearby Chinese pagoda, **Eng An Kiong**, on the corner of Jl. Martadinata and Jl. Zainul Zakse, welcomes curious visitors.

On the west side of the *alun-alun* is Malang's central mosque, **Mesjid Agung Jami'**; during Friday noon prayers, people spill out across the *alun-alun*. The **City Hall**, built in 1926, can be seen on Taman Tugu, near the Hotel Tugu.

On the western edge of Malang, in *desa* Karangbesuki, is **Candi Badut**, a small reconstructed Shaivite temple which is usually associated with a stone inscription – the Dinoyo inscription – dated to 760, which indicates that the temple was dedicated to Agastya. If so, it is the oldest temple in east Java. It was rediscovered in 1923 in very poor condition, and was rebuilt soon after.

It displays similarities to early central Javanese *candi*, such as those at Dieng and Gedong Songo: the same simple, flat base; the *kala-makara* motif, now partially damaged, round the cella doorway and niches; and the lower section of the roof. Inside is a *linga*, defaced with graffiti. The interior walls, heavily repaired, contain five empty niches. In a niche on the north exterior wall is a damaged, headless image of Durga slaying the buffalo-demon. To the southwest are the

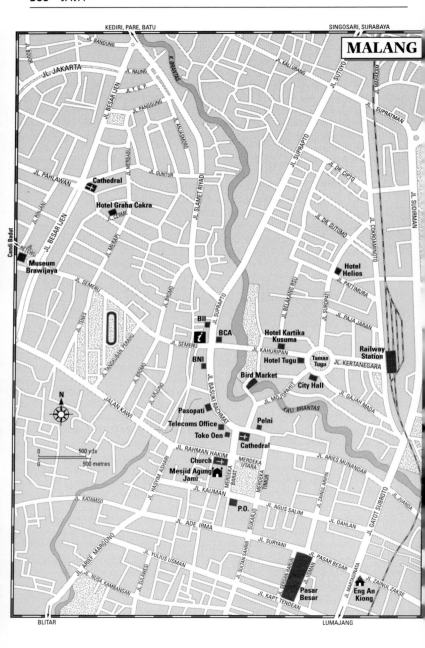

KEDIRI, PARE, BATU

SINGOSARI, SURABAYA

MALANG

JL. BANDUNG

JL. BOGOR

JL. JAKARTA

JL. RAUNG

K. BRANTAS

JL. KALI URANG

JL. SUTOYO

JL. MALIKAM

JL. SUPRATMAN

JL. BESAR IJEN

JL. Y. G. P.

JL. PANGGUNG

JL. ANJASMORO

JL. RINJANI

JL. PAHLAWAN

JL. MERBABU

JL. GUNTUR

JL. SUPRAPTO

JL. DR. CIPTO

JL. BESAR IJEN

Cathedral

Hotel Graha Cakra

JL. CERME

JL. SLAMET RIYADI

JL. DR. SUTOMO

JL. SUDIRMAN

Candi Badut

JL. SEMERU

JL. MERAPI

JL. SEMERU

Museum Brawijaya

JL. KELUD

JL. TENES

JL. BROMO

TANGKUBAN PERAHU

JL. ARJUNO

JALAN KAWI

JL. DR. SUTOMO

JL. COKROAMINOTO

Hotel Helios

JL. PATTIMURA

JL. BELAKANG RSU

JL. SUROPATI

JL. PAJA JARAN

BII

i

BCA

JL. SUPRAPTO

Hotel Kartika Kusuma

JL. KAHURIPAN

Hotel Tugu

Taman Tugu

Railway Station

JL. KERTANEGARA

BNI

Bird Market

City Hall

JL. MOJOPAHIT

KALI BRANTAS

JL. GAJAH MADA

Pasopati

Telecoms Office

Toko Oen

JL. BASUKI RACHMAT

Pelni

Cathedral

JL. RAHMAN HAKIM

JL. HASTYM ASHARI

Church

Mesjid Agung Jami

MERDEKA UTARA

MERDEKA BARAT

MERDEKA TIMUR

JL. ARIES MUNANDAR

JL. JUANDA

N

0   500 yds
0   500 metres

JL. KAUMAN

JL. KATAMSO

JL. ADE IRMA

P.O.

SUKARJO

JL. AGUS SALIM

JL. ZAINUL ARIFIN

JL. DAHLAN

JL. GATOT SUBROTO

JL. ARIEF MARGONO

JL. YULIUS USMAN

JL. SULTAN SAHIRIR

JL. SURYANI

JL. PASAR BESAR

JL. NUSA KAMBANGAN

JL. SULAWESI

JL. TERUSAN HAMID

JL. USMAN

Pasar Besar

JL. MARTADINATA

Eng An Kiong

JL. ZAINUL ZAKSE

BLITAR

JL. KAPT. TENDEAN

LUMAJANG

foundations of a subsidiary shrine, which may have housed the now-damaged Nandi image that lies in the courtyard.

To get there, take an 'A–T' (Arjosari–Tidar) *mikrolet* to the Tidar terminus, then walk 100m to the site.

Many excursions are possible from Malang. Detailed below are five of the most interesting.

CANDI JAGO, CANDI KIDAL, AND BROMO VIA GUBUGKLAKAH

Take the main highway north from Malang and turn east (right) to Tumpang (16km) along Jl. Adisucipto. In Tumpang, just before the *mikrolet* terminal, a signed lane to the left leads after 300m to Candi Jago.

Candi Jago

The date of Candi Jago's construction is not clear, though there is evidence from Old Javanese texts which indicate that it was built in 1268 or 1280. It is likely that its modern name derives from Jajaghu, the name of a temple built in memory of King Vishnuvardhana (d. 1268), father of the last Singosari king, Kertanagara. It may have been built then, or 12 years later, when a memorial service was held for him.

It seems likely, however, that the excellent reliefs – or some of them at least – date from the mid-14C, when the temple was partially rebuilt. Research by Marijke Klokke in the 1980s showed some reliefs here to be consistently similar to others at Panataran (see p 359), which clearly dated from 1375. The reliefs and the statuary originally found here indicate both Shaivite and Buddhist beliefs – an indication of the religious syncretism of the period, which had Vishnuvardhana deified both as Shiva and the Buddha.

The *candi* comprises three terraces, with the now-ruined temple body above. The **walls of the lowest terrace** show a series of narrative reliefs, many severely weathered, some depicting scenes from Tantri themes. One of the clearest is in the corner to the left of the southern staircase, showing the tale of the goat who fools a tiger. On the left stands a goat with its left foreleg raised, facing a monkey on the right, standing upright. On the panel round the corner to the right is a tiger, walking to the right, but looking back towards the monkey. The story is familiar from Candi Mendut, where it also appears (see p 320).

Two stairways lead on to the **first terrace**. Between the first and second terraces is a low 'belt' of reliefs, and further sequences are found on the walls of the second terrace and the third.

In the enclosure in front of the *candi* is a now faceless, 2m-high statue in high relief of Amoghapasha Lokeshvara, a bodhisattva who took care of the deceased. This was the principal image of the sanctuary, which originally would have been in the cella, flanked by his four attendants, Bhrikuti, Hayagriva, Sudhanakumara and Tara, all of which are now in the National Museum in Jakarta.

Also in the enclosure are three large, fierce *kala* faces, which would once have decorated the temple body.

At a T-junction c 1km beyond Tumpang, past the livestock market (*pasar hewan*) where cattle and goats are traded, turn right to Candi Kidal or left to Gubugklakah and Gunung Bromo (see below). The *candi* is most easily reached by *ojek* or *dokar* from Tumpang; the 6km road is rough.

Candi Kidal

Renovated most recently in the 1980s, Candi Kidal is a small mid-13C Hindu temple, the funerary monument for King Anushapati (d. 1248), father of King Vishnuvardhana, for whom Candi Jago was built. Similar in style to Candi Sawentar near Blitar (see p 362), it has a huge *kala* face above the doorway. The base is decorated with images of Garuda, the mount of Vishnu, which on the south side is portrayed carrying the *naga* entwined round Mount Meru, which was pulled back and forth by the gods at its head and demons at its tail to churn the sea of milk; on the east, Garuda clutches a vessel holding the elixir of eternal life which emerged during the churning; and on the north Garuda supports a female divinity (above his head) – probably Lakshmi, the first of the *apsaras* which came forth from the churning.

In a shed beside the *candi* are photos from the recent renovation.

Gunung Bromo: the west approach

Mikrolet operate from Tumpang as far as Gubugklakah, from where the traveller must charter a jeep or *ojek*.

From the Tumpang junction, follow the Ngadas road through pretty scenery towards **Gubugklakah**, an important apple-growing area; orchards flank the road below and above the village. Above Gubugklakah, a parking lot and *warung* on the right mark the path to Pelangi waterfall, a pleasant 10–20-minute walk away. The road beyond becomes a very narrow, winding, overgrown lane flanked by forest, with fine views of incredibly steep, cultivated hillsides. The road enters a gateway marking **Bromo-Tengger-Semeru National Park** and finally reaches the small settlement of Ngadas c 8km above the waterfall.

In **Ngadas** you can rent a jeep and driver to descend to the sandy ash-covered floor of the 10km-wide caldera in which Gunung Bromo and Gunung Batok sit (see below), or to **Ranupane**, the starting point for an ascent of Java's highest mountain, Semeru (see below).

The rim of the spectacular **Tengger caldera** is reached 2km beyond Ngadas, where the road forks. The left fork descends very steeply on an extremely rough track to the caldera floor; the right track continues south to Ranupane. Only a sturdy 4WD vehicle should be used on either route; the alternative is to hike. Just before the junction is a high viewing tower from which Bromo can be seen clearly on a cloudless day.

CANDI SINGOSARI, AND BROMO VIA NONGKOJAJAR

Take the main road north from Malang, and c 4.5km beyond the Arjosari bus station turn left in Singosari to Candi Singosari, 600m further.

Candi Singosari

This Shaivite temple dates from the very late 13C or very early 14C and has little ornamentation, probably because it was never completed. The only remaining statue is a damaged image of Bhatara Guru in the south cella, representing Shiva as a hermit. The statues of Mahakala and Nandishvara which once stood in the niches flanking the west cella, as well as Durga from the north cella and Ganesha from the east, were removed in 1804 by the Dutch official, Nicolaus Engelhard, who had rediscovered the temple the previous year.

Above each cella is a badly weathered *kala* face. Along the west boundary of the enclosure are pedestals and damaged statues, some of them depicting rows of now headless horses pulling chariots, which once carried a large statue. Some of these may have come from other structures discovered in the vicinity in the early 19C, which have now completely vanished.

Two huge stone kneeling, club-wielding **dvarapalas** lie 200m further west, flanking the road. Thought to have been the guardians for royal gardens to the west of here, they are depicted as terrible giants with sharp teeth and bulging eyes, with a serpent entwined round them, symbolising the passion to destroy.

At the intersection beside Candi Singosari, a lane leads north towards **Candi Sumberawan**. Follow this 4km to a junction, and turn left along a rough lane to the *candi*; there is a parking space on the right after 400m, from where it's an easy 5-minute stroll along a footpath between a small watercourse and rice fields to the *candi*. It comprises the remains of a simple, square-based Buddhist *stupa*, which probably dates from the 14C. Possibly it marks a resting place of King Hayam Wuruk of Majapahit (r. 1350–89) during his travels round the kingdom.

Purwodadi Botanical Gardens and Coban Baung

The main highway north from Singosari leads after c 13km to a turning on the east side to Nongkojajar (not signed), for the northwest approach to Gunung Bromo (see below). 500m further north is the entrance to the **Purwodadi Botanical Gardens** (Kebun Raya Purwodadi).

Created in the 1940s, the gardens are too large to explore without a vehicle, though in fact most of the interesting plants are close to the main road: the first turn to the left inside the gates leads to palms and succulents. In the far northeast corner is a large collection of banana varieties. The orchid house is through another entrance 100m south along the main highway; visitors are welcome to look.

Immediately north of the gardens, a dirt lane runs east off the highway c 1.3km alongside the gardens' boundary fence, to **Coban Baung**, a large waterfall. It's a 5–10-minute walk from the parking area, though it can be clearly seen from there. Swimming is not permitted, as there have been several deaths – mostly, it must be said, caused by falling from the top of the cliff, not by swimming in the bottom pool; if you want a cooling dip, probably no-one will stop you.

Gunung Bromo: the northwest approach

Transport

Public transport runs as far as Nongkojajar, but from there to Tosari and Wonokitri traffic is very scarce, as most minibuses to Tosari take the main road from Pasuruan; it is easiest to charter an *ojek* from Nongkojajar to Tosari (12km) or to Wonokitri (3km further). From the park gate, just beyond Wonokitri, four-wheel drive jeeps can be chartered to the viewpoint (9km) or down to the caldera floor and Bromo; for the caldera route they are essential (unless you choose to walk); for the viewpoint, which is accessible to any vehicle, it would be much easier to find another *ojek* in Wonokitri.

Take the Nongkojajar road east off the main Malang–Surabaya highway. At the main junction in the centre of Nongkojajar turn left and follow this lane through Mororejo, reaching a T-junction after c 10km; turn right there to Tosari, a further 2km.

To the left in Tosari, the road descends to the ✩✩✩✩ *Hotel Bromo Tosari*, a large, overpriced and rather soulless hotel at the bottom of the village, with clean, comfortable rooms. To the right, you come to a T-junction after c 300m. To the left here is the main road down to Pasuruan (c 40km); to the right is **Wonokitri** (c 3km), where there is extremely basic and shabby *penginapan* accommodation, and the route to the fine Gunung Penanjakan viewpoint overlooking the Tengger caldera.

Just beyond Wonokitri you enter the **Bromo-Tengger-Semeru National Park** (entry fee); the viewpoint is c 9km further, along a twisting lane. On a clear day, the panoramic view from here is one of the most spectacular in Java.

Between the park gate and the viewpoint, a very rough road turns off right to Cemoro Lawang and Gunung Bromo; without a 4WD jeep, you must walk this route. It is in fact a pleasant, though tiring hike to Cemoro Lawang, on the northeast rim of the caldera, where there is a wide choice of accommodation (see below).

Gunung Bromo: the northern approaches

The most popular and accessible route to Gunung Bromo is from **Probolinggo**, northeast of the Bromo-Tenggg-Semeru massif, from where frequent minibuses run all the way to the caldera rim at Cemoro Lawang. Less used is the road from Pasuruan to Tosari and Wonokitri, from where you must either walk or hire a 4WD jeep to reach Cemoro Lawang (see above). Beware of fast-talking touts at the Probolinggo bus terminal, who may try to charge outrageous prices. On the coastal highway between Pasuruan and Probolinggo is the **Kedawung sugar mill**, which invites visitors to view its beautifully maintained steam locomotives.

The Cemoro Lawang road climbs gradually from Probolinggo, passing after c 22km a road to the right to the high **Madakaripura waterfall** and Tongas. The waterfall is to the left in Lumbang, c 6km along here. If you wish to visit it, there is a Probolinggo–Tongas–Sukapura bus service which passes it; it is suggested that you visit it on the way back from Bromo, assuming that you return this way.

On the main road, just beyond the junction, you pass through the small market of **Sukapura** and then reach the huge, grossly overpriced ☆☆☆☆/☆☆☆☆/☆☆☆ *Hotel Raya Bromo* (☎ 0335 23103; fax 23142). There's little reason to stay here, as it is far from Bromo, and there is a wider choice higher up.

Continue c 10km to **Wonokerto**, where ☆☆/☆ *Yoschi's* (☎ 0335 23387) provides the nicest accommodation on this approach to Bromo, with simple, but cosy and well-furnished rooms, friendly staff, and generally reliable food.

At **Ngadisari**, c 2.5km further up, is the entrance to the **Bromo-Tengger-Semeru National Park** (entry fee); a final 3km climb brings you to the caldera rim at Cemoro Lawang.

Accommodation

There are several choices in Cemoro Lawang, all very close together. The ☎ code is 0335. The lane to the first three listed is c 250m beyond the minibus terminal.

☆ *Hotel Bukit Lava* (☎ 23458/20272). Reasonable rooms in an airy setting; the best ones have views over the caldera.

☆ *Puri Lava* (☎ 23458/20272). A cheaper *losmen* under the same ownership, a few metres away; very basic rooms.

☆☆☆/☆☆/☆ *Hotel Bromo Permai I* (☎ 23459). Very expensive compared to the competition, and devoid of any atmosphere.

☆ *Hotel Cemara Indah* (☎ 23457). Highest up the road to the caldera, and probably the worst of all, with fairly squalid rooms.

Gunung Bromo and the sand sea

The early-morning ascent of Bromo is a magical experience, even in the knowledge that people have done it almost every day of the year for decades. You are woken by hotel staff at the appointed hour (usually 04.00), and there follows a 1–2-hour walk down the caldera wall from beside the *Hotel Bromo Permai*, and across the sand sea to the stairway which ascends to Bromo's crater rim (2392m). It can be a very chilly experience; frosts occur several times a year, so bring warm clothes. The intention is to reach the rim around sunrise, when the sky is usually clearest and the gently smoking crater of Bromo appears at its most ethereal; but of course the walk can be done at any time of day, even in the midday heat if you take plenty of water. Ponies can be hired to save tired feet.

Beside Gunung Bromo is a flat-topped, extinct cone, **Gunung Batok** (2440m), with steep, fluted ridges; in the hollow between the two is a **Hindu temple**, the focus of an annual festival for the Tengger people.

The scenery round Cemoro Lawang and the Tengger caldera is characterised by extremely steep hill slopes planted with cabbages, carrots, potatoes, onions and garlic; unlike the Dieng plateau, however, there is very little terracing to prevent soil erosion, which occurs here on a massive scale.

Many hiking routes are possible. Suggested walks include the track beyond Cemoro Lawang, which climbs along the northern caldera rim to the viewpoint; the energetic hiker can complete a circuit by taking the Wonokitri road from there, and then descending down to the caldera floor, and back to Cemoro Lawang via Gunung Bromo; allow a full day and take plenty of water and sun protection.

From Gunung Bromo's rim, it is possible to follow other ridges south and west to the less distinct summits of **Gunung Kursi** (2581m) or **Gunung Watangan** (2601m). A circuit of the flat sand sea is possible, with the option of exiting either southwest to Ngadas (for Malang), south to Ranupane (for Lumajang), or north to Wonokitri (for Malang, Pasuruan or Surabaya). The adventurous may be able to find a way up the fluted ridges of Gunung Batok for an excellent view of Bromo.

Pantai Ngliyep and the south coast

Transport

On public transport, take a *mikrolet* from Malang's Terminal Gadang to Kepanjen, another from there to Donomulyo, and a third from there to Ngliyep. On Sundays they run direct from Kepanjen to Ngliyep, but the beach can be very crowded. A recommended alternative is to charter a vehicle from Malang for the day.

Take the main highway south from Malang past the Kebonagung sugar factory to Kepanjen. Here, turn west (right) along the main Blitar road, past the Taman Wisata Karangkates and the wonderful **Arca Ganesha Karangkates** (see p 363). Just beyond the reservoir dam, turn south (left) on the road signed to Kalipare, which passes round the west and south sides of the reservoir through plantations of teak and pine. Turn right in **Kalipare** and climb steadily through dry terrain over several low ridges; there are excellent views back to the north over the Brantas valley, with Gunung Kawi-Butak behind.

Beyond Donomulyo, the Ngliyep road turns off right, signed 11km to the beach.

One of Java's most beautiful south coast beaches, Ngliyep is a charming white sand cove, with a rather worrying signboard which lists those who have drowned here. The main beach is flanked by low, jagged limestone cliffs; paddling is possible, swimming is heavily discouraged – in fact, it is forbidden. A simple *pesanggrahan* offers very basic accommodation. The site is very peaceful in midweek, with just the odd woman selling young coconuts, a few courting couples chatting in the shade, and one or two *warung* open to catch the occasional passer-by. This is a wonderful picnic spot, but note that at weekends it can be busy and noisy.

To the east of the main beach, over a low ridge, is a very small, sandy bay, **Teluk Putri**. To the west of the main beach, you come first to a small sandy cove separated from the main beach by a massive rock outcrop. Then a 100m walk through forest leads to **Pantai Panjang**, a broad beach with a strong swell. If you can put up with the basic accommodation of the *pesanggrahan*, it's a good place to come for a day or two of quiet relaxation.

The asphalt road continues past the beach to **Gunung Kombang**, a low headland reached by a raised walkway.

Further east along the coast is **Balekambang**, where a small Balinese temple, Pura Ismoyo, stands on a rock outcrop on the beach. Built in 1985, the temple is usually closed, except during its annual festival. Balekambang is more visited than Ngliyep, with scores of *warung* along the sea front; it is much less attractive, however.

To get there, return north to the junction 4km before Donomulyo, and instead of turning back west, turn east (right) c 16km through Sumbermanjing Kulon, and turn south (sharp right) shortly before Bantur; from there it is a further 12km to the beach.

Gunung Semeru from Lumajang

Transport

The ascent of Gunung Semeru starts from Ranupane, which – for normal 2WD vehicles – is only accessible from Lumajang, along the winding asphalt lane through Senduro; the alternative route, via Ngadas (see above), is only open to 4WD jeeps or walkers. Frequent buses run between Malang and Lumajang, from where there are minibuses to Senduro. There you must charter an ojek to Ranupane (27km).

Take the main road south of Malang from the Gadang terminal through Bululawang, and turn east at the Krebet sugar factory on to the Turen road. Just beyond Turen, join the main Blitar–Lumajang highway, a rather slow, winding and busy road which only becomes scenic after c 40km, when it begins to climb through dense forest. Further on there are good views of Semeru on a clear day, and then the road starts to descend steadily, crossing a couple of deep ravines.

From Lumajang, take the road west to Senduro, c 17km. Just above Senduro centre is a Balinese Hindu temple, **Pura Mandaragiri Semeru Agung**, which was consecrated in July 1992. The *pura* was planned by the prince of Ubud, Tjokorda Gede Agung Suyasa, and funds were raised by readers of the *Bali Post*. It was to be a *pura kayangan jagat* – a status equal to the nine most important temples on Bali itself. Visitors are required to wear a sarong and sash, as they would in temples on Bali.

From the *pura*, turn back c 350m to the centre of **Senduro**, where a very scenic narrow lane turns off (to the right as you descend towards Lumajang) to Ranupane.

The lane's condition is deteriorating fast as a result of poor maintenance. After c 10km, you pass the entrance gate to the **Bromo-Tengger-Semeru National Park**, and c 15km further on is a footpath to the left, clearly signed to Gunung Semeru (28km). Just beyond is the national park **information centre**, then the lake itself, **Ranu Pane**, and finally you arrive at the rather shabby little village of **Ranupane**.

There is very simple accommodation c 200m past the lake, at the *Family Homestay*, run by 'Pak' Tasrip. The road continues through the village and on towards Ngadas, but eventually becomes impassable to all but 4WD vehicles. A short walk from Ranu Pane is another lake called Ranu Regulo.

Gunung Semeru is best climbed between June and September; climbers should try to bring all supplies with them, as there is little choice in Ranupane. Guides or porters, tents and sleeping bags can be hired through the *Family Homestay*.

It's a tough, but enjoyable, three-day hike to the summit and back, but if Semeru is active, pay great attention to advice you receive from guides or park officials. A foreign tourist was killed and another injured in late 1997 when they ignored local warnings not to venture too close and were struck by rocks; it can be extremely dangerous. Some maps show a route up Semeru from the south; this should not even be considered, either for ascent or descent.

The path south from Ranupane climbs gently to **Ranu Kumbolo** (2390m), an attractive lake, and then skirts **Gunung Kepolo** (3035m) to **Arcopodo**, the usual campsite, c 6–7 hours from Ranupane. The second day it's a tough, slippery climb through volcanic ash and lava to the summit. Return along the same route on the third day.

Gunung Semeru has erupted frequently in the past few decades, causing immense destruction. An eruption in 1911 destroyed 200 houses; another in 1946 killed six people and flattened more than 80 dwellings. A major eruption in 1981 caused a lahar (mud flow) which killed more than 250 people and damaged 16 villages; another eruption in May 1993 destroyed two villages, while a third in February 1994 spewed out perhaps eight million cubic metres of ash, destroying six villages.

Gunung Penanggungan, Trowulan and vicinity

Highlights. This chapter covers a rather ill-defined area in the triangle between Malang, Pasuruan and Jombang, which includes the ancient capital of Majapahit (see p 379) at Trowulan; the site museum here has an excellent but small collection of artefacts. Surrounding the sacred mountain of Gunung Penanggungan (see p 376) are several notable temple sites, and hikers may enjoy climbing to others dotted across the mountain's upper slopes. Other isolated sites of antiquity are scattered across the area; of them all, the elegant Candi Jawi (see p 377) near Prigen should not be missed.

Practical information

Travel advice

For the sights round Pacet, Trawas, Gunung Penanggungan and Gempol, it is suggested that visitors charter a vehicle in Malang for a day, to save time waiting for scarce public transport. This has the added advantage of enabling you to use picturesque country lanes instead of the congested highways. Mojokerto, Trowulan, and Candi Rimbi are easily accessible by bus from Malang.

Accommodation

Malang is the suggested base, although the area could be explored equally well from Surabaya. Along the way, there are scores of hotels in Tretes and Trawas; however, neither place is recommended. Mojokerto has the closest hotels to Trowulan's sights.

Malang to Pacet

The recommended approach from Malang is via Batu, in the hills c 17km to the west. Turn north here, past Selekta and Junggo, along a road lined with plant nurseries. Beyond Junggo the road climbs for c 6.5km through terraced fields of vegetables to Sumberbrantas, which is the starting point for an ascent of **Gunung Welirang** (3156m) and **Gunung Arjuno** (3339m).

Beyond Sumberbrantas, the road descends steeply past the bathing pools at the Cangar hot springs (Air Panas Cangar), and then winds through forest to **Pacet**, a small, lively market town.

Detour to Candi Kesiman Tengah

Take the Mojokerto road northwest from Pacet c 3.5km, and just beyond the 'Pacet 3km, Pugeran 6km' stone, take the lane to the right signed to **Candi Kesiman Tengah**. After c 900m, at an intersection, a rough but driveable track to the right is signed 750m to the *candi*, an easy walk through emerald-green terraced rice fields.

Candi Kesiman Tengah, a Shaivite temple, has one of the loveliest settings of any east Javanese *candi*, perched above a stream and surrounded by rice terraces, with views of Gunung Penanggungan to the northeast and Gunung Welirang to the southeast; but the temple itself is small and incomplete, and the enclosure locked. Anyone who can find the caretaker (*juru kunci*), please let me know.

The *candi* base is decorated with reliefs, but some half-finished panels attest to the theory that the temple was never finished; little remains of the temple foot and temple body above.

The road beyond the *candi* continues to Mojokerto and Trowulan, but travellers are strongly recommended to take the more circuitous route detailed below, if time permits; there are many fine sites along the way.

Pacet to Jolotundo and Candi Jawi

From Pacet, which has a few dull hotels, follow the road towards Trawas. After 8km, you reach a T-junction where Trawas lies c 1km to the right. A steep lane to the right just before Trawas leads to **Reco Lanang**, a large, badly weathered stone statue of the Buddha, on the left side after 850m.

Returning downhill from there, the first house on the right has in the garden, over to the far left, a toppled stone figure, which is believed to have once made a pair with the Buddha image. It is considered locally to be the female partner, but the origin of both is unknown.

In Trawas a road to the left is signed to Candi Jolotundo, 8km. Follow this c 5km to a turning on the right signed 7km to **Candi Selokelir**; the steep, rough track is impassable to all but the most sturdy of vehicles. Selokelir (also known as Antiquity no. XXIII) is one of more than 80 ancient sites scattered across the slopes of Gunung Penanggungan and its subsidiary peaks; two inscribed stones found in the vicinity indicate that it dates from the first half of the 15C.

It is a tough but enjoyable walk to the site, though it would be of interest only to specialists or hikers seeking to stretch their legs. If you are lucky, you might find an *ojek* in the village willing to take you most of the way.

Continue north along the asphalt road c 3km to a lane on the right signed to the **Pusat Pendidikan Lingkungan Hidup** (PPLH; 'Environmental Education Centre') and Candi Jolotundo (1.4km).

PPLH is a non-governmental environmental centre which runs educational programmes, mainly for local students, but also for the occasional foreign tour group; ✩✩✩/✩✩/✩ accommodation is available (☎ 031 561 4493), but advance booking is usually necessary. It's a very pleasant place to stay for those wishing to explore the area, especially the antiquities of Gunung Penanggungan; PPLH can often help to arrange a guide from the nearby government archaeology office (Dinas Purbakala).

Candi Jolotundo, up the lane beyond, is a bathing pool dating from 977—the earliest dated antiquity in east Java, built in the reign of Udayana, father of King Airlangga. It was rediscovered in 1817 and partially restored in the 1920s, when some stone fragments were retrieved from the mud-clogged basin. Reliefs which originally stood above the water spouts have now been removed to the National Museum in Jakarta.

Gunung Penanggungan, because of its four almost symmetrical subsidiary peaks, became identified from the 10C with the cosmic mountain, Meru, from which flowed the elixir of eternal life; the water flowing from Penanggungan was thus considered sacred.

A path beyond Candi Jolotundo continues up the mountain to several minor 15C sites, including **Candi Kendalisodo**, a site comprising the remains of two buildings and four terraces, with an altar upon the highest. Most of the sites dotting the mountain are simple altars and terraces; many are heavily overgrown and are now difficult to reach.

From Jolotundo, return to Trawas, and turn left to Prigen along a steep road lined with villas and hotels. In **Prigen**, the right turn leads to **Tretes**, a rather depressing hill resort that caters to Surabayan weekenders and single men in search of a good time; the left turn leads to Candi Jawi and then descends to the Malang–Surabaya highway.

Candi Jawi

The elegant east-facing, 25m-high tower of Candi Jawi, c 4.5km below Prigen, stands on a very high stone foot upon a broad brick base surrounded by a moat. Above the doorway and three empty niches in the temple body are fine *kala* faces; inside is a *yoni*. Much of the **temple body** is actually built of new stone, installed during a restoration in the 1970s. A heavily weathered frieze has been carved round the walls of the temple foot; parts of it are clear enough to identify people, buildings and animals, and on the north side one part illustrates a temple complex that looks remarkably similar to Jawi itself.

Candi Jawi is unusual in that it comprises a Shaivite temple, with Shaivite sculpture, but is topped by a Buddhist *stupa*. It was perhaps built to commemorate King Kertanagara (r. 1268–92), the last Singosari king, whose father, Vishnuvardhana, was commemorated by Candi Jago near Malang (see p 367) – though some scholars have argued that Jawi is not a funerary temple.

Excavations carried out in the 1930s brought to light a magnificent 1m-high statue of Durga slaying the demon Mahisha (Mahishasura), a fine image of Nandishvara, and a damaged Shiva; none are now on site.

To the west is the remains of a brick split gateway; on the southwest side is a storage room with fragments of images from the site.

A few metres beyond Candi Jawi, on the other side of the road, is *rumah makan Sri*, which serves good food; 2.5km further, the road joins the main highway in Pandaan. Malang is c 45km to the south. To the north, after c 7km you reach a road signed west to **Candi Belahan**, another 10C bathing place; the final 1.5km is up a steep, rocky track.

Smaller than the basin at Jolotundo, Belahan is still in regular use by local villagers. The two statues here – Lakshmi (from whose breasts water spouts) and Sri, the goddesses of wealth and fertility – originally flanked an image of Vishnu seated on his mount, Garuda; this is now in the Trowulan Museum (see below). It is thought that the ashes of King Airlangga were interred here after his death in 1049.

Further north along the main highway, pass through Gempol (5km), and turn west in Porong (1km further), beside the Photo Agung shop, to find two minor sites, **Candi Pari** and **Candi Sumur**.

Follow this side road c 3.5km to a turning on the right signed to Candi Pari; this leads through sugar-cane fields to an intersection in *desa* Candi Pari, where the *candi* lies to the right.

This very large brick *candi*, renovated in the 1990s with much new brickwork, has been dated to 1371, but little is known about its history. The cella is empty and there is no decoration to be seen; statuary found here has been removed to Jakarta.

Due south of Candi Pari, just 50m away, is the very dilapidated Candi Sumur, a smaller brick structure.

Back on the main highway, turn south towards Malang, cross back over the Porong river and take the first main turn to the left a short way beyond – the

Pasuruan road – which leads directly, after 3km, to the new Surabaya–Malang expressway; cross this at the traffic circle and continue east 1.7km to a turning on the south side signed to **Candi Gunung Gangsir**. Turn left at an intersection after 1.3km, and right after a further 1km.

The very large brick *candi*, built on a 5m-high foot, dates probably from the 14C (though some scholars suggest the 10C–11C) and is now in poor condition. Several terracotta reliefs decorated with floral designs, flower vases and goddesses remain, though most are damaged.

Return west to Gempol and take the Mojokerto road west off the main highway. After 7.5km, an indistinct sign indicates a lane to the north (right) leading to **Candi Bangkal**, signed 1.6km but in fact a bit further. At a fork after c 700m, keep right (straight ahead); the *candi* is on the right side.

This minor brick *candi* is surrounded by the low remains of a brick enclosure wall. On the west side is a raised rectangular brick platform which probably once contained wooden shrines. Above the lintel and niches are kala faces of stone.

Further west along the Gempol–Mojokerto road is the extensive Ngoro Industrial Park (NIP: Ngoro Industri Persada). A turning south just before the main gate of NIP leads through the park to **Candi Jedong**, c 3km south on the lower slopes of Gunung Penanggungan.

Under renovation since 1992, Candi Jedong comprises two stone, roofed gateways dating from the 14C. The upper (finer) one has four magnificent kala faces. The remains of brick walls can be seen linking the two gateways, and several other brick structures, including a tunnel to a well.

The rough track beyond Candi Jedong climbs up to other temple sites on Gunung Penanggungan.

MOJOKERTO

From the 10C–14C, Mojokerto was an important port on a major estuary; as a result of sedimentation over the centuries, it is now 30km from the sea. There is little to see here, though it makes a useful base from which to explore the nearby ruins of the Majapahit capital at Trowulan. The only possible point of interest in the town itself is the shabby **Archaeological Museum** (Museum Purbakala) on Jl. Yani, which has a small dusty collection of stone statues and fragments, mostly from sites at Trowulan; the best pieces have been removed to the Site Museum at Trowulan (see below).

Practical information

Transport
The main **bus terminal** is far from the town centre on Jl. Pahlawan. The **train station** is on Jl. Bhayangkara, near the Hotel Wisma Tenera.

Accommodation and services
☆☆/☆ *Hotel Wisma Tenera* (☎ 0321 22904) Jl. Cokroaminoto 3, is central, with a good range of rooms. *BCA* next door can change money. The **post office** is on Jl. Yani near the museum.

Trowulan

The site of the late-14C court of Majapahit, Trowulan village today is dotted with remnants from that era, some of them restored recently in a rather heavy-handed fashion.

History

Majapahit was a Hindu-Buddhist kingdom founded in 1293 or 1294 by Raden Vijaya (Kertarajasa), son of the last Singosari king, Kertanagara. On Kertanagara's death in 1292 at the hands of Jayakatwang, Viceroy of Kediri, Raden Vijaya led an army against the Viceroy. Inscriptions on a set of six copper plates discovered in the late 18C on Gunung Butak, west of Malang, record how, after initial victories, Vijaya was forced to flee to Madura, only to return with a larger army and establish himself on the site of Majapahit at the end of 1292.

Unknown to him, the Mongol ruler Kublai Khan had already launched an expedition against Vijaya's father, who had earlier refused Mongol demands to send a member of the royal family to the Peking court. The Chinese fleet, assembled in Tuban on Java's north coast in early 1293, sent a messenger to Singosari to gather news; he reported the death of Kertanagara and the seizure of power by Jayakatwang. The Chinese then captured Jayakatwang's fleet off the Surabaya estuary, caught his army as it advanced on Vijaya at Majapahit, then marched on Jayakatwang's palace at Kediri; he surrendered in April 1293, was imprisoned, and died soon after. Vijaya, freed from the threat of Jayakatwang, now turned on his new-found Chinese allies and forced them back to their ships; they set sail for China in May.

Vijaya took the name Kertarajasa (r. 1293–1309) and quickly restored relations with China; his son, Jayanagara (r. 1309–28), unfailingly sent annual embassies to Peking.

Majapahit's golden age was during the reign of Hayam Wuruk (= Rajasanagara; r. 1350–89), when the kingdom expanded its suzerainty throughout most of the territory of modern Indonesia and the Malay peninsula; Bali was conquered in 1343 and given to his uncle to rule.

After Hayam Wuruk's death, Majapahit fell into decline, partly as a result of Malacca's growing importance, and partly because of a succession war between Hayam Wuruk's son-in-law, Vikramavardhana, and Virabhumi, a son of Hayam Wuruk by a concubine; the five-year war ended with the death of Virabhumi and left Majapahit greatly weakened, with many tributary states transferring their allegiance to China.

Majapahit survived for another century, overcoming an invasion attempt in 1478, and moving – perhaps under a new dynasty – to Kediri between 1486 and 1512; by 1527–28 it had come to an end, a victim of military expansion by the Muslim kingdom of Demak.

In the early 19C, a Dutch official had investigated the sites at Trowulan and tentatively suggested the link to Majapahit; then in 1894, during the sacking of the Cakranegara palace in Lombok by a Dutch expedition, a copy was discovered of a poem, the Nagara-Kertagama, written by Prapañca in 1365, during the reign of Hayam Wuruk, which described Majapahit's palace and city in detail. Intensified investigations by the Dutch at Trowulan followed, and in 1924 Henri Maclaine Pont began his research there.

From the centre of Mojokerto the main road runs south towards Trowulan and Mojoagung. A turn to the west after c 7.5km is signed to **Kekunaan Bhre Kahuripan**, of interest for its colossal *yoni*. Follow the lane c 2.5km to a T-junction, then turn right; to the left after 350m can be seen a small walled enclosure set back in a field of sugar cane. Inside is a small courtyard containing the massive, beautifully decorated *yoni*, dated to the equivalent of 1372; its original purpose and location are unknown. An adjacent room contains a huge stela. Bhre Kahuripan was a son of King Rajasawardhana of Majapahit (r. 1451–53); local myth associates this site with the prince.

Back on the main highway, continue south c 3.5km to the north edge of Trowulan, where a turning to the east near the 'Jombang 19km' stone leads to **Gopura Wringin Lawang**, a brick gateway almost 14m high.

Continuing c 1.4km along the main road, turn south (left) at an intersection and follow the lane 600m to the corner of the **kolam segeran**, a large rectangular reservoir. Its function remains unclear, though it may have been simply a recreational lake. A left turn at the corner of the reservoir leads to **Candi Menak Jinggo**, comprising the overgrown remains of a brick temple base, with carved stone blocks scattered in the vicinity.

At the reservoir corner, the main road bears right along the west side of the basin to the **Trowulan Site Museum** (open Tues–Sun 07.00–16.00), which houses a small but excellent collection, including small terracotta figurines and stone statuary from Trowulan and other Majapahit sites in the vicinity; old pots, coins, kris blades, bells and gongs, jewellery and porcelain. Of particular note are the animal-shaped money boxes from Majapahit. The main exhibit in the left room is a magnificent decorated clay pot which was used for holding water. Of note among the statues behind are a beautiful but damaged stone Garuda from Menak Jinggo, and the statue of Vishnu riding his mount, Garuda, from the Belahan bathing pool (which perhaps is a portrait statue of King Airlangga).

South of the museum you reach an intersection after c 500m. Candi Tikus and Candi Bajang Ratu are to the left; **Candi Sumur Upas** (Candi Kedaton), a very minor site, is 450m straight on, and 700m beyond that is **Makam Troloyo**, an ancient Muslim cemetery dating from the late 14C to early 17C—an indication of the tolerance that Majapahit's Hindu rulers had for other religions.

The lane east from the intersection reaches **Gopura Bajang Ratu**, another large brick gateway, after c 1.7km. Dating from the 14C, it is decorated with a few badly weathered reliefs from the *Ramayana*, and is believed to have been the entrance to a shrine commemorating the death of Jayanagara (r. 1309–28). Above the gateway are *kala* faces.

Outside the old city wall, 850m further along the lane, is **Candi Tikus**, a brick-built bathing place with fine gargoyle waterspouts, which was discovered in 1914 by local villagers digging up a large rats' nest (hence the modern name, *tikus*, meaning rat).

Return to the main highway and cross straight over along a lane on the far side. After c 750m turn left at a T-junction and follow the road past the excavation site of **Candi Gentong**, where there is little to see except foundations of old walls, to **Candi Brahu**. This is a large brick temple which has undergone a hideously heavy-handed renovation.

At Candi Brahu the road swings left and leads back to the main highway, passing on the way several cottage industries (*pengerajin patung*) that produce small metal statuettes and ornaments from scrap metal for the tourist industry in Bali; visitors are welcome to look.

Opposite the highway junction is the government's **regional archaeological office** (Suaka Peninggalan Sejarah dan Purbakala Jawa Timur), where hundreds of statues and carved fragments are laid out in the garden. Among them are two very large, heavily restored, 2.4m-high images of Bhairava, the demonic form of Shiva. The house here was built in 1929 as a field museum by Maclaine Pont, who constructed an experimental roof using bamboo stakes with a span of nearly 25m and a height of 20m; remarkably, this roof lasted till the 1960s, despite an expected lifespan of just 10 years and a complete lack of maintenance after 1938.

Detour to Candi Rimbi

Candi Rimbi, an interesting and rarely visited temple, lies c 16km beyond Trowulan. Follow the main road south from the archaeological office for c 3km to Mojoagung, and turn left opposite the mikrolet terminal on to the Wonosalam road (take a Wonosalam mikrolet from the terminal). Follow this road c 13km, and just beyond *desa* Pulosari, Candi Rimbi can be seen on the right – a Shaivite temple, dating probably from the second half of the 14C.

Most of the temple body is missing, but there are excellent reliefs in good condition round the base, comprising narrative scenes alternating with raised panels depicting floppy-eared animals; the latter are very similar to those found at Candi Surowono (see p 354). Some of the narratives are identifiable: the panel at the east corner on the north side shows a man with his hand on the back of a reclining tiger. This may refer to a Tantri tale about a brahmin and an ungrateful tiger, in which a student brahmin has learnt how to revive dead animals; he revives the tiger, which then kills the brahmin. The next narrative panel to the west shows a man putting his hand on a Garuda's head, which may be Garuda being blessed by his father, Kashyapa, before fetching the elixir of eternal life.

Scattered round the site are stones from the temple, among them, in the southwest corner of the enclosure, a damaged statue of Agastya comprising head and torso only. An image discovered here of Parvati, Shiva's consort, is now in the National Museum in Jakarta.

Surabaya

Java's second largest city is a humid, polluted urban sprawl covering nearly 300 sq km and housing more than four million people. It is not a place to go on holiday, and unless you have already explored the rest of east Java very thoroughly, it is best avoided. It is, however, a useful transit point for public transport, and provides the simplest route to Madura (see p 388). It also offers all the services a weary traveller could possibly want, with excellent hotels, well-stocked shops and markets, and plenty of evening entertainment.

Surabaya is a city built for commerce, and not one of great cultural and artistic wealth. Old architectural delights are torn down without a second thought to make way for new glass-and-steel towers; the city's museum houses a dusty, seldom-visited collection which has barely changed in decades. The city holds few specific attractions for the casual visitor; a day or two will suffice to see the little there is.

Practical information

Inter-city transport
Trains

Most services depart from **Gubeng station** on the east bank of the river, or from **Pasar Turi station** on the northwest side of the city. Overnight trains to Jakarta include the *Argo Bromo* (c 9 hours) and the *Sembrani* (10 hours), both from Pasar Turi, and the slower *Bima* (12 hours) from Gubeng. The *Sembrani* and *Argo Bromo* services are booked in a separate, smart and quiet office at Pasar Turi station. Travel agents can make bookings for a small surcharge.

Buses

Most inter-town buses depart from the **Bungurasih terminal** (= Purabaya terminal), 10km south of the city centre. There are frequent services to all major towns in Java, and regular buses to Denpasar in Bali, and towns in southern Sumatra.

Ships

Surabaya is one of the main hubs for *Pelni* passenger ships travelling through the archipelago, with frequent services to Ujung Pandang, and fewer to Bawean, Lombok, and ports on the south coast of Kalimantan. Bookings can be made at the office on Jl. Pahlawan or through travel agents. Wisata Bahari (☎ 031 336963/ 334594) runs sailing trips of up to two weeks through Nusa Tenggara to Flores and back on a converted pinisi.

Flights

From Surabaya there are direct international flights to Hong Kong and Singapore. Direct domestic destinations include Balikpapan, Bandung, Banjarmasin, Denpasar, Jakarta, Mataram, Semarang, Ujung Pandang and Yogyakarta; there are indirect flights to a dozen more towns. Many airlines have offices in Surabaya. International airline offices. Many airlines have offices in Surabaya; for details (see p 14).

Domestic airline offices

Bouraq Jl. Sudirman 70/II, t 545 2918-22. Jl. Genteng Kali 63, t 534 4940, 532 6538.
Garuda Graha Bumi Modern, Hyatt Regency, Jl. Basuki Rachmat, ☎ 545 7747.
Mandala Jl. Diponegoro 73, ☎ 567

8973. Jl. Genteng Kali 63, ☎ 534 4940, 532 6538.

Merpati Gubeng train station, Jl. Stasiun Gubeng 1, ☎ 535 3993/4 (= city check-in). Jl. Raya Darmo 111, ☎ 568 8111.

Local transport
Taxis

Taxis are metered and provide the most comfortable transport around the city.

City buses

Buses are extremely crowded and generally uncomfortable, but are very cheap.

Harbour cruises

are operated by *Wisata Bahari* at lunchtime or sunset.

Car rentals

Toyota Rent a Car (☎ 031 546 2500) on Jl. Basuki Rachmat, almost opposite the Hyatt Regency, has well-maintained vehicles for rent. Driving in Surabaya is no more fun than in Jakarta, but a rented car is the most comfortable way of touring eastern Java. Travel agents can provide vehicles for day trips; other local rental agencies can be found in the phone book.

Hotels

Surabaya has a huge number of hotels, many of the better ones catering mainly to the business market. These offer generally impeccable service and excellent comfort, and are no different to top-class hotels anywhere in the world. The area ☎ code is 031. They include the ✵✵✵✵✵ *Hyatt Regency* (☎ 531 1234; fax 532 1508) Jl. Basuki Rachmat 106–28; the ✵✵✵✵✵ Shangri-la (☎ 566 1550; fax 566 1570) Jl. Sungkono 120; the ✵✵✵✵✵ *Sheraton Surabaya* (☎ 546 8000; fax 546 7000) Jl. Embong Malang 25–31; and the ✵✵✵✵✵ *Westin Surabaya* (☎ 545 8888/3333; fax 535 3034) Jl. Embong Malang 85–89. The glut of rooms means discounts are always available;

expect to negotiate 20–50 per cent off the rack rate. Below are listed some cheaper, or more unusual hotels.

✵✵✵✵✵/✵✵✵✵ *Hotel Majapahit* (☎ 545 4333; fax 545 4111) Jl. Tunjungan 65. A magnificently renovated hotel, with many original 1910 features, lovely garden and pool; very good food and excellent service. Highly recommended.

✵✵✵✵✵/✵✵✵✵ *Garden Hotel* (☎ 532 1001; fax 531 6111) Jl. Pemuda. Shares facilities with the Garden Palace Hotel next door, but is slightly cheaper. Reasonable rooms in a central location.

✵✵✵✵✵/✵✵✵✵ *Novotel* (☎ 568 2301; fax 567 6317) Jl. Ngagel 173–75. Far from the city centre, but a bright and fun hotel with pleasant, light rooms, a good pool and garden. Has discounted weekend rates.

✵✵✵ *Hotel Ibis Rajawali* (☎ 339994; fax 339995) Jl. Rajawali 9. Pleasant air-con rooms with TV; no pool.

✵✵✵/✵✵ *Hotel Remaja* (☎ 534 1359/531 0045; fax 531 0009. Jl. Embong Kenongo 12. Good-value air-con rooms.

✵✵ *Hotel Ganefo* (☎ 311169; fax 361390) Jl. Kapasan 169–71. An old and rather neglected colonial building with some cavernous rooms.

✵✵/✵ *Hotel Paviljoen* (☎ 534 3449) Jl. Genteng Besar 94–98. A colonial-era building with simple but good-value rooms round a central courtyard, close to the city centre; highly recommended.

Restaurants and cafés

The food at the major hotels is usually excellent; the restaurants at the *Hotel Majapahit* are especially recommended, serving international, Japanese and Chinese cuisine in pleasant surroundings. Numerous cafés, bakeries and snack bars can be found in the city centre, including *Es Krim Zanandi* on Jl. Yos Sudarso; *Café Venezia* on Jl. Ambengan; the *Surya Ahimsa* vegetarian restaurant at the corner of Jl.

Sudarso and Jl. Walikota; *Granada Bakery* on the corner of Jl. Pemuda and Jl. Sudirman; and *Chez Rose* on Jl. Polisi Istimewa. There are many fast-food restaurants in the various shopping plazas, including *Dunkin' Donuts*, *KFC*, and *McDonald's*.

Information and maps
The **tourist information office** (Kantor Penerangan Pariwisata) on the corner of Jl. Pemuda and Jl. Kayun is generally of little help, but can advise on public transport and city sights. Local street maps of Surabaya, and the Surabaya/east Java map by Periplus, are sold at Gramedia on Jl. Basuki Rachmat.

Money
BII is in Wisma BII on Jl. Pemuda; *BCA* and *Bank Bali* are on Jl. Tunjungan; *Bank Duta* is on Jl. Gubernur Surjo. All the above can change foreign currency or travellers cheques and provide a cash advance on credit or direct debit cards; some have ATMs which accept foreign cards.

Post and telecoms
A convenient **post office** is the sub-office on the corner of Jl. Gubernur Surjo and Jl. Taman Apsari. A 24-hour **wartel** is on Jl. Walikota Mustajab, near the river.

Travel agents
Reputable travel agents include *Haryono* at Jl. Sudirman 93

(☎ 532 5800); Pasopati at Jl. Raya *Darmo 1* (☎ 567 4000/5000); Pacto at the *Hyatt Regency* (☎ 531 1234); and *Vayatour* in Plaza Tunjungan I on Jl. *Basuki Rachmat* (☎ 531 9235). All the above can arrange flights, car rentals, discounted hotel rooms, and train, bus or ship tickets.

Consulates

The **British consulate** (☎ 532 6381) is at *Hongkong Bank* in Graha Bumi Modern at the *Hyatt Regency*. The **US consulate general** is at Jl. Sutomo 33.

Shopping
Market lovers should visit the dark and cramped *Pasar Pabean* off Jl. Songoyudan in the north of the city. Plaza Tunjungan on Jl. Basuki Rachmat has a department store and supermarket, a branch of *Gunung Agung*, a bookshop with a small selection of English-language books; and dozens more shops and restaurants. *Sarinah* and *Siola* are two other department stores on Jl. Tunjungan. Plaza Surabaya on Jl. Pemuda has a supermarket and more fast-food restaurants. The huge *Mal Surabaya* on Jl. Kusuma Bangsa is another shopping plaza with scores of shops.

Cultural events
The *Centre Culturel Français* on Jl. Darmo Kali holds occasional art exhibitions and other events, as does the *Goethe Institut* (Yayasan Goethe) on the corner of Jl. Embong Ploso and Jl. Taman Nasution

History

Surabaya has been an important trading port since at least the 10C. In the shadow of Majapahit in the 15C and Demak in the 16C, it had become, in the early 17C, one of three major political centres on Java, together with Mataram in central Java and Banten in the west. A VOC report dated 1620 depicts Surabaya as a powerful, wealthy city state surrounded by a canal and defended by cannon.

In the 1620s the city was repeatedly besieged by Mataram forces under Sultan Agung, and was finally defeated in 1625, its population starved into submission by Agung's policy of destroying the city's crops.

The city was seized from Mataram in 1675 by Trunojoyo from Madura, but he in turn was driven out by the VOC two years later, to whom the city was finally ceded in 1743 by Pakubuwono II.

In recent history, Surabaya was the site of the bloodiest battle of the revolution. After the Japanese surrender in 1945, the city was effectively in Republican hands until the arrival in September of a British paratrooper unit which set up base on the roof of the Oranje Hotel (now the Hotel Majapahit). A group of young Surabayans, not prepared to see their hard-won independence lost, were incensed by the actions of a group of Dutch nationalists who provocatively raised the Dutch flag on the hotel roof; the flag was torn down and one of the Dutch protagonists killed. The Surabayan youths then went on the rampage, killing Japanese prisoners and Europeans.

On 25 October, 6000 British Indian troops arrived under Brigadier-General Mallaby. Fighting soon broke out, with huge mobs attacking the Indian soldiers. The British flew in Sukarno and Hatta in a bid to restore order, and a ceasefire was arranged for 30 October. Soon after Sukarno and Hatta had departed, Mallaby was killed by a car bomb. On 4 November more British troops arrived, demanding the surrender of the local Republican leaders. When this didn't happen, the Allied forces began a bloody sweep through the city on 10 November, supported by a heavy air and naval bombardment which razed much of the city; the fighting lasted three weeks, during which more than 6000 Indonesians died and many thousands more fled the city.

Exploring Surabaya

South of the city centre along Jl. Raya Darmo is the **Museum Negeri Mpu Tantular** (open Tues–Thur 08.00–14.30; Sat–Sun 08.00–13.30), the provincial museum housed in the former Javasche Bank, built in 1921. The collection includes fossils and stone age and bronze age tools, old weaponry, wayang and topeng; ceramics and money; of note is a 19C steam-powered bicycle.

A few metres south from the museum is Surabaya's **zoo** (*kebun binatang*; open daily 07.00–17.30), best visited in the early morning (07.00–08.00) when the air is still cool and the animals are most active. Many cages are reminiscent of 19C European zoos, though an effort has been made to improve conditions for some, notably the orang-utans. The collection includes Sumatran tigers, anoa and babirusa from Sulawesi, rhino and a small herd of Bawean deer, as well as African and North American mammals; the aquarium and nocturnal house are worth a look.

Off Jl. Raya Diponegoro to the northwest of the zoo is the **Kembang Kuning cemetery**, part of which is a Dutch war cemetery, Ereveld Kembang Kuning, with more than 5000 graves.

Close to the city centre, on Jl. Taman Apsari, is a small park containing a fig tree, at the foot of which lies a small stone statue, known affectionately as **Joko Dolok** ('Brother Fatty'), inscribed with a date equivalent to 1289. It is believed to be a portrait statue of King Kertanagara, last of the Singosari kings (r. 1268–92), who was consecrated as a Buddha during his lifetime; the damaged face has been poorly restored. Other statue fragments lie nearby.

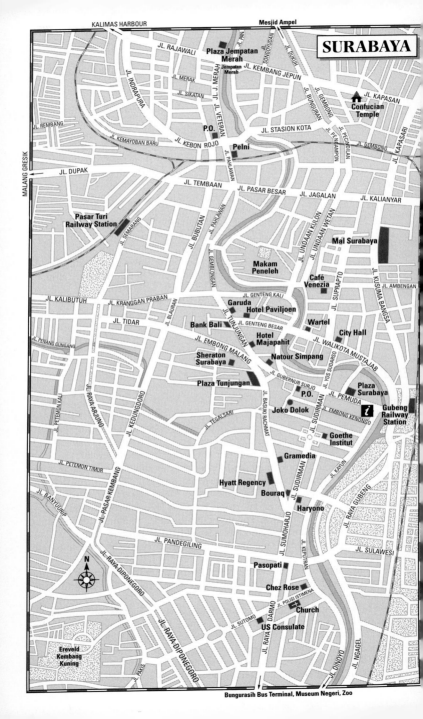

Nearby on Jl. Gubernur Surjo is a **statue of Surjo**, the city's Governor in 1945, who negotiated with General Mallaby prior to the latter's murder in October and the subsequent battle of Surabaya.

Further east along Jl. Pemuda is the **Monumen Kapal Selam**, a submarine celebrating the role of the navy, which is based in Surabaya.

On Jl. Sudirman, across the river to the north is a **statue of Sudirman**, and beyond lies the City Hall, a Dutch-era building dating from the 1920s.

Further to the northwest, off Jl. Makam Peneleh in a quiet residential neighbourhood, is an old and heavily overgrown European cemetery, **Makam Peneleh**, dating from the 19C and early 20C. Many of the tombstones have been defaced or the graves broken open.

To the north along the river is Jembatan Merah; the area on the east bank here is Surabaya's Chinatown, with dozens of old warehouses and several Confucian and Buddhist temples. The **Pasar Pabean** on Jl. Songoyudan is worth a wander; nearby is the **Mesjid Ampel** (Ngampel), the burial site of Sunan Ngampel, one of the *wali songo* who propagated Islam through Java in the 15C. It's an extremely popular pilgrimage site, entered along a narrow alley off the west side of Jl. Nyamplungan, which is lined with stalls selling religious merchandise. Also worth a visit is the *klenteng* **Dukuh**, a Chinese temple entered off Jl. Dukuh Gg. II, which on Sunday afternoons holds traditional puppet shows.

The **Kalimas harbour** (Pelabuhan Kalimas), off the east side of Jl. Kalimas Baru, has a very long wharf usually lined with many Bugis *pinisi* and wooden-hulled coastal tramps. Visitors are welcome to look.

Dotted around the city are a number of architecturally impressive, **colonial-era buildings**, among them the now rather dilapidated Gedung Soerabaiasch Handelsblod with cupolas, near the Pelni office on Jl. Pahlawan; and the Gedung Internatio on the west side of the square in front of the Jembatan Merah Plaza; other fine buildings can be seen on Jl. Jembatan Merah, Jl. Merak and Jl. Veteran.

Sights near Surabaya

Much of Surabaya's hinterland is an industrial sprawl, but there are a couple of places worth visiting if time permits.

Two **Muslim tombs** at **Gresik** attract a steady stream of pilgrims from across Java. Most important is the grave of Sunan Giri, one of the *wali songo*; the other, Maulana Malik Ibrahim, was probably a Persian or Arab trader from Iran, who died here in 1419. Both are clearly signed in Gresik, which is a grim, polluted and busy town over which hangs the odour of nearby petrochemical plants.

At a junction c 5km beyond Gresik, a road to the left signed to Bunder leads after 1.2km to Gua Pongangan (Gua Kelelawar), a cave inhabited by thousands of bats.

Birdwatchers may appreciate the important **heronry** at **Ujung Pangkah**, on the Bengawan Solo estuary a short distance north of Sedayu. To reach it, charter an *ojek* from Sedayu to Suaka Burung Ujung Pangkah (Ujung Pangkah bird reserve). From the guard post you can arrange a boat onto the mud flats.

In Paciran, further west along the coast, a road turns south to **Makam Sendang Duwur**, a mid-16C Muslim cemetery with a magnificent winged stone gateway and containing the tomb of Sunan Sendang.

The lane from the main highway climbs gently through dry limestone scenery to the village. The path to the main tomb passes through a split gateway and then an arched gate to the remarkable winged gate; they were partially restored in the 1930s. The winged gate is decorated with a *kala* face above the doorway, but in place of the usual *makaras* that flank the opening are deer. The views from the site are spectacular.

The coast road 6km west of Paciran passes through **Blimbing** and **Brondong**, two small fishing villages where scores of brightly painted fishing boats are drawn up on the roadside beach. Beyond, the road continues through the coastal towns of Tuban, Lasem and Rembang. There is little to see of interest along the coast beyond Sendang Duwur, though serious textiles enthusiasts may wish to visit the **villages round Kerek**, c 20km west of Tuban, where small amounts of distinctive *batik tulis* are still made using handwoven cotton and organic dyes.

Madura

Highlights. The reason most outsiders visit Madura is to watch the **ox racing** between July and October; otherwise, there are few specific attractions. It is, however, a tranquil island, with quiet country lanes, fine beaches and safe swimming, a low-key but important batik industry, and a people who, while brusque by reputation, are in fact friendly and welcoming to visitors.

Practical information

Travel advice
There are two **ferry routes** to the island: a regular shuttle that leaves every few minutes from Surabaya to the main port of Kamal, taking up to 1 hour; and a much longer sailing from Jangkar, near Java's northeast tip, to Kalianget at the east end of Madura (usually daily).

Accommodation
Accommodation is generally extremely basic; Sumenep has the best choice, but there are also hotels in Bangkalan, Pamekasan and Sampang, and on the north coast in a simple, friendly guesthouse.

Madura and the Madurese

The island of Madura, c 150km long and 35km wide, is a dry, rather barren, limestone island slightly larger than Bali. More than 80 per cent of the population live in villages; most are engaged in fishing or dry-land agriculture—growing peanuts, cassava, maize, rice and fruits such as salak, mango and watermelon. Salt-making and tobacco-growing are carried out on a commercial scale, and cattle are a major export.

The c 3.5 million Madurese comprise the third largest ethnic group in Indonesia; several hundred thousand have migrated to eastern Java and Kalimantan in search of better land and greater wealth. Considered rather uncouth by the Javanese, who are rather fearful of them, they certainly do not suffer fools gladly, and *carok* – murder to revenge humiliation or defend one's honour – still existed in the 1990s, though is usually hushed up from outsiders. The *carok* may result from squabbles over women, fishing or even cheating at the ox races. As a local saying explains: 'It's better to have white bones than white eyes.'

Despite this element of aggression, the Madurese are generally welcoming to visitors, and courteous without the excessive politeness found among Javanese.

While on Madura, try some of the **local food**: *soto Madura*, the local soup, is served in most restaurants; *sate laler* ('fly satay'), so-called because the size of the meat pieces is so tiny, is served with *lontong* and comes in portions of 30–35 sticks, not the usual 10; and *kaldu* is a thick soup made with mung beans.

Ox racing

The Madurese racing ox is a cross between the banteng – a wild ox found throughout Java and other Indonesian islands – and the zebu, an Asian humped ox; the best traditionally have been bred on Pulau Sapudi, an island in the Kangean archipelago to the east of Madura.

Ox racing (*kerapan sapi*) began on Madura perhaps as early as the 15C, and today is the island's major sport. From July to September regional heats are held in the island's districts, with the finals taking place in Pamekasan in late September or October.

The race is always between just two pairs of animals, each pair yoked to a wooden plough-like sled on which the jockey perches. The course is c 120m; the race lasts about 10 seconds. The animals are lovingly cared for by their proud owners; a winning ox is worth many thousands of dollars, and brings enormous prestige to its owner and village.

History

Despite its reputation today as a religiously conservative Islamic society, Madura was not Islamised until 1528, when Kediri, the last Hindu-Buddhist kingdom in eastern Java, fell to the Muslim forces of Demak. Little else is known of Madura till 1624, when Sultan Agung of Mataram conquered the island and briefly established a unified government under one princely line, based at Sampang.

From the mid-17C to the mid-18C, Madurese princes played an immensely important role in Javanese politics, twice sacking the royal court of Mataram. The island's most famous son is Trunojoyo, nephew of a lord of west Madura, Cakraningrat II (r. 1680–1707).

In 1656, Trunojoyo's father had been killed at the Mataram court by Sultan Agung's successor, Amangkurat I, who had also murdered the family of his own son's mother. As a result, the crown prince (later to be Amangkurat II) and Trunojoyo united in an attempt to depose Amangkurat

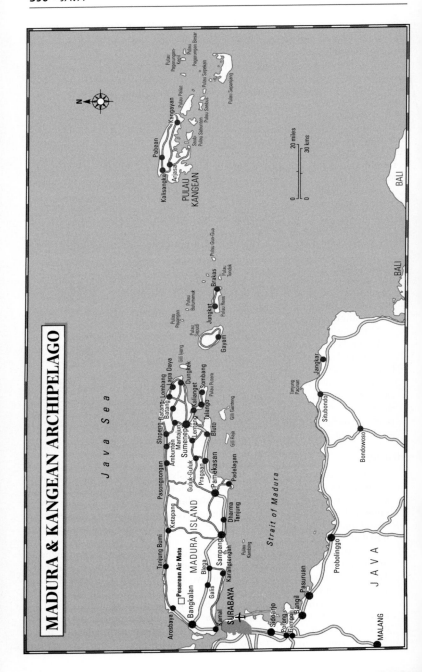

MADURA & KANGEAN ARCHIPELAGO

I; in return, Trunojoyo would be rewarded with control over all Madura and parts of eastern Java.

Trunojoyo began his rebellion in Madura in 1670, and by the following year controlled the whole island. In 1675 the revolt spread to Java, with Trunojoyo winning a string of victories and defeating the Mataram army near present-day Paciran, on the coast to the west of Surabaya.

In 1677 the VOC intervened, worried by the threat Trunojoyo caused to the Mataram court. Trunojoyo's forces were driven out of Surabaya and forced inland; in retaliation, he attacked and sacked Mataram's court at Plered, then withdrew east to Kediri with the royal treasury.

The Dutch army responded in 1678 by marching on Kediri in a concerted attack with the forces of Amangkurat II, Trunojoyo's erstwhile comrade-in-arms who had now succeeded to the Mataram throne and made his peace with the VOC. Kediri was eventually seized; Trunojoyo fled and in late 1679 was captured and taken before Amangkurat II, who personally stabbed him to death. The rebellion was over; Madura once more came under Mataram's control.

Madura's second assault on the Javanese court came under Cakraningrat IV, lord of west Madura (r. 1718–46), who had little time for the court of Mataram and instead sought to become a vassal of the VOC. By 1738, he was defying the king's orders by refusing to come to the Mataram court when summoned, but his repeated requests to the VOC to make him a vassal were refused.

By 1741, however, the VOC was reeling from a spreading Chinese rebellion, and when it appeared that the Mataram court might join the revolt, the VOC turned to Cakraningrat for help. Hoping that his long-sought request would be granted, he provided an army, which swept through east Java in 1741–42, and in December 1742 he sacked the Mataram court at Kartosuro.

The VOC, however, far from granting Cakraningrat his request, now feared his ambitions might threaten their own position; the VOC handed back Kartosuro to Mataram and broke off negotiations with Cakraningrat, declaring him a rebel in 1745. He eventually was forced to flee to Kalimantan, was betrayed, handed over to the VOC and exiled to South Africa. Ironically, his son became a vassal of the VOC in west Madura—which had been Cakraningrat's aim from the start.

In the 19C, Madurese vassals provided mercenary troops for the Dutch colonial army, but never again intervened directly in Java; it was these soldiers which in 1830 defeated Diponegoro in the Java War.

BANGKALAN

From the ferry port at Kamal, the main road runs north c 17km to Bangkalan, a small town with little of special interest, but with the only accommodation to be found on Madura's west coast.

Hotels and services

The only decent hotel is the clean ✰✰/✰ **Hotel Ningrat** (☎ 031 309 5888/ 5507) on Jl. Kholil, c 1km south of the *alun-alun*. Advance booking is advisable, as the other accommodation options in Bangkalan are awful. There are several simple, friendly *depot* nearby, serving cheap, reasonable food.

BNI on Jl. Trunojoyo changes money.

The small **Musium Pemda** (open Mon–Thur 08.00–14.00), on the east side of the *alun-alun*, has a dull and dusty collection of musical instruments, ceramics, coins, weapons, and other oddments.

Considerably more interesting is the **Pesarean Air Mata**, a cemetery near Arosbaya that contains the tombs of many of the rulers and princes of the Cakraningrat dynasty which ruled much of Madura in the 15C–16C.

From the *alun-alun* in Bangkalan, take the coast road or catch a minibus north, and turn off east at a point c 400m south of the 'Arosbaya 1km' stone. After 1km, turn right in *desa* Tengket, and follow this road 2.2km to the market of Bunten Tambegan, where the tombs are clearly signed to the left.

A donation is requested before you climb the stairway to the tombs, where a group of beggars is always to be found loitering.

The first group of tombs includes those of princes of west Madura, among them Cakraningrat V (r. 1746–c 1770) and Cakraningrat VI (r. c 1770–80), who ruled as vassals of the VOC.

Those in the section behind include that of Panembahan Cakraningrat II, lord of west Madura (r. 1680–1707); and another which claims to be that of Pangeran Cakraningrat IV (r. 1718–46)—which is doubtful, as he was exiled to the Cape of Good Hope in 1746 by his former allies, the VOC, after he mounted a rebellion across Madura.

In the highest part of the complex is the tomb of Ratu Ibu, wife of the first ruler of a temporarily unified Madura (1624–48), which is considered the most important tomb in the complex and attracts a steady stream of pilgrims who pray at the grave. Many of the tombstones are decorated with intricate carving, some in the form of *cakra*, the stylised wheel symbolising the Wheel of Buddhist Law.

An **ox-racing** stadium on the main road c 2km south of Bangkalan's *alun-alun* is used at weekends from July to October for trials and district heats for the important island-wide championship, held at Pamekasan in October.

The Bangkalan–Sampang road

The main road east from Bangkalan is generally less scenic than the north coast road. Galis, c 27km from Bangkalan, is the site of a busy, colourful livestock market on Tuesdays, with a large general market held on Tuesdays and Saturdays.

East of Blega, a lane to the north leads to the Sumber Api Alam Konang, a tiny and unexciting 'eternal flame' of gas seeping from the ground; a visit is not recommended.

SAMPANG

The capital of Madura in the 17C, Sampang today is a small, busy town and district capital, which offers the visitor little more than some decent lodgings and food.

Hotels and services

☆/☆ **Hotel Trunojoyo** (= Hotel PKPN; ; ☎ 0323 21166) at Jl. Rajawali 9, lies south of the bus terminal on the southern extension of Jl. Teuku Umar; rooms are small, but clean and good value. On the main Pamekasan road on the southeast side of Sampang is Hotel Rahmat (☆☆/☆ ☎ 0323 21302) at Jl. Agus Salim 31, with pleasant rooms.

The **bus terminal** itself lies c 900m southeast of the *alun-alun*, on Jl. Teuku Umar. *BNI* is on Jl. Wahid Hasyim, just east of the *alun-alun*; nearby is a *wartel*. The town market is c 650m east of the *alun-alun*, on Jl. Wahid Hasyim.

On the south side of Sampang is the **Gopura Madegan**, a small brick gateway dating from 1536. To find it, take Jl. Rajawali past the Hotel Trunojoyo to a T-junction. To the left here is the **ox-racing stadium**, used at weekends from July to October. To the right is Jl. Mangkubumi, which leads after 1.4km to a mosque on the right side; the old *gopura* is in its grounds, near the ornate tomb of Ratu Ibu Madegan.

Gua Lebar is a cavernous hole in the ground on a hillside above Sampang. To get there, take Jl. Pahlawan north from the Mesjid Agung, and after a few metres turn right, uphill, along Jl. Pahlawan Gg. V. While it is potentially a good viewpoint, the view itself is nothing special; still, there's not much else to do in Sampang.

The Sampang–Pamekasan road

East of Sampang the road comes down to the sea shore, here planted with mangrove; there is no beach. ☆☆/☆ **Pondok Wisata Camplong** (☎ 0323 21586/ 21570), 9km east of Sampang on a regular minibus route, has quite pleasant cottages close to the sea, but is poorly maintained with goats grazing on the litter-strewn grounds, and an uninspiring view of oil storage tanks. Nevertheless, it remains some of the best accommodation on Madura.

At a bridge c 1km beyond, the river below is filled with brightly painted Madurese fishing boats. Along the coast from here are many small stone harbours built to shelter the huge number of boats. In the busy fishing village of *desa* **Dharma Tanjung**, c 8.5km beyond Pondok Wisata Camplong, scores of boats can be seen moored along the beach front, with fish drying on racks by the roadside.

The road eventually turns inland once more, passing another 'eternal flame' (*api abadi*) signed to the left c 5km before Pamekasan; this is a highly overrated attraction which is best ignored.

PAMEKASAN
• • • • • • • • • • • • • • •

A small, friendly town which hosts the island's ox-racing championships in October each year, Pamekasan is also an important centre for local batik production.

Hotels and services

☆☆/☆ **Hotel Trunojoyo** (☎ 0323 22181) at Jl. Trunojoyo 48—on the main road into town from Sampang—has simple but adequate rooms. ☆☆/☆ **Hotel Garuda** (☎ 0323 22589), on the corner of Jl. Trunojoyo and Jl. Mesigit beside the *alun-alun*, has very cheap and basic, but cavernous rooms. Next door is the **post office**.

A 24 hour ***wartel*** is on the north side of the *alun-alun*. *BCA* is on Jl. Jokotole, off the east side of the *alun-alun*.

Pamekasan and the surrounding villages are renowned for good quality *batik tulis* made in the local style. On Jl. Jokotole, a short distance east of the *BCA*, is Batik Kristal, a small manufacturer and dealer, where you can see the different stages of *batik tulis* production, or buy local pieces; prices are high, the quality varies.

In the countryside near Pamekasan are several batik-producing villages. One group can be found round *desa* Toket, on the southwest side of Pamekasan. To find them, follow Jl. Trunojoyo south from the town and turn west across a bridge along Jl. Teja, through *desa* Teja Timur and *desa* Teja Barat; c 5.5km from the Jl. Trunojoyo junction, a lane to the south leads to *desa* **Toket**, where there are many batik tulis producers.

Another group can be found to the northwest of the town in the hamlets of *desa* **Banyumas**. To get there, take Jl. Diponegoro west from the north side of the alun-alun and after c 1km turn north (right) on to Jl. Pintu Gerbang. After a short way, the Proggo road turns off west (left); take this as far as a sign advertising '*Sentra Industri kecil batik desa Klampar*' (batik cottage industry of *desa* Klampar). Turn right here and follow this lane c 3km to *desa* **Banyumas**, where batik can often be seen hanging out to dry; further on are other batik producers in desa Klampar. Some makers produce strikingly original, modern designs as well as more traditional patterns.

Though it is interesting to visit the producers in their villages, one can more easily purchase their batik from the **Pasar 17 Agustus** on Jl. Pintu Gerbang, a market held on Thursday and Sunday mornings. It lies a few hundred metres further north along Jl. Pintu Gerbang from the Proggo road turn-off. There is a huge selection of Madurese batik, but quality and price vary hugely; let the buyer beware.

There is much at the market besides batik, including livestock and fresh produce; a visit is recommended.

The Pamekasan–Sumenep road

The road comes down to the shore briefly c 14km east of Pamekasan, where you can see many fishing boats. **Karduluk**, c 14km further on, is home to dozens of cabinet-makers, whose wares can be seen on the roadside. There is little else of interest before Sumenep.

SUMENEP

The most attractive of Madura's four district centres, Sumenep has enough of interest to merit an overnight stay.

Hotels and services

☆☆/☆ *Hotel Wijaya* (☎ 0328 62433) Jl. Trunojoyo 45–47, is Sumenep's best hotel, with decent rooms, efficient staff and a good restaurant. ☆☆/☆ *Hotel Wijaya II* (☎ 0328 62532), owned by the same family, is at Jl. Wahid Hasyim 3, a few metres west off Jl. Trunojoyo.

☆ *Hotel Safari Jaya*, on the main road c 1km south of Sumenep's centre, has cheap, basic rooms.

BCA is c 200m south of *Hotel Wijaya*. The **post office** is c 1.5km southeast of the town centre on Jl. Yani.

The **Mesjid Jami'** (Mesjid Agung), on the west side of the *alun-alun*, is noteworthy for its fine gateway.

East of the *alun-alun*, the mid-18C **Keraton Sumenep** is open to the public, and houses a few dusty cabinets of exhibits; the oddments include the skeleton of a whale washed ashore in the 1970s. Perhaps most interesting are a few damaged Hindu statues in a small grassy courtyard, which supposedly accompanied an early invasion attempt from Java. A small bathing pool, fed by a natural spring, is now full of fish. The whole place is extremely ramshackle and charmingly dilapidated.

The **Museum Daerah Kabupaten**, across the street from the *keraton* entrance, has a couple of fine carriages from the *keraton* and a few other odds and ends.

The town's main market is the sprawling **Pasar Anom Baru**, 400m south of the town centre along a lane to the east. East of the *keraton* are several 'antiques' shops, mostly owned by ethnic Arabs, which produce reproductions of traditional furniture. One is *Prima Antiques* (no signboard), on the east side of Jl. Yani; the workshops of Ahmad Abdul are in an alley off the west side a bit further on. Just beyond this alley is a narrow lane, Jl. Abdullah, with a couple of similar shops.

The graveyards of **Asta Tinggi**, c 2km west of Sumenep along Jl. Diponegoro, contain the tombs of many lords of east Madura. The lane from the main road climbs past several tombs of princes, regents and holy men to the main burial chamber, a large domed structure housing eight members of the ruling family; pilgrims come to pray here and at the more important graves in neighbouring courtyards.

On the main road 1km past the lane to Asta Tinggi, a tree can be seen on the left side, surrounded by clay pots and plastic buckets; these contain the umbilical cords of babies, left by their parents in thanks for a safe birth.

Southeast of Sumenep is the port of **Kalianget**, from where a vehicle ferry to Jangkar on Java's northeast coast departs every morning, returning in the afternoon. The road to Kalianget passes several old Dutch-built, porticoed mansions, now in poor repair and hemmed in by modern bungalows; these were once the property of salt barons. Salt production remains an important business at Kalianget, which has a processing factory.

Separated by a narrow channel from Kalianget is **Pulau Puteran**. On the south side of Talango, the main settlement overlooking the strait, is a shipyard where traditional wooden Madurese *perahu* are made. The crossing from Kalianget takes a few minutes.

Boats also depart from Kalianget to Kalisangka, the main port on Pulau Kangean, the largest island of the Kangean archipelago.

Dungkek and the eastern tip

The most scenic part of the island is found at the eastern end. Public transport is very infrequent, so it is preferable to charter a vehicle in Sumenep; the hotels can sometimes help arrange this, but otherwise it is often possible to talk to motorcycle owners in town, who may wish to supplement their income. A half-day is enough to explore the quiet lanes round Dungkek and the north coast beaches.

Take Jl. Kusuma north from the town centre, and after c 500m turn off east onto the Gapura road. The route runs through quiet villages and wooded country for c 28km to **Dungkek**, a sleepy port of whitewashed cottages, from where there are boats to the nearest islands of the Kangean archipelago.

Boat services

There are two daily boats to Pulau Sapudi, and a twice-weekly service to Pulau Raas (Thur and Sun, though liable to change), both in the Kangean Archipelago to the east. You can also charter a boat to Gili Iyang, just off Madura's easternmost tip, where there is a beach frequented by hawksbill turtles.

The road northeast from Dungkek is one of the loveliest on the island, passing through coconut plantations planted with watermelons, peanuts and mango trees. The area round *desa* Lapa Daya and *desa* Lapa Taman is especially attractive, with goats and cattle grazing by the roadside, and children and chickens running wild. In the area round *desa* Bunginbungin, cassava and peanuts are grown.

The road reaches an intersection at Lombang after 9.5km, where a right turn leads to the beach, **Pantai Lombang**, 1400m away. This is a fine spot, shaded by cemara trees; *warung* sell bowls of spicy *rujak*, washed down with fresh young coconut water. The sandy beach stretches for many kilometres in both directions, and is safe for swimming.

From the Lombang intersection, the main road continues northwest to desa Legung Timur; the coast road beyond here is in a poor state, and it is advisable to turn south to Batang-Batang unless you are travelling by cycle or motorbike.

The road to the right in Batang-Batang leads after c 16km to a T-junction in desa Mantajun; turn right here to reach the north coast and the spectacular sand dunes at Slopeng, or turn left to return to Sumenep.

The **Slopeng dunes**, fringed by lontar palms, are a popular recreation spot at weekends, when the *warung* beside the beach are busy; in midweek, the place is virtually deserted.

Slopeng to Arosbaya: the north coast road

West of Slopeng the road runs between the sea and coconut palms. At Ambunten, dozens of fishing boats can be seen moored downstream of the Ambunten river bridge.

In the market of **Pasongsongan**, c 10km west of Ambunten, a lane to the north leads to the simple ☆ *guest-house* of Pak Taufik Rahman. Anyone in the village can show you the way; he is well-known here, and any foreigner wandering through the village is assumed to be looking for him. This is the most agreeable place to stay on the north coast, and allows you to have a good look round a typical Madurese fishing community; guests must register at the police station, however, which is an irritation.

West of Pasongsongan, the scenery is less varied and interesting, passing through fishing communities and small market towns at regular intervals. Drivers should note that the only petrol station on the north coast lies just west of Ketapang, c 43km from Pasongsongan.

At the market in *desa* **Telaga Biru**, c 24km west of Ketapang, and at the adjacent **Pasar Tanjung Bumi**, c 600m beyond, are several dealers and producers of Madurese *batik tulis*.

A turning to the north, 2.5km west of Tanjung Bumi, leads to the beach of **Siring Kemuning**, a rather grubby recreation beach, considerably less attractive than Slopeng or Lombang to the east.

The road reaches Arosbaya (see above) after a further c 24km.

The eastern salient: Argopuro and Ijen

Highlights. A region of great natural beauty, the eastern salient offers the hiker or outdoors enthusiast a tremendous selection of walks and wonderful scenery. Especially recommended are the forests round **Taman Hidup** (see p 398) on the slopes of Gunung Argopuro, the wonderful **Kawah Ijen** (see p 401) and the coffee plantations of the **Ijen plateau** (see p 399) , and the three national parks at Java's eastern end—**Baluran**, **Alas Purwo**, and **Meru Betiri** (see pp 403)—all of which receive far too few visitors.

Practical information

Travel advice

A recommended route across the eastern salient from the Lumajang–Probolinggo road is via the north coast from Probolinggo. To the south here, you can visit the marvellous Yang plateau of Gunung Argopuro and a couple of old temples, then go on to Bondowoso, which is the best approach for the delightful Ijen plateau and Gunung Raung. Descend from there to Banyuwangi, from which three national parks are within easy reach: Baluran, the most accessible, on Java's northeast corner; Blambangan on the small southeastern peninsula, which is a mecca for surfers; and Meru Betiri National Park on the south coast.

Should you take the route east from Lumajang to Jember, you can visit the beach south of Jember at Watu Ulo, and be sure to stop off at Kalibaru's very pleasant guest-house.

Accommodation

Accommodation is widely available: a simple *penginapan* at Bremi, for visitors to Taman Hidup; very pleasant hotels in Bondowoso; the lovely guest-house at Blawen on the Ijen plateau; and simple accommodation in the three national parks. Kalibaru, on the Jember–Banyuwangi road, has one of the region's most delightful hotels; others can be found in Glenmore and Jagjag. Banyuwangi and Jember both have a large choice.

East from Probolinggo

Travellers needing to stay overnight in the vicinity of Probolinggo are advised instead to take the road up to **Wonokerto** (c 35km) and **Cemoro Lawang**, where there are several hotels close to the magnificent Tengger Caldera (see p 370). Probolinggo itself is a dull, busy town and cannot be recommended.

At Pajarakan, c 20km east of Probolinggo along the busy main highway, a road turns south signed 37km to **Candi Kedaton**. It is a long detour for a small temple, but the scenery is delightful, and the trip can be combined with a visit to the very beautiful Yang Plateau and Taman Hidup, high on the Gunung Argopuro massif.

Detour to Candi Kedaton and Taman Hidup

For travellers with their own transport, this is a wonderful area to explore; those relying on public transport should take a minibus as far as **Bremi** (Bermi), and charter *ojek* from there as needed. Very basic *penginapan* accommodation is available in Bremi, and it is best to spend the night there and start early the next morning on the hike to Taman Hidup.

From the coastal highway junction, follow the road south c 22km to a fork, where Bremi is signed to the left (for Taman Hidup) and Tiris to the right (for Candi Kedaton).

The Kedaton road reaches Tiris after c 10km. Follow the road straight through the village, over the river bridge, and at a fork c 500m beyond, take the left turn. After 1km, a lane to the left is signed 5km to **Candi Kedaton** (though in fact it's more like 7km). This follows the side of a valley floor, beside emerald-green paddy fields and a meandering river, and after c 5km becomes too rough for most vehicles; walk or charter an *ojek* for the final stretch to the *candi*, which lies amidst thick vegetation a few metres to the left of the track.

Candi Kedaton consists of the stone base of a small, northwest-facing temple, dated 1370 and decorated with reliefs. The inscribed date can be seen on the left balustrade. The reliefs, still generally in good condition, are from a narrative called the Arjunavivaha, telling the story of Arjuna.

From Candi Kedaton return to the Bremi/Tiris fork, and take the Bremi road to the right, through Pasar Krucil. In **Bremi** (c 10km), a guide can be hired for the c 3-hour climb to the beautiful lake of Taman Hidup on the west side of the 15,000ha **Yang Plateau Reserve** – a beautiful walk through coffee plantations, apple orchards and pine forest. With camping equipment, it's possible to climb to the summit of **Gunung Argopuro** (3088m), a further c 6-hour hike to the northeast, where the remains of 15C temples can apparently be found. Spend the night at Taman Hidup and start early the next morning for the summit, where there are sulphurous vents.

Further east along the coastal highway, the road passes through Kraksaan. In *desa* Jabung, c 6.5km further east, a lane to the south leads after 500m to **Candi Jabung**, a Buddhist temple dating from 1354.

Above the very high brick base is a very unusual temple body with curved walls; the *kala* face above the doorway is now missing, but those on the other three sides remain. The site is kept locked, but the caretaker (*juru kunci*) will soon hear of your presence from local children; a small donation is appreciated.

The main road to the east passes the huge Paiton power stations, and shortly after Besuki, the Bondowoso road turns off south – a beautiful route that climbs past tobacco fields with fine views back to the north, across the coastal plain.

The coastal road continues east through **Pasir Putih**, a rather drab beach resort which attracts crowds at the weekends, to Situbondo. Unless you are heading directly for **Baluran National Park** or Bali, there is little reason to travel this road, though there are a couple of sugar mills close to Situbondo which would be of interest to steam railway enthusiasts. The **Olean** mill (*pabrik gula Olean*), c 5km north from the *alun-alun* in Situbondo, is one of the best places to see steam locomotives working in the fields during the day; an afternoon visit is recommended. The nearby **Wringinanom** mill also uses steam engines, but the cane fields are less accessible to the visitor.

Bondowoso

An excellent overnight stop on the way to the Ijen plateau, Bondowoso has very pleasant hotels and is one of few towns in Java to stage ox races, which are held at an arena c 16km northeast of town, just past Tapen.

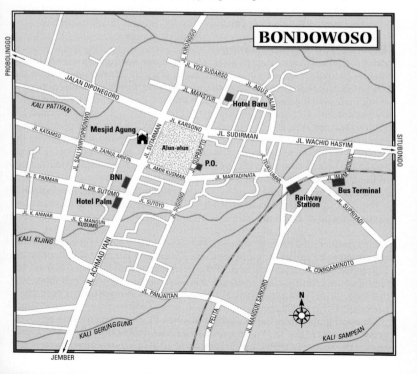

Practical information

Hotels

☆☆/☆ *Hotel Palm* (☎ 0332 2505/21201) at Jl. Yani 32 is the town's best hotel, with spotless rooms and a pool. ☆ *Hotel Baru* (☎ 0332 21474) at Jl. Kartini 26 has cheaper, good-value rooms, and is run by very amicable staff.

Services

BNI is just north of the *Hotel Palm on* Jl. Yani; nearby is a **wartel**. *BCA* is on Jl. Wachid Hasyim. The **post office** is on Jl. Suprapto, near the junction with Jl. Martadinata.

The Ijen Plateau

One of the most interesting and beautiful parts of Java's eastern salient, the Ijen Plateau is well worth a visit, if only to see the magnificent pale-green crater lake of Kawah Ijen.

From Bondowoso, take the Situbondo road northeast through Wonosari, and turn off right c 2km beyond, soon after the 'Situbondo 25km' stone. After 11km the road comes to **Sukosari**, the only settlement of any size on the way to Ijen and the last place to stock up on food and drink. Minibuses go as far as Sukosari, after which you must hire an ojek. At a junction 2km further on, the road to Ijen is to the left; straight on, the lane climbs to Sumber Wringin and the start of the climb to Gunung Raung (3332m).

Excursion to Gunung Raung

Among the most impressive of all Java's volcanoes, Raung is rarely climbed— mainly because it's a very tough walk; the glorious summit views from the edge of the jagged caldera are ample compensation, however. Climbers need to bring their own food and bivouac gear; it's a long day up and a long day down the mountain.

From Sumber Wringin, charter an *ojek* or walk for c 2 hours to Pondok Motor. From there it's an exhausting c 8–10-hour walk through forest, straight up the flank of the volcano to the open grassy slopes above. A further hour's walk brings you to the barren crater rim at c 3213m; the highest summit lies on the far side of the 500m-deep caldera, but there is no path.

Gunung Raung erupted in mid-1997, sending out ash clouds to a height of c 5km. Until 1938, there was a crater lake in the huge caldera, but this vanished in the eruption of that year.

Follow the Ijen road through desa Sukorejo, and c 20km beyond you reach a barrier (small entry fee) at the entrance to the Kalisat and Jampit coffee plantations.

Sempol, on the northwest edge of the Ijen plateau 5km further, is a small village of coffee estate workers' cottages, with several warung and small shops selling food, drink and essentials. The *Pesanggrahan Sempol* offers very basic accommodation (if it's open).

The road to the left in Sempol goes to **Kalisat** (1.2km), where there are overpriced lodgings at the ☆☆ *Penginapan Kalisat*. The road to the right a few metres beyond the Kalisat junction goes to **Jampit**, a village on the southwest side of the

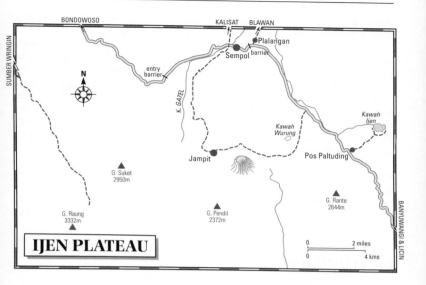

BONDOWOSO
KALISAT BLAWAN
Plalangan
Sempol barrier
entry barrier
SUMBER WRINGIN
N
K. GATEL
Kawah Ijen
Kawah Wurung
Jampit
Pos Paltuding
G. Suket 2950m
BANYUWANGI & LICIN
G. Raung 3332m
G. Pendil 2372m
G. Rante 2644m
IJEN PLATEAU
0   2 miles
0   4 kms

plateau near a small volcanic cone. It's a pleasant walk from Sempol.

Beyond Sempol, the main road comes to a barrier at a junction after c 1.7km; turn right for the Ijen crater. The road to the left passes through Plalangan, another estate workers' village, to the Blawan coffee-drying factory and the charming ☆☆/☆ *Catimor Homestay*. This guest-house is the former estate manager's house, built in the 1920s; it's the finest place to stay on the Ijen Plateau.

Beyond the factory, the road passes through Blawan estate workers' village and then descends very steeply on a rough, rocky track to some hot springs and a thunderous waterfall, fed by a mixture of hot and cold water.

The main Ijen crater road continues south through coffee plantations, c 12km to **Pos Paltuding**, the guard post where the path to the Ijen crater begins.

On the way to Pos Paltuding, a rough track to the right after 5.5km, signed to Kawah Wurung, leads eventually to Jampit, past a couple of small volcanic craters.

At Pos Paltuding, extremely basic accommodation is available at the guard post; the staff are friendly and can sell you instant noodles, rice and biscuits, tea, coffee and bottled water; there is no electricity.

Kawah Ijen

(There is a small entry fee to Kawah Ijen or Ijen crater.) From the guard post at Pos Paltuding, it's a 30–50-minute walk to the sulphur-weighing station on the way to the crater. Along the way you will pass wiry men weighed down by baskets containing up to 60kg of bright yellow sulphur, mined from the crater above.

Just above the weighing station, the path forks; the left route descends to the dam at the lake's edge (45–60 minutes), built to regulate the level of the crater lake; the path to the right climbs to the rim of the crater (c 30–40 minutes), above the sulphur-extraction area. Both routes are highly recommended, but on the former, beware of sharp, slippery scree on the descent to the dam. To the west from the dam is a fine view of Gunung Raung; on a clear evening, the sunset can be beautiful.

From the crater rim, you can descend to watch the sulphur miners at work near the shore of the pale-green lake. To the southeast are the wooded slopes of Gunung Merapi, which has its own, unseen crater behind the ridge.

Note that the Ijen crater area is potentially very dangerous: during June–August 1997 it was closed to the public after birds, overcome by poisonous gas, were seen falling into the water, and some sulphur miners suffered severe dizziness; at the same time bubbling, upwellings and a strong smell of sulphur were reported from the lake, which changed colour. The sulphur from Ijen is taken to a factory in Licin, on the Banyuwangi road, to be used in sugar refining and medicine.

The road east from Pos Paltuding to Banyuwangi (32km) is rough in places and in need of repairs. It's a scenic descent from the plateau, through forest to Licin and Glagah, and finally Banyuwangi. If relying on public transport, you must walk as far as Licin, from where there are minibuses to Banyuwangi; start early in the morning.

BANYUWANGI

A transit town for those crossing to and from Bali, Banyuwangi is a bustling trading centre with no specific attractions. The small and dull Museum Daerah Blambangan on the north side of the *alun-alun* is worth a visit only if you are extremely bored.

Practical information

Transport
Buses

Buses depart from Banyuwangi to most major towns in Java, and to Denpasar in Bali. If you are heading straight for Denpasar or the resorts of south Bali, it is considerably quicker to take a direct Banyuwangi–Denpasar bus, rather than a local bus to the ferry, followed by another local bus from Gilimanuk.
Trains

Trains leave from **Banyuwangi Baru** train station, c 100m north of the Ketapang ferry terminal. There are slow services to Yogyakarta, Malang and Surabaya, with fast connections from Surabaya to points further west.
Ferries

Ferries to Bali leave from the **Ketapang terminal** c 8km north of Banyuwangi. The crossing takes 45–60 minutes; ferries leave every few minutes.

Passenger ships. Several Pelni ships call at Pelabuhan Tanjung Wangi, the main port 1km north of the Ketapang terminal, mostly on their way to Denpasar and the islands of Nusa Tenggara. The Pelni ticket office is there, but agents in town or opposite the Ketapang terminal can arrange tickets for a small surcharge.

Hotels

Hotels in Banyuwangi. The ☎ code is 0333.

☆☆/☆ *Hotel Ikhtiar Surya* (☎ 21063/ 23631) Jl. Gajah Mada 9, c 2km from the town centre. Probably the best hotel, with large rooms and a rather quaint atmosphere.

✩✩/✩ *Hotel Kumala* (☎ 23287/23533) off Jl. Yani. Pleasant rooms round a central court with restaurant.

✩ *Hotel Baru* (☎ 21369) Jl. Haryono. Friendly place with good-value, cheap rooms and a restaurant across the street; justifiably popular with budget travellers.

Hotels outside Banyuwangi. Again, the ☎ code is 0333.

✩✩✩/✩✩ *Hotel Manyar* (☎ 24741/ 27374; fax 24742) on the highway c 900m south of the Ketapang ferry terminal. Reasonable rooms, but not especially good value.

✩✩✩✩ *Hotel Ketapang Indah* (☎ 22280/22281; fax 23597/23252) on the coast c 2km south of the Ketapang ferry terminal; swimming pool; can arrange diving trips direct to Pulau Menjangan, off the northwest coast of Bali.

✩✩✩/✩✩ *Pesanggrahan Wisata Irdjen* (☎ 24896, fax 410482, or contact the Banyuwangi office at Jl. Ngurah Rai 17; advance bookings only), at the Kaliklatak plantation, c 12km from Banyuwangi. The best place to stay in the vicinity of Banyuwangi; the price includes full board and a tour of the plantation, to see coffee, cacao, rubber and several spices including vanilla, cloves and nutmeg.

Information and services

The tourist information centre at Jl. Diponegoro 2 can provide a town plan and information about public transport; the **post office** is almost opposite. *BCA* and a *wartel* are on Jl. Sudirman

Baluran National Park

An easily accessible national park on the northeast corner of Java, Baluran has pleasant hiking trails, coastal scenery, coral reefs and accommodation, and you are likely to see banteng, feral water buffalo, monkeys and several types of deer without much difficulty, and c 200 bird species have been recorded, including the Java sparrow, a beautiful endemic species. You should bring your own food.

Take the main highway north c 36km from Banyuwangi through Bajulmati to the clearly signed entrance on the east side. On the approach, there is a good view of Gunung Baluran, the long-extinct Holocene-epoch volcano in the park.

The park is very dry and dominated by savanna and acacia trees – the latter an introduced species which is now out of control, to the detriment of animal viewing in the park. At **Bekol**, the park headquarters, is a ✩ guest-house, a watchtower and a track to the beach at Bama, where there is more accommodation.

Alas Purwo National Park

The Blambangan peninsula at Java's southeastern tip is hard to reach—and very tedious by public transport – but rewarding for those who make the effort. Surfers have long regarded the waves at Plengkung on the west side of the peninsula as some of the best in Indonesia, and the site is now well established on the world surfing circuit. For the non-surfer, this 43,500 hectare park has beautiful isolated, white sand beaches, mangrove forest and dry savanna, banteng, macaques, wild dogs, muntjak deer and turtles, as well as peafowl, hornbills and kingfishers.

Take the main road south from Banyuwangi to Rogojampi, and there turn off south (left) to Srono and Benculuk. Here, turn south towards Grajagan, and after c 10km, turn east (left) at an intersection towards Plengkung. At Tegaldlimo, after c 7.5km, turn south (right) and follow the signs, first to the beautiful sandy beach of **Trianggulasi**, and then on foot to **Plengkung**, a further c 8km; there is basic *penginapan* accommodation at Trianggulasi, and during the surfing season (May–September) at Plengkung – at least for those who book through surf camp agents in Bali. At **Sadengan**, a short walk from Trianggulasi, is a viewing tower from where you may be able to see large herds of banteng and Java deer. Much of the rest of the peninsula is rugged and inhospitable, with no easy access.

Meru Betiri National Park

On the south coast between Banyuwangi and Jember, Meru Betiri is accessible from both the east and west sides; access is easier from the east, via **Jagjag**, where good accommodation is available at the very reasonable ☆☆/☆ *Hotel Surya* (☎ 0333 36141/36041), which has a pool and tennis court.

Approaching from Banyuwangi, turn off the main highway in Rogojampi, and continue through Benculuk to Jagjag; if coming from Jember, turn off in Genteng.

In the centre of Jagjag, turn south and follow the signs to Sukamade (c 61km). Much of the route is in poor condition, though no problem for a four-wheel-drive vehicle or motorcycle. On public transport, take a bus first to Jagjag, then a minibus to Pesanggaran; from here it easiest to charter an *ojek* to Sukamade, though there are a few trucks each day.

Pantai Rajegwesi is a fishing beach east of Sukamade, but not especially attractive. In **Sukamade** itself is a decent ☆ guest-house (full board). From here you can hike to various quiet beaches and coves, including the secluded **Teluk Ijo**, and a grazing area where you may see Java deer and the occasional muntjak; staff can arrange a tour of the local plantation enclave within the park, where rubber, coffee, cacao and coconuts are grown.

The beach at Sukamade is an important turtle-nesting beach, mainly for green turtles; staff here tag female adults and release protected hatchlings into the ocean. But despite the huge numbers released, the rationale for this protected hatchery is questionable. Since the gender of turtles depends on the temperature at which they are incubated, human interference – through reburial of the eggs in a specific protected location – may unknowingly skew the results. Furthermore, although the numbers released are impressive, the turtles may in fact be weaker than they would be in normal circumstances; young turtles can live for a week on built-in food reserves, which see them through the journey to the water's edge and the first few days of ocean life; the hatchery's young are usually kept a few days in the pen for visitors to see before being released directly into the sea with most of their food reserves already used, leaving them more vulnerable.

To reach the west side of the park, which is not linked to the east section by roads within the park, you must either hike from Sukamade through the park to Bandialit, or take the main highway round the periphery from Genteng, through Kalibaru to Jember. For the walk, you must take a guide, as well as food and water; it takes two days. More than **180 bird species** have been recorded in the park.

The Genteng–Jember road

Accommodation on the main highway is available in Glenmore at the ☆☆/☆ *Hotel Minak Jinggo*, which has pleasant rooms and a pool.

In **Kalibaru**, c 23km west of Genteng, is the ☆☆ *Hotel Margo Utomo*, one of the very nicest hotels in eastern Java. Tucked away on the north side of the road behind the train station, it has a fine garden and decent rooms and restaurant. Staff can arrange rather expensive tours to nearby coffee, cacao and rubber plantations. On the east side of Kalibaru, south of the main road, are *Margo Utomo Cottages*, owned by the same hotel, and offering equally pleasant accommodation.

West of Kalibaru the road winds for c 8km through the beautiful Gumitir forest, and then passes through pine plantations, where the trees are tapped for resin.

JEMBER

Jember is a large town with all the services a traveller needs, though the hotels at Kalibaru are preferable.

Practical information

Transport
The main **bus station**, Terminal Tawang Alun, lies c 8km west of the *alun-alun* on the Rambipuji–Jember highway. A steady stream of Damri city buses runs between the town centre and the terminal, from where buses go to Surabaya, Probolinggo and Banyuwangi, as well as further afield.

Hotels
The ☎ code is 0331.
☆☆☆/☆☆ Hotel Bandung Permai (☎ 84528/84530) Jl. Hayam Wuruk 38. Cavernous and somewhat jaded, with a pool; on the west side of town.

☆☆/☆ *Hotel Safari* (☎ 81882) Jl. Dahlan 7, off Jl. Trunojoyo; has adequate rooms.
☆☆/☆ *Hotel Seroja* (☎ 83905/85580) Jl. Sudirman 2, near the *alun-alun*, has simple, pleasant rooms.
☆ *Hotel Widodo* (☎ 86350) Jl. Suprapto 74, off Jl. Yani on the southeast side of town; an excellent little low-budget hotel.

Services
BCA is on Jl. Gajah Mada. The **telecoms office** is next to the old Jami' mosque at the *alun-alun*. The **post office** is on the north side of the *alun-alun*.

Watu Ulo and Tanjung Papuma

On the coast south of Jember, just outside Meru Betiri National Park, is the charming sandy beach of **Tanjung Papuma**.

To get there, take the main highway southwest from Jember to Mangli (2.5km east of the Tawang Alun bus terminal), and there turn south, straight through Ambulu to **Watu Ulo**, a long black sand beach of little interest. Far more beautiful is the white sandy beach near Tanjung Papuma, over the headland at the west end of Watu Ulo beach, reached along a steep lane. Swimming here is safe and pleasant; in midweek, it is extremely quiet. A few *warung* beside the parking lot produce simple food; trees behind the beach provide shade. There is rather dismal accommodation at Watu Ulo, but visitors are advised to make a day trip from Jember.

Meru Betiri National Park: the west approach

In Ambulu on the Mangli–Watu Ulo road, turn east and follow the road through Wonosari and into a large rubber plantation. The badly maintained road continues to Curahnongko, from where it is c 20km to the Bandialit enclave, where there is a simple guest-house. This side of the park receives very few visitors, but there are interesting walks in the vicinity, notably to the viewing tower at the Nanggelan grazing area, and to the beach at **Teluk Meru**.

One of the stupas found on the upper terraces of Candi Borobudur

LOMBOK

West Lombok: Ampenan, Mataram, Cakranegara and Senggigi

This chapter covers Lombok's capital and its prime beach resort, **Senggigi** (see p 413), on the coast to the north. The island's greatest range of accommodation is found in these two areas, either of which makes a convenient base from which to explore the island.

THE AMPENAN-MATARAM-CAKRANEGARA CONURBATION

At some stage during their visit to Lombok, almost all visitors pass through the three towns that make up Lombok's capital, which now have merged into a contiguous, leafy, low-density sprawl linked by broad boulevards.

On the coast at the west end is **Ampenan**, the old trading port, with formerly distinct Malay and Arab quarters—the latter to the south of Jl. Yos Sudarso, the former to the north. Pertamina, the state-owned petrochemicals company, has now built a large oil storage depot to the north; behind it on the coast is a grubby fishing village with dozens of *jukung* drawn up on the beach. Today Ampenan is the most dilapidated part of the conurbation, with ramshackle warehouses and neglected shop-houses.

Mataram, in the centre, is the administrative capital, where are to be found government offices, the district hospital, the sprawling campus of Mataram University, and some of the capital's better hotels.

The modern commercial centre is **Cakranegara** (often shortened to Cakra), at the east end—a bustling, noisy district of markets and shops, restaurants and hotels, surrounded by a compact grid of quiet residential streets. Here there are several textile factories and some of the city's few historical sites.

Practical information

Transport
City minibuses

Small yellow minibuses swarm along the streets throughout the city from dawn till dusk for a fixed fare; simply flag one down going in your direction.

Cidomo

These pony traps with car wheels, are slower and more expensive round town, but are also more enjoyable.
Inter-town buses and bemo

For journeys to most destinations outside the Mataram area, **bemo** and **buses** start from Terminal Mandalika, c 3km east of Cakra; for destinations to north and south, you may be able to pick up the same vehicle nearer the city centre. Local hotel staff are usually well informed and can advise for specific destinations. From the smaller Terminal Kebon Roek in Ampenan there are **bemo** to Senggigi and other towns in the north.

Ferries

Ferries to Bali leave from Lembar, 19km south of Cakra. The shabby vehicle ferries depart every two hours for Padangbai (4–5 hours); the crossing can be extremely rough in bad weather. The *Kencana Express* is rather more comfortable for passengers but not much faster. The more expensive *Mabua Express* passenger catamaran (2.5 hours) leaves in the late afternoon for Benoa Port (an extra midday service runs during Christmas and New Year, Chinese New Year, July and August).

Passenger ships

A few *Pelni* ships call at Lembar on their regular circuits round the archipelago, usually on their way to or from Surabaya, Ujung Pandang or ports further east in Nusa Tenggara. The office at Jl. Industri 1 in Ampenan can provide tickets and the latest schedules.

Flights

Lombok's Selaparang Airport, c 2km north of Mataram via Jl. Udayana, is served by several airlines. Direct destinations include Denpasar, Jakarta, Singapore, Sumbawa Besar, Surabaya and Ujung Pandang.

Airline offices

Bouraq in the Hotel Selaparang on Jl. Selaparang; *Garuda* in Hotel Lombok Raya; *Merpati* on Jl. Pejanggik; *SilkAir* is at Senggigi.

Accommodation

Most of the more expensive hotels are in Mataram, and the cheaper ones in Cakranegara. The ☎ code is 0370.

☆☆☆☆/☆☆☆ *Hotel Lombok Raya* (☎ 632305; fax 636478) Jl. Panca Usaha 11, Mataram. Comfortable rooms, pool, friendly staff.

☆☆☆/☆☆ *Hotel Graha Ayu* (☎ 635697/ 636514; fax 626291) Jl. Ismail Marzuki, Mataram. Reasonable rooms, large pool.

☆☆☆/☆☆ *Hotel Granada* (☎ 636015/ 622275) Jl. Bung Karno, Mataram. Looking rather worn, but remains popular; has swimming pool.

☆☆☆/☆☆ *Hotel Nitour* (☎ 623780/ 625328) Jl. Yos Sudarso 4, Ampenan. Decent rooms in a mature but cramped garden.

☆☆ *Hotel Pusaka* (☎ 634189) Jl. Sultan Hasanudin 23, Cakra. Pleasant air-con rooms, but on a busy street.

☆☆/☆ *Hotel Karthika* (☎ 633129) Jl. Jayengrana 20, Cakra. Good-value rooms on a quiet street.

☆☆/☆ *Hotel Pesaban* (☎ 632936) Jl. Panca Usaha 30, Cakra. Very clean rooms round a garden courtyard.

☆☆/☆ *Hotel Wisata* (☎ 626971; fax 621781) Jl. Koperasi 19, Ampenan. The attached restaurant is popular.

☆ *Dunia Homestay* (☎ 636736) Jl. Pisang 12, Cakra. In a very lovely garden, but rather far from the centre.

☆ *Lily Homestay* (☎ 633679) Jl. Abimanyu 4, Cakra. Four simple, very clean rooms in a rather drab setting.

☆ *Oka Homestay* (☎ 622406) Jl. Rapatmaja 5, Cakra. Exceptionally friendly family; slightly shabby, basic rooms in pleasant garden.

Restaurants and cafés

Café Candung at Jl. Cendrawasih 18 has excellent food served on a charming bamboo *bale*. The simple, family-run *Warung Mobil 'Ri-lan-ida'* on the corner of Jl. Panca Usaha and Jl. Abimanyu does only a few dishes, but very well and at rock-bottom prices (open 17.00–23.00 only). *Aroma* on Jl. Palapa I is a justifiably popular Chinese-run restaurant with many seafood dishes. The food at *Putri Duyung* on Jl. Alengka is only average, but there is a pool table. In Ampenan, *Betawi Restaurant*, overlooking the main intersection, has reasonable food served on a pleasant shaded balcony; it is best in the evening when traffic is quieter.

Information and maps

The **tourist office** (Dinas Pariwisata; closed Fri afternoon and Sun) on Jl. Langko has a map of the Mataram area and Lombok, but offers little else. *Dunia Ilmu* at Jl. Yos Sudarso 108 and *Duta Ilmu* at Jl. Yos Sudarso 56 are two bookshops in Ampenan which usually stock the excellent *Lombok & Sumbawa* map by Periplus, as well as postcards. *Jabal Rahmah*, a small bookstore just east of Hotel Mataram in Cakra, frequently has the *Jakarta Post* on sale by mid-afternoon.

Money, post and telecoms

In Cakra, *Bank Danamon* (M, V) and *BCA* (M, V) offer full services, but *Bank Danamon* in Ampenan and *BNI* in Mataram change cash only. The **post offices** in Cakra on Jl. Kebudayaan, or in Ampenan on Jl. Langko are easier to reach than that in Mataram, but the latter has a poste restante service. On Jl. Langko is a 24-hour **telecoms office** with full services; there are many **wartel** in the three towns, including one in Cakra on the corner of Jl. Pejanggik and Jl. Rapatmaja.

Travel agents and tours

Bidy Tour at Jl. Ragigenap 17 can arrange flight tickets and local island tours; staff are friendly and generally efficient. **Edi Ardius** at *Lombok Mandiri*, Jl. Gunung Kerinci 4 (☎ 0370 621793; fax 636796), can organise 'alternative' tours with guests staying in private houses in Sasak villages and meeting farmers' and women's community groups; accommodation is simple, but the tours are highly rated by those who have taken them. He needs a group to make it financially viable, but is happy to provide information to lone travellers. *Perama*, at Jl. Pejanggik 66, runs regular tourist shuttle buses to Senggigi, Bangsal port and Kuta, as well as combined bus-ferry tickets to destinations in Bali. It also offers good value boat-and-bus excursions lasting 2–7 days through Sumbawa and Komodo to Flores.

Exploring the capital

The **Museum Negeri Nusa Tenggara Barat** (West Nusa Tenggara Museum; open Tues–Thur and Sun 08.00–14.00; Fri 08.00–11.00; Sat 08.00–12.00; nominal charge) on Jl. Panji Tilar Negara has an interesting assortment from the province, largely of ethnographic artifacts. Highlights in the main gallery are two bronze kettledrums, lontar palm manuscripts, a selection of unusual amulets, and a small, but very fine collection of Balinese and Sasak krises, although the best of these are rather poorly displayed behind an iron grille. Other items include fishing implements and replica boats, traditional hunting traps and agricultural tools, basketry, pottery and children's simple toys. Notable is the very widespread use of bamboo, rattan, wood and palm leaves.

Also displayed are fine examples of textiles from Lombok, Sumbawa and Bali, mostly *songket* fabrics, but among them a double-*ikat geringsing* cloth from Tenganan Pegeringsingan in Bali; weaving tools and a body-tension loom; old

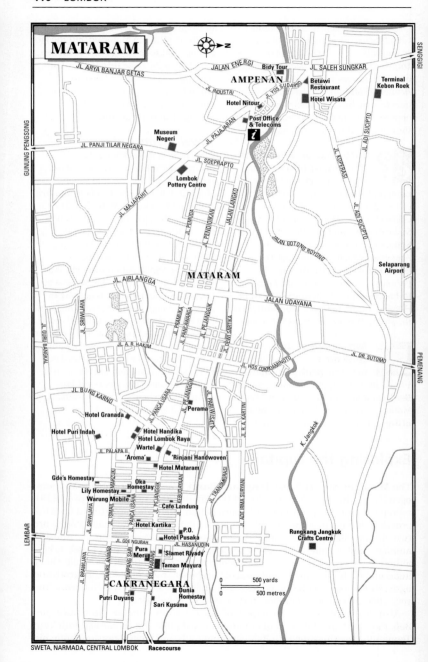

MATARAM

N

JL. ARYA BANJAR GETAS

JALAN ENERGI   Bidy Tour

AMPENAN   JL. SALEH SUNGKAR

JL. INDUSTRI   JL. YOS SUDARSO   Betawi Restaurant

Hotel Nitour   Hotel Wisata   Terminal Kebon Roek

SENGGIGI

Post Office & Telecoms   *i*

JL. ADI SUCIPTO

GUNUNG PENGSONG

Museum Negeri

JL. PANJI TILAR NEGARA   JL. PAJAJARAN

JL. SOEPRAPTO

JL. KOPERASI

Lombok Pottery Centre

JL. MAJAPAHIT

JL. PENDIDIKAN

JALAN LANGKO

JALAN GOTONG ROYONG

JL. AIRLANGGA   **MATARAM**

JL. SRIWIJAYA

JL. GURU BANGKAL

JL. PRAMUKA   JL. PANCAWARGA   JL. PELANGGIK   JL. DEWI CARTIKA   JALAN UDAYANA

Selaparang Airport

JL. A. R. HAKIM

JL. HOS COKROAMINOTO   JL. DR. SUTOMO

PEMENANG

JL. BUNG KARNO

JL. PANCA USAHA   JL. PELANGGIK   JL. PARIWISATA   JL. R.A. KARTINI

K. Jangkok

Hotel Granada

Hotel Puri Indah

Perama

Hotel Handika   Hotel Lombok Raya

JL. PALAPA II.   Wartel

'Aroma'   'Rinjani Handwoven'

Hotel Mataram

Gde's Homestay

JL. MAZUKI   Oka Homestay

JL. PANCA USAHA   JL. PELANGGIK   JL. KEBUDAYAAN   JL. TRANSMIGRASI   JL. ADE IRMA SURYANI

Lily Homestay

Warung Mobile

Cafe Landung

LEMBAR   JL. SRIWIJAYA   JL. USMAN   Hotel Kartika

P.O.

Hotel Pusaka

Rungkang Jangkuk Crafts Centre

JL. GDE NGURAH   JL. HASANUDIN

JL. BRAWIJAYA   JL. CHABIL ANWAR   JL. DUMPANG SARI   JL. SELAPARANG   Pura Meru   'Slamet Riyady'

Taman Mayura

CAKRANEGARA

0   500 yards

0   500 metres

Putri Duyung   Dunia Homestay

Sari Kusuma

SWETA, NARMADA, CENTRAL LOMBOK   Racecourse

courtly clothes; Sasak shadow puppets; and instruments used in the circumcision ritual.

A short stroll to the northeast brings you to the **Lombok Pottery Centre** (open Mon–Sat, 08.00–17.00) at Jl. Majapahit 7, the central office for a very successful community development project operating in three villages in Lombok. With assistance from New Zealand advisers, potters in these villages have improved their techniques to create a thriving industry producing beautiful handmade earthenware. Staff at the office encourage visitors, and can show a video highlighting the project's progress. Examples of the pottery are sold in the showroom.

In **Cakra** are several **weaving factories** that use shaft looms to produce a variety of textiles. While they concentrate on modern *ikat* and *songket* yardage for clothing and use bright industrial dyes, some do weave the occasional piece of *ikat* with traditional motifs and using natural vegetable dyes. *Sari Kusuma* at Jl. Selaparang 45 has some of the more original textiles, and visitors are welcome to watch the weavers; mid-morning is usually the best time to catch them at work. Others to consider are *Slamet Riady* on Jl. Tenun, and *Rinjani Handwoven* on Jl. Pejanggik.

Taman Mayura (Mayura garden and water palace; open daily; small entry fee), entered from the west, provides a moment of tranquillity amidst the bustle of the city. The large rectangular pool with its island *bale* was built in 1744 for the Balinese raja of Lombok. When the first Dutch expeditionary force invaded Lombok in 1894, they camped at Taman Mayura, where they were surrounded and defeated by the Balinese.

At the entrance to the *bale* are two small Dutch cannon, left behind from their military excursions, and round the edge of the *bale* are small statues. At the east end of the compound are a couple of Balinese Hindu *pura*.

The rather overgrown **tomb of General Van Ham**, a leader of the first Dutch expeditionary force who died in the Balinese attack, can still be seen across from the Hotel Handika on Jl. Panca Usaha; a small engraved obelisk stands inside a walled enclosure beside the road.

Directly across Jl. Selaparang from Taman Mayura is **Pura Meru** (open daily; donation to rent a sash), the largest Balinese *pura* on Lombok, built originally in 1720. Except during festivals, there is little to see except for the three high, multi-tiered *meru* to Shiva, Vishnu and Brahma.

On Jl. Peternakan, to the east of Pura Meru, is the **Selagalas racecourse**. Races are held infrequently, usually during public festivals, but are well worth attending should your visit coincide; the jockeys are young boys and the 'horses' are in fact ponies, but the spectacle is highly entertaining.

Also on Jl. Peternakan, 450m beyond the racecourse is **Pasar Ternak**, Mataram's main livestock market (Thur), which attracts farmers from all over Lombok, particularly in the weeks prior to Ramadan, when demand and prices rise.

Visitors interested in Lombok's handicrafts can go to the **Rungkang Jangkuk crafts centre**, c 2km north of Cakra along Jl. Sultan Hasanudin. In this hamlet are a dozen or more shops selling items of bamboo, rattan, lontar, wood and pandanus leaf: baskets, boxes, furniture, masks, and all sorts of trinkets. The place is geared up for tourists, and you must bargain tirelessly. In the back rooms, you can usually find the creators at work.

On Jl. Saleh Sungkar, just north of **Ampenan**'s centre, are several **curio shops** selling a few antiques and a lot of artfully aged furniture and ornaments.

East of Mataram

To reach **Taman Narmada** (Narmada water palace and gardens; small entry fee), c 8km east of Cakra, follow the main road past Sweta and the Mandalika bus terminal. Any bus or *bemo* will pass the gardens, which lie on the south side of the road; the entry gate is tucked away along the west side.

The gardens were built in 1805 by Mataram's Balinese raja, and were modelled on Gunung Rinjani, which he could no longer climb. To the casual observer, there is no resemblance whatsoever to Rinjani, but popular myth has it that the Balinese *pura* on the east side is supposed to represent the summit. The pool below it to the west represents Segara Anak, the crater lake. The wooden pavilion high on the west side represents the accommodation for the king's retinue on the mountain. The gardens are very pleasant to wander in, with swan-shaped pedalos for hire on the lake; however, there are many souvenir vendors, and at weekends Narmada can be crowded and noisy.

The road to the north directly opposite Taman Narmada leads to **Pura Suranadi**, a Balinese *pura* which would be of little interest but for its sacred eels. To find it, follow the road north, turn right after 1km and continue 4.5km further.

In the *pura* compound (donation for a sash) are some freshwater springs which gently bubble up into a couple of rectangular pools. These contain large but shy eels which lurk beneath rocks round the pool edges. They can usually be coaxed into view with fragments of hard-boiled egg, on sale at the entrance.

Just beyond the *pura* is ✩✩✩/✩✩ *Hotel Suranadi* (☎ 0370 633686), a sadly neglected Dutch colonial relic. The setting is charming, with views over rice terraces. It sorely needs a coat of paint, but has a pleasant garden with a swimming pool fed by the nearby spring, inhabited by small fish, and lined with river rocks. In midweek, you might have the hotel to yourself and be given a 50 per cent discount. The pool is open to the public, and so can be busy at weekends.

Head back towards Narmada, and at the junction after 4.5km turn north (right) once more. After 1.5km, the road divides: the left fork leads after 2km to Pura Lingsar; the road straight on runs c 3km to **Karang Bayan**, a village visited by many tour groups because of its traditional bamboo-and-timber architecture. Many of the villagers here make attractive, tightly woven baskets for sale to passing tourists.

Pura Lingsar (entry by donation) is of little visual interest; however, it is one of the most important religious sites for both the Islam Wetu Telu Sasaks and Hindu Balinese. A *pura* was first built here by Balinese in 1741; when it was rebuilt in 1878, the Balinese and Sasaks symbolised their political unity by sharing the site. The main part comprises two compounds: the northern one, **Pura Gaduh**, for the Hindus; and the *kemaliq*, to the south, for the Wetu Telu believers, which contains sacred stones wrapped in cloth, and a pool of eels.

Lying empty most of the year, Pura Lingsar comes alive during its *odalan* festival in November or December each year (the full moon of the sixth Balinese lunar month), when the two religious groups stage a 'rice war', *perang topat*, which involves hurling little leaf-wrapped parcels of rice at each other. It is part of a series of ceremonies to encourage a successful rice crop. For several days beforehand, there are bouts of ritual fighting, *peresehan*, between two Sasak men armed with rattan sticks and cowhide shields; despite the presence of a referee, these can be bruising and bloody encounters. A few days before the rice war, the sacred stones in the *kemaliq* have their cloth wrappings renewed and bouts of cockfighting are held. On the final day the main religious ceremony takes place, followed by the rice war. The tourist office can provide a programmme of events for the festival.

From Pura Lingsar, the road continues west back to Cakra.

South of Mataram

Banyumulek, south of Cakra along Jl. Gde Ngurah, is one of the villages to have benefitted from the initiative of the Lombok Pottery Centre (see above). Follow the road southward and after 6.5km turn west to the village centre, 1.2km further. Here there are numerous small showrooms displaying the wares of Banyumulek as well as other villages in Lombok: not only the distinctive flecked terracotta earthenware, but painted and glazed pots too. Most afternoons the somewhat primitive, but clearly effective kiln is filled and fired up. In the morning, there's a good chance you'll find some potters at work, or one may be happy to demonstrate the traditional methods they use.

To reach **Gunung Pengsong**, a low hill to the south of Mataram offering sweeping views to the south, west and north, take Jl. Gajah Mada south from Mataram (or, if coming from Banyumulek, turn back north then west). The busy, narrow road from Mataram passes through Pagesanan, which at the end of the 18C was one of the Balinese principalities in western Lombok; today it is just an insignificant suburb of Mataram. After 5km, turn west at the Perampuan market T-junction, and continue c 1.2km to the parking lot at the foot of the hill (entry by donation).

It is a 10–15-minute climb up an easy path to the summit, where there is a Balinese *pura*. This is only of real interest during the temple's *odalan* festival, on the Tuesday of Prangkabat, the 24th week of the 30-week, 210-day Pawukon calendar (the next dates for this are 31.10.00; 29.5.01; 25.12.01; 23.7.02, 18.2.03, 16.9.03, 13.4.04). The panorama over the coast, fields and nearby hamlets is excellent; Gunung Rinjani can be seen on a clear day, and the sky at sunset can be spectacular.

SENGGIGI

Lombok's main beach resort, on the west coast c 9km north of Ampenan, is a suitable alternative to the Mataram area for visitors seeking a base from which to explore the island. Here are most of Lombok's best hotels, spread along a pleasant sandy beach.

From the busy five-way junction in the centre of Ampenan, take Jl. Saleh Sungkar north through flat countryside. On the edge of the city are two huge **Chinese cemeteries**; some of the tombs are recent, but many date from the anti-Chinese pogrom which swept through much of Indonesia in 1965–66 as part of the anti-communist backlash to the September 1965 coup attempt.

The road beyond passes through coconut plantations, occasionally alongside the sea, and 5km from Ampenan passes the southernmost of the Senggigi resort hotels. The heart of Senggigi is a further 4km, though developers are slowly but relentlessly filling in the gaps with more and more hotels.

Makam Batu Layar, c 2km before central Senggigi, is the tomb of one of the missionaries who brought Islam to the island. The shrine lies up the slope to the east of the road at a headland with good sea views. **Pura Batu Bolong**, on the next airy promontory 1km further, is a diminutive Balinese shrine close to the water's edge. The gatekeepers here have no scruples about demanding ridiculously high donations; take no notice, and give what you believe is merited.

The heart of Senggigi comprises a string of closely packed hotels, restaurants, dive operators, money changers, travel agents and shops, spread along c 1.5km. The resort has a chequered history, involving land-grabbing by government officials and greedy speculators at the expense of often untitled villagers who had lived there for decades, but today is a relaxed and pleasant – if not outstanding – holiday centre.

The beach is generally good, although not very wide, and in the peak season (July–August and Christmas) Senggigi appears to be a thriving, vibrant resort town. For much of the rest of the year, however, it is extremely quiet, many hotels are nearly empty, and the place takes on a rather mournful air; huge discounts on accommodation are available, especially during the rains (January–March).

Practical information

Transport
There are frequent public *bemo* to Mataram, and always drivers looking for passengers to charter privately. Several agents have Suzuki jeeps and small motorcycles for rent; the price varies with demand and bargaining skills. For flights, the *SilkAir* office is in central Senggigi, and tickets for the *Mabua Express* catamaran to Bali can be bought from agents here, who also sell tourist shuttle bus tickets to Mataram, Lembar, Kuta and Bangsal.

Accommodation
Bookings are advised for July–August, Christmas and New Year. The ☎ code is 0370. Distances are from central Senggigi.

☆☆☆☆☆ *Sheraton Senggigi Beach* (☎ 693333; fax 693140) central Senggigi. Beautiful design with outstanding pool. Full facilities.

☆☆☆☆/☆☆☆☆ *Holiday Inn Resort* (☎ 693444; fax 693092; e-mail: hirlo@mataram.wasantara.net.id) c 4km to the north. Extensive grounds with large pool, pleasant rooms, and a full range of facilities.

☆☆☆☆/☆☆☆☆ *Jayakarta* (☎ 693045–9; fax 693043) 4.5km south, nearer Ampenan than Senggigi. Modern and spacious, with pool and pleasant garden.

☆☆☆☆/☆☆☆☆ *Lombok Intan Laguna* (☎

693090; fax 693185) central Senggigi. Rather bland international resort hotel with full range of facilities.

✩✩✩✩✩/✩✩✩✩ *Senggigi Aerowisata* (☎ 693210; fax 693200/693339; e-mail: hsa@mataram.wasantara.net.id) central Senggigi. Prime location with tasteful rooms, mature garden and many sports facilities.

✩✩✩ *Nusa Bunga* (☎ 693035; fax: 693036) c 5km to the north. Delightful, low-key hotel with large garden, small pool, beach and friendly staff.

✩✩✩ *Maskot Berugaq Elen Cottages* (☎ 693365; fax 693339) central Senggigi. Spacious bungalows in huge, quiet garden with beach access; pool.

✩✩ *Santai Beach Inn* (☎ 693038) in Mangsit, c 2.5km to the north. Charming setting in magnificent garden; simple rooms, often full.

✩ *Traveller Hostel* (☎ 693414) c 4km to south. Extremely basic rooms in relaxed setting; quiet beach, bicycles and boats; pool.

Restaurants and cafés

The menus at most of Senggigi's cafés and restaurants are full of fine-sounding Western dishes, but they can be disappointing. *Kafe Wayan*, 1km south of central Senggigi, is reliable and does excellent cakes and coffee. *Kafe Alberto* at the Pasar Seni (art market) provides fairly authentic Italian pizzas, and there are several other cafés and food stalls nearby that offer seafood and Chinese cuisine. *Kafe Espresso*, close by on the main road, makes good but overpriced coffee; don't expect much from the food. The *Alang-alang bar* and restaurant, c 3km north, has a pleasantly secluded beach-side location.

Money, post and telecoms

Bank Danamon and *BNI* accept travellers' cheques and change cash. The former accepts credit cards but at huge cost. The **post office** is in central Senggigi and there is a small 24-hour **telecoms office** opposite the Sheraton

The coast road

The road continues north from Senggigi along the spectacular coast, climbing steeply from one narrow cape to the next, with sharp descents to the bays in between. Some of the finest views are from **Tanjung Rumbeh**, a dramatic headland c 9km north of central Senggigi; the sandy bays to the north—Malimbu and Nipah—can be seen, separated by another sharp promontory, Tanjung Serombong. Two islands just offshore, **Gili Trawangan** and **Gili Meno**, are also in sight.

Winding inland through small hamlets and coconut plantations behind the bays, the road emerges on the coast again at **Tanjung Serunggal** after c 8km, from where all three small islands lying close by can be seen together with Pantai Sira, the fine sandy beach on the mainland opposite Gili Air. The road then descends gently to the intersection in Pemenang.

1.2km to the left here is the small port of Bangsal, from where boats depart to the three islands—Air, Meno and Trawangan (see p 420).

Central Lombok: Mataram to the east coast

The main road running east from Mataram through Kopang and Terara divides at Masbagik, forking southeast to Selong, the administrative centre for east Lombok, and northeast to Labuhan Lombok, the main east coast harbour. This is the spine of Lombok's road network and the busiest stretch on the island. For the visitor, it usefully links a network of minor roads to interesting, if minor sites: villages of weavers and artisans, waterfalls and natural springs, ancient tombs and areas of tremendous natural beauty, some of them offering simple but delightful accommodation and providing a glimpse of Sasak village life.

For exploring some of the minor roads, the Periplus *Lombok & Sumbawa* map is generally accurate, and is strongly recommended.

Practical information

Travel advice
The visitor is advised to rent transport in Senggigi (or Mataram) to explore the back roads of this area; this enables you to spend less time on the rather dull and sometimes busy main highway. It is possible to reach the sites listed below by public transport, but it can be frustratingly slow.

Accommodation
The best choice of accommodation in central Lombok is found in the pretty villages of Tetebatu and Sapit. Alternatives are a simple homestay at Lendang Nangka and beach-front cottages in the quiet village of Labuhan Haji. Almost all lodgings in this section are cheap and basic.

Take Jl. Selaparang east from Cakranegara, and continue past Sweta and Narmada. Public buses and bemo depart regularly from the Mandalika terminal, east of Sweta. The Japanese-owned ✫✫✫✫✫/✫✫✫ *GEC Rinjani Country Club*, with an 18-hole golf course and comfortable accommodation, lies to the north c 5km east of Narmada.

At Terara, c 29km east of Narmada, a road to the north leads to Montong Betok, and then east to Kotaraja. Between these two villages a lane climbs northwards to **Otak Kokok Gading**, a natural spring in a pleasant forest setting; its water is believed locally to have curative powers, but the bathing pools are not terribly inviting.

From the intersection in Kotaraja, the road south leads after 1.8km to **Loyok**, a small hamlet producing crafts of bamboo and basketry. In nearby **Rungkang**, 550m east of Loyok, the villagers make charming but simple pottery, dark and unglazed, but with a rich sheen.

Tetebatu

The road north from the Kotaraja intersection leads after c 3.5km to Tetebatu, a village of no special interest except that the surrounding countryside is of exceptional beauty. The terraced rice fields and magnificent views of Gunung Rinjani on a clear day have led to a dozen or more guest-houses and simple *penginapan* opening in the area.

The cool climate of Tetebatu led to it becoming a popular health spa during the early 20C, when a Javanese doctor named Soedjono built his house here. This is now the rather shabby ☆☆/☆ *Soedjono Hotel*, at the road head 1.3km north of the village's main junction; the grounds round the original house are cluttered with ugly newer rooms, and there is a slight air of decrepitude.

If you wish to stay in the Tetebatu area, the rustic ☆ *Mentariku Bungalows*, 1.6km east from the main junction, are recommended for the excellent views of Rinjani and friendly staff, not for the rooms. ☆ *Lentera Indah*, just 250m east from the same junction, is reasonable, and ☆ *Wisma Rambutan*, 750m further east at the Kembang Kuning intersection, has a pleasant garden. All these are very basic places.

Tetebatu is a good area for hiking, with several waterfalls and scenic footpaths in the area. The largest of the waterfalls is **Jeruk Manis**, c 6km north of the Kembang Kuning intersection (the last 1.5km on foot only). However, there have been muggings in the area in the past, so check the current situation with local guest-house staff.

Lendang Nangka

From the Kotaraja intersection, the road east leads after 3.5km to Lendang Nangka, a small village which, like Tetebatu, has become a tourist destination of sorts simply because there is accommodation here. There is nothing particular to see, but for interested visitors it offers the surprisingly rare chance to stay in an Indonesian (and more specifically, Sasak) village. Recommended is ☆ *Haji Radiah Homestay*, on the north side of the road 150m west of the main intersection. Set up by the eponymous Haji Radiah, a local teacher who was keen to show his village to curious outsiders, it has extremely simple rooms, though smarter new ones have been built in the centre of some paddy fields nearby. The family can suggest numerous walks in the neighbourhood and give tours explaining the local farming crops and methods. Comforts are few, but the villagers are friendly and the experience is recommended. Two other guest-houses, *Pondok Wira Homestay* and *Sasak Homestay*, a few metres further west, are rather grim and best avoided.

Pringgasela

East of Lendang Nangka, a lane branches off northeast to Pringgasela, c 4km, an important but low-profile weaving centre. Along each of the roads from the central Pringgasela intersection are small showrooms with a selection of locally woven fabrics. Almost all textiles produced here are high-quality, brightly dyed *songket* woven on body-tension looms, but a few pieces of plain *ikat* can be found. The weavers can be found in the alleys behind the streets; visitors are free to wander, but often showroom staff are happy to give you a tour of the processes. *Songket Lombok*, a shop just east of the intersection, has friendly, relaxed staff.

Masbagik Timur

South of Pringgasela, the road rejoins the main east-west highway at Hikmah. Turn west from here c 1km to **Masbagik Timur**, where a string of hamlets sprawls for 750m along a lane off the south side of the road, producing a huge range of pottery. This is one of the three potters' communities to receive support from the Lombok Pottery Centre (see p 411).

From the market of Masbagik, 1.3km further west on the main highway, a road runs southeast to **Selong**, the undistinguished capital of East Lombok, and on to Labuhan Haji on the coast.

Labuhan Haji

This small fishing village, c 15km from Masbagik, has quiet and clean beachfront accommodation at ☆ *Pondok Meliwi Beach Cottages*; there is safe swimming and snorkelling off the black sand beach.

From Labuhan Haji a quiet road runs south along the coast to Tanjung Luar (see p 430).

Sapit

Continuing east from Masbagik or Hikmah, the main highway comes to Aikmel; here it turns sharply southeast, but a lane branches off northeast to Swela, a small but busy market. In the centre of Swela, a road turns off north to the beautiful rice-growing area round Pesugulan and Sapit, 5km from Swela on Gunung Rinjani's southeastern slopes. ☆ *Hati Suci Homestay*, 450m east of Pesugulan on the Sapit road, and *Hati Suci Indah*, owned by the same family, a short way beyond, have some of the finest panoramas of any accommodation on Lombok. The rooms are clean but simple, and the views north to Gunung Rinjani and east to Sumbawa and Lombok's coast are magnificent.

From Pesugulan, the road climbs onward through forest towards Sembalun Bumbung (see p 424).

Selaparang

To find the **tombs of the Selaparang kings**, the Sasak princely line which ruled eastern Lombok in the 16C–17C, take the road southeast from the junction in Swela and turn off left after 1km along a narrow asphalt lane. After 3km, a tomb known as **Makam Tanjung** is rather indistinctly signed on the west side of the road, 150m along a grassy track. Here are two graves inside a walled enclosure. Far more impressive is the main group of tombs, **Makam Selaparang**, 450m further south on the east side of the lane.

The graves, consisting of multi-tiered bases of river rocks with Islamic grave markers, have clearly been rebuilt in recent times, but local tradition has it that some of those buried here are the Selaparang kings. More fanciful are the local beliefs that the large one in the northeast corner, with four inscribed markers, is that of Arung Palakka of Bone, Sulawesi, and that another belongs to Gajah Mada.

Beyond the graves the lane rejoins the main road down from Swela, which descends to the main east–west highway at Pringgabaya. From here, Labuhan Lombok lies to the northeast (see p 424).

North Lombok and Gunung Rinjani

Practical information

Travel advice

There is a choice of two parallel routes from Mataram to Pemenang, the small market town which marks the approximate start of the north coast; for details of the coastal route through Senggigi and beyond, see p 415. The inland route, equally scenic, climbs up a forested pass and then descends in a series of sharp curves to the valley floor and Pemenang.

Accommodation

In general, the accommodation found along the coast is very simple and cheap; the exception is the *Oberoi*, one of Lombok's finest luxury hotels. The three gilis – the small islands offshore from Pemenang – have several dozen *losmen* and bungalow groups; on the coast road there are rooms at Jambianom and Labuhan Pandan; inland there is a choice of places at Senaru and at Sembalun Lawang, at each end of the Gunung Rinjani hiking trail.

The inland route

From Mataram, take Jl. Cokroaminoto north c 4km from Bumi Gora, the governor's office on Jl. Pejanggik, to reach **Gunung Sari**, a village with a thriving trade in bamboo products. Workshops line the main street, churning out simple and often rather uncomfortable hand-made chairs with amazing precision and speed. Beds, tables and couches, from many different varieties of bamboo, are bound with rattan threads. Woven bamboo walls and floors are assembled, together with cheap roofing from sugar-palm and coconut-palm fronds or the better quality *alang-alang* grass; roofs made from the latter can last up to 15 years if the roof pitch is sufficiently steep and they are exposed to the sun. These can be seen all over Lombok.

Beyond Gunung Sari the road starts climbing, passing through Sideman, where there is a busy Monday market, then running beside a boulder-filled stream on the east side, glimpsed through shady fruit trees and palms. At the **Pusuk Pass**, c 10km beyond Gunung Sari, there is a restaurant with a fine view north to the sandy coastline of Pantai Sira. The forest at the pass is a popular haunt for scores of bold macaques, who get fat on hand-outs from travellers. The road beyond descends to the flat cultivated valley floor at Pemenang, c 10km further.

GILI AIR, GILI MENO AND GILI TRAWANGAN

These three small islands, hugely popular with young Western tourists attracted by the simple living, white sand beaches and colourful fringing reefs, are just a short boat ride from the shore. In July, August and at Christmas it is not unusual to find all rooms full, and visitors may need to spend a night on the beach; in the low season, however, there may be just 30 tourists on Gili Meno. The inconsistencies of tourism are such that many of the locals prefer the reliability of seaweed cultivation over the seasonal tourist trade.

Each island has roughly similar facilities: simple raised bungalows, traditionally built of bamboo and timber with roofs of *alang-alang* grass, but increasingly of brick, concrete and tile. Restaurants and *warung* offer standard tourist fare and show recent video releases to attract customers; dive operators run beginners' courses and lead dives on the local reefs, which generally are not outstanding. Money changers, postal agents and *wartel* provide services at inflated prices.

Gili Air is the most popular with day trippers because of its proximity to Bangsal; it also has the largest permanent local population. **Gili Meno** is the quietest of the three. Much of its fringing reef is now used for seaweed farming, and swimming is only really good at high tide; the best sandy beach is found along the southern part of the east shore, while snorkelling is best on the north side. Furthest out is **Gili Trawangan**, the largest and liveliest island. Several dive operators are based here, and there is a fine beach on the northeast side. A walk round the island's perimeter track takes 1–1.5 hours; a sunset stroll to the summit of the low hill at the south end can provide fine views across to Bali's Gunung Agung.

Practical information

Transport

Boats leave from Bangsal, the small port at Pemenang, where there are money changers, cafés, persistent T-shirt vendors, souvenir shops and secure storage for motorcycles. Cars parked here overnight are not necessarily safe; they are best left in Senggigi or Mataram.

There is a choice of **public boat**, **private charter**, or usually a twice-daily **shuttle boat** which calls at each island.

The private charters depart on demand, and are the most expensive. The public boats are cheapest, but wait for the requisite number of passengers to turn up – usually between 15 and 30; your name is put on a list, and you must then await an announcement, so – for Gili Meno especially – this can be a lengthy wait. The scheduled shuttle boat should depart at 10.00 and again at 16.30, visiting each island in turn. On the islands, transport is limited to the odd **bicycle** and *cidomo*; all can be easily covered on foot.

Accommodation

With a dozen or more places to stay on each island, the choice appears large. In reality, most are very similar, with quality of staff and food being the major distinguishing features; personal recommendations from recent visitors can be useful. The area ☎ code is 0364. On Gili Air, ✰✰✰/✰✰ *Han's Bungalows* at the northeast corner, and ✰✰✰/✰✰ *Gili Indah*, on the south coast near the landing point, are both better than the average. On Gili Meno, ✰✰✰ *Gazebo Meno* (☎ 635795) has pleasant air-conditioned bungalows and a restaurant in a spacious garden of coconut palms; ✰✰ *Penginapan Janur Indah* has attractive, simple bungalows and friendly staff; ✰ *Pondok Meno*, near the northeast corner, is extremely quiet and low-key, with basic bungalows in an unkempt garden. Many of Gili Trawangan's bungalows are in cramped compounds on the southeast side. More spacious are those on the south coast, which include ✰ *Sunset*, ✰ *Pondok Santi* and ✰ *Dewi Sri*; the beach here, however, is covered with coral fragments and swimming is awkward because of seaweed cultivation offshore.

The north coast

Continuing north along the coast from Pemenang, the road passes after 2.5km an earth road on the left to **Tanjung Sira**, a small peninsula of coconut palms with a long but narrow white sandy beach, deserted save for a few fishing boats.

One of Lombok's finest hotels, the ✰✰✰✰✰ *Oberoi* (☎ 0364 638444; fax 632496; e-mail: oberoi@indosat.net.id) lies on the west side of Tanjung Medana, 2km further on. Elegant furnishings, enthusiastic service from local staff and, if you wish, a villa with its own swimming pool, make this an exceptional hotel; prices start at c US$300.

In the village of **Jambianom**, 2km further, is the laid-back ✰ *Club des Explorateurs* (☎ 0364 626879), run by the irrepressible Yves Magnin. The simple rooms, just behind the beach, are often filled with European groups, but in the low season walk-in guests are welcome. The friendly family will include you in their trips to the market or to their neighbours, lend you their small boat or suggest other excursions. This is a very good opportunity to experience Sasak village life, and the beach is excellent for swimming.

The shady road continues northeast through the busy market at **Tanjung**, and 7km beyond reaches a right turn to the **Tiu Pupus waterfall**, along a rough road. In the rainy season this has a delightful but chilly swimming pool at the foot. 2km further along the main road is another turning signed to the **Gangga waterfall**. This asphalt lane climbs gently through hamlets and wooded hills for 9km to the poorly signed parking lot, from where it is an easy walk to the falls; it is not, however, as impressive as Tiu Pupus lower down.

Segenter

The coast road continues through increasingly open terrain of rice and maize fields, with views to both the sea and the Rinjani massif. Just before Sukadana, and 28km beyond the Gangga waterfall turning, an indistinct sign indicates a track south to Segenter, 2.5km, a village of Wetu Telu adherents which has maintained very traditional ways of house construction and layout. The rough track passes the village primary school, a simple bamboo structure on the left side, and just beyond is the entrance to the village enclosure on the right.

One of the most interesting villages in Lombok, Segenter's houses are built of bamboo with pitched roofs of *alang-alang* grass, and are arranged in tidy rows, each pair sharing a *bale* which stands between them. An amicable guide will usually emerge to show visitors round and answer questions in halting English; few of the older villagers speak even *bahasa Indonesia*. The village is impeccably tidy compared to most in Lombok, but this should not be taken as a sign of prosperity; this is a dry part of Lombok, drought is a persistent threat, and the village relies on maize and cassava as well as rain-fed rice, while livestock are kept in pens on the village perimeter. You will be asked politely for a donation as you leave.

At Anyer, the main road turns inland, and 5km beyond, a lane branches off to the right to Senaru, the starting point for the northern approach to Gunung Rinjani.

Senaru and Gunung Rinjani

A good road, steep in places, ascends the lower slopes of Gunung Rinjani to Batu Koq and **Senaru**, the enclosed village compound at the road head. Senaru has kept its traditional architecture, and is similar to Segenter, though considerably smaller. Visitors are welcome to wander round, and someone will probably come forward to invite a donation; the money is spent in an egalitarian way on community projects.

Beside *Pondok Senaru*, a lodging 1km before the road head, a footpath descends to the charming **Sendang Gile waterfall**, where two main cascades and many smaller ones tumble from the cliff face through a tangle of ferns and creepers. Far more dramatic—and much better for swimming—is the magnificent thunderous torrent of **Tiu Kelep waterfall**, a 20-minute walk upstream.

To find it, climb back up the steps from Sendang Gile waterfall towards the narrow irrigation channel, and take a footpath to the left several metres below the point at which this channel emerges from a small tunnel. Cross the river on the concrete aqueduct and follow the channel upstream to where it joins the river, then follow the river's right bank. At one point it may be necessary to wade through the water, but the path then continues along the same bank to the falls. Beware of very slippery, slime-coated rocks near the falls. The pool beneath provides a most invigorating swim.

At the end of the asphalt above Senaru, a track continues due south; this is the start of the path to **Gunung Rinjani**'s caldera rim.

Climbing Gunung Rinjani
There are at least three routes up to Gunung Rinjani, of which the path from Senaru is the most frequently used. While it is not the easiest route to Rinjani's summit, which is best approached from Sembalun Lawang to the east (see below), it is the simplest way to the caldera rim, from where there is a magnifi-

cent view over the lake, Segara Anak, and the young active ash cone, Gunung Baru. A third approach – from the south – is rarely used these days.

From Senaru to the rim is a 5–7-hour hike of gradual but relentless ascent, beginning through fields of shoulder-high *alang-alang* grass, then for much of the rest of the way through shady forest, with a couple of extremely tatty, litter-strewn shelters en route. If you wish to go only to the rim, it is worth climbing up one day, then rising early the next morning for the sunrise before descending again. While a porter is very useful, the path to the rim is obvious and a guide is not necessary.

From the caldera rim to the summit is another whole day of strenuous walking and scrambling, via the caldera floor and soothing hot springs; a guide is essential. The view from the summit (3726m) – the highest point in Indonesia outside Irian Jaya – can be sensational on a clear day, but the final steep scramble through soft ash and sand is exhausting and definitely not enjoyable.

For a round trip from Senaru to the summit and back, you should allow at least three days: day one from Senaru to the caldera floor; day two to the summit and back to the caldera floor; and day three back to Senaru. Alternatively, to avoid retracing your steps, it is possible to descend to Sembalun Lawang (see below), if you arrange this with your guide prior to departure; you will then have to pay his transport costs back to Senaru. If you have time, an extra day allows for an exploration of the caldera itself.

Porters or guides and some camping equipment can be hired through the guesthouses near Senaru. Although possible, it is not advisable to climb Rinjani in the rainy season, since the path through the forest to the caldera rim can be slippery in places and blocked with fallen trees; more importantly, the extremely steep path down from the rim to the caldera floor becomes potentially dangerous; there have been fatalities. There is also a greater chance of clouds obscuring any views.

Accommodation in Senaru

There are at least four very basic guesthouses on the road between Batu Koq and Senaru, offering similar facilities. ☆ *Pondok Senaru* has a pleasant view of Sendang Gile waterfall, but is 1km below the road head, adding unwanted distance to the Gunung Rinjani trek. ☆ *Bale Bayan*, with simple rooms round a garden, is closest to the mountain and is run by a friendly young couple.

Bayan and the northeast

Back on the main coast road, 1km east of the Senaru turn-off, is the small village of **Bayan**, and an interesting old mosque, **Mesjid Kuno Bayan Beleq**, on the north side. One of Lombok's oldest mosques, it is built with bamboo walls and a magnificent bamboo shingle roof supported by coconut palm pillars, all on a base of river rocks. Surrounding it are similar bamboo structures housing old graves. The mosque is said to be at least 300 years old, though clearly it has been renovated recently.

The main road divides at a junction 9km east of Bayan, just after crossing the small gorge of the Kali Putih, the outflow stream for Gunung Rinjani's caldera lake. To the south (right) lies **Sembalun Lawang**, the recommended starting point for a climb to Gunung Rinjani's summit (see below), while to the left the road continues round the coast.

Sembalun Lawang

The road to Sembalun Lawang climbs to a high plateau lying between the main massif of Gunung Rinjani to the west and a lower range to the east. After 5km, a track to the right leads to a small waterfall; beyond, the road narrows and begins to climb very steeply c 11km to Sembalun Lawang.

Just before the centre of the village are ☆ *Pondok Sembalun Bungalows* on the right side, the most pleasant place to stay, with clean, simple rooms in a beautiful setting surrounded by hills. The track to Gunung Rinjani starts from the entrance; equipment and guides can be hired here, though rental costs are much higher than at Senaru.

Even if you do not wish to climb Rinjani, there are plenty of very pleasant walks in this area. Recommended is the airy climb up the ridge of Gunung Sengkor on the east side of Sembalun Lawang, or, for the very adventurous, the steep-sided Gunung Bau behind the bungalows.

From Sembalun Lawang, the road runs south c 3km across the flat plateau to Sembalun Bumbung, past fields planted in the rainy season with rice, and in the dry with garlic and onions. From there it climbs c 5km to a narrow craggy pass, which periodically falls victim to landslides. If the way is clear, and bridges further down have not been washed away, you can follow this extremely picturesque route all the way south on asphalt road through natural forest and plantations c 11km to Pesugulan and Sapit (see p 418).

Continuing round the coast, the main road comes down to the sea at Obel-Obel after c 8km, and runs beside the black sand beach for much of the next 11km before climbing inland once more. Offshore can be seen the flat, uninhabited islands of Gili Lawang and Gili Sulat.

Beyond Sambelia the road returns to the coast, passing through coconut plantations. ☆☆/☆ *Pondok Siol* in Labuhan Pandan, c 4km beyond Sambelia, has simple bungalows beside a quiet beach. Staff here can arrange snorkelling and camping trips to the nearby islands of Gili Petagan, Gili Lampu and Gili Bidara.

The next settlement of any size is **Labuhan Lombok**, on a broad sheltered bay c 15km to the south. This is a busy market town and fishing port, and the main harbour on Lombok's east coast. Along the water's edge are rows of raised stilt houses of Bugis origin, and you may see here large wooden *pinisi* under construction.

Ferries to Sumbawa
Vehicle ferries to Poto Tano depart from Kayangan port, c 3km from the centre of Labuhan Lombok at the end of a curving peninsula. Boats depart every hour from 06.00 to 20.00.

From Labuhan Lombok, a fast road leads west across central Lombok back to Mataram.

South Lombok

South Lombok has some of the island's most beautiful coastal scenery, with clear seas and bright white sandy beaches. There are two main roads to the south coast from Mataram, though travellers equipped with a good map and their own transport can explore any number of back lanes on the way there.

Practical information

Travel advice

The most frequented route lies through Praya and Sengkol to Kuta, where most of the south coast's accommodation is to be found. In the far southeast is the flat, dry Ekas peninsula, difficult to reach by road. The southwest peninsula is much more accessible, with a generally good road running along its northern coast.

Accommodation

The main place to stay in southern Lombok is Kuta, a small coastal village with half a dozen rather rickety lodgings. Nearby is the very comfortable Novotel; other up-market resorts are under construction in the vicinity. Further west, there are rooms at Selong Belanak. On the southwest peninsula, simple rooms are available at *Sekotong Indah Cottages* and on the small island of Gili Nanggu.

The southwest peninsula

This is an area offering fine coastal views, small fishing hamlets and white sandy beaches; offshore are three easily accessible islands, which on a weekday you would probably have to yourself. From Lembar to the end of the track is c 56km; beyond is a beach popular with surfers. *Bemo* operate infrequently along this route, but it is recommended that travellers rent their own transport. Although a journey along here necessitates retracing your steps, this is an excellent day trip from Mataram.

Take the main road south from Cakra towards Lembar, and turn off east beside the bemo terminal just before Lembar harbour. 3km along here the road divides: the main road continues south, climbing sharply over low hills before descending past steep slopes covered with banana groves and coconut palms, to rice fields on the valley floor and the tiny village of Sekotong Timur; the alternative—and recommended—road to the west hugs the meandering coastline round the east side of the bay, providing excellent views across the water and of the many bagan, the floating bamboo fishing platforms; at night the fishermen shine a bright light from these to attract fish. The coast road rejoins the main road after c 9km.

At a junction in *dusun* Sekotong, c 6km further on, a road turns off south across the peninsula to Teluk Sepi on the south coast (see below). The road to the north leads back to the shore of Teluk Lembar after c 2km, before cutting across a narrow neck of land to Medang Barat. Along the coast here are more bamboo *bagan* and views of the small islands of Gili Tangkong, Gili Sudak and Gili Nanggu, all three fringed with beautiful white sandy beaches and reefs.

In *dusun* Batukijuk, a man named Guntur can organise a boat to the islands for snorkelling or swimming; only on **Gili Nanggu** is there ✩✩ accommodation. Guntur is well known in the hamlet; foreigners who stop here are assumed to be looking for him.

Northwest of *dusun* Tawun, a tiny shrine can be seen on rocks in the shallow water just offshore; 850m further are ✩ *Sekotong Indah Cottages*, the only accommodation on this stretch of coast, with very basic rooms. There are nice beaches nearby, however, the restaurant is pleasant, and staff can arrange boats to the three islands, although at a higher price than Guntur in Batukijuk.

The road beyond passes through **Pandanan**, a small fishing settlement with a long row of boats drawn up on the beach, and 1km beyond climbs to an airy viewpoint overlooking **Gili Poh**, a flat sandy island with a large beacon. 700m further, a sandy track to the north leads through a coconut palm plantation to a beautiful narrow white sand spit; at low tide, you can wade through warm, shallow water to the tiny island hill at the northern tip. Locals fish here, and gather sackfuls of bleached coral fragments for making lime.

The route further west skirts the southern end of **Gili Gede**, a large island with several hamlets, then heads inland to the junction in *dusun* Pelangan. Here a lane turns south 6.5km across the peninsula to the huge south coast beach on **Teluk Mekaki**, flanked by rocky islands at the headlands; the descent to the bay is extremely steep. In midweek, the beach is usually deserted, except for the occasional fisherman. There is no shade, nor facilities of any sort, but the water is clear and swimming pleasant.

Continuing along the north coast, the asphalt ends after c 12km, but a drivable track continues c 3km to the cliffs of Tanjung Bangko-Bangko, descending past maize fields to the water's edge, and then through grassy meadows to the stony beach and low cliffs. This final stretch of beach has a surfing break known to surfers as Desert Point; there are no facilities, but this is a fine picnic spot.

THE SOUTH COAST ROUTES

The main road from Mataram to the beautiful southern beaches runs through Praya and the pottery centre of Penujak. Here the road divides, offering two main routes to the coast (and numerous back-road alternatives); one runs direct to Kuta, where most of the accommodation is to be found; the other, more circuitous, goes via Selong Belanak, passing the magnificent beach at Teluk Mawun. It is suggested that the traveller takes the main road to Kuta and returns via the Selong Belanak route.

Sukarara

Take Jl. Teguh Faisal south to Kediri from the main Sweta intersection, and then take the clearly signed road to Praya. Sukarara, an important weaving centre, lies to the southwest at an intersection in Puyung, 11.5km from Kediri. Being so close to Mataram, Sukarara is well established on the tour-bus circuit; partly as a result, prices tend to be high and vendors can be unusually pushy and sometimes rude. Nevertheless, there is a huge range of textiles on show here, some made locally, some not. Most of the local weaving is done not by the smiling women sitting at their looms in front of the shops, but in the surrounding hamlets. To find them, continue past the showrooms and ask around; it helps to speak Indonesian, but purchases from the makers may be no better value than from the showrooms.

Penujak

Beyond Puyung the road continues to **Praya**, the pleasant administrative centre for South Lombok, where there are banks, *wartel*, a post office, and a very large Saturday market. Turn off southwest here to **Penujak**, c 7km, one of Lombok's largest pottery centres. Most of the workshops and showrooms lie along a lane off to the right immediately after crossing the large girder bridge. As at Banyumulek (see p 413), the potters of Penujak have benefited from the attention of the Lombok Pottery Centre project, which has improved the firing of the pots and helped with marketing advice.

This lane continues southwest to the coast at Selong Belanak (see below), but the most direct route, described below, continues southeast from Penujak to Kuta via Sengkol.

Rembitan

In Rembitan, a small village 3.5km south of Sengkol, is an interesting old mosque of bamboo and timber, with a roof of *alang-alang* grass; many of the houses in the village are in traditional style, also of bamboo, with rock-hard, pounded-earth raised floors and grass roofs. A guide will usually come forward to show you round and invite a donation; as elsewhere, many of the exaggerated donation entries in the guest book do not reflect what has actually been given.

Sade

Sade is a much-visited village 1km further south, which has maintained its traditional style of architecture in an almost museum-like setting to attract tourists; within are numerous persistent textile vendors and 'guides', but the architecture is nevertheless interesting and you are free to wander at will. There are several *lumbung*, the old style of rice barn which has become a dreadfully overplayed architectural symbol of Lombok, used widely and often tastelessly in modern hotels and government offices.

KUTA
• • • • • •

Further south, the road follows a winding roller-coaster route down to Kuta, c 7km, through verdant hills. This tiny village has become a low-key, low-budget resort, catering primarily to surfers. Kuta's coastal scenery is pleasant, although the beach in front of the village is rocky and not good for swimming; to west and east are some truly magnificent bays.

Accommodation

Almost all the south coast accommodation is in Kuta, and most of it, unfortunately, is dismal. This is largely because for most of the 1990s there has been a great deal of uncertainty about whether powerful individuals in the government or well-connected businessmen were going to seize the land for their own greedy purposes; not surprisingly, bungalow owners have been reluctant to invest further in their properties. The ☎ code is 0370.

The only high-quality accommodation is the ✭✭✭✭✭ *Novotel* (☎ 653333; fax 633555), c 1.5km east of Kuta at Pantai Putri Nyale, a beautiful curving white sand beach with clear water. In Kuta itself, ✭✭✭/✭✭ *Kuta Indah Hotel* (☎ 653781/2; fax 654628) is clean but overpriced and rather far from the beach; ✭ *Anda*, on the beach front, is popular but run-down; ✭ *Cockatoo* is friendly but dilapidated.

East of Kuta

The beautiful beaches at Tanjung Aan, 5km east of Kuta, are justifiably popular. Food and drink vendors set up stalls during the day, and you can climb to the headlands to watch the sunset. The road continues east to **Gerupuk**, a grubby fishing village 1.3km further, where seaweed is cultivated on racks offshore.

A road inland from Kuta heads east c 15km to **Awang**, a predominantly Bugis fishing village on the west side of Ekas Bay. On a clear day there is a fine view of Gunung Rinjani to the north. Of note are the Bugis houses, raised on stilts and painted.

From Awang it is possible to continue northeast on good asphalt roads round Ekas Bay to Batu Nampar, and eventually join the main Praya–Tanjung Luar road at Ganti or Tangun; the landscape is flat and the journey somewhat tedious, although you can see fine examples of traditional architecture well away from the 'prepared' atmosphere of Sade.

West of Kuta

To the west, the road climbs after c 3km to a high viewpoint with excellent views back over Kuta, Seger and Tanjung Aan. **Pantai Mawun**, possibly the most beautiful beach on Lombok, lies c 6km further west, clearly signed. The swimming is excellent off this curving bay of white sand, which is protected by craggy headlands.

Another beach, just as fine but less easily accessible, is **Pantai Mawi**, along a lane to the left c 7km further west. The first 1.4km is on asphalt, but then the route becomes a narrow, overgrown dirt track, often impassable after heavy rain.

At **Selong Belanak**, a further 3km west, is yet another fine beach, in front of a tiny hamlet. Here the road turns inland, passing ☆☆/☆ *Selong Belanak Cottages* c 2km from the beach, which have basic wooden bungalows in a garden.

At a junction c 2km further north, the road straight ahead leads directly back to Penujak and Praya; the shady lane to the west meanders through forest and plantations to Montong Sapah, and from there to Teluk Sepi and eventually Sekotong. This alternative but longer route back to Mataram, which avoids repeating the roads from Praya or Penujak, is detailed here.

The Montong Sapah route

This is a reasonable road, 7.5km to Montong Sapah, although the second half is on a rocky surface. Turn left in this isolated village and follow the winding road across terraced hills; in the dry season, the land appears barren and desolate; in the rains, when the terraced fields are filled with rice and glisten with water, the scenery can be dramatic. Shortly before Pengantap, the road descends steeply to the coast; beyond, it passes the mangrove-fringed **Teluk Sepi** before climbing steeply over the spine of the Sekotong peninsula and descending through a lush valley flanked by rock outcrops to the junction in *dusun* Sekotong (see above). Lembar (13km) and Mataram (32km) are to the right.

The southeast corner

Most easily reached from Praya on the main road to Tanjung Luar, this isolated corner of Lombok receives few visitors.

From Praya, instead of turning south to Kuta, continue straight on through Mujur to Ganti (which can also be reached from Kuta on the south coast; see above). To the south here, 1.2km along the Batu Nampar road, is **Batu Rintang**, a village of traditional houses and rice barns; be prepared for excited, shouting children asking for money and cigarettes.

To the north of the main road c 3km is the village of **Beleka**, a centre for rattan and bamboo crafts.

Further east on the main road, shortly before the centre of Keruak, a road to the south signed to Kaliantan leads through flat dry terrain to the isolated Ekas peninsula.

Detour to the Ekas peninsula

The route passes the small settlement of Jor on the north side of Teluk Jor, where the road turns due west. At a junction c 6km further, a road to the west leads to **Ekas**, a small, unkempt fishing village, to the south of which are the remote ☆☆/☆ *Laut Surga Cottages* which are best avoided; rat-infested, run-down and at times lacking electricity and/or water, they are distinctly overpriced, which is a shame because the coastal setting is magnificent.

The main road on the peninsula continues south towards Kaliantan, but quickly deteriorates. Although some of the beaches down here are very beautiful, facilities for tourists are non-existent and it requires a huge effort to reach them. The nearest decent accommodation is at Labuhan Haji on Lombok's east coast (see p 418).

Continuing east through **Keruak**, where there is a big Friday market, the road reaches the coast and bears northeast towards Labuhan Haji. A turning to the southeast c 4km beyond Keruak leads to **Tanjung Luar**, a small but wealthy fishing port with a large fleet; the village, viewed from the main jetty, is surprisingly picturesque. It is possible, though not cheap, to charter a boat from here for a day trip to Tanjung Ringgit at the eastern tip of the Ekas peninsula, or any of the adjacent bays and islands visible in the distance from the jetty.

Glossary

abhaya mudra (Skt.), the gesture of dispelling fear and bestowing protection, one of several frequently seen ritual hand gestures of the Buddha. The hand is raised with palm outwards and all digits pointing upwards.

adat (Ind.), traditional custom, accepted as law within a specific community.

Agastya, a legendary sage and a form of Shiva, accredited with the spread of Shaivism in India; often depicted in Java as a bearded, pot-bellied guru dressed in simple garb.

air terjun (Ind.), waterfall.

Akshobhya, the *jina* Buddha presiding in the east, making the *bhumisparsha mudra*.

alun-alun (Ind.), the town square, usually a grassy area, where public rallies and fairs are held; found in every Javanese town.

Amitabha, the *jina* Buddha presiding in the west, making the *dhyana mudra*.

Amoghasiddhi, the *jina* Buddha presiding in the north, making the *abhaya mudra*.

angklung, Javanese musical instrument made out of bamboo.

apsara (Skt.), celestial dancer who entertains the Hindu gods.

arca (Ind.), statue or image, usually sculpted from stone.

Arjuna, the principal hero of the *Mahabharata*.

atap (Ind.), thatched roof of woven palm fronds.

Atavaka, the male counterpart of Hariti.

Avalokiteshvara, the bodhisattva of the present era in Mahayana Buddhist teaching; the lord of compassion.

bajaj (Ind.), three-wheeled, motorised taxi in Jakarta.

banjar, village-sized administrative unit on Bali.

batik, method of colouring cloth by applying wax, before dyeing, to the parts to be left uncoloured; or the cloth created in this way.

becak (Ind.), pedal-powered tricycle used as a taxi in towns.

bemo (Ind.), public minibus transport found throughout much of Indonesia.

benteng (Ind.), fortress.

Bhatara Guru, a form of Shiva as the 'perfect teacher'.

Bhoma, mythical son of the forest in Bali-Hinduism, with huge fangs and bulging eyes; his face is frequently carved above the inner gateways in Balinese temples to keep away evil spirits.

bhumisparsha mudra (Skt.), the gesture of calling the Earth to witness the Buddha's victory over the devil Mara. The left hand is on the lap, palm upwards; the right hand is touching the ground with the back of the hand facing outwards.

bodhisattva (Skt.), a person in Mahayana Buddhism who has achieved Buddhahood but who chooses to remain in the world to help others to achieve understanding. In Theravada Buddhism, is one who has reached the state preceding the final liberation and attainment of Buddhahood.

Brahma, the four-faced, four-armed creator of the universe, and with Vishnu and Shiva one of the Trimurti, the trinity of principal gods of Hinduism; his mount is the goose, Hamsa.

bupati (Ind.), senior local administrator, roughly equivalent to a mayor.

cagar alam (Ind.), nature reserve.

candi (Ind.), any ancient temple or ruins or site of a now-vanished temple.

candi bentar (Ind.), the split gateway found in most Balinese temples.

cap (Ind.), stamp of copper or tin used in making batik designs.

cella, internal section of a temple often containing a statue.

chakra (Skt.), the wheel or solar disc, one of the attributes of Vishnu.

Chandra, Hindu god of the moon.

cidomo (Ind.), pony trap with car tyres, used as public transport on Lombok.

curuk (curug) (Ind.), waterfall.

danau (Ind.), lake.

desa (Ind.), village-sized administrative unit in the countryside.

dharmacakra mudra (Skt.), the gesture of setting the Wheel of the Law in motion at the first sermon of the Buddha in the Deer Park at Sarnath. The right hand, representing the wheel, is raised with the thumb and forefinger joined at the tips and almost touching the same digits of the left hand, which is turning the wheel.

dhyana mudra (Skt.), the gesture denoting deep meditation, with both hands resting, palm-upwards, in the lap.

dokar (Ind.), a two-wheeled pony trap used as a taxi in towns.

Durga, the consort of Shiva in her terrible aspect; often seen in Javanese sculpture as Mahishasuramardini, slayer of the buffalo-demon, Mahisha.

dvarapala (Skt.), door guardian; figure of a deity placed at the entrance to a temple to keep away evil spirits.

gamelan (Ind.), Indonesian classical orchestra comprising primarily of tuned gongs, with some woodwind and stringed instruments.

Gandavyuha, a Buddhist text telling the story of the young prince Sudhana and his quest for enlightenment.

Ganesha, the child of Shiva and Parvati in Hindu mythology, portrayed as having a plump human body and an elephant's head; the god of wisdom and the remover of obstacles. In the Shaivite temples of Java he appears—with Durga and Agastya—as one of the three principal deities adjacent to Shiva, usually in the west-facing chamber; he is occasionally found standing alone, and is the most commonly represented deity in records of Indonesian statuary.

gang (Ind.), alley; on maps abbreviated to 'Gg'.

Garuda (Skt.), a mythical creature, the king of the birds; the mount of Vishnu.

geringsing, double-ikat textile made in a single village in eastern Bali.

gili (Ind.), small island.

gua (goa) (Ind.), cave.

gunung (Ind.), mountain; on maps often abbreviated to 'G'.

Hamsa (Skt.), the sacred goose, the mount of Brahma.

Hariti, Mythical ogress turned Buddhist goddess of fertility and protectress of children. In Bali she is called Men Brayut, and is usually thought to have had 18 children.

harmika (Skt.), box-like, cube-shaped element between the bell-shaped chamber of a *stupa* and the conical spire.

ikat (Ind.), method of tie-dying cloth to create random patterns; or the cloth made in this way.

jalan (Ind.), road or street; on maps abbreviated to 'Jl.'

jamu (Ind.), traditional medicine and health tonics made from herbs, roots and spices.

jataka (Skt.), the story of the former lives of the Buddha in which he achieved perfection in the practice of different virtues.

jina (Skt.), five 'conqueror' Buddhas who preside over the zenith and four quarters of the universe: Vairocana, Akshobya, Ratnasambhava, Amitabha and Amoghasiddhi.

juru kunci (Ind.), caretaker of shrines, *candi* and other sites.

kabupaten (Ind.), regency; the highest administrative division within a province.

kaja (Bali), the direction upward, mountainward, towards the realm of the Balinese gods.

kala (Skt.), demon mask frequently carved over temple doorways, windows and niches to protect the temple from evil spirits.

kampung (Ind.), a neighbourhood in a city.

kawah (Ind.), volcanic crater

kecamatan (Ind.), district; an administrative division within a *kabupaten.*

kelod (Bali), the direction downward, seaward, away from the realm of the Balinese gods.

keraton (kraton) (Ind.), fortified palace at the political and spiritual heart of a traditional Javanese kingdom; several remain in the old courtly centres on Java.

kijang (Ind.), a species of deer; but much more widely used as the generic name for several marques of 'people-carrier' types of vehicle.

kinnara (Pali), mythical creature, half-human, half-bird, dwelling in the Himavanta Forest.

klenteng (Ind.), Chinese temple or joss-house.

kris, a double-edged dagger, often with a wavy blade, traditionally considered sacred or possessing supernatural abilities.

Krishna, an avatar or incarnation of Vishnu, and the charioteer of Arjuna in the *Mahabharata.*

kulkul (Bali), bell or drum tower in a Balinese temple.

Kuvera, Hindu name for the god of riches; known as Jambhala to Buddhists.

labuhan (Ind.), port or harbour.

Lakshmi, the consort of Vishnu in Hindu mythology; the goddess of fortune.

lalitasana, seated posture with one leg pendant, the other drawn up.

Lalitavistara, the text narrating the life of the historical Buddha from the time of his descent to Earth from the Tushita heaven until his death or *parinirvana*.

linga (Skt.), symbolic representation of Shiva as a stylised phallus, usually of stone.

losmen (Ind.), a cheap and simple hotel.

Mahabharata, one of two great Indian epic poems, telling the story of rivalry between the Pandava and Kaurava brothers.

Mahakala, the Buddhist god of death; often found flanking the doorway to a temple together with Nadishvara.

Mahishasura, the buffalo-demon slain by Durga in numerous tableaux found in Javanese temples.

Maitreya, a benevolent bodhisattva, now living in the Tushita heaven, who will be the future Buddha.

makam (Ind.), tomb or grave

makara (Skt.), a mythical, aquatic monster resembling a crocodile, often with an elephant's trunk, and spewing forth flowers. Is frequently seen in association with the *kala*, carved round windows and niches of Javanese temples.

Mardijker (Dutch), a Christian Asian, originally from Portuguese-held Asian territories captured by the Dutch in the 17C and taken to Batavia.

menara (Ind.), minaret of a mosque.

Meru, mythical cosmic mountain, axis of the world round which the continents and oceans are grouped, and abode of the gods.

meru (Skt), shrine—usually many-tiered, in a Balinese temple, through which deities descend for their visits to Earth.

mesjid (masjid) (Ind.), mosque.

mikrolet (Ind.), small minivan used as public transport in towns.

moko, ancient bronze drums of Nusa Tenggara.

naga (Skt.), chthonic serpent deity.

Nandi (Nandin), the sacred bull mount of Shiva.

Nandishvara, a manifestation of the god Shiva; often found as a deity guarding the entrance to a shrine together with Mahakala.

odalan (Bali), Balinese temple festival to celebrate the anniversary of the temple's founding.

ojek (Ind.), motorcycle taxi in rural areas, where the paying passenger rides pillion.

padmasana (Skt.), a shrine found in most Balinese temples, surmounted by an empty seat reserved for Shanghyang Widhi Wasa.

padma tiga, a triple throne found in some Balinese temples for Brahma, Shiva and Vishnu.

paduraksa, arched gateway to the inner courtyard in many Balinese temples.

pantai (Ind.), beach.

pasar (Ind.) market.

pendopo (Jav.), open-sided, roofed pavilion, found in palaces and the houses of wealthy Javanese; traditionally used for giving audiences.

penginapan (Ind.), a type of cheap hotel with simple facilities.

PHPA, Directorate-General of Forest Protection and Nature Conservation.

pinisi (Ind.), traditional two-masted, wooden-hulled sailing ship originating from the Buginese traders of South Sulawesi.

Prajnaparamita, female form of the bodhisattva Avalokiteshvara.

pralambapadasana (Skt.), posture when seated on a throne, with both legs pendant; sometimes known as the European posture.

prasada (Skt), tower-sanctuary found in a few Balinese temples.

pulau (Ind.), island; often abbreviated on maps to 'P'.

pura (Ind.), general name for a temple in Bali.

Ramadan, Muslim month of ritual fasting.

Ramayana, one of the two great Indian epic poems, probably written in two parts between 500 BC and AD 200, which recounts the adventures of Rama and his wife Sita.

Rangda (Bali), mythical witch representing evil and negative aspects; is often depicted in Balinese temple carvings with a huge tongue and pendulous breasts.

Ratnasambhava, the *jina* Buddha presiding in the south, making the *varada mudra*.

rijsttafel (Dutch), a buffet comprising a range of different dishes.

Sanghyang Widi Wasa (Bali), the creator god of Bali-Hinduism, of whom all other deities in the Balinese pantheon are manifestations.

sawah (Ind.), rice fields.

Shakyamuni, the historical Buddha.

Shiva, one of the *trimurti* or trinity of Hindu deities; Shiva is associated with cosmic destruction, asceticism and creative powers, and is usually distinguished by a third eye in the centre of his forehead, and by wild coiling hair crowned with a skull crescent headdress. His attributes usually include a trident, *kendi*, and a flywhisk; his mount is the bull, Nandi.

songket (Ind.), a method of weaving using a supplementary weft thread of gold or silver, once common on Bali but now fairly rare; or the completed fabric.

stupa (Skt.), usually a dome-shaped monument surmounted by a conical spire; traditionally a reliquary to house Buddhist relics.

subak (Ind.), water users' association in Bali, essential for the fair distribution of water for rice cultivation.

sunan, Javanese Muslim holy man.

Surya, Hindu god of the sun.

tanjung (Ind.), headland, cape or promontory.

Tara, the female counterpart of Avalokiteshvara in his role as the Saviour from the Eight Perils. She gradually came to assume many different forms and ultimately became the supreme goddess of Buddhism and the female counterpart of Amoghasiddhi.

teluk (Ind.), bay.

tephra, fragments of rock and dust thrown into the air by a volcanic eruption.

tsunami, undulating oceanic wave caused by earthquakes, volcanoes or undersea disturbances.

Vairocana, the *jina* Buddha of the zenith making the *dharmacakra mudra*.

vajra (Skt.), thunderbolt.

Vajrapani, a *bodhisattva* who converted the Hindu gods Shiva and Sati to Buddhism by slaying them and then restoring them to life.

varada mudra (Skt.), gesture of bestowing favours and charity. Hands similar to *bhumisparsha mudra*, but right hand rests on knee, palm outwards.

vihara (Pali), Buddhist temple or monastery.

Vishnu, one of the Hindu *trimurti* or trinity; the god of re-creation, tradition and preservation. He has ten avatars or incarnations, including Krishna.

vitarka mudra (Skt.), gesture of preaching. The left hand is in the lap, the right hand is raised with palm outwards, thumb and forefinger touching at their tips and the other three digits pointing upwards. (This is sometimes performed with both hands.)

VOC, (*Vereenigde Oost-Indische Compagnie*) (United East India Company), the Dutch trading company which founded Jayakarta (Jakarta) in 1611.

wali songo, the nine saints of Muslim legend who introduced Islam into Java.

wartel, telephone office found in every town and city, from which national and (usually) international calls can be made.

warung, small shop or food kiosk.

wayang, puppet or the art of puppetry. There are many regional variations, such as *wayang golek*, *wayang kulit*, etc.

yakhsa (Skt.), benevolent or evil demigod, often depicted as a giant, frightening guardian at Javanese temple doorways.

yoni, female sexual emblem, found as a stone pedestal for the *linga* in Javanese temples, and usually indented to receive the waters used in ritual libations.

Index

A

Affandi 310
Agung Rai Museum of Art 130
Air Sanih 165
Alas Kedaton 171
Alas Purwo National Park 403
Ambarawa 282
Ambunten 396
Amed 158
Amlapura 155
Ampenan 407
Ancol 180, 206
Anyar 218
Anyar Kidul 218
Arca Ganesha Boro 357
Arca Ganesha Karangkates 372
Arca Gopolo 332
Arca Totok Kerot 353
Arjasari 250
Arosbaya 392
Asta Tinggi 395

B

Baduy, the 216
Balekambang 373
Baluran National Park 403
Bandung 235
Bandungan 283
Bangkalan 391
Bangli 143
Bangsal 415
Banten 209
Banten Girang 209, 215
Banyumas 271
Banyumulek 91, 413
Banyuwangi 402
Batavia 60
Batuan 131
Batur caldera 160
Baturaden 270
Bayan 423
Bekol 403
Belahan 78
Blawan 401
Bledug Kuwu 293
Blimbingsari 175
Blitar 359
Bogor 223
Bogor Botanical Gardens 224
Bondowoso 399
Borobudur 76

Bremi 398
Bromo-Tengger-Semeru National Park 370, 371, 373
Bugbug 153, 154
Bukit 117
Buleleng 61
Bunutan 158

C

Cakranegara 91, 407
Campuhan 120
Candi Abang 332
Candi Asu 322
Candi Badut, 365
Candi Bangkal 378
Candi Banon 74
Candi Banyunibo 331
Candi Barong 332
Candi Belahan 377
Candi Borobudur 312
Candi Boyolangu 356
Candi Canggal
    see Candi Gunung Wukir 323
Candi Cangkuang 255
Candi Ceto 344
Candi Cibedug 234
Candi Dadi 356
Candi Gambar Wetan 362
Candi Gambirowati 334
Candi Gebang 324
Candi Gunung Gangsir 378
Candi Gunung Wukir 75, 323
Candi Ijo 77, 332
Candi Jabung 79, 398
Candi Jago 79-81, 367
Candi Jawi 79, 377
Candi Jedong 378
Candi Jolotundo 376
Candi Kalasan 76, 325
Candi Kedaton 81, 398
Candi Kesiman Tengah 375
Candi Kidal 79, 368
Candi Kotes 362
Candi Kuning 167
Candi Lor 351
Candi Loro Jonggrang 326
Candi Lumbung 322
Candi Lumbung (Prambanan) 329
Candi Mendut 76, 320
Candi Mirigambar 81, 357
Candi Muncul
    see Candi Ngempon

Pringapus 284
Candi Ngampel 357
Candi Ngawen 323
Candi Ngempon Pringapus 284
Candi Ngetos 351
Candi Panataran 80, 81, 359
Candi Pari 377
Candi Pawon 319
Candi Pendem 322
Candi Planggatan 344
Candi Plaosan 77
Candi Plumbangan 362
Candi Pringapus 75, 280
Candi Rimbi 81, 381
Candi Sambisari 73, 325
Candi Sanggrahan 356
Candi Sawentar 362
Candi Selogriyo 73, 280
Candi Selokelir 376
Candi Sewu 77, 329
Candi Simping 357
Candi Singosari 79, 80, 369
Candi Sojiwan 77, 330
Candi Songgoriti 355
Candi Sukuh 343
Candi Sumberawan 369
Candi Sumberjati
    see Candi Simping 357
Candi Sumur 377
Candi Surowono 81, 354
Candi Tebing Jukutpaku 127
Candi Tebing Kalebutan 136
Candi Tebing Kerobokan 137
Candi Tebing Tegallinggah 133
Candi Tebing Tembuku 144
Candi Tegowangi 353
Candi Wringin Branjang 362
Candidasa 152, 153
Canggal 323
Carita 218
Celuk 132
Cemoro Lawang 370, 371
Cemoro Sewu 345
Cepu forest 349
Ciampea 231
Ciater hot springs 247
Cibeureum waterfall 233
Cibodas Alpine Gardens 228
Cibolang hot springs 250
Cigugur 268
Cihanjuang 253

Cilacap 263
Cimacan 228
Cimahi falls 254
Cimanggu hot springs 251
Cipanas (Garut) 256
Cipanas (Puncak) 230
Cipari 268
Cirebon 264
Citarum valley 250
Ciwalini hot-water swimming pool 251
Coban Baung 369
Coban Rondo 355
Colo 295
Culik 157
Curug Citiis 256
Curug Sewu 287

D

Danau Selorejo 354
Demak 292
Denpasar 62, 100, 101
    Bali Provincial Museum 103
    Pura Agung Jagatnatha 103
    Pura Maospahit Gerenceng 105
    Werdi Budaya Museum 105
Dieng 73, 75, 273
Diponegoro 304
Dungkek 396

E

Ekas 429

G

Galis 392
Gede Pangrango National Park 229
Gedong Songo 73, 283
Gelgel 148
Gianyar 90, 133
Gili Air 415, 420
Gili Iyang 396
Gili Meno 415, 420
Gili Nanggu 426
Gili Trawangan 415, 420
Gilimanuk 176
Glenmore 405
Gondang 332
Grojogan Sewu 344
Gua (Guwo) Tabuhan 346
Gua Gajah 134
Gua Gong 346
Gua Langse 334
Gua Lawah 149, 271

Gua Pasir 356
Gua Petruk 264
Gua Selomangleng (Kediri) 352
Gua Selomangleng (Tulungagung) 81, 356
Gubugklakah 368
Gunarsa, Nyoman 146
Gunung Abang 161
Gunung Agung 83-84
Gunung Argopuro 398
Gunung Arjuno 375
Gunung Batok 371
Gunung Batur 163
Gunung Bromo 82, 368, 370, 371
Gunung Ciremai 268
Gunung Galunggung 260
Gunung Gede 229
Gunung Guntur 256
Gunung Halimun National Park 47
Gunung Kawi 137
Gunung Lawu 345
Gunung Malabar 248
Gunung Merapi 78, 336
Gunung Merbabu 48, 282
Gunung Papandayan 250, 256
Gunung Patuha 251
Gunung Penanggungan 78, 376, 378
Gunung Raung 400
Gunung Rinjani 422
Gunung Salak 231
Gunung Sari 419
Gunung Semeru 373, 374
Gunung Slamet 271
Gunung Sumbing 279
Gunung Sundoro 279
Gunung Tampomas 253
Gunung Tangkuban Perahu 247
Gunung Telomoyo 282
Gunung Welirang 375

H

Ho-ling 57

I

Imogiri 333, 334
Indramayu 267

J

Jagjag 404
Jakarta 178
    Adam Malik Museum 180, 203

Armed Forces Museum 180, 205
Batavia 180, 189
Bina Graha 180, 196
Chinatown 180, 202
Church of Zion 180, 201
City Hall 180, 196
Ereveld Menteng Pulo 180, 205
Fine Arts Hall and Ceramics Museum 180, 200
Galeri Foto Jurnalistik Antara 187
Galeri Lontar 187
Garden of Inscriptions 180, 195
Glodok 180, 202
History Museum 180, 200
Immanuel Church 180, 196
Istana Merdeka 180, 196
Istana Negara 180, 196
Jayakarta 180, 188
Klenteng Sentiong 180, 205
Kota 180, 197
Lapangan Banteng 180, 196
Lapangan Merdeka 180, 192
Maritime Museum 180, 197
Mesjid Istiqlal 180, 197
Museum of National Archives 180, 202
Museum of the Revolutionary Hero Gen. A. Yani 180, 203
Museum Waspada Purbawisesa 180, 205
National Monument 180, 192
National Museum 180, 187, 194
Old City Hall 180, 199
Pancasila Building 180, 196
Puppet Museum 180, 187, 200
Sunda Kelapa 180, 188, 197
Taman Fatahillah 180, 199
Tasman Mini Indonesia Indah 180, 207
Textile Museum 180, 205

Toko Merah 180, 199
War Cemetery 180, 205
Wayang Orang 'Bharata' 187
Jambianom 421
Jangkar 395
Jember 405
Jepara 295
Jimbaran 114
Jimbaran Bay 100
Jolotundo 78
Junghuhn, Franz Wilhelm 246
Jungut Batu 151

K

Kalak 347
Kalianget 395
Kalibaru 405
Kalijogo, Sunan 293
Kalipucang 263
Kalisat 400
Kaliurang 336
Kamasan 87, 148
Kampung Naga 258
Kampung Pulo 255
Karang Bayan 412
Karang Kamulyan 261
Karangasem 61
Karimunjawa National Park 296
Karsten, Thomas 245
Kawah Ijen 400, 401
Kawah Putih 251
Kawah Telaga Bodas 257
Kebun Binatang Ragunan 180, 208
Kedewatan 121
Kekunaan Bhre Kahuripan 380
Kelampok 91, 271
Kepulauan Seribu 180, 208
Kerambitan 173
Keraton Ratu Boko 331
Kerek 388
Kopeng 281
Kornel (Kusumahadinata) 252
Krakatau 218
Kudus 293
Kusamba 149
Kuta (Bali) 110
Kuta (Lombock) 428

L

Labuan 217
Labuhan Haji 418, 430
Labuhan Lombok 424

Lake Bratan 167
Lake Buyan 167
Lake Tamblingan 167
Legian 100
Lembang 246
Lembongan 150, 151
Lendang Nangka 417
Linggarjati 267
Lombok 149
Loro Jonggrang 73, 75, 77
Lovina 165
Loyok 416
Lubang Buaya 180, 207
Lumajang 373

M

Madiun 348
Madura 90
Majapahit 59, 79, 80, 82, 378, 379
Makam Sendang Duwur 387
Malang 364
Mandra, I Nyoman 146
Mantingan 296
Margarana monument 171
Mas 88, 131
Masbagik Timur 91, 418
Mataram 57, 92, 407
Mengwi 141
Merprès, Adrien-Jean Le Mayeur de 108
Meru Betiri National Park 48, 404, 406
Mojokerto 378
Muara Angke 180, 207
Munduk 168
Museum Haji Widayat 319
Museum of Classical Balinese Painting 146
Museum Rudana 130

N

Negara 174
Ngadisari 371
Nganjuk 351
Nieuwenkamp, W.O.J. 134, 135, 165
Nusa Dua 100, 116
Nusa Kambangan 263
Nusa Lembongan 151
Nusa Penida 149, 151
Nyoman Gunarsa 310

P

Pacet 375
Paciran 387
Pacitan 347

Pajajaran 180, 188, 210, 216, 239
Pakis Baru 296
Palasari 175
Pamekasan 90, 393
Panataran 79, 81
Padangbai 149
Pande Sari 158
Pangalengan 248, 249
Pangandaran 261
Pangandaran Nature Tourism Park 262
Panjalu 260
Pantai Biastugal 150
Pantai Lombang 396
Pantai Mawun 428
Pantai Ngliyep 372
Pantai Rajegwesi 404
Pantai Saba 132
Pantai Suluban 118
Parangkusumo 335
Parangtritis 335
Pare 353
Pasongsongan 396
Payangan 121
Pejeng 135
Pekalongan 285
Pelabuhanratu 233
Peliatan 131
Pemuteran 177
Penebel 172
Penestanan 120
Penujak 91, 427
Perean 141
Petulu Gunung 140
Pintu 249
Pohsarang 353
Praya 427
Pringgasela 91, 417
Probolinggo 398
Pulau Dua 213
Pulau Kangean 395
Pulau Menjangan 175
Pulau Puteran 395
Pulau Raas 396
Pulau Rambut 180, 208
Pulau Sangiang 218
Pulau Sapudi 396
Pulau Serangan 108
Puncak 227
Pura Agung Jagatnatha 83
Pura Beji 165
Pura Besakih 144
Pura Dalem Jagaraga 165
Pura Lempuyang Luhur 156
Pura Lingsar 412
Pura Luhur Batukaru 172
Pura Meduwe Karang 165

Pura Pasar Agung 159
Pura Suranadi 412
Pura Tegeh Koripan 162
Pura Ulun Danu Batur
   (Kintamani) 161
Pura Ulun Danu Batur
   (Songan) 163
Pura Ulun Danu Bratan 167
Purwodadi 369
Purwokerto 270

R

Raffles, Thomas Stanford
   304, 344
Rajapolah 260
Rangkasbitung 215
Ranupane 373
Rawa Danau 215
Reco Lanang 376
Rembitan 427
Rungkang 91, 416

S

Sade 427
Sampang 392
Sangeh 141
Sanggingan 121
Sangiran 342
Sanur 62, 100, 105
Sapit 418, 424
Sarangan 345
Sawahan 351
Sayan 120
Sebatu 139
Segara Anakan 263
Segenter 422
Selabintana 233
Selaparang 418
Selekta 355
Selong Belanak 429
Semarang 287
Semarapura 147
Sembalun Lawang 423
Sembungan 277
Seminyak 100, 110
Sempol 400
Senaru 422, 423
Senggigi 413, 414
Serang 214
Shrivijaya 72, 78
Sideman 90, 159
Singaraja 90, 164
Singosari 59, 79
Situ Cangkuang 255
Situ Lembang 254
Situ Lengkong 260
Situ Patengan 251
Situgunung 233

Situs Payak 333
Slopeng 396
Solo
   see Surakarta 337
Spies, Walter 87, 95
Sragi 286
Stutterheim 135
Suharto 66
Sukapura 371
Sukarara 91, 427
Sukarno 62, 64
Sukawati 132
Sumedang 252
Sumenep 394
Surabaya 64, 382
Surakarta 337

T

Tabanan 170
Taman Hidup 398
Taman Narmada 412
Taman Ujung 155
Tanah Aron 156
Tanah Lot 170
Tanjung 421
Tanjung Bumi 90
Tanjung Papuma 405
Tanjung Sira 421
Tapen 399
Taro 139
Tarumanagara 57
Tasikmalaya 260
Tawangmangu 344
Telaga Menjer 273
Telaga Ngebel 349
Telaga Tista 158
Telaga Waja 137
Teluk Amuk 152
Teluk Meru 406
Tenganan Pegeringsingan
   90, 152
Tetebatu 416
Tibubiyu 173
Tihingan 147
Tirta Gangga 155
Tiu Kelep 422
Tiu Pupus waterfall 421
Toya Bungkah 162
Trangkil 296
Trawas 375
Trinil 349
Trowulan 78, 80, 378, 379
Trunyan 162
Trusmi 267
Tulamben 157
Tulungagung 355

U

Ubud 118
   Campuhan 125
   Museum Neka 124
   Museum Puri Lukisan
      127
Ujong Kulon National Park
   221
Ujung Genteng 234
Ujung Kulon National Park
   47

W

Wangon 269
Wates Tengah 158
Watu Karung 347
Watu Ulo 405
West Bali National Park 175
West New Guinea 64
Wonokerto 371
Wonosobo 271

Y

Yang Plateau 48
Yang Plateau Reserve 398
Yeh Gangga 173
Yeh Pulu 135
Yogyakarta, 90, 297
   Affandi Museum 310
   Air Force Museum 311
   Army Museum 310
   Biology Museum 308
   Diponegoro Museum 311
   Gembira Loka Zoo 309
   Keraton Ngayogyakarta
      Hadiningrat 305
   Kota Gede 302, 311
   Monumen Yogya Kembali
      311
   Museum Batik Yogyakarta
      309
   Museum Benteng 308
   Museum Sono Budoyo
      305
   Museum Wayang Kekayon
      309
   Sasmita Loka Panglima
      Besar Jenderal Sudirman
      309
   Semaki Heroes Cemetery
      309
   Taman Sari 307

2

JAVA SEA

Pulau
Rambut
☐ **Bird Sanctuary**
Tanjungpasir

Soekarno-Hatta
Airport
JAKARTA
Tangerang

Ciputat

Serpong
Parungpanjang
Parung
Depok
Cibinong
Cileungsir

Bekasi Cikarang

Karawang

Cikampek

Jatisari Sarengseng

Pamanukan

Pagadenbaru

Cipeundeuy

Campaka **Purwakarta**

Subang

Kedawung
Batujaya

Rengasdengklok

Ciampea
Leuwiliang

Bogor

Cisarua
Ciawi Puncak Pass
Gibodas Cipanas
Alpine Gardens ☐ Pacet
G. Pangrango
3019m 2958m
▲ G. Gede

Jatiluhur
Jatiluhur
Reservoir
Plered

Wanayasa Sagalaherang

Ciater
2076m
G. Tangkuban Perahu
Cisarua Lembang

Maribaya

Bandung
Cimahi
Bojongloa
Tanjung Sa
Ujungberu
Ci
Buahbatu
Rancaekek
Daeyeuhkolot

2211m
G. Salak
Cianten
Cicurug
Gunung
Halimun
Nat. Park Kalapanunggal
Parangkuda
Cibadak
Sukabumi
Cikembar

Cimerang

Cisolok

Pelabuhanratu
Cikadal
Cisaat Selabintana
Gede-
Pangrango
National Park

Cibeber

Cianjur

Cipatat

Rongga

Soreang

Ciparay
Majala
Kawah Kamoja
G. Malabar Pacet
2350m

Pangalengan

Cikembang
Kertasari

Sa
Cisur
G. Papanda
2622r
Ci

Ciwidey
2040m
▲ G. Tilu
2434m
▲ G. Patuha
G. Wayang
▲2182m
Pintu Santosa

Rancabali

Pasir Malang

Arjuna

Sagaranten
Kadupandak

Cibinong

Cisewu

Cipandak Bandarwaru

Jampangkulon

Surade

Cikadal

Ujung
Genteng
Muaregede Sindangbarang

Cikelet
Pameungpe

INDIAN OCEAN

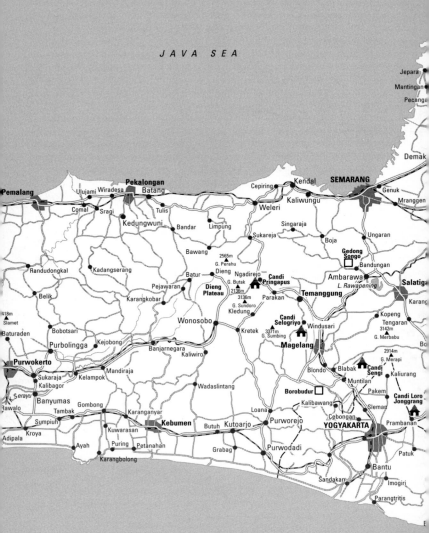

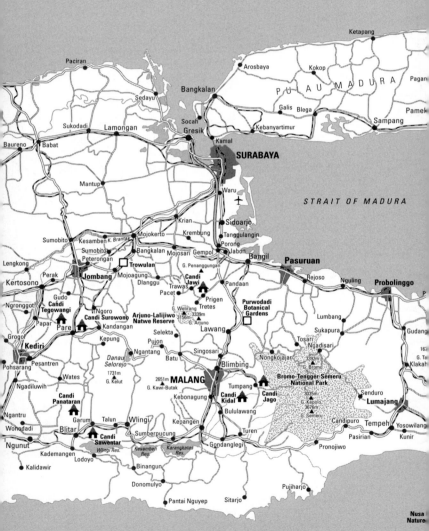

6

JAVA SEA

Paciran

Sedayu

Ketapang

Arosbaya
Kokop

Bangkalan
P U L A U   M A D U R A   Pagan

Sukodadi   Lamongan
Gresik

Galis   Blega
Pamek

Socah   Kebanyartimur
Sampang

Baureno   Babat
Kamal

Mantup
SURABAYA

Waru

STRAIT OF MADURA

Krian

Sumobito   Kesamben K. Brantas   Mojokerto
Sidoarjo

Tanggulangin
Porong

Lengkong   Sumobito   Bangkalan   Mojosari   Gempol   Jabon   Bangil
Peterongan   Mojoagung   □ Trowulan   G. Penanggungan   Pasuruan

Kertosono   Perak   JOMBANG   Dlanggu   Trawas   Candi Jawi   Rejoso   Nguling   Probolinggo
Gudo   Ngoro   Pacet   Prigen   Tretes   Pandaan   P
Ngronggot   Candi Tegowangi   Candi Surowono   G. Welirang 3339m   Purwodadi Botanical Gardens   Lumbang   Gudang
Papar   Pare   Kandangan   Arjuno-Lalijiwo Natwe Reserve 3156m   Lawang   Tosari   Sukapura   167
Grogol   Kepung   G. Arjuno   Ngadisari   G. Ta
KEDIRI   Selekta   Nongkojajar   3392m   Klakah
Pohsarang   Pesantren   Danau Selorejo   Ngantang   Batu   Singosari   G. Bromo   Senduro
Ngadiluwih   Wates   1731m   Pujon   Blimbing   Bromo-Tengger-Semeru National Park   3035m   Lumajang
G. Kelut   2651m   Tumpang   Candi Kidal   Candi Jago   G. Kepolo 3676m   Candipuro   Tempeh   Yosowilang
Ngantru   Candi Panataran   G. Kawi-Butak   MALANG   Kebonagung   G. Semeru   Pasirian   Kunir
Wonodadi   Garum   Talun   Wlingi   Bululawang   Pronojiwo   Tempeh
Blitar   Candi Sawentar   Kepangen   Turen
Ngunut   Sumberpucung   Gondanglegi
Kademangan   Wlingi Res.   Kesamben Res.   Karangkates Res.
Kalidawir   Lodoyo   Binangun   Pujiharjo
Donomulyo   Sitarjo

Pantai Nguyep
Nusa Nature

INDIAN OCEAN

N

0   30 miles
0   50 kms

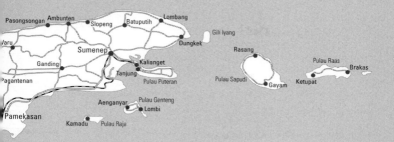

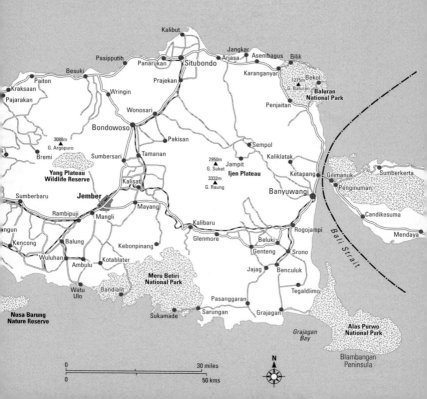

Pasongsongan   Ambunten   Batuputih   Lombang
Slopeng
Jaru   Sumenep   Dungkek   Gili Iyang
Ganding   Kalianget   Rasang
Pagantenan   Tanjung   Pulau Puteran   Pulau Raas   Brakas
Pulau Sapudi   Gayam   Ketupat
Aenganyar   Pulau Genteng
Pamekasan   Lombi
Kamadu   Pulau Raja

STRAIT OF MADURA

Kalibut
Pasipputih   Jangkar
Situbondo   Arjasa   Asembagus   Bilik
Panarukan
Besuki   Karanganyar
Paiton   Prajekan   1276m   Bekol
Kraksaan   Wringin   G. Baluran   Baluran
Pajarakan   Wonosari   National Park
Penjaitan
Bondowoso   Pakisan
3088m
G. Argopuro   Sempol
Bremi   Sumbersari   Tamanan   2950m   Kaliklatak
Jampit
G. Suket
Yang Plateau   Ijen Plateau   Ketapang   Sumberkerta
Wildlife Reserve   Kalisat   3332m   Gilimanuk
Jember   G. Raung   Penginuman
Sumberbaru   Mayang   Banyuwangi
Rambipuji   Mangli   Candikasuma
Kalibaru   Rogojampi
ngun   Kencong   Balung   Kebonpinang   Glenmore   Beluki   Mendaya
Wuluhan   Kotablater   Genteng   Srono
Ambulu   Jajag   Benculuk
Meru Betiri
Watu   Bandialit   National Park   Tegaldlimo
Ulo   Pasanggaran
Nusa Barung   Sarungan   Grajagan   Alas Purwo
Nature Reserve   Sukamade   National Park
Grajagan
Bay
Blambangan
Peninsula

0   30 miles
0   50 kms

N

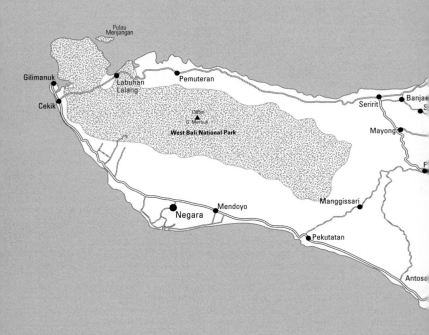

Pulau
Menjangan

Gilimanuk

Labuhan
Lalang

Pemuteran

Seririt

Banja

S

Cekik

1365m
G. Merbuk
West Bali National Park

Mayong

P

Negara

Mendoyo

Manggissari

Pekutatan

Antosa

INDIAN OCEAN

BALI

N

0
0

20 miles

30 kms

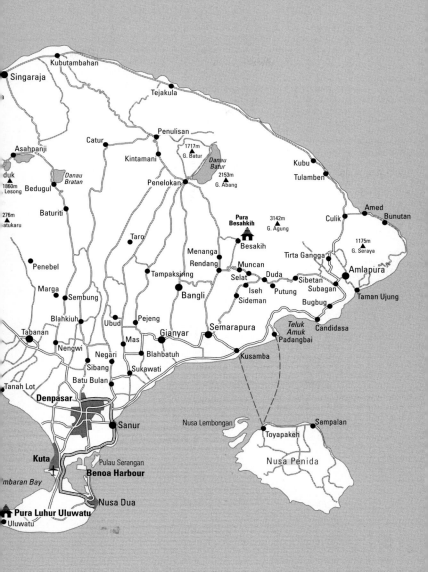

LOMBOK

N

INDIAN OCEAN

0
0

15 miles
20 kms

Gili Lawang
Gili Sulat
Labuhan Pandan
Gili Petagan

Kayangan
Kayangan Peninsula
Labuhan Lombok
Pringgabaya

Sambelia
Obel-obel
Tanjung Ringgit

Sembalun Lawang
1491m G. Senghor
Sembalun Bumbung
Sapit
Pesugulan
Swela
Selaparang
Labuhan Haji

Anyer
Bayan
Sukadana
Segenter
Senaru

Sendang Gile Waterfall

Danau Segara Anak
2351m Baru 2726m G. Rinjani

Jeruk Manis Waterfall

Tetebatu
Kotaraja
Aikmel
Pringgasela
Landang Nyangka
Masbagik Timur
Selong
Tanjung Luar
Keruak
Jor
Ekas Peninsula
Kaliantan

Masbagik
Loyok
Terara
Ganti
Batu Rintang
Tanjung
Sapikmateng
Ekas

Tiu Pupas Waterfall

Tanjung
Jambianom

Pemenang
Tanjung Sih
Sideman

Gili Air
Tanjung
Bangsal
Gili Meno
Gili Trawangan
Tanjung Rumbeh

Pusuk Pass

Gunung Sari
Karang Bayan
Pura Lingsar
Narmada
Lengkong
Montong Betok
Kopang
Beleka
Mujur
Sengkol
Rembitan
Sade
Kuta
Tanjung Aan

Ekas Bay
Awang
Gerupuk

MATARAM
Cakranegara
Kediri
Banyumulek
Sukarara
Praya
Penujak

Ampenan
Gunung Pengsong

Senggigi
Lembar
Sekotong Timur
Montong Sapah
Selong Belanak
Mawun
Pengantap
T. Semu
T. Gerupuk
Selong Balanak T. Mawi

Barukjuk
Sepi
Sepi
Gili Nanggu
Gili Tangkong Sudak
Gili Gede

Sekotong

Bangko Bangko
Pelangan

Teluk Mekaki